Law, Society and Business

Textbook

Robert W. Emerson
J.D., Harvard Law School
Member, Maryland Bar
Rapporteur, Conseil Scientifique, Union Internationale des Huissiers de Justice
Advisory Editor-in-Chief, American Business Law Journal
Huber Hurst Professor of Business Law
Warrington College of Business Administration
Affiliate Professor, Center for European Studies
University of Florida
    Some of my articles are on the Social Science Research Network at
    http://ssrn.com/author=86449

Copyright (c) 2016 Robert W. Emerson
All rights reserved. Except for the quotation of short passages for the purposes of criticism and review, no part of this publication may be reproduced, stored in a retrieval system, or transmitted, in any form or by any means, electronic or mechanical, photocopying, recording or otherwise, without permission of the author.

Manufactured in the United States of America

ISBN 978-1-938315-54-1

Library of Congress Cataloging-in-Publication Data

Emerson, Robert W.
Law, Society and Business / Robert W. Emerson

1. Law. I. Title.

Table of Contents

Table of Contents

ARTICLE I: LEGAL SYSTEMS & BUSINESS FORMATIONS — 1

A. INTRODUCTION TO STUDYING BUSINESS LAW — 1

B. LAW AND LEGAL SYSTEMS — 4
- I. LAW AND ETHICS — 4
- II. HISTORY OF LAW — 11
- III. PURPOSES OF LAW — 17
- IV. CLASSIFICATIONS OF LAW — 19
- V. THEORIES OF LAW — 34
- VI. LEGAL SYSTEMS IN THE WORLD — 59

C. INTELLECTUAL PROPERTY — 64
- I. INTRODUCTION — 64
- II. CYBER PIRACY — 66
- III. WHAT DOES INTELLECTUAL PROPERTY PROTECT? — 68
- IV. PATENTS — 69
- V. COPYRIGHTS — 75
- VI. TRADEMARKS — 81
- VII. TRADE SECRETS — 87
- VIII. KNOW-HOW — 88

D. AGENCY — 89
- I. INTRODUCTION — 89
- II. ACTUAL AUTHORITY — 90
- III. APPARENT AUTHORITY — 92
- IV. THE PRINCIPAL'S LIABILITY FOR THE AGENT'S ACTIONS — 99
- V. THE MASTER/SERVANT RELATIONSHIP — 102
- VI. THE INDEPENDENT CONTRACTOR RELATIONSHIP — 103

VII. THE AGENT'S DUTIES TO THE PRINCIPAL . . . 106

VIII. THE AGENT'S POWERS ON BEHALF OF THE PRINCIPAL . . 110

E. ESTABLISHING A BUSINESS 111

    I. INTRODUCTION TO BUSINESS ENTITIES 111

    II. SOLE PROPRIETORSHIPS 114

    III. NON-CORPORATE BUSINESS ENTITIES: PARTNERSHIPS
AND LIMITED LIABILITY COMPANIES 116

    IV. CORPORATIONS 125

F. THE FIRST AMENDMENT AND FREEDOM OF SPEECH . . . 156

    I. THE FIRST AMENDMENT GENERALLY . . . 156

    II. FREE SPEECH 156

ARTICLE II: MAKING DEALS 169

A. CONTRACTS: INTRODUCTION 169

    I. BASIC CONTRACT LAW FORMATION . . . 169

    II. OFFER 198

    III. ACCEPTANCE 208

    IV. CONSIDERATION 214

    V. MUTUALITY (REALITY) OF ASSENT . . . 222

    VI. ETHICS IN THE DEAL-MAKING PROCESS: A BRIEF DISCUSSION 236

    VII. CAPACITY 239

    VIII. LEGALITY (PUBLIC POLICY) 245

B. SPECIAL RULES ABOUT WRITTEN AGREEMENTS . . . 258

    I. WHY DO WE LIKE WRITTEN AGREEMENTS? . . 258

    II. THE STATUTE OF FRAUDS 258

    III. THE PAROL EVIDENCE RULE (PER) . . . 265

C. THIRD PARTIES AND CONDITIONS 268
    I. THIRD PARTIES 268
    II. CONDITIONS 272

D. DISCHARGE OF CONTRACTS AND REMEDIES FOR BREACH . . 275
    I. PERFORMANCE 275
    II. BREACH 278
    III. DISCHARGE BY AGREEMENT OF THE PARTIES . . . 280
    IV. DISCHARGE BY OPERATION OF LAW 281
    V. DAMAGES AWARDS. 285
    VI. EQUITABLE REMEDIES 293

E. EMPLOYMENT DISCRIMINATION LAW 298
    I. COMPETING THEMES AND COMPETING PHILOSOPHIES . . 298
    II. THE EMPLOYMENT AT-WILL DOCTRINE . . . 299
    III. WHISTLEBLOWING OR RETALIATION CLAIMS . . . 301
    IV. DISCRIMINATION STATUTES AND REGULATIONS . . 303
    V. SPECIAL TOPICS: RELIGION, THE WORLD, AND SEXUAL ORIENTATION 306
    VI. TITLE VII PRELIMINARY INFORMATION 308
    VII. THREE THEORIES FOR PROVING A TITLE VII VIOLATION . 311
    VIII. TITLE VII DEFENSES 314
    IX. SEX DISCRIMINATION, ESPECIALLY SEXUAL HARASSMENT . 317
    X. THE AMERICANS WITH DISABILITIES ACT . . . 323

ARTICLE III: RIGHTS AND WRONGS   327

A. KEY LEGAL PLAYERS: LAWYERS AND JUDGES . . . 327
    I. LAWYERS 327
    II. JUDGES 350

B. LITIGATION 368
    I. SUING AND SETTLEMENTS 368

II. PLEADINGS	376
III. DISCOVERY	379
IV. MOTIONS AND OTHER MATTERS	385
V. PROCEDURAL FAIRNESS	387
VI. THE TRIAL	390

C. ALTERNATIVE DISPUTE RESOLUTION 410

I. EMPIRICAL STUDIES	411
II. NEW ARBITRATION APPEALS PROCEDURES	412
III. COMPARATIVE LAW ON *ADR*	412

D. CRIMINAL LAW 413

I. TERMINOLOGY: THE GENERAL, LEGAL CATEGORIZATION OF CRIMES	413
II. CRIMINAL LAW COMPARED TO TORT LAW	415

E. TORTS 424

I. INTRODUCTION	424
II. THREE MAIN DIVISIONS OF TORT LAW: NEGLIGENCE, INTENTIONAL TORTS, AND STRICT LIABILITY	424
III. NEGLIGENCE	425
IV. INTENTIONAL TORTS	452
V. STRICT LIABILITY, PRODUCT LIABILITY, AND WARRANTIES	477

ARTICLE I: LEGAL SYSTEMS & BUSINESS FORMATION

©Robert W. Emerson, 2016

A. INTRODUCTION TO STUDYING BUSINESS LAW

> WHY STUDY LAW?
> *Quotations from two of our two most intellectual Presidents:*
> "The study of the law qualifies a man to be useful to himself, to his neighbors, and to the public." Thomas Jefferson
> "The worst enemy of the law is the man who knows only the technical details." From page 441 of Woodrow Wilson's book, "Legal Education of Undergraduates"

There are many reasons to study business law. Certainly, acquiring some knowledge about the legal system, particularly the American system as it affects business, is a crucial focus of any course of study. Besides knowledge generally, one may pursue specific topics of vital interest to most businesspersons, such as contracts, torts, and corporations, to name just a few. The author's role for this text is to present information acquired in his dual roles as a lawyer and as a university professor who teaches and researches business law. The text is intended to give information not only about law itself, but to consider the law in its societal context, especially as the role of law relates to business.

A theme of this text is: do not leave law entirely to the "pros" - the judges and lawyers. Learning law can make the learner a better citizen - to be a more productive and insightful businessperson. The author's role is to describe, to discuss trends, but not necessarily to defend the system.

    1. We should consider alternatives and possible reforms.
    2. We should not be bashful about saying, "What's wrong here?" And
    3. We should always "get the Big Picture." That is, we should learn pertinent legal particulars, but – most important – we must not get bogged down in legal minutiae and thereby miss the forest for the trees. As poet T.S. Eliot (1888-1965) lamented, "where is the knowledge we have lost in information?"

Still, we must know the basics of law and the legal system to make informed decisions – about our duties, our rights, and our possible remedies for wrongs to us. We may hire others for assistance, but that is certainly not always practical or economically feasible. And we need to know enough to know whether to hire a lawyer. Even experienced laypersons often miss that.[1]

---

[1] Robert W. Emerson, *Fortune Favors the Franchisor: Survey and Analysis of the Franchisee's Decision Whether to Hire Counsel*, 51 SAN DIEGO LAW REVIEW 709 (2014). You can find this article and many others by the author on the Social Science Research Network at http://ssrn.com/author=86449.

Example: *Miranda v. Arizona*

> Joke: Police Officer to Criminal Suspect – "You have the right to an attorney . . ."; Suspect's interjection – "Isn't that cruel and unusual punishment?"

You have to know your rights before you can waive them (give them up). *Miranda v. Arizona*, 384 U.S. 436, 444 (1966), is a classic example of this notion ensconced in constitutional law. In *Miranda*, the court wrote:

> "[T]he prosecution may not use statements, whether exculpatory or inculpatory, stemming from custodial interrogation of the defendant unless it demonstrates the use of procedural safeguards effective to secure the privilege against self-incrimination. By custodial interrogation, we mean questioning initiated by law enforcement officers after a person has been taken into custody or otherwise deprived of freedom of action in any way."

Sometimes, a defendant will say that the case "should be dropped because the cops didn't read me my rights." If law enforcement officers do not ask any questions, they do not have to read the defendant any rights. The requirement to read the defendant his or her rights has created a new verb: "to Mirandize."

Miranda Warnings (required by the Supreme Court decision): (1) You have the right to remain silent; (2) Anything you say may be used as evidence against you; (3) You have the right to speak to an attorney before being questioned and to have an attorney present during questioning; (4) If you cannot afford an attorney, you have the right to have an attorney appointed for you prior to questioning; (5) Do you understand these rights?; (6) Understanding these rights, do you wish to answer my questions?

The Supreme Court further stated: "The defendant may waive [give up] effectuation of these rights provided the waiver is made voluntarily, knowingly, and intelligently. If however, he indicates in any manner and at any stage of the process that he wishes to consult with an attorney before speaking, there can be no questioning."

Confessions and *Miranda v. Arizona*

Confessions can implicate legal balancing tests: society's best interest, and the defendant's rights (which actually are tied in with society's interests).

What concerns are raised by Miranda? Why is there a protection from self-incrimination? What would we think if the police bought to the police station a man whom they thought guilty of a burglary, and did the following:

1. Seated him on a padded office chair, offered him a cup of coffee and use of the lavatory, told him the evidence they had linking him to the crime, and within five minutes he confessed? We would probably think that was all right.

2. Placed him on a hard unpadded stool, in a room with no windows, two detectives questioned him for 35 minutes, and then he confessed? We might think that was "not too bad."

3. Took down his pants, set him on a block of ice, and questioned him for 55 minutes until he confessed? Now we wonder whether the defendant confessed because he was guilty or just because he was very uncomfortable

4. Put him on the rack and tortured him for two hours until he confessed? Clearly, such a confession is unacceptable.

It is very difficult to know why a person confessed, and it is much easier simply to say that no person can ever be required to incriminate himself or herself at all: then we do not need to get into a detailed examination of the circumstances under which the confession was made. (If a person does confess, he/she may still argue later that the confession was not voluntary. The argument may be difficult to win, assuming police followed appropriate procedures and thoroughly and fairly recorded the confession.

In practice, confessions – inadvertent or intended – are very rare in court itself. We see it much, much more in television and movies than in real life.

> Confessions may happen in investigative and other pretrial work – *Miranda* is among many cases speaking to these matters.
>
> Here is one example of an inadvertent "confession":
>
> Charles Taylor was on trial for robbing a shoe store at knifepoint. He was identified by a store clerk as the man who stole a pair of tan hiking boots and $169. " I leaned over and stared," said Judge James Fleetwood, presiding. Taylor had been propping his feet on the defense table; he was wearing some tan hiking boots! "I thought," Judge Fleetwood recalled, "surely nobody would be so stupid to as to wear the boots he stole to his trial." But the judge was wrong.
>
> Prosecutors asked the shoe store employee for more information about the stolen boots. Everything matched: color, brand, style, size, and even product lot number. Tan L.L. Bean hiking boots Size 10 ½ from Lot No 1046 – precisely the same as the boots Taylor wore to trial. His boots "confessed" for Taylor, and he was, of course, convicted of robbery.
>
> Here is another example of an accidental "confession":
>
> At San Diego Superior Court, two men stood trial for armed robbery. An eyewitness took the stand, and the prosecutor moved slowly and cautiously: "So, you say you were at the scene when the robbery took place?"
>
> "Yes," she responded.
> "And you saw a vehicle leave at a high rate of speed?"
> - "Yes," she answered.
> - "And did you observe the occupants?"
> - "Yes, two men," she volunteered.
> - "And," the prosecutor boomed, "are those two men present in court today?"
>
> At this point, before the witness could say anything, the two defendants sealed their fate. They raised their hands. Apparently, the two defendants thought they were back in school – they were very helpful; they raised their hand and waved to the witness – without speaking still declaring to the witnesses, "Here we are!" The defendants were convicted of armed robbery.
>
> Here is a third, final example:
>
> Occasionally, a witness gives descriptions that result in a sketch artist's drawing of a perpetrator that looks remarkably like the witness himself. It turns out the witness must have been, at least subconsciously, describing himself. When there is other evidence as well, this indirect "confession" has led to the witness' own arrest!

An Explanation of Case Citations

Brown v. Board of Education, 347 U.S. 483 (1954), is "translated" as follows:

(1) Brown is the party (the appellant) who appealed a lower court decision, or was the plaintiff at the trial, or both.

(2) Board of Education is the party (the appellee) who was appealed against (e.g., the appellee won the lower court's decision), or was the defendant at the trial, or both.

(3) 347 U.S. 483 means that the official court decision is in the 347th volume of the U.S. Reports, starting at page 483; if the 483 were followed by a comma and then another number – e.g., 505, that would mean the citation refers to the case starting at page 483, with the quotation or paraphrasing derived from the court opinion at page 505.

(4) 1954 is the year of the decision. Only U.S. Supreme Court cases do not need, in the parenthesized statement of the date, an indication of the particular court that issued the opinion – Here are examples, with the court named before the year of the decision:

(2nd Cir. 1987) – Second Circuit Court of Appeals – a federal appellate court

(S.D. Fla. 1999) – Southern District of Florida – a federal trial court, with this one being in Southern Florida, typically Miami). Few *state* trial courts have many reported court decisions; California and New York are exceptions.

(Ill. 2005) – the Illinois Supreme Court; whenever the court name is solely the abbreviation of a state, that indicates the highest state court for that state.

(Mich. Ct. App. 2010) – the Michigan Court of Appeals; most states have a lower court of appeals, below the state's highest court- these lower appeals courts will usually have an "App." along with the abbreviated name of the state, and perhaps some other court abbreviation such as "Ct." (for Court) or "Cir." (for Circuit).

Law is pervasive

As Alexis de Tocqueville (1805-1859) observed when he visited the United States in 1831-1832 and authored the book, "Democracy in America" (written from 1835 to 1840), "There is hardly a political question in the United States which does not sooner or later turn into a judicial one." For the sake of good government generally, not just one's own individual well-being, all citizens should have some basic understanding of law and the legal system.

Study of law usually emphasizes analytical skills, critical thinking, public policy, ethics, decision making under conditions of complexity and uncertainty, and effective communication. As A. Bartlett Giamatti observed when he served as President of Yale University (before he became Major League Baseball Commissioner): "The law is not simply a set of forensic or procedural skills. It is a vast body of knowledge, compounded of historical materials, modes of textual analysis and various philosophical concerns. It is a formal inquiry into our behavior and ideals that proceeds essentially through language" and draws on many disciplines also relevant to business: economics, psychology, accounting, politics, philosophy, history, sociology, language, literature, and other subjects. Indeed, some business school scholars recommend that business schools, especially MBA and doctoral programs of business, emulate the most innovative law schools, with their focus on teaching and pragmatic writing and research.[2]

B. LAW AND LEGAL SYSTEMS

I. LAW AND ETHICS

Examine criminal law, business ethics, regulation of business, etc. to test what type of theories about law/ethics you have. Engage in self-analysis and ask yourself, "What are my beliefs? Why?"

A. What Is Law?

> "There are two, and only two, foundations of law, . . . equity and utility." (fairness and efficiency) Edmund Burke (1729-1797), TRACT ON PROPERTY LAWS, Part 1, Chapter 3.

"Few questions concerning human society have been asked with such persistence and answered by serious thinkers in so many diverse, strange, and even paradoxical ways as the question, 'What is law?'"[3]

The American Law Institute states, law is "the body of principles, standards, and rules which the courts . . . apply in the decision of controversies coming before them." So, law is a mechanism for humans to order their lives and force adherence to societally acceptable norms.

---

[2] Warren G. Bennis & James O'Toole, *How Business Schools Lost Their Way*, HARVARD BUSINESS REVIEW (May 2005).
[3] H.L.A. Hart, The Concept of Law 1 (1961).

Law has been compared to life plans (Spinoza). It has been defined as the norms established by government (Locke), as a body of precepts (Hume), as individual, free will harmonized with universal rules (Kant), or as the unfolding of or reaching justice (Hegel). Most concepts of law can be grouped into one of three categories: social order,[4] institutionalism,[5] or justice.[6] But there are weaknesses in all three approaches, as realized by observers going back to Socrates nearly 2,500 years ago: (1) Settled rules and binding customs seem like law, but that brings in all of social life; (2) Decisions of the state are law, but some decisions are unjust, unworthy of law; and (3) Law must be just, but opinions differ on justice and right.

1. Notions of Morality and Etiquette: Are they law?

"There is a big difference between what we have the right to do and what is right." Potter Stewart, US Supreme Court Justice, 1958-1981.

Etiquette, morals, and ethics can be and usually are distinguished from law. When we talk about the decline of civil society, in a general sense we speak of a decrease in civility that encompasses all three.

Here is an example: When people wait in a line at a fast food restaurant, that is an example of people following a social norm rather than a law.

2. Law as *Enforced* Rules

Law can be defined as those rules which are enforced. What will a court enforce? "The prophesies of what the courts will do in fact, and nothing more pretentious, are what I mean by the law." *Oliver Wendell Holmes, Jr., "The Path of the Law," 10 Harvard Law Review 457, 461 (1897) (arguing that the objective of legal study is to predict a judge's decision).* Holmes further declared that the law is "a statement of the circumstances in which the public force will be brought to bear through courts." In short, the law encompasses *rules that the courts will enforce.*

A law must be enforced; otherwise, what is its meaning? A contract, a will, a corporate charter, and other legal documents have meaning because of enforceable rules (Law) concerning the documents. They have special meaning because these documents represent rights and duties a court could enforce.

Suppose that there is a "No Spitting" Sign. Is that sign a law? Does it, at least, evidence a law? An answer may be revealed by determining whether the sign's statement is actually enforced. To understand better whether it may have risen to the level of a law, we often need to know more about the society in which this sign was created. We must know more about the circumstances leading to the erecting of this sign, about the culture and habits of the people.

---

[4] In Ancient Athens, Plato spoke of law as a form of social control, a method to discover social structures and to attain "the good life," while Aristotle held that law is a rule of conduct or decision, a contract, an ideal of reason or a form of order. Modern theorist Eugen Ehrlich and others incorporated ideas about custom. Earlier, English jurist Francis Bacon (1561-1626) opined that the main need for law, and of law, is certainty.

[5] This theory looks at the state and was expounded upon by the English legal theorists John Austin in the 19th Century and H.L.A. Hart in the 20th Century, as well as by social scientists such as Max Weber and Paul Bohannan. Philosophers have, echoing Plato, referred to law as characterized by societal structures (Leibniz).

[6] To Cicero in ancient Rome (1st Century B.C.), law is commands and prohibitions, but it is also the merger of nature and reason as well as the distinction between the just and the unjust. This emphasis on what is moral or just is seen from the Stoics of Ancient Greece to Thomas Aquinas of the Middle Ages to Harvard's Lon Fuller and John Rawls in the 20th Century. For example, Aquinas concluded that law is an ordinance of reason for the common good.

To back up a law, to make a rule appear to all concerned that it indeed does have the force of law behind it, signs or forms or other documents may have additional information on them citing the applicable law and/or the consequences of a violation. For example, underneath the words "No Littering" a sign may further state "by order of [naming a governmental body]," note that violators face $500 fines (or some other specified dollar amount or jail time), and cite the relevant Florida statute or municipal ordinance. Legal forms often include oaths with a friendly (?!) printed reminder of the relevant statutes on perjury and the consequences for violators of these statutes (felony convictions, fines, and possible imprisonment). With a reminder of the consequences of littering or lying, the makers of the signs or the forms say, in effect, "It's the law, and we are serious!"

B. Competing Definitions of Law

1. Hobbes

After witnessing Europe's religious wars, the great English philosopher Thomas Hobbes (1588-1679) became deeply pessimistic about human nature and concluded that only one law prevailed in a world of *Homo Homini Lupus* — Latin for "every man is a wolf to every other man."[7] In Hobbes' classic work,[8] he defined law as a social construct that should provide stability, order, and security. People relinquish, in essence, all of their rights to the state, with an emphasis upon social controls – restraining people's "base instincts" (i.e., law *is* order).

2. Montesquieu

Another great legal and political philosopher, the French writer Charles de Secondant, known as Montesquieu (1689-1755), supported freedom. In 1748, Montesquieu published *The Spirit of Laws.* He believed that political liberty (the opposite of tyranny) involves separating the legislative, executive, and judicial powers of government. Montesquieu contended that liberty and respect for properly constituted law could exist together. Montesquieu's concepts helped to spur the writing of constitutions throughout the world, including the U.S. Constitution. Perhaps his most notable idea is the notion of checks and balances as well as the separations of powers concept, ideas which Montesquieu propounded and the Founding Fathers adopted.

---

[7] As you read this text, you will quickly discover that Latin is a favorite language for law. One reason is that the greatest Code in history – the one with the most influence throughout time, even to the present – is that of the great Roman Emperor, Justinian. Much of Roman law, including even its terms in the original language (Latin), survives to this day in the Civil Code found throughout most of the world. More important, though, for our purposes in studying principally American law, is the fact that Latin survives even disconnected from the Roman law. Long after the Roman Empire fell, jurists from England, America, France, or other Western nations discussed their own laws or customs using terms themselves coined in Latin, not in their own "vulgar" tongue of English, French, or whatnot. That practice lent these newly described or recommended concepts more panache and also gave them the benefit of being more accessible across borders, as Latin is, or at least was, a common language for the educated of Europe and the Americas. Yes, Latin is a "dead" language, no longer the first language of anyone; even the few hundred residents of Vatican City - where Latin is the official language - learned the language as their second (or third, or fourth . . .) language. But it is the mother tongue for the Romance languages (e.g., French, Italian, Portuguese, Romanian, and Spanish), and it has also strongly influenced many other languages, such as English. So, albeit "dead," Latin remains a universal, or at least an accessible and common language useful in many fields, from science to the arts to law. It is still a language lawyers, physicians, judges, and others often invoke. Still, in spite of many professionals' reliance on Latin, numerous persons, from tiny schoolchildren to fully grown scholars, have decried the often difficult and even discouraging study of an ancient language, great for vocabulary but not for everyday speech. As the schoolyard ditty goes, "Latin is a dead language./ It's plain enough to see./ It killed off all the Romans./ And now it's killing me!"

[8] Thomas Hobbes, *LEVIATHAN, OR THE MATTER, FORM, AND POWER OF A COMMONWEALTH, ECCLESIASTICAL AND CIVIL (1651), at Chapter XXVI.*

3. Locke
"The end of law is not to abolish or restrain, but to preserve and enlarge freedom."[9]

John Locke (1632-1704) wrote of law as a liberator, as a promoter of freedom; to inspire or spark liberty; and to improve society. People give up some rights to the government, but they retain other, inalienable rights, Locke concluded

Locke believed that the task of any state is to protect people's rights. Because governments inconvenience people in various ways, the justification for a state's existence is its ability to protect human rights better than individuals could do on their own. And if a state does not do that, then the people should overthrow it.

Both John Locke and Thomas Hobbes wrote of a social compact or social contract - the agreement among people who had lived "in a state of nature" to form the *body politic* - a government making rules binding on all of them. A government's *constitution* may represent the social compact.

Locke's writings were very influential at the time of the American Revolution and the development of the U.S. Constitution.

4. Blackstone (see pg. 8; Emerson BL)[10]
Sir William Blackstone (1723-1780), was an English jurist who gave up his law practice to become a law professor at Oxford University. In his *Commentaries on the Common Law* (published in 1769), Book I, 44, states that law is "a rule of civil conduct prescribed by the supreme power in a state, commanding what is right, and prohibiting what is wrong" ("the superior [commands, and] the inferior is bound to obey").

To this day, sources of information (e.g., books, the Internet) are very important: what lawyers and judges can do to access and learn the law has always been at the core of common law development. Lawyers (and judges) are paid for knowing what to do with the resources.[11]

C. What Are Ethics?

> "Always do right. This will gratify some people, and astonish the rest."   Mark Twain, address to the Young People's Society, Greenpoint Presbyterian Church, Brooklyn, New York, Feb. 16, 1901.

The confluence of law and ethics have eternally beguiled and defied philosophers.

Lord Chief Justice Coleridge (England) in 1893 wrote, "It would not be correct to say that every moral obligation involves a legal duty; but every legal duty is founded on a moral obligation."

1. Law and Morals (see pg. 5; Emerson BL)
The term "legal ethics" is not an oxymoron.

Is the term "legal ethics" an oxymoron? Like jumbo shrimp, airline schedule, Justice Thomas, postal service, smart economist (picture of Mark Rush)

---

[9] John Locke, TWO TREATISES OF GOVERNMENT, Book II, Chapter VI (1690).

[10] Throughout the body of this text, cross-references to a page or pages from the book - Robert W. Emerson, *Business Law*. NY: Barron's Educational Series (6th ed., 2015) – are indicated by the phrase, **(see pg. ___; Emerson BL)**. In the footnotes of this text, the above book is cited with the full reference.

[11] Besides FindLaw.com, Lexis, Westlaw, and Google searches, a few other mechanisms for legal research include: Legal Information Institute (LII), a site maintained by Cornell Law School, http://www.law.cornell.edu/; Zimmerman's Research Guide, http://www.lexisnexis.com/infopro/zimmerman/; LLRX.com on United States law, http://www.llrx.com/category/1048 ; and the Library of Congress Law Library, http://www.loc.gov/law/index.php (the largest legal library in the world, and especially useful for those interested in historical perspective).

There is the story of a lawyer visited by a client with a question about ethics. The lawyer, in a huge office with shelves of hundreds and hundreds of law books, responds, "Ethics? Hmmm… Let's see… I think I have a *pamphlet* on that around here somewhere." Obviously, ethical matters should be more than just a solitary pamphlet.

> YOUTUBE – Law And Ethics (3mins23secs) at robertwemersonufl
> Ethics and law are intrinsically connected. They are not the same by any stretch, but one would have to be a fool, to somehow think that one could behave in a despicable, completely immoral fashion and would not have to worry about legal consequences because of some sort of technical interpretation of the law. The law tends to be conservative by nature, and tends to trail behind ethical consensus. But the law does in some way track our moral notions. So, what we see historically tends to be situations in which we as a society grow philosophically and morally, and thus our laws are impacted.
> Occasionally we see the reverse; the law actually precedes the ethics. Courts go out in front of the populace and decree something – say, find that segregated public schools are unconstitutional; over time, perhaps also the ethics and morality change. What we are talking about is, in essence, a notion of what's fair and what's right. While some people say "legal ethics" is an oxymoron, a contradiction of terms, I would say that's not really true. I think we just have impressions sometimes given to us by people who may be "lower on the totem pole," closer to the least common denominator.
> The impression we sometimes get, for instance, watching legal advertisements, is that a lawyer (1) demonstrates his/her legal acumen by showing a bunch of nice books behind him/her there in the advertisement, (2) shows his/her knowledge by wearing a dark suit, (3) shows his/her capability and competence by wearing such a suit, and (4) shows that he/she is in fact a good person by having quite obvious photographs of perhaps family members; and we thus get a cynical notion that it is all a game, all a manipulation. But, in fact, there is a strong correlation between philosophy and morals and law, and it behooves us all to do a bit of reading and thinking in this area. That is because – usually - if you follow your conscience and do what most people looking at it objectively would say is the right thing to do, you are probably <u>not</u> going to get into trouble with the law; and, conversely, if you do something most people would look at and say, "that's really bad, that's really wrong, there OUGHT TO BE A LAW," then there probably is a law (or there will soon be one!) to take care of such immoral, inappropriate behavior. So don't be a dunce.

2. Ethics and Law

> *Earl Warren (Chief Justice of the United States, 1954-69): "In civilized life, law floats in a sea of ethics."*

a. Related, Not Synonymous

A risk of considering law and ethics to be co-extensive is that we "sink to the *lowest common denominator*" - <u>the law, which is supposed to be something almost all of us are capable of obeying, is all that is expected of us, even though we might otherwise expect much more from ourselves - higher standards,</u> beyond simply legal requirements. Ethics is not just for business or our own self-concept, but also for society at large: our view of the prospects for human progress. The <u>maintenance of high ethical standards may be good business; it may be a tonic for good health.</u> But beyond these, it is a <u>measure of our sympathy with our fellow humans,</u> an <u>affirmation</u> that <u>we exist here to serve more than ourselves,</u> that <u>there is some larger purpose at work.</u> If we are unethical and cynical, we cannot have confidence in the perfectibility of humanity. If we are without confidence in the larger purpose, we certainly cannot contribute to its realization, and we are left merely to "strut and fret our hour upon the stage."

b. Law as a Time-Saver

In his essay, "Why Law Is Indispensable," George Bernard Shaw (1856-1950) examined how law is meant to decide things for us (so we can think of other things), and to give us dependability (so we know what others will do), Shaw opined that morality is <u>not</u> an issue for most areas of the law. As he puts it:

> **important principle: Conduct that a reasonable person conscientiously deems moral + just is unlikely to collide with law**

Law is never so necessary as when it has no ethical significance whatever, and is pure law for the sake of law. The law that compels me to keep to the left when driving along Oxford Street is ethically senseless, as is shown by the fact that keeping to the right answers equally well in Paris; and it certainly destroys my freedom to choose my side; but ==by enabling me to count on everyone else keeping to the left also, thus making traffic possible and safe, it enlarges my life and sets my mind free for nobler issues.== Most laws, in short, are not the expression of the ethical verdicts of the community, but pure etiquette and nothing else. What they do express is the fact that over most of the field of social life there are wide limits within which it does not matter what people do, though it matters enormously whether under given circumstances you can depend on their all doing the same thing. The wasp, who can be depended on absolutely to sting you if you squeeze him, is less of a nuisance than the man who tries to do business with you not according to the customs of business, but according to the Sermon on the Mount.

> **Law is easier to enforce when citizens yield to govt for moral reasons**

c. ==Morality is more likely to influence law than vice-versa==

In medieval times, the European church and state usually were inseparable. The church guided people's morals. Since the church also, in many ways, wrote the law, public morals and the law tended to coincide. Even in more modern times, though, we can find many examples of morals affecting law, including:

(1) <u>Slavery</u> – moral viewpoints helped lead to war and a change in the law;
(2) <u>Sexual harassment</u> – a gathering of opinion that it is wrong;
(3) <u>Attitudes towards smoking</u> - now seen as a wrongful action toward others: secondhand smoke; and
(4) <u>Attitudes toward drunk driving</u> – a growing consensus that it is not funny but dangerous and even immoral. Old views of drunkenness, even perhaps while operating machinery, as being cute and silly – to a newer view of its being quite foolish, wrongful, risky behavior. Penalties for drunken driving have risen significantly.

3. Civil Disobedience

> "Good men must not obey the laws too much." Ralph Waldo Emerson, American philosopher (1803-1882)

People are free to break the law as long as they are willing to take the consequences. Using morally-based challenges to urge changes in the law were these great thinkers/activists agitating against the law, but in pursuit of highly moral purposes.

(1) Henry David Thoreau (1817–1862) - wrote the book WALDEN POND and the essay "Civil Disobedience"; opposed slavery and the Mexican War; therefore, refused to pay his poll tax and, therefore, spent a night in jail (until, without Thoreau's approval, an anonymous source paid the tax).
(2) Mohandas Gandhi (1869-1948) – great Indian leader and moral philosopher who helped bring his country to independence from Britain.
(3) Martin Luther King, Jr. (1929-1968) – leader of the American Civil Rights movement defying legally-mandated segregation.

4. Law Affecting/Preceding Morals

==It is harder to show that law has affected morality than it is to show that morals have affected law== (although laws certainly can strengthen or weaken social norms by signaling an official stance toward them). Three examples of law perhaps preceding morals are:

(1) The <u>Civil Rights Movement</u> - e.g., *Brown v. Board of Education*, 347 U.S. 483 (U.S. Supreme Court, 1954) – the Court unanimously rules against "separate but equal" public schools segregated by race, but it takes a long time for the public to agree, overwhelmingly, that legally-mandated racial segregation is morally wrong;

(2) The accessibility of abortion - *Roe v. Wade*, 410 U.S. 113 (U.S. Supreme Court 1973) – by a 7-2 vote, the U.S. Supreme Court finds a constitutional right to choose to have an abortion, particularly in the first trimester and – subject to some regulation – in the second trimester. Perhaps, the argument goes, the availability of abortion has impacted the views of its morality, women will have had an abortion. 25% of those favoring abortion rights, according to polls, list as their main reason for approval their personal experience involving abortions, while only 6% of those opposing abortion rights list their personal experience as their main reason for opposing such rights; and

(3) Insider trading and financial markets manipulation - scholars have noted that the securities statutes and regulations started in the 1930s helped to develop a "financial morality" perhaps absent, and certainly not a consensus, before that time.

Once one (law or ethics) causes the other (ethics or law) to change, the latter may – in turn – cause more changes in the former – i.e., there is a cycle of effects. For example, social norms may have led to laws against smoking. In turn, a law thereby passed against smoking in public places may have a dramatic effect on smokers, not because of the formal penalty for public smoking (which is hardly ever imposed) but because it empowers nonsmokers to levy social sanctions on smokers.

d. Ethical and Practical Dilemmas for Attorneys

1. General Concepts

The lawyer's role is not to pass judgment, but to do what is legal to help the client. The lawyer cannot legally destroy evidence or condone perjury, nor can he/she ethically engage in courtroom "antics."

The Lawyer has dual roles as a zealous advocate versus as an officer of the court.
Can a lawyer defend a client if the lawyer knows his/her client is guilty?
Does the lawyer "really" know?
Perhaps a more important question for a lawyer, besides would he/she defend a guilty client(?), is:
How would the lawyer defend that client?

The defense lawyer's "standard spiel" to his/her potential client is an implied warning to that client. As an officer of the court, the lawyer notes, he/she cannot suppress evidence or condone perjury.

A defense lawyer may never ask clients if they "did it." Instead, he/she may ask them, "If this matter were to proceed to trial, what is our defense?"

Many defense attorneys acknowledge that they do not want to hear clients confess to a crime, because that would hamper the defense. Lawyers often advise a confessing client to find another attorney. If a client has confessed, and if the defense attorney has reason to believe that this client will lie on the witness stand, the attorney should try to keep the client from testifying. Because an attorney should not suborn perjury, if the client insists on testifying the defense counsel should not participate in questioning but should only allow the client to ramble on.[12]

---

[12] Almost all defense counsel also would agree that ordinarily counsel has no duty to – and likely has a duty not to – report the client's perjury. To do so would, for instance, probably breach attorney-client confidentiality. Of course, ongoing frauds may be another matter (requiring a report, or at least some serious soul-searching), as demonstrated by the whistleblowing duties under the Sarbanes-Oxley Act (2002).

2. Whistleblowing

Ordinarily, there are no whistleblowing duties for attorneys, but the Corporate Responsibility Act more popularly known as the Sarbanes-Oxley Act (SOX) (**see pgs. 434; Emerson BL**). This law obliges a corporation's lawyers to alert senior officers, such as the chief legal counsel or chief executive officer, of evidence of corporate misconduct. That duty arises despite the fact that the attorney represents the corporation. And if the corporate officials to whom the lawyers report fail to address the problems, then the lawyers are required to report the misconduct to the board of directors.

3. Lawyers Revealing Confidences

Lawyers may reveal to the court a client's spoken criminal intent. In the ABA's Model Rules of Professional Conduct, Rule 1.6 says, "a lawyer *may reveal* [emphasis added] such information to the extent the lawyer reasonably believes necessary: to prevent the client from committing a criminal act that the lawyer believes is likely to result in imminent death or substantial bodily harm. . ." When that rule was adopted, some lawyers argued for a mandatory disclosure rule, but the ABA made it optional.

II. HISTORY OF LAW

A. Pre-History (Before Any Writings)

In the beginning, "law" might have been – (a) sheer brute power (a strong cave man with a big club); or (b) cunning – primitive "patent holders" for the Wheel or Making Fire. Perhaps the most primitive form of law was a big man – let us call him "Grok" – with a big stick. Because Grok and his stick could impose order, they represented the first rule of law for humanity, there among the clansmen. Or there may have been a very bright person who had figured out how to make fire. Or to make a wheel, or to plant crops. This knowledge, and the application of that knowledge, as long as it remained with this cave "genius," became a form of property, a type of ancient patent right.

The origins of law are as obscure as the origin of society because the existence of law, in some form, is a precondition for society. Law arises as hierarchies develop, even within the most primitive of governing structures, such as families, clans, and tribes.

For any modern understanding of ancient law, and for law best to serve as a guide to future legal developments, recorded (written) laws are essential. Until we had writing, how could we be sure what the law was? We can only pass it down easily and precisely to others when we go beyond oral traditions and customs and have written texts for reference.

B. Codes (see pg. 3; Emerson BL)
A Code is a collection of laws into a single, organic whole.
Some reasons for learning about Codes are:
(1) it provides background on how law developed generally;
(2) international/comparative law is increasingly important;
(3) there is a stronger "global" orientation in both business and law; and
(4) throughout the world exists a trend toward the mixing and coming together of the Code Law and Common Law approaches.

Four of the most important codes ever are discussed below.

1. Code of Hammurabi

[handwritten note: designed to promote justice but based on lex talionis]

Hammurabi reigned in ancient Babylon from before 1792 B.C. to 1750 B.C. The first known law book dates from 2100 B.C.; it was unearthed in 1902 at Um Nammar (also called Susa), in the land of Ur (Mesopotamia, what is now Iraq). Hammurabi had the earlier law revised and expanded.[13]

Hammurabi's Code contained some laws on individual rights, and there were 285 chapters, in a well-ordered system, on various topics from false accusation to witchcraft to military service to land and business regulations, to family law to property, tariffs, wages, trade, debts, partnerships, and many other concepts important even to the present-day and beyond.[14]

The Code's general purposes were essentially the same as in today's law: *"To cause justice to prevail, to prevent the strong from oppressing the weak, to enlighten the land and to further the welfare of the people."* Even some things that seem very primitive may have been improvements for their time, such as *lex talionis*, the law of retaliation. The Code of Hammurabi says, "If a man destroy the eye of another man, they shall destroy his eye." "If he breaks a man's bone, they shall break his bone." "If a man knock out a tooth of a man of his own rank, they shall knock out his tooth." "If he knock out a tooth of a common man, he shall pay one-third mana of silver."

Lex talionis is also found, for instance, in ancient Hebraic law. The Bible, Old Testament, Exodus 21: 23-25, states, "And if any mischief follow, then thou shalt give life for life, eye for eye, tooth for tooth, hand for hand, foot for foot, burning for burning, wound for wound, stripe for stripe." By this reasoning, the "responding" violence is not initiated, but is merely a repayment of violence in equal measure. Law thus sanctions the retribution impulse.

Lex talionis is perhaps not so primitive as it may now seem, at least when compared to what used to be the approach taken when someone felt aggrieved: Rampant revenge. *Lex talionis* puts limits on the scope of vengeance, to avoid what Francis Bacon (1561-1626), wrote about in ESSAYS: ON REVENGE, "Revenge is a kind of wild justice, which the more man's nature runs to, the more ought law to weed it out."

The Code of Hammurabi supposedly was passed down to Hammurabi from the Babylonian Sun God, Shamash (who was also the Patron of Justice).

The effect of having Law come from the Gods is that it invests great power in (respect for) the Law, but it also means that challenging the Law becomes practically impossible. So there is extreme difficulty in changing laws; a society such as that in Babylon found it nearly impossible to adapt these God-given laws to meet social, economic or technological changes.

> You're a Heretic! Blasphemy, arguing with / disobeying the word of the law of God!

2. Code of Solon

[handwritten note: Rules imposed by citizens, which were equal under the law]

Solon of Athens, Greece – His code rested upon the premise that Laws do not simply come from the Gods, but can be a product of human reason. So, in our Western system, going all the way back to the Greeks, Religion and Law (or Philosophy and Law, or Ethics and Law) are not the same.

The Code of Solon was adopted in 594 B.C. It encouraged law's adaptability and people's power to shape the law. Other notions found in the Code of Solon were state protection of property; a rudimentary form of democracy, the notion of law springing from and dependent upon a consenting citizenry: A consenting citizenry rules itself. But it is a primitive form of democracy - no rights, or even limited rights (certainly no voting) for slaves, women, or even non-property owning free men.

---

[13] The Code of Hammurabi, therefore, was not the first recorded code of law, but it built upon what had gone before it in ancient Mesopotamia. For example, in about 1860 B.C., a few generations before Hammurabi's Code, there was the Sumerian Code of Lipit-Ishtar.

[14]

Also, there is to be equal application of law to all citizens - the same restraints and penalties (Rule of Law). A key concept was that the ruler himself is subject to the law: a well-ordered society is "when the people obey the rulers, and the rulers obey the law."

3. The Justinian Code

Emperor Justinian (of the Byzantine Empire – the Eastern Roman Empire) collected and published in a systemic whole the Roman Law. It is the beginnings of **the Civil Law** *(Lex Civilis)* (presently found in Europe, Latin America, parts of Asia and Africa, and elsewhere).[15]

Justinian's Code is an all-encompassing code, from 533 A.D. It is a systematized series of laws; legal scholars from that time gathered up the existing laws from prior centuries and from throughout the empire. This Code was an attempt to systematize what the Greeks had partially developed and what Roman law already had covered extensively in many areas of business and family law, particularly under law-oriented emperors such as Augustus (27 B.C. - 14 A.D.), Hadrian (117-138 A.D.), and Constantine (306-337 A.D.).

4. The Code Napoleon

Napoleon influenced Western Europe, French colonies, and even former colonies such as Louisiana. His patchwork code, the Code Napoleon (official name, "Code Civil"), with 2,281 articles, went into effect in 1804. (Other "Codes" under Napoleon were the Code of Commerce (1807), Penal Code (1808), and Administrative Code (1811). The Code Napoleon draws its roots from the Roman Law (including the Code of Justinian) predominant in southern France and from the customary law of northern France. The Code Napoleon was a compromise between the ideals of the French Revolution (1789) and older principles. New liberties were provided, but old ideas, such as inheritance, were retained.

C. Common Law (see pgs. 9-11; Emerson BL)

> "The common law is not a brooding omnipresence in the sky, but the articulate voice of some sovereign or quasi-sovereign that can be identified." Oliver Wendell Holmes, Jr.

Common law is distinct from the Civil Law (Code system – the Roman Law). In judge-made law (the common law system), the law bubbles up from court cases, as decisions are written down and put in yearbooks. The result is that the law increasingly becomes universal, understood, and spread throughout the kingdom.

1. The Norman Invasion

There were English origins of the Common Law long before William I of Normandy and his fellow French Norsemen (Vikings) ruled England. Customs, including understandings of legal duties and rights as stated by Anglo-Saxon, Jute (Danish) and other judges, developed as principally oral traditions in the centuries after the Romans abandoned Britain in the Fifth Century A.D. This pre-Norman, Medieval England did not have a unified system of courts. The courts were run quite differently in different locales, and they were usually somewhat susceptible to corruption. Furthermore, the courts were not particularly objective or "rule-based," and they must have been unsatisfactory to many, if not most, parties ensnared in either litigation or criminal matters.

Into this judicial hodgepodge came William I (1027?-1087), better known as William the Conqueror. In October 1066, William defeated in battle the last Anglo-Saxon ruler, Harold Godwinson, and seized the English crown. During the years thereafter, William ruthlessly consolidated his rule, yet he still had trouble in certain areas. William realized that he needed to create incentives for people to go along with

---

[15] But, in today's Civil Law world, there is not necessarily as much commonality as one might think. For example, even to this day, there is little, international communication among legal scholars and jurists in the Spanish–speaking world and little effort has been made to standardize terminology.

[handwritten: Equity as an independent legal system, based on fair play (Barron pg 11)]

the new government, and one way to do that was to establish a new set of courts, the Royal Courts.[16] These courts initially had very limited powers, but they began to hear some cases of direct and indirect trespass, which could have been trespass upon land or upon another person (e.g., battery). The Royal Courts' authority expanded slowly, and eventually there was a well-established system of courts which adjudicated cases and written decisions based not so much on statutes (although they were required to follow statutes in the relatively rare circumstances where a statute applied), and not just upon customs (tradition), but on precedent (prior court decisions) and general principles of justice.

So, while not starting the common law,[17] William I and his successors helped to systematize and make "common" the common law. These Norman kings did not replace or eradicate the common law. However, through the courts and the new Year Books, William and his descendants helped to make law universal, that is, *common* throughout the realm – the same in Northumberland, Cornwall, Dover, or wherever. In these Year Books and other recorded sources, more and more law was recorded (written down) and thus systematized.

> YOUTUBE – Battle of hastingsfirstnutcrackertheninclass andymycommentary10min6secs (http://www.youtube.com/watch?v=r2jQRza5GQ8) at robertwemersonufl.

2. The Common Law Today

Nowadays, the common law is found principally in English-speaking countries: the United Kingdom, the United States, Canada, Australia, New Zealand, and – to a lesser extent – India and some Asian, African and Caribbean nations colonized by the British.

Note that, in the United States, Oliver Wendell Holmes, Jr.'s The Common Law (1880) is, for most jurists, the most important book on American law, if not for all time, then certainly for the first 150 years of our national existence.

3. *Stare Decisis* (see pg. 9; Emerson BL) *[handwritten: decision made by the highest court]*

Stare decisis (Latin for "standing by the decision") is the common law doctrine that courts follow (abide by) the precedents.

> Without *stare decisis* and with all the power of judges to make law, there would be chaos.

It *is usually the wise policy, because in most matters it is more important that the applicable rule of law be settled than it be right. The Court bows to the lessons of experience and the force of better reasoning, recognizing that the process of trial and error, so fruitful in the physical sciences, is appropriate in the judicial function."* Louis Brandeis (Supreme Court Justice, 1916-39). Stare decisis binds all of the lower courts of a jurisdiction to determinations rendered by the highest court in that same jurisdiction. But the high court that issues a decision can itself change its mind, and – unless a decision is based on the national or state constitution – the legislature can overturn a court opinion via new legislation.

Reasons for *stare decisis* (following precedent) include:
(1) Guidance - no "reinventing the wheel" is necessary;
(2) Stability - people can rely on the law as presently stated; and
(3) Restraint - it is a method for restraining judges in a judge-made law system (thus avoiding idiosyncrasy).

However, if there is already a precedent, *stare decisis* may thwart potentially necessary changes in the law by restricting judges' abilities to alter it.

---

[16] Much legal jargon goes back to the Old French of Norman times, including the Royal Courts, who – for several centuries - heard cases only in French!

[17] The common law, as the great English legal commentator William Blackstone wrote, goes back to "time immemorial."

Overcoming *stare decisis* is rare. We hear about it because it is so unusual and often very important [e.g., *Brown v. Board of Education*, 347 U.S. 483 (the 1954 Supreme Court decision overturning "separate but equal" segregation of the races in the public schools)]. Arguments for overcoming *stare decisis* are: (1) changed times (e.g., business practices); (2) changed attitudes (society) and norms; (3) new technology and science; (4) error in the prior case; (5) conflicting precedents; and (6) changes in statutes.

> A risk of almost blindly following precedent is **stagnation**.

Much more likely than overturning precedent is a distinguishing of cases (to get around, but not directly overcome, a precedent). Common law seems to offer, compared to civil law, more room for argument- hence, more room for lawyers.

> PRECEDENT – or DISTINGUISHING A CASE
> The present case must be very similar to the earlier case that is supposedly a precedent. Otherwise, it is likely to be distinguishable.

4. Dicta

Another way to counter language in an opinion is to demonstrate that the language constitutes *dicta*. While holdings are propositions - along a decisional path of reasoning - that are actually decided (based upon the facts of the case, and leading to the judgment). Any other propositions in a case, if they are *not* holdings, are *dicta*.

Dictum is the singular form, while *dicta* – the typical usage – is plural. Note that there are two forms of word usage in a judicial decision – *ratio decidendi* are the words which constitute the reason for the decision. They may serve as precedent. *Obiter dicta* are the non-binding words – the explanation or commentary. Instead of saying *obiter dicta* (*obiter dictum* in the singular), judges and lawyers often simply shorten the term to *dicta*. So, if statements in a past judicial opinion concern a rule of law or legal proposition not necessarily involved nor essential to determination of the case in hand, these statements lack force of adjudication and are *dicta*. The commentary in an earlier decision may involve an issue briefed and argued by the parties in the current case, but if this commentary were not needed to resolve the current case, then, again, its use in a judicial opinion for the current case would be *dicta*.

Here are two typical examples of dicta:
(1) A court's discussion on how the case, if it involved different facts, might be decided (perhaps differently) by either that court or the court in another jurisdiction.
(2) A court's analysis of how a different set of rules, ones not applicable to the facts in this case, might call for a different decision.

5. Mandatory versus Persuasive Authority

Opinions from another state (another jurisdiction) furnish guidance, but not precedent. For example, courts in Florida are not bound by what a Georgia court did. They can adopt all or part of the Georgia decision, but the Florida courts do not have to do so. "Even if based upon identical facts, decisions of courts of other jurisdictions are no more than persuasive, and then only to the extent that their meaning is regarded as logical." *Gary v. Helmerich & Payne, Inc.*, 834 S.W.2d 579 (Tex. App. 1992).[18]

As for federal court holdings, a U.S. Supreme Court holding is binding on all other federal courts, as well as on state courts for purposes of federal constitutional or statutory interpretation. A federal court of appeals ruling is precedent for the federal courts within that circuit (e.g., the Court of Appeals for the 11th

---

[18] As stated above in discussing Blackstone, opinions of a federal court may be binding for other federal courts. The analysis can become quite complex, as one must consider the facts, the level of the court (district court, circuit court of appeals, supreme court), and the law to be decided.

Circuit issues holdings that federal district courts in Alabama, Florida, and Georgia must follow). Just as at the state trial court level, U.S. trial court opinions do not bind other trial courts, although they may be persuasive guidance.

See page 38 of Emerson BL for examples of national or state regulatory powers; pages 42, 43, 51 and 54 of Emerson BL concerning federal or state court jurisdiction; and pages 49-50 & 52-53 of Emerson BL for diagrams of the federal and state court systems.

6. Precedent, and Why Blackstone Matters More to American Law than to Other Common Law Systems

Common law focuses on precedents. Under that approach, judges look to past decisions in similar cases. The precedent must be from the same jurisdiction (e.g., state trial courts in Florida are bound by prior Florida state appeals court cases; a federal trial court may be bound by a federal appeals court holding).

Here is what it means to have a precedent binding a court – a prior court decision (case A) that binds a court in the same jurisdiction as it resolves a current dispute (case B): the case B court must follow the case A precedent if is "directly on point" when (1) the question resolved in case A is the same as that to be decided in case B, (2) the resolution of that question was necessary to decide case A; and (3) the significant facts of case A are also found in case B, with no important, additional different facts in case B. (So often the facts can be distinguished somehow, that the so-called precedent does not bind but is, at best, guidance.)

In any common law jurisdiction (e.g., a state or country), the line of cases that may be precedent go back to the holdings, court opinions, or other authoritative writings issued by judges or other governing officials with the power to rule (make law) for that society. So, while we may look to other nations, including their court decisions, for guidance, and while we have a common legal heritage with other English speakers that makes American law often tracking, or at least similar to, the laws of those other nations (e.g., England or Canada), we are not bound to follow those laws from outside our nation (unless we actually agreed to them, such as via a treaty).

But what of so-called precedents from long, long ago? William Blackstone's Commentaries on the Common Law (1769) is so important to the development of American law because it is the last overall statement of common law as it existed before the colonies broke away from England. James Madison, "Father of the Constitution" (1787), described Blackstone's work as "a book which is in every man's hand." When we became an independent nation, law was not created on a blank slate. We built upon the law as it existed in the colonies, taken from the British. Because Blackstone's work is the last, best summary of that law which we took from the British, it is authoritative in this country.

It is more popular, and useful, in the United States than in England, where more recent works superseded it. But, for the United States, Blackstone remained the best source of early American law – what we had taken from our English roots – at the time we split away from the Mother Country.[19] It is especially ironic that Blackstone's book was so important in America (but of quickly preceding import in England) in that Blackstone never visited America, took his cases from England – not the barbarians in the New World – and certainly never intended his book to be a guidepost for independent American judges to build their own, distinct common law system (separate from the English). English law in a relatively young system, the United States; that was especially so in earlier times such as throughout the 19th Century.

---

[19] The books in England after Blackstone contained cases from after our independence, and so had principles of law – while interesting and perhaps applicable to our system – were not a body of precedent (or close thereto), as were the cases in Blackstone's book.

III. PURPOSES OF LAW

Most nations have similar purposes for their legal systems, although emphases vary. The main purposes are justice (fairness), order, the influencing of conduct, honoring expectations, assisting compromises, and promoting equality.

> "A thousand policemen directing the traffic cannot tell you why you come or where you go." T. S. Eliot

> "We live in a society of laws. Why do you think I took you to all those Police Academy movies? For fun? Well, I didn't hear anybody laughing, did you?" Homer Simpson

A. Justice/Fairness

It is very important that most people agree with the law, that is, agree that the law is fair - otherwise, there will be tremendous problems in enforcing the law. We need a system in which the vast majority obey the law because they believe it is right to do so; therefore, we can concentrate our enforcement resources on the small percentage that break the law.[20] Tyranny (obedience to law only via fear) is far more costly than laws with a moral imprimatur. The collapse of communism in Eastern Europe and Russia may be an example of how a social, legal, and economic system divorced from moral support cannot be sustained.

> "Justice must not only be seen to be done. It must be seen to be believed." J.B. Morton (1893-1979).

In the legal systems found in many Arab and other Islamic countries, the legitimacy of the law lies not solely in its religious attachments but in its direct employment of common-sense concepts about persons, relationships, and consequences. Even the idea of justice accords with such an emphasis, for justice is said to reside not in equality but in equivalence - in the ability to place a person in context and to appraise the implications of his or her actions through conceptualizations that can be applied to anyone (yielding not the same result but the same mode of appraisal).

> "The love of justice is, in most men, nothing more than the fear of suffering injustice." François, Duc de la Rochefoucauld (1613-80), French writer, moralist. Sentences et Maximes Morales, no 78 (1678).

B. Order/Stability

> "Law is order, and good law is good order.... In all well-tempered governments there is nothing which should be more jealously maintained than the spirit of obedience to law, more especially in small matters; for transgression creeps in unperceived and at last ruins the state, just as the constant recurrence of

---

[20] Consider Prohibition in the 1920s. There, "the manufacture, sale, or transportation of intoxicating liquors within, the importation thereof into, or the exportation thereof from the United States and all territory subject to the jurisdiction thereof for beverage purposes" was prohibited in the United States. This was significantly ignored by many, and that led to the dramatic expansion of organized crime. Soon, the public came around to the abandonment of the great experiment, Prohibition, and the passage of the 21st Constitutional Amendment in 1933 effectively overturning the 18th Amendment for Prohibition that was ratified only 14 years earlier (and leaving laws restricting or prohibiting alcohol sales up to the states, where some localities may be "dry" (no sales permitted) or have "Blue Laws" banning or limiting sales on Sunday.

small expenses in time eat up a fortune."   Aristotle (384-322 B.C), Greek philosopher and teacher. POLITICS, <u>Book 5, Chapter 1</u>.

"All religions, laws, and moral and political systems are but necessary means to preserve social order." Ch'en Tu-Hsiu.

"Law and order exist for the purpose of establishing justice and when they fail in this purpose they become the dangerously structured dams that block the flow of social progress." Martin Luther King, Jr.

LAW AS ORDER: Escalus, Prince of Verona and embodiment of law-as-order -
<u>REBELLIOUS SUBJECTS</u>
"Rebellious subjects, enemies of peace, profaners of this neighbor-stained steel –
What, ho! You men, you beasts, that quench the fire of your pernicious rage
With purple fountains issuing from your veins,
On pain of torture, from those bloody hands
Throw your mistemper'd weapons to the ground,
And hear the sentence of your moved prince . . .
If ever you disturb our streets again
Your lives shall pay the forfeit of the peace."
THAT IS DIRECT LAW-GIVING: LAW AND ORDER.

C. Influencing Conduct

For example, tax law, via deductions and credits, affects business' and individuals' behavior. More specifically, the tax law encourages people to buy homes (the mortgage interest deduction) and may encourage businesses to manufacture in the United States (the domestic production activities deduction).
Law may not only cause people to change behavior, but also to internalize certain ideas. A major theme of law is to affect (mold) behavior, either beforehand (prevention) or afterwards (punishment).

D. Honoring Expectations

To support a law-abiding person's rightful hopes that others likewise will obey the law is for business an especially important purpose of law. For example, the law may offer rewards or punishment concerning the upholding or breaking of promises (No "weaseling out of a contract!").
The ability to honor expectations in business dealings contributes to market efficiency. Knowing that contract law gives people the right to compel enforcement of a contract should make it easier for businesses, employees, and consumers to act based on the deals that have been reached; the high degree of certainty makes the markets more efficient as both transaction costs and enforcement costs diminish.

E. Assisting Compromises

The legal system serves as an outlet for resolving disputes. The law provides a forum through legislatures and courts and other governmental agencies.

F. Promoting Equality

This is a relatively new notion in many societies.

Emphasis on different purposes <u>may differ from place to place, and from time to time</u>; but, overall, despite differences from culture to culture, all societies tend to agree that the law should be just, should be seen to be just, should provide order, and should uphold people's legitimate expectations.

An example is Singapore, with its emphasis on preventing vandalism and maintaining order (stability), and evidently less concern with a criminal suspect's or convict's rights; the legal system in the United States would have different emphases.

> The great French philosopher Voltaire (1694-1778) supposedly wrote, "I do not agree with what you have to say, but I'll defend to the death your right to say it." The equality of the law in the United States applies to everyone. For example, freedom of speech protects everyone's opinions, including those voiced by the few or those contrary to popular beliefs.

IV. CLASSIFICATIONS OF LAW

CLASSIFYING LAW THROUGH "DYADS": The Microscope Analogy: we sometimes can learn more about a subject by taking it out of context – with an artificial construct or viewpoint that is nonetheless necessary in order to understand more. The Law is a "seamless web." Dissecting it, dividing it into categories creates an artificial construct.

The analogy, in science, is to slicing and placing something under a slide, to be examined through a microscope. But this process - microscopic viewing/or categorizing of the law - helps us to learn.

A. Public/Private

<u>Public law</u> (<u>government, in its role as government</u> - representing society) involves relations <u>between people and their government;</u> it affects the interests of society as a whole; examples are administrative, constitutional, criminal, and tax law.

<u>Private law</u> involves <u>relations between persons (individuals or business entities)</u>. Examples include most of the areas discussed in this text - torts, contracts, corporations, agency, partnerships, and employment – as well as commercial paper, wills, trusts, estates, property, and family law.

In private law, the government provides a forum, a decision maker.
Generally, there is not as much governmental stake in private law compared to public law. The government's primary interest tends to be the maintaining of order via the resolution of problems (i.e., maintaining courts, enacting appropriate laws that govern procedures, correcting substantive/procedural law impediments to justice).

B. Criminal/Civil

The criminal/civil law distinction is distinguished from the code law/common law dichotomy. All systems (common law, Civil Law, or whatever) have both criminal law and civil law. <u>Criminal law encompasses wrongs prohibited by society;</u> <u>civil law</u> (noncriminal) law concerns <u>alleged wrongs between individuals or businesses (</u>lawsuits may be filed).[21]

---

[21] As you may recall, in October 1995, after a lengthy, highly publicized criminal trial, a California jury acquitted former football star O.J. Simpson for the June 1994 murders of his ex-wife Nicole Brown Simpson and her friend Ronald Goldman. In February 1997, in a California civil case, a jury unanimously found Simpson liable for the wrongful death of Ronald Goldman, battery against Ronald Goldman, and battery against Nicole Brown. Simpson was ordered to pay $33,500,000 in damages, although little of that has been paid.
In a totally different case over a decade later, Simpson was found guilty of numerous felonies arising from his leading a group of men who broke into a room at Las Vegas' Palace Station hotel-casino and took sports memorabilia at gunpoint.

Criminal Law and National Constitutions

In most systems, the main sources of law for criminal procedure are the constitution, legislation, and – at least for common law countries - case law. The constitution of South Africa is noteworthy because of its extensive and detailed list of principles and rules. This is in marked contrast to the U.S. system, where the vague, broad wording of constitutional amendments has been fleshed out by an extensive case law, especially U.S. Supreme Court holdings. It is these judicial opinions that, in effect, contain detailed rules.[22]

> *Joke*
> *Newcomer to town:* "I'm looking for a criminal lawyer. Got one here?"
> *Long-time resident of town:* "I'm sure we do. But we can't prove it on him!"

C. Statutory/Case

Statutory law is based on statutes (legislative enactments). Examples include some criminal, administrative, employment, labor, and commercial law (e.g., the UCC - Uniform Commercial Code).

Case law is based on court cases (whether interpreting prior cases or statutes, or both). Statute books may be annotated with notes about court decisions interpreting particular statutes.

> The book volumes, Florida Statutes Annotated, represents an interplay between statutory and case law.

The Civil law has systematic statutes. Our common law is essentially "pure" case law, but with statutes grafted on and altering/pruning the common law. Increasingly, common law nations have some areas that are governed partly, if not mainly by statutory law.

What Do Americans Know about the Common Law

Most Americans do not understand how the common law works. They know that there are three branches of government: Congress passes laws, the President enforces them, and the Judiciary interprets. But there is much more to it, of course.

The law is comprised of both statutes (laws passed by the legislature) and common law. Courts create the law when they decide cases, because lower courts are bound to follow appellate or supreme court rulings. This legal precedent can be overridden by statutes passed by the legislature, but courts are still free to interpret these statutes as narrowly or broadly as they deem fitting (although they usually follow certain standards of "statutory construction," meaning statutory interpretation).

Courts also may take into account abstract principles, ethics, morals, the concept of justice, and even precedent outside our judicial system. In fact, since the common law system began in England, countries colonized by England considered the English cases as valid precedent, and still do. I have read cases from the 1800's wherein the judge cites Roman law as the rationale for his holdings. This is rare, of course, but not unheard of.

There are large areas of law still only covered by common law, not by statutes. Sometimes statutes overriding common law are later repealed because they cause problems the common law avoided.

However, the most important thing to realize about all this is that the law as stated by the legislature is not really something you can rely on without an understanding of how courts will view it. The real law is the collection of decisions by the courts interpreting a statute, or stating the common law rules, because these are what dictate future decisions.

Convicted of all charges - criminal conspiracy, kidnapping, assault, robbery, and using a deadly weapon – Simpson was sentenced in December 2008 to 33 years imprisonment, with a minimum of nine years before becoming eligible for parole. Simpson thus is serving his sentence at the correctional center in Lovelock, Nevada.

[22] While many common law systems turn to a constitution for their penultimate law on crimes (Canada, South Africa, and the United States, for example), some nations, such as England and Israel, simply turn to statutes and court holdings; they have no constitution with a higher status than their regular legislation has.

D. Foreign/Domestic

Foreign laws are those outside of the relevant, lawful authority's borders (e.g., outside the state or national borders). If the matter is one of state law, then foreign law would be from another state or nation. If the matter concerns national law, then it would be the law of another nation.

Domestic law is law from within a lawful authority's borders – e.g., law from Florida for state law matters within Florida; U.S. (national) law for legal matters within the United States.

Comparative law compares the domestic laws of various nations. For purposes of comparison, the laws of nations in addition to those of the United States are frequently discussed in this book. Almost always, those laws – from England, France, Germany, China, India, Japan, Russia, Brazil or wherever – are provided as a comparative law approach.

The term "International law" is distinguishable from the term "comparative law." As stated in Emerson BL at page 709, international law govern relations, both public and private, between nations.

E. Federal/State

In this text, we study mainly state law. Although most of what we study is state law, generalizations can be made: (a) there are similarities between the states' laws - there is a *trend toward uniformity* (e.g., uniform law proposals or enactments, such as the UCC); and (b) Except for some states' rights decisions by the U.S. Supreme Court since 1995, more and more areas have been taken over, or at least increasingly influenced, by federal (national) law.[23] (And that trend toward national laws has continued, almost inexorably, since the beginning of our republic.[24])

1. Precursors to the Drafting of the Constitution (1787)

The Revolutionary War had nearly bankrupted the former colonies, and both credit and currency were almost worthless. The independent states quarreled fiercely over economic resources, such as oyster-harvesting rights in the Chesapeake Bay, and Congress had no effective power to keep the peace. The country was racked with large debts, with tariffs between states, with some states printing almost worthless paper money, and with Shays Rebellion by former Revolutionary soldiers demanding payment of what they had been promised.

The Articles of Confederation (1781) provided some federal authority on foreign affairs and on dealing with Native Americans (but not much else). Presidents had one-year terms and were chosen by Congress. Other than borrowing money or operating a postal service, the national government had no real power. There was no power over interstate or foreign commerce, over coining money, on taxes or duties, or on the creation of an army (no power to draft). There was no national court system and no executive power to enforce acts of Congress.

As in the U.N. General Assembly nowadays, the Confederation recognized sovereign states, each with one vote. Nine of thirteen votes were needed to pass any law, and all thirteen were needed to amend the Articles of Confederation.

The Articles contemplated a "firm league of friendship," but each state was to maintain its "sovereignty, freedom, and independence." The arrangement proved faulty. The only significant law in

---

[23] For example, in 1935, with the enactment of the National Labor Relations Act (also called the Wagner Act), the national government took over most areas of labor law from what previously had been almost entirely state law. The growth of national governmental power often relates to commercial matters (e.g., the Commerce Clause giving power to Congress under the Constitution's Article I, Section 8). Also, under the Constitution's Article VI, the supremacy clause clearly states that federal law (assuming it is, in fact, lawful – in compliance with the Constitution)) is above state law.

[24] There is still a reservoir of powers held by the states – state law on matters such as contracts, torts, agency, partnerships, marriage, and corporations.

those years was the Northwest Ordinance enacted in July 1787 (and reaffirmed by the new Congress in 1789).[25]

> **History and the Experimental Perspective**
>
> In the United States, there were 13 sovereign states before there was a federal government. In the aftermath of the American Revolution, thirteen colonies transformed into states independent from Britain; this was contemporaneous to or even predating any national government. Thus, it should be easy to see why (1) state governments retain some sovereignty, and (2) why – as much as some might prefer otherwise – states cannot simply be dissolved![26]
>
> Indeed, state sovereignty can be useful for effective governance and reform. Justice Louis D. Brandeis called the states in our federal system "laboratories of democracy." "Denial of the right to experiment may be fraught with serious consequences to the nation," Brandeis warned. "A single courageous state may, if its citizens choose, serve as a laboratory, and try novel social and economic experiments without risk to the rest of the country."[27]

2. State Constitutions

Just as the United States Constitution establishes the responsibilities and powers of the national government and guarantees basic freedoms, each state has its own constitution, which is its fundamental law. The state constitution establishes the basic framework of state government and addresses areas untouched in the federal Constitution, such as education, local finance, and voter qualifications. Each state constitution also includes provisions comparable to the Bill of Rights, protecting the basic rights of its citizens, and covers a variety of other matters.

The U.S. Supreme Court determines the scope of protections under the U.S. Constitution; likewise, a state's supreme court is the final arbiter of its constitution. A state cannot deprive citizens of federal rights, but it can extend protections beyond those in the federal document. In recent years, the Supreme Court has limited federal constitutional protections for criminal defendants, but some state courts have interpreted comparable clauses in their own constitutions to provide more extensive rights. The Supreme Court has no jurisdiction to review a state court's interpretation of its constitution as long as "the state court decision indicates clearly and expressly that it is alternatively based on bona fide separate, adequate, and independent grounds."[28]

State constitutions can be the basis of substantial rights unavailable under federal law.[29]

---

[25] Under the Ordinance, the Eastern states abandoned their claims to territory in what is now the Midwest and instead provided for admission of new states.

[26] Under a unitary system, states or other smaller governing units can be dissolved or rearranged, as was done in China in 1997 - ordering that the city of Chongqing split off from the populous province of Sichuan. In 2014, France's national government started a reconfiguration of the 22 regional governments into only 14 regions. This is because, in a unitary system the lesser units are simply tools for implementing the national plan of governance.

In a federalist system, the national government could not unilaterally make such changes among the lower units (although nominally federalist India could do so); that is because provinces or states also have their own limited sovereignty. Even if a vast majority of the U.S. citizenry, and of every other state, favored the elimination of, say, Alabama, that does not mean Alabama could be dissolved. Alabama has its own sovereignty, and - unless it agrees to self-annihilation – Alabama cannot be eliminated. (Of course, the really cruel comment might be, even if Alabama could be dissolved, and thereby divided among other states, who would want it? The author disassociates himself from such a sentiment, which could be extended toward any state in the Union by those who view it as a sacred duty to uphold a historic, political, cultural, or sports rivalry until the end of time!).

[27] *New State Ice Co. v. Liebmann*, 285 U.S. 262, 311 (1932) (Brandeis, dissenting).

[28] *Michigan v. Long*, 463 U.S. 1032, 1041 (1983).

[29] For example, in *Sheff v. O'Neill*, 678 A.2d 1267 (Conn. 1996), the Connecticut Supreme Court held that the state constitution required the integration of the school districts of Hartford and its suburbs. A year earlier, litigants in another

State courts may carve out, and some have done so (e.g., in California, New York and New Jersey), *state* constitutional rights above and beyond what the federal constitution guarantees to criminal defendants.

Although state constitutions are similar in function to the U.S. Constitution, in some ways they are quite different. The U.S. Constitution is a venerable, concise document (fewer than 7,500 words) that has been amended only 27 times since its ratification in 1789. All state constitutions are longer and almost all are newer (the average state constitution now in effect is just half as old as the U.S. Constitution).[30] Most state constitutions tend to be far longer and much more detailed than the federal constitution, and they are amended and revised regularly (an average of ten times as often as amending the U.S. Constitution). Nineteen states still operate under their original constitutions, but all of these nineteen (except for Alaska's fairly recently adopted constitution, effective in 1959) have been amended more than 90 times. It is far easier to put an amendment before the voters of a state than it is to seek approval by three-quarters of the states to amend the U.S. Constitution.[31]

Even wholesale revision is a simpler matter at the state level. Some states have had several constitutions in their history, with Louisiana's 11 constitutions taking the lead. Since 1960, ten states have adopted new constitutions. Many states have commissions that study constitutional issues and recommend needed changes, but the normal mode of revision is through a constitutional convention. A proposal to call a convention generally requires approval from the voters.

3. Jurisdictions

Jurisdictions are governments (with their courts) having the power to "Speak the Law" (as the word "jurisdiction" indicates). Nations have sovereignty: their own power-base. In a federal nation, states or provinces also have sovereign power. So federalism involves dual sovereignty – both National *and* Provincial (e.g., the 50 states in the United States, the 16 German states (called "Lander"), the 23 Swiss cantons, and the 10 Canadian provinces).[32]

Therefore, while some American areas are primarily state law or – at most – areas of shared federal-state jurisdiction (e.g., education, tort law, most areas of business regulation), there are some topics where federal law is exclusive (or nearly exclusive). A prime example of this federal exclusivity is foreign policy.

4. Confederacies and Unitary Systems

There has been some degradation of the nation-state.

In Europe, from Belgium to Denmark to France to Italy to Moldova to Russia to Serbia to Spain to Ukraine to the United Kingdom;

---

case before the same court had claimed that the state had an obligation under its constitution to provide indigent citizens with a minimal level of subsistence, but the court disagreed. *Moore v. Ganim*, 660 A.2d 742 (Conn. 1995). Both court opinions were extremely long, with vigorous dissents and discussions of various constitutional sources over 200 years old.

[30] The only two state constitutions older than the federal constitution, albeit with well over 100 amendments each, are Massachusetts' (1780) and New Hampshire's (1784).

[31] A popular vote is not even required in Delaware, where the constitution can be amended by the legislature.

[32] To a lesser extent than is the case for Canada, Switzerland, or the United States, the six Australian states have some sovereignty. To an even lesser extent, with comparatively more national power, there is some sovereignty in the 31 Mexican States, the 26 Brazilian states, and the 23 states in India. In other words, the division of powers is different between the National and State governments in different federalist countries. For example, while most American law is state law, the German Lander's (states') main legal powers concern just law enforcement and education; Germany's primary laws, including criminal, civil, family, labor, and tax laws, are federal laws.

in Asia from Azerbaijan to China to Cyprus to Georgia to India, to Indonesia, to Iran, to Iraq to Myanmar to Papua New Guinea to the Philippines to Syria to Turkey;

in Africa from the Congo Democratic Republic to Ethiopia to Morocco to Nigeria to Somalia to South Sudan to Sudan;

in North America from Canada to Mexico to Nicaragua to the United States; and

in South America from Argentina to Bolivia to Brazil to Colombia to Venezuela – many countries face the internal demands of sub-state (regional) nationalism and the external push of globalization, with the nation-state in the middle. Regions ask for more power, international organizations seek more authority, and the nation-state loses power in both directions. "Devolution" thus would place more power in super states (e.g., the EU, WTO, NAFTA), more in regional governments (e.g., provinces), and less in the middle - the nation-state (the UK, USA, etc.).

There are few <u>confederacy systems, in which state sovereignty is supreme over the nation's power</u>. One example, where the provincial powers are supreme over the larger group's authority, is the Commonwealth of Independent States, created in 1991. It is a grouping of former Soviet republics and includes Armenia, Belarus, Georgia, Russia, Turkmenistan and Ukraine.

On the other end of the governing spectrum are unitary systems, where all sovereignty rests with the national government. Unitary systems still are, by far, the most prevalent system worldwide. Most nations, such as China, France, and Japan, have a <u>unitary system</u> of government. There, it is just a matter of efficiency to devolve some powers on the states/local governments. Indeed, the people of these nations sometimes find it difficult to understand how a federal nation's national government might not have control over a matter of law, as it is under the purview of the local/provincial authorities.

Secession

The U.S. Civil War resolved not just the death of slavery, but also the outlawing of secession. Federalism involves state power; but it is not absolute – it does not, in the United States, permit secession. That is unlike the former Soviet Union and Yugoslavia, in which secession occurred, and perhaps Canada, in which secession of Quebec may occur (although it appears improbable – indeed, much less likely - than two decades ago).

pg 26 Ramon

F. Internal Checks and Balances
[Internal – within one sovereign power (e.g., a state government) as opposed to
External – between two different sovereign powers, usually at different levels
(e.g., national vs. provincial powers)]

Federal/state conflict is one check on power. This is a kind of external check in that, within a larger system, there are checks outside a sovereign's (i.e., a state's or national government's) power.

These checks, though, are internal – that is, within a particular sovereign government – between the branches within that one government (i.e., in that state government or that national government). The three branches are found in the states and in the U.S. government, with the latter exemplified below:

The Three Branches

Legislative	*Executive*	*Judicial*
(Congress)	**(President)**	**(Courts)**
House of Reps. & Senate	Executive Agencies	Supreme Court
make the laws	(e.g., U.S. Department of State)	Circuit Courts of Appeal
	enforces the laws	District Courts
		interpret the laws

There are checks and balances within the federal government (between branches of the federal government). For example, the President can veto bills passed by Congress and is responsible for selecting judges. And Congress (both the House of Representatives and the Senate acting together) may override the President's veto, conduct hearings and compel the attendance of executive branch witnesses, while the Senate decides whether to confirm judicial and high-level executive branch nominees. The judiciary may limit or invalidate Congressional statutes or Presidential actions, while Congress, in turn, can limit the scope of judicial review and increase the number of judges, including the number on the U.S. Supreme Court.

There are also checks and balances between governments and individuals. For example, the government is supposed to be restrained from conducting warrantless searches (4th Amendment), of barring certain types of speech or peaceful gatherings (1st Amendment), of compelling criminal defendants to testify 5th Amendment), of carrying out any sort of cruel or unusual punishment (8th Amendment) or violation of due process (5th or 14th Amendments). As examples from the other angle, the people cannot, simply via a majority vote (i.e., not a constitutional amendment), make the government support or undermine a particular religion (1st Amendment), take away the smaller states' right of equal representation in the U.S. Senate (1st Article), interfere with the tenure of federal judges (3rd Article), or secede from the Union (the Civil War).

The Bill of Rights

The most famous check on the government's power over the people is the Bill of Rights (**see pg. 32; Emerson BL**).

The Constitution drafted in the summer of 1787 was finalized and proposed for state ratification in September 1787. It had no Bill of Rights. An argument against including a Bill of Rights was that by spelling out some rights, other rights – if not specified – might be deemed to NOT exist (not be protected under the Constitution). However, in order to get enough states to ratify the Constitution, the Constitution's proponents relented and promised that the first Congress elected under a ratified Constitution would send to the states a proposed Bill of Rights.

After the Constitution came into effect in early 1789, the 1st Congress convened and in September of that year proposed a Bill of Rights (in the form of 12 recommended amendments). By 1791, the necessary number of states ratified 10 of the 12 proposed amendments. Thus, the Bill of Rights, as enacted, became the first ten amendments the Constitution.[33] In line with the argument about the risk of having a Bill of Rights (that it omits other rights), the 9th Amendment says that, even with the stating of some rights, other unstated rights may be present.

The protections in the 1st, 2nd, 4th, 5th, 6th, and 8th Amendments are almost entirely incorporated into the due process clause of the 14th Amendment which became part of the Constitution in 1868. Thus those provisions apply to the states as well as the national government.

Here are the Ten Amendments, as ratified:

1st: Congress shall make no law respecting an establishment of religion, or prohibiting the free exercise thereof; or abridging the freedom of speech, or of the press; or the right of the people peaceably to assemble, and to petition the Government for a redress of grievances.

2nd: A well regulated Militia, being necessary to the security of a free State, the right of the people to keep and bear Arms, shall not be infringed.

3rd: No Soldier shall, in time of peace be quartered in any house, without the consent of the Owner, nor in time of war, but in a manner to be prescribed by law.

4th: The right of the people to be secure in their persons, houses, papers, and effects, against unreasonable searches and seizures, shall not be violated, and no Warrants shall issue, but upon probable cause, supported by Oath or affirmation, and particularly describing the place to be searched, and the persons or things to be

---

[33] Only 17 more amendments – up through the 27th Amendment) have been ratified since 1791.

seized.

5th: No person shall be held to answer for a capital, or otherwise infamous crime, unless on a presentment or indictment of a Grand Jury, except in cases arising in the land or naval forces, or in the Militia, when in actual service in time of War or public danger; nor shall any person be subject for the same offence to be twice put in jeopardy of life or limb; nor shall be compelled in any criminal case to be a witness against himself, nor be deprived of life, liberty, or property, without due process of law; nor shall private property be taken for public use, without just compensation.

6th: In all criminal prosecutions, the accused shall enjoy the right to a speedy and public trial, by an impartial jury of the State and district wherein the crime shall have been committed, which district shall have been previously ascertained by law, and to be informed of the nature and cause of the accusation; to be confronted with the witnesses against him; to have compulsory process for obtaining witnesses in his favor, and to have the Assistance of Counsel for his defence.

7th: In suits at common law, where the value in controversy shall exceed twenty dollars, the right of trial by jury shall be preserved, and no fact tried by a jury, shall be otherwise re-examined in any Court of the United States, than according to the rules of the common law.

8th: Excessive bail shall not be required, nor excessive fines imposed, nor cruel and unusual punishments inflicted.

9th: The enumeration in the Constitution, of certain rights, shall not be construed to deny or disparage others retained by the people.

10th: The powers not delegated to the United States by the Constitution, nor prohibited by it to the States, are reserved to the States respectively, or to the people.

Comparative Law on Separation of Powers as well as Checks and Balances:
Many other systems - e.g., in parts of Africa and the Middle East, in China, and in the former Soviet Union - still have difficulty accepting the notion of an independent judiciary, one not controlled by the executive branch.

G. Procedural/Substantive (see pg. 11; Emerson BL)

The <u>Track and Field Example</u> - Emerson and the Hurdles.

Procedural Protections: The role of procedure is an honorable role (with both procedure and substance intersecting and having crucial roles to play). Substantive law cannot effectively be enforced and develop without procedure. Justice encompasses *both* concepts: substance *and* procedure.

Procedure versus substance
If you have to say one is more important, it would be substantive. One needs some substance- without it, the flawless following of procedure is pointless. Still, procedure is very important.

Which is more important - procedural or substantive law?

<u>Substantive law</u> is the law that defines legal relations, rights, and obligations.

Procedural law is a means of enforcing substantive law. Examples of procedural law include the rules for conducting litigation, such as discovery, and the rules of evidence for the trial itself. Attorneys, as alter egos for their clients, act for people who have insufficient information about the rules, the procedures. The client is entitled to act for himself, but has a lawyer do that because the lawyer knows the procedures, whether for litigation[34] or any number of other legal topics.[35] Otherwise, as the old saying goes, "He who represents himself has a fool for a client."

If the client knew the procedures, etc., then he/she might not need a lawyer. A criticism of the system is: Unnecessary complexity results in heightened transactional costs (e.g., paying lawyers) more than it does any genuine, systemic increase in fairness.

Without knowledge of procedure - one can end up shafted, by one's own ignorance. The convoluted nature of the law and legal procedure may cause too many difficulties and may compromise efficiency and fairness. Often one needs another person as one's lawyer, for objectivity and expertise.[36]

So, an efficient system sometimes makes things unfair on an individual level: Efficiency versus Justice? To seek absolute fairness in every case might require abandonment of procedural order and risk the anarchy of never knowing whether processes actually must be followed. Thus, sometimes a person with a substantively valid claim or defense may nonetheless lose because the system demands *procedural consistency* (e.g., adherence to the statute of limitations or to notions of *res judicata*). Indeed, if legal substance can be freely changed, then procedure itself is the law: it is what protects us.

Procedural law is a means of enforcing substantive law
We know this from UF, Gov't agencies (e.g., Motor Vehicles Admin.) - there are procedures that must be followed; and failure to do so puts substance at risk. E.g., failed to fill out a form, to get the right signature, to file something on time. Failed to do correct procedure--> sent back to the end of the line, or even (e.g., because of the Statute of Limitations) blown away!

But, at its core, procedure is – again – a necessary protection. Most of our fundamental rights may be considered procedural in nature (e.g., many of our constitutional rights).

Pursuing the Devil: The Law is our final, secular protection.
In Robert Bolt's magnificent play, "A Man for All Seasons," the great historic figure, Thomas More, loses his head because he is the only man in England who will not lie about sexual relations (not his own, but King Henry's VIII's). At one point, Sir Thomas hears his son-in-law assert that he would cut down every law in England to beat the devil. To which Sir Thomas objects.

From *A Man for All Seasons*
ALICE [More's wife, speaking of a man named Rich, who was a former servant of the More household] Arrest him!
MARGARET [More's daughter, and Roper's wife] Father, that man's bad.

---

[34] Litigators are able to cram substantive law into their brains and then – after a trial is over – flush it away. But the litigator keeps procedures (how to introduce evidence, and how to proceed) on his "hard drive" (to liken a litigator to a computer). So the substantive law can be compared to software (just there for the trial that a lawyer must handle, or for the test that a student must handle), while the "hardware" of procedural law is always around for the litigator to call upon: It is the litigator's knowledge of and facility with procedure that trial clients most desire and need.

[35] A lawyer may be needed not just for litigation, but also any number of matters, such as corporate law, administrative processes, and taxation.

[36] Without a lawyer, a layperson may be analogized to an athlete trying to play a game without knowing the rules of the sport. No matter how great the physical skills of the athlete, he/she can accomplish little without the intelligence to play the game with clever short-term tactics and a wise long-term strategy.

> MORE There is no law against that.
> ROPER There is! God's law!
> MORE Then God can arrest him.
> ROPER Sophistication upon sophistication!
> MORE No, sheer simplicity. The law, Roper, the law. I know what's legal, not what's right. And I'll stick to what's legal.
> ROPER Then you set man's law above God's!
> MORE No, far below; but let me draw your attention to a fact - I'm not God. The currents and eddies of right and wrong, which you find such plain sailing, I can't navigate. I'm no voyager. But in the thickets of the law, oh, there I'm a forester.
> ALICE (Exasperated, pointing after RICH) While you talk, he's gone!
> MORE And go he should, if he was the Devil himself, until he broke the law!
> ROPER So now you'd give the Devil benefit of law!
> MORE Yes. What would you do? Cut a great road through the law to get after the Devil?
> ROPER I'd cut down every law in England to do that!
> MORE (Roused and excited) Oh?

Comparative Law on the Exclusionary Rule (a criminal procedural matter)

In most systems, procedural sanctions, most notably exclusion of evidence or something similar ("nullite"), may apply when the police or other agencies have obtained evidence in an unlawful manner, whether via searches and seizures or via interrogation. In many of those systems, the rationale for sanctions is not deterrence of the police - preventing the police's unlawful conduct - as it is in the United States, but fairness of the proceedings: the safeguarding of integrity in the administration of justice. This integrity notion is found in, among other nations, Argentina, Canada, England and Wales, France, Germany, Italy, South Africa and - although less clearly - Russia. However, in some systems (e.g., China and Israel), only considerations of reliability determine whether evidence is admissible.

The U.S. system seems to be the most rigid system insofar as unlawfully obtained evidence must be excluded, and American courts have no discretion over whether somehow to admit the illegally obtained evidence. However, this total exclusion of evidence does not arise for all kinds of police misconduct, nor does it apply in all kinds of proceedings. For example, the American exclusionary rule does not apply in the grand jury or in deportation proceedings.

In other systems (elsewhere in the world), the court has some discretion whether or not to admit illegally obtained evidence, depending on the rules violated (e.g., France and Germany) or on considerations of fairness and integrity (e.g., Canada, England and Wales, and South Africa). Insofar as information is derived from evidence that was unlawfully obtained (this information the courts refer to as "fruits of the poisonous tree"), various systems differ considerably. In Argentina, Canada, and the United States, this secondary evidence ("fruits") is excluded in the same manner as primary evidence. In South Africa, the result depends on the nature of the illegality, whereas in Germany in principle secondary evidence is not excluded.

Another problem is whether evidence can only be excluded when it has been obtained in violation of a right of the accused ("standing"). While that approach is relevant in the U.S., Canada, and - in principle - Argentina, that approach is generally not the law in France and Germany (there, the defendant's "standing" is not necessary to exclude illegally obtained evidence).

> YOUTUBE – CriminalLawInterrogation_ComparativeLaw_andanOperaAria.wmv at robertwemersonufl (5mins53secs) - In a Foreign Land, a Nasty Interrogation and a Demand that the Accused Confess! (Special Guest Star: Opera singer, Pinar Dőnmez, of Turkey – music by Giuseppe Verdi)

> NOT JUST AT, BUT BEFORE TRIAL, ONE HAS RIGHTS (whether in civil or criminal cases). Discovery is one of those procedural rights.[37]

Technicalities or Fundamental Rights?

Many criminal law policy debates concern whether something is a "technicality" or a fundamental right. What is a use/abuse of provisions intended to protect not just criminal defendants, but all of us? We do not want innocent people to be incarcerated. Moreover, the constitutional and other protections are for all (even the guilty). The exclusionary rule (concerning searches, arrests, statements) restrains the authorities. It bars the use of evidence against the defendant that might otherwise be probative (useful and relevant and credible). The rule thus provides the authorities (e.g., police and prosecutors) with incentives to do their job properly. We want checks on the government (e.g., ordinarily no searches are allowed without warrants); we do Not want a police state. In a small percentage of cases, the exclusionary rule may, in effect, help a guilty party obtain a lesser punishment or even go free, but that is held to be the price we pay for upholding fundamental rights. Obviously, for such serious consequences to occur, (1) the rights being upheld genuinely should be fundamental, (2) the application of exclusionary rule principles, or the like, really must have a strong connection to upholding these fundamental rights, and (3) the "unhappy" outcome (freedom, reduced charges, another trial) for someone who seems guilty should be as rare as possible. In *United States v. Leon* (1984), the U.S. Supreme Court did establish a "good faith" exception for searches conducted with an invalid warrant.

"A search is not to be made legal by what it turns up."[38] But, in *Illinois v. Wardlow*, 528 U.S. 119 (2000), the U.S. Supreme Court held, 5-4 (Stevens, Souter, Ginsburg, and Breyer partly concurring and dissenting), that police may stop and question a person who fled at the sight of a law-enforcement officer. Chief Justice Rehnquist, writing for the Court, stated: "Nervous, evasive behavior is a pertinent factor in determining reasonable suspicion" to justify stopping and questioning a suspect. In this case, William "Sam" Wardlow fled after seeing Chicago police officers patrolling "an area known for heavy narcotics trafficking." When the officers conducted a pat-down search, they found a 38-caliber handgun and arrested Wardlow.

H. Constitutional Law
(as opposed to "lower" law such as *ordinary* case law or statutory law)

---

[37] Here is a *brief summary of some of what happens*:
Emerson, as a cop, is pacing and swinging his nightstick. He tells Pinar, who is on a stool:
"Young Lady, you are in a lot of trouble. You have NO right to stay silent. I am zee Assistant Deputy to the Deputy Assistant to the Associate Deputy Vice Minister of Justice for this Subprefect, and I ask you - Where do you think you are, Miss? America?!!
"We can hold you indefinitely. And don't tell me you need a lawyer. What you need is some common sense. now, and we won't have to beat it out of you! Ha ha ha. Only kidding."
"Seriously, you need to speak. Can't you say something? Tell us what happened."
"You have no choice. Right now I have - on my own authority - as Assistant Deputy to the Deputy Assistant to the Associate Deputy Vice Minister of Justice for this Subprefect, ordered a thorough search of your apartment and of your workstation. We'll plant, er, find, some evidence, you can be sure of that."
"Also, we'll make you answer both HERE and then later on the witness stand, assuming that you have a trial. AND if you continue to hesitate, we'll use that hesitation against you, also! So give me what I need to hear. Sing, woman, sing!"
Then there is a dimming of the lights as Pinar comes forward to sing. Emerson cries for joy to hear it all.
When Pinar is done, Emerson says, "My my, that's the most beautiful confession I've ever had the privilege to hear. " Then he shrugs his shoulders, puts Pinar in handcuffs, and leads her away, saying, "Guilty as charged. Come along."
[38] Robert H. Jackson, 1892-1954 (U.S. Supreme Court Justice, 1941-54).

The need for a more national system of governance was a driving concern behind the creation of the U.S. Constitution. A worry of the Founding Fathers was the need for a more centralized government than the extremely weak Articles of Confederation provided; on the other hand, though, the Founding Fathers knew that power can lead to despotism. So they tried to calibrate between insufficient power (leading to anarchy) and too much power (leading to tyranny).

1. Some Basic Information

a. Ignorance

A majority of adult Americans misunderstand many of the basic provisions of the nation's most important governmental document, according to numerous public surveys. Here is a sample of these misunderstandings –

On basic knowledge of the Constitution:
- Nearly half of the American public cannot identify the purpose of the original U.S. Constitution.
- Nearly 60% do not know what the Bill of Rights is.
- Nearly two-thirds of Americans mistakenly believe the Constitution establishes English as the national language.

On understanding of institutional authority:
- Nearly half of Americans mistakenly believe the President can suspend the Constitution in time of war or national emergency.
- Half of the public incorrectly say local schools may order a moment of silence for the purpose of prayer.
- Four in 10 Americans do not know the Supreme Court is the final authority on constitutional interpretation.
- An overwhelming majority mistakenly believe any important court case can be appealed from the state level to the U.S. Supreme Court.
- Less than one in five know who the current U.S. Chief Justice is.

YOUTUBE – administrative law compared to constitutional law4mins43secs (with a black robe, and a white wig, and a tricorner hat!) at robertwemersonufl

ADMINISTRATIVE LAW, ACCESS TO INFORMATION, AND CONSTITUTIONAL LAW

When people think about the Constitution, they often think of the founding fathers. They think of the history in which the Constitution was actually framed. And that is certainly an appropriate perspective, but it is certainly not the full perspective in terms of what our Constitution is today. For the Constitution is not simply a document that owes its origins to the late eighteenth century; it is much more than simply what this tri-cornered hat represents from colonial or early revolutionary times. The Constitution today is frankly most dependent upon present day persons in the law, most notably judges, hence the incredible judicial robe here, and the lovely wig (which is really more appropriate to the English than the American experience).

It is the judicial interpretation of the Constitution that is so important in terms of what the Constitution means presently. The Constitution is a living, breathing document, given its vitality by the interpretation people have given to it over the years. Yes, it has been amended, but most of the amending has not actually been through the formal process - the 27 amendments to date that have been added - but through the informal process of interpreting what the Constitution means through case law and through popular consensus.

Now, sometimes of course the Constitution is given short shrift. I recall a cartoon, which featured two politicians, and apparently they are doing something that is probably inappropriate and one of them turns to the other and says, "What's the Constitution between friends?" Or a cartoon that shows two men dressed in colonial garb and they are drafting our Constitution and one says to the other, "Look, we'll call it

[Handwritten note at top: 2 types of laws that cannot be passed by Congress or the states
① ex post facto – laws making criminal past action, that were not defined as criminal when they occurred
② bills of attainder – laws intended to single out an individual and/or punish him/her w/o benefit of a trial]

the Constitution but we'll leave a few loopholes." Well, any Constitution that is as short and as old as ours is dependent on, for vitality today, interpretation by people today. I wouldn't call them loopholes as much as simply necessary *openings* so that the Constitution can breathe, can give, can grow over time. And that is the role, not just of the judges, but of everybody that has any interest in our governing structure. So, in our system, judges have incredible power because they help to implement and inform us as to what the Constitution really means.

The other development that is of such significance is a little bit more recent. It is a 20th century development, and that is the incredible growth of administrative law. You can trace this back in some ways to the 1930s and the New Deal - certainly to the 1960s and the Great Society - legislation which created a host of administrative agencies, a host of programs at the federal and state level. The idea is to create an abundance of law and bureaucracy, in which a lot of the power wielding is no longer necessarily judges in robes but government officials creating and interpreting rules. And one of the biggest areas of real dispute in this burgeoning field of administrative law is the whole question of information. We are inundated with information; all of us are. How do we access that information, and who should have access to that information? And so there are all sorts of new rules, perspectives, case rulings, and the like in this area. It's just one example in the field of administrative law, which is an outgrowth, one might say, of constitutional law, which goes all the way back, but is still vital to us today, even though it goes back to the late 1700s.

2. Sources to Understand the Constitution

The most famous contemporaneous sources are the Federalist Papers, 85 essays written and published during the years 1787 and 1788 in several New York State newspapers in order to persuade New York voters to ratify the proposed constitution. The authors were Alexander Hamilton (about 52 of the essays), James Madison (about 28 essays), and John Jay (the remaining five).

Comparative Law: The British Do Not Have a Written Constitution

The United Kingdom, unlike the United States and most other nations, does not have a written constitution, yet it has a body of constitutional law. The courts there recognize three kinds of rules: statutory law, case law, and custom or constitutional convention. Statutory law, which comes from Parliament, is potentially limited in scope. That lack of a fixed constitutional protection convinced the founders of the United States that a written constitution was desirable.

British courts may not strike down statutes because of constitutional restrictions, as may U.S. courts. Nor is there official separation of powers in Britain; the courts in the United Kingdom cannot use constitutional custom to overrule parliamentary law. Also, by custom, the monarch cannot veto laws. So the legislative branch (Parliament) rules supreme.

In the United Kingdom, constitutional customs change over time, just as the United States Supreme Court at different times infers different standards from the Constitution, often reflecting changes in social values and economic realities. An interesting development is that membership in the European Union (EU) has brought to the UK the possibility that a British statute may be found unconstitutional, not because it violates a higher UK "law" but because it is counter to a higher law for the EU.

3. Debating the Constitution's Meaning: Slippery Slope Arguments –

For want of a nail the shoe was lost;
For want of a shoe the horse was lost;
And for want of a horse the rider was lost;
For the want of a rider the battle was lost;
For the want of the battle the kingdom was lost
And all for want of a horseshoe-nail

Benjamin Franklin, Poor Richard's Almanac (1758).

Franklin's phrasing may exemplify a **Slippery Slope Argument,** *an argument that an action apparently unobjectionable in itself would set in motion a train of events leading ultimately to an undesirable outcome.*[39] The metaphor portrays one on the edge of a slippery slope, where taking the first step down will inevitably cause sliding to the bottom. For example, it is sometimes argued that voluntary euthanasia should not be legalized because this will lead to killing unwanted people, e.g., the handicapped or elderly, against their will. Another example is the slippery-slope argument against gay marriage: that if we allow a man to marry a man (or a woman to marry a woman), then we will not be able to restrict marriage to two people; that is, a man could have several wives, or a woman several husbands, and a man or woman could even marry his or her dog.

In some versions of the slippery-slope argument, the argument aims to show that one should intervene to stop an ongoing train of events. For instance, it has been argued that suppressing a communist revolution in one country was necessary to prevent communism's spread throughout a whole region via the so-called domino effect.

Slippery slope arguments with dubious causal assumptions are often classed as fallacies under the general heading of "the fallacy of the false cause."

The slippery slope argument sometimes is called the *wedge argument*. Rhetoricians, politicians, and others disagree about the breadth of coverage for slippery slope arguments. Some people would restrict the term to arguments with evaluative conclusions, while others construe it more broadly so as to include other *sorites* arguments (arguments with several premises and one conclusion - a number of syllogisms, the conclusion of each being the premise of the next).

Here is another "Slippery Slope" Definition:
In order to show that a proposition, P, is unacceptable, a sequence of increasingly unacceptable events is shown to follow from P. A slippery slope is an illegitimate use of the "if-then" operator.
Examples:
1. If we pass laws against fully-automatic weapons, then it will not be long before we pass laws on all weapons, and then we will begin to restrict other rights, and finally we will end up living in a communist state. Thus, we should not ban fully-automatic weapons.
2. You should never gamble. Once you start gambling, you find it hard to stop. Soon you spend all of your money on gambling, and eventually you turn to crime to support your earnings.
3. If I make an exception for you, then I have to make an exception for everyone.
4. A Classic Example, concerning Nazis - Who did they come for? First, the Jews, then the Gypsies, then the Communists, then, etc. Finally, having never complained before, I had no real ground to stand on when the Nazis came for ME!

Proof to Refute Slippery Slopes: Identify the proposition P being refuted and identify the final event in the series of events. Then show that the final event (the end result of the sliding slope) need not occur as a consequence of P.

---

[39] Here is an example of the slippery slope argument in the form of a test question –
If Sam's mother lets him stay home from school one day because he wanted to go to a concert, Sam will then start skipping every day for other fun things. Then he will not graduate and will not go to college. He will become homeless and have to beg on the streets. If Sam's mother uses that scenario as reasoning for not letting him skip school that one day, she is engaged in:
a. Slippery Slope Argument
b. Legal Dicta
c. Self-Restraint Principle
d. Causal Chain of Proximate Events
e. Checks and Balances

The answer is "Slippery Slope Argument" – arguing against a policy or action because it may set in motion a train of events leading ultimately to an undesirable outcome.

Slippery slope arguments abound throughout constitutional case law. The slippery slope argument is that if one allows small incursions on liberty, that may start a slippery slope (slide) into the loss of larger liberties.[40] Note the Pessimistic nature of these arguments: that we cannot draw the lines, that we cannot make distinctions. Then we cannot establish any standards→ Anarchy?

On the other side: Majorities cannot always be trusted. Some poor choices lead, ultimately, to far worse scenarios.

Here is a "Slippery Slope" Notion: "I believe there are more instances of the abridgement of the freedom of the people by gradual and silent encroachments of those in power than by violent and sudden usurpations." James Madison ("Father of the Constitution"), 1788.

4. Amending the Constitution

Over the past two centuries, more than ten thousand proposed Constitutional amendments have been introduced in Congress.

There have been long stretches without formal amending of the Constitution - only 27 successful Amendments, and ten were in the Bill of Rights by 1791. So there have been only 17 Amendments in the last 225 years. No amendments were enacted from 1804 to 1865, only eight have been enacted since 1920 (with only one of those since 1972).

An interesting book, Richard B. Bernstein & Jerome Agel's AMENDING AMERICA (1995), discusses how, when, and why Americans have used the Constitution's Article V amending process and, more importantly, how - even without any formal revision - the Constitution constantly changes in the way that judges, lawmakers, and ordinary citizens interpret and apply it.[41] The book deals not just with the 27 formal changes (amendments) actually ratified and placed in the Constitution, but with the thousands of proposals that have failed.[42]

As a practical matter, the most common way to change the constitution is through judicial opinion. The Constitution could not have survived this long if we did not constantly recast the way we think about the meaning of those few pages of eighteenth-century parchment. This old document sends different signals to different generations, and often it is hotly debated within the same generation. The Civil War was fought by a North that saw the Constitution as an irrevocable contract between the American people and their self-created government and by a South that believed it to be the charter of a league of states, with any member free to leave. The Northern view won, and the victors' heirs subsequently re-imagined the Constitution as the charter of an industrial nation, a welfare state, a world power. Behind the literal reading of the text was, and is, a mobile, "unwritten" Constitution.

To understand this idea of change through interpretation, not formal amendment, let us consider how the Constitution is interpreted via a balancing of interests.

Imagine Three Drawings

1. Man supplicating before a table with a valentine-shaped rock on it.

2. The man goes to an open window, armed with the strength of a loyal servant and he jettisoned it out from the top window of a six-story apartment building.

---

[40] Analogies, besides sliding down a slope, are to the camel's nose getting into a tent (once the nose gets in, one cannot keep out the rest of the animal) or to a wedge (once the point gets into position, the rest surely follows).
[41] This is why Presidents want the opportunity to appoint new justices to the Supreme Court. They can leave a legacy through their selections that can significantly change our country's future.
[42] Two recent examples of the relatively few proposed amendments passed by Congress but not enacted by the necessary three-fourths of state legislatures are the Equal Rights Amendments (for equality based on sex) and the Washington, D.C. statehood amendment; both received too few supporters in the 1970s and 1980s.

3. Below is Priscilla Plaintiff, working and happy – a good potential claimant.

Consider how, for this example, the Constitution says, in the First Amendment, "Congress shall make *no law* respecting an establishment of religion, or respecting the free exercise thereof . . ." (emphasis added). However, the Constitution is almost never interpreted in absolute terms, even if the text's language appears to bar any exceptions. (Freedom of Religion – free exercise – although worded absolutely, is interpreted under a balancing test.)

The free exercise rights can be limited, by law. There is an old saying: "Your right to swing your arms, to punch your fists, ends somewhere between your fist and my nose!"

In *Reynolds v. United States*, 98 U.S. 145 (1879), the Court ruled that while laws "cannot interfere with mere religious beliefs and opinions, they may with practices." Therefore, the federal territorial law against bigamy could be applied to Mormons in the Utah territories. Likewise, in *Cantwell v. Connecticut*, 310 U.S. 296 (1940), Jehovah's witnesses were going door to door distributing religious materials and soliciting donations. Their defense against charges of unlawful solicitations was that it was their constitutional right to do so. The Supreme Court stated that the Free Exercise Clause "embraces two concepts-- freedom to believe and freedom to act. The first is absolute, but in the nature of things, the second cannot be."

So, some restrictions on the free exercise of religion approved by courts have been:
(1) the subjecting of children to medical treatment (e.g., inoculations), despite their parents' religious objections;
(2) requiring children to go to school, again despite religious objections;
(3) a ban on polygamy (*Reynolds v. United States*, 98 U.S. 145 (1878));
(4) restrictions on the use of a sacramental hallucinogen.[43]

A Review of Categories of Law, Via Six Examples is at pgs. 20-21; Emerson BL).

Law can be a whole series of above categories. In this text, we study mainly private, civil, state, domestic, case, substantive, "ordinary" – that is, lower than constitutional - law. Although unlikely to be at issue, a matter would be more likely to involve internal law checks and balance than external. And most
All examples involving foreign law are used for comparative purposes, not to discuss "international" law involving treaties or international conventions.

V. THEORIES OF LAW

> "But what according to you is a true philosopher?, he asked. He, I answered, who loves to contemplate truth. . . who is able to arrive at what remains ever constant. He who is capable of seeing the Whole is a philosopher; he who is not, is not." Plato (Raphael, <u>Initiation into the Philosophy</u> 1 (1999)).

Jurisprudence is the science or philosophy of law. Jurisprudence includes subjects such as philosophy, economics, psychology, religion, and sociology. Nearly any theory/inquiry can relate to law. Everyone, knowingly or not, tends to have a philosophy.

---

[43] In *Employment Division v. Smith,* 494 U.S. 872, (1990), the Supreme Court ruled that the *Free Exercise Clause* permits the State to prohibit sacramental peyote use. The Court ruled, "if prohibiting the exercise of religion… is not the object… but merely the incidental effect of a generally applicable and otherwise provision, the First Amendment has not been offended."
Therefore, the question may simply be: Was a prohibition targeting a specific religious group?

A. The Historical School

Here are some basic Historical School concepts:
- We build the law in increments, based upon experience.
- To understand law, one must understand history.
- A society's laws naturally derive from that society's past.
- In developing laws, we do not write upon a blank slate. We must deal with, work through, what was done already by prior courts, legislators, and the people generally.

"The law is the only profession which records its mistakes carefully, exactly as they occurred, and yet does not identify them as mistakes." Elliot Dunlap Smith.

The Historical School considers law as custom, tradition, what has gone before. Prominent proponents have included Germany's Friedrich Karl von Savigny (1779-1861) and the United States' Oliver Wendell Holmes, Jr. (1841-1935). The common law emphasis on precedent reinforces an historic approach to law.

The law seeks contradictory goals: stability and certainty (tradition) versus the need for change; there is dynamic tension between those forces.

"No written law has ever been more binding than unwritten custom supported by popular opinion." Carrie Chapman Catt (1859-1947) (American suffragist).

The following is a very famous statement about the law and how we must understand the past in order to understand our society, to know the law:

"The life of the law has not been logic; it has been experience. The felt necessities of the time, the prevalent moral and political theories, institutions of public policy, avowed unconscious, even the prejudices which men share with their fellow men, have had a good deal more to do than the syllogism in determining the rules by which men shall be governed."[44]

Holmes continued as follows, "The law embodies the story of a nation's development through many centuries, and it cannot be dealt with as if it contained only the axioms and corollaries of a book of mathematics. In order to know what it is we must know what it has been, and what it tends to become. We must alternately consult history and existing theories of legislation. But the most difficult labor will be to understand the combination of the two into new products at every stage. The substance of the law at any given time pretty nearly corresponds, so far as it goes, with what is then understood to be convenient; but its form and machinery, and the degree to which it is able to work out desired results, depend very much upon its past."[45]

As a judge, Holmes made the same point quite succinctly: *"Upon this point [what the case was all about] a page of history is worth a volume of logic."* New York Trust Co. v. Eisner, 256 U.S. 345, 349 (1921).

B. Utilitarianism

Bentham was a philosopher on law, politics, and economics. He founded utilitarianism.

---

[44] OLIVER WENDELL HOLMES, JR., THE COMMON LAW 37 (1880) (emphasis added).
[45] As Benjamin Cardozo (himself a great Supreme Court Justice) wrote of that passage – the famous opening passage in Holmes' work – "Here is the text to be unfolded. All that is to come will be development and commentary."

> John Stuart Mill refined and extended Bentham's ideas.

Utilitarianism's prominent proponents include Jeremy Bentham (1748-1832) and John Stuart Mill (1806-1873). A key utilitarian concept is THE GREATEST GOOD FOR THE GREATEST NUMBER (a Bentham notion).

Utilitarians believe that we should judge institutions, ideas, and actions based upon their *overall USEFULNESS*. We look at the impact on all affected persons, not just the individual decision makers; the latter would be "ethical egoism" - the theory that one should simply maximize one's own benefit (and "to hell with everyone else").

But how can one determine what is best for one, or for all? In looking at 100 people in a society, some people may feel that the key to a moral assessment of how these people are treated is not just how everyone, as a whole (or as a near-universal majority), is treated. The morality, instead, may rest as much on how the solitary individual is treated – particularly the one that is testing the patience and the good humor of the many. It is, for example, the teacher's or parent's discipline of and/or love for the one student, the one child, that communicates love for the others. It may be how you treat the one that reveals how you regard the ninety-nine, because everyone is ultimately a one. There is the Biblical parable of the lost sheep – the shepherd has 100 sheep, but, with 99 safe, focuses his energy on the one that is wayward.

English jurist James Fitzjames Stephen published "Liberty, Equality, Fraternity" in 1873 (the year John Stuart Mill died), still perhaps the best criticism of Mills' theories about liberty and society, as most prominently found in Mills' book, "On Liberty" (1859).

Utilitarianism and Sugar Imports: An Example

Laws restricting the importation of sugar into the United States make more expensive the sugar and products containing sugar sold in America. These laws greatly benefit a small number of U.S. sugar farmers and refiners.

Utilitarianism - the greatest good for the greatest number – would likely hold that these laws should be repealed. (Remember, though, that utilitarianism is not simply majority-rule. If the advantage to the minority is extremely great and the disadvantage to the majority is so small (perhaps infinitesimal), utilitarianism takes that into account and may find more useful and efficient the laws favoring a minority.)

Utilitarians helped lead to >>>> The Law and Economics School.

C. Law and Economics

Law and Economics' prominent proponents include Richard A. Posner, Ronald Coarse, and Gary Becker (all of "the Chicago school"). Its emphasis is on economic efficiency and market analysis.

This school concerns how law does incorporate or, if it does not, should incorporate economic efficiency, market analysis, and other economic matters. This school maintains that law cannot be evaluated in a vacuum. It should include economics. Proponents say, "Let us recognize economic reality: how markets behave." But watch out, others note: empirics can become imbued with normative notions.

The Law and Economics school holds, among other things, that lawmakers should apply and follow economic principles whenever practical, that one can almost always reduce a case or law to economic analysis. This school has had enormous influence in antitrust law, much influence for some aspects of tort law and administrative law, and some influence in many other topics.

Here is an example of the application of economics to law: In Gary S. Becker's Book, *The Economic Approach to Human Behavior* (1976), at pages 3-14, economist Becker asserts, under orthodox (neoclassical) economic theory, that people are rational, self-interested, and calculative. Becker broadly defines as an "economic" question any question that can be stated as a choice between rational alternatives.

Theories of Economics put forth the notion of a mythical, economically efficient person - people as "profit maximizers" (more concern with economic "efficiency" and utility). Similarly, law upholds the notion of the Hypothetical Reasonable Person (the "reasonable person" standard). However, economists and legal theorists can be wrong.[46] In the law, it is very difficult, usually, to get emotional or psychological satisfaction in a case. To make it worthwhile, generally there must be real compensation (e.g., money). Remember: in economics, the goal of a firm is to maximize profit, while the goal of an individual is to maximize utility.

But are people rational? Many studies indicate they are not. Suppose two people, who have not met before, have to split one day's average wage for that society. The offeror solely decides how much goes to himself/herself and how much to the other person (the respondent), who in turn decides whether to accept the division or to refuse it (have no money for either the offeror or the respondent). The respondents tended to offer between 35% and 40%, and to reject offers below 23%. Interestingly, this average varied across cultures: Spaniards offered the least (around 26%); Japanese offered the most (44%). The French had one of the highest thresholds for acceptance - most would reject offers of 30%. Most Germans, on the other hand, were willing to accept 10%.[47]

A broad definition of utility may encompass fairness. Alleged unfairness (in receiving the smaller portion of the money) might be viewed as *negative* utility. **Economists try to refute the above example by saying that we must attach an economic value ("utility," if you will) to revenge. That if it exceeds what I am willing to share with you, then the economically-wise approach (whether profit-maximizing or utility-maximizing) is to have the entire $10,000 sent back.**

Comparison to People Who Want to Sue or Defend a Lawsuit:
In the law, it is very difficult, usually, to get psychic satisfaction in a case. To make it worthwhile, generally there must be real money as compensation. In law, and in life: Know when to "play the game," and know when to quit.

Do not think these choices are entirely fanciful.
As a lawyer, I have had several clients/ potential clients whom I'd advise either to drop a matter or compromise, instead hire me. And then . . .

D. Positivism –
Positivism has had prominent proponents, including legal theorists such as John Austin (1790-1859), Hans Kelsen (1881-1973), and H.L.A. Hart (1907-1992). Positivism is who the State has **posited** (what it has stated, put forth); it is the command of a governing authority.
Austin said that positive law consists of three parts:
(1) A rule
(2) from a political superior to a political inferior
(3) with sanctions imposed if the rule is broken.

But positivism risks an emphasis on power.
Positivists believe that to go beyond the posited law (e.g., via a "supra-morality" used to override or otherwise change the stated law) is to risk idiosyncratic notions of justice, to have after-the-fact decisions which "muck up" the system by reducing its clarity - making it harder for people to understand the law and for government to enforce the law. Professor Andrei Marmor of the University of Chicago Law School argues that law is founded on constructive conventions, and that consequently moral values cannot

---

[46] P.J. O'Rourke, in "Eat the Rich: A Treatise on Economics," ATLANTIC MONTHLY, Sept. 1998, wrote this satire: "Microeconomics concerns things that economists are specifically wrong about, while macroeconomics concerns things that economics are wrong about generally. Or to be more technical, microeconomics is about money you don't have, and macroeconomics is about money the government is out of."
[47] *The Civilizing Effect of the Market*, WALL ST. J., Jan. 24, 2002, at A1, available at http://online.wsj.com/article/SB1011885700476777840.html.

determine what the law is. He further contends that many aspects of law and of moral values are metaphysically objective.[48]

1. "Functional" Law and Economics: A Bridge Between Stark Positivism and Interventionist Law and Economics

Originating in the public choice school of economics, *"functional" law and economics* stands as a bridge between the strictly positivist and normative approaches to law and economics. While the positive school emphasizes the inherent (naturally evolving) efficiency of legal rules and the normative school often views law as a solution to market failure and distributional inequality, functional law and economics recognizes the possibility for both market and legal failure. In other words, while economic forces sometimes lead to market failures, structural forces may limit the law's ability to remedy those failures on an issue-by-issue basis.

The functional approach uses economic tools to analyze market and legal behavior and create rules limiting the extent of any market or legal failures. These rules are meant to induce individuals to reveal their preferences in cases where collective choices are necessary, and to internalize the effects of their actions generally. This functional approach to law and economics focuses on social welfare maximization – and thus has an approach similar to utilitarianism.

2. A Red Traffic Signal, at 2:00 a.m. in Kansas: An Example

The light just stays red. How many students have been in a similar circumstance?
What if you go through the light?
What if you go before a judge? Do you win anything by arguing that the law in
these circumstances, has no moral standing? Very LIKELY NO.[49]

How many have gone through the light?
Some persons certainly believe that there is value in obeying law, just for sake of
obedience. They have put implied moral notions into positive law. It is moral to
obey the law generally even though in that particular case no moral framework.
"A law is a law is a law." It is good for society that we have some such persons
obeying the law (just as, maybe, it is good that we have persons disobey a law –
assuming, of course, that the law should be eradicated or at least reformed).

The morality of a violation may depend on the situation.

Is there a lawyer-like approach?

E. Natural Law
Natural Law's proponents declare that there is something "beyond" positive law.
Natural Law is controversial because, on rare occasions, natural law proponents believe that this absolute law may have to overturn positive law. Prominent Natural Law advocates have included numerous writers, such as Marcus Tullius Cicero in Ancient Rome (106-43 B.C.), St. Thomas Aquinas in the Middle Ages (1225?-1274), and Lon Fuller at Harvard Law School (20th Century). Aquinas taught that "the natural law is nothing other than the light of understanding placed in us by God; through it we know what we must do and what we must not do."

---

[48] ANDREI MARMOR, POSITIVE LAW AND OBJECTIVE VALUES (2001).
[49] Traffic Control devices are there for a reason, according to the UF Police Department. "[Let's say you come] to a stop light at University Avenue at three in the morning...You look both ways, see nothing and run the light. Would you consider that breaking the law?" THE INDEPENDENT ALLIGATOR, August 26, 1997, at 7. [The answer almost all judges would state, is: you have definitely violated the law.]

Here are two examples of natural law:

1. *"There is but one law for all, namely, that law which governs all law, the law of our Creator, the law of humanity, justice, equity - the law of nature, and of nations." Edmund Burke (English statesman, 1729-1797).*

2, William Lloyd Garrison, a prominent Massachusetts abolitionist, spoke in opposition to some of the U.S. posited law – specifically that part which permitted, indeed protected and even promoted, slavery. He once thundered, "The Constitution is a pact with Hell." Indeed, Garrison, in 1831, wrote this opening salvo in his abolitionist tract, "The Liberator": "That which is not just is not law."

So how might one define Natural Law? It is the theory that law arises from certain values or judgments that never change. These values or judgments come from an absolute source - God, reason, or nature - but humans can understand these values/judgments. Once discovered, these fundamental points of law overrule any contradictory positive law. As Cicero wrote over 2,000 years ago:

> *"Those who formulated wicked and unjust statutes for nations, thereby breaking their promises and agreements [to formulate laws for national preservation and for the citizens' safety, tranquility, and happiness], put into effect anything but `laws'. . . . [Just as the rules adopted by a band of robbers do not deserve to be called Laws; and an ignorant or unskillful man's prescribing of deadly poisons instead of healing drugs `cannot possibly be called physicians' prescriptions'] neither can an unjust statute be called a law - even though the nation has accepted it."*

Therefore, Natural Law involves: The moral, the just – "A Higher Law" Some Natural Law scholars believe that we must imbue the law with moral notions. Indeed, many, if not most, Natural Law philosophers would say that we need do no such thing – that the law inherently incorporates moral concepts. And all Natural Law proponents would agree: Certain fundamental notions are so correct, so universally true that it does not matter what the posited law is. Cicero put it this way:

> *"Law is the distinction between things just and unjust, made in agreement with that primal and most ancient of all things, Nature; and in conformity to Nature's standard are framed those human laws which inflict punishment upon the wicked but defend and protect the good. . . . The very definition of the term `law' inheres the idea and principle of choosing what is just and true."*

The French philosopher, Montesquieu (1689–1755), in his major work, The Spirit of the Laws (1748), and other works, contended that laws underlie all things human, natural, and divine. While Montesquieu conceded that the laws governing human nature are complex and often difficult to discern, he believed that empirical (experimental) investigative methods could help us discover and know those laws. Such knowledge then would ease the ills of society and improve life.

1. Natural Law Documents

Three documents evincing Natural Law concepts are: The United States' Declaration of Independence (1776); The French Declaration of the Rights of Man and of the Citizen (1789); and The United Nations' Universal Declaration of Human Rights (1948).

2. War Crimes and Divine Law

An example of Natural Law in action could be war crimes trials. For example, after World War II, the Nuremberg Trials took place in Germany. An underlying reason obviously was the invocation of "A Higher Law": That some conduct (e.g., genocide) is so beyond any sense of fairness and decency that it should be punishable at law.[50]

---

[50] A permanent international war crimes court was established in 2002 in the Dutch city of the Hague (although trials can occur elsewhere). As of July 30, 2015, 123 nations had ratified the 1998 treaty creating the court, with some of the nonratifying nations including China, India, Israel, Russia, and the United States. Very few nations in the Middle East or Asia have ratified the treaty, while essentially all of Europe and Latin America have done so.

Another example of Natural Law is the Divine Law principle propounded by John Locke (1632–1704). Locke believed that God had established divine law. This law could be discovered by reason, and to disobey it was morally wrong. Locke believed that people by nature had certain rights and duties. These rights included liberty, life, and ownership of property. And if a government failed to protect adequately the rights of its citizens, Locke declared that these citizens had the right to find other rulers. Locke's belief that the people should decide who governs them – a right under divine law – strongly influenced Thomas Jefferson's writing of the Declaration of Independence.

3. Duties, Rights, Egalitarianism, and Consequentialism: Kant, Rawls and Others

While not necessarily classified as Natural Lawyers, a number of philosophers have spoken about rights and duties in a focus that is morally-based and – at the very least – analogous to some Natural Law concepts.

German philosopher Immanuel Kant (1724-1804) had a duty-based (deontological) view of human conduct and ethics. To judge the propriety of actions, look at obligations, not just consequences: Duty (a categorical imperative) is more important than consequences. A concern about Kant's views is that they may justify a simplistic "duty for duty's sake."

Other philosophers, instead of speaking of duties, speak of consequences. Behaviors or approaches such as hedonism (does it taste good, feel good, and look good?!), egoism (a counter to Immanuel Kant's categorical imperative[51]), altruism, and utilitarianism are all closely connected to consequentialism (also called the teleological approach): the ends justify the means. (The emphasis is on the ultimate product – not worrying about the method to obtain the results.) In the extreme were certain 19th century German thinkers, such as Max Stirner. Stirner wrote: "No one is my equal, but I regard him, equally with all other beings, as my property." In Stirner's view, other people are objects in one's quest for the ultimate good, "total independence." This absolute stand is perhaps the opposite of Natural Law, which often is concerned about Duties, about Methods, and about overall Justice and Fairness.[52]

A modern, Harvard philosopher, John Rawls (1921-2002), one of the most important jurists of the 20th Century, had some duty-based ideas and a moral, natural law focus. (Note: the two neither naturally coincide nor are they necessarily opposites; however, most philosophy seems to result in a duties focus being in a different camp than is a moral focus.)

Rawls put forth a natural law idea concerning "original position": If each of us did not know what position we were starting from in society (if we thus operated from a "veil of ignorance") our race, sex, nationality, income, intelligence, physical abilities, occupation, wealth, etc. - what would we want the law to be? This starting point, the *original position*, is the viewpoint from which we judge the law. Risk-averse persons at the original position presumably would want strong legal protection for persons at a disadvantaged position: the better situated persons need less protection, and - perhaps more important - what

---

The approach used now is more solicitous of defendants than was the case for the Nuremberg trials, where former Nazi leaders chose lawyers from a list of German attorneys unschooled in the British and American legal procedures the court used; the Hague court lets defendants pick almost any lawyer they want.

[51] "Act only according to that maxim whereby you can at the same time will that it should become a universal law." Immanuel Kant.

[52] There certainly is no teleological approach when one speaks of a community, of moral standards derived from human connections. That may be at the heart of Natural Law.

> "All mankind is of one author, and is one volume; when one man dies, one chapter is not torn out of the book, but translated into a better language; and every chapter must be so translated.
> ... As therefore the bell that rings to a sermon, calls not upon the preacher only, but upon the congregation to come: so this bell calls us all: but how much more me, who am brought so near the door by this sickness. . . No man is an island, entire of itself . . . any man's death diminishes me, because I am involved in mankind; and therefore never send to know for whom the bell tolls; it tolls for thee."

John Donne (1572-1631), in *Devotions Upon Emergent Occasions, Meditation XVII.*

if one were to end up, upon entering society (from the original position), to be one of these disadvantaged people? Better have those legal protections in place![53]

According to Rawls, therefore, the two basic principles of justice are:

(1) Each person has an equal right to the most extensive scheme of equal basic liberties compatible with a similar scheme of liberties for all.
(2) Social and economic inequalities are to meet two conditions. They must be: (a) to the greatest expected benefit of the least advantaged, and (b) attached to offices and positions open to all under conditions of fair equality of opportunity.[54]

Rawls' and others' notions of fairness and equality are perhaps encapsulated in this statement of U.S. author James Baldwin (1924-1987) in "The Price of the Ticket" – NO NAME IN THE STREET (1972): "If one really wishes to know how justice is administered in a country, one does not question the policemen, the lawyers, the judges, or the protected members of the middle class. One goes to the unprotected—those, precisely, who need the law's protection most!—and listens to their testimony."

4. Natural Law in Action: Animal Rights

When an animal is lost, is it (a) the animal's right to be returned to its proper owner? Or is it (b) the owner's right to have the animal returned? In the last few centuries, the common law's answer could only be (b).

In our Western system of law, only humans - or things that humans have created - have any legal rights. People have rights, and corporations do, and infants, and the estates of dead persons, and even incompetents (e.g., the insane or intoxicated). But muskrats have no rights, unless we consent to give them some by declaring their homes "protected areas." Likewise, the trees in the forest have no rights. This stems from a completely anthropocentric view of the world: that it is here to be used by and for humans, such as to make money or to provide us sport. We may choose to protect certain places or animals, but that is our choice. It is not the places' or the animals' right or privilege.

The law, though, is always in flux. Animal rights may be a major development of 21st Century law. In 1972, three U.S. Supreme Court justices endorsed a remarkable concept: that "trees should have standing." Justice William O. Douglas (who served on the Court from 1939 to 1975) suggested that the courts adopt a rule "that allowed environmental issues to be litigated before…courts in the name of the inanimate object about to be despoiled, defaced, or invaded by roads and bulldozers…. Environmental objects [should be able] to sue for their own preservation."[55] As law professor Christopher D. Stone observed in his famous and influential essay, "Should Trees Have Standing?,"[56] such an idea is not outlandish: one hundred years earlier, women did not have standing, and neither did children. Now both do.

If environmental objects had recognizable rights, debate about the merits or demerits of exploring for oil in the Arctic National Wildlife Preserve would take on new meanings. So would controversies involving power lines, roads, coal mining, housing and resort developments, golf courses, and many other projects.

So, how far should the law go to compensate an owner for a pet's injury or death? What do you think is fair compensation for harm to a pet?

It is hard to generalize how much money is fair. If a pet owner was negligent and the dog leash broke causing the dog to run into the street, it is hard to blame a driver, unless perhaps he/she was driving

---

[53] This is why the defense gets to go last in trial. This is why prosecution must prove beyond a reasonable doubt in criminal trial. Still, even though defense counsel is guaranteed to all defendants, many question the quality of these attorneys. Are we giving those in disadvantaged positions adequate representation?

[54] John Rawls, "A Kantian Conception of Equality," CAMBRIDGE REV. 96 (Feb. 1975); JOHN RAWLS, A THEORY OF JUSTICE (1971), p. 83. (Rawls thus rejected utilitarianism because it might permit an unfair distribution of burdens and benefits.)

[55] *Sierra Club v. Morton*, 405 U.S. 727 (1973).

[56] 45 S. Cal. I., Rev. 2 (1972). Stone later expounded on the subject in a book.

drunk or speeding. In our case, we know the neighbor did not like Scooter, but he did not intentionally hurt the dog. Should the neighbor's feelings be included in the case? Because he did not directly act on his intention, so he would not be liable for the dog's death. (Contrast that with the case of *Propes v. Griffith*, where the defendant intentionally shot the plaintiff's dog and punitive damages were awarded.)

What if the pet served a functional purpose, by providing protection (a watchdog) or vision guidance (a Seeing Eye dog)? The value likely would increase. The pet's age or time with the family becomes a factor. Surely if a pet owner had the dog only one week versus ten years that makes a difference in the court's award. (However, an old dog would have a shorter life span remaining.) All of these factors play a role.

An Example of Positivism Versus Natural Law: The Scottish Man and the Stray Cats

Positivists - like others, can urge change in law (e.g., enact statutes), but no <u>ex post facto</u> laws (which would apply new law to past conduct).

For Natural Lawyers, the questions may be:
   a. How do you feel about cats?
   b. How immoral, how fundamentally wrong, was what the man did to the cats?
       Is it so vital that is must be seen as a higher law---> Natural Law?

Natural Law (one can sometimes go beyond posited law) or
Positive Law (one must find posited law on point for morality to have a <u>legal</u> impact)
To the positivists, if there is no positive law, then one cannot create other law. That would be too risky, especially with juries – risking idiosyncratic legal interpretation.

Transatlantic correspondence between Lon Fuller (Natural Lawyer) of Harvard Law School and H.L.A. Hart (Positivist) of Cambridge University) - these two most renowned scholars of their era debated what could be done to the Scottish man.

    Who has rights? Just people?

    Ulysses S. Grant: "The best way to get rid of a bad law is to enforce it"

Positivists - like others, can urge change in law (enact statutes), but no ex post facto law (**pg. 691; Emerson BL**) - cannot apply new law to past conduct.

F. Legal Realism

"The law, in its majestic equality, forbids the rich as well as the poor to sleep under bridges, to beg in the streets, and to steal bread."
Anatole France, CRANQUEBILLE

This philosophy started with American thinkers such as Karl Llewellyn of Columbia Law School (1893-1962) and John Dewey (1859 -1952).[57] It owes its origins to the idea of law (as expressed by John Dewey) as a means to serve social ends. In the 1920s and 1930s Legal Realism was a dynamic new theory - a novel approach to law, adjudication, and legal education.

Legal Realists believe that, to understand the law, one must go beyond the "Black-Letter Law" approach; one must understand the connection between people and the law. We have got to account for the way people really are – the way they really act and react.

---

[57] Dewey, an American educator and philosopher, led a philosophical movement called Pragmatism, which emphasized using intelligence and experimentation to bridge the gap between thought and action.

The great New York judge and jurist Benjamin Cardozo espoused Legal Realism when he wrote the following:

> Forces which they do not recognize and cannot name have been tugging at [judges] for their entire lives - inherited instincts, traditional beliefs, acquired conviction; and the result is an outlook on life, a conception of social needs. . . . In this mental background every problem finds its setting. We may try to see things as objectively as we please. Nonetheless, we can never see them with any eyes except our own. To that test they are all brought - a form of pleading or an act of parliament, the wrongs of paupers or the rights of princes, a village ordinance or a nation's charter.[58]

To understand and predict the law, Legal Realists believe that one must look to the players (how the rules are actually enforced), not just the rules themselves. So one should consider: (1) people's conditioning, training, and background; and (2) how the law is actually applied and enforced.

For example, there is discretion at every level of the criminal justice process. The police may target certain individuals or activities and overlook others, the prosecuting attorneys decide which arrests to pursue, and juries and judges have preconceived notions which influence how they approach a particular individual or allegation.

More generally, as the legal scholar Kenneth Culp Davis wrote in his seminal work, *Discretionary Justice: A Preliminary Inquiry* 20 (1969), "[P]erhaps the most significant twentieth-century change in the fundamentals of the legal system has been the tremendous growth of discretionary power."[59]

Legal Realists consider how human nature affects the creation and implementation of the law. Here is some Legal Realism reasoning: Reading the rules without reviewing or looking at the "players" is like reading about the beach without ever going to the beach - your "understanding" of the beach (the law) is rather limited.[60]

Legal Realism called into question three basic cherished ideas: (1) The notion that, in the United States, the people (not unelected judges) select the rules by which they are governed; (2) The conviction that the institution of judicial review reinforces rather than undermines representative democracy; and (3) The faith that ours is the government of laws, not of men.

Most schools of American legal theory which have developed since World War II have tried to meet the Legal Realism challenge: to somehow demonstrate that, if courts behave responsibly, adjudication can be reasonably constrained, the courts' role (judicial review) can be legitimate, the rule of law can be a reality, and justice can be secured.

A basic example of "legal realism" in action is the important role played by nonprofessionals (nonlegally trained people) in the legal system. Understanding their beliefs and actions within the legal system is an important way to evaluate the effectiveness and fairness of that system. We should look, for example, at people proceeding *pro se* (representing themselves) in lawsuits and – most importantly – at the jury: ordinary people ("laypersons") with an extraordinary role in the legal system.

1. Laypersons Generally

---

[58] BENJAMIN CARDOZO, THE NATURE OF THE JUDICIAL PROCESS 12-13 (1921).

[59] The judge's discretionary power is more readily acknowledged in common law nations than in Civil Law countries. However, the trend throughout the world tends to be toward greater freedom for judges to manage litigation (i.e., more discretion). *See* Burkhard Hess, "Judicial Discretion," in *Discretionary Power of the Judge: Limits and Control* (Marcel Storme & Burkhard Hess, eds. 2003).

[60] But legal realism can reach the point of absurdity: What the judge ate for breakfast, and whether the judge had an argument with his/her spouse, and whether a witness reminds the judge of someone he really likes (or detests!). Can these things really impact a judge? Certainly, but at some point judges presumably should be able to rise above these very superficial, possible impacts on their decision making. The process becomes extremely haphazard if even matters so peripheral and tangential to the case at hand are still to be considered to determine why a judge may have ruled the way he/she did.

A key to understanding the legal system is understanding the people in the system. Ordinary people have roles as parties (plaintiffs and defendants), witnesses, and jurors. A commonly raised complaint, by academics, judges, some lawyers and politicians, and – especially – by business interests and insurers, is that there are too many plaintiffs and too many lawsuits. In effect, the complaint is that too many people are somehow involved in the system in that some cases are brought that should never even have been raised, and that other cases get to trial that should have been settled long ago.

a. What to Wear?

There is an unofficial dress code for court, sometimes explicit, such as when jury notices tell men they are expected to wear a coat and tie (and, at least implicitly, tell women to dress nicely as well). For parties and witnesses, lawyers often go into some detail discussing all aspects of the trial process, including the roles of all the court personnel, the layout of the courtroom, and the types of attire and attitude expected from people attending court and perhaps testifying.

Of course, sometimes courts can go overboard. One Florida judge was disciplined for pulling out a baseball bat and threatening a badly attired party. And, in late August 1998, Florida's Hillsborough County Judge Elvin Martinez, then age 64, ordered a misdemeanor marijuana possession defendant to quit disobeying a bailiff who had told the defendant to button his shirt. Defendant Tony Arnette Cole, a landscaper and maintenance worker, said that he had not understood the bailiff's instruction. Cole was dressed in new sneakers, khaki pants, a tucked-in T-shirt, and an unbuttoned shirt worn over the T-shirt like a jacket. Later, Judge Martinez admitted that he overacted at the pretrial hearing when he told Cole's lawyer to remind Cole of the following: (1) that this was not a barroom or recreational hall, and (2) that in a courtroom the defendant's manner of dress should not include casting a T-shirt open "like him throwing his cojones at me, because I'll step down from here [the bench] and knock the hell out of him if he doesn't button that shirt."

b. Attractiveness Can Have an Effect on Trial Outcomes

Physically attractive clients have an advantage over others. As in other areas of life, jurors and judges often are psychologically predisposed to favor them, without even perhaps knowing it. The scholarly evidence is far from absolute, and one may need to also look at the relative attractiveness of the jurors or judges (not just the parties); for example, some studies show attractive people are harsher on the less attractive, while the less attractive jurors may not be predisposed to favor the more attractive. Furthermore, if a criminal defendant appears to have used his/her attractiveness to further himself in his wrongful conduct, that may actually magnify the likelihood of a conviction and a stiff sentence. Still, the evidence seems to be that – without anything else to differentiate two parties – it is generally better to be considered attractive.[61] Likewise, it is better to be a thin plaintiff, not an overweight one.[62]

2. A. Self-Representation

The Federal system and the U.S. states have constitutional provisions, statutes, rules, or court decisions that expressly or by interpretation permit self-representation (handling a matter *pro se* – for oneself). Someone's ability to proceed without an attorney in bringing or defending a lawsuit varies depending on the court and the positions of the parties. For example, normally corporations cannot be represented by non-attorneys, as the corporation is a "person" distinct from its officers and employees. Moreover, a nonattorney parent usually cannot sue on behalf of his/her child. Also, unless the executor of a dead person's estate is an attorney, he/she cannot represent himself in matters other than probate

---

[61] Sandie Taylor, *Can't be him your honour - he's gorgeous!* 13 Psychology Review (Issue 3), pp. 31-33 (2008).
[62] Trial consultants note that jurors have preconceived, negative perceptions about overweight and obese plaintiffs. Those prejudices can cost plaintiffs verdicts and decrease damages in personal injury cases. Even overweight jurors will tend to disfavor the overweight or obese party.

proceedings.

There are many *pro se* resources: local courts, which may offer limited self-help assistance; public interest groups that sponsor reforms and promotes self-help resources; and commercial services, which sell forms so that parties have formally correct documents. Self-help legal service providers must be careful to not give advice, in order to avoid "unauthorized practice of law" (which is nonlawyers giving legal advice). Every U.S. state has some forms available on-line for most common filings.

The percentage of matters handled *pro se* is no doubt large, but varies tremendously from state to state and type of proceeding. In 2010, approximately 26% of actions filed, 93% of prisoner petitions and 10.5% of non-prisoner petitions in federal court were filed by *pro se* litigants. Most of them probably go *pro se* because they think they cannot afford a lawyer, while a smaller number – perhaps 20% to 25% each - said they did not wish to spend money on lawyers or that they believed that their case was simple and thus an attorney was not needed. About half of the *pro se* proponents further feel that lawyers are more concerned with their own self-promotion than their client's best interest.

3. Jury Trials

A jury trial involves a *petit jury* (usually 12 or 6 members).[63] Many state trials have as few as six jurors, though many still have twelve. In Florida, there are six jurors, unless a capital crime or eminent domain is involved; then there are twelve.[64]

Numbers for Criminal Trials

For criminal trials involving felony charges, a vast majority of states has 12 jurors and requires a unanimous decision. Exceptions from the 12-juror standard only arise for cases where the death penalty is not possible, and they only are found in about five states: six-person juries for non-death penalty cases in Connecticut, Florida, and certain lower Massachusetts courts; and, in Arizona and Utah, eight-person juries. Oregon only requires agreement of 10 out of the 12 jurors, as long as it is not a murder case. Louisiana likewise only requires 10 out of 12 jurors for a non-death penalty case. And Puerto Rico only requires 9 jurors out of 12 to agree upon a conviction, whether for felonies or misdemeanors.

For misdemeanor criminal cases, about half of the states only require 6 jurors: Arizona, Colorado, Connecticut, Florida, Georgia, Idaho, Indiana, Iowa (for non-serious misdemeanor cases), Kansas, Louisiana, Minnesota, Mississippi, New Hampshire, Oklahoma, Oregon, Utah (just four jurors for less serious cases), Wisconsin, and Wyoming; some states have 12 jurors for their highest level trial court and six jurors for lower trial courts – Alaska, Kentucky, Massachusetts, Michigan, Montana, Nebraska, Nevada, New Mexico, New York, South Carolina, Texas, Washington, and West Virginia. Ohio has eight jurors for misdemeanor cases, and Virginia has seven jurors. The rest of the states – about half - have 12 jurors. Almost all states still require a unanimous decision, with Oregon being the only exception for six-person juries – requiring only five out of six jurors to agree.

Numbers for Civil Trials

For civil cases, a small majority of the states have 6-person juries, with most of the rest using 12 jurors. Only Alabama, Arkansas, Missouri, New Hampshire, Tennessee, and Vermont require twelve jurors for all civil cases, with California, Hawaii, Louisiana, North Carolina, Pennsylvania, and South Dakota providing for twelve civil trial jurors unless the parties agree to a lesser number. Iowa, Maine, Ohio, and Utah have eight jurors for civil trials. The rest of the states thus have six jurors for many or perhaps all civil

---

[63] At English (and then American) common law, the number of jurors was 12; in Scotland, the number remains 15.
[64] Federal and state trials often have one or two alternate jurors who also sit in a case and only help decide a verdict if a regular juror has been removed or otherwise cannot participate in jury deliberations. These alternates usually are not told their status until the trial is over (perhaps so they will take their job seriously!), and it thus may look as if a trial has one or two more jurors sitting in on a case (e.g., seven jurors at a Florida trial) than is actually needed.

jury trials (otherwise, they usually have 12 jurors). Three Western states – Montana, Nevada, and Utah – even permit civil trials with as few as four jurors.

Puerto Rico does not have juries for civil trials.

> A 2004 ABA-sponsored poll found that 75% of Americans said they would prefer to be judged by a jury than by a judge.

The petit jury decides whether the defendant is guilty in criminal cases or is liable in civil cases; in most state courts, the jury's decision must be unanimous.[65] Unanimity is required for all federal jury verdicts, in any criminal or civil case. All federal criminal cases heard by a jury are before twelve jurors, and six jurors decide civil jury trials unless a twelve-member panel is demanded. About six percent of all jury trials end in a hung jury.[66] The result is no verdict, and the case may, but need not, be retried.

Businesses and lawyers must know their audience: How will things play? A long discussion, let alone a diatribe (a bitter and abusive criticism or denunciation) is quite unusual for a verdict. Indeed, that may even make the verdict more susceptible to an appeal. Usually the jury just says "guilty" or "not guilty" (in criminal law) or "liable" or "not liable" (in civil cases) and perhaps it specifies damages amounts (in civil cases). The judge can poll the jurors individually, but that is it. It is very difficult to find the reasoning behind the jury's decision.

But it is in the United States, where the <u>right</u> to a jury, and the actual use of juries, is so common.

> ### Vikings and other origins of trial by jury
> Danes, Norwegians, and Swedes (collectively known as Norsemen or Vikings) harried the coasts of their neighbors from the 8th to the 11th centuries. They occasionally took large expeditions inland! These Vikings attacked and sometimes settled in places from Ireland, Iceland, Greenland and (briefly) North America in the West to Russia and the Caspian Sea in the East, and from the Arctic Circle in the North to the Mediterranean Sea and North Africa in the South. Their influence extended throughout almost all of Europe, including, most importantly for our study of law, England.
> Throughout the 9th and 10th centuries almost half of present-day England was ruled by Scandinavians, with fantastic names such as Ivar the Boneless and Eric Bloodaxe, in what was called the **Danelaw** (in effect, land ruled by the laws of the Danes – i.e., the Vikings). Most of the rest was held by Anglo-Saxon rulers such as the leader whose army stopped the Vikings' advancement in the 870s, Alfred the Great (king of Wessex, 871 to 899).
> As the new millennium (after the year 1000) dawned, the Anglo-Saxons and the Norsemen continued to fight for dominance in England, and the Scandinavian cultural and legal hegemony reached its zenith with the rule of King Canute the Great (king of all England from 1016 to his death in 1035, with an empire that also included Canute's native Denmark, neighboring Norway, and part of Sweden). It was only with the rise of the Norman French rulers of England, starting with William the Conqueror (king of England

---

[65] For all civil jury trials, Alabama, Colorado, Connecticut, Delaware, the District of Columbia, Florida, Georgia, Illinois, Indiana, Maryland, New Hampshire, North Dakota, Oklahoma, Rhode Island, South Carolina, Tennessee, Vermont, Virginia, West Virginia, and Wyoming require unanimity. The other 31 states permit civil jury trial verdicts to be reached by a majority vote of two-thirds, three-fourths, five-sixth, or seven-eighths of the jurors, depending on the state and the size of the jury.

[66] In a 2002 study of hung juries, the National Center for State Courts found that complex cases, ambiguous evidence, poor advocacy and jurors' perceptions of unfairness often played a role in failed deliberations. But the typical hung jury is not an 11-to-1 split. Jurors tend to view a hung jury as a failure, so the inability to reach a verdict usually occurs, if at all, when the juries are split more evenly and individual jurors do not feel outnumbered.

> from 1066 to 1087) and his successors, that the British Isles became decreasingly tied to Scandinavia and more aligned - culturally, linguistically, and legally - with western Europe, especially France.

Jury use in the United States compared to other nations is typically more common than in other countries with juries, even England (which uses juries, in effect, only for some criminal cases). In fact, most countries do not even have a jury system. However, most Civil Law nations use "lay" judges – citizens who hear evidence, have access to the dossier, and vote along with the professional judges. And some Civil Law nations – e.g., Germany, Italy and Russia - use juries in some types of criminal cases.

Still, in the United States, jury trials tend to be much rarer than judge (non-jury) trials. On average, about 93% of state court cases are dismissed or settled before trial, 6% go to a trial by judge, and only 1% are tried before a jury. (That is an average – some states with a much higher percentage of civil cases going to trial are Indiana (20%, with 19% before a judge, 1% before a jury), Texas (14.5% - 11.5% judge, 3% with jury), Massachusetts (13.5% - 12% judge, 1.5% jury) and Pennsylvania (12.5% - 8% judge, 4.5% jury); and two places with a relatively large percentage of trials going before a jury are South Dakota (7% of cases go to trial, with 6% going before a jury and only 1% before a judge) and Washington, D.C. (just 0.5% of its cases going to a trial, but almost all of those cases going before a jury). *Source: National Center for State Courts.*

Juries are not favored in the rules. A reason is that jury trials take more time (thus, cost more) than do nonjury trials. A study published in 2004 found that, in the 75 most populous counties of the United States, a bench (nonjury) or jury disposition affected the length of time in trial. Jury trials lasted 4.3 days on average compared to 1.9 days for bench trials, and the longest jury trial recorded in the sample of 12,000 trials lasted 70 days, while the longest bench trial was just 18 days long.[67]

It is very difficult to overturn jury verdicts; Judges cannot do so based solely on emotions, on a different reading of the evidence - it has to be fraud, bribery, or a completely erroneous (completely irrational) interpretation of the law. For example, suppose that during the midst of a lengthy jury deliberation a juror for a criminal case cries out, with both anguish and anger, "We've been cooped up in this place for four days; no way are we gonna let him go scot-free!" As outrageous as that statement is, it is just one statement in the long decision making process and – by itself (assuming that the statement is even reported to lawyers or the judge) probably is *not* grounds for successfully appealing a conviction.

Do juries run amok? Studies indicate that such behavior is quite rare. For example, Elizabeth McNaughey of the Manhattan Institute studied 3,750 cases (Holy Cow! That's a high number!). She determined that judges would have decided a case differently than the jury did in only about 2% of the cases; also, even for those 2%, judges usually would have conceded that the jury had a reasonable basis for doing what it did (it is just that the judge disagrees on its findings of fact). The vast majority of American judges

---

[67] U.S. Department of Justice, Office of Justice Programs, Bureau of Justice Statistics, CIVIL TRIAL CASES AND VERDICTS IN LARGE COUNTIES, 2001 (published in 2004), http://bjs.ojp.usdoj.gov/content/pub/pdf/ctcvlc01.pdf.

evidently support the jury system.[68] Indeed, some studies contradict conventional wisdom and seem to indicate that juries may be less pro-plaintiff than judges operating without a jury (bench trials).[69]

Little can be done to a jury that may have made a wrong decision. One cannot do much to overcome a jury verdict simply because one feels that the jury "messed up" (unless there was outrageous behavior, such as bribery of jurors).[70]

> In *Young*, Queen's Bench 324 (England 1995), Stephen Young had been convicted of murder. On appeal, Young's lawyers told the court they had received anonymous information from another juror about a séance in the hotel where the jury was sequestered the night before it found Young guilty of shooting newlyweds Harry and Nicola Fuller. At the séance, three jurors drank "too much alcohol" while the spirit of Harry Fuller appeared in a hotel room and spelled out his killer's name via a Ouija board.
>
> The 12 jurors went on to convict Young unanimously. Young's lawyers argued that the séance showed that the jurors did not reach their verdict solely on the basis of evidence in court.
>
> The appeals court decided that the matter could not be written off as "merely a drunken game." A retrial was ordered, and the defendant was again found guilty (presumably with no séance this time).[71]

As long as the instructions and the verdict format are okay, it is very hard to overturn a verdict.[72]

---

[68] So do lawyers, especially plaintiffs' attorneys. Indeed, the author has known some lawyers with such strong (extreme?) faith in juries that at trial they, on occasion, purposely make a mistake (against their own client!) because they are so confident that these mistakes will be obvious to at least a few bright, attentive jurors. The "purposely mistaken" lawyer is convinced that these attentive jurors will certainly make sure to "correct" the mistake for purposes of jury deliberations (e.g., place a decimal figure in the correct column, so as to not deprive the lawyer's client in the calculations of damages). Moreover, what the lawyer really seeks is, in effect, to enlist the attentive juror as a kind of self-appointed advocate for his/her client. In the jury chambers, perhaps the juror will take up the cause of the client, consciously or unconsciously driven by a concern that the lawyer's client is represented by a nincompoop ("what an obvious mistake that lawyer made!") and that somebody (i.e., the juror) needs to help even things out – to help that client! "My gosh! I gotta help that person; his lawyer's a fool!"

[69] A 2004 study of 12,000 civil cases in the 75 most populous counties of the United States finds that, among other things, plaintiffs won more often in bench trials (65%) than in jury trials (53%), http://bjs.ojp.usdoj.gov/content/pub/pdf/ctcvlc01.pdf

[70] The tradition in the United States and elsewhere (e.g., under the United Kingdom's Contempt of Court Act 1981), is that it is inappropriate to force the disclosure of details concerning a jury's deliberations. So, even if a jury allegedly decided matters by tossing a coin or drawing lots, the court may do nothing about it. But if jurors come forward, of their own volition, most American judges would undertake an inquiry and – in egregious cases - consider ordering a new trial.

[71] Information about these and other Ouija cases can be found at http://www.museumoftalkingboards.com/stories.html

[72] Here is an example of how mistakes about who serves on a jury may not be grounds for overturning a verdict.

In Miami, in September 1999, a teenager who was convicted of first-degree murder sought a new trial because the wrong man was sitting in the jury box. Twelve jurors had been selected from a pool of fifty for the trial of Travis James, charged with a 1997 shooting death and summoned to the courtroom o Circuit Judge Daniel True Andrews. At the end of voir dire, when a bailiff called for the juror named "Burns," Fred Burtz misunderstood and stepped up to perform his civic duty. The real Robert Burns apparently didn't hear (or saw Burtz step forward and quietly said to himself, "Alleluia!"). Burtz, a supermarket produce clerk, sat through the entire four-day trial that ended September 2, 1999; Burtz even served as foreman and signed his own name to the verdict form.

Only after 19-year-old James had been sentenced to life in prison, shackled, handcuffed and hauled away as his family sobbed did anybody realize that the jury foreman was not supposed to be on the panel. No one recalled any similar incident in the courts.

As jurors were addressed by name during the proceedings, court officials decided Burtz must have thought court officials simply were mispronouncing his name when they called him "Burns." At a September 7, 1999 hearing defense attorney Kayo Morgan argued for a mistrial, while prosecutor Ken Padowitz contended the jury's verdict should stand: "You're entitled to 12 people on your jury. Not 12 names. We had 12 people."

A few days later Judge Andrews decided that the conviction should stand. His decision was upheld on appeal. That Burtz served on the jury was a mistake, but the defense had a chance to see who was on the jury and never objected

A jury verdict may be internally inconsistent (based on what the jurors believed), but as long as it is not externally contradictory (with obvious contradictions in the jury's reported findings), then it is very difficult to challenge successfully.[73] Individual jurors, of course, can get in trouble for wrongful behavior, such as lying during voir dire, or violating a judge's orders, or taking a bribe. The usual remedy for noncriminal misbehavior is typically limited to dismissal from a jury.[74]

The Sleeping Juror

What would you do, if you were the judge, in dealing with this, perhaps the most mistaken juror ever? At a rape trial in Snaresbrook (U.K.) county court, on an unusually warm and sultry day, a juror fell asleep just as the prosecutor started to question the alleged victim. "Would you," the prosecutor asked, "tell the court precisely what the defendant said to you before the attack?" She declined to do so on the grounds that what the defendant said "was far too crude and shocking."

The prosecutor then asked, "Would you be prepared to write it down?" And she did, with every sign of distaste (it was, broadly speaking, a promise that nothing in the history of sexual congress compared with what the rapist planned to do to his victim). The paper was passed to the judge, then to the prosecutor and defense counsel, then to the clerk of the court, and – finally – to the jury. In the second row of the jury box, the sleeping juror slumbered on until he was suddenly woken by a sharp nudge from the smiling brunette juror next to him. She passed the note to him. He read the message thereon, gazed in wonder at his neighbor, read it again, winked at the woman, and slipped the note in his pocket. When the judge demanded the note back, the juror refused. It was, he said, "a private matter." STEPHEN PILE, BOOK OF HEROIC FAILURES (1979).

States are trying to make jury duty less onerous: one trial and out, so that there is usually just one or two days of service. More jurors are being called, but for less time. (Courts are trying to move away from the cynical view, sometimes found in popular culture, where, say, a judge bangs his/her gavel, looks down at the defendant, and says: "The prison cells are full. Therefore, I'm sentencing you to six months of jury duty!")

Although, by far, the summons for jury trial most commonly arrives by mail and gives prospective jurors some time to prepare, courts may use other methods to obtain jurors. To avoid declaring a mistrial for lack of jurors, courts throughout the United States, especially rural courts, have periodically authorized deputies to obtain a fill-in, last-minute juror, known as a *talis* juror (from a Latin phrase meaning bystander). Deputies have summoned people in stores (Wal-Mart seems to be a favorite), along sidewalks, and in other public locales.

Originally, talis jurors were plucked from the courtroom itself. Now the best source for fill-in jurors is outside the courtroom. Unless a prospective juror has a very good reason why he/she could not serve right then as a possible juror (and thus persuades the deputy not to hand him/her a summons), then he/she is summoned and goes – with the deputy – off to court!

---

until after the trial, when it saw the actual juror names. The mistake simply was not serious enough to overturn the jury's verdict.

[73] Can authorities arrest the entire jury? With jurors, no matter how stupid, there is no personal liability for a "bad" decision. As a group, juries do not face legal consequences for their decisions (as opposed to individual jurors getting in trouble for taking bribes, lying about their bias/knowledge in a case, or other transgressions). One apparently unique case of collective jury responsibility certainly was an extremely odd matter. In Los Angeles, during the Prohibition Era a jury that had heard a bootlegging case was itself put on trial after it drank the evidence. The jurors argued in their defense that they had simply been sampling the evidence to determine whether or not it contained alcohol, which they determined it did. However, because they consumed the evidence, the defendant charged with bootlegging had to be acquitted. N.Y. Times, Jan. 7, 1928.

4. Empanelling a Jury: Voir Dire

If you are called, you must respond.

> Voir Dire Answers
> *Judge: Is there any reason you could not serve as a juror in this case?*
> *Potential Juror: I don't want to be away from my job that long.*
> *Judge: Can't they do without you at work?*
> *Potential Juror: Yes, but I don't want them to know it.*

a. Origins and Processes

The original idea for juries was that jurors often were also witnesses - people with information about the parties and the facts. In the last few centuries, the idea has reversed: except in extreme cases (in which everyone has heard or read something about the case), jurors are not to have any specific knowledge about the facts of a case, nor have any knowledge or feelings about the parties or their lawyers. The present approach is thus to emphasize no knowledge about the case or – at the very least – no bias: the ability to disregard what one has heard or read and restrict a holding to the evidence submitted at trial.

The process of empanelling a jury involves written questionnaires and oral questions from judges and lawyers.[75] All states require that jurors must be U.S. citizens. To derive the master list for calling potential jurors, almost all states use voter registration lists, with most states also using driver license registrations and a few states supplementing with other lists, such as utility customer lists (AL, CA, ID, IA, and WI), tax rolls (AL, CT, HI, ID, IN, NJ, NY, PA, TN, VA, WV, and WI), motor vehicle registration (AL and ID), customer mailing lists (CA), city/county directories (CO, IN, PA, and VA), telephone directories (CA, IN, PA, VA, and WI), motor vehicle registration (AL, IN, and RI), unemployment and welfare lists (NY and WI), actual voters (ND), chauffeurs licenses (WV), state issued non-driver's license identification cards (IL, KS, ME, MI), high school graduates (WI), volunteers (FL, ME, NY, OK, PA, and VT), numbered resident files (MA), homestead rebate filers (NJ), and other lists approved by the state supreme court (AZ, ID, MA, ND, OR) or other authorities such as a board of jury commissioners (CT, DE, GA, IA, LA, MD, NV, SC, TN, and VA).

> Voir dire is a jury selection process in which the judge and the lawyers question potential jurors **(see generally pg. 72; Emerson BL).**
>
> Confessions or Inadvertent Admissions: In Court, the former is <u>extremely</u> rare and the latter is uncommon. But jurors, preconditioned by popular culture, may very much expect, or at least want, those confessions or admissions.
>
> Jury instructions - errors here are significant grounds for appeal. Via court rulings on evidence, initial instructions to the jury, and occasionally subsequent instructions (after jury deliberations began), judges try to have juries follow the law and render justice. Infrequently, instead of accepting the jury's ruling, a judge may instead issue further instructions or otherwise continue the proceedings. For example, the judge may issue a partial verdict (dismissal of the jury for some purposes; holding it together - refusing to dismiss the jury - for other purposes). This may be seen as better than simply accepting a verdict, rejecting a verdict, or having no verdict at all (a hung jury).

---

[75] The federal courts and a majority of states conduct voir dire with attorneys and judges asking questions, but a small minority only allow attorneys (Connecticut, North Carolina, Texas, and Wyoming) or only allow judges (Arizona and Delaware) to conduct voir dire. In California, Illinois, Massachusetts, and New Jersey, judges conduct voir dire but may permit lawyers to participate.

> race or sex as a basis for a peremptory challenge is unconstitutional

b. Driver's Licenses, Voter's Registration Lists, and Felons

For summoning jurors, many states, including Florida in 1998, have switched from voter registration rolls to the driver's license list (or now use both, not just the voter rolls). Legislators hoped to expand the overall jury pool and boost voter registration among people who would not register to avoid jury duty. They also saw it as a way to make juries more representative of their communities.

But there are some problems with the switch. Even though more people are called in, fewer people show up for jury duty. Prosecutors tend to dislike, while defense attorneys like, the new list because they deem it a more "pro-defendant" sample. The theory is that many more people in those larger jury pools have had negative encounters with law enforcement officers and are less likely to believe their testimony. Prosecutors even fear that some jurors may have an "agenda" against the state and are not looking at the evidence in the case but are making decisions based on their own past interactions with the legal system.

An ongoing political and public policy battle over who could be jurors (whether in civil or criminal trials) involves the criminal justice system. People cannot serve on a jury if they are felons and their civil rights have not been restored, are under prosecution for any crime, do not live in the county where the jury is being picked, or are not a U.S. citizen. In many states, civil rights are restored (namely, the rights to vote and to serve on a jury) as soon as a felon is released from jail, while – on the other end of the spectrum – some states do not restore voting rights (and potential jury service) to felons, even upon their relapse from jail or completion of any parole, unless they apply for and receive from the state government that restoration.

Typically, when called for possible jury service, potential jurors are informed of the restrictions on jury eligibility, are asked if they fall under these restrictions when they come into court, and are again questioned by attorneys during jury selection. Because some people fail to give the required information, prosecutors will frequently run criminal background checks to prevent convicted felons from ending up on a jury.

c. Empanelling: Challenges and Jury Consultants

Judges or attorneys do not pick a jury; instead, they just eliminate some potential jurors and arrive at a process whereby jurors remain (generally are randomly determined from the group of non-removed people). Voir dire (old French, "to speak the truth") answers not only tell us whether someone should be removed from the panel of potential jurors, but the answers also tell us information, give us clues, about people who should serve on the jury.

> Voir dire also is important in criminal cases. There, too, it may be revealing.
> One Too Many Questions
> In February 1989, this exchange took place in the courtroom of Michael T. McSpadden, presiding judge of the 209th District Court in Houston, Texas.
> The defense lawyers in a criminal case wanted to show that the witness had been coached by the prosecutor as to the location of the different parties in the courtroom.
> The defense lawyer pointed at the prosecutor and asked, "Do you know what his job is?"
> "Yes, sir," said the witness. "He's a lawyer."
> "And do you know my job?"
> "Yes, sir, you're also an attorney."
> "And do you know his job?" the defense lawyer asked, pointing at the defendant.
> "I guess he's the criminal"

The jury selection/elimination process involves social sciences, demographic data - information on each potential juror's income, race, religion, political registration, credit status, neighborhood, job, etc. Jury consultants work in cooperation with a lawyer during jury selection, during the actual trial, and possibly post-trial as a reviewer of the lawyer's effectiveness with a jury. They advise lawyers on how to dress, sit, walk, and talk as well as what kind of car to drive to the courtroom. Many complain that this approach is too much like show business, where form and style are more important than substance.

Similarly, businesses may advertise to counter the poor publicity arising from lawsuits against them. Not incidentally, the advertising reaches potential jurors and perhaps interferes with the right of plaintiffs to fair trials. So the overall battle is the defendant's First Amendment free speech rights versus a plaintiff's constitutional right to a fair trial (impartial jurors).

"For Cause" challenges of potential jurors are based on contentions such as bias. Lawyers must have some proof, some basis for asserting "bias." It is not enough simply for a lawyer to say, "I looked in the prospective juror's eyes and didn't like what I saw," or "Excuse him, Your Honor - he works for an insurance company (and we're the plaintiffs)."

To make a "for cause" challenge one needs much more than a "gut feeling" or speculation about possible bias.[76] But, for example, close relations are sufficient to excuse a potential juror "for cause." A potential juror who is best friends with, or a relative of, or otherwise close to a case's lawyer, party or witness is ordinarily subject to a "for cause" challenge.

Each party has a limited number of peremptory challenges, where specific reasons for seeking a potential juror's exclusion from a jury panel need not be provided. Most states allow numerous peremptory challenges for capital punishment murder cases (a median average of twelve peremptory challenges each for the defense and for the prosecution) and about half that number in less serious felony cases (a median average of six peremptory challenges each for the state and the defense). A small number of states allow more challenges for the defense than for the prosecution; otherwise, the number is the same for the state and the defense. For misdemeanor charges and civil cases, state jury trials have a median average of either three or four peremptory challenges each for the defense and, also, for the prosecution.

In Florida, each side has ten peremptory challenges in cases where a death penalty or life imprisonment is possible, with six each for any other felony case and three for each side in misdemeanor or civil cases. For federal courts, each side has 20 peremptory challenges for death penalty cases; in other felony cases, the prosecution has six peremptory challenges and the defense has ten; in misdemeanor cases and civil matters each party has three peremptory challenges.

Peremptory challenges of potential jurors can be undertaken without giving reasons. However, citing the Constitution's 14th Amendment (specifically, the Equal Protection Clause), the U.S. Supreme Court has imposed severe restrictions on peremptory challenges based on race (*Batson v. Kennedy*, 476 U.S. 79 (1986)) or sex (*J.E.B. v. Alabama ex. rel. T.B.*, 511 U.S. 127 (1994)); if the opposing party convinces the judge(s) that racial or gender considerations motivated the other side's exclusion of a potential juror, then a judgment can be overturned.[77]

An approach to evaluating peremptory challenges is *comparative analysis*. Look at the transcript from the voir dire and compare, for example, the blacks kept off the jury with the

---

[76] Judges, though, sometimes simply dismiss potential jurors before the lawyers even ask for a removal from the jury pool. For example, here is a case of what Memphis, Tennessee criminal defense attorney Leslie Ballin called "the jury pool from hell" (featuring sex, drugs and bias). On January 10, 2005, the prospective jurors were summoned to hear a case of trailer park violence, with a woman accused of hitting her brother's girlfriend in the face with a brick. Right after voir dire began, one man got up and left, announcing, "I'm on morphine and I'm higher than a kite." (Although the judge certainly could have ordered the man to remain seated, apparently the judge decided that the man's departure was a good idea.) Then, when the prosecutor asked if anyone had been convicted of a crime, a prospective juror said that he had been arrested and taken to a mental hospital after he almost shot his nephew. He claimed to have been provoked because his nephew just would not come out from under the bed. A third would-be juror said he had had alcohol problems and was arrested for soliciting sex from an undercover officer: "I should have known something was up; she had all her teeth." And a fourth potential juror volunteered that he probably should not be on the jury: "In my neighborhood, everyone knows that if you get Mr. Ballin [as your lawyer], you're probably guilty." He was not included among the empanelled. (Does it signify anything that all four of those excused "prospects" were male?) Ballin's client was found not guilty.

[77] Some judges - including Justice Stephen Breyer – have argued for eliminating peremptory challenges entirely and only permitting "for cause" challenges.

whites who were seated. Look for the similarity, or not, in these potential jurors' responses. "If a prosecutor's proffered reason for striking a black panelist applies just as well to an otherwise similar nonblack who is permitted to serve," Justice Souter wrote for the majority in *Miller-El v. Dretke*, 545 U.S. 231 (2005), "that is evidence tending to prove purposeful discrimination." The California Supreme Court, in effect, bans such comparative analysis, while the 9th U.S. Circuit Court of Appeals in San Francisco allows it. A future U.S. Supreme Court may have to decide whether such analysis must be used to test the legitimacy of peremptory challenges allegedly based on sex or gender discrimination.

> Note: Courts are less concerned about peremptory challenges for other reasons, such as the religion or national origin of potential jurors. Also, the Constitution's Sixth Amendment does not require representative juries, but simply requires impartial juries.

5. Expanded Functions of Juries

Few states outright ban juror note-taking or expressly permit jurors to take notes during trials.

The fear has been that while taking notes a juror may lose track of what is presently happening at the trial. Of even greater concern is that the juror and perhaps other jurors will refer to the notes rather than to more reliable sources, such as a transcript of the testimony (but rules, such as in Mississippi, often prevent that by allowing note-taking but barring jurors from bringing them to the jury deliberations).

However, proponents contend that note-taking jurors feel more engaged, are more likely to be attentive to the trial, and actually take rather accurate notes.

Some states (Arizona, California, Colorado, Massachusetts, New Jersey, Ohio, and South Carolina) now allow jurors to question witnesses. Ordinarily, the judge consults with both parties' lawyers before deciding whether to pose to a witness a juror-suggested question (and screen and edit even those questions they allow). Still, jurors must not carry out their own investigation of the facts. And jurors making online posts during trials is a new problem that is increasingly being punished.

6. Jury Nullification

At many points in American history, juries have refused to convict even when a defendant's actions are unquestionably unlawful; the jury refused to convict because it apparently believed that the law was unjust. That is known as jury nullification. Although most jury instructions explicitly prohibit jury nullification, there is a burgeoning jury nullification movement. For example, the Fully Informed Jury Association, with 6,000 members, encourages jurors to act according to their own moral code and to veto unjust laws. While still a small proportion of jurors, these nullifying jurors are growing in number. Some judges and lawyers even believe that the growth of jury nullification poses a strong threat to the American court system.

A study 30 years ago indicated that a 5% hung jury rate is the norm. But that figure has, in recent years, doubled or even quadrupled, depending on the location (e.g., some California state courts report a higher than 20% hung jury ratio; and federal criminal cases in Washington, D.C. averaged 15% hung juries in 1996, three times the rate in 1991). Experts believe that the increase in hung juries stems less from differences over the evidence than over the law itself - whether the law that a defendant violated is a fair law. Indeed, a Decision Quest/National Law Journal poll in October 1998 found that three out of four Americans eligible to serve on a jury say they would act on their own beliefs of right and wrong regardless of legal instructions from a judge.

Cases often leading to jury nullification include drug possession charges, cases with convictions leading to stiff mandatory sentences, and ones in which African-American jurors believe that "social justice" demands the acquittal of a factually guilty black defendant. That is an approach advocated by George Washington University Law Professor Paul Butler.

Few trial judges have publicly voiced concerns about jury nullification for fear that doing so would give the movement legitimacy or would appear to tread on jurors' independence. Two ways to counter nullification are: (1) permit non-unanimous verdicts, and (2) spend even more time in voir dire trying to weed out jurors who would use their jury service to protest laws or otherwise make a statement.

On November 5, 2002, South Dakota residents voted by a three-to-one margin against Constitutional Amendment A, which proposed to allow criminal defendants to challenge the merits, validity and applicability of the law which the defendant allegedly broke, including the sentencing laws for any violation. Libertarian organizations especially, but also some liberal and conservative groups, supported the amendment. South Dakota officials, lawyers, candidates for attorney-general, and the legal community generally opposed the amendment and said that it invited anarchy.

> Jurors' rationales for nullification may fall into four categories: (1) the law is unjust; (2) an otherwise fair law is being unfairly applied in a particular case; (3) the prosecutors engaged in misconduct; and (4) the jurors are biased in favor of the accused person or against the prosecutor. Only the last category definitely contravenes the rule of law.

G. A Classic Example to Consider Legal Philosophies:
Regina v. Dudley and Stephens, *Queen's Bench 61 (England 1884)*
("Regina" is Latin for Queen)

Four men waited for rescue in a lifeboat after the yacht, the *Mignonette,* which they were transporting from England to Australia, sank in the South Atlantic: Captain Thomas Dudley, First-Mate Edwin Stephens, a third experienced seaman named Edmund Brooks, and cabin-boy Richard Parker. Horror happens!

Various legal theories could apply to the Dudley and Stephens case.

1. Positivism -
    Laws against murder
    No self-defense, even if failure to kill means all die. Parker had not placed their lives in danger. (For example, Parker was not trying to sink the boat, nor throw out water or food, or come after others with a knife).

2. Utilitarianism
    All of us die vs. just one die
    The boy was the sickest, so least likely to live anyway.
    The death with the least harmful impact – Parker was just a teenager; he had no dependents.

3. Economics and Law
    Supply and Demand?   Optimal Time   Earning Potential

4. Natural Law
    "Thou shalt not kill"
    Murder? What of extreme circumstances?
    Not a fair way of deciding. Two persons make self-serving determination that a third should die. Why Not Draw Lots?

What would you do? Judges themselves acknowledge extreme circumstances -- but hold you to a high, noble standard -- matter of Honor and Duty. The Law sets a standard.]

Any other defenses? E.g., malnutrition leading to insanity?
No insanity defense was raised.

> Legal Realism
> > Victorian England – attitudes. Lower Classes vs. Upper Classes
> > The Lower Classes-see a legal system; run by the upper class (upper-crust barristers and judges); lower class men sometimes pressed into Naval Service.

"Necessity" was argued as a defense: that a situation posed such an overwhelming urgency that a person was permitted to break the law; that the response was justified as necessary. The defense is almost exclusively satisfactory when the response is relatively minor compared to the emergency itself (e.g., driving over the speed limit to reach medical care; damaging property in order to escape a flood, fire or some other natural catastrophe).

From the Court's Opinion:

To preserve one's life is generally speaking a duty, but it may be the plainest and the highest duty to sacrifice it. War is full of instances in which it is a man's duty not to live, but to die. The duty, in case of shipwreck, of a captain to his crew, of the crew to the passengers, of soldiers to women and children . . .; these duties impose on men the moral necessity, not of the preservation, but of the sacrifice of their lives for others, from which in no country, least of all, it is to be hoped, in England, will men ever shrink, as indeed, they have not shrunk. . . .

It would be a very easy and cheap display of commonplace learning to quote from Greek and Latin authors, from Horace, from Juvenal, from Cicero, from Euripides, passage after passage, in which the duty of dying for others has been laid down in glowing and emphatic language as resulting from the principles of heathen ethics; it is enough in a Christian country to remind ourselves of the Great Example whom we profess to follow. . . .

It must not be supposed that in refusing to admit temptation to be an excuse for crime it is forgotten how terrible the temptation was; how awful the suffering; how hard in such trials to keep the judgment straight and the conduct pure. We are often compelled to set up standards we cannot reach ourselves, and to lay down rules which we could not ourselves satisfy. But a man has no right to declare temptation to be an excuse, though he might himself have yielded to it, nor allow compassion for the criminal to change or weaken in any manner the legal definition of the crime.

Result - the appeals court upheld the convictions and the death sentence; but Queen Victoria commuted the sentences to the time in prison already served.

Jurisprudence: Twelve Review Questions or Examples

1. As a former volunteer sheriff, Dwight Shroot has a strong belief that laws are in place to be followed. Even if a law is unjust or against common morality, Dwight believes that one must still abide by the laws set by the governing body. Dwight has a(n) _____ approach to law
A. Natural law
B. Positivist
C. Utilitarian

D. Deontological
E. Legal Realist

2. Four sailors are out at sea and stranded on a boat. It has been several weeks, and the crew is severely dehydrated and on the verge of starvation. Three of them make the decision to kill off the last person and eat him, because he is very old, the closest to death, and has no family. The next day, a ship passes by their boat and rescues the three men. The ship's captain soon realizes what has happened, and he takes the men to jail. What theory of law best explains an outcome for the case which is based solely on the judge's background and prior experience with cannibalism?
A. Utilitarianism
B. Law and Economics
C. Natural Law
D. Legal Realism
E. Positivism

3. Congress, concerned over the poor economy in domestic purse production, has recently passed a law that makes it illegal for any U.S. citizen to possess or use a Louis Vuitton (LV) purse. (LV is based in France.) Alexandra hates this law and daydreams about kidnapping the President so that he will call for eradicating this statute. Alexandra cries out to all who may hear her, "A Louis Vuitton purse brings only happiness to its owner! No one is harmed. People have a God-given right to get one if they want!" Congress and Alexandra are least likely to be following which principles, respectively:
A. Congress – utilitarianism; Alexandra - utilitarianism
B. Congress – utilitarianism; Alexandra - positivism
C. Congress – law and economics; Alexandra – utilitarianism
D. Congress – law and economics; Alexandra - natural law
E. Congress – natural law; Alexandra – legal realism

4. Which statement(s) about the teleological theory is(are) false?
A. Teleological theory is concerned with consequences.
B. Teleological theory judges the ethical good of an action by the effect of the action on others.
C. Teleological theory focuses more on the motivation and principle behind an action.
D. Teleological theory is concerned with consequences AND teleological theory judges the ethical good of an action by the effect of the action on others.
E. None of the above. (All are true.)

5. As a proponent of natural law, St. Thomas Aquinas contended that the only true laws were those that followed _____.
A. reasoned law
B. customary law
C. eternal law
D. localized law
E. none of the above

6. For the *Regina v. Dudley and Stevens* case, if Dudley and Stevens argued in their defense that more good than harm was done eating Parker, what legal theory are they invoking?
A. Utilitarianism
B. Legal Realism
C. Natural Law
D. Positive Law

E. Law and Economics

7. According to the Kant's theory, the ethical worth of an act is determined by whether one
A. would want such a rule applied to minority members of society
B. would want everyone to perform in this manner
C. could get away with such an action
D. could live with the results of such an action
E. could justify the act before God

8. Which of the following is part of Kant's categorical imperative?
A. The form of an action rather than the intended result determines the ethical worth.
B. No one person's interest is given more weight than another.
C. Distribution favors the person getting the worst share.
D. Both that no one person's interest is given more weight than another and that distribution favors the person getting the worst share.
E. Majority vote should determine legal principles.

9. True or False: According to John Rawls, it is easier for a person to understand (that is, assess the fairness of) a system when that person is part of the system.

10. Rawls believed that social policies developed due to the veil of ignorance would create a system that most benefits the
A. Majority
B. Minority
C. Least well off
D. Most well off
E. cultures that value education

11. Jimenez decides to donate leftover food from his restaurant to a homeless shelter. One of his employees claims that Jimenez decided to donate the food only for publicity and that Jimenez did not really care about homeless people.
Upon which of the following would Jimenez most likely rely in contending that he donated the food because he was motivated to help the poor?
A. Rawlsian moral theory
B. Teleological theory
C. Deontological theory
D. Positive Law
E. Utilitarianism

12. Assume the same facts in the previous question. Another of Jimenez's employees, Monica, disagreed with her coworker; Monica contended that, regardless of his motivation, Jimenez was acting ethically because of the consequences involved and the number of people helped. What should Monica rely upon to support her argument?
A. Rawlsian moral theory
B. Historical School
C. Deontological theory
D. Positive law
E. Utilitarianism

> **Answers:**
> 1. B
> 2. D
> 3. E
> 4. C
> 5. C
> 6. A
> 7. B. This is part of Kant's theory of universality.
> 8. A
> 9. False. Rawls contended that a "veil of ignorance" gives one a better sense of what is fair.
> 10. C
> 11. C
> 12. E. Teleological theory likely would also apply. Utilitarianism focuses on the greatest good for the greatest number (here, the feeding of many homeless people), and the teleological theory focuses on consequences.

H. Overall, the Role of Judges and Lawyers

Ordinarily, American judges and lawyers are not boxed in as adherents to a particular theory of law. In most situations, lawyers and trial judges do not think much about legal theory, probably because for most of their cases it seems irrelevant: Any underlying theory is simply a basic part of the legal edifice's basic architecture (like the forces of gravity or electromagnetism affecting all objects in nature – it is always there, but how much thought do we give to it?). The lawyers or judges, let alone the parties, may not think much about the individual aspects of a case, with the case's legal or factual issues' real but seemingly remote connection to legal theory.

<u>Judges and Lawyers may adopt more than one theory</u>, and many do not think too much about jurisprudence. An example of that might be the great American jurist, Benjamin N. Cardozo (1870-1938), New York Court of Appeals Judge (1914-1932) and then Supreme Court Justice (1932-38): "My analysis of the judicial process comes then to this, and little more: logic, and history, and custom, and utility, and the accepted standards of right conduct, are the forces which singly or in combination shape the progress of the law."

Judges and lawyers still may be Renaissance men and women: artists and poets, not just technicians. Indeed, all businesspersons, and all professionals, should aspire to be more than mere technicians, but also to have a vision. These people should have a sense of the artistic (an appreciation for beauty, for esthetics), and a feel for the grand scope of an activity - its place in the larger context. One must see the big picture, how things fit together, not just focus on "getting things done": *"A lawyer without history of literature is a mechanic, a mere working mason: If he possesses some knowledge of these, he may venture to call himself an architect"* (Sir Walter Scott, 19th Century lawyer and novelist - e.g., "Ivanhoe"). For an example of a poetic judicial opinion, see <u>In re Robin E. Love</u>, 61 Bankr. 558 (S.D. Fla. 1986) (denying a debtor's request to avoid his debts).[78] Another example of a poetic court opinion is *Fisher v.*

---

[78] The opinion is online at: http://www.lclark.edu/~lotl/volume5issue5/love1.html
For another poetic decision, *see* Jenkins v. Commissioner (Conway Twitty and the bankrupt Twitty Burger enterprise), 47 T.C.M. (CCH) 238, 247 n.14 (1983),
http://scholar.google.com/scholar_case?case=10329305433284389410&hl=en&as_sdt=2&as_vis=1&oi=scholarr, in which the tax court wrote,
"We close with the following 'Ode to Conway Twitty':
Twitty Burger went belly up
But Conway remained true

Lowe, 333 N.W.2d 67 (Mich. App. 1983) (denying a man's suit against a careless driver on behalf of a "beautiful oak tree" harmed by the driver).[79]

The U.S. Courts have issued a glossary of "Commonly Used Terms," http://www.uscourts.gov/library/glossary.html.

VI. LEGAL SYSTEMS IN THE WORLD

Even within a particular "legal system" there are extensive differences from nation to nation. But, despite their differences, the nations within that same "system" share a common set of characteristics – a tradition. A legal tradition is "not a set of rules, but a set of deeply rooted, historically conditioned attitudes about the failure of law, about the role of law in society and the polity…the legal tradition relates the legal system to the culture of which it is a partial expression. It puts the legal system into cultural perspective."[80]

He repaid his investors, one and all
It was the moral thing to do.
His fans would not have liked it
It could have hurt his fame
Had any investors sued him
Like Merle Haggard or Sonny James.
When it was time to file taxes
Conway thought what he would do
Was deduct those payments as a business expense
Under section one-sixty-two.
In order to allow these deductions
Goes the argument of the Commissioner
The payments must be ordinary and necessary
To a business of the petitioner.
Had Conway not repaid the investors
His career would have been under cloud
Under the unique facts of this case *Held:*
The deductions are allowed."

[79] Below is the entire opinion in *Fisher v. Lowe:*
"We thought that we would never see/ A suit to compensate a tree.
A suit whose claim in tort is prest/ Upon a mangled tree's behest;
A tree whose battered trunk was prest/ Against a Chevy's crumpled crest;
A tree that faces each new day/ With bark and limb in disarray;
A tree that may forever bear/ A lasting need for tender care.
Flora lovers though we three,/ We must uphold the court's decree.
Affirmed. (Footnote 1)
Footnote 1. Plaintiff commenced this action in tort against defendants Lowe and Moffet for damage to his 'beautiful oak tree' caused when defendant Lowe struck it while operating defendant Moffet's automobile. The trial court granted summary judgment in favor of defendants …. In addition, the trial court denied plaintiff's request to enter a default judgment against the insurer of the automobile, defendant State Farm Mutual Automobile Insurance Company. Plaintiff appeals as of right. The trial court did not err in granting summary judgment in favor of defendants Lowe and Moffet. Defendants were immune from tort liability for damage to the tree pursuant to … the no-fault insurance act…. The trial court did not err in refusing to enter a default judgment against State Farm." Since it is undisputed that plaintiff did not serve process upon State Farm in accordance with the court rules, the court did not obtain personal jurisdiction over the insurer. . . .

[80] John Henry Merryman, "Major Traditions in the Contemporary World" (pp. 2-11), in COMPARATIVE LAW: WESTERN EUROPEAN AND LATIN AMERICAN LEGAL SYSTEMS, CASES AND MATERIALS (John Henry Merryman & David Clark, eds. 1978), at 3.

A. Civil Law and Common Law

Civil Law and Common Law are the predominant systems in most of the World. Other countries, e.g. in the Muslim World - Iran, Saudi Arabia, Sudan, and some others - follow Islamic Law (the Sharia, based on the Koran).

Civil Law (Code Law) has its origins in Roman law, with many developments and elaborations since, such as the Code Napoleon and other more modern codes. The Civil Law depends almost entirely upon (or, at least, profoundly emphasizes) systematized statutes (codes).

The Common Law is found almost exclusively in English-speaking countries. It is law developed through court cases. It involves the use of *stare decisis* (precedent) when a case is from the same jurisdiction and is, in fact, a precedent.

Common Law principles do not change as much as do the facts - the technology and the society. We can still follow a Medieval legal case: wording is antiquated, but concepts are similar (e.g., do not lie, obey your word, do not harm others). We cannot do that for texts on Medicine from even a century ago.

In the United States and other common law nations, there has been a process of codification (especially for the criminal law). Conversely, among Civil Law countries, many are tentatively adopting aspects of our common law approach and letting at least a rudimentary form of case law develop.

The Common Law Tradition, Greater Freedom, and Prosperity

Why do the way in which countries such as the Unites States and Great Britain conduct business differ so greatly in comparison to countries in Latin America and Asia? The answer lies in the different legal traditions that emerged in England and France in the 12th century, which spread through their colonies.

Western commercial law comes from a combination of the common law with roots in England and the civil law used in ancient Rome. Countries using this type of law use independent judges and juries and "legal principles supplemented by precedent-setting case law," while in Civil Law countries such as those in most of Latin America, judges are often life-long civil servants who "administer legal codes packed with specific rules." Civil law countries tend to distrust their judges and arbitrators while common law countries "venerate and empower them."

On average, Civil-law countries have heavier regulation, weaker property right protection, more corrupt and less efficient governments and less political freedom then do common-law countries. What is the significance of this difference? As "financial markets outgrow national borders," economies based on different legal foundations must reconcile their differences because markets and prosperity do not exist independent of the law and the institutions of government but are intertwined with them.

B. Inquisitorial Approach and Adversarial Model (see pgs. 83-85; Emerson BL)

| Civil Law Judges > Facts ****** | Common Law Judges > Law |

1. Introduction

The treatment of facts and law are generally quite different in most common law nations than in Civil (Code) Law regimes. Common law judges have more of a role developing the law than do Civil Law judges; but - as part of an adversarial system - common law judges usually have less of a role finding and developing the facts in a case than do Civil Law judges presiding under an inquisitorial system.

The *Adversarial Approach* is prevalent in most Common Law nations, including some countries in Asia and Africa such as Israel and South Africa. But the adversarial system is especially predominant in the United States. Under this approach, judges ordinarily develop law more than they develop facts. The latter is for the parties, with their lawyers, to do.

The *Inquisitorial Approach* is found in most Civil Law nations. It features an inquiry into the facts, directed from above, by the judge or magistrate.[81]

(Court-appointed assistants are known as "huissiers" in France and other French-speaking countries; there are comparable officials in most nations following the Inquisitorial approach.)

2. Potential Disadvantages of Inquisitorial System
(1) Judicial bias - affecting fact investigations;
(2) Judicial laziness - affecting the fact determinations;
(3) Judicial overload - inadequate time and other resources (and income and career advancement generally does not depend on success for either side); and
(4) Judicial incompetence - affects not just reversible legal findings, but the very hard to overcome or recreate establishment of the factual premises for a case.

American courts have reversed criminal convictions because the trial judge engaged in prolonged questioning of witnesses. This may intone overt skepticism about that witness's testimony. *People v. Carter*, 40 N.Y. 2d 933, 934 (1976). Such behavior may deny the accused his Constitutional right to a fair trial before an unbiased court and an unprejudiced jury. To ensure this impartiality, the verdict must be the result, solely, of the evidence adduced on the witness stand. *Shepard v. Maxwell*, 384 U.S. 333, 350-51 (1966); *Estes v. Texas*, 381 U.S. 532, 540-41 (1965).

---

3. Federal and State Procedures
Although rarely invoked, the Federal Rules of Evidence **(see pg. 74; Emerson BL)** and the state rules provide for court appointment of neutral experts.[82] Moreover, in many state courts, an emphasis on problem solving has led to specialized courts with many of the characteristics of inquisitorial bodies. The results have, perhaps, been generally positive, but this "therapeutic" approach is certainly controversial.

VIDEO: "The Sad, Sad Tale of the Allegedly Big Bad Wolf"

---

[81] The inquisitorial approach sometimes has been notorious, such as in the Spanish Inquisition of the late 15th Century. Such inquisitions against outcasts, such as religious minorities, have not been confined to Civil Law systems. The English, for example, had their own witch-hunts, starting under the rule of James I (1603-1625) and, with the Puritans, even spreading to colonial settlements in America.

Historical note: Witchcraft was viewed as a genuine threat across Europe in the fifteenth, sixteenth and seventeenth centuries. Many people - perhaps those seen as odd or outsiders - were accused of being witches, and often they were tortured and executed.

Evidence of witchcraft was often presented through documentation in the form of the testimony of a fellow witch, the suspected witch's contradicting himself/herself when being questioned, the common belief/accusation of those who lived with the suspected witch, cursing or quarrelling (followed by some mischief or mishap), or the suspect's having the Devil's *mark* (perhaps a birthmark or deformity).

The process was often unfair starting from the very top, with the judge inquisitor himself having strong incentives to declare the accused a witch. For example, in eastern England, one Matthew Hopkins set himself up as Witch-Finder General, and from 1644 to 1646 he had over 200 people hanged. In his search for witches, Hopkins was paid, for each execution, the handsome sum of one pound. No wonder there were so many witches!

[82] A comprehensive analysis of the French approach to employing legally-trained judicial officers as investigators, and its potential use in the American system of justice, is in this long (!) article: Robert W. Emerson, *The French Huissier as a Model for U.S. Civil Procedure Reform,* 43 U. MICHIGAN JOURNAL OF LAW REFORM 1043-1135 (2010), available at http://ssrn.com/author=86449.

> The Wolf tells his side of the story, concerning the three little pigs:
> > Was trying to make a cake for granny
> > Needed some sugar
> > Went to the first little pig
> > But was allergic to straw
> > Sneezed
> > . . . .
> > Went to the second little pig
> > Sneezed
> > . . . .
> > Went to the third little pig, a rude little porker
> > ("Get Lost, Wolf! . . .")
> > Encountered cops and then reporters
> > Was subjected to vicious, fictitious accounts
>
> How is that for an adversarial system?
>
> Before, based on the traditional story, the Wolf is as bad as they come.
> Now, after hearing the other's side (the Wolf's story), what do we think?
>
> If one watches a court proceeding with good lawyers, when one speaks we think, "He's absolutely right!" Then the opponent speaks, and we think, "And she's absolutely right, too!"

4. In the Adversarial System, Attorneys/Parties Develop and Present the Facts

Adversarial lawyers have a personal stake in the case (fees, reputation), more so than controlling, neutral, inquisitorial magistrates. Both adversarial sides are strongly committed to get the facts.

The idea is that, as sides clash, the truth will arise. So, how events are described often depends drastically on who is telling the story. In our system, lawyers thus have been criticized as *Hired Guns* practicing "the tricks of the trade"; adversarial system lawyers also often are strong advocates for individual rights.

Adversarial approach lawyers may play the part of actors and/or psychologists. Social scientists have studied <u>body language</u> since the 1960s. For example, standing across a courtroom from a witness your side calls – that supposedly enhances the witness' credibility – the jury's and judge's focus on the witness. On the other hand, the lawyer may get in the face of a witness that he/she cross-examines, in order to create an opposite effect (showing conflict and reducing the witness' credibility). And using a lectern may give the speaker an appearance of authority, OR it may seem to show the speaker has something to hide.

Lawyers increasingly accept the message on how to be expressive - to persuade with eye contact and voice intonation. Or they learn how to perform a stunt; for example, during a meeting with his lawyer a client accidentally spilled many pills and then the light went on the lawyer's brain: Wouldn't it be marvelous to have that client, while testifying in the courtroom, somehow repeat the performance by spilling a large container of all the prescription pain medicines that he needed to take? What a way to illustrate pain and suffering: All those pills to pick up – with bailiffs and others to help – makes a real, and lengthy, visual impact on the jury!

In highly choreographed proceedings, a lawyer's actions – his/her facial gestures and all the rest - can amount to a kind of unsworn testimony that disrupts the search for truth. Sometimes, a judge's own body language may be challenged - judges turning their backs, shaking their heads, pounding their fists, falling asleep. Increasingly, some judges try to rein in the lawyers; these judges bar smirking, shaking of the head, loud sighs, rolling eyes, snickering, turning their back on a witness, and even overly emotional questioning of witnesses or dramatic readings from deposition transcripts. Some judges require lawyers to stand behind lecterns, not roam the courtroom.

> **Skills Are Good, But Not Always Crucial – Someone Else Can Still Win, So Be Prepared**
> A turkey was chatting with a bull. "I would love to be able to get to the top of that tree," sighed the turkey, "but I haven't got the energy."
> "Well, why don't you nibble on some of my droppings?" replied the bull. They're packed with nutrients."
> The turkey pecked at a lump of dung, and found it actually gave him enough strength to reach the lowest branch of the tree. The next day, after eating some more dung, he reached the second branch. Finally, after a fourth night, the turkey was proudly perched at the top of the tree.
> He was promptly spotted by a farmer, who shot him out of the tree.
> Moral of the story: Bull Sh-- might get you to the top, but it won't keep you there.

5. Potential disadvantages of the adversarial system (see pgs.83-85; Emerson BL)

Truth and justice may go in one direction while the courtroom proceeds, amid adversarial trickery, in the other direction. For close cases, simply having a better lawyer could make the difference, so, the adversarial system may exacerbate the potential for unfair results due to inequality of resources and/or experience.[83] The adversarial method is also considered much more expensive to operate in comparison to the inquisitorial system.[84]

6. The Adversarial System and the Reputation of Lawyers

The adversarial system often seems to revolve around not justice, but "legal games" (Manipulations). The role of the main "gamesmen," the major "players," thus is crucial. "There was a society of men among us, bred up from their youth in the art of proving, by words multiplied for the purpose, that white is black and black is white, according (to) as they are paid."[85]

The effects of the adversarial system may especially impact the reputation of lawyers as a group. Compare the American lawyer's role and function against the other three "ancient professions": medicine, education, and the ministry. The doctor joins with patient and society in a common effort to fight pain and suffering and delay death. The educator joins with students to defeat ignorance, and the minister joins the flock to subdue evil and corruption (to try to ascertain God's will).

The lawyer, on the other hand, only joins a client against another party. The lawyer is principally an advocate whose general position is to press the good side of his/her client's position to the extreme and omit the warts. It is the rare client who likes the opposing side's attorney.

The attorney's position in public esteem will always be precarious. Unlike the physician who may save a life, the clergyman who may save a soul, or the educator who may save a mind, the attorney deals with making or losing our money or gaining or losing our freedom, matters more close to the hearts of many than mere matters of life or death. Yet attorneys are officers of the court, their functions are essential in our societal system, and their challenges are great.

---

[83] If a lawyer is no good in a criminal case, then the criminal defendant may be unconstitutionally deprived of his/her right to counsel (as if he/she had no lawyer at all - thus unconstitutional). The criminal defendant is entitled to a reasonably competent lawyer, not a brilliant one. In civil cases, there tend to be no constitutional issues associated with having an inadequate lawyer.

[84] That is one reason for a number of commentators' arguing for reforms which might incorporate elements of the inquisitorial system. See, e.g., Robert W. Emerson, *The French Huissier as a Model for U.S. Civil Procedure Reform*, 43 U. MICHIGAN JOURNAL OF LAW REFORM 1043-1135 (2010); Robert W. Emerson, *Judges as Guardian Angels: The German Practice of Hints and Feedback*, 48 VANDERBILT JOURNAL OF TRANSNATIONAL LAW 707 (2015). Both articles are available at http://ssrn.com/author=86449.

[85] JONATHAN SWIFT, ON LAWYERS, IN GULLIVER'S TRAVELS (1726).

C. INTELLECTUAL PROPERTY (see pg. 605; Emerson BL)

> The rulers of renaissance Venice were apparently the first to guarantee inventors a limited monopoly, as a method of attracting new technology to the city–state.
>
> A few centuries later, the U.S. Constitution put it clearly in Article 1, Section 8: "The Congress shall have the power – to promote the sciences and useful arts, by securing for limited time to authors and inventors the exclusive rights to their respective writings and discoveries."[86] The idea was that the law must not stifle either genius or motivation. As Abraham Lincoln said, U.S. patent law lights a "fire" to the practical genius of mankind.
>
> It is predicted that corporations increasingly will define more of their value by intangibles – the creativity of their designs, the proficiency of their software architects, the knowledge of markets, and even the strength of their internal culture. Those may all be examples of intellectual property.
>
> Encouraging intellectual development is very important because, while land, money, and other property (e.g., oil and other minerals, water) are far from evenly distributed among nations, presumably the capacity for intellectual progress is found everywhere. And that potential can be nurtured. While some property can simply be harvested (crops are picked) or mined (iron ore is gathered) or manufactured (steel is produced), great strides in intellectual property depend on a culture - including an educational system and laws – that inspire and sustain the life of the intellect.

I. Introduction

Intellectual property ("IP") is a special type of intangible property, arising from the creative endeavors of the human mind. After it has been created, intellectual property either can be used or licensed. This form of property is often crucial to business start–ups and to businesses' continued success.

Intellectual Property Law is a legal system intended to provide private rights that serve the public good (induces creativity, production, improvement). Intellectual property rights for individuals should help create a better social and economic structure for a society.

For most businesses, crafting a wise IP strategy requires a deep understanding of their industry, the relevant markets, the competition, what IP protection is or is not available, and the effects of IP protection (including remedies for infringement) – Companies race against their competition to obtain more patents (thousands each year for many very large research oriented firms such as IBM, Samsung, Canon, Sony, and Microsoft): Much of this is to hedge the exposure of their existing products from competitors' claims.

> **THE POOR EFFECTS OF INADEQUATE PROTECTION FOR INTELLECTUAL PROPERTY, AND RESPONSES THERETO**
>
> If we reward intellectual endeavors, we get more such productivity.
>
> If we punish intellectual endeavors (with inventors taking risks, spending money, taking time, etc., and with everyone else able to be a freeloader on any successes and not pay for any failures) → we get less such productivity.
>
> In the 21st Century, ideas and technological discoveries appear to be the driving force behind economic growth, more so than land, machinery, labor, or capital. The last four suffer from diminishing

---

[86] Definitions have changed since the Constitution was written. "Sciences" corresponds more closely to what we would call knowledge; the useful arts are essentially technology.

returns (less output per additional outlays), but ideas do not, concludes economist Paul M. Romer. When legal systems fail to provide adequate patent/copyright protections for inventors/authors, those systems:

(1) Suffer brain drain (the best and brightest go to countries – e.g., the United States – where intellectual property is protected and leave their less protective nations (e.g., many Russians are now in the American computer industry).
(2) Discourage venture capital (financing) – Less risk taking occurs because the risks are too great (e.g., too subject to theft).
(3) Cause fewer Multinational Corporations to invest (again, because of too high risks).
(4) Make it harder for Native, Domestic Firms to grow and develop.

World Comparison

Western nations (Europe and the Americas) have, historically, given far more protection to intellectual property than have other countries. A result has been far more robust growth in Western science and, arguably, the arts.

Non–western industrial powers tend to have adopted Western norms on intellectual property (Japan) or have faced the need to do so in order to sustain their expansion into fields with more value–added characteristics, such as from manufacturing to information services. (China probably falls under this latter grouping.

Many Third World (less developed) countries, the old Soviet Union, and other nations have not, or do not, foster intellectual progress. There simply has not been a tradition of strong cultural support – legal, economic or social – for those who create or invent.

Some cultures little value the individual property interest; so these societies have fewer laws (scant legal protection) and less protection culturally (less popular support) for any property interests in intellectual expression.

However, developing nations increasingly do more than just sell simple products while purchasing from abroad the products that are highly value–added with technological innovation (e.g., with computer technology). Instead, more countries and businesses in the developing world are demanding the technology be passed on so that they can manufacture their own high–value goods. Thus has grown the need for the technique of "technology transfer," usually through licensing.

Intellectual property may be stolen – e.g., outright stealing of a design (pretending that something is the authorized product, when it is not) or, more subtly, leeching off the public goodwill associated with a particular intellectual property.[87] Is it really an authentic Rolex watch? Is it an authorized copy of a movie, or is it a pirated version? Is something so similar to a protected work that a license (and royalties) should be required?

Not only are there possible actions for fraud, breach of contract, or intellectual property infringement, but counterfeit products may have defects for which a product liability action may be brought. For example, knockoff toys may be unsafe, car replacement parts may not perform properly, and supposedly "designer" shampoo could actually cause hair loss! Counterfeit products almost never come with guarantees. And, in worst–case scenarios, such as with bootlegged music or movies, even the purchaser, not just the counterfeit item's producer or seller, may face legal action.

"Blonde to Blonde" (5:23) is a YOUTUBE *video* – BlondetoBlonde_5mins23secs at robertwemersonufl

---

[87] Consideration of a key franchising issue – who owns the goodwill (the franchisor or the franchisee?) – leads to an extensive discussion of the nature of business goodwill generally. Robert W. Emerson, *Franchise Goodwill: "Take a Sad Song and Make It Better,"* 46 U. MICH. J. LAW REFORM 350 (2013), available at http://ssrn.com/author=86449.

> The Playwright urges everyone: Please, Just Say No to Knockoffs.
> With that in mind, RWE Legal Eagle Flicks presents:
> BLONDE TO BLONDE: FIFI AND SHARI DISCUSS BOGUS HANDBAGS
> Two Little Rich Girls are Disturbed by Knockoffs & Palming Off!
>
> Shari: Hey, Fifi, is that a new purse?
> Fifi: Oh, hey, Shar…yeah, it sure is!
> Shari: A Real one?
> Fifi: Well, what else? Like I would really carry a knockoff!
> Shari: Or a palming off!
> . . . .
> Shari: Don't blame me, Fifi. You're the one who bought the fake handbag!
> Fifi: It's just - I don't understand how this could have happened. I mean, the sidewalk vendor… he just, he seemed so nice. I mean . . .
> Shari: Well, how much did you pay for it?
> Fifi: Well, I, I paid, I only paid 50 dollars. But, I mean, he threw in a wallet [he should have thrown in a hot dog!] and everything!
> Shari: For an authentic Louis Vuitton purse?
> Fifi: Uh huh, uh huh. Well, see, he knows, the guy whose, whose brother's sister's cousin, I think, maybe mows the, the yard of Louis Vuitton, or, maybe his mom. I don't know. I mean, but he said I was getting a really, really good deal. I believed him!
> Shari: Oh, did he!
> Fifi: [Nodding] Uh huh.
> Shari: And what would become of the artists, of the design innovators, and the leather engineers, and the handbag scientists if everyone bought a fake Louis Vuitton.
> . . . . .
> Shari: And, without strong legal protection, all those high-quality purse producers may have to shut down production lines. Think: all those high quality purses—gone! All the trendy looks – gone!
> . . . .
> [And there is so much more to see in the video itself!]
>
> Conclusion: Cash spent on designer fakes (e.g., faux Burberry, Kate Spade, and Coach handbags) supports several worldwide organized-crime syndicates. Sales of fakes have been traced to the Born to Kill gang in Los Angeles, as well as gangs in New York, Niger, and China. While selling designer counterfeits may seem a wimpy way to make money (at least compared to drugs, gambling, prostitution, etc.), it is an excellent way for crime syndicates to make money. First, such bags often are poorly constructed in sweatshops where the child workers remain impoverished. Second, the bags can easily be shipped all over the world.

II. Cyber Piracy (Stealing IP- Software, Movies, Books, Designs.: A Problem of Enforcement Internationally)

The Internet has become designer labels' worst enemy. Online shopping involves an estimated $100 billion (or more) of "cyberfakes." And, of course, much of the fakery concerns computer software. Large entities such as Microsoft Corporation devote substantial resources pursuing piracy, via - world–wide - hundreds of lawsuits as well as asking authorities to file criminal charges. Companies have forced "takedowns" of counterfeit sales on the Web.

For example, in China there has been *almost identical packaging of many protected marks. Two instances were "Kongalu Cornflakes" and "Cologate Toothpaste."*

> In small, "regular" letters is the E-MAIL ADVERTISING "Kudos Kopies" (spam to the author, from what may be an online fraudster); and in ALL CAPITAL LETTERS is the author's commentary.
>
> There may be many reasons for you to purchase a replica from Kudos Kopies: GOOD THAT THE COMPANY ACKNOWLEDGES IT IS NOT THE "REAL" THING, BUT A REPLICA – SO THERE IS UNLIKELY TO BE AN ISSUE ABOUT KNOCKOFFS, WHILE THERE IS PERHAPS ONE ABOUT PALMING OFF
>
> a) You want a genuine Rolex or Breitling watch, but the price is too ridiculous.   *"TOO RIDICULOUS?"* ISN'T PLAIN "RIDICULOUS" BAD ENOUGH?
>
> b) You want to impress your friends or business clients. PROBABLY NOT THE BEST MOTIVE, BUT NOT ITSELF UNLAWFUL
>
> c) You want to keep your original safe, while using the replica for daily wear and tear.   AN UNDERSTANDABLE MOTIVE (BUT THE NEXT STEP MAY BE TO NEVER GET THE "ORIGINAL" IN THE FIRST PLACE)
>
> Our finely crafted replicas are created with the utmost care, and using only state of the art workmanship and finishing. The result is a timepiece that is guaranteed to be meticulous in its finish, and impeccable in style and quality. THAT IS FINE. BUT IS IT A "REPLICA" THAT SPONGES OFF OF THE GOODWILL THE MORE EXPENSIVE PRODUCT HAS ACQUIRED? OR DOES IT STAND ALONE BASED ON ITS OWN QUALITY?
>
> The main reason why you should select to purchase from Kudos Kopies is because it is almost impossible to tell the difference between our replicas and the real thing.   HERE IS THE CRUX OF THE ISSUE - WHAT THE COMPANY SAYS SHOULD BE THE BASIS FOR YOUR PURCHASE: ITS "PRODUCTS" CAN FOOL PEOPLE. IS THE BASIS FOR THIS FOOLING OF PEOPLE THE USE OF SOMETHING (E.G., THE DESIGN, LOOK, "FEEL" OF THE PRODUCT) THAT RIGHTFULLY BELONGS TO THE ROLEX OR BREITLING BRAND? IF SO, THEN IT IS TREADING INTO INFRINGEMENT OF INTELLECTUAL PROPERTY.

<u>Names – even numbers – can have intellectual property powers – imaginary personalities. E.G., 727, 747, 767. Airplanes. People –Betty Crocker, Jolly Green Giant, Poppin' Fresh Pillsbury Doughboy.</u>

> YOUTUBE – Intellectual_Property_1min59secs at robertwemersonufl
> "There are several types of intellectual property, and there are numerous sites you can find information about intellectual property, including sites devoted to copyright law, trademarks, trade secrets, and patent law. Obviously, my costume is devoted to patent law. One might think of me as some sort of mad scientist, perhaps. Obviously when one puts glasses on you raise your I.Q. by 10 points, my I.Q. is now up to at least, say, 85. I am perhaps mixing all sorts of ingredients, doing all sorts of things in a scientific manner, and the stereotype that we have of patents, that they are associated with scientific or engineering principles is really not off the mark by much. If you're looking at intellectual property, you tend to think of

> the science, the engineering, and the practical applications as things that tend to be in the field of patents. You tend to think of areas which are more artistic in nature - performance arts, literature, fine arts - those tend to be copyright fields. Things that are specially geared towards marketing, public recognition, logos, and packaging tends to deal with trademarks. Trade secrets are sort of far afield because essentially don't register for a trade secret; you just try to keep something secret and, if you do so, you might be able to retain ownership rights over it indefinitely."

III. What Does Intellectual Property Protect?

Intellectual property protects – gives ownership over – not ideas, but tangible *expressions of ideas*.[88] Consider Country music themes and titles. Any intellectual property therein?[89]
The "intellectual" property is distinct from the physical property associated with it.

Example:
You buy a book. You acquire that physical property, and you can resell that book itself. But you cannot sell the intellect behind it (e.g., run off photocopies of the book). You have bought the physical item, but <u>not</u> its intellectual property.
Intellectual property ("IP") includes patents, copyrights, trademarks, and trade secrets. IP law often concerns itself with fighting infringement of those property rights.
Consider the world of dolls for examples of IP infringement.
Whether Cabbage Patch dolls or Barbie dolls, or any other trendy doll or "action figure," a similar doll likely to cause customer confusion about who is the doll's maker, could be palming off, a type of infringement.[90]

---

[88] "The concept of intellectual property came about as it became necessary to protect inventors, authors of literary works, and composers from having their work pirated." Robert W. Emerson, *Business Law*. NY: Barron's Educational Series (6th ed., 2015), at 605-606.
[89] Here are some examples of Country music titles:
I've Got Tears In My Ears From Lyin' On My Back And Cryin' Over You
I Haven't Gone To Bed With Any Ugly Women, But I've Sure Woke Up with A Few!!
Please Bypass This Heart
She's Actin' Single and I'm Drinkin' Doubles
She's Looking Better After Every Beer
Her Teeth Was Stained, But Her Heart Was Pure!
If You Leave Me, Can I Come Too?
My Every Day Silver Is Plastic
My John Deere Was Breaking Your Field, While Your Dear John Was Breaking My Heart
Oh, I've Got Hair Oil On My Ears And My Glasses Are Slipping Down, But Baby I Can See Through You
I Been Roped And Thrown By Jesus In The Holy Ghost Corral
I Changed Her Oil, She Changed My Life
I Fell In A Pile Of You And Got Love All Over Me
I Would Have Wrote You A Letter, But I Couldn't Spell Yuck!
I'm Just A Bug On The Windshield Of Life
I'm The Only Hell Mama Ever Raised
I've Got The Hungries For Your Love And I'm Waiting In Your Welfare Line
If Love Were Oil, I'd Be A Quart Low
I Bought A Car From A Guy Who Stole My Girl, But It Don't Run So We're Even!
[90] Mattel's doll, Barbie, dates back to 1959 and is the most successful doll in history. Sometimes miscreants build a niche for a new doll by copying Barbie themes. Mattel will pursue such knockoffs. And Mattel will pursue others trading off Barbie's fame (even if the consumer likely does not misunderstand that somehow Mattel actually is behind this doll or other toy or advertisement. Mattel and other companies aggressively purse those who undertake disparaging

IV. Patents (see pgs. 606-607; Emerson BL) Law of Inventions

The patent system has evolved as an attempt to balance public and private interests in obtaining the benefits of inventions. Supreme Court Justice Felix Frankfurter explained the delicate balance this way: "The average person reaps the benefits of this form of property because the inventor has created it under a patent system that rewards the inventor *only* if society *does* derive benefit from it." In other words, one is not paid just for inventing something; one only gets paid if someone manufactures and can actually sell your invention to the public. In Germany, at one time, this requirement was codified in even stricter form. If a German patent holder did not commercialize his/her invention, he/she could lose the rights before the term was up. On the other hand, some societies have denigrated this commercialization of patents as a tool of monopolists; in the 1960s and early 1970s, many federal courts were quite receptive to the antitrust claims or other contentions of parties challenging patents. Many scholars blame these judicial attitudes for a concomitant drop in innovation. Only as industrial and international competitiveness became a hot topic in the mid to late 1970s did patents swing back into favor, and private sector innovation increased.

The U.S. Patent and Trademark Office allows free searches of its patent database. The database can be accessed through the agency's website, http://www.uspto.gov/
See also YOUTUBE – patents_5mins0secs at robertwemersonufl

The importance and activity of patents as intellectual property has increased as we become more technologically-advanced and competitive in business. Top-ranking organizations, each with thousands of new patents every year, have included IBM, Samsung, Canon, Panasonic, Toshiba, Microsoft, Sony, Seiko, Hitachi, and General Electric.

A Slight Miscalculation:
"Everything that can be invented has been invented."
–Charles H. Duell, Commissioner, U.S. Office of Patents, 1899

Many people's impression of the economic worth of a patent is an inordinately inflated one. A patent is by no means tantamount to a ticket to the millionaires' club. A patent is *negative* right, to prevent others from making or doing something (others need to get a license from the patent holder).

Patents (exclusive rights to sell) are grants – rights to charge royalties – based on the practical application of an insight.

Patents Convey Unique Power
Patents can cover everything from abstract concepts to detailed designs (unlike copyright).
Patents exclude third parties who independently develop their own embodiments.
Unpatented know-how erodes rapidly as the world catches on, but patents create legal barriers to competitive entry.

Patents concern inventions – designs, manufacturing processes, machinery, electronics, chemical compounds, computer programs, genetically–modified life forms (generally, plants and seeds), and other devices. Indeed, patent law is the law of inventions. Not patentable are naturally occurring phenomena, laws

---

actions, such as linking a Barbie-like doll or picture to smoking cigarettes or drinking champagne (hardly the wholesome image for the doll).

of nature, abstract ideas,[91] perpetual motion devices, or simple "mental steps." Discovery itself is insufficient; there must be <u>applied science</u>.

Philo T. Farnsworth (1906-1971), Idaho farm boy, in early 1920s saw how the scientists of prior decades had tried to send pictures through the air with spinning dishes and mirrors. He replaced all the moving parts with the invisible electron. Farnsworth demonstrated it and applied for a patent in 1927. In 1930, his patent was granted for his patent #1,773,980 describing the sending of an electrical image counterpart to an optical image.

David Sarnoff's company, RCA, fought Farnsworth with RCA's chief scientist, Vladimir Zworykin. Finally, in 1939 RCA capitulated and accepted a license from Farnsworth for use of his patents - the first such license for RCA, a company determined to collect patent royalties, not pay them.
But who ultimately "won," Farnsworth or RCA?

Patent Case Statistics

Patent cases are expensive and lengthy.
Average duration for patent litigation is two years and costs about $3 million.
Appeals can add another year and an additional $2 million.
Examples of highly prolonged litigation:
1. 15 years: Polaroid vs. Kodak for Polaroid's instant camera patent. (Kodak paid $925 million to Polaroid as an out-of-court settlement).
2. 12 years: Inventor Robert W. Kearns vs. Ford Motor Company over windshield wiper patent infringement. (Ford agreed to pay $10.2 million to settle the lawsuit from the inventor, Robert W. Kearns).
3. *Apple v. Samsung* (ongoing).

On January 9, 2007, Apple shook the mobile phone market with the announcement of the iPhone. After much anticipation, in June 2007, the iPhone became available to U.S. customers, with estimated 475,000 units sold in the first weekend alone. Four days before the release of the iPhone, Apple filed four design patents covering the basic shape and appearance of the phone. Later that year, Apple followed up with a design patent that included 193 screen shots of various iPhone graphical user interfaces.

Samsung Galaxy S Release

In June 2010, Samsung released its new phone, the Galaxy S. The similarities between the two phones were undeniable. In April 2011, Apple sued Samsung for patent infringement, unfair competition, trademark infringement, and trade dress rights. Samsung, denying that it copied Apple, countersued Apple in various countries, alleging that Apple infringed upon Samsung patents. 2

Patent and Trademark Infringement Court Verdicts

On September 9, 2011, the German court ruled in favor of Apple, with a sales ban on the Galaxy Tab 10.1. The court found that Samsung had infringed Apple's patents and concluded that there was a "clear impression of similarity." 2

In late August 2012 a three-judge panel in Seoul Central District Court delivered a split decision regarding business in South Korea. It ruled that Samsung violated one of Apple's utility patents over the "bounce-back" effect in iOS, and that Apple was violating two of Samsung's wireless patents.

In 2012, Apple filed a lawsuit in U.S. courts against Samsung, claiming violations of seven overall patents, and trade dress, in various Samsung smartphones. Samsung responded to the lawsuit with a counterclaim that two of their patents were infringed upon with the iPhone. Apple succeeded in swaying the jury, who awarded Apple $1.05 Billion of Samsung's profits. Apple won with the help of pictures comparing Samsung's designs before and after the release of the iPhone, as well as with internal Samsung memos which implicated the company of willful infringement.

---

[91] While physical designs must function correctly under real–world physics, and that requires extensive upfront design and prototyping before these designs can be turned into mass–produced products, abstract ideas can be developed mentally, and the upfront work required before the idea can be put down on paper usually is trivial by comparison.

Today, the battle between the two companies continues. The final implications of this battle are yet to be seen, but results likely will foretell future technology industry developments.

A. Timing for Patents

Most patents ("regular" utility patents and plant patents) are for 20 years from when applied for; Design Patents are for 14 years from the date the design patent was granted. After the time lapses, then all that was patented falls into the public domain.

For plant patents, the protected property is a hybrid plant that, to be protected must be distinctive. To be protected, the plant patent must be granted to anyone who invents, discovers, or asexually produces a distinctive and new plant variety. Over 120,000 plant patents are granted annually. **pg. 732; Emerson BL.**

Bowman v. Monasanto, 569 U.S. ___ (2013) - **pg. 606; Emerson BL**

Monsanto Company sued Indiana farmer Vernon Hugh Bowman for patent infringement. Monsanto invented and patented Roundup Ready soybean seeds, which contained a genetic alteration that allowed them to withstand exposure to the herbicide glyphosate. This genetic alteration is passed on from the planted seed to the harvested soybeans. These beans can be planted to grow another plant and then those beans can be replanted and so on. The seeds were purchased under the agreement that farmers were to plant the purchased seed in only one growing season. The farmers were free to consume or sell the resulting crops, but were not to save any of the harvested seeds to be re-planted.

Bowman purchased the patented soybean seeds and sold the crop it produced, thus following the terms associated with the agreement. However, for his second crop of the season, Bowman purchased "commodity soybeans" from a grain elevator that got the soybeans from other local farmers, most of whom used Roundup Ready seeds. He planted the beans and treated the plants that grew with glyphosate, killing the plants without the Roundup Ready trait. He then harvested the resulting soybeans that survived and contained the trait and planted them during the next season.

Monsanto sued Bowman for patent infringement on the account that Bowman breached the agreement stating that he could not re-plant the seeds for a second growing season. Bowman used the defense that the patent was exhausted because he got the soybeans from the grain elevator, which in turn received them from other farmers. According to the patent doctrine, "the initial authorized sale of a patented article terminates all patent rights to that item." Bowman further argued that he was using the seeds in the way that farmers normally do, however what he was asking for was the right to make copies of the patented item in an indirect way. He was copying the seeds by planting and harvesting soybeans from the grain elevator, without the patent holder's permission.

The District Court rejected Bowman's argument, and awarded damages to Monsanto. The District Court stated that the fact that Bowman grew a Roundup Ready plant from the grain elevator's soybeans was in fact making a new item based on the template of the original, the original item being the patented Roundup Ready soybean seeds by Monsanto.

Had the District Court sided with Bowman, then Monsanto's patent would provide little benefit. The farmers would only need to buy the seed once, and then could multiply the initial purchase the way Bowman had. There would be no need to continue to purchase from Monsanto, depriving its monopoly.

In 2009, the district court ruled in favor of Monsanto. The Federal Circuit upheld the verdict on appeal and Bowman appealed to the United States Supreme Court. On May 13, 2013, the Supreme Court unanimously affirmed the Federal Circuit's decision. The patent on genetically modified soybeans remained in force.

Bowman v. Monsanto sets precedent for other patent infringement cases and empowers business to protect intellectual property from being copied and reproduced without permission. It affirms that patent exhaustion does not permit a farmer to reproduce patented seeds through planting and harvesting without said permission.

For design patents, the protected property (a design) – to be protected – must be ornamental. The design patent is granted to anyone who invents a new, original, and ornamental design for an article of commerce (pg. 681; Emerson BL).

> In *Pfaff v. Wells Electronics, Inc.*, 525 U.S. 55 (1998), the U.S. Supreme Court unanimously ruled that the one–year time clock on applying to patent an invention begins once there is an accepted purchase order, even if the invention has not yet been perfected (has not yet been fully tested).

Patent applications are growing at about a 10% annual rate. More than five million patents have been granted in the United States since the first national law on patents was enacted in the 1790s. The website to search the U.S. patent databases, and for comprehensive information about patents, is http://www.uspto.gov/main/patents.htm See a database at http://www.uspto.gov/patft/

B. Three Elements Needed to Obtain a Utility Patent

Patents are granted only upon the application's meeting an objective, three–part test. Ninety–nine percent of patent applications initially are denied. (Compared to copyrights, patents offer stronger protections, but patents are much less likely to be granted.)

Three elements needed to obtain a utility patent (covering processes, machines, compositions of matter) are: useful – not eventually, but now; new (novel); and nonobvious. "Although the range of patentable subjects is broad, some things cannot be patented: natural phenomena (e.g., photosynthesis, or a newly discovered plant or mineral), abstract ideas, perpetual motion devices, or simple 'mental steps', and so-called laws of nature. Discovery itself is insufficient: there must be applied science."[92]

C. Comparing Novelty and Nonobviousness

"Novelty" asks whether an invention was known or used by others in this country, or was patented or described in a printed publication in this or a foreign country before the new invention – in essence, novelty asks whether the new invention was anticipated by a prior invention. For example, what if I patent an invention comprising the elements A, B and C and someone tries to patent an invention comprising just the elements A and B? The new invention is anticipated by my invention because I already patented an invention comprising all the elements of the new invention. Therefore, the new invention is not novel and the new inventor will not receive a patent.

In contrast, non–obviousness asks whether it would be obvious to a person of ordinary skill in the relevant art to add the new element (at the date of the new invention). For example, what if I patent an invention comprising the elements W, X and Y and someone tries to patent an invention comprising the elements W, X, Y and Z? The new invention IS novel because the new invention is not anticipated by my invention (my invention does not comprise all the elements of the new invention). However, if adding the element Z to my invention would be obvious to a person of ordinary skill in the relevant art, the new invention is obvious and the new inventor will not receive a patent.

D. Purposely Seeking Narrower Patent Rights

One may purposely seek narrower patent rights, so that there is more cumulative innovation and greater licensing fees.

For some businesses, there may be a strategic advantage in obtaining narrow patents and publishing, in an unprotected way, information about their research and development (R&D) output. Broad patents might stifle follow–on improvements by deterring potential cumulative innovators, who fear being held up by the initial inventor when they seek their own patent or license.[93] By opting for a narrower patent and

---

[92] Robert W. Emerson, *Business Law*. NY: Barron's Educational Series (6th ed., 2015), at 606.
[93] Many R&D departments depend upon building upon their own prior work, as well as others work. This continual accretion of innovation means that the "cutting–edge" is protected while the other, older work (what is built upon) falls under the public domain.

Isaac Newton is reputed to have said upon admission to the Royal Society: "If I have seen further than other men, it is because I have stood on the shoulders of giants." (Gracious as that sounds, some say Newton meant it

unprotected publication, the initial patent holder commits not to hold up follow–on inventors, thus promoting sequential innovation and generating lucrative licensing fees for the initial patent holder.

    This approach, less protection to produce more earnings, is counterintuitive. Furthermore, it demonstrates that for intellectual property the divergence between private interests (property rights) and social objectives (information revelation) is not as great as conventionally believed.

THE STORY OF THE STEAM ENGINE: PATENTS

Do patents hinder incremental innovation and others ability to innovate upon existing ideas? In the absence of patents, would people still be willing to take the risk to innovate without the protections offered under current patent law?
 	
    The story of the steam engine - Cornwall, England (1772-1852) - used in the copper and tin mines. Measurement of work delivered was referred to as a "duty."
 	
    The Newcomen steam engine produced a duty of 10 million foot-pounds (10M). Invented by Thomas Newcomen and put into operation in 1711 to pump water out of the mines (as much power as 500 horses, but consumed much energy).
    In 1777, the partnership of entrepreneur Matthew Boulton and inventor James Watt produced and began selling a steam engine with a "separate condenser" called the Watt engine with a duty of 18M and peaking at a duty of 26M.
    From 1792 to 1813, the engine's performance plateaued: The annual increase in the max duty of the steam engine through the years 1777-1813 was only 3.8%. Due to patents held by Boulton & Watt, unless someone constructed an engine substantially different in design than the Watt engine, he was not legally permitted to make improvements.
 	
    <u>An entirely new engine</u>
    In 1814, Richard Trevithick invented the high-powered pressured steam engine.
    He did not pursue any patents and, as a result, during the ensuing years many different, improved variations of his original engine were brought to market. During the next 34 years improvements and adaptations to the Trevithick engine resulted in an average annual increase in duty twice as fast, at a rate of 8.5%.

E. The Shop Rights Doctrine (see p. 610; Emerson BL)

Depending on when and where an employee develops an idea, ownership may vest in the employer. This concept of employer ownership is *the shop rights doctrine.*

    To decide whether an invention/creation is owned by the employer, not the employee (because the worker's invention/creation was "within the scope of employment"), a court may consider not only the employee's job description and any contracts he/she signed, but also whether he/she used office equipment, did the work during business hours, or violated company rules.

F. Reform: The America Invents Act (2012) (see p. 607; Emerson BL)

    Pres. Obama signed the Leahy-Smith America Invents Act ("AIA") on September 16, 2011. AIA represents the most significant change to the U.S. Patent system since the Patent Act of 1952. With the AIA, the U.S. patent system changed from a "first to invent" system to a "first to file" system which is the same system as the rest of the world. AIA applies to fillings after March 16, 2013. If the inventor/business

---

sarcastically, but we will ignore that for now.) The argument runs that inventions are not made in a vacuum; almost all progress is made building on work that has gone before. If an inventor wants to take fair advantage of all earlier work, then he must be willing to make his own work available for others.

publicly discloses patent-pertinent information even before a patent application is filed, then that inventor/business has a one-year grace period to file for the patent before other entities can act.

An Example of the Impact of Reform

Who gets the patent?

Example: Tom at Company XYZ develops an invention in May and files the corresponding patent application in August. At the same time, Tim at Company AAA independently develops the same invention in June and files for a patent in July.

Before AIA:

Company XYZ can secure the patent because its employee invented it first.

Under AIA:

If Company XYZ does not make any public disclosures regarding the invention before the August filing, Company AAA can obtain the patent by virtue of its earlier filing date.

If Company XYZ provides disclosure before Company AAA. Company XYZ can get the patent even though it filed after Company AAA.

G. International Patent Law: The Paris Convention versus the Patent Cooperation Treaty

The Paris Convention for the Protection of Industrial Property is a treaty agreed to by 176 nations – nearly every country in the world. It provides that an applicant for a patent from one of the signatory nations can use that first filing date as the effective filing date in any of the other 175 nations if the applicant files a subsequent application within six months for industrial designs and trademarks or twelve months for patents. Patent applicants that file under this convention are granted the same intellectual property rights in each member country that they would receive in their home country.

For applicants that want to file for industrial designs, patents or trademarks in several countries or want to keep open the option of doing so, the Patent Cooperation Treaty (PCT) application[94] - as operated by the World Intellectual Property Organization (WIPO) - is the more cost-efficient route. For applicants that know they only want to obtain patents, industrial designs, or trademarks in a few countries, filing directly in those countries via the Paris Convention is almost always easier and less expensive.

The PCT is a much more elaborate process than simply filing in one Paris Convention nation, and thereby having a protected time frame for filing in the other Convention countries. A PCT procedure includes an International Search Report, which may assist the applicant in determining what prior "art" (designs, inventions, marks, etc.) the application may face in one or more national patent offices. In effect, a PCT application is submitted to all nations or world regions in which the applicant is interested. An optional international examination procedure allows the applicant to present amendments and arguments in its applications proceeding in various countries.

The deadline for filing a PCT application is 12 months from the earliest priority date (basically, the time frame of the Paris Convention). Then the PCT applicant has 18 months (19 months in some countries, such as in Europe) before the application must enter the national phase in each country or region of interest.

In essence, the PCT application buys time. You file a single application with fairly high fees, which reserves your rights for about 2.5 years from the priority date. Ultimately, the PCT application can be custom-tailored for each jurisdiction and then proceed as a normal patent application in each such country or region.

H. Exceptions to Infringement – Not Nearly as Large as Copyright's Fair Use

There are exceptions to alleged patent infringement, but not nearly as large as copyright's fair use exception (which is discussed in the copyright part of this section). Here are those two exceptions:

(1) A common law research exception

---

[94] Almost 150 nations are signatories to the PCT, with Argentina, Pakistan, Taiwan, and Venezuela being prominent nonsignatories.

(2) Food and Drug Administration (FDA) regulatory compliance (the Hatch-Waxman Exemption)
This exemption, generally reserved for drug companies, allows generic drug manufacturers to prepare generic drugs in advance of the patent expiration. It applies to tests while preparing for FDA approval (the exception being granted before the end of a patent term).

I. Infringement Actions

A patent infringement may be direct, indirect, or contributory.

<u>Direct Patent Infringement</u>: the making, use, or sale of any patented invention within the U.S. during the term of the U.S. patent. This is generally a *literal* type of infringement that exists when the wording in the patent is directly violated (infringed upon).

<u>Indirect Patent Infringement</u> (also known as "Inducement to Infringe"): a party's active inducement of another party to infringe a patent.

<u>Contributory Patent Infringement</u>: occurs when one party knowingly sells an item with one specific use that will result in the infringement of another's patent.

Note that Direct Infringement can be committed innocently and unintentionally, while Indirect and Contributory Infringement require some intent or knowledge that a patent will be infringed. That type of willful infringement involves intentional disregard for the patent holder's rights and the continued production of the infringing product.

Legal Implications

Patent holders must file infringement cases within six years of the occurrence. As usual, the plaintiff, in this case the patent holder, bears the burden of proof – by a preponderance of evidence - that a legal wrong (here, infringement) has occurred. Specialized legal assistance is HIGHLY recommended for patent holders seeking damages for patent infringement!

Rights do not always lead to riches. Philo T. Farnsworth as exemplary.

V. Copyrights (see pgs. 608-612; Emerson BL)

Literally, copyrights are "copy rights": the right to make copies (to reproduce, distribute, perform publicly, and display publicly the work, and to authorize others to do so).

Although filings with the Copyright Office are preferable,[95] common law copyrights may be created without a filing.[96] E.g., putting on a work, especially before you distribute or show it: © Name, 2011. That is not necessary for protection, but at least it helps to show others that you are maintaining all your rights (you are not somehow abandoning them).

> **Copyrights:** Protective rights usually dealing with the arts.

Copyrights involve the law of authorship: a personal way of presenting something concretely (Subjective Considerations). So copyrights give legal protection to the authors of original literary, dramatic, musical, artistic, and certain other intellectual works. A copyright, as held by a natural person (e.g., an individual) lasts for the life of the creator, plus 70 years. For a corporate-held copyright, the rights last for 95 years.

A. Common Law Copyright (Without Filing) and Moral Rights: A Different European Approach

You cannot copyright music in your mind, only the notes written on the paper → the expression of an idea, not the idea itself, is protected.

Key is putting something in tangible form! Into a concrete recorded form.

---

[95] The violation of a registered copyright increases the potential type of damages to include statutory damages often worth tens of thousands of dollars per infringement and not limited to the actual harm provably suffered by the plaintiff.
[96] Moreover, suits for violation of a common law copyright can still result in actual damages.

In Europe, authors/creators often have moral rights: they retain certain rights not to have their work undermined, even though they may no longer "own" the copyright. For example, a book author who sells his copyright to a publisher still has moral rights. As stated in the Berne Convention for the Protection of Literary and Artistic Works (discussed later), in defining a moral rights concept found in most of the world besides the United States, "moral rights" encompass "the right to claim authorship of the work and the right to object to any mutilation, deformation or other modification of, or other derogatory action in relation to, the work that would be prejudicial to the author's honor or reputation."[97]

In Europe, there is more emphasis on the Natural Rights – the absolute "Moral Rights" of the Creator/Author. The American system has had shorter periods of protection. The French Revolution's heritage is absolute rights, while the American Revolution and resulting law took a more practical, accretionist (built upon precedent) tack. America is supposedly more pragmatic, prudent and property-oriented (encourage creativity, but do not insulate it with protections after the creation to such a degree that competition is stifled for the long-term). But what about the 1998 Sonny Bono Copyright Term Extension Act (named for the late entertainer and Congressman) extending corporate copyrights from 75 years to 95 years (called the "Disney extension" because so many Walt Disney copyrights from the 1930s were about to expire), and extending natural persons' copyright from "life of the author, plus 50 years" to "life of the author plus 70 years"? That brought American copyright length in line with European law, although we still do not hold to the European "Moral Rights" concept.[98]

B. *Elder v. Ashcroft*

In *Elder v. Ashcroft*, 537 U.S. 186 (2003), by a 7-2 vote (Justices Stevens and Breyer dissenting), the U.S. Supreme Court upheld the constitutionality of the "Disney extension" 1998 statute against a challenge by a group of individuals and companies that were creating free Internet libraries or publishing works in the public domain. In appealing to the Supreme Court, the challengers said the Constitution gave Congress authority to "promote the progress of science" by giving protection to authors for only "limited times." But by extending copyrights, they said, "Congress has now found a clever way to evade this simple constitutional command" and violate the First Amendment. Noting that Congress has extended existing copyrights 11 times in the past 40 years, they had argued that the Sonny Bono Act "rendered meaningless" the Constitution's "plain and express intent to restrict the duration of monopolies over speech." But they lost.

The stakes were high. Walt Disney Co., which faced losing exclusive rights to Mickey Mouse in 2003 and to cartoon characters Pluto, Goofy and Donald Duck in 2009, had been a leader in pushing for the legislation, along with other entertainment and media companies. On the other hand, eliminating the extension would have freed up vast amounts of material for Internet libraries.

C. Elements of Copyright

> The "labanotation" example from the world of dance: Tangible preserved explanation is necessary to obtain IP rights.

To be copyrighted, creations (e.g., art) must be placed in a tangible preserved expression; they cannot just be "all in my mind." Ideas alone are not copyrightable. A copyright is for the original expression

---

[97] Summary of the Berne Convention, at http://www.wipo.int/treaties/en/ip/berne/summary_berne.html.
[98] For example, challenges on "moral rights" notions against the colorization of classic black-and-white films (e.g., "It's a Wonderful Life" (1946)) are more successful as a matter of public relations than of American case law. For a consideration of moral rights as instructive to American law, *see* Robert W. Emerson, *Franchises as Moral Rights*, 14 WAKE FOREST J. BUS. & INTELL. PROP. 540 (2014), available at http://ssrn.com/author=86449.

> Although U.S. copyrights are usually valid in other countries due to the Berne convention (signed by almost every nation), trade secrets, patents + trademarks have no protection elsewhere unless it's also in compliance w/ other countries' laws

<u>of ideas, not the ideas themselves.</u> One must put the idea into expressible form. Even a short, catchy phrase may be copyrighted,[99] although the actual enforceable rights associated with that copyright may be limited.

Elements Required for a Copyright: the creator's work must be:
1. original;
2. in a tangible medium of expression;
3. with some minimal level of creativity.

Copying Examples

A Poem on a Website

I compose a poem. I post the paper on my website. You read the poem on the website. You print the poem without indicating that I wrote the poem, and you put it in a nice frame and hang it in your home.

Have you infringed my copyright?

Yes, a court could find that to be the case, as you have copied the work. Only the copyright owner has the right to reproduce it under Copyright Act § 106(1). (Of course, it may not be worth suing over, in terms of being able to prove actual damages, or because it may just prove to create a public relations firestorm.)

Recited Poetry

I compose a poem. I then memorize it and put the paper with the poem on it in my desk. I stand in front of the poetry bulletin board and recite the poem from memory. You write it down

Have you infringed my copyright?

Yes, a court could find that to be the case, as you have copied the work. Copying the work does not require access to the tangible medium of expression in which the work is embodied (here, the paper on my desk). The fact that you have not seen the paper is irrelevant to infringing, as you know there is a created work which you are copying. Again, the owner has the exclusive right to reproduce the work under § 106(1). Also, as in the previous example, there may be no practical value in suing, and it may actually prove counter-productive (e.g., a suit costs money and time without providing a significant damages award, and it produces a backlash).

A Poem on a Bulletin Board

I compose a short poem (Poem X). I physically tack the paper to a bulletin board.

You never see my poem; you compose a poem with the same words, in the same order and cadence as my poem. You write this poem (Poem Y) on a document stored in your computer.

Have you infringed my copyright? No, because there is no "copying" here. Independent creation is not copying.

Do you have a copyright on Poem Y? That seems doubtful. Although not copied, one could argue that Poem II was not an original work of authorship (a necessary element for obtaining a copyright) because it does not add to previous expressions. (One could argue that it does not even rise to the level of a "derivative work," which would fall under my zone of protection from others engaged in copying.)

To determine what is "original," courts look at the general understanding – a new creation of something heretofore not produced (something not the case here) – versus the independent basis of the work (that it is original to you, even if not original generally). Patent law has a much stricter approach. If a patented work extends to these matters, then your independent production of the already invented work does not protect you from a claim of patent infringement. Also, the nonobviousness requirement for patents may make it even harder to not infringe when what one is doing should, obviously, be seen as something already out there in either the public domain or among protected intellectual properties.

Bouchat v. Baltimore Ravens Football Club, Inc.

---

[99] It may seem hard to believe, but one can trademark a phrase such as "Let's Roll" from 9/11 (with a trademark application in late September 2001 by Lisa Beamer, the widow of the brave passenger Todd Beamer's last recorded words on Flight 93, which crashed in Shanksville, Pennsylvania). Likewise, Donald Trump in 2004 filed for a trademark for the phrase, "You're Fired," as used in the television show, "The Apprentice."

346 F.3d 514 (4th Cir. 2003), cert. denied, 541 U.S. 1042 (2004)

Amateur artist Frederick Bouchat established that the National Football League (NFL) and the Baltimore Ravens football team had infringed his copyright in a drawing for the Baltimore Ravens logo. However, Bouchat often showed his artwork to people passing through the main entrance where he worked, at the State of Maryland Office building in downtown Baltimore. He even gave away drawings, such as many he drew in late 1995 and early 1996, shortly before his drawing of the Ravens logo.

Bouchat claimed damages based on a variety of sources of revenue to the team, including merchandise sales and broadcast income. The Fourth Circuit held that there must be a more than a speculative causal link between the infringement and the revenue.

Note: If there had been registered copyrights, that may have led to statutory damages awards: substantial amounts provided under the U.S. copyright statutes for willful infringements of registered works.

D. Licensing

Licensing is a means to spread the protected work to others, while the licensor gathers fees or royalties from the licensee.

Example: In the 1904 US presidential campaign, Theodore Roosevelt had just been nominated by the Republican Party and his campaign posters were all set for printing. In fact a few thousands had already been printed. Then disaster!

E. Rephrasing or Truly Distinct?

Merely rephrasing a copyrighted work does not protect the rephrasing from charges of copyright infringement. On the other hand, if the work is altogether different from a prior work, then there is no copyright infringement. For example, in April 2006 British trial judge Peter Smith found no copyright infringement by Dan Brown's best–selling novel, THE DA VINCI CODE (2003). Michael Baigent and Richard Leigh, the authors of a 1982 nonfiction book about many of the same religious and historical matters discussed in the Brown book complained that the similarities were, in effect, too much. However, the judge disagreed. The fact that the older book, THE HOLY BLOOD AND THE HOLY GRAIL, and Brown's book both dealt with the same theory that Jesus and Mary Magdalene married and have a line of descendants to the present day, does not itself constitute infringement.

F. Listings

Here is an example of a non-copyrightable work. In *Feist Publications, Inc. v. Rural Telephone Service Co.*, 499 U.S. 340 (1991), the U.S. Supreme Court held that alphabetical listings of names, addresses, and telephone numbers in the "white pages" are not protected under federal copyright law. As stated in the copyright statute, 17 U.S. C. § 103(b), "The copyright in a compilation or derivative work extends only to the material contributed by the author of such work, as distinguished from the preexisting material employed in the work, and does not imply any exclusive right in the preexisting material." As the Court observed in *Feist*, 499 U.S. at 345, the act of collecting and compiling facts or other public domain materials does not transform them into a copyrightable product: "[c]ommon sense tells us that 100 uncopyrightable facts do not magically change their status when gathered in one place."

G. Derivative Works

A copyrighted work's protections do extend to works derived from those copyrighted materials. In *Sobhani v. @radical.media, Inc.*, 257 F. Supp. 2d 1234, 1238–39 (C.D. Cal. 2003), the U.S. District Court rejected the plaintiff's attempt to invoke fair use as a "sword," rather than as a defense to an infringement claim, because the plaintiff claimed a copyright in what was actually an unauthorized derivative work. The courts tend to construe broadly the derivative works rights afforded a copyright holder: his/her right to control what works may be derived from his/her copyrighted works. The U.S. District Court in *Los Angeles*

Times v. Free Republic,[100] considered how a website operator had allowed subscribers to post stories from various newspapers and then encouraged readers to discuss the articles, including critiques of any alleged biases by the articles' authors. The court rejected the defendant's contention that, by encouraging others to post their own criticism, its use was "transformative" and therefore more likely to be considered a fair use. The court wrote, "verbatim posting of plaintiffs' articles is 'more than necessary' to further defendants' critical purpose."[101] It also found that the use was commercial and that the use, if permitted, would impair the plaintiff's ability to license its works. Simply adding some commentary, changing some words, and introducing some examples does not transform a theft of copyright (an unauthorized derivative work) into something lawful.[102]

H. Fair Use (see pg. 609; Emerson BL)

Copyrights not only last much longer than patents, but also are easier to obtain than patents. However, in return for copyrights lasting longer and being easier to get than patents, copyrights have somewhat less protection than patents.

Fair Use, a concept put in the federal copyright statutes at Copyright Act Section 107, allows use without copyright holder's permission. Fair use is an exception to copyright protection. It involves a balancing of interests: (1) educational purpose, instead of commercial purpose, for the use; (2) the nature of the work; (3) proportionality and importance of the use (compared to the work as (4) no reasonable expectation of compensation for the copyright owner, as we consider the use's effect on the value of the work, including its potential market.[103]

Parody is usually upheld as fair use. For example, Paramount Pictures Corporation's use of a posed photo similar to that of actress Demi Moore's pregnant pose on the cover of Vanity Fair – only this new photo, to promote Paramount's movie, "Naked Gun 33 1/3: The Final Insult," features a supposedly pregnant male actor, Leslie Nielsen (the white–haired star of the Naked Gun movies). *Leibovitz v. Paramount Pictures Corp.*, 137 F.3d 109 (2d Cir. 1998) (upholding a decision by federal district court judge Loretta Preska, in favor of Paramount and against the copyright owner of the Vanity Fair picture).[104]

---

[100] 54 U.S.P.Q.2d (BNA) 1453 (C.D. Cal. 2000).

[101] Id. at 1464.

[102] Likewise, copyright protection for a compilation of facts is very thin, with infringement only when the selection, coordination, or arrangement is copied, not when merely the factual material is copied. Indeed, the more comprehensive the compilation of data, the less likely it is protected from copyright law. If the selection or arrangement of data is merely the inclusion of the entire relevant universe, there is arguably very little or no "creativity" involved. As the Eleventh Circuit explained in Warren Publishing, Inc. v. Microdos Data Corp., "Just as the Copyright Act does not protect 'industrious collection,' it affords no shelter to the resourceful, efficient, or creative collector." 115 F.3d 1509, 1520 (11th Cir. 1997), cert. denied, 522 U.S. 963 (1997).

[103] In *Zacchini v. Scripps Howard Broadcasting*, 433 U.S. 562 (1977), a television station broadcast entertainer Hugo Zacchini's "human cannonball" act at the Geauga County Fair in Burton, Ohio, against Zacchini's objections. The entire act – Zacchini being shot 200 feet through the air into a net – was broadcast. The commentary accompanying the film clip on the 11 o'clock local news was as follows: "This . . . now . . . is the story of a true spectator sport . . . the sport of human cannonballing . . . in fact, the great Zacchini is about the only human cannonball around, these days . . . just happens that, where he is, is the Great Geauga County Fair, in Burton . . . and believe me, although it's not a long act, it's a thriller . . . and you really need to see it in person . . . to appreciate it." The Supreme Court held that, inasmuch as the broadcast deprived Zacchini of the economic value of his performance, the First Amendment freedom of the press did not insulate it from Zacchini's tort action. This ruling is similar to copyright rulings where partial excerpts for reviews are permitted under fair use, but a complete reprinting or rebroadcasting of some material would be copyright infringement.

[104] Barney v. San Diego Chicken (Lyons Partnership, L.P. v. Giannoulas), 14 F. Supp. 2d 947 (S.D. Cal. 1998)

Barney may love you and he may love me, but he doesn't love the San Diego Chicken.

The red-and-yellow chicken mascot, Ted Giannoulas, was first notified in 1994 that using the Barney-like costume in his act constituted infringement of Lyon's trademarks and copyrights and violated state and federal law.

More recently, in *Bourne Co. v. Twentieth Century Fox Film Corp.*, U.S. District Judge Deborah Batts of Manhattan ruled that creators of the television show, "Family Guy," did not infringe copyright when they transformed a song made famous in Walt Disney's cartoon, "Pinocchio."[105] The song from 1940, "When You Wish Upon a Star" (winner of the 1940 Academy Award for Best Original Song) was parodied with the cartoon's protagonist, Peter Griffin, singing "I Need a Jew" in an episode entitled "when You Wish Upon a Weinstein." Judge Batts ruled that the lyrics and tone of the song used in "Family Guy" were "strikingly different" from the original work. Among other conclusions, she wrote:

> Defendants' use of "When You Wish Upon a Star" calls to mind a warm and fuzzy view that is ultimately nonsense; wishing upon a star does not, in fact, make one's dreams come true. By pairing Peter's "positive," though racist, stereotypes of Jewish people with the fairy tale world-view, "I Need a Jew" comments both on the original work's fantasy of stardust and magic, as well as Peter's fantasy of the "superiority" of Jews. The song can be "reasonably perceived" to be commenting that any categorical view of a race of people is childish and simplistic, just like wishing upon a star.[106]

The judge also held that the "Star" song, recorded by more than 100 different singers in the past seven decades, was ripe for a humorous imitation spoofing the very thing the music publisher had benefited from: the song's association with other more "wholesome" shows like "Pinocchio." "It is precisely that beneficial association that opens the song up for ridicule by parodists seeking to take the wind out of such lofty, magical, or pure associations," Judge Batts ruled.[107]

I. Global Copyright Protection? Copyright Law Throughout the World

There is no such thing as an "international copyright" that protects copyrighted materials around the world. Copyright protection is a matter of national law. However, most countries protect foreign works via two international copyright conventions, the Berne Convention for the Protection of Literary and Artistic Works, adopted in 1886 and amended as late as 1979, as well as the Universal Copyright Convention. The United States has been a member of the Berne Convention since 1989 (168 signatory nations as of December 2015; see http://www.wipo.int/treaties/en/ShowResults.jsp?treaty_id=15) and of the Universal Copyright Convention since 1955 (100 signatory nations as of December 2015; see http://www.wipo.int/wipolex/en/other_treaties/parties.jsp?treaty_id=208&group_id=22). Under both conventions, if one holds a protected work in a nation that is a member, then protection applies in all countries that are members of the conventions. The Universal Copyright Convention requires use of the copyright symbol, ©, along with the name of the copyright owner and the year of publication. The Berne Convention is the same as U.S. law, which has no formal notice requirements, but, as in the United States, there are advantages for publishing a copyright notice to help defeat claims of innocent infringement. The United States has treaties with some other nations that are not members of either convention. In other countries, one would have to follow national law.

International copyright protection was further strengthened by the World Intellectual Property Organization (WIPO), which added the Berne Convention protection for "works in digital form" (e.g.,

---

The complaint said that because Barney consumers are young children, they aren't likely to know the difference between the real Barney and the one getting knocked around by San Diego's infamous fowl.

The federal court dismissed the suit with prejudice, holding that "Although plaintiff does not appreciate defendant's intent, there is no doubt that parody is intended. Defendants' act is not an effort to confuse consumers, but rather to amuse."

Parody is given wide leeway. Barney loses! Most people who say the staged fight would realize that this was not really the purple dinosaur, "Barney."

[105] 602 F.Supp.2d 499 (S.D.N.Y. 2009).
[106] Id. at 506.
[107] Id. at 511.

websites are copyrighted at the time of development). Protection for digital on–line materials was strengthened and clarified in U.S. copyright law by the Digital Millennium Copyright Act of 1998.

Here is the Berne Convention's summary of its coverage and protections:

> The Berne Convention . . . . is based on three basic principles and contains a series of provisions determining the minimum protection to be granted, as well as special provisions available to developing countries that want to make use of them.
>
> (1) The three basic principles are the following:
>
>   (a) Works originating in one of the Contracting States (that is, works the author of which is a national of such a State or works first published in such a State) must be given the same protection in each of the other Contracting States as the latter grants to the works of its own nationals (principle of "national treatment") .
>
>   (b) Protection must not be conditional upon compliance with any formality (principle of "automatic" protection) .
>
>   (c) Protection is independent of the existence of protection in the country of origin of the work (principle of "independence" of protection). If, however, a Contracting State provides for a longer term of protection than the minimum prescribed by the Convention and the work ceases to be protected in the country of origin, protection may be denied once protection in the country of origin ceases.
>
> (2) The minimum standards of protection relate to the works and rights to be protected, and to the duration of protection:
>
>   (a) As to works, protection must include "every production in the literary, scientific and artistic domain, whatever the mode or form of its expression" (Article 2(1) of the Convention).
>
>   (b) Subject to certain allowed reservations, limitations or exceptions, the following are among the rights that must be recognized as exclusive rights of authorization:
>   the right to translate,
>   the right to make adaptations and arrangements of the work,
>   the right to perform in public dramatic, dramatico-musical, and musical works,
>   the right to recite literary works in public,
>   the right to communicate to the public the performance of such works,
>   the right to broadcast (with the possibility that a Contracting State may provide for a mere right to equitable remuneration instead of a right of authorization),
>   the right to make reproductions in any manner or form (with the possibility that a Contracting State may permit, in certain special cases, reproduction without authorization, provided that the reproduction does not conflict with the normal exploitation of the work and does not unreasonably prejudice the legitimate interests of the author; and the possibility that a Contracting State may provide, in the case of sound recordings of musical works, for a right to equitable remuneration),
>   the right to use the work as a basis for an audiovisual work, and the right to reproduce, distribute, perform in public or communicate to the public that audiovisual work.[108]

VI. Trademarks   (see pgs. 612-615; Emerson BL)

> "MY BUNS HAVE NO SEEDS": *Customer reliance for trademark –*
> *What do you think when you see McDonald's golden arches?*
>
> Cleo McDowell, played by actor John Amos in the Eddie Murphy movie , "Coming to America," was the owner of a "McDowell's" fast-food restaurant that looked quite similar to McDonald's. Cleo

---

[108] Summary of the Berne Convention, at http://www.wipo.int/treaties/en/ip/berne/summary_berne.html.

> McDowell certainly seems to use unfair business tactics to confuse customers into who they were dealing with (McDowell's or McDonalds?). This quotation from Mr. McDowell demonstrates this point:
>> "Look…me and the McDonalds people got this little misunderstanding. See, they're McDonald's…I'm McDowell's. They got the golden arches, mine is the golden arcs. They got the Big Mac, I got the Big Mick. We both got two all-beef patties, special sauce, lettuce, cheese, pickles and onions, but their buns have sesame seeds. My buns have no seeds."[109]

The U.S. Patent and Trademark Office began allowing free searches of its trademark database, including both registered trademarks and pending trademarks. The database can be accessed through the agency's website, http://www.uspto.gov/

Patents and copyrights are oriented toward the creator; trademarks are oriented toward the end–user. So trademarks depend on what a consumer believes. "A trademark is a distinctive symbol, word, letter, number, picture, or combination thereof adopted and used by a merchant or manufacturer to identify his/her goods."[110] **Customer recognition and reliance** is the *Focal Point of Trademark Law*. Businesses look to create visual reminders, to protect an item in the customer's eyes (the mind's eye).

Consider "Emerson Electronics": How common is the name? The more common it is, perhaps the less protection there is. Also, if the name is also a common word, that diminishes the chances for protection. What if I, Robert Emerson, decide to form my own electronics company - Emerson Electronics? But there is an already existing "Emerson Electric Company" (NYSE stock exchange symbol: EMR).[111] I can introduce evidence that my last name - Emerson - goes back to England's King Henry VIII in the early 16th Century. That Henry had a relationship with a commoner named Emma, who had a son, called Emma's son, soon transformed through bad pronunciation into "Emerson." A ludicrous story, but – true or not – the descendants over the centuries still cannot use my name to name a business which would cause confusion with customers about the already established Emerson Electric Company.

"The *protection of trademark* is the law's recognition of the psychological function of symbols. If it is true that we live by symbols, it is no less true that we purchase goods by them" (emphasis added). Felix Frankfurter, 1892–1965 (U.S. Supreme Court Justice, 1939–62).

Trademarks are distinctive symbols, designs, words, devices, shapes, letters, numbers, pictures or a combination thereof to identify goods – to distinguish the source of goods of one person from another. Even particular colors may be associated with a product/company.

Other types of marks are (1) service marks, which identify services rather than goods,[112] **(2) collective membership marks, adopted to indicate membership in an organization (e.g., Better Business Bureau), and (3) certification marks.**

In *Qualitex Co. v. Jacobson Products Co.*, 514 U.S. 159 (1995), a U.S. Supreme Court decision, the court held that businesses can obtain trademarks for colors associated with their products. That had led to

---

[109] Somewhat ironically, comic writer Art Buchwald won an award from persons who produced the movie because they violated his copyrighted work – his expressed ideas for the move.
[110] Robert W. Emerson, *Business Law*. NY: Barron's Educational Series (6th ed., 2015), at 612.
[111] It is an American multinational corporation founded in 1890 by John Wesley Emerson. The first business to sell electric fans, in 1892, now headquartered in Ferguson, Missouri, this Fortune 500 company makes products and provides engineering services for a wide range of industrial, commercial, and consumer markets. The Emerson Electric Co. has approximately 115,000 employees and 220 manufacturing locations worldwide.
[112] In addition to trademarks, the Lanham Act also recognizes service marks. These marks, denoted by "SM," apply to services rather than to goods, but the law is the same as it is for trademarks. Service marks are distinctive symbols, words, letters, numbers, pictures, or combinations thereof that a business adopts and uses to identify its service. These marks can apply to services such as advertising, insurance, hotels, restaurants, and entertainment. For example, the International Silk Association uses the motto "Only silk is silk." That is a service mark. "Burger King" is a trademark. The phrase "Home of the Whopper" is a service mark owned by Burger King.

some interesting trademark battles, such as one that started in 1997 Revlon Inc. and a new company (Urban Decay) over "street–smart" nail polish colors with names such as "Uzi," "Gash," "Blood," "Acid Rain," "Bruise," "Spare Change," "Road Stripe," and "Shattered."

> **International Business and the Significance of Trademarks**
> Many companies, especially large, multinational businesses, depend upon a bundle of trademarks to project and maintain their name and products in various markets.

A. Trademark Lawsuits

Trademark law usually does not concern the sale of genuine goods bearing the true trademark, even though the sale occurs without the trademark owner's consent. Instead, in such a case, the owner's claim is for breach of licensing arrangements, unfair competition or other tort or contract claims.

Trademark claims usually involve misstatements about a good's true origins or ownership, knockoffs without furnishing the correct trademark, the use of misleading marks, etc. Examples would be to label falsely the origins of onions as "Vidalia Onions," of potatoes as "Idaho Potatoes," of oranges as "Florida Oranges," and of apples as "Washington State Apples." Another example: professional sports leagues and major colleges with prominent sports programs fight trademark infringement.

B. Trademark Time Period and Registration

To apply for a trademark, an applicant (usually through its attorney) should research the current database at www.uspto.gov to ensure there would be no infringement on an existing trademark. One can apply for a trademark at the same website using the Trademark Electronic Application System (TEAS).

To apply for a trademark, an applicant (usually through its attorney), should

Trademarks last as long as they are protected. There is a federal ten–year term, but trademarks are renewable indefinitely. In addition, there is a state registration system: as with the federal system, the terms for state trademarks are ten years and, without limitation, are renewable.

The advantages of registration of trademarks with the U.S. Patent and Trademark Office (http://www.uspto.gov/), rather than relying only on common–law protection of trademarks, include: (a) nationwide notice of the trademark owner's claim; (b) evidence of ownership of the trademark in the event of a dispute; (c) federal court jurisdiction, if desired; (d) forming the basis for obtaining registration in other nations; (e) filing the registration with U.S. Customs Service may help prevent importation of foreign goods that infringe on the trademark.

You can make sure people know a mark is protected by stating "Registered in U.S. Patent and Trademark Office" or using the ® (circled R). You also see the symbol "TM," which puts people on notice but is not specified in the Lanham Act. However, lack of notice that a mark is a trademark does not mean the owner of the mark is not due legal protection for the mark. Since 1995, international protection of trademarks has been encouraged by the World Trade Organization.

C. Trademarks Cannot Substitute for an Expired Copyright

In *Dastar Corp. v. Twentieth Century Fox Film Corp.*, 539 U.S. 23 (2003) **(see pg. 613; Emerson BL)**, the U.S. Supreme Court ruled 8–0 in a dispute between two filmmakers that once the copyright on a creative work has expired others may copy it and pass it off as their own without incurring liability under a provision of a federal unfair trade law. Twentieth Century Fox Film Corporation ("20th Century"), which more than 50 years ago had made a television series from Dwight D. Eisenhower's World War II memoir, "Crusade in Europe," sued the Dastar Corporation for using much of the footage without attribution in a current video series that Dastar calls "World War II Campaigns in Europe." 20th Century had allowed the copyright on its series to expire, so it sued Dastar under the Lanham Act, a federal trademark law that prohibits "any false designation of origin" in the sale of "any goods or services." 20th Century contend that

Dastar, in offering its video set as its own product, with only its own employees listed in the screen credits, falsely described the videos' "origin."

But, writing for the court, Justice Antonin Scalia said that "origin" in the Lanham Act referred only to "tangible goods" — a counterfeit watch, for example — and not to the content of a creative work like a book or film. To hold otherwise, Justice Scalia said, would amount to the judicial creation of "a species of mutant copyright law." Instead, patents and copyrights offer a "carefully crafted bargain," a temporary monopoly after which "the public may use the invention or work at will and without attribution." If Congress wants to expand intellectual property protection, Justice Scalia said, it must do so explicitly, as it did when it created new rights for visual artists in a 1990 law.

D. Lapse of trademark

Trademarks can cease for any number of reasons, including: (1) Product itself simply disappears (therefore, any trademark died); and (2) Trademarked term becomes a generic term (i.e., product works so well the term becomes generic). This is called, "genericide." Examples are aspirin, cellophane, shredded wheat, March Madness, kleenex, escalator, and brassiere.[113] Terms that remain protected include Xerox and Rollerblade.

Generic use of a trademark is the use of a mark to describe the product or service with which it is associated, and not as an indicator of a source for that type of product or service. It may cause the mark to become generic and thus lead to a loss of trademark rights.

In some nations, such as the United States, the United Kingdom, and France, aspirin is the common name for the chemical acetylsalicylic acid, and any company may use that name to describe its product. But "aspirin" is a registered trademark of Bayer AG, Germany, in approximately seventy countries worldwide. And in Canada, it is a registered trademark used exclusively to identify analgesics manufactured and distributed by Sterling–Winthrop, Inc. In *Bayer Co. v. United Drug Co.*, 272 F. 505 (S.D.N.Y. 1921) (opinion by the great federal judge, Learned Hand), the trademark "aspirin" was held to be generic for the general public but still had trademark significance for manufacturing chemists, physicians and retail druggists. Today, numerous U.S. companies make aspirin under various trade names.

Another example of a generic term is cellophane. In *DuPont Cellophane Co. v. Waxed Products Co.*, 85 F.2d 75 (2d Cir. 1936), DuPont's famous cellophane mark was held to have become generic. The French inventor of cellophane, one Brandenburger, coined the word as suggesting a cellulose transparent film and registered "La Cellophane" as a trademark in France. However, he immediately used the word generically, i.e., as a noun describing certain material, and with a lower case "c." Thereafter, his American agent distributed advertising circulars to customers describing "La Cellophane" as "the most interesting article put on the market in many years a transparent parchment tissue of the highest merit" (emphasis added) and repeatedly used the words to describe the cellulose product throughout advertising distributed between the years 1912 through 1924. Likewise, after its acquisition of the patents for cellophane in 1923, DuPont itself published several articles in its company magazine using the term "cellophane" generically. From all this evidence, Justice Augustus Hand found that "cellophane" had become generic: "[Cellophane] would have served as a useful trademark, at least in the beginning, if it had not almost immediately lost ground as such because it was employed to describe the article itself." Id. at 77.

Avoiding Genericide

---

[113] Other famous trademarks held to have become generic through improper use include shredded wheat (Kellogg Company v. National Biscuit Company, 305 U.S. 111 (U.S. Supreme Court, 1938)) and thermos (KingSeely Thermos Co. v. Aladdin Industries, Inc., 321 F.2d 577 (2d Cir. 1963)). A more recent example of a mark becoming generic occurred in Illinois High School Ass'n v. GTE Vantage, Inc., 99 F.3d 244 (7th Cir. 1996). There, the term "March Madness," used by the Illinois High School Association since the early 1940s to describe the Illinois state high school ? basketball tournament, was held to have become generic and therefore unenforceable as a trademark against CBS's use with respect to its broadcast of the NCAA championship basketball tournament.

To avoid genericide, Intellectual Property (IP) managers should consider developing a brief manual setting forth the rules of proper use of the company's trademarks. There is, of course, a certain irony in these concerns regarding genericism. After all, managers want people to think of their good as "the good," but not have them use the name of their good to describe all such goods.

E. Terms That Are Best Trademarked

Some terms or phrases are much better(i.e., grant stronger or wider protection) to the trademark holder) than are other, more mundane terms or phrases.
- Best terms (unique) – <u>Made–up</u> (Exxon, Polaroid, Kodak, Lexus, Valspar);
- Good terms – Common words, but an <u>unusual connection or suggestion</u> (Apple Computers);
- Little Protection – Merely <u>descriptive</u> terms (Tastee salad dressing, Premier Motors, Great Steaks).[114] Unlike the made-up or unusual connection or "suggestive" terms above, the descriptive terms are only protected if they have acquired a secondary meaning (e.g., Home Depot). See **pg. 613; Emerson BL**. The term, "secondary meaning," indicates that the mark has a meaning beyond just the language itself – that it creates or evokes an association between the mark and the product in question.

Incontestability rules distinguish separate generic terms and descriptive terms. Generic terms are always contestable, even after five years of registration; on the other hand, even if "merely descriptive," a mark that is registered and unchallenged for five years becomes incontestable.

<u>An Example: A Dry Cleaning Business</u>

Good names (for trademark purposes)

"G Guys & Gals Cleaners" – it is arbitrary, fanciful.

"Summer's Day Dry Cleaners" – it is suggestive, so can be registered without showing secondary meaning.

Poor names (for trademark purposes)

"Quick and Tidy Dry Cleaners" - probably merely descriptive, so no registration should work unless there is a showing of secondary meaning. A solution: Change the name or advertise greatly and create secondary meaning.

"Dry Cleaning Business" - generic, so any application should be bounced (i.e., rejected!).

What about a term such as "chicken tenders"? Burger King each year warns dozens of businesses to stop using that, or a similar, term. Burger King holds a trademark on the term, "chicken tenders," and it won a jury verdict in 2005 against an infringing use by a chicken processing company.

Menashe v. V Secret Catalogue, Inc., 409 F.Supp.2d 412 (S.D.N.Y. 2006)

The lawyers of trademark holders often send letters demanding that an individual or business immediately cease-and-desist from using a picture, phrase, logo, or some other alleged mark. This case is an example of a "defensive" action: a plaintiff's preemptively seeking to have a court end the other party's "cease-and-desist" efforts. Here, two women sued to stop Victoria's Secret from squelching the women's new product launch.

Former Sports Illustrated swimsuit model Audrey Quock appeared in the sports magazine's annual swimsuit issue between 1998 and 2003 and was also featured in other magazines and advertising campaigns. She and publicist Ronit Menashe alleged that they came up with the term "Sexy Little Things, Sexy Little Things" in July or August 2004 and registered a domain name to build a website. After sending a manufacturer diagrams for the production of "Sexy Little Things" labels and preparing publicity, the pair

---

[114] One cannot trademark terms too similar to existing trademarks, that imply government approval, or that are obscene. See, e.g., In re Rundsdorph, 171 U.S.P.Q. 443 (1973).
In April 1999, a three–judge panel of the US Trade and Patent office withdrew trademark protection for football's Washington Redskins on the grounds that the name "may disparage Native Americans and may bring them into contempt or disrepute."

received a letter from Victoria's Secret telling them their line would constitute trademark infringement. Menashe and Quock then stopped development of the clothing line and sought relief in court, saying no one had registered the trademark when they checked with the Patent and Trademark Office in September 2004.

U.S. District Judge Harold Baer concluded that between March 2004 and June 2004 the Victoria's Secret marketing department decided to use the "Sexy Little Things" phrase for its panties collection. More important, Victoria's Secret acquired priority in the trademark use of "Sexy Little Things" because, since July 28, 2004, it had placed "Sexy Little Things" signs in its stores and used the "Sexy Little Things" label on panties displayed for sale under those "Sexy Little Things" signs. Judge Baer also held that the phrase "sexy little things" was suggestive, entitling it to greater legal protection than if it were merely descriptive: "While the term describes the erotically stimulating quality of the trademarked lingerie, it also calls to mind the phrase 'sexy little thing,' popularly used to refer to attractive lithe young women."

Marketed to females in their 20s or 30s willing to wear their pants low enough to expose "decorated bottoms," the "fun, flirty and playfully sexy" panties earned Victoria's Secret $119 million in revenues from July 2004 through November 2005.

F. Trade Dress

Trade dress is a commercial symbol also protected by trademark law and the Lanham Act, although it is often not registered. Trade dress involves distinctive packaging or appearance, such as a particular color and style of uniform for servers at a chain of restaurants (e.g., Hooters). It does <u>not</u> extend to a functional part of a product, for which, instead, patent protection may be available.

Trade dress concerns the "look and feel" of products and of service establishments. This includes the size, shape, color, texture, graphics, and even certain sales techniques of products. This has been applied to many products such as teddy bears, luggage, greeting cards, romance novels, and folding tables.

The U.S. Supreme Court supported a trade dress claim made in *Two Pesos, Inc., v. Taco Cabana, Inc.*, 505 U.S. 763 (1992). A Mexican-style restaurant could not copy its competitor's decor, which included distinctive exterior decorations and interior design. Trade dress that is "inherently distinctive" is protected under the Lanham Act and by common-law principles concerning unfair competition.

An overlap between patent law and trade dress law is demonstrated when a former design patent tends to undermine a present trade dress claim. In *TrafFix Devices, Inc. v. Marketing Displays, Inc.*, 532 U.S. 23 (2001), Marketing Displays of Framingham, Michigan made and sold road signs (e.g., "Road Work Ahead") with a patented dual-spring mechanism that kept them upright during windy conditions. After the patent expired, TrafFix Devices of San Clemente, California began selling signs with the same device. Marketing Displays sued TrafFix Devices for, among other things, trademark and trade dress infringement. However, the claim of unlawful copying of appearance or packaging involved the dual-spring mechanism that allows roadside signs to pop back up on windy days. So, in the *TrafFix Devices* case, the U.S. Supreme Court unanimously ruled that the existence (or former existence) of a company's design patent provides "strong evidence" that the design was functional and therefore not entitled to trade-dress protection. For the Court, Justice Anthony Kennedy wrote, "Where the expired patent claimed the features in question, one who seeks to establish trade-dress protection must carry the heavy burden of showing that the feature is not functional." The effect of the decision is to deter patent holders, such as for durable consumer goods, from obtaining protection for the look of an invention and, therefore, extending intellectual property rights in the invention beyond the life of the patent.

Remember: patents have a finite term, while trade dress (in effect, a type of trademark) has an indefinite duration.

G. Victor's Little Secret and the Trademark Dilution Revision Act

What is too similar a term? Victoria's Secret brought an unsuccessful action against Victor's Little Secret, an Elizabethtown, Kentucky strip–mall shop selling lingerie and adult videos and "novelties." In *Moseley v. V Secret Catalogue, Inc.*, 537 U.S. 418 (2003), a unanimous U.S. Supreme Court decision, the

> Trade names: cannot be federally registered, infringement is still subject to injunction + damages

Court found that use of the name Victor's Little Secret "neither confused any consumers or potential consumers, nor was likely to do so."

The opinion interpreted a 1995 Congressional amendment of the Trademark Act to cover "dilution of famous marks," with such dilution defined as "lessening of the capacity of a famous mark to identify and distinguish goods and services."[115] But the Court in *Moseley* noted that federal trademark law still requires some proof of real harm, which Victoria's Secret did not provide.[116]

The decision upset large businesses with strong trademarks. In 2006, Congress enacted, and President Bush signed, the Trademark Dilution Revision Act, which states, in part: "the owner of a famous mark that is distinctive, inherently or through acquired distinctiveness, shall be entitled to an injunction against another person who, at any time after the owner's mark has become famous, commences use of a mark or trade name in commerce that is likely to cause dilution by blurring or dilution by tarnishment of the famous mark, regardless of the presence or absence of actual or likely confusion, of competition, or of actual economic injury." This law clarified the "blurring" and "tarnishment" standards that courts had been dealing with for many years, and it also dealt with other matters concerning dilution, including "acquired distinctiveness,"[117] the definition of "famous," and issues of "trade dress" and "fair use."

Still remaining is the question whether marks famous only in a particular geographic area or channel of commerce ("niche" marks) qualify for dilution protection under the statute. Also, should dilution be limited to marks that are inherently distinctive (i.e., marks that consumers recognize as brand symbols immediately upon use). This limitation would exclude from federal protection those famous marks that acquired distinctiveness through use (e.g., McDonalds, Coca Cola).

VII. Trade Secrets (see pgs. 614-616; Emerson BL)

Trade secrets typically relate to or can be acquired via access to methods of production – they are particularized to a business, not just general aspects of all businesses or an industry, such as ideas on payroll, controlling inventory, etc. Almost any business-specific information (e.g., a formula, process, customer list, or method of operation) that has economic value, is secret, and is subject to reasonable efforts to maintain secrecy could qualify as trade secrets.

The trade secret is the oldest and simplest form of intellectual property. It remains a widely used form of intellectual property protection, in part because patents and copyrights eventually expire while trade secrets (similar to trademarks) have no maximum period of duration (one can lawfully hold onto and own a trade secret as long as it is kept secret); even more important, unlike patents or other registered works, which usually require making public company-specific information and property interests, the trade secret is to be kept completely confidential.

The trade secret's indefinite duration and simplicity do come with drawbacks. Keeping something secret obviously requires extensive commitments of time and energy and the results may still be out of one's hands. If someone else either independently stumbles on the same idea, or can figure out the secret by reverse engineering the product, then all protection is lost. Indeed, trade secrecy is *not* suited to an environment in which skilled employees who work with or develop secret technology are highly mobile and

---

[115] Congressional debate on this change cited such examples as Buick Aspirin, DuPont Shoes, and Kodak Pianos. The 1995 law is the Federal Trademark Dilution Act (FTDA), at 15 U.S.C. 1125(c).

[116] The Supreme Court noted various types of evidence used to prove actual harm where the parties' marks are not identical. For example, a plaintiff may submit surveys, expert testimony and/or consumer testimony on the impact of a defendant's use on the plaintiff's mark.

[117] So protection goes beyond the inherently distinctive (marks that consumers immediately recognize as brand symbols) to also cover famous marks that acquired distinctiveness through use (e.g., McDonald's, Coca Cola).

are frequently inclined toward independent innovation and business development – conditions that characterize the computer industry and, at times, other high-tech fields.[118]

Two of the most famous trade secrets involve the Coca-Cola classic drink formula and the Kentucky Fried Chicken (KFC) original chicken recipe. On January 29, 2001, it was announced that a note found in the basement of a home once owned by KFC founder "Colonel" Harland Sanders did not contain his secret recipe. This was a welcome relief to the company because 16 months earlier restaurateurs Tommy and Cherry Settle, who bought the home in the 1970s, had found a leather-bound 1964 date book containing the note - a recipe listing 11 herbs and spices in specific proportions. If it had proven to be the recipe, that would have been the end for the KFC trade secret. (There have been instances where people have threatened to reveal the Coca-Cola formula, only to have it become clear that they were bluffing and did not really have access to the tightly controlled trade secret.)

A YOUTUBE *video* – "Senior Thesis" (8 minutes, 31 seconds) is at robertwemersonufl

A trade secret may be defined as confidential, privately made and owned information, such as a formula or process or something else whose secrecy enhances its value. It may simply be a business' guarded information about customers and suppliers, or on pricing, marketing, services or manufacturing.

But secrets often are fleeting.

William Congreve wrote in his play, *Love for Love*, "I know that's a secret, for it's whispered everywhere."

And Ben Franklin observed, in *Poor Richard's Almanack*, "Three may keep a secret, if two of them are dead!"

So, with pride, Emerson Productions Presents: "THE SENIOR THESIS" – Based on *Real Events* leading to a lawsuit in fine, fair, friendly Phenix City, Alabama.

The scene is Chimera Chemical Company: "chimera" - pronounced "Kye-MEER-uh" – something impossible or fanciful, the monster of Greek mythology (half-lion and half-snake?) – fancy, dream, daydream, whim, castle in the air, pie in the sky, fool's paradise, pipe dream, fantasy, illusion, delusion.

[There is so much more to see in the video itself!]

When Chimera Chemical discovered what those miscreants were doing, a huge lawsuit followed for theft of trade secrets. Who won? The case had an ironic twist, involving a *defendant's* trade secrets: Because the plaintiff managed to access, during the lawsuit, some of the defendant's trade secrets, the trial court dismissed the plaintiff's suit!

VIII. Know-How

American courts and legislatures have collaborated to safeguard know-how, a subject closely related to trade secrets. This has especially been the case for **franchising**. Such protections also are found in many other countries, including throughout Europe.

Know-how has no precise definition that applies in all cases, but can be considered information which is business or systems specific (not something simply used in all similar businesses). Elements may exist that when considered individually, do not attain the degree of originality constituting know-how, but

---

[118] Those fields are more often characterized by registered intellectual property, such as patents and trademarks. For patents, as discussed previously, the state offers its protection for patented works only if the intellectual property registrant agrees to "give the invention away" after having had a fair chance to profit from it during the 20-year period of exclusivity.

when organized as a system and considered holistically, have the specificity of know-how. It is, in other words, the entire set of knowledge that collectively must have a degree of originality, not necessarily parts of the set – such as a franchise "package" - which may be similar to what is found in other businesses.

Even if not a trade secret, it is something only readily available to those who are specifically provided access to that information. In the franchising context it is associated with system-wide skills and practices, generally transmitted from franchisor to franchisee and part of the franchise network. In the Civil Law tradition as found in France, Germany and many other nations, know-how's required characteristics are fourfold:
1. substantiality (significant and useful to the know-how's recipient for use, sale or resale of goods or services);
2. experimentation (the analysis of experience and then formulating a system from the resulting conclusions);
3. identification (sufficiently described so that it can be transmitted to and adopted by others); and
4. secrecy (not generally known, readily accessible or easily learned).

While American courts and regulators have not usually followed this more detailed approach for cases considering know-how, the increasing globalization of business and legal concepts may contribute to a uniform approach world-wide, as has already been the case for more established forms of intellectual property such as patents, trademarks, copyrights, and trade secrets.[119]

D. AGENCY

[Handwritten note: Agency is state common law. Neither federal law nor the Uniform Commercial Code deals w/ the subject of agency]

> "Oh world! world! world! thus is the poor AGENT despised. O traitors and bawds, how earnestly are you set a-work, and how ill requited! Why should our endeavor be so loved, and the performance so loathed?" William Shakespeare, "Troilus and Cressida, Act V, scene ten, line 36.

All sorts of problems are associated with possible vicarious and direct liability: Respondeat superior, disclosed or undisclosed agency, frolics, detours, negligent hires, disloyal agents, fiduciary duties, and functions too personal to be handled through an agency.

I. INTRODUCTION

All of us can be agents either for good or evil. American business could not function without agents. In agency, a person represents another person; authorized acts of the representative are, in effect, the acts of the one he/she represents. Agency is a paramount topic in the law of partnerships and corporations (e.g., to function, corporations must have agents).

A. Key Terms
Principal (P) – any legal entity (a person) who authorizes an agent to act on his/her (P's) behalf (example: CEOs are agents for the corporation (the principal)).

Agent (A) – any legal entity that has the capacity to act as a representative of the principal and is, in the present situation, authorized to bind the principal when it (A) acts within the scope of his/her/its authority.
Examples: Others paying Agent (A), delivering goods to A, receiving goods from A, signing contract with A – it is as if these acts were done to or for the Principal.

Creation of Agency – As with creation of a contract, look to the parties' words and conduct, and to the overall circumstances.

---

[119] For a comprehensive discussion of know-how law in the United States and France, *see* Robert W. Emerson, *Franchise Savoir-Faire,* 90 TULANE L. REV. _ (Dec. 2015), to be added and available at http://ssrn.com/author=86449.

Agency is similar to (but not identical to) contract law – consent is required for an agency to be created, and for it to remain in existence. But consideration may be unnecessary.

B. Agency Law Applicability to Directors and Corporate Managers

In Anglo–American law, fiduciary duty is the core legal concept to address conflicts among directors/managers and shareholders. The concept is developed and constantly refined by courts in the process of adjudication.

By contrast, most civil law jurisdictions, including many transition economies, either lack the procedural rules that would enable parties to bring such cases to courts, or have not developed a sufficient body of case law to determine the contents and meaning of this concept. As law in a fast–changing world often is incomplete, and the expected harms of certain behaviors are recognizable and can be contained through court decisions causing no significant externalities, courts sometimes must have the right to define and enforce fiduciary duty principles. Economists might say that to allocate the lawmaking and law enforcement functions to courts in those circumstances is not simply a common law tradition, but – regardless of the legal system, is optimal. Breaches of fiduciary duty pose harms typically limited to the principal (e.g., the corporation/shareholders for whom officers/directors work). While courts in transition economies may have difficulties living up to the task of exercising lawmaking rights, there may be no workable alternative.

II. ACTUAL AUTHORITY

Actual authority means an actual agency, either express or implied.[120]

A. Example of an Actual Agency: The Hotel Room with a Stopped-Up Shower Drain

Alice, Manager for a Hotel, is supposed to collect payments, check guests in and out, and generally keep guests satisfied. Alice was hired to carry out anything necessary. Gustav Guest tells Alice that his shower drain is stopped up. Alice attempts to clean and unclog the drain, but Alice is unsuccessful and determines that a professional is needed. So Alice hires Perry Plumber to do the required plumbing.

Plumber clears the drain and bills the hotel owner. Plumber should be paid.

Hotel owner to Alice: What is this? I never gave you authority to hire a plumber. (Perhaps the owner wants to take the plumber's bill out of Alice's pay.)

But Alice has Implied Authority (owner is liable for the plumber's bill; Alice and Owner apparently never talked directly re this area – plumbing).
(1) To do what is reasonably necessary to accomplish the Principal's purpose (a good, safe, sanitary, profitable hotel). Therefore, Alice was acting within her implied authority, and the owner must pay the plumber.
(2) To carry on the business in the usual and customary way.
(3) To take necessary action in an emergency.
(4) The Agent may be restricted, but can follow common sense as to what is implicit.
Ordinarily implied authority must be within reason.

Suppose Owner says to Alice, "I never told you to hire a plumber this way. My cousin's a plumber. When work need to be done, I use him." That will not keep the Owner from being responsible for the work the Agent previously authorized. But, from now on, Alice's authority is limited to hiring the owner's cousin.

---

[120] An implied agency (one inferred from the words or conduct the principal manifested towards the agent) could include custom, the ways an arrangement has always been. Of course, an express agency is based on oral or written words from the principal to the agent. Robert W. Emerson, *Business Law*. NY: Barron's Educational Series (6th ed., 2015), at 305.

B. Actual Authority: Three Other Brief Examples of Implied Authority

> Two agents for a bar: a bouncer & an accountant
>
> Each one is an agent, authorized to represent the bar. But each has different areas of authority (different implied authorities). The bouncer is authorized to bounce. Within reason, the bouncer may eject unruly bar patrons or otherwise act to maintain order in the bar. As for the accountant, he/she has the authority to fill out tax forms and carry on other stimulating accountancy work on the bar's behalf. Each one could bind the principal in the agent's area of expertise, for which the agent had been hired. But neither could bind the principal beyond the agent's area of representation. For example, the bouncer could not bind the principal with a tax form, and the accountant could not "bounce" and thereby bind the principal. In summary, in most cases, if an agent should take it upon himself/herself to deviate from his/her realm of expertise (the purpose of his/her agency for the principal), his/her resulting actions ordinarily cannot bind the principal.
>
> Big City Firm: a messenger and the firm's car
>
> Even in an age of instant messaging, e–mail, and other electronic wonders of instantaneous communications, there remain businesses and areas of employment requiring physical delivery of documents or other materials (e.g., FedEx, UPS). Many firms in large cities have employees, or hire outside delivery contractors, whose job is to take items from the firm (point A) to another location (point B) and vice–versa (from point B to point A). These delivery people often use bicycles, mopeds or other quick and easily maneuverable means of transport. But what if there is a vital document that absolutely must get to an office, clear across the city, before that office closes? Because that office will soon close, the messenger must get there much quicker than via the usual means (bicycling); the messenger thus likely has the authority to take a cab, or to commandeer the firm vehicle, in order to make a timely delivery. That authority is based on the implied power of the agent to do whatever is reasonably necessary to make timely deliveries and pick–ups on behalf of the principal.
>
> A waiter's discretionary authority to lower a bill
>
> Authority arises from the situation at hand. Servers at restaurants often have, depending on the circumstances, the power to make adjustments to placate disgruntled customers.[121] Such adjustments in a bill would, as authorized actions of the server–agent, bind the employer–principal.

C. Unauthorized Contracts Formed by an Agent

The agent is liable to the third party if the agent lacks authority to make a contract with the third party. Now, if it is clear, or should be clear, to the third party that the agent lacks authority, the agent alone is liable.

Suppose that Abner Agent presents a letter of introduction and authority from Paula Principal indicating that Abner is authorized to purchase antique dining room furniture for her. Abner and Theodore Third Party make a contract, ostensibly binding Paula, for Abner to buy an antique automobile. Abner alone is liable: Theodore should not have made such a contract, which is clearly outside the express or implied authority to buy furniture.

However, if Paula told Abner, "Buy antique furniture for me, but no drop–leaf tables," and Abner did buy a drop– leaf table from Theodore, Theodore could expect that Paula would pay. Knowledge of secret and unexpected (unreasonable) limitations on the agent's authority is not imputed to the third party. (If Abner made a good deal, however, Paula could accept it – she could ratify the unauthorized contract.)

Actually, what is happening is this: when an agent acts, she makes an implied warranty to the third party. The warranty is "I have authority to act on behalf of my principal." If the agent does not have

---

[121] Servers (waiters, waitresses, waitpersons) often pop by and ask customers, "How is the food?" What if a customer angrily responds, "No good; it stinks!"

authority, or if she exceeds her authority, she has breached her contract with the third party. (In this example, with Abner making an unauthorized but ostensibly reasonable contract, although Theodore will bill Paula and Paula will have to pay, Abner has breached his duty to Paula, and Paula has the right to pursue Abner for indemnification.)

III. APPARENT AUTHORITY Bamon pg 305

A. Two Different, Exemplary Cases Involving Apparent Authority

In *Croce v. Bromley Corp.*, 623 F.2d 1084 (5th Circuit, U.S. Court of Appeals, 1980), the next of kin sued the tour operator for the Jim Croce band.

Jim Croce, the singer of such songs as "Operator," "Big Bad Leroy Brown," and "Roller Derby Queen" – died with the rest of his band in an airplane crash. The band had even more hits after he died. The band's next-of-kin sued the tour operator, which had led Croce and his band to assume the tour company was in charge of everything related to the tour. (Of course, the airplane company likely was directly liable; but the next-of-kin's alleged agency, presumably because there are bigger pockets from which to collect.)

The court held that even though an independent company controlled the airplane and the pilot, Jim Croce and his band reasonably believed they were under the tour operator's control (that the operator was in charge of it all).

The following case had a different result from that of the Croce case. In *CSX Transp., Inc. v. Recovery Express, Inc.*, 415 F.Supp.2d 6 (D. Mass. 2006), the court dealt with this issue: Is a company–issued e–mail address enough to imply authority?

IDEC and Recovery Express shared email services. An employee of IDEC, Albert Arillotta, sent e–mails which appeared to be from Recovery Express; he negotiated a contract with Len Whitehead, Jr., who was acting as a representative of CSX. Allegedly, the contract involved the use of CSX's railcars. When Recovery Express refused to honor, CSX sued for breach, but the Court held "Whitehead and CSX were unreasonable, as a matter of law, in their reliance solely on an e–mail domain name. Such a manifestation by Recovery cannot be sufficient to sustain a claim of apparent authority. Granting an e–mail domain name, by itself, does not cloak the recipient with carte blanche authority to act on behalf the grantee. Were this so, every subordinate employee with a company e–mail address – down to the night watchman – could bind a company to the same contracts as the president. This is not the law."

The Court then wrote: [T]he results in analogous low–tech situations confirm this conclusion. The Court could find no cases where, for example, giving someone a business card with the company name or logo, access to a company car, or company stationery, by themselves, created sufficient indicia of apparent authority. [Citing five pro–apparent authority cases with these holdings – (1) issuance of a company credit card, business cards with company logo, possession of company paraphernalia, and appearing in company advertisements was insufficient to create apparent authority); (2) issuance of a business card and display of a plaque insufficient to create apparent authority); (3) permitting the occupation of offices, the use of telephones and receptionist, the receipt of mail at company offices, and access to stationery was insufficient to create apparent authority; (3) putting a purported agent in an electric company vehicle, when plaintiff knew that volunteers were assisting crews, was insufficient to create apparent authority; (4) providing nitrogen tanks with company logo, billing for services with invoices bearing company logo, sending postcards claiming to be a company representative, distributing business cards indicating representative status, and giving out calendars with company logo was insufficient to create apparent authority; (5) supplying forms and business cards were the only actions of defendant and were not sufficient to create apparent authority. But citing cases where courts found support for apparent authority – (1) agent used business card designating him as vice president, agent met with plaintiff's representatives, and agent directed and negotiated contract terms with plaintiff; (2) detailing the sharing of website and e–mail addresses, the use of identical business cards, and "collectively behav[ing] 'as a single production and sales team'," as well as other facts "too numerous to detail."]

An e–mail domain name is sufficiently analogous to business cards, company vehicles, and letterhead for these cases to be persuasive. Those indicia of apparent authority all convey some degree of association between the purported principal and agent. By themselves, however, no reasonable person could conclude that apparent authority was present. The same is true with e–mail domain names.

In the end, CSX and Whitehead should have been more suspicious of an unsolicited, poorly written e–mail that arrived late one Friday afternoon. There are means by which CSX could have protected itself (e.g., requiring a purchase order form from IDEC or Recovery). Before delivering goods worth over $115,000 to a stranger, one reasonably should be expected to inquire as to the authority of that person to have made such a deal. Given the anonymity of the Internet, this case illustrates the potential consequences of operating–even in today's fast–paced business world–as did CSX.

B. Apparent Authority Is An Agency By Estoppel

Apparent authority – creating an apparent agency – is by estoppel. It is not a "true" agency, but treated as such re: third parties.

Apparent authority is a communication or signal directly from the principal to a third party…[that] arises out of actions or the conduct of the principal which causes a third party to reasonably believe that the agent has the authority to make contracts for the principal.[122]

The Elements of Apparent Authority are twofold:
(a) The apparent principal has by its acts or omissions created, or allowed others to create, a third person's reasonable belief that someone (the apparent agent) is the apparent principal's agent (although in reality this apparent agent is not an actual agent); and
(b) the third person relies on the apparent agency. The third person cannot rely on the presumed agency to an extreme – there may be some duty to verify the agency. We hold a supposed principal accountable if the victim reasonably thought an agent was acting with authority and the supposed principal helped create that belief.

So, to sum up this key matter: The third party's belief must be reasonable, and the supposed principal must somehow be responsible for letting the third party come to that belief. The defendant must have fostered the trappings (appearance) of authority in order to be bound.

C. Apparent Authority: Franchising as an Example

The most famous franchised system in the world is almost certainly McDonald's. A franchisee has a contractual relationship with McDonald's. The franchisee of McDonald's typically is, at most, an apparent agent because ultimately the franchisee, not McDonald's, tends to control the restaurant.

Robert W. Emerson, *Franchisors' Liability When Franchisees Are Apparent Agents: An Empirical and Policy Analysis of "Common Knowledge" About Franchising*, 20 HOFSTRA L. REV. 609–685,[123] concerns the issue of apparent authority in the franchising context. It noted that judges may presume "common knowledge" about franchising – that the general public must by now know that many gas stations, stores, restaurants, etc. have a national name, but are actually independently owned and operated. The article shows that while maybe people should know this, most do not; therefore, a basis for defeating "apparent" agency (via so–called common knowledge) is missing.

Blood Transfusion Example

Warner v. Hillcrest Medical Center, 914 P.2d 1060 (Okla. Civ. App. Nov. 20, 1995), cert. denied April 1, 1996, was a suit by the estate of Norma Levitt.

---

[122] Robert W. Emerson, *Business Law*. NY: Barron's Educational Series (6th ed., 2015), at 305.
[123] This article will be added and available at http://ssrn.com/author=86449.

> Levitt died on the operating table at the hospital in Tulsa following successful hip replacement surgery. A nurse anesthetist gave Levitt a unit of Levitt's own blood that had been warmed in a microwave oven located in the employees' lounge. Heating blood that way destroys the red blood cells, resulting in "gross hemolysis" of the blood, releasing large amounts of potassium, an often fatal event.
>
> The practice of warming intravenous (IV) fluids, other than blood, in the microwave was an accepted practice at the hospital, as reflected in its written procedures. However, Abbot Laboratories, the manufacturer of the IV solutions, had mailed Hillcrest telling it that microwaving the solutions was not recommended.
>
> The plaintiff's expert, a neurosurgery and anesthesiology prof at Stanford, testified in a deposition that the Anesthesiologists at Hillcrest, especially the one who supervised the giving of anesthesia to Mrs. Levitt, had deviated below a national standard of care. By not prohibiting the warming of blood in a microwave oven (rather than using the slower, but safer blood warmers that were available).
>
> Levitt died minutes after receiving the blood. The defendants argued that Levitt died from a blood clot, while the plaintiffs pointed to the hemolysized blood.
>
> **Bottom line: should we consider it to be <u>common knowledge</u> that the fast-action microwaving method of heating does things differently than the slower stove method?**

D. *Serbin v. Walt Disney World:* Reliance on Supposed Authority Must be Reasonable

In *Serbin v. Walt Disney World*, 386 A.2d 1372 (N.J. Super. 1978), the New Jersey Superior Court, a state court, found in favor of Walt Disney World. Plaintiff Richard Serbin, a New Jersey lawyer, attended a convention of the New Jersey Bar Association held at Disney World in Orlando. There, Richard, his wife Kathy Serbin, and their minor sons Jonathan and Jeffrey were arrested for allegedly passing a counterfeit $20 bill. The plaintiffs sued Walt Disney World in New Jersey. On appeal, the Superior Court found no personal jurisdiction over the defendant because the New Jersey based travel agency, Rosenblatt Travel Agency, which had promoted the convention, was not an agent of Disney World – even though it had said so in small print on brochures, as the court wrote "proof of agency cannot rest solely on the declarations of the person whose agency is sought to be proved, without other evidence." Because Rosenblatt was not an agency of Disney,

Disney succeeded in having the court dismiss the case. There were none of the minimal contacts in New Jersey necessary for personal jurisdiction (no incurring or paying of taxes, no agent for service of process, no advertising in local N.J. media, no listing in any N.J. telephone directories, no commissions to any travel agent in N.J. for booking reservations at Disney World, and no assets, office, or place of business in N.J., as well as no offices, agents, salesmen, or reps. in N.J.).

E. The Government and Its Supposed Agents

<u>The Government Usually Cannot be an "Apparent" Principal:</u> It is better for one person to suffer due to (be screwed over by!) a government error than the entire country being bound by the mistake.

Apparent or even Implied Authority claims ordinarily fail against the government. The classic, often–cited case for this proposition remains *Federal Crop Ins. Corp. v. Merrill*, 332 U.S. 380 (1947), in which an employee of the federal agency accepted a wheat farmer's crop for coverage under the federal regulations. The employee did not know that the farmer's acreage was not eligible. When the crop was destroyed and the farmer was denied insurance, he complained, asserting that the representations made by the FCIC's agent bound the agency, just as such representations would have bound a private insurance company if made by its agent. The Supreme Court of the United States held that the agency was not bound: innocent ignorance of the regulations could not enlarge the administrative agency's congressionally granted powers.

F. Clauses in a Third Party's Contract with Someone Who Is, Not, In Fact, an Agent

Even if a supposed agent turns out to have no authority, contractual clauses asserting such authority (in contracts between the "agent" and a third party) may help claims of apparent authority or – at the very least – a claim of fraud against the "agent." Here is a sample "corporate authority" contract clause:

"<u>Corporate Authority (if Representative is a corporation)</u>. Representative represents and warrants that the execution and delivery of this Agreement by said Representative has been authorized by proper corporate action, and that the officers of the corporation whose names appear hereafter have been duly elected or appointed and are presently serving as such officers."

G. Lingering Authority (see pg. 312; Emerson BL)

Lingering authority involves an actual agency transformed into an apparent agency. For the lingering authority to arise, the actual agency would be gone, but the agency would reasonably "linger" in the minds of third persons (this lingering thus constitutes apparent authority).

But – per the skit – required payments in cash, receipt to be issued later, no uniform or other indicia of company connections all point to the absence of reasonable signs of agency to rely upon.

LINGERING AUTHORITY SKIT: "ARNIE AGENT, THE BAD BAD BRUSH BROKER"
It is a question of lingering authority.
Question: Does Arnie have express authority to act for the Pure Brush Company?
Answer: No. The company has not authorized him to act.
Question: Does he have implied authority?
Answer: No, because his actions were not reasonably necessary to accomplish an authorized act.
Question: Does he have any authority? (Obviously, Arnie is liable for his own malfeasance or other wrongs, but what if his venture goes bust and he bought a lot on credit (or misled his customers)? Can the creditors or customers collect from the Pure Brush Company?
Answer: Apparent authority. The principal has not authorized him to act but perhaps the principal has done something to make an innocent third party believe Arnie was authorized to act.
Question: What has Pure Brush Company done to make Customer believe Arnie is authorized to act? (The customer had prior dealings with Agent.)
Answer: It did not retrieve his samples and forms. Many companies require their sales staff to put down a substantial deposit so that they will have an incentive to return samples and forms.
Question: Is there anything else the company could have done?
Answer: It could notify its customers that Arnie no longer works for it. That would have prevented the problem with Customer, since she had been a customer previously.

A somewhat similar example: An agent, a Resort's Sales Representative, is fired or quits, but pretends the agency still exists as a way to set up her own business. She orders and puts goods and equipment in her own warehouse while raising capital to acquire a real property.

To prevent lingering authority, the company should give actual notice to the former employee's customers. That is because if a customer reasonably believes the former employee still works for the company, then the company could be stuck as responsible for the former employee's actions.
To avoid lingering authority, notice must be given (but one need not tell everyone in the world). In the notice, one need not go into particulars. One does not have to say, "we fired her!" Just say: "Ms. __ is no longer our agent."

Two types of notice given to kill the chances for lingering authority are constructive notice and actual notice.

Constructive notice is adequate for those with whom the agent did not have dealings (the "no–past–dealings people"). The notice is good if in newspapers or trade journals, regardless of whether the no–past–dealings people read the notice.

Actual notice is the preferred method for people who actually dealt with the Agent. That is because such notice provides direct notice to everyone with whom an agent dealt. Other information sources may work. But we cannot be sure that will happen. So the safe thing (once an agent is terminated) is for the principal to give actual notice.

Of course, if a third party already knew that there was no longer an agency, then no direct notice to that third party would be necessary to forestall an appearance of authority; there would be no reasonable basis for the third party to believe in a former agent's apparent authority if the third party somehow knew that the agency had, in fact, been terminated. In cases such as these, one may err on the side of caution by making confirmation with the third party, preferably leaving some physical proof (e.g., a paper trail).

H. Ratification

Even if there was no agency at first, there may be an after–the–fact authorization (ratification). So an agency was created, albeit after–the–fact (ex post facto). Such ratification can be either express or implied (just as agencies and contracts can be express or implied).

Here are some examples of the principal later ratifying an agent's unauthorized acts.

Express Ratification

A minister had no permission, nor even any apparent authority, to undertake alone significant business decisions for his church. But he went ahead and, in the name of the church, obtained a mortgage for some new real property. The vestry (board of directors) was upset that the minister acted first without consulting it, but at its next meeting the vestry decided that the deal the minister obtained looked good. Therefore, the vestry passed a resolution reminding the minister that he had no authority to act as he did, but also agreeing to pay the mortgage. Later, when the church runs into financial difficulties and seeks to stop paying the mortgage on the grounds that it is not bound (that the minister acted without any actual or apparent authority), that claim is no longer tenable. The church is stuck with the contract because it expressly ratified the minister's actions after–the–fact.

Implied Ratification: Two Examples

1. A Vice–President for personnel proceeds with a marketing idea on behalf of her company. The people with whom she dealt knew that she was in her company's personnel department and had no authority in the marketing sphere. (The old saw about some industries – e.g., banking – is that everyone becomes a Vice–President within six months after being hired. Titles do not necessarily confer authority – express, implied, or apparent!)
So the Vice–President had no actual OR apparent authority. But company officials with authority over marketing, after finding out about what she did, continue the arrangements with the outside parties (e.g., keep paying on certain deals). Later, if it turns out the VP was not in marketing because she really didn't know that sector (her marketing arrangements, in retrospect, stunk (!), then it is too late for the company to back out. By, at least for a time, going with her idea the company implicitly ratified her actions.
2. A store clerk exceeds her authority when a manufacturer's sales representative persuades her to order a number of goods for the store. The sales rep knows that the clerk simply sells goods and is not a buyer for the store, or otherwise authorized to buy goods for re–sale. So the clerk had no authority, actual or apparent, to bind the store in this instance.

But suppose that the storeowner (after berating the clerk!) decides to not send the goods back but to "see if they sell." Months later, long past any time when the store ordinarily could return goods to wholesalers/manufacturers for reimbursement, the storeowner again berates the clerk (this time, not so much because the clerk had no authority, but just because her idea turned out to be stupid!). But the storeowner cannot win a claim that the clerk's acts do not bind the store: By holding onto the goods to "see if they sell," the owner implicitly ratified the clerk's ordering of the goods from the manufacturer.

I. Examples Concerning An Agent's Authority

1. Calvin and Bobo

Calvin is the owner of "Calvin's California Rolls" (CCR), where he sells one product: a particular type of sushi roll. Calvin's roll contains the traditional four ingredients: cucumber, crab meat, avocado, and – of course - rice. Bobo works for Calvin.

a. Calvin tells Bobo, "We're out of avocados. Go get some from the grocery store." Does Bobo have authority to buy avocados on behalf of Calvin? If so, what kind?
Answer: Yes, Bobo is authorized. This is <u>actual, express authority</u> - from the words of Calvin.

b. While at the grocery store, Bobo remembers that CCR is low on cucumbers, too. Does Bobo have authority to buy cucumbers on behalf of Calvin?
Answer: Yes, probably so. While Bobo was not explicitly authorized to buy cucumbers, he probably has <u>actual, implied authority</u> to do so - especially if he has done so before, or if these type of workers normally do buy cucumbers along with avocados.

c. Bobo takes all of his items to the checkout register. The grocery store manager says, "Hey Bobo! Buying some stuff for the CCR today?" Is Calvin a disclosed principal or an undisclosed principal?
Answer: <u>A disclosed principal,</u> as discussed earlier in this text. The third party (the grocery store, through its agent) knows for whom Bobo is acting.)

d. While at the grocery store, Bobo goes down the unicycle aisle ("wow – what a cool grocery store!" he says to himself). Bobo decides it would be fun to ride a unicycle while working at CCR. Does Bobo have authority to buy the unicycle on behalf of Calvin? If so, what kind of authority?
Answer: <u>Bobo probably does not have authority</u>. He was not expressly authorized to buy unicycles, and he is not implicitly authorized to do it either, because riding unicycles does not naturally go with making and selling sushi. <u>If Calvin had made it known to the grocery store that Bobo is acting on his behalf with respect to purchases generally, then – even though in fact Bobo had no actual authority with respect to buying a unicycle - Bobo could have apparent authority</u>; it is a question of whether the store reasonably believed Bobo was authorized to buy the unicycle (not just the avocados and cucumbers) for CCR.

e. Bobo takes the items back to CCR. He presents the avocados and cucumbers; then Bobo dismounts from the unicycle and announces to Calvin, "And this is yours, too!" Calvin stares in amazement, then gets on the unicycle, rides it smoothly, and proclaims, "This will be great for our publicity! Good idea, Bobo!" This an example of authority based on _____?
Answer: <u>Ratification</u>. Although Bobo did not have any actual authority to buy the unicycle (and very likely did not have apparent authority, either), Calvin has ratified the purchase after-the-fact.

f. For the next three weeks, Bobo rides the unicycle to deliver sushi on the CCR premises to customers waiting for their California Rolls. While making such a delivery, on Day 21 of the "Great Unicycle *Experiment*," Bobo accidentally runs over a customer's foot. She screams in pain, and her boyfriend drives her to the hospital, where she requires medical treatment. Calvin fires Bobo. The next day, Bobo goes to the grocery store, buys crab and rice, and – as he always did while working for CCR – put it on a charge to CCR's account. Is Bobo authorized to make this purchase (in the eyes of the grocery store)? If so, what type of authority does Bobo have?

> Answer: Bobo made the purchase with a type of apparent authority (lingering authority) to act on behalf of CCR. To destroy any lingering authority, Calvin would have to contact the grocery store and tell authorized agents there that Bobo is no longer authorized to act for CCR. That would destroy any alleged reasonableness on the part of the store in letting Bobo charge CCR's account.

An agent must have capacity (agents are fiduciaries), so not every person can be an agent.

Any legal entity can be a principal. Not unincorporated associations – they are not principals (or agents) because they have no independent, separate legal existence.

2. Social arrangements, Not Legal Entities

Two examples of being just a social institution, not a legal entity (a matter of ethics, perhaps, but not law, that the friends pay/reimburse another person) are:

a. The "Monday Night Poker Club" is not a chartered club or any other formally or legally recognized group. It is just an informal collection of men who gather regularly, on most Monday nights, to play cards and socialize. If they gather one Monday night at Mort's house, and Mort calls a pizza place for a delivery, then Mort is responsible for the contract with the pizza shop. The others – based on what they have said or on past arrangement – may be legally responsible to Mort to help defray the pizza costs, but that is simply a matter of individual (albeit informal) contracting among the club "members." There is no legal entity for Mort to bind as an agent. (There is No partnership either, as the "club" is not a business.) So the pizza place's contract is with Mort, not the "club." As for other individuals, the pizza place only has a contract with other individual "members" of the club if – as individuals – they effectively authorized Mort to be their agent.

b. The Saturday morning tennis group is not in any way licensed, chartered, or otherwise legally recognized. It is just a number of women who gather on the tennis courts almost every Saturday morning to play tennis and socialize. Barbara buys from a sporting goods store some tennis balls for group play. As with the poker club example, perhaps the other members of the group are obliged, as individuals, to help reimburse Barbara, and perhaps they individually were principals who "hired" Barbara to be their agent for purposes of buying the balls, but there is no Group Entity/principal for whom Barbara acts. Thus, Barbara, as is the case with Mort, is individually liable on the contract for buying balls from the sporting goods store.

And here is an actual court case: The Little League Baseball Sponsors: Example of a Non–Existent Principal.[124]

Twelve business people joined together to sponsor several Little League teams and create a league for them – "The Golden Spike Little League." These 12 sponsors bought uniforms and equipment from a sporting goods store. They ran up a $4,000 bill.

The sporting goods store demanded payment, and the sponsors' defense was: "We were only agents."

The Utah Appeals Court rejected the defense and found that the League was not a legal entity (so could not be a principal) – just "a loosely formed voluntary association." So the twelve sponsors were

---

[124] *Smith and Edwards v. Golden Spike Little League*, 577 P.2d 132 (Utah 1978).

individually liable. "When a person enters into a contract and represents that he's acting as an agent for a principal, when there is in fact no such principal, the person entering the contract is personally liable."

The Individual Is Always Personally Liable for His Torts

Note that, even though the "business" is not liable in these cases – because there is no legal entity for which the individual has acted - an individual is always responsible for his/her torts.[125] Also, if one's actions are on behalf of something that is, in fact, *not* a legal entity, then one might be held responsible personally in *contract law* as well. The analogy could be to an extended hand: if extended on behalf of someone else, then the other person (the principal) is the only one responsible for the contract if it is breached. But if there is no other person (no principal), then the law abhors a vacuum and holds the would-be agent (the one extending the hand) personally liable on the contract.

IV. THE PRINCIPAL'S LIABILITY FOR THE AGENT'S ACTIONS

There are three key elements to winning a lawsuit (or a settlement)[126] and obtaining a recovery: 1. A Wrong. 2. Damages. 3. Deep Pockets (money, or access to money).[127]

With any one element missing, as a practical matter the suit is <u>not</u> a success. For example, sometimes a plaintiff's strongest legal case is against a defendant who has little ability to pay damages. The plaintiff therefore seeks a defendant with deep pockets (who meets the third element, above – ability to pay a damages award). Proving a wrong (liability) usually is more difficult, because these defendants' liability, if any, is indirect. This leads, for instance, to cases against principals, based on the agent's negligence, breach of contract, or otherwise.

A principal's liability for the agent's actions is based on two assumptions: that the principal has the right and duty to control the agent, and that the principal is often better able to absorb losses than is the agent (and, in effect, the harmed third person).

> Special rules concerning agents who are professionals, specifically attorneys acting in their professional capacity, are addressed later in the text, in Article III's discussion of lawyers.

A. Torts (see pgs. 447–468; Emerson BL)[128]

Regardless of whether there is or is not an agency (whether the tortfeasor is/was an agent), the tortfeasor himself/herself is always liable. Usually, an agent would be liable to the principal for any money the principal has to pay the injured third person (principal's right of indemnification).

Conversely, the principal has a duty to reimburse and indemnify the agent for the agent's authorized actions, such as in reaching a contract on the principal's behalf. That means that every agent has a corresponding right against his/her principal to be reimbursed for all expenses and to be indemnified against all losses and liabilities incurred in the execution of his/her authority. The right is either contained in the express terms of the agency or it is implied. Without any express terms, the principal's liability to the agent

---

[125] Torts are discussed near the end of this text. See also Robert W. Emerson, *Business Law*. NY: Barron's Educational Series (6th ed., 2015), at 447-471.
[126] Via the threat of a lawsuit.
[127] The "deep pockets" element may be furnished by insurance. Plaintiffs tend to go after the biggest, ripest target. And that is why third persons go after the alleged principal. (Let the Principal worry about obtaining indemnification (reimbursement) from the Agent for the Plaintiff's judgment–award; the Plaintiff simply collects directly from "Mr./Ms. Moneypants," the Principal.)
[128] "A tort is a private wrong, a trespass against a person or his/her property. Aside from certain limited circumstances, all torts arise from either an intentional wrongful action or from a negligent action." Robert W. Emerson, *Business Law*. NY: Barron's Educational Series (6th ed., 2015), at 447.

depends upon the nature of the authority granted to the agent. As usual, a contract may limit such a right of reimbursement, as in this clause between a sales agent and the company (principal) for whom it sells products: "Agent's Expenses. Agent shall, at her own expense and without reimbursement from Company, incur such travel, product promotion and service, advertising, entertainment, office and administration expenses as may be necessary in order to perform her agency duties."

The principal's duty to reimburse or indemnify the agent, though, does not extend to an agent who has acted unlawfully, or negligently, or in breach of duty.

1. What is within the P's zone of control?

If the agent was in the zone of control of the principal, then the principal is accountable for the tortious actions of the agent.

The question often becomes: <u>Is A genuinely acting on behalf of P</u> (within his scope of authority), or is he instead engaged in a *frolic and detour*? The English Judge Baron Parke uttered the classic phrase: <u>a master is not liable for the torts of his servant who is not on his master's business but is "on a frolic of his own."</u> *Joel v. Morrison*, 172 Eng. Rep. 993 (1834).

a. What Is a Frolic, and What Is Simply Doing the Master's Bidding, Albeit in a Roundabout Way?

FROLIC AND DETOUR EXAMPLE: TOMMY TRUCKDRIVER VISITING HIS GIRLFRIEND

Long-haul (3000 mile cross-country) truck trip - ten miles out of the way, and hundreds of miles out of the way

---

A Burger King Example: Not a "Frolic and Detour"

A Burger King manager went to the bank, then to KFC to pick up his lunch. The accident occurred on the return trip (the way back). Is the Burger King owner also responsible? YES! The employee was making a deposit on his principal's behalf, and his slight excursion to get lunch was reasonably within the agency's zone of activities.

Commuting

<u>An employee's negligence while commuting to or from work is not a basis for employer liability.</u>

b. *Respondeat Superior*

The concept of *respondeat superior* (Latin for "<u>Let the superior respond</u>") goes all the way back to before Roman times – the belief that if a person tries to increase his wealth through the work of slaves, he should be responsible for the slaves' actions, for the harm their work may have caused. Indeed, vicarious liability – imposing liability on one party because of the acts of another party – was quite frequently practiced in ancient times. The "torts" of spouses, servants, slaves, pets, other animals, and even inanimate objects were charged to the other spouse, the employer, or the owner.[129]

The main vestige of the vicarious liability approach now is only found in the area of employment. <u>Three reasons given for why the employer is held vicariously liable for employees' torts are:</u>

1. The employer hires and trains employees and should be expected to take care that good people are employed and that they receive appropriate training. (Of course, a failure in this area would probably lead to direct liability for the employer because of the employer's own negligence in hiring, supervising, or training the employee.)

2. The employer obtains the benefits of the employees' labor, which helps the employer to earn revenues, and so the employer should pay the cost when, as sometimes happens, one or more employees commit a tort. While accidents are to be avoided whenever possible, sheer numbers indicate that – at least for larger employers – they are bound to occur sometimes; therefore, liability for these accidents should simply be a cost of doing business for the employer.

---

[129] WILLIAM E. PROSSER, THE LAW OF TORTS 458 (1971).

3. The employer is almost always the party with "deeper pockets" than the employee. Why should the innocent third party injured by a tortfeasing employee be limited to the pockets of an often–impecunious employee? Why shouldn't the employer have to pay the third party and –instead of the third party – be the one stuck with the task of being paid(indemnified) by the employee for his/her torts?

Here are three policy and ethics questions about *respondeat superior*:
1. Does it seem fair that an employer is liable for his/her employees' negligence?
2. Who should bear the risk of loss (assuming, as is often the case, that the employee has inadequate funds or insurance to cover a third person's losses)?
3. Does the respondeat superior doctrine encourage employers to hire and train careful workers? Without it, would the workplace be appreciably more dangerous (unsafe conditions, poor products and services, etc.)?

The Restatement of Law on Agency[130]

Restatement (Second) of Agency, § 229, lists six general issues that courts should consider when deciding whether a particular act occurred within the course and scope of employment:

a. the "Zone of Risk" test – what was the time (e.g., normal working hours), place (e.g., the usual place of employment), and purpose of the act;
– If within the "Zone of Risk," then the employer may be liable under respondeat superior

b. was the act authorized by the employer (implied emergency powers are viewed as authorized);
– Even if not, would the act have been authorized if there had been time? If yes, then more likely to indicate that the "Act was Within the Course and Scope of Employment" – hereinafter "AWCSE."

c. was the act commonly performed by employees on behalf of the employer (if the situation was unusual, the question may be – was the employee's response a "common," reasonable response to that unusual situation);
– If yes, then more likely to indicate that AWCSE.

d. how much did the act serve the employer's interests directly or indirectly; e.g., in this case, did the action create goodwill for the employer?
– The more it serves the company's interests, the more that is likely to indicate that AWCSE.

e. how much were the employee's private interests involved (was he/she acting for reasons of self-interest);
– The more it was for the employee's own interests, the less the act may have been AWCSE.

f. did the employer furnish the means or the instrumentality by which the injury was inflicted (could the employer have anticipated, and thus prevented or specifically disallowed, that use of such means or instrumentalities).
– If yes, then more likely to indicate that AWCSE.

B. Contracts

The Principal can be held liable for contracts entered into by his/her Agent.

1. Disclosed Agency

If the fact that the Agent is acting on behalf of the Principal has been disclosed to the other side (the party contracting with the Agent), and if the Agent has authority to act on behalf of Principal in this particular matter, then the Agent is not liable for breach of contract (that is different from tort law on the agent's liability). Only the Principal is liable for the breach. >>

Example: Agent, as the Principal's right hand, for example, as a corporate treasurer. This officer of the corporation sign checks of that corporation as the treasurer, thus as agent (disclosed) of that named corporation. Therefore, she signs the contract, "Annie Agent on behalf of Paul Principal."

Must one disclose his agency? Generally not – only if a statutory requirement, if it would be fraud not to disclose, or if the contract is of a personal nature (thus, who are the actual parties to the contract is a crucial fact).

---

[130] For information about Restatements of Law generally, see Robert W. Emerson, *Business Law*. NY: Barron's Educational Series (6th ed., 2015), at 20.

2. Partially Disclosed or Totally Undisclosed Principals

If Arthur Agent says to a landowner, "I am an agent, but I have been requested not to tell you who my principal is," then the principal is a partially disclosed principal.

If Arthur does not tell the landowner that he is an agent, so that the landowner thinks that Arthur himself is the principal, the principal is an undisclosed principal.

In either case, Arthur is liable on any contract reached with the landowner. Because the landowner dealt with Arthur and knows no one else to pursue, she has a right to remedies against the person with whom she made the contract. If the landowner discovers the principal's identity, the principal could become liable. And if Arthur, with authority, makes a contract in such circumstances, intending to bind the principal, then Arthur has remedies against the principal if Arthur is sued.

3. Undisclosed Agency

If a third–party does not know you are an agent and relies on your actions to his/her detriment, there is a substantial risk of personal liability for you (as the agent). Contracts with an undisclosed agent tend to be "legal" and enforceable – i.e., the other party cannot get out of them – unless there were special grounds on which the agency should have been disclosed, but was not.[131]

V. THE MASTER/SERVANT RELATIONSHIP

The master/servant relationship is a highly controlled form of employment. Servants are told what to do, how to do it, what hours to work. The employer furnishes the tools, etc. Master (to servant): "Do what I say, when I say it." The master exercises over the servant control of all important areas. Under this common law control test, for example, each of the following six factors is relevant to the inquiry whether someone (e.g., a shareholder) is an employee:

1. Whether the organization can hire or fire the individual or set the rules for the individual's work;
2. Whether and, if so, to what extent the organization supervises the individual's work;
3. Whether the individual reports to someone higher in the organization;
4. Whether and, if so, to what extent the individual is able to influence the organization;
5. Whether the parties intended that the individual be an employee, as expressed in written agreements; and
6. Whether the individual shares in the profits, losses, and liabilities of the organization.

So, an employer is the person, or group of persons, who owns and manages the enterprise. The employer can hire and fire employees, can assign tasks to employees and supervise their performance, and can decide how the profits and losses of the business are to be distributed. The mere fact that a person has a particular title—such as partner, director, or vice president—should not necessarily be used to determine whether he or she is an employee or a proprietor. Nor should the mere existence of a document styled "employment agreement" lead inexorably to the conclusion that either party is an employee. As is true in applying common law rules to independent–contractor–versus–employee issues, the answer to whether a shareholder–director is an employee depends on all aspects of the relationship, with no one factor being decisive.

The Alleged Employment Relationship and Coverage under Employment Discrimination Laws

In *Clackamas Gastroenterology Associates, P.C. v. Wells*, 538 U.S. 440 (2003), the U.S. Supreme Court considered whether the director–shareholder physicians in a professional corporation (PC) would be counted as "employees" of that PC. The decision affected whether the PC would be considered as having 15 or more employees and thus have to abide by the Americans with Disabilities Act (ADA). In a 7-2 holding (Justices Ginsburg and Breyer dissenting), the Court focused on the common law touchstone of control and the six–factor inquiry, above; it found such director-physicians to *not* be employees for ADA purposes. The *Clackamas* effect is that businesses with over 15 full–time "workers" may still not be covered by the ADA

---

[131] The European Union's Directive on Commercial Agents is discussed in Robert W. Emerson, *Business Law*. NY: Barron's Educational Series (6th ed., 2015), at 313.

(or similarly with respect to other employment discrimination laws, which also have minimum-number-of-employee thresholds); that is because the "workers" who are shareholder–directors or partners are treated as employers and thus not counted as employees.

VI. THE INDEPENDENT CONTRACTOR RELATIONSHIP
(see pgs. 298–299; Emerson BL)

New developments: A disruptive economy – Uber, Airbnb, etc. There will likely be major new developments by the time you are reading this book!

A. The Independent Contractor and the Agency Relationship

"An independent contractor is hired to achieve a purpose, to do a job, to undertake a contractually defined result."[132] An agent is hired to be, in effect, a representative. An agency relationship may arise whether one is an employee or not.

Along a continuum Servanthood (S) – the most controlled form of employment - is at one end and Independent Contracting (IC), a non-employment arrangement, is at the other. Both employees and independent contractors may or may not be agents (representatives).

```
<—— Agency (or not) all along the S<--->IC continuum ——>
  M/S <-------------------------------------> IC
```

Agents can be anywhere along the above continuum.[133]

Self-Employment

The self–employed are independent contractors and, just like those who are employees, may or may not be agents (it depends on the hiring arrangement – the circumstances).

When academics and commentators discuss self-employment, there tends to be two opposing viewpoints. On one hand, the self-employed are seen as dispirited, atomized victims, beyond the help of unions or governments. On the other hand, self-employment is seen as liberating. Most people probably fall somewhere between the two views and leap from project to project both in hope and in desperation. Realities of free agency include a small percentage (less than 10% of the self-employed) who are temp "slaves" with bad pay and demoralizing work and "perma-temps" that never get a permanent job.
But for many self-employed the serious drawback of their position is a lack of health benefits, arbitrary zoning laws making work from home problematic, and tax difficulties. Some businesses, such as Starbucks and FederalExpress/Kinkos, depend on a customer base including numerous self-employed persons.

An Example: Lawyers as Agents and Also In-House Counsel or Independent Contractors
An agent has authority to bind the principal. That agent may be an employee or he/she may be an independent contractor. Therefore, for instance, a large business may have its own general in-house counsel (one or more lawyers) who represent the business (act as agents) and also are employees of that business. In effect, the business is that lawyer's only client. Most lawyers, though, work in outside firms and thus are independent contractors; they are agents for their clients, such as for purposes of dealing with administrative agencies, the courts, other businesses, etc., but they are not employees of their clients and – presumably – have many clients for whom they act as agents. (All the while, these lawyers must make sure to have no conflicts of interest in their representation of the various clients.)

---

[132] Id. at 286.
[133] However, the most controlled form of employee – the "servant" – tends to not be an agent.

B. The Independent Contractor Clause in a Contract; Incentives to Classify the Hired Party as an Independent Contractor, Not an Employee

An agreement may specify that a party is an independent contractor and may further indicate that this party is not an agent. Here is an example of such a clause, found in a contract between a sales representative and the company for whom the sales rep tries to sell products:

> "Representative acknowledges that Representative is an independent contractor not controlled by Company in the operation of Representative's business and that Representative shall not be considered or hold itself out as an employee or agent of Company. Representative shall not, without prior written consent of Company, sign Company's name to any document, contract or agreement."

To determine whether a relationship is employment or independent contractor relationship, look at the parties' actions, at circumstances, not just at the labels used in the document that the parties signed, not just the written agreement between the parties, but – much more important – what is/was actually done. That is because <u>there are all sorts of incentives to claim (pretend) that hired persons are not employees, but are independent contractors.</u> The hiring party's claim that the persons it has hired are independent contractors is often made to avoid:

- <u>taxes</u> (social security, unemployment compensation, workers' compensation, and other payroll taxes applicable to employers);
- <u>labor laws</u> (e.g., the FLSA, the NLRA) which only extend protections to employees, not independent contractors (YOUTUBE – Labor Law 1min48secs is at robertwemersonufl);
- <u>OSHA , Title VII of the 1964 Civil Rights Act, Americans with Disabilities Act, Age Discrimination in Employment Act and other laws</u> dealing with <u>employee</u> rights; and
- <u>tort law liability</u> under the doctrine of <u>respondeat superior</u> (employees' negligence binds the employer under respondent superior, but, there ordinarily is no such vicarious liability concerning independent contractors' negligence).

But there are some disadvantages to having someone truly be an independent contractor: less control over a worker's performance and over his/her use of the hirer's proprietary information, potential liability beyond workers' compensation limits, and the possibility that misclassification will result in penalties costing far more than simply classifying, initially, someone as an employee.

C. Hirers Have Been Penalized by Administrative Agencies (e.g., the IRS) for Pretending that Employees Are Independent Contractors

The analysis of whether someone is, in fact, an independent contractor, not an employee, looks at a number of questions, such as:

(1) Is the hired person really *independent*? Look at the parties' actions and circumstances, not just what the parties say, but what is actually done.
(2) Does the hirer only determine ultimate goals, while the hired person decides how to do the job? (If so, that is an indication that the person is an independent contractor.)

Each year, the Internal Revenue Service audits thousands of companies that it finds have wrongly classified, altogether, tens of thousands of workers as independent contractors or temporary employees. The IRS thus annually has assessed, collectively, well over a hundred million dollars in back taxes and penalties on these companies.

Some local governments (e.g., King County, Washington) and universities (e.g., Texas A&M), many smaller businesses, and some very large corporations (e.g., Microsoft) have had to pay large fines or settlements – often millions of dollars - for pretending that their employees were independent contractors (often calling them "temporary workers" or "freelancers").

> ### An Adult Entertainment Case
> In *303 West 42nd Street Enterprises v. IRS*, 916 F. Supp. 349 (S.D.N.Y. 1996), rev'd on other grounds, 181 F.3d 272 (2d. Cir. 1999), Show World, an "adult entertainment" enterprise in New York, provided booths known as one–on–one fantasy booths, where customers could communicate with performers termed "visual telephone communicators." What happened inside the booths was private, determined both by the number of coins the customer deposited and by the customer's conversation with the performer.
>
> "At the end of the day (or night), when the performer has finished her shift, the tokens are collected and the visual telephone communicator is paid 40% of the coins deposited; Show World keeps the additional 60%. The performers are then asked to sign a purported lease agreement…..Show World argues that as a result of this lease , the visual telephone communicators are tenants."
>
> The IRS argued that the performers were employees, not tenants. Show World argued that if they were not tenants, they were independent contractors. Not so, held Judge Sand, who ruled that the IRS is right: the visual telephone communicators are employees, not tenants or independent contractors. Show World had to pay $290,000 in back taxes.

However, courts, including U.S. Circuit Courts, have upheld well–drafted, clearly–delineated differences in the treatment of "leased," or contract, workers from the "regular" workforce. For example, in January 1997, employee benefits at DuPont Corporation were found, by court opinion, to not extend to temporary workers. Also, in 2009, FedEx truck drivers were found to be independent contractors and thus not able to form a union (something only employees may do).[134]

D. Two Tests: The Right to Control Test and the Economic Realities Test

Statutes and rules rarely define employees or independent contractors. However, real estate agents and direct sellers are classified as independent contractors under 26 U.S. Code Section 3508; and professionals such as physicians, lawyers, dentists, and contractors are usually considered to be independent contractors under 26 Code of Federal Regulations Section 31.3401(c).

1. "Right to Control" Test

This test is a common law approach. It focuses on the right to control rather than the actual exercise of that control. The "right to control" is determined by considering these traditional agency law principles: whether the worker is engaged in a distinct occupation or business; whether the work involved is usually done under an employer's discretion or by an unsupervised specialist; the degree of skill involved; who supplies the instrumentalities, tools, materials, and place of performance; the length of employment; the method of payment (by the time or by the job); whether the work is part of the employer's regular business and/or is necessary to it; the intent of the parties creating the relationship; who designates the time and place at which work is to be done; and the right to hire and fire.

2. The Economic Realities Test

The economic realities test uses many factors. Essentially, economics is used to evaluate the nature of a hiring relationship.

Slight variations in tests for employee/independent contractor are found in, among other things, the federal law as propounded under the National Labor Relations Act, the Fair Labor Standards Act, the Social Security Act, the Internal Revenue Service regulations, and the Occupational Safety and Health Act, and the state law for torts and workers' compensation.

E. Typical Characteristics of Independent Contractors Versus Those of Servants

---

[134] That is the same approach toward franchisees and other presumed independent contractors – they can join associations for some dealings with the franchisor, but not have many of the unionization rights that employees do. Robert W. Emerson, *Franchising and the Collective Rights of Franchisees,* 43 VANDERBILT L. REV. 1503 (1990). Perhaps Uber drivers and others in the new, disruptive economy are also in the same situation.

(pp. 298-99; Emerson BL)

Characteristic	Independent Contractor	Servant (Employee)
Nature of work	Is engaged in distinct enterprise Often involving a specialized or skilled occupation	Performs work that is a part of the employer's regular business
Method of payment	Is paid for a completed job	Is paid on regular basis by salary or hourly wage
Duration of employment	Works long enough to complete a particular job	Works regular hours as part of continuous working relationship
Materials/place of work	Provides own tools, equipment, and materials: often works at own place of business	Uses tools, equipment, and materials supplied by employer, often works at employer's workplace
Right of control	Works without supervision; not subject to control of employer; generally determines time, place and manner of performing the job	Works under supervision of employer who has power to control, including setting, time, place, and manner of performing work

F. Tort Liability of Hirer (Even If an Independent Contractor)?

Unlike an employer's vicarious liability (under respondeat superior) for the negligence of an employee, ordinarily, a hirer is not liable for his/her independent contractor's actions. The exceptions are:
(1) Public Policy – a hirer cannot subcontract away responsibility involving inherently dangerous activities;
(2) Negligent Hiring – the hirer's own negligence in hiring the independent contractor (hirer's direct liability—not vicarious liability, not respondeat superior).

You can be liable to injured persons if you hired someone (even if he/she was an independent contractor) who seemed to be, for example, violence–prone and he/she later committed acts of violence. Even if someone is an employee at will, there may be implied contractual restraints on their being fired. That is, there may be a public policy against such termination, and the firing thus constitutes an abusive discharge. These concepts are discussed below, in this text's discussion of discrimination.

The Negligent Hiring Example of the House Painter Who Goes Berserk

A House Painter/Hotel Painter usually is an Independent Contractor because he brings his own drop cloths, paint brushes, and spray guns, sets his own hours, pays his own taxes.

When the painter is hired, the home owner takes that painter because his bid is the lowest. Hires him even though he smells of liquor, is slurring words, has a nervous tic, fidgeting – "Pets and kids really set me off" – Homeowner assures him no children in the home, or pets.

But across the street is a nursery school, with a playground; and just caddy-corner (diagonally opposite) are the pet shop and veterinarian office.

VII. THE AGENT'S DUTIES TO THE PRINCIPAL (see pgs. 302-304; Emerson BL)

The agent's duties to the principal include obeying instructions, acting with skill, and avoiding conflicts of interest. These duties include generalities such as loyalty and more specific obligations such as protecting confidential information, providing notification, and giving an accounting.

The agent is a fiduciary.[135] He/she may hold items in trust or otherwise act on behalf of the dependent party. Fiduciary relationships are present in many types of relationships besides agency, such as: Parent for child, priest for member of congregation, lawyer for client, doctor for patient, spouses for each other, etc.[136] The agent's first concern should be for the principal.[137]

Some common subjects are an agent's financial investments on behalf of the principal, an agent's misuse of his/her official position as the principal's agent (e.g., insider trading of securities, misuse of proprietary data), an agent's receiving bribes, kickbacks, gifts or entertainment (e.g., from suppliers to the principal).

Three duties encompassed within the agency relationship are loyalty, obedience, and care.

> YOUTUBE – two videos – "employment conditions duties skit" (3:52 long) (EMPLOYMENT CONDITIONS & DUTIES - THE DRY CLEANERS EXAMPLE) and "employmentconditionsdutiespostvideo8mins3secs" - are at robertwemersonufl
>
> One reason we have OSHA & Workers Compensation: Employees are entitled to a safe working environment. Therefore, employers must take reasonable measures to provide a safe workplace.
>
> Laura would have a claim against Paul if he refuses or fails to provide a reasonable, safe workplace.
>
> - Could the employee quit because of the nasty comment? If the parties are in a long-term contract and all the employer says is one nasty comment, that is probably insufficient grounds for the employee's terminating the contract. (But how horrible was that one comment? It is within the employer's rights to furnish safety goggles and say, "Wear them or be fired"; and the employee's spilling detergent is probably grounds for firing.)
>
> Employers have the right to request safety compliance from the employees, e.g., wearing safety goggles, if needed to ensure employee safety. Indeed, the employer ordinarily *must require* compliance with regulations and statutes; especially insofar as it is a matter of life and limb, it is the employer's legal *and moral* responsibility to order compliance. Thus, the employer can fire employee for not complying.
>
> - In this case, is the equipment appropriate for the task? Yes, in general safety goggles make sense, but perhaps this particular equipment was not necessarily appropriate; these goggles may not have been what was needed for this worker's (Laura's) safety.
>
> - So, what if the goggles did not fit and thus were defective? Laura should have told Paul that she could not see through them. Indeed, Laura and Paul might have claims against the goggles manufacturer; it would be harder to hold the government itself liable.

---

[135] "The obligations of a fiduciary are very strict; failure of the fiduciary to account for monies collected for his/her principal, commingling of such monies with the fiduciary's own, or appropriation of the principal's property to the fiduciary's own use may be not only a breach of the agency contract, but also a criminal act." Robert W. Emerson, *Business Law*. NY: Barron's Educational Series (6th ed., 2015), at 302.

[136] An example of a relationship that is almost never found to be fiduciary is the franchise relationship. Partly because franchise contracts almost uniformly state that the franchisor is *not* a fiduciary, and partly because of the nature of the business-to-business, arm's length relationship between the franchisor and franchisee, for a franchise to vest fiduciary rights in the franchisee is exceedingly rare. *See* Robert W. Emerson, *"Franchise Contract Interpretation: A Two-Standard Approach,"* 2013 MICH. ST. LAW REV. 641 (Dec. 2013), available at http://ssrn.com/author=86449.

[137] "IT'S NOT EASY BEING A FIDUCIARY" is a video featuring a 4 minute skit and then a taped 9-minute discussion afterwards. Both are YouTube videos at robertwemersonufl: It_Is_Not_Easy_Being_a_Fiduciary.wmv (https://www.youtube.com/watch?v=nV7wmgphrz4) and
It_Is_Not_Easy_Being_a_Fiduciary_postvideo_discussion.wmv
(https://www.youtube.com/watch?v=2h1QtTZl_EQ).

> (As for Laura's pursuing Paul, other than in workers' compensation, if Paul was legally required to use the goggles then that probably absolves Paul of liability.)
>
> In return for compensation paid to the employee, the employer buys obedience - an expectation of loyalty from the employee. The employer also has a right to expect the employee's reasonable care and skill in doing his/her job.
>   - The employee's primary duty to the employee is to produce a satisfactory work-product. Laura's carelessness (messing up Daniel's "lucky" jacket), her clumsiness, could be grounds for dismissal. Paul could probably fire, demote, and dock the pay of Laura.
>
> What about Paul's words and actions against Laura?
>
>   <u>Paul calling Laura a "clumsy fool"</u>
>   We would all probably agree that it was poor behavior, probably an ineffective, counter-productive management tool. You do not motivate or inspire with that language. But it is an opinion, not defamation. And just because Laura's treatment by Paul is harsher than expected, or her tasks are more difficult than expected, is not grounds for Laura's breaking her employment contract with Paul.
>
>   <u>Paul's pushing Laura</u>
>   This constitutes a battery. Paul cannot lawfully batter Laura, and Laura can quit from a long term contract that otherwise would have bound her. Paul, in effect, breached his contract with Laura by carrying out an assault and/or battery. Certainly there is inappropriate behavior by Paul (not just verbal (berating) but a physical assault). Laura can recover compensatory and punitive damages for Paul's outrageous physical mistreatment of her. It goes beyond workers' compensation, into punitive damages (court suits), because it was intentional misconduct.

If you think the skit is "all silly" and completely far-fetched, with no legal substance behind it – that a case could never have such outrageous facts - here is just one case among many to choose from that should change your mind: The Louisiana Appeals Court case involving a Dairy Queen manager upset over poorly prepared hamburgers returned by a customer (<u>England v. S & M Foods, Inc.</u>, 511 So.2d 1313 (La. Ct. App. 1987)).

    Betty England worked at a Dairy Queen owned by S & M Foods in Tallulah, Louisiana. One day while she was at work, her manager, Larry Garley, became upset when several incorrectly prepared hamburgers were returned by a customer. Garley allegedly expressed his dissatisfaction by shouting profane language and threw a hamburger that hit England (the employee) on the leg. England filed a battery suit against Garley and S & M won a $1,000 judgment. Garley and S & M appealed. This is what the Louisiana Appeals court wrote in upholding the trial court's judgment:

> Defendants contended no battery was committed because Garley did not intend to inflict bodily harm upon England. They argue Garley was disgusted about the returned hamburgers and threw one towards the trashcan and it advertently splattered on her and Alice Rash, another employee. They contended that England's embarrassment was caused as much by her overreaction to the situation as by Garley's conduct.
>
> England said that Garley used profane language when he told her to prepare the hamburgers correctly. She said Garley, while looking straight at her, then threw the hamburger which hit her in the leg. She testified that she argued with Garley about the matter and that several patrons observed the incident which caused her to cry and become emotionally upset.

Rash said that she did not see Garley throw the hamburger, but observed it hit the floor and splatter mayonnaise and mustard on her and England.

A battery is any intentional and unpermitted contact with the plaintiff's person or anything attached to it. In the area of intentional torts, intent means the defendant either desired to bring about the physical results of his act or believed they were substantially certain to follow from what he did. Mental distress and humiliation in connection with a battery are compensable items of damage.

The totality of the evidence provided a substantial basis for the trial judge to conclude Garley must have been substantially certain the hamburger would hit England or splatter on her when he threw it toward her. His contact with her was, therefore, intentional and unpermitted and constituted a battery.

A. Loyalty

Loyalty is probably the most important, fundamental duty. It involves (a) protection of confidential information, (b) noncompetition, and (c) refusal and/or disclosure of gifts or favors received within role as agent. Whenever a conflict, the agent sides with the principal.

Penalties for a disloyal agent: He/she will not be compensated, he/she will be required to disgorge (return) profits he/she derives from disloyal acts, and he/she derives from disloyal acts, and he/she may be fired. E.g., Agent takes a kickback – must give that and profits therefrom to the principal, and also probably will be fired.

If at all in doubt, the agent should <u>fully disclose</u> facts to the Principal and seek the Principal's consent.

<u>An Agent's Breach of Duty: An Example of Wrongly Seizing the Principal's Opportunity</u>
Solitaire works as the manager of Mr. Big's Tarot Card Shop in Harlem.

One day James Bond enters the shop and informs Solitaire that he would be interested in financing a Mr. Big shop in London. Solitaire takes Mr. Bond's card, and instead of passing the information along to Mr. Big, she visits James Bond that evening. By the following morning they have agreed that Solitaire will manage the London tarot card shop. After learning what has transpired, Mr. Big wishes to know what recourse he has against Solitaire. Is it okay for Solitaire to open a Tarot store in London?

Mr. Big may sue Solitaire for breach of contract because Solitaire violated her duty of loyalty in failing to disclose Bond's offer and in taking advantage of Mr. Big's opportunity.

To avoid a disloyalty claim, Solitaire should clear it with Mr. Big.

Some penalties for a disloyal agent are: he/she will not be compensated, he/she will be required to disgorge (return) profits he/she derives from disloyal acts, and he/she may be fired. For example, the Agent takes a kickback and therefore must give that and the profits therefrom to the principal (and the agent also probably will be fired).

The agent almost always can avoid a breach of duty to the principal if the agent gives the principal a full and timely disclosure of possible problems (e.g., of a potential conflict of interest).

Gussin v. Shockey, 725 F. Supp. 271 (D. Md. 1989): A Duty of Loyalty (No Conflicts of Interest)
Frederic Gussin and his father, Paul Gussin, entered into an arrangement with the defendant, Richard Shockey, under which Shockey agreed to assist the Gussins in buying, maintaining, breeding and selling thoroughbred horses. The Gussins, who were inexperienced "in horses," relied on Shockey's twenty years' experience in buying and selling horses.

For every horse Gussin purchased, the price Shockey quoted to them included a "commission" that the seller would pay to Shockey. Overall, the Gussins purchased seven horses using the advice of Shockey, and of the $2.7 million the Gussins paid for these horses at least $575,000 were direct "commissions" to Shockey.

When the Gussins discovered that Shockey had taken what they characterized as kickbacks from sellers on transactions in which Shockey was representing the Gussins as buyers, the Gussins sued Shockey. Shockey's defense was that the Gussins still got good deals on the horses, even with the kickbacks included, better than what they could have gotten on their own. Is that a good defense?

No. As the Gussins' agent, Shockey had a duty of loyalty that required him to pass on any benefits he received incidental to the agency relationship. Shockey got great prices on behalf of the Gussins, so Shockey had to pass on all these benefits to the Gussins. That is the case even if the Gussins would not otherwise have obtained such good deals. Also, Shockey violated his duty of disclosure: As an agent of the principal, the Gussins, Shockey violated fiduciary duties owed to the principal when he purchased racehorses for them without disclosing that he was receiving "commissions" on the sales.

The court required the agent, Shockey to pay to the Gussins the "commissions" he had received.

In an unpublished disposition of the case, the appeals court affirmed the trial court's decision. 933 F.2d 1001 (4th Cir. 1991).

B. Obedience

Much more obedience is expected from employee–agents than from IC–agents (independent contractors who are agents). The Duty of Obedience includes the duty *not* to exceed actual authority.

C. Care

> Hammurabi's Code – "If the agent be careless and do not take a receipt for the money which he has given to the merchant, the money not receipted for shall not be placed to his account."

The duty of care brings to the fore the concept of reasonableness. The agent should not sub–agent any personal duties without principal's approval (in big accounting or law firms, it usually is understood that the hirer is hiring the firm, not just one person).

The principal has a right to an accounting.

The principal has the right to inspect books.

> Here is a sample contract clause about inspections, when a sales agent acts on behalf of a company (the principal):
> "Books and Records. Representative agrees, upon request, to make its books, documents and records available for inspection to Company or its duly authorized representatives during normal business hours, and to provide Company in writing, within ten (10) days of receipt of any request therefor, all Materials, documents and facts which may be required or requested by Company relating to sales of Products or other matters. Time shall be of the essence for this provision."
> Note that "time is of the essence" is specifically stated in this provision, signifying that a so–called slight breach is, in fact, a material breach. (These concepts are discussed in Article II (Contracts) in this text.)

D. An Agency's Duty of Exclusivity?

Ordinarily, there is no duty of exclusivity. But agents should not breach their duties of loyalty, obedience, or care while working for multiple principals (No Conflicts of Interest). In the past few decades, the number of part–time, income–generating home businesses has skyrocketed, with the number (perhaps over 20 million, with some people owning more than one such business) continuing to rise and many people now working for numerous employers/principals.

VIII. THE AGENT'S POWERS ON BEHALF OF THE PRINCIPAL

The agent has power to do most legal tasks as an agent (e.g., to sell real estate; to be an attorney–in–fact, through a power–of–attorney; to hire employees; to perform clerical duties). However, an agent cannot do purely personal matters (e.g., cannot go to jury duty instead of the person summoned to jury duty). Therefore, while some functions are inherently human and personal, for which you cannot hire someone else's performance (e.g., to eat for you, to sleep for you, to romance someone for you), one generally can contract out *business* duties.

A. Attorney-at-law and Attorney-at-fact

There are important differences between an attorney–at–law and an attorney–at–fact. Powers–of–attorney are documents that create attorneys–at–fact. Attorneys–at–law are agents who, because of their license from the state, are able to represent the principal (the client) in legal proceedings. The attorney–at–fact is someone (usually a close friend or relative) who the principal trusts to be able to handle certain functions on behalf of the principal, such as handling certain financial transactions or overseeing certain business matters.

Powers–of–attorney are often granted from aged or infirm persons who need some assistance. Also, people who are going to be out of the country or otherwise indisposed for a lengthy period may want someone "back home" to be able to handle certain tasks, such as paying bills, reviewing correspondence, etc. For special needs involving, for example, lawsuits, a particular type of "attorney" (a lawyer) is needed.

> "Let every agent trust for itself and trust no agent." William Shakespeare, MUCH ADO ABOUT NOTHING

B. Governmental Administrative Agencies

The government ordinarily is not liable when a governmental agent either misstates his/her authority or mischaracterizes the law. For example, Internal Revenue Service (IRS) agents can repeatedly tell taxpayer Tina a wrong deadline, yet – when Tina follows their advice and thus misses the true deadline – the courts will tell Tina that the correct calculation of the deadline was the taxpayer's responsibility, and thus bar Tina's appeal. It would likely be different if the decision to aid an innocent, wronged private party, by reversing a governmental agent's mistakes, does not leave the government – hence the taxpayer – accountable. That is, when such a reversal works to the detriment solely of another private party.

E. ESTABLISHING A BUSINESS

I. INTRODUCTION TO BUSINESS ENTITIES (see generally pgs. 319-351; Emerson BL)

> "Drive thy business or it will drive thee." Benjamin Franklin.

YOUTUBE – Partnerships 2mins34secs at robertwemersonufl
YOUTUBE - TypesBusOrgs_2mins46secs at robertwemersonufl

"This is an area of law in which there has been tremendous change, tremendous flux in the past decade or so. For instance, in the late 1990s we moved in the direction of what is called a "check the box" approach, which essentially means, for smaller businesses, no matter what their actual status is, they're able to (for tax purposes) check a box and pick which sort of treatment they want. Do these businesses want to be treated like a partnership with all the pluses and minuses of that, or for tax purposes do they want to be treated like a corporation? So, with that check-the-box approach, we have moved toward much greater flexibility. There are estimates that perhaps in the next 10 or 20 years, this flexibility is going to lead to overwhelmingly dramatic changes in the types of businesses that are being formed. For instance, old assumptions that most of the time people's businesses grow and go from partnerships to corporations may no longer hold true. In fact, many people now, and perhaps far more in the future, will simply be forming limited liability companies, or limited partnerships, or limited liability partnerships, and never proceed to corporate status no matter how large their business may grow.

"There's so much more flexibility in this area that I think, sometimes, people get too out of joint or needlessly worried about "what business do I form now?" They know that they have so many different

> options. They ask, "What format do I choose?" and they're overlooking the fact (a good fact) that flexibility continues even after you have opted for a particular business status. Oh sure, it's better to start out with the right business status in the first place, but as your business needs change, you may change the status of your business; you're always free to change from one format to the other. The classic example of this is the many, many people who form sole proprietorships (they don't even think about it, they just go into business themselves) and then only later, as they start to think about tax issues, as they start to worry about personal liabilities, do they consider whether they want to, in fact, form some sort of other status, such as a limited liability company, an S corporation, or some other such entity."

A. Comparison of Sole Proprietorships, Partnerships, Corporations, and Limited Liability Companies

1. Sole Proprietorships

The sole proprietorship is the simplest business format in which an individual owns and operates the company, paying taxes at the individual income level. "The sole owner and his business are not legally distinct entities." [138] As an example, Ed's Eats is not distinct from Ed himself; Ed is personally responsible, with potentially unlimited personal liability.

2. Partnerships

Two or more people may operate a business as partners, "having expressly or implicitly agreed to establish and run a business for profit." – to share in profits or losses.[139] Many circumstances affect whether there is a partnership, and parties may not even know whether there is a partnership. The format is adaptable, and partners – as in sole proprietorships – have equal potential personal liability for the business debts.

The partnership itself does not pay taxes – taxes are paid by each partner at the individual level.[140]

3. Corporations

Corporations are "persons" in the eyes of the law. Typically created under state law, they are distinct legal entities with their existence separate from the shareholders. Corporations are only 20% of all U.S. businesses, but 90% of all sales go through corporations. Corporations "incorporate" to protect its owners from potential lawsuits at the individual level. Owners share limited liability and lawsuits must be brought against the corporation as a whole. Corporations pay taxes at the business income level.

Most corporations are fairly small. Over 90% of all corporations have fewer than ten shareholders; and less than 1/10 of 1% of all corporations have more than 5,000 shareholders. There are some huge corporations, of course, nationally and internationally.

4. Limited Liability Companies

It is a new format with both corporate and partnership characteristics. Limited liability protects owners from losing more than their investment in the company. In a LLC, personal assets cannot be seized to pay for the company's debt.

B. Small Business (see generally the U.S. Small Business Administration, www.sba.gov/)

A little less than 30 million businesses operate inside the United States, with over three-fourths of them having no employees. "Small" firms (those with under 500 workers) employ about half of the U.S. private sector workforce. Fewer than 20,000 large businesses (employing more than 500 persons each)

---

[138] Robert W. Emerson, *Business Law*. NY: Barron's Educational Series (6th ed., 2015), at 320.
[139] Id.
[140] A partnership files an *informational* return (Form 1065). Schedule K-1 is furnished to each partner so they can 'pass-through' the income/loss on their personal returns.

employ the other half.

> **The Corporate Veneer: An Illusion of Bigness**
> One reason to incorporate is to feed on the illusion that when one thinks of a corporation, one thinks of Big Business. Most consumers view Big Businesses as successful and thus less risky for investments. Another strategy small businesses have used is having a private mailbox at a mailing service store such as UPS and tacking on a "suite" or other number to the stores street address, without mentioning the store's name. This gives customers the impression the business operates in a big office building, with spacious suites, not a 5-inch wide mail slot at the UPS store!
> Nevertheless, in March 1999, the U.S. Postal Service (after first proposing the rule in mid-1997) began requiring mail to these private rental mailboxes to include the designation PMB, for "private mailbox." After a six-month grace period, mail addressed without a PMB, would not be delivered, these new rules stated.
> Renters of the more than one million private rental mailboxes in the nation and owners of the 10,600 pack-and-send stores asserted that the post office was acting out of spite. The Postal Service responded that criminals increasingly used private mailboxes for illegal activities, such as credit card fraud and identity theft; the Service was simply trying to reduce deception – let senders know the PMB address was not an office or a home.
> Estimates were that the cost of changing letterhead, business cards, and other items informing people about "PMB" would cost over $1,000 per business. A bill to rescind the rule was taken to the House Appropriations Committee. In August 2000, the Postal Service amended the requirement so that using "PMB" or "#" in the address box would suffice to specify that someone uses a private mailbox at a Commercial Mail Receiving Agency.[141] So businesses or individuals with a PMB could, for example, receive mail to:
> John Jones
> Large Business Corp.
> 525 8th Avenue, #100
> Gainesville, FL 32601

C. Hybrid Business Categories

Hybrid business categories include cooperatives, syndicates, joint ventures, associations, and limited liability companies. The legal foundations of these hybrids tend to be based on a combination of partnership and corporate law principles.

One example of a "hybrid" business category is the joint venture. Joint ventures have the substance of regular partnerships, and they arise where parties have agreed to act jointly for a limited purpose. This could range from sharing expenses on a long trip to selling a shipment of salvage goods that lay unclaimed at a receiving dock. A joint venture could include three construction companies, usually corporations, building a 30-story office building.

Each corporation would be a partner (or joint adventurer) with the other two corporations. Some nations may require joint ventures for foreign direct investment (FDI) within their borders. This may effectively limit the home country (where the business originated) to less than 50% ownership in order to ensure the host country maintains control.

D. Franchises (see pgs. 348-351; Emerson BL)

The franchise is not a form of doing business, like a corporation or partnership. It is a type of relationship involving a number of elements, including a trademark license. The parties to the franchise

---

[141] "Mail Box Service, Private Mail Boxes, PMB, and Mail Forwarding Service USA Los Angeles News." *Mail Box Service, Private Mail Boxes, PMB, and Mail Forwarding Service USA Los Angeles*. 16 Aug. 2000. Web. 27 Oct. 2010. <http://www.mailservicecenter.com/news.php>.

relationship – the franchisor and franchisees – are business entities whose individual structures, like those of other businesses, tend to be in the form of sole proprietorships, limited liability companies, partnerships, or corporations." [142] Occasionally franchisees allege that they are, in effect, employees, not independent contractors. Courts usually deny that claim. However, in extreme cases a franchisee may be deemed so much under the franchisor's control that the franchisee is actually an employee. [143]

II. SOLE PROPRIETORSHIPS (see pgs. 320-325; Emerson BL)

A. Advantages of the Sole Proprietorship
Some advantages are:
- Ease of formation – fast and inexpensive "to organize, with few requirements"[144] (just go into business!)
- No filing requirements – taxes reported at the individual income level
- There are no special laws regarding business format; any laws to follow would be, simply, industry standards that *all* businesses in that industry (no matter their format) must obey. The sole proprietor must obtain only whatever licenses are needed (and follow the regulations required) for that industry and for employers generally – e.g., workers' compensation.
- Permission to operate using a fictitious name. Any business, including a sole proprietorship, which operates under a fictitious name, must file with the state for permission to use that name (and to provide information to others as to the true name and address of the person(s) actually operating the business using that fictitious name).
- Not having to share profits (except with taxing authorities and spouse/dependents).
- Exclusive control over the business – no shareholders, no board of directors, no co-owners; control and decision-making rest in the individual (there tends to be no one you need to consult except possibly a spouse, an insurer, a lender.)
- Very flexible management - In the late 1990s and early 2000s, tax rules became more favorable for sole proprietors. On his own income taxes, the sole proprietor ordinarily reports his business matters on a Schedule C, which is used to determine the proprietor's net profit or loss from the business. (A Schedule C-EZ is used if expenses are no more than $5,000.00.)[145]

B. Disadvantages of the Sole Proprietorship
Some disadvantages are:
- Too easy for owner to take action quickly, without forethought (a limited viewpoint and experience, trotting down the wrong path too easily- *fools go where angels fear to tread!*) - e.g., May try to cut corners by not hiring/using lawyers.
- Very unstable business format – the business, in a sense, dies when the owner dies; there often is a huge disruption when the owner becomes ill or dies.
- Rules of succession often are unclear – *like many Third World dictatorships!*
While 80% of business owners have a will, as few as about 40-50% of them have a succession plan

---

[142] Robert W. Emerson, *Business Law*. NY: Barron's Educational Series (6th ed., 2015), at 348. The author has written numerous law review articles about various franchise law topics involving, among other things, contracts, torts, agency, legal ethics, collective bargaining, comparative and international law, antitrust law, territories, community expectations, bankruptcy, goodwill, unions, discrimination, independent contracting, non-compete covenants, and trademarks. A number of these may be downloaded at http://ssrn.com/author=86449.

[143] *See* Robert W. Emerson, *Assessing Awuah v. Coverall North America, Inc.: The Franchisee as a Dependent Contractor*, 19 STANFORD J. LAW, BUS. & FINANCE 203 (2014), available at http://ssrn.com/author=86449.

[144] Robert W. Emerson, *Business Law*. NY: Barron's Educational Series (6th ed., 2015), at 320.

[145] See IRS Publication 334, "Tax Guide for Small Business."

for their entity. Such plans cover what is to happen when the owner dies, retires, or otherwise must relinquish command.
- Unlimited personal liability – personal and business assets are not separate. Personal assets are liable for seizure if the business cannot pay off its debt.
- It can be difficult to raise capital, whether short-term or long-term financing (because the owner usually is small, and lenders are wary of the owner's unlimited liability)[146]
- They are more likely to be audited to verify accuracy in their reporting of taxes to the IRS. Small-businesses, especially those with large cash receipts, have a relatively high rate of tax "noncompliance"—underreporting income and inflating deductions. So, for example, in the past decade the IRS has audited nearly 3% of sole-proprietor returns (a percentage higher for returns showing receipts more than $100,000.00), but audited only less than 1.3% for Form 1040 returns overall.

There are other disadvantages which may not simply be inherent problems of the proprietorship model insomuch as they are just a byproduct of the type of people (the entrepreneurs) that start small businesses:
- High business failure rate - "termination by sale, insolvency, or voluntary cessation of business; or by death or incapacity of proprietor."[147]
- Owner often has little experience.
- Owner often receives insufficient advice[148] regarding the operation and control of the entity

However, if any of the many problems or disadvantages become too much, one can usually switch from a sole proprietorship format to another form fairly easily and quickly. One cannot, after the fact, negate current liabilities, but – anticipating future problems – one may change the format to, for example, a corporation or a limited liability company.

Different legal systems' treatment of agency, respondeat superior, partnership –
Some General Information

Lebanon
While Sharia law permits contracts to be oral, written contracts are preferred. As in many Civil Law countries, such as France (which greatly influenced many Arab countries such as Lebanon, Algeria, Morocco, and Tunisia), a commercial agency must be in writing. While in France there is some case law for apparent authority as to contracts, there is none for torts. Moreover, in Arab countries there is no apparent authority doctrine. It is thus difficult in Arab countries even to recognize respondeat superior, let alone apparent authority.

Mexico
Partnerships are governed by the law of July 28, 1934 as amended (the General Law of Commercial Companies), which applies to all of Mexico.
All partnership agreements must be in the form of a public document, which must be recorded in the Public Registry of Commerce. All partnerships are regarded as legal entities.

Saudi Arabia
Except for some cases involving nationals of the GCC – the Gulf Cooperation Council (besides Saudi Arabia, the other five GCC members are Bahrain, Kuwait, Oman, Qatar, and the United Arab Emirates),

---

[146] Of course, if the owner is already well off, then financing should prove easy (e.g., Bill Gates seeks a loan!), but then the old saying is apt: *The only folks who could get a decent loan are those who don't need one!*
[147] Robert W. Emerson, *Business Law*. NY: Barron's Educational Series (6th ed., 2015), at 325.
[148] Sole proprietors rarely have an *in-house* lawyer, and they may not even have an *outhouse* lawyer! In-house lawyers operate within the business. Outside lawyers are exactly that – outside the business and appointed for legal proceedings.

non-Saudi natural persons or entities not wholly owned by Saudis are prohibited from engaging in trading activities in Saudi Arabia. While "trading activities" in this context is not expressly defined in any Saudi legislation, in practice that term has been taken to mean import, sale of or trading in goods. Therefore, it has been a long established practice for foreign manufacturers to appoint Saudi agents or distributors to trade and distribute their products in local markets.

Commercial agents as well as distributors and franchisees must have valid commercial registrations and must also register with Ministry of Commerce each time that an agency/distributorship/franchise relationship is entered into.

As part of such registration, agent or distributor must submit its agreement with its non-Saudi principal to Ministry of Commerce, which traditionally has taken expansive view of its ability to require substantive changes in that agreement. Such agreements, which stipulate non-Saudi law as governing law will not be accepted.

Failure of the Saudi agent or distributor to register with the Ministry of Commerce could lead to fines and other penalties for that agent or distributor, but would not render the agency or distributorship agreement invalid or otherwise subject the non-Saudi principal to any penalties except that, in certain circumstances, the principal could not participate as a supplier for some public sector activities.

For partnerships, Saudi Arabia has some strict filing requirements, but in other ways seems to have a flexible approach similar to the American and English common law.

Some brief statements about partnership or agency law in various countries

In South Korea and Thailand, lingering authority is the way that apparent authority can occur. Apparent authority is possible in China, Japan, Nigeria, Taiwan, Indonesia (called "mandates"), and Pakistan.

In Thailand, an ordinary partnership may be required to be in a written format, but the state does not always require that.

India and Nigeria have the same flexible partnership law as in England.

Columbia requires written documents. China requires for partnerships a writing, with some form of yearly reports. However, the law is generally flexible.

Indonesia and Netherlands (both call partnerships "Maatschap") do not require a writing, nor does South Korea.

Panama, Peru, and most other countries in Latin America generally adhere to a formal set of requirements for partnerships, including putting things in writing.

Russia allows for apparent authority in partnership law. Filings of partnerships are required, as for all "legal entities" except sole proprietorships.

In France, the general partnership is a "société en nom collectif" or "SNC" and is in writing.

III. NON-CORPORATE BUSINESS ENTITIES: PARTNERSHIPS AND LIMITED LIABILITY COMPANIES (see generally pgs. 320-325; Emerson BL)

TOPICAL LECTURE: Partnerships

Introduction to Topical Lecture:
There are no formal requirements, such as a written agreement or a filing, for a partnership (a general partnership - GP) to arise. If two or more persons carry on, as co-owners and joint operators, a business for profit, then that ordinarily is a GP. Partners in the GP are fiduciaries – entitled to survivorship rights, agents for and principals of their fellow partners. Limited partnerships, with two kinds of partners (general and limited partners), are of an entirely different order.

A. General Partnerships (see pgs. 329-342; Emerson BL)

> *PARTNERSHIPS 2mins34secs* is a YOUTUBE video at robertwemersonufl
> (again, a pirate costume, with a puffy shirt)
> "Shiver me timbers, mateys! In marriage and in partnership, one wants someone who is trustworthy and competent, and I believe partnership is probably the best example (among business formats) where you really need to trust and be able to trust the people that you're working with (your fellow partners). It is kind of like a piracy arrangement where, if you studied the pirates of ancient yore, they often had a rather democratic organization and they would "share and share alike" in the risks, and they really were dependent upon one another. The problem is, "pirates being pirates," they often were cutthroats and double-crossed one another.
> "If that happens in a partnership situation, you can be in extreme danger. The reason for that is partnerships (at least general partnerships) - each member of the partnership, each partner, is both an owner and an agent of that arrangement and that means essentially everything a partner does on behalf of the partnership is ascribed to all the other partners. If one partner screws up, the others can be held accountable. If one partner behaves in a malfeasant manner, then - if he cannot be found or is otherwise judgment-proof - then his fellow partners can be held accountable.
> "Because of these risks, a lot of people look to other business formations. General partnerships are wonderful because they're so easy to form; they don't need to file anything with the state, and often people have them without even knowing they were established. But if you're worried about that risk, you can have a limited partnership and be a limited partner in such an arrangement.
> Alternatively, you could form a corporation and have the limited liability available to corporate status. You could form a limited liability company, and there are limited liability partnerships: there are so many forms out there."

The history of general partnerships goes all the way back to Hammurabi's Code nearly 4,000 years ago. Provisions on partnerships are thus older than laws concerning corporations (dating from Ancient Rome over 2,000 years ago).

Partnership law is state law. The Uniform Partnership Act (UPA) has been adopted in most states (including Florida in 1972). The UPA essentially retains much of the old common law doctrine on partnerships.

This is the UPA's definition of a general partnership: "An association of two or more persons to carry on as co-owners of a business for profit."[149] Key elements thus are common ownership, sharing of profits/losses, and management rights for all partners. — *implied agreement, express agreement pg 329 Barron*

1. Essential Characteristics of General Partnerships

- Partners equally share in both the risk of losses and the potential for gains (some form of agreement, implied or express) - "one for all, and all for one"[150]
- Limited life span - i.e., death of one partner can mean death of partnership
- Common ownership - each partner with control over the business' assets (each partner is a principal) – each partner is an owner of the partnership (with right to real estate, inventory, equipment, etc.) and has the right to control the entire property (like a marriage)
- Mutual agency - liability risks for all partners (each partner is an agent) – a partner had better trust his partners; it is a great problem if business (or marital!) partners are incompetent or, even worse, dishonest – *respondeat superior* (each partner is bound by the acts of the other partners, insofar as

---
[149] So, while a charitable institution can be a corporation, it cannot be a partnership. Partnerships are "for profit," although a partnership may, of course, not end up making any profit.
[150] The sharing means that each partner will either make a profit or a loss. The amount of the loss or profit can vary from partner to partner, depending on his/her/its ownership stake (i.e. a partner owning 30% of the business will make or lose three times more than one owning just 10% of that business).

those acts are within the scope of partnership authority)
- They have shared profits and management rights
- Partners are fiduciaries for each other –"one for all, all for one"

2. The Partner as Fiduciary (see pg. 302; Emerson BL)

In the most famous case in partnership law, *Meinhard v. Salmon,* Judge Benjamin Cardozo wrote that partners owe to each other not simply a duty of honesty, but something much greater: "the punctilio of an honor the most sensitive." A business partnership is no arm's length transaction; it is an embrace.

> **Meinhard v. Salmon** (1928)
>
> Suppose that Jo and Jill own a business in which they lease an office building and then sublease the offices to others for a profit. When their lease is up, Jo decides that she wants to renew the lease on her own behalf and not on behalf of the two as partners. Can Jo do this?
>
> No. It is a violation of the fiduciary duty and of the duty of loyalty not to offer Jill the opportunity to renew the lease. This was the situation in the classic case of *Meinhard v. Salmon,* 164 N.E. 545 (N.Y. 1928).
>
> In the *Meinhard* case, in order to finance a twenty-year lease on a building, Salmon entered into a joint venture with Meinhard. Meinhard would provide the investment capital, Salmon would manage the business, and the two of them would divide up the profits. When the lease expired, Salmon entered into a new lease between himself and the property owner, without informing or involving Meinhard. When Meinhard learned of this deal, he sued to be let into the deal on the grounds that the opportunity to renew the lease belonged to the joint venture.
>
> New York's highest court, in a 4-3 ruling – Cardozo for the majority and Andrews for the dissenters - found that Salmon had breached his fiduciary duty by lining up new opportunities for the property in the months before the lease was to end. The reason for the holding was that the defendant's efforts were not disclosed to the other joint venturer, Meinhard. There was no indication of bad faith or fraud, the court commented, but the innocent venturer, Meinhard, nonetheless was entitled to an equitable interest of just one-half of a share fewer than the shares held by Salmon in the venturers' enterprise. So the plaintiff, Meinhard, ended up with almost half of the new business interest Salmon had lined up while the old lease was expiring.
>
> This decision extended the duties of partnership far beyond duties under a contract. It determined that in such a relationship, loyalty must be undivided and unselfish, and that a breach of fiduciary duty can occur by something less than fraud or intentional bad faith. Judge Benjamin Cardozo, the future U.S. Supreme Court Justice and then Chief Judge of the New York Court of Appeals, wrote: "Many forms of conduct permissible in a workaday world for those acting at arm's length, are forbidden to those bound by fiduciary ties. A trustee is held to something stricter than the morals of the marketplace. Not honesty alone, but the punctilio of an honor the most sensitive, is then the standard of behavior." *Id.* at 546.

3. A Fiduciary Relationship

A partnership is a fiduciary relationship similar to that existing between trustee and beneficiary, principal and agent and director and corporation. The fiduciary duty of loyalty imposes an obligation upon each partner to act solely for the benefit of the other partners or the partnership in matters within the scope of the partnership relation. "As such, he/she owes the other(s) a high, fiduciary duty of care similar to that required in any principal/agent relationship." [151]

The relationship is one of strict trust and confidence, requiring the partner generally to subordinate personal interests to those of fellow partners. The Revised Uniform Partnership Act (RUPA) holds a partner liable as a fiduciary by requiring every partner to:

---

[151] Robert W. Emerson, *Business Law*. NY: Barron's Educational Series (6th ed., 2015), at 334.

1. Account to the partnership and hold as trustee for it and property, profit, or benefit derived by the partner in the conduct and winding up of the partnership property, including the appropriation of partnership opportunity;
2. Refrain from dealing with the partnership in the conduct or winding up of the partnership of the business as or on behalf of a party having an interest adverse to the partnership; and
3. Keep from competing with the partnership in the conduct of the partnership business before the dissolution of the partnership. RUPA Section 404(b).

Many litigated cases involve breach of a partner's fiduciary duties (see pg. 302; Emerson BL). Prohibited conduct includes, for example:

a. A partner may not secretly use or deal in the partnership assets for personal benefit, personally acquire a partnership asset, or otherwise use the partnership or its property in ways not contemplated by the partnership agreement.
b. A partner may not compete with the partnership in transactions within the scope of partnership business, and must account to co-partners for all "secret" profits realized in transactions injurious to partnership interests.

1. **Advantages and Disadvantages of the General Partnership**

Advantages
- Ease of formation – simply agreeing to do something as co-owners, could result in a partnership (so partnerships arise expressly or implicitly). Nothing written is required, unless the partnership business itself involves something that must meet the Statute of Frauds by being explicitly stated in writing (e.g., real estate sales).
- Profits connected to control/management – direct rewards. Motivating owners/managers tends to be easy.
- Very flexible operations - usually free to form any sort of business - an extremely adaptable business format.

Disadvantages
- Unlimited liability (but, as a practical matter, the order of proceeding after partners individually or after partnership assets may afford individual partners some protection). A partnership creditor - who dealt with, and is owed money by, the partnership – must first proceed after partnership assets before he can seek the assets of individual partners. And a creditor of an individual partner ordinarily must first proceed after that partner's assets before seeking to go after his draw or interest or other connection to the partnership (thereby not, at least at first, interfering with the other, *innocent* partners who had nothing to do with that partner's debt). Creditors are free to proceed after a partner's interest in the partnership through the process of attachment or garnishment. Attachment involves seizing partner's property and placing it under a court's control. Garnishment involves the court's holding a partner's wages to pay off a lawsuit settlement.
- Unstable business life. (A possibility of limited life for the business if a partner dies or becomes disabled – need to contractually account for that, with specificity.) One possible solution to business life instability is: A Buy/Sell Agreement.
- Difficult to raise capital.
- Ordinarily, buying out a partner is difficult unless there is a written provision outlining precisely the steps to be taken. Without a written clause on point, the handling of ongoing arrangements for "buying out" partners may be like going to court in a divorce case. (Accounting and law firms often have such clauses in their partnership agreements.)

> The Revised Uniform Partnership Act that 37 states follow provides that a partner can leave a partnership and not disrupt a partnership; instead, it is a *dissociation*. However, if death, withdrawal, or expulsion of a partner is not covered in a

> partnership agreement, the partnership is transformed. So, to definitely avoid a dissolution (the elimination of the existing partnership), the partnership agreement should provide that a partner's withdrawal does *not* dissolve the partnership.

5. Partnership Formation

There are no special formalities for forming a general partnership. The key factors that determine whether a set of individuals are indeed behaving like co-owners of a business are:

- Whether the individuals <u>jointly owned</u> the business,
- Whether the individuals <u>shared in the profits and losses</u> of the business, and
- Whether the individuals had <u>equal management rights</u> in the business.

Generally, there must be some evidence of all three factors.

Express Partnerships are formed in words.
Implied Partnerships are formed through conduct.

<u>Two Examples</u>

1. Bill & Bob's Roadkill Bar and Grill ("Swamp Water on Tap") – discussed in the "Partnerships" Topical Lectures

2. Roommates selling T-Shirts Together (discussed in the "Partnerships" Topical Lectures): If you and others run a business as if it were a partnership, even though you don't call it that and don't think of it as a partnership, you likely nonetheless have a partnership.

<u>In partnership law, agency concepts predominate. Partners are both agents and principals.</u>

Choose a Straight Shooter for a Business Partner

Be careful in choosing a partner, so your business does not suffer.
Ask yourself these questions:

(1) Has he/she been sued? Investigate at the local courthouse.
(2) Does he/she provide what you do not bring to the business? Balance your skills between you and your partner. And do not just take his/her word; check with his/her former employers and associates.
(3) Does his/her management style fit your business? Watch how the prospective partner interacts with customers and other people in general. Make sure that you and your employees can work with him/her.
(4) Does he/she rage about a former partner, employer, or employee? Problems from the past often reoccur.
(5) Does he/she have a bad credit history? Check with the credit bureau; you do not want a partner with problems handling finances.
(6) Does he/she want to do everything on a handshake? Get it in writing; memories can be fleeting.
(7) Has he lied about anything? Lying can be a habit. There is a Latin legal expression sometimes invoked by courts when reviewing the statements of someone who has been shown to have misrepresented the facts in at least one aspect of his/her testimony: *Falsus in uno, falsus in omnibus* ("false in one, false in all"). The doctrine is that if the decision maker (the judge or the jury) believes that a witness' testimony on a material issue is intentionally deceitful, the decision maker may disregard all of the witness' testimony.

So, just as you would not want to marry a liar, so you should not go into business with one. Run away!

6. The Partnership Agreement and the Statute of Frauds

For partnerships, the Statute of Frauds governs whether writing is required. So, just like contracts generally, most partnership agreements do not have to be in writing. For practical reasons, all important partnership agreements should be in writing.

7. Partnership by Estoppel (see pg. 331; Emerson BL)

Partnership by estoppel is similar to the concept of apparent authority (agency by estoppel) found in agency law.[152] The key question is: Did partners create or permit third parties' reasonable belief and reliance on a partnership [the belief that a person was acting as a partner-agent on behalf of his/her supposed co-owners/partners (the supposed partnership)]? If the answer is "yes," the third party may, for that context, be able to treat the business like a partnership even if it was not an actual partnership (e.g., the so-called partner was actually not a partner and thus not actually able to bind his/her "partners").

8. Partnership Property

Each partner owns all of the property. This ownership, similar to marriage's tenancy by the entireties or joint tenancy, is known as *tenancy in partnership*, and the partners are termed "tenants in partnership."

A somewhat comparable ownership concept, that a husband and wife may own property in a "tenancy by the entirety," bars a creditor of just one spouse from satisfying the spouse's debts by trying to attach (collect on) the property held "by the entirety." When is a tenancy by the entirety created? Some banks and other creditors contend that there should be written proof, but lawyers representing debtors note that – on their account forms – banks often do not offer depositors the option of tenancy-by-the-entirety ownership. (That is because banks themselves want to be able to collect debts from joint accounts, in case of holder defaults on a loan.) The Florida Supreme Court ruled in favor of debtors in that creditors generally must prove that a tenancy-by-the-entireties did not exist. Even if a bank signature card said that there was a joint account (with right of survivorship), since the card was not an express disclaimer of a tenancy-by-the-entireties, the account holders could still try to prove that a tenancy by the entireties did exist. *Beal Bank, SSB v. Almand and Associates*, 780 So. 2d 45 (Fla. Supreme Court, 2001).

Another important partnership concept concerns transferability and survivorship. Again, the notion is similar to what is found in marriage: Upon death, the partnership *property* (and the control of the property), pass to the surviving partners, while the *interest* in the property passes to the dead partner's heirs. So, for heirs or creditors, a partner – on his/her own (without seeking or needing his/her fellow partner's approval) - can allocate to the heirs or creditors a partnership *interest*. But the partner cannot make an heir or creditor a partner without the existing partners' approval.

> A Survivorship Vignette - The Ice Cream Partnership (discussed in the "Partnerships" Topical Lectures)
> If you bring in a new person, there is usually a new partnership.
> If this 3rd person "leaves," there is a new partnership again.
> But one can spell everything out in a writing; that is often done in law firms' or accounting firms' partnership agreements.

9. Partnership Funds and Partner Salaries

For what can partnership funds be used? Whose debts may they pay? There are stricter legal principles here than for sole proprietorships (the owner/partner cannot just use the business' money to pay his/her personal debts).[153] Also, in a partnership, partners ordinarily are not entitled to a salary (to be paid

---

[152] Robert W. Emerson, *Business Law*. NY: Barron's Educational Series (6th ed., 2015), at 331.
[153] However, even concerning sole proprietorships, it is wise, for tax and accounting purposes, to separate personal assets from business assets.

something other than or in addition to profits) unless specified in the written partnership agreement.

10. Capital Contributions compared to Labor

Courts often recognize money contributions more than labor contributions (unless the value of labor is spelled out in the partnership agreement).

> You, with great perspicacity, line up with someone who has big bucks, to form a partnership. WATCH OUT! Money – property – is more "quantifiable" than are labor contributions – "sweat equity" (Every partner in a partnership has the right to work really hard – an equality of rights, even if not in terms of actions. So courts "look to the money!").

B. Limited Partnerships (LPs) (see pgs. 342-343; Emerson BL)

The medieval commenda was an arrangement by which a traveling trader could raise capital by teaming up with, and using the money of, a local merchant. The commenda, a French concept, is the precursor of the modern limited partnership: the traveling trader was the equivalent of today's general partner, and the local merchant was equivalent to today's limited partner.

> Sometimes the purpose for limited partnerships is to create paper bonuses, for tax purposes.

1. Taxes and a Comparison to General Partnerships

The theory of tax shelters is based on taking advantage of provisions in the tax code that allow certain bookkeeping entries (such as depreciation and depletion) to be deducted from the profits of specific investments. If economically viable and properly set up, these projects can have a negative taxable income plus a positive cash flow for a period of years, thus offering shelter from taxation to some part of a wealthy person's income.

Comparison with general partnerships: In LPs, there are two different types of partners: At least one general partner and one limited partner. General partners have unlimited legal responsibility, whereas limited partners share the liability for debt.[154] "A general partner in a LP has essentially the same rights and duties as do partners (i.e. general partners) in a general partnership (GP)."[155]

2. Characteristics of Limited Partners

> A LIMITED PARTNERSHIP DRAWING - discussed in the "Partnerships" Topical Lectures
> Man pulling on rope;
> Fans cheering = limited partners;
> Man with rope = general partner

Limited partners are investors, somewhat similar to corporate shareholders, not managers. "Limited partners contribute capital and receives a special share of the LP's profits." However, limited partners only risk what they put in. In return for risking only their investment, limited partners have no management or control of the business "and are not held personally liable for partnership obligations beyond the amount of his/her capital contribution."[156]

Traditionally, the secondary market for limited partnerships has been extremely inefficient, with only about dozen outfits acting as brokers and information often hard to come by. But all that is likely to

---

[154] "Garnishing Definition." *InvestorWords.com - Investing Glossary*. Web. 27 Oct. 2010. <http://www.investorwords.com/2150/garnishing.html>.
[155] Robert W. Emerson, *Business Law*. NY: Barron's Educational Series (6th ed., 2015), at 343.
[156] Id.

[Handwritten note at top: LP do not need to create a partnership agreement stating what happens to the partner if he/she dies]

change with the Internet.

> Florida's version of the Revised Uniform Limited Partnership Act (RULPA), enacted in 2005, is at http://www.leg.state.fl.us/Statutes/index.cfm?App_mode=Display_Statute&Search_String=&URL=0600-0699/0620/0620PARTIContentsIndex.html

The effect of the RULPA is to "loosen" the law - to permit limited partners to become somewhat more involved in the business of the limited partnership without losing limited liability. Limited partners still cannot run the business on a day-to-day basis, but they have more flexibility than formerly was the case under the older statutes on limited partnerships.

Limited partnerships must be written down and comply with statutory disclosure requirements: a filing with the state. There must be notice to other parties that the business entity is a limited partnership. For instance, the limited status must be disclosed in the name of the business. Not only should one not let limited partners run the LP, but one should not let it *appear* that limited partners run the LP. For example, there must be no limited partner's name in the LP's name.

This notion of giving notice via the name is found in other countries, also. For example, limited partnerships in Germany must contain the term "kommanditgesellschaff" or a generally known abbreviation of that term; also, a limited partner's name may not figure in the name of these German firms.

End of Topical Lecture on Partnerships

C. The Limited Liability Company (see pgs. 368-370; Emerson BL)

A business format that is neither a partnership nor a corporation, but has some characteristics of one and some of the other, is the limited liability company. LLCs must file articles of organization with the state. "Unlike the S corporation, the LLC has no restrictions on the number or kinds of owners, the class of stock, and the owning of subsidiaries. Unlike general or limited partnerships, the LCC permits investors to manage the business yet not be personally liable for the business debts. The LCC thus is a *partnership-corporation* hybrid."[157]

The limited liability company (LLC) is a format mechanism for avoiding double taxation (why S corporations aren't as popular anymore - LLCs are more flexible).[158]

The early LLC laws were in Florida (1982)[159] and Wyoming (1977). An IRS tax ruling in 1988 led to LLC laws in all 50 states (plus Washington, D.C.). These laws authorize LLCs, which can allocate income and losses as partnerships do (thus similar to S corporations). While LLP (Limited Liability Partnership) ownership is not a security, LLC membership/ownership may be (that is an unsettled point in the law).

LLCs can be run informally. LLCs do not have to have the corporate mechanisms of control such as boards of directors. (Unless also a close corporation, an S corporation must follow those formal structures.)

Here are three problems with LLCs:

(1) while both partnerships and LLCs are not subject to federal income tax, LLCs (as are S

---

[157] Id. at 350.
[158] Id.
[159] Florida adopted a Limited Liability Company (LLC) Statute in 1982 (Florida Statutes, Chapter 608), then only the second state to do so. The LLC Statute was substantially revised in 1993, but few Florida LLCs were created because Florida subjected LLCs to the Florida Corporate Income Tax. On May 22, 1998, Florida enacted modifications to its LLC Statute which allowed for single member LLCs and provided that LLCs in Florida would not be taxed as corporations under Florida's corporate income tax if they were classified as partnerships for federal income tax purposes. While other states have passed similar acts, each state is unique.

corporations) are sometimes subject to a state income tax (e.g., in Florida and Texas), which partnerships are not;

(2) a LLC may not be permitted to merge directly with a non-LLC, so that the only way to effectuate a merger is for the LLC to dissolve, form a corporation, merge with the other entity and then revert back into a LLC - each such business format transformation tends to create tax liabilities;[160] and, most significantly,

(3) the law on business management, liability, dissolution, and other matters is still relatively new and unclear, especially compared to more established forms such as corporations and partnerships. Uniform laws have been proposed, but none have been enacted. Leading business law states have influence, but obviously do not control the law. For example, many states have followed Delaware's approach with LLC governance rules imposing *no* fiduciary duties between LLC members, but some states hold LLC members to a fiduciary status comparable to that of partners.

> LLCs are growing rapidly in number, in the United States and worldwide. Indeed, under the Civil Law, many European and Latin American nations had permitted the formation of limited liability companies since long before the United States had the LLC. (Germany started the process in 1892, followed by, for example, Austria in 1906, England 1907, Brazil in 1919, France in 1925, Cuba in 1929, Argentina in 1932, Luxemburg in 1933, Mexico in 1934, Belgium in 1935, and Switzerland and Italy in 1936, and Greece in 1945.) With the rapid growth in the United States, the LLC has gotten a tremendous boost in overall numbers internationally, also.

Check-the-Box

An IRS "check-the-box" income tax regulation permits most one-owner business entities to choose, to be taxed either as proprietorships or as corporations, while entities with two or more owners can decide to be taxed either as partnerships or as corporations.

> The "check-the-box" approach is also found, in effect, in some other countries. So, for example, a German GmbH (limited liability company) and a Dutch CV ("Commanditair Vennootschap" – a limited partnership) are business forms that can be treated as either a corporation or a partnership for tax purposes.

Pursuing Judgments Against the Limited Liability Company

Judgment-creditor remedies are highly diverse among the 50 states, ranging from none to a sale foreclosing the lien.

Unless the case goes to a bankruptcy court, the debtor member usually can, with planning, avoid paying the creditor from any LLC assets or distributions. However, the Florida Supreme Court's decision in *Olmstead v. FTC*, 44 So. 3d 76, 2010 WL 2518106 (Fla. June 24, 2010) takes a new, pro-creditor approach towards SMLLCs. The court, in a 5-2 decision, fashions a remedy not clearly intended by the legislature (full transfer of any distribution without any foreclosure procedural protections for the LLC or the LLC's sold owner). Specifically, the court held that courts can order a judgment debtor to surrender all right, title, and interest in the debtor's SMLLC to satisfy an outstanding judgment.

Olmstead encourages those who create or have SMLLCs to add a second member (even if it is just an owner of simply, say, 1% of the LLC). Alternatively, in Florida (and the 20-plus other states with Florida-like LLC statutes), *Olmstead* encourages a SMLLC to instead form under a state LLC law that is more protective, such as Delaware's LLC law. Under Delaware law, it is clear that the charging order is the exclusive remedy and its lien may not be foreclosed against the LLC. Inevitably, even this approach (e.g., a Florida-based LLC setting up its LLC in Delaware) will eventually result in law conflicts as creditors obtaining judgments in one state may seek registration of those judgments in other states with different policy approaches.

---

[160] This is a problem in, e.g., South Carolina., which has not drafted laws to "correct" the problem.

So the ultimate solution is greater clarity and uniformity in the law. Or for the Florida legislature to overturn, in effect, the holding in *Olmstead*.

Review Summary of Key Non-Corporate Business Formats

Sole Proprietorship - the simplest business format. An individual owns and operates the company, paying taxes at the individual income level; the owner and his/her business are not legally distinct entities, with him/her having potentially unlimited personal liability.

General Partnership (GP) – two or more co-owners and co-managers of a business-for-profit, with the key elements being: (1) a partnership agreement, express or implied, (2) common ownership and control of the business' assets (each partner is a principal), (3) shared management rights for all partners (each partner is an agent for his/her other partners, with corresponding liability risks for all partners – *respondeat superior*), (4) shared profits or losses for all partners, (5) fiduciary duties of each partner to his/her other partners, and (6) potentially unlimited personal liability for the partners.

Limited Partnership (LP) - In LPs, there is at least one general partner and one limited partner. The general partners have unlimited legal responsibility, whereas limited partners share liability for debt. General partners in a LP have essentially the same rights and duties as do partners (i.e., general partners) in a general partnership. Limited partners have limited management rights, but also limited liability – somewhat akin to corporate shareholders.

Limited Liability Company (LLC) - A business format that is neither a partnership nor a corporation, but a partnership-corporation "hybrid," with some characteristics of one and some of the other. More flexible than the S corporation, the LLC has no restrictions on the number or kinds of owners, the class of stock, and the owning of subsidiaries. More flexible than general or limited partnerships, the LCC permits investors to *manage* the business yet not be personally liable for the business debts.

IV. CORPORATIONS (see generally pgs. 357-443; Emerson BL)

YOUTUBE – Corporations 3mins6secs at robertwemersonufl

"'Salve, Salve.'[161] Welcome, students. We have gone all the way back 2000 years to the Roman era, and I am your Caesar directing you to the ancient law of corporations. Corporations are artificial beings, but they are recognized in the law as persons, having almost all the same rights and duties of natural flesh and blood persons. Corporations go back at least to Roman times, if not earlier, and in fact the word, "corporation," owes its origin to the Latin *corpus,* meaning body. So a corporation is something which has been given a body. It has been given a body by the state.

"Corporations are at the heart of a lot of the growth in the domestic product, in trade, in services of the 19th century, the 20th century, and well into the 21st century. One of the interesting questions, as we are in a new century, is, "Will the corporation continue to be at the forefront, or will some other entity take its place?" Contenders to take its place include the limited liability company, or forms of partnerships, particularly limited partnerships and limited liability partnerships.

"Another interesting question is, "Will society continue to accept the relatively limited liability of corporations for their actions, particularly in a multicultural global context, where it sometimes appears as if corporations are less accountable for things going wrong than are governments or individuals?" It's an ongoing debate that certainly cannot be resolved by looking up a few sites on the Internet, but I certainly think by looking into these issues, one becomes a more informed citizen. We thus are better able to make

---

[161] Latin for "welcome, welcome."

> choices in terms of our own personal decisions and our social policy analysis (e.g., in terms of our political voting) or what we think ought to be done in terms of business regulation and formation."

A. Introduction
1. A Business as a Collective or as an Entity

Since ancient times, there have been two main views about the legal structure of business entities. One view has been that "corporations" existed first as a concept of associated, collective (group) rights that predated any concept of the "corporation" as a distinct entity, endowed with its own individual rights and separate from the various members/owners of the corporation.[162] The other view looks to the "corporation" as being an invention of individuals and thus, from the outset, a separate, distinct entity. In our system, we tend to respect the individuality and separateness of the corporate entity rather than consider it to be just a bundle of the collective rights of its owners/members. However, the law did not always view things that way. (And it still may not do so in other, less individualistic societies.)

2. Corporate Powers

The following are some corporate powers:
"CLAMS"
- **C** ontract in its own name
- **L** end/Borrow money and make political/charitable contributions
- **A** ct as a partner
- **M** ortgage and hold title to (acquire and dispose of) property in its own name
- **S** ue and be sued in its own name

> *A corporation is "an artificial being, invisible, intangible, and existing only in the contemplation of the law. Being the mere creature of law, it possesses only those properties which the charter of its creation confers upon it, either expressly or as incidental to its very existence… [Among its properties] "are immortality; and if the expression be allowed, individuality."*
> Chief Justice John Marshall, *Dartmouth College v. Woodward, 17 U.S. 518 (1819).*

B. A Distinct Legal Entity

A corporation is separate and distinct from its "shareholders, directors, officers, and employees. This separation gives the corporation a life of its own and the responsibility and accountability to the law that are attributable to a natural person."[163] Its true owners are the shareholders who are issued shares of stock to represent their stake in the company. "In all of the states, corporations are created by state corporation commissions, although the management of corporations is left to internal controls within the corporate structure."[164] A corporation can, among other things:

1. The Three Basic Corporate Advantages

Perhaps partnerships have these qualities, also - but only corporations offer these advantages – (1) limited liability for the owners (the shareholders),[165] (2) greater ease of ownership transferability, and (3) the ability to opt for perpetual existence.

> YOUTUBE – corporation's three distinct elements (2:42 long) at robertwemersonufl

---

[162] This view is probably closer to the approach taken toward general corporations.
[163] Id. at 341.
[164] Id.
[165] Note, though, for small new companies, creditors typically require personal guarantees from owners.

> "Originally, all corporations were created, in effect, directly by the state to serve the state's purposes. For instance, in Roman times, you might have had a salt-mining operation, or you might have had a tax farmer, someone who went out, he was "incorporated," by the state, to collect taxes. Or you might have had a colony, which was incorporated by the state. And this trend continued throughout the Middle Ages - you started to have incorporated entities, such as guilds. The ancient guilds were, in effect, incorporated, as also were the church and universities.
>
> "And then there was the more modern era (and, in honor of that, I will don my Abe Lincoln hat). It was not until the modern era, basically the 1800s, in the United States and England and other common law countries, that we finally went to the point where we recognized all of the major elements associated with corporate status: Those three elements being 1) that it is a <u>distinct separate entity from the owners</u> or members of the corporation, 2) that the <u>membership in this corporation could be sold to others</u> and 3) that there is <u>limited liability for the shareholders</u>, the owners of the corporation, and that last concept took a long, long time for the government to accept. But, by the mid-1800s, it was becoming established in the United States and then Britain (1862), and is now found throughout the world, this notion that if you are a mere shareholder, you are not liable for the debts of the corporation. You have to be something more than a shareholder to be personally liable. All you can lose is your investment.
>
> "That [limited personal liability] is a very, very important concept. It's at the heart of why so many people form corporations: the fear that they might be personally liable, and they don't want to put everything at stake in running a business. They want to establish a separate entity where they can shield some of their personal assets from the business' assets."
>
> Questions for Possible Exploration on Your Own:
> 1. Some people blame the rise of huge, multinational corporations for evils such as child labor, pollution, famine, and even war. What do you think?
> 2. Why has every country in the world agreed to the principle that shareholders are not personally liable for corporate debts?
> 3. Do you agree with this notion of limited liability for shareholders? If so, is there a good reason why it should not be extended to other non-corporate business entities?

2. Financing: Another Corporate Advantage?

With corporations, it is usually easier to raise capital (e.g., can sell more shares), assuming that there is a market for the corporation's securities. Are there any potential buyers? At what price?

Another caveat (besides whether there is a genuine market for the securities): Bringing in investors can lead to management's ultimate loss of control. (For example, in August 1999 Towne Services' founding CEO placed an angry telephone call to an institutional investor. That led to that investor's huge sell-off of stock. And that, in turn, led the board of directors to force CEO Drew Edwards to resign.)

Initial Public Offerings (IPOs) are sometimes used to demonstrate the viability of a corporation, at least as much as to raise capital. For example, some tech firms have gone public to boost their credibility with potential customers.

C. Disadvantages of the Corporate Format

Corporations:
- Are more expensive to form,
- Require more documentation - One must account to the people (the state and the shareholders), such as in meetings. That is the way the system works. The owners do have a voice.
- More hierarchy is mandated – Perhaps creates inefficiencies – wasting of time; that is more a problem of management and organizational behavior than law. Corporations can suffer from bureaucracy just like the government does.
- Necessitate more dealing with lawyers (oh, no!) than simpler formats do.

- Double taxation (for the typical, C-Corporations – general corporations).

1. Pretense
More pretense (fiction) may be needed. That is because corporations are subject to more regulation (regulation of the business format itself).

2. Managerial Rigidity
Corporations are susceptible to rigid centralization and difficulty in adapting to firms' varying circumstances. It may be unsuitable for new economy firms that rely on markets and networks over integration. (Conversely, a partnership's greater flexibility and freedom from government interference arguably make it a better choice than a corporation for many publicly held firms.)

3. More Opportunities for Lobbyists and Politicians
So, the persistence of incorporation may owe more to politics and regulation than to efficiency. The rigidity of the corporate form makes it easier to regulate and therefore provides more rent-seeking opportunities for politicians and interest groups than if parties were left to freely choose their business form. Also, by protecting managers' power, preserving the corporate form co-opts the interest group that is best able to lobby for change. However, new corporate tax rules, increased federal regulation of corporate governance and the changing nature of U.S. business may give firms new incentives to use the partnership form. Lawyers may be the agents of change, as they have been in promoting partnership-based business forms for closely held firms.

4. Incentives for Managers, and Bureaucracy
With corporations, there are potential problems with work incentives because management is distinct from ownership. Managers may not get profits, so one may have to create other incentives for better work performance. (Sole proprietors and partners/managers already have inherent incentives (profits/risk of losses) to work very hard.)

Large corporations can suffer from bureaucracy similar to the government's problem (more meaningless meetings and less risk-taking?). Because corporations are more geared toward the delegation of authority, that can lead to inertia and systemic lethargy. Remember: A committee is a group that keeps minutes and loses hours! For example, a huge gap has sometimes separated many large corporations from the freewheeling Internet culture. Old-line companies often have moved slowly, appeared to be overly risk-averse, seemed too absorbed in protecting their established lines, and were viewed as too meddlesome for the tastes of up-and-coming movers and shakers. In the late 1990s, for example, large companies such as Disney became a "Poacher's Paradise" as smaller companies beckoned with stock options and their "freewheeling" ways.

Tax Principles[166]
Albert Einstein allegedly complained that preparing his own tax return was *"too difficult for a mathematician. It takes a philosopher."*

An old-fashioned approach is for the probable use of the partnership format for prospective early losses[167]; and the probable use of the corporate format for prospective early gains.[168] But businesses,

---

[166] Taxes have been a driving concern, such as for small business in deciding whether or not to incorporate, but less so with the "check the box" discussed earlier in this text.

[167] E.g., until the Tax Reform Act of 1986, limited partnerships often were notorious instruments for creating, and passing onto investor-partners, paper losses deductible from real income. The reform law closed many loopholes, and people learned the merits of the old saying that – to enjoy or respect sausage or laws, one should not know how they were made!

particularly small businesses, if they get in tax trouble, often do so for rather obvious failures on their part:
- Failing to send in payroll taxes withheld from the employee, such as income tax or FICA (social security).
- Failing to pay the matching or otherwise required employer contributions, such as FICA (7.65% of wages), sales taxes, use taxes, or unemployment compensation taxes (.008% of income).
- Failing to file a required tax return.
- Failing to deposit taxes in an account.
- Failing to pay the taxes.

5. Double Taxation

There are some tax advantages of corporations, (e.g., they can take advantage of certain deductions and credits), but there is **double taxation.** The term, "double taxation," refers to the fact that corporations pay income tax on earnings and then shareholders are taxed on the same assets when they receive dividends on their investments.[169]

So, with double taxation, the portions of income that are dividends are taxable as income for the corporation and also are taxable as income for shareholders. In other words, that income is taxed twice, at the corporate **and** individual levels. At least for smaller businesses, that may be avoided by not forming a corporation (staying as a partnership or sole proprietorship)[170] or by forming an S corporation or a Limited Liability Company. And sometimes it can be avoided simply by not issuing dividends.[171]

Strategies to reduce or eliminate double taxation involve maximizing the benefits owners receive and minimizing the corporate profits (which otherwise may need to be passed onto the shareholders as dividends).

One tactic is to pay large salaries and provide substantial benefits to owners/officers of the business. But the IRS only permits the corporation to deduct *reasonable* salaries and benefits. For tax-exempt groups, the IRS has the power - albeit little exercised - to revoke the tax-exempt status if the group pays exorbitant salaries to its top officers. In defining what pay is reasonable, tax-exempt groups should look at comparable private-sectors firms and at other tax-exempt groups. (However, a uniquely qualified, experienced executive can receive what for many people might appear to be excessive pay. It would be "reasonable" because of the executive's unique characteristics.)

Another tactic is to have owners lend the firm money and receive interest. (Nevertheless, the IRS can disallow (not permit the deduction of) excessive interest payments. A business funded 100% with debt provided by its owner(s) would not pass IRS muster, but a 50% debt/ 50% equity ratio would probably appear reasonable.)

These efforts to avoid double taxation are more likely to stir internal dissent if some shareholders are not employees, lenders, or otherwise receiving "dividend substitutes." And the IRS may force disgorging of dividends (and even order penalties) if a shareholder who also is an employee/officer/director has an unreasonably high salary. Also, as a practical matter, some shareholders invest expecting

---

[168] Corporations often can reinvest (without taxation) most gains – most profits. Traditionally, the corporate format is more suitable for deductions and credits than is the partnership format.

[169] Capital gains-increases in stock prices are a sign of cash flows the company could pay out, but holds for future growth.

[170] Partnerships are not taxable entities. Sole proprietorships are not even distinct entities. But all businesses tend to have the duty to file an informational return (Form 1065) detailing the firm's expenses and distributions to owners/partners.

[171] The IRS can tax excess accumulated earnings, which it defines as corporate earnings accumulated not for business-related reasons but for tax-avoidance purposes. Usually, before the IRS can levy the tax, several million dollars of earnings must accumulate without future plans for expansion or other such legitimate reasons for retaining earnings.

dividends,[172] and a corporation's paying higher salaries or rent or interest in lieu of dividends may not make business sense.

Six distributions from a corporation to its shareholders that the IRS classifies as dividends:
1. A bargain sale of corporate property to shareholder(s).
2. Shareholders' use of corporate assets without paying full value.
3. Corporate payment of shareholder debts.
4. Corporate "loans" to shareholders that were not bona fide (good faith) loans.
5. A corporate loan in good faith to shareholders, but without a fair rate of interest.
6. A corporate payment of excess rent to a shareholder for use of his/her property.

If the IRS detects these subterfuges, the money will be re-classified as a dividend and tax penalties also will be assessed.

D. Early forms of "Corporations"

Unlike partnerships, which go back at least 4,000 years – to Sumerian and Babylonian law, the earliest forms of corporations seem to go back only 2,000 years – to Ancient Rome. Thus, corporate concepts go back to Roman times; universities, salt mining colonies, ore extraction, tax collection.

1. Rome and Medieval Europe

In Latin, *corpus* means, "body." To incorporate is, in effect, to breathe life into, that which would otherwise remain inanimate. Early forms of corporations included the Roman "universitas" and the Roman salt mining enterprises. The university as a "corporation" carried over to early post-Roman schools such as England's Oxford University and Cambridge University.

In Medieval times other prominent "corporations" were:
- The Church ("ecclesia universalis"; the church as a person, as "the mystical body of Christ," as the "body corporate in the mystical body and blood").
- Ancient and Medieval Towns - predecessors of the modern municipal corporation
- Guilds - authorized by governments, since the 1400s, to regulate trade in particular industries (merchants and craftsmen, haberdashers, fishmongers, vintners, tailors, carpenters, etc.)

> Corporations were and are formed under the express authority of the government – a king's decree or a state statute.
> So corporations were and are *state creatures (creations)*

2. Development of the Basic Corporate Elements

As stated previously (IV Corporations, B(1)), there are **three main concepts concerning corporations** (sole proprietorships and partnerships do not have these characteristics) – (1) perpetual existence, (2) greater ease of ownership transferability, and (3) limited liability for owners. These elements come into play when looking at the development of corporations as an Anglo-American legal phenomenon.

a. Perpetual Existence for an Entity Distinct from Its Creators and Owners

First accepted was the notion of members/founders/shareholders are distinct from the entity they created/own. "Most modern corporations are usually granted *perpetual existence* as a routine charter provision, although corporation existence may be for a stated or limited period of time."[173]

This key notion is that the corporate/LLC entities are artificial beings, separate from the people who

---

[172] Many investors, such as retirees, have stock in a company because they need the cash flows from dividends (they need the cash and still hope for further capital gains). Banks and utilities typically are, compared to other companies, large dividend payers.
[173] Robert W. Emerson, *Business Law*. NY: Barron's Educational Series (6th ed., 2015), at 361.

made them or who are their members (e.g., donations of property could go directly to the university or the church - the university chancellor or the church's bishop did not really own the entity's land - rather, he just held it in trust for the true owner, the university or church itself). Because the entity is distinct from its flesh-and-blood owners/managers, one result is that the entity need not die; it can live forever.

b. Ease of Transferring Ownership

In the late 1500s and in the 1600s and 1700s, "corporations" added to their characteristics: now, in addition to being a distinct entity, the corporation also could include the idea of ease of transferring ownership (including with it the notion of individual profits). These ideas developed with respect to Joint Stock Companies (entities often created to help explore and settle the New World, such as the East India Company in 1600 and a company created in 1670 and still in existence in Canada - "the Governor & Company of Adventurers of England Trading into Hudson's Bay"). We know it as the Hudson's Bay Company. At this time, though, corporations were still seen as requiring a "public" purpose. Explorers, colonists, and traders were all agents for a corporate endeavor. The state, in effect, subcontracted out colonization to those hardy entrepreneurs. So America got its start via corporations!

c. Limited Liability of Shareholders/Members, with Shareholders
Not Personally Liable for Corporate Debts

Now universally accepted, limited liability was the last of the three notions (legally separate entity, selling of ownership, and owners' limited liability) accepted concerning corporations. Worries about the liability of a corporation and its owners led decision makers to retreat from the possibility that shareholders have limited personal liability. The worry about protecting innocent third parties meant that genuine, limited personal liability for shareholders was not put in the law until the early to mid 1800s (first in England, then the United States, then the rest of the world!).

An early 19th Century American (later, also the British, in 1862) addition to the corporate law was the notion of limited liability for stockholders. (The limited liability idea applied first to public corporations and only later covered purely private (for profit) corporations.)

Limited Shareholder liability was difficult for governments to accept at first, especially given a history of stock scandals, crashes, and other problems.[174] For an account of one huge such scandal, in the early 1700s, involving a complex scheme to privatize the national debt of England and concerning England's South Sea Company, see Christopher Reed, "'The Damn'd *South Sea*': Britain's Greatest Financial Speculation and Its Unhappy Ending, Documented in a Rich Harvard Collection," HARVARD MAGAZINE, May-June 1999, at 36 (http://harvardmagazine.com/1999/05/damnd.html).[175]

> Daniel Defoe, who authored the book, Robinson Crusoe, in the early 1700s, described in verse the problem of irresponsible corporate management:
> *Some in clandestine companies combine;*
> *Erect new stocks to trade beyond the line;*
> *With air and empty names beguile the town,*
> *And raise new credits first, then cry 'em down;*

---

[174] There had been lots of scandals – "speculations," they were often called. In the Netherlands, there was a scandal over stupendously high tulip bulb prices.

[175] See also EDWARD CHANCELLOR, DEVIL TAKE THE HINDMOST: A HISTORY OF FINANCIAL SPECULATION (1999). The South Sea bubble had some similarities to all of the bubbles – the booms and busts (e.g., the High Tech/Internet/Stock Market Bubble of the late 1990s): Many people were convinced we were living in an unprecedented moment in history – i.e., no collapse could happen. In London coffeehouses in 1720, you could buy puts and calls. You could even invest in business plans that described no real business besides investing in other businesses. During the Internet bubble, those were called "incubators."

After the Bubble "popped," the British Parliament passed the Bubble Act of 1720.

> *Divide the empty nothing into shares,*
> *And set the crowd together by the ears.*
>
> These worries, though, did not stop the incredible growth of private corporations as the Age of Exploration led to the Industrial Revolution, first in the West and then throughout the world. As stated in a comprehensive, scholarly work, TIMO RAPAKKO, UNLIMITED SHAREHOLDER LIABILITY IN MULTINATIONALS 423 (1997), "The corporate form and shareholders' limited liability has been universally adopted. This universal acceptance suggests that there are significant benefits which can be derived from the limitation of shareholders' liability."

TOPICAL LECTURE: Corporate Law and Delaware

Introduction to Topical Lecture:

Delaware is the leading state for corporate law. There, and in many states, are numerous management-friendly provisions: (1) Few restrictions on selling/mortgaging assets, merging businesses, or fighting takeovers; (2) Strong indemnification rights for officers and directors; (3) Weak rights for dissenting shareholders; (4) Staggered elections for board of directors; (5) Less mandatory disclosure about personnel and purposes; (6) Debtor-friendly courts for corporate bankruptcy cases; and (7) No corporate income tax for corporations formed in the state if they do not transact business in the state. Delaware is the only state with a separate business court (special recognition of corporate law needs); the state's most notable advantages include an experienced bench and bar for bankruptcy and corporate law, and the relative certainty of the corporate law.

E. Most Corporate Law Is State Law

At the federal level, laws predominate in a few sectors greatly affecting corporations. Key examples are securities laws (impacting finance), antitrust laws (impacting competition and mergers), and some employment and labor laws (impacting fields such as employment discrimination and management-union relations).[176] But the laws governing corporate set-up and governance are generally state laws.

There are similarities from state to state, but the corporate laws are not uniform. Many states adopted the Model Business Corporation Act (MBCA) (the 1946 and 1950 drafts) in the 1950s and 1960s. The MBCA was greatly changed in 1969, with many states adopting those changes.

A Revised Model Business Corporation Act (RMBCA, proposed in 1984) has been adopted by some states, including Florida in 1990. Florida's adoption of the RMBCA contains some exceptions, notably for state anti-takeover laws and corporate measures in that same area. (From 1976 to 1990, Florida followed the MBCA.)

The MBCA or RMBCA have been enacted in most states. But they have not been uniformly enacted and most states have made at least some changes to the model act. The effect is that while the MBCA and RMBCA can give some guidance on general corporate law principles, neither has created anything even close to a uniform law of corporations; that is – as usual – distinct from the one true instance of uniformity in state law – the Uniform Commercial Code (the UCC). "Still, the state corporation commission, by whatever name it may be called, is little more than an issuer of the corporate charter at the beginning of the corporate life; in practice, the state rarely takes any interest in the actual corporate function. Nevertheless, a corporation must be a good citizen. It may be punished for its crimes, sued for its torts, and held accountable for its contracts. *At all times it must be operated for the benefit of its shareholders, who are its owners.*"[177]

---

[176]There are important federal laws that greatly affect corporations, such as the Sherman Act (1890), Clayton Act (1914), Federal Trade Commission Act, Robinson-Patman Act, and other antitrust laws, the Securities Act of 1933, the Securities Exchange Act of 1934, other securities laws and the federal labor laws. However, the direct law of incorporating, managing, and terminating corporations is state law.

[177] Robert W. Emerson, *Business Law*. NY: Barron's Educational Series (6th ed., 2015), at 358.

F. Modern Corporation Statutes and Early American Law (see pg. 358; Emerson BL)
Purposes of modern corporation statutes are to:
- Simplify and clarify the law
- Provide a general, corporate form for
- Conducting business, with businesses usually free to modify that form
- Recognize close corporations, other special corporate formats

Before 1800, in the United States, 330 corporate charters had been issued, mainly in New England and usually for public interest ventures.[178] In early American corporate law, well before the founding of the United States, the corporation not only shaped economic development, but also wove the American political and social fabric. In the early 1600s, for example, the Virginia colony's royally-chartered company (the Virginia Company) authorized the new colony's first general assembly.

Over time, corporations no longer were restricted to just "public" purposes. But – as the Industrial Revolution got a head of steam – the time and expense of seeking a special state legislative enactment (to get a corporate charter) was increasingly burdensome, not only for businesses but also for state legislatures.[179] This bottleneck was accentuated by the fact that legislatures and courts were starting to let corporations form for any lawful purpose (far beyond the requirement that the company must be "in the public interest").

Then, starting with New York in 1811, and continuing throughout the mid-1800s, every state enacted a General Corporation Statute. So incorporators no longer had to petition the state legislature for a special act of legislation in order to be incorporated.

G. Delaware Corporate Law
(see Delaware Law & The Policy Foundations of Delaware Corporate Law), http://digitalcommons.law.umaryland.edu/cgi/viewcontent.cgi?article=1006&context=blc_2006

1. Introduction
Delaware is the state of choice for many large businesses (with thanks to Woodrow Wilson, progressive Democratic governor of New Jersey, 1910). Despite having a population of less than one-third of one percent of the United States, Delaware has almost three-fourths of all initial public offerings, over 80% of all out-of-state incorporations (companies not incorporated in the same state as where they are headquartered), and about two-thirds of all Fortune 500 companies. One of corporate law's enduring issues has been the extent to which state-to-state competitive pressures on Delaware make for a race to the top or the bottom. States, or at least some of them, are said to compete with their corporate law to get corporate tax revenue and ancillary benefits. Delaware has continued to "win" that race, however.

Two principle reasons for incorporating in Delaware are, compared to most other states:
1. Freedom for management; and
2. Relative certainty in the law - Not always the best answer for corporations, but at least there are some answers in Delaware law.

Tax advantages are not a usual basis for incorporating in Delaware, but certainly are not a disincentive. Delaware imposes on corporations an annual Franchise Tax based on the number of authorized

---

[178] Public-Purpose Companies included Turnpikes, Canals, Bridges, Ferries, Insurance, with a special act of the state legislature required for each corporation. However, in the 1700s, corporations began to replace partnerships as the most fundamental unit for larger forms of American commerce.

[179] The corporate chartering process imposed severe strain on legislatures; they could not enact each proposed charter, so grants sometimes appeared to result from happenstance or far worse (unfair connections and perhaps even bribery). The businesses that could get a charter seemingly gained a great, unfair advantage over the many whose hopes for a charter were delayed or denied.

shares. But there is no corporate income tax for corporations formed in Delaware if they do not transact business in the state. (Most other states follow that principle, also.) Delaware is the tenth cheapest state in which to incorporate; and there is no sales tax, personal property tax, or intangible property tax.

Delaware's revenue from its Corporation Department is nearly one-fourth of its total revenue and is exceeded only by income taxes. So the state depends on attracting a high volume of corporations and has a great incentive to keep its laws and fees favorable to Delaware-based corporations (e.g., no Delaware estate tax or any other Delaware tax on shares of stock held by non-residents).

2. Counterarguments against the Generally Accepted Reasons for Delaware Dominance in American Corporate Law

But some experts contend that Delaware's chief competitive pressure comes not from other states but from the federal government. When the issue is big, the federal government takes the issue or threatens to do so. Delaware players are conscious that if they misstep, federal authorities could step in. This possibility has conditioned Delaware's behavior. Moreover, even if Delaware were oblivious to the federal authorities, those authorities can, and occasionally do, overturn Delaware law. That which persists is tolerable to the federal authorities.

3. State Corporate Law: Delaware or Elsewhere?

> Corporate law in Delaware is one of the most flexible in the USA. It permits firms and their shareholders maximum flexibility in ordering their affairs and is written with a bias against regulation. The must lucrative reasons to incorporate in Delaware are the overall legal benefits due to Delaware's Court of Chancery specializing in corporate law allowing for developed procedures for firms to easily follow in order to avoid potential lawsuits. Delaware usually has little of great note in other areas of law, but for corporate law the Delaware Bar and its judges are among the leaders worldwide.
>
> Inertia: Many corporations incorporate in Delaware because this has been done by so many corporations for so many years.

There is more flexibility now, even for small entities, in choosing where to incorporate. Before, for small companies, it probably made sense just to incorporate where located. Now, with more mobility and the Internet, one may simply incorporate in Delaware or wherever else one prefers. Forms and information can be downloaded off the web.

For decades, American legal scholars have debated over the implications of allowing corporations to choose the state in which they will incorporate, irrespective of where they do business. Until recently the debate has centered almost exclusively on whether the managers who choose where to incorporate have the incentive to choose a state whose laws favor managers to the disadvantage of shareholders (the "race to the bottom" thesis) or whether their incentives are to choose states whose laws treat shareholders properly (the "race to the top" thesis).

Recently, some scholars have questioned whether the state charter competition process will necessarily lead to an optimal choice from the point of view of corporate decision makers, whatever the incentives of those decision makers might be. The presence of a variety of network effects may cause corporations to incorporate in a state which already has taken the lead in the charter race, even if some other states might offer better substantive law. For instance, corporations may prefer a state which has a well-developed, and hence more predictable, body of corporate law, or they may prefer to appear before judges who have much experience and familiarity with corporate law. These effects may cause the whole system to get stuck with sub-optimal laws dominating. Is that what we have with so many corporations staying in, or "going to," Delaware?

End of Topical Lecture on Corporate Law and Delaware

H. Types of Corporations (see pgs. 363-367; Emerson BL)

A public corporation is formed to meet a governmental or public purpose, an example is municipal corporations (historically, all corporations were "public purpose" corporations.)

A private corporation tends to be a for-profit corporation, created for private purposes. The private corporation is the status for most corporations. The Florida Business Corporation Act is in the Florida Statutes, at Chapter 607.

In all of the states, there are still some special incorporation statutes for financial institutions and insurance companies. Non-Profit Corporations are much more common today than in earlier generations. These corporations have members rather than shareholders. An example, at the federal level, is the American Red Cross. Most are at the state level, such as Blue Cross & Blue Shield. The Florida Not For Profit Corporation Act is in the Florida Statutes, at Chapter 617.[180]

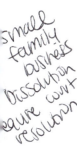

In close corporations stock is held by a limited number of persons in management and run like a partnership, "sometimes with no board of directors, or with other informalities not permitted to general stock corporations for profit" [181] (e.g., do not have to have directors or officers). Close corporation statutes are intended to combine the management flexibility of a partnership with the liability protection of a corporation.

> Many small, family-owned businesses are incorporated as close corporations. Close corporations typically can suffer the same problems as partnerships can: Management often must be by consensus, and business dissolutions are often like divorces and require a court resolution. "To permit such loose organization, the laws of most states limit the number of stockholders and permit restrictions on stock transfer by agreement among the shareholders or by charter provision."[182]

Professional Corporations are often formed for tax advantages. Examples include P.A. (Professional Association), P.C. (Professional Corporation), some law firms, accounting firms, etc. According to the Florida Professional Service Corporation Act is in the Florida Statutes, at Chapter 621, individuals/members may still be responsible for torts/contracts of others, as if it were a partnership. (So it may not insulate individual member/shareholders of the corporation from malpractice liability; joint/several liability for fellow professionals' wrongs may still exist, as if it were a partnership.)

> For new companies, the creditors typically require personal guarantees from owners so often there is no effective limit on personal liability.

A domestic corporation is "domestic" in the state where it is incorporated. For lawsuit purposes, a corporation's domicile (place in which it is a citizen) may be somewhat different. A corporation's domicile, at least for federal diversity jurisdiction, is the state in which it is incorporated and also in its principal place of business (so the corporation is domiciled in one or two states). Taxes and lawsuits are not generally avoided because of one's domicile. **Foreign corporations should register in states where they do business so that they can qualify to receive "other benefits" when registered; a foreign corporation generally has the same rights and duties as do domestic corporations.**

---

[180] Due to the availability of insurance and the large size of many charitable organizations, charitable immunity is generally a thing of the past.

Suppose there is a lawsuit for negligence against a hospital run by the eleemosynary society - "OMMMMM" (slogan - "Everyone who cares about anyone is chanting "Ommmmm!"), the Order of Merciful Medical Missionaries of Middle Minnesota. Decades ago, the suit likely would have been dismissed, as the society would have charitable immunity (similar to the sovereign immunity protecting governments from lawsuits). But now the case could be tried, and OMMMMM potentially answerable for a damages award.

[181] Robert W. Emerson, *Business Law*. NY: Barron's Educational Series (6th ed., 2015), at 366-367.

[182] Id.

Foreign corporations are "foreign" in that they are not incorporated in the state where they are operating. Because the United States is a federal nation, and corporations almost always are incorporated at the state level, even U.S. corporations are foreign corporations in 49 states, the states other than where they are chartered. So, for example, the Coca-Cola Company, which has its headquarters in Atlanta, Georgia, but has been incorporated under Delaware law since 1919, is a foreign corporation everywhere but in Delaware. Of course, a corporation need not be from some "foreign" locale as Delaware (or even Georgia) to be a foreign corporation in, say, Florida. It could be from another country, making it, again, a foreign (or alien) corporation.

Lawsuits in Florida against foreign corporations are governed by Florida Statutes, beginning at § 607.15101. (Serve process on the corporation's registered agent, located in Florida, or - if such service cannot reasonably be expected - on the corporation's Secretary at the corporation's principal, out-of-state office by registered or certified mail, return receipt requested.)

Penalties for failure to qualify or register can be severe: loss of the privilege of using state courts to file a lawsuit; a fine for every day of failure to register while doing business; and personal liability of officers, directors, and agents for actions in the foreign state.[183]

I. S Corporations (see pgs. 367; Emerson BL)
1. Opting for S Corporation Status

The S Corporation has a different tax treatment than does the regular (C class) corporation. Opting for S corporate status is a way to avoid the problem of double taxation (while still having, as a corporation, the limited liability for the business owners/shareholders)

For tax purposes, S corporations are treated like a general partnership. There is no taxing of the business entity - profits and losses are passed on through to the owners/shareholders for their individual income taxation. (If the S corporation must also want the corporation to be run/managed like a partnership, then they must adopt the close corporation status.)

For shareholders to choose S corporation status, an officer of the corporation must file IRS Form 2553, http://www.irs.gov/pub/irs-pdf/f2553.pdf (Instructions to Form 2553 - http://www.irs.gov/pub/irs-pdf/i2553.pdf) with the Internal Revenue Service.

To obtain and maintain S corporation status, no more than 100 shareholders are allowed, all owning the same class of shares, with no regular corporations or foreign citizens as shareholders. For purposes of the shareholder count, all shareholders who are family members (for up to six generations!) count as just one shareholder; so, another 99 are allowed.[184]

---

[183] In 1998, a classified ad in the Independent Florida Alligator's "Help Wanted" section stated: "Actresses/Models - $2,000 per day. Needed for upcoming film project."

A man in a business suit told each woman who showed up at his hotel room that he represented "Media World," a company making a sex-education video instructing Malaysian high school students how to insert a female condom, masturbate, and have safe sex. To complete the audition, the man explained, the applicant would have to disrobe, masturbate, and have sex with him.

Four women complained to the authorities. One of the women ("Pam") had completed the "audition."

Police concluded that the man did not use or threaten force and thus committed no sexual battery: Pam was an adult, had consented to sex, and even signed a contract saying she agreed to it. However, if the man was not conducting a legitimate job interview, he was guilty of fraud (and could also be sued for fraud). He was also guilty of misleading advertising, a first-degree misdemeanor, if he advertised for a job that did not exist.

Florida had no listing for the company. The man's most definite offense – even if there really was a company and a job - was the failure to register a corporation, a second-degree misdemeanor. Biggest problem: finding the man.

[184] In other words, the "family" is defined very broadly - every lineal descendent (including adopted children) as well as spouses and former spouses of the descendants, tracing back to up to six generations to a common ancestor.

The IRS reports that S corporations are the most widespread style of corporation.[185] Still, almost all S corporations tend to be small businesses – about 80% of all S corporations have just one or two owners (shareholders). At a certain size, S corporate status may not be possible; that is one reason for the rapid growth in Limited Liability Companies, where there may be no such practical difficulties. Even with reforms expanding the S corporation availability, it is still very rare for a large business to become or remain an S corporation.

2. Comparison with Close Corporations

S Corporation status is something that a corporation may be able to opt for under federal law. A close corporation is a special corporate format available only under state law. A business may be both an S corporation and a close corporation, or it can be either of the formats but not the other, or it may be neither format. While the close corporation is managed like a general partnership – with informality and the need for consensus (e.g., no board of directors; perhaps no officers) – the S Corporation is taxed as if it were a general partnership. S corporation shareholders can own different amounts of shares (not share and share alike, as if often found in general partnerships).

J. Stakeholders in Corporations

Who are stakeholders? Shareholders who legally own the corporation and have many rights,[186] but also others (employees, managers, suppliers, customers, dealers, distributors, and the community as a whole) who have an interest in the corporation.[187] There is a lively debate over whether a corporation's proper purpose always is to maximize shareholder wealth, or whether directors sometimes can consider the interests of creditors, employees, and other corporate stakeholders.[188]

The law provides few, if any, protections to these stakeholders as somehow being "owners" of a piece of the corporation. Lynn A. Stout, UCLA law professor, argues that two of the arguments traditionally used to justify strict shareholder primacy - that (1) shareholders own the corporation and (2) that shareholders are the sole residual claimants of corporations - are bad arguments from both an economic and a legal perspective. Instead, Prof. Stout opines that there is a better, third argument for shareholder primacy: requiring corporate directors to serve only shareholders is the best way to keep directors from imposing excessive agency costs on firms.[189]

This agency cost argument recognizes that, in an ideal world, directors would take into account the interests of both shareholders and other stakeholders (and that could benefit shareholders by encouraging nonshareholder groups to make firm-specific commitments to corporate team production). However, a rule of strict shareholder primacy is preferable because it permits corporations to monitor and reward director performance according to a single, easily observed metric: stock price. The biggest weakness in this agency cost argument is that it ignores actual business practice: the business world's clear preference for corporate governance rules gives to directors the discretion to serve stakeholder groups, even at the shareholders' expense.

State Law
Most corporate law is state law. (There are important federal laws the greatly affect corporations,

---

[185] Form, By. "SOI Tax Stats - S Corporation Statistics." *Internal Revenue Service*. 1 Apr. 2010. Web. 05 Nov. 2010. http://www.irs.gov/taxstats/bustaxstats/article/0,,id=96405,00.html .

[186] If anyone is the primary stakeholder, it must be, under law, the shareholder.

[187] Worker stakeholders could be present employees, prospective employees, and unions. Societal stakeholders could be local, national, and governmental, with these community stakeholders including persons such as local businesses dependent, in part, for their business upon those who make money as workers or suppliers for the corporation.

[188] Mark J. Roe, "The Shareholder Wealth Maximization Norm and Industrial Organization (ISSN 1045-6363, Harvard Law School Center for Law, Economics, and Business – Discussant Paper No. 339 (Nov. 2001) - http://www.law.harvard.edu/programs/olin_center/papers/pdf/339.pdf

[189] Lynn A. Stout, *Bad and Not-So-Bad Arguments for Shareholder Primacy*, 75 S. CAL L. REV. 1189 (2002).

such as the Sherman Act (1980), Clayton Act (1914), Federal Trade Commission Act, Robinson-Patman Act, and other antitrust laws, the Securities Act of 1933, Securities Exchange Act of 1934, and other securities laws, and the federal labor laws, but the direct law of incorporating, managing, and terminating corporations is state law.[190]

Proposals re: a Federal Corporate Law– intended to alleviate the states' competition in attracting and retaining corporations, their business, their jobs and taxes, etc. Meant to stop an unseemly and nationally inefficient "race to the bottom of the gutter" – The claim is that it is <u>Not</u> good for the nation as a whole, to have this internal domestic competition between the states, to have these "givebacks" from states to corporations. So one idea is to have chartering, at the national level, for very large corporations; charters could be in addition to, or instead of, state charters. An alternative proposal is to have a "Federal Minimum Corporation Standards Act," which would eliminate forum shopping and could compel corporations to become "socially responsible."

A counterargument is that any such proposal, if enacted, would just be more burdensome regulation.

A Hierarchy of Responsibility for Corporations:
At the top – Philanthropic Responsibility;
then, Ethical Responsibility;
then, Legal Responsibility (a fundamental duty);
and, at the bottom (but the base of it all, because a corporation must be profitable to survive and do anything else), Economic Responsibility.

K. Ethical Concerns: The Corporation and the OECD

1. Ethics and Corporations – Some Anecdotes

It is cynical to assume that law and ethics often contradict one another, or that businesses succeed by operating without many moral compunctions. Nonetheless, business law professors have often looked with some amusement at students who have the dual "impediment" of interests in both business and law: there is an old story about the corporate lawyer's spouse, called for voir dire in a criminal case, who was asked whether his wife is a criminal lawyer, and he said, "Yes, she works for corporations!"

Others have had a more positive view of law and business. Who said, "The business of America is Business"? It was one of our presidents. He was very taciturn (extremely quiet), one of Reagan's favorite presidents, and well-known for refraining from doing much; this President had no difficulty getting ten hours of sleep daily. That must be another reason Pres. Reagan admired our 30th President, Calvin Coolidge. In the 1980s and perhaps also the 1990s, society glorified business much as occurred in Coolidge's era, the 1920s.

Coolidge was so quiet and uncommunicative that everyone was always trying to get him to say something, <u>anything</u>. One lady came up to him at a party and said, "Mr. President, it's such a pleasure to be here at the White House. I feel so honored. And I don't care what the papers say about your being "Silent Cal": I know you'd talk about many things if given the right chance. Why, I have a bet here with one of the other guests that I can get you to say more than two words." To which Silent Cal simply started to leave the party, after first telling the lady, "You lose." Two words, and that was all!

2. International Business and the OECD

There are burgeoning legal and ethical issues for international business formation. The

---

[190] Each of those Acts is discussed in the book, Robert W. Emerson, *Business Law*. NY: Barron's Educational Series (6th ed., 2015).

Organization for Economic Cooperation and Development (OCED).[191] has adopted the Guidelines for Multinational Enterprises - a code of conduct to regulate relations among multinational corporations, international corporations, host countries, and home countries.

A number of economic, political, historical, and cultural issues must be faced when businesses operate internationally. It is a dynamic combination of issues beyond simply "law," and it may furnish a rationale for treating businesses differently in developing countries than in developed nations. In other words, the needs of developing nations are different, and these OCED Guidelines or other principles may mean that courts and multinational businesses should understand these differences and adjust for them. Should such a relaxed, differentiating approach be followed internationally, is there no reason to do the same within a large nation, such as the United States, with regional differences? Still, many believe uniformity – internationally and most certainly among the states, is the corporate law wave of the future.

L. Corporate Structure and Organization

1. Promoters of a Corporation (see pgs. 361-362; Emerson BL)

a. The Risk for the Promoter

"In the course of forming the corporation, the promoter may incur costs, make contracts, and do other acts [e.g., lines up employees and suppliers] in furtherance of the corporation."[192] Because the corporate entity is not yet created, the promoter is potentially liable for his actions – not protected by a corporate shield. (This is the same as the little-league-coach-as-agent-for-non-existent-principal example).

One cannot ascribe to a corporation anything occurring before the corporation was incorporated. "However, *it may ratify, adopt, or accept them, provided that there is full and open disclosure by the promoter to the corporation.*"[193]

b. Promoters or Others (e.g., Accountants) Issuing Stock: *Due Diligence*

Three defenses for non-issuer defendants (e.g., accountants, lawyers, and other experts acting on behalf of a corporations) are (1) that the misstatement proved immaterial, (2) that the investor knew about the mistake but purchased anyway, and (3) the "Due Diligence" Defense.

"Due Diligence" is roughly a defense that "I did what was expected of someone (e.g., an accountant) in my position – I was not negligent." The "due diligence" defense requires "proof by the defendant (the defendant's burden of proof) that after a reasonable investigation the defendant had reasonable grounds to believe, and did believe, that the registration statement was true and contained no material omission."[194]

Due diligence ordinarily is not expected of investment bankers advising companies about mergers; that is because financial advisers typically do not look behind the numbers in audited financial statements, and — as a standard practice — the investment bankers (or other financial advisers) state in documents known as "fairness opinions" that they have relied on the merging companies to tell the truth (and thus have not conducted their own investigations into the numbers supplied by the companies). Instead, it is the auditors who are at risk, such as in the Enron scandal, when then huge Houston-based energy, commodities, and services corporation collapsed in late 2001 and key persons subsequently went to jail.

---

[191] The OECD consists of the 30-plus leading economic trading nations; it is headquartered in Paris. In its other official language, French, it is l'Organisation de coopération et de développement économiques (OCDE).
[192] Robert W. Emerson, *Business Law*. NY: Barron's Educational Series (6th ed., 2015), at 362.
[193] Id.
[194] Id. at 404.

For accountants to be held liable, their misdeeds could be a failure to disclose important information or, when a disclosure is made, a significant misstatement. To sue successfully for common law fraud, a plaintiff must show that it reasonably relied on false statements or on omissions to disclose.[195] However, some claims based on violations of statutes do not require reliance; for example, reliance is unnecessary for plaintiffs to sue and win damages when the defendant has violated Section 11 of the 1933 Securities Act (e.g., by failing to include the information meant to be found in a securities registration statement).[196]

2. Articles of Incorporation: The State Charter (see pg. 371; Emerson BL)

So that the corporation has flexibility and does not have to amend and refile its Articles of Incorporation; keep its articles of incorporation very large and flexible, like a constitution.

"The charter (sometimes called the articles of incorporation, or articles) is the grant of corporate existence, the birth certificate of the corporation. This formal document, executed by the state through its corporate commission, is the source of corporate authority."[197]

"The incorporators are the persons who make application for the charter. Their only function is to lend their names and signatures to the incorporating documents."[198] Incorporators should usually make articles of incorporation broad – and, therefore, provide the corporation with maximum flexibility and less need for numerous authorizations of new powers. Other than some tax you may have to pay on the total number of authorized shares, there is usually no good reason why a corporation should not authorize a very large number of shares – far more than it actually plans on initially selling.

For the pertinent Florida Statute concerning the Florida Articles of Incorporation, see Florida Statute § 607.0202.

charter - grant of corporate existence

Among the provisions that must be set forth in the Articles of Incorporation are:

- A satisfactory name and the principal office or mailing address of the corporation. *Note: even unincorporated business can choose to use a distinct business name, generally so long as it does not infringe others' intellectual property and as long as a proper Fictitious Business Name form was filed with and approved by either state or county officials.*

- The total number of shares the corporation is authorized to sell (one reason not to have too many authorized shares - many states levy a yearly tax against the authorized shares of corporations chartered in the taxing state; there is absolutely no such tax ordinarily for owning a "piece" of a partnership).

- If the shares are divided into classes, the designation of each class and a statement of the preferences, limitations, and relative rights for the shares in each class.

- The same type of particular information about any preferred or special class issued in series, including a statement of the board of directors' authority to establish series and determine variations in the relative rights and preferences between series.

- If there are to be any shareholder preemptive rights, a provision granting such a right.

- The street address of the corporation's initial registered office and the name of its initial registered agent at that office. [State laws require that a location which is open and staffed during business hours be designated in the state of incorporation to receive and forward all official documents from the state, service of process, and other legal notifications.]

---

[195] For more on fraud, *see* id. at 106-10 and this text's discussion of contract law and mutuality of assent.
[196] Section 12 violations of the 1933 Act involves selling nonexempt securities without a registration.
[197] Id. at 353.
[198] Id.

- The name and address of each incorporator.[199]

- For a **de facto corporation** (a corporation "in fact"), there is a glitch in the formation of the corporation.[200] Only the state can come after the corporation to rectify the situation (which is ironic because the state regulator perhaps should have noticed the irregularity in the first place). A **de jure** corporation is a completely lawfully formed corporation (it meets all of the requirements in terms of it being established and maintained). For a de facto corporation, since the incorporators tried in good faith to form the corporation correctly, the entity is treated like a corporation. Third parties cannot hold a shareholder liable for the glitch.

In corporations there are three main groups -
Shareholders > Board of Directors > Officers
elect appoint
(see pgs. 384-400; Emerson BL)

If the board will not replace officers, shareholders can choose new directors *(shareholders cannot directly choose officers).*

When you buy shares, ordinarily it is <u>not</u> important that you actually have the stock certificate. Most brokerages actually hold any stock you buy in "street name" (i.e., their own name) instead of putting the shares in your name and mailing you the certificates. This is routine and the shares still belong to you. It is a good system for most people, as it means shares can be sold more quickly. You do not have to find and mail back the certificates to the brokerage.

Other people have some lesser interests, but the law is not clear on protections for these stakeholders. For **"stakeholders"** - e.g., employees, suppliers, the community, customers, many others - protection tends to be a matter of Ethics & Economics, not just Law.

A trend is for pensions, mutual funds, or other institutional investors to increasingly play a role in rendering management susceptible to a takeover or some other change in the Board. For example, many institutional investors use the 1995 Private Securities Litigation Reform Act to pursue improvements. Large

---

[199] The following Corporate Data Sheet lists some basic information that attorneys, accountants or other advisors usually require in creating a corporation.
1. Name, Address, Telephone, FAX, and e-mail for the Corporation and all of its professional advisors.
2. Officers and Directors: Names, Addresses (both home and business), and Titles.
3. Stock - a. Classes & amount (i) authorized, (ii) issued b. Par value c. Owners d. Capitalization
4. Annual meetings of: (a) Stockholders, (b) Directors
5. Corporate Books: Custodian(s) of Minute Book and Stock Book
6. Incorporation: Date, Close status (?), State in which incorporated, Amendments to Articles of Incorporation (Date & Purpose), Resident Agent (Name, Address, and Telephone Number)
7. Foreign Qualifications: for each one, the State, Date of Qualification, and Resident Agent
8. Tax Status: ID Number, S Corporation status (?), "Check-the-Box" filing or other significant filings affecting tax status
9. Bylaws: Amendments (including Date and Purpose), Fiscal Year adopted by the corporation.
10. Bank Accounts and Insurance - for each policy, the type of insurance, the broker, and the insurer
11. Subsidiaries and Parents.
12. Agreements by the Corporation and also Stockholders' Agreements: Title and Type of Document, Date, Parties, Term, and Other Provisions.

[200] Perhaps the articles of incorporation left out required names or addresses, or stock classification, or procedures in electing directors. Problems could be that the articles did not list all of the incorporators or did not list the resident agent's address. Or a difficulty could be that the corporate secretary failed to sign a corporate document or that the corporation did not classify stock properly.

pension–fund managers have won leading roles in class-action suits and have garnered settlements worth much more (e.g., over 40% of the estimated damages suffered by investors) than the typical settlements (averaging 14% of investor damages), and also have kept attorneys' fees to about 18% of the settlement (far below a 32% average). Also, unions representing shareholders sometimes have fostered a change in management policies, such as better benefits for workers, by using the unions' shares to access corporate documents, to align with other shareholders or bondholders, and otherwise seeking reforms such as through proxy fights. Unions, environmental activists, and other institutional investors have been leaders in attacking corporate deals, corporate officers' compensation, and other activities felt detrimental to the workers or other stakeholders.[201]

M. Shareholders (see pgs. 384-391; Emerson BL)

Shareholders have no real "duty" except, perhaps, to their own financial well-being; so there are *some shareholder rights, but no duties*. "The primary right of the shareholder is to attend meetings of the shareholders and to vote on matters properly brought before such meetings, including the election of directors and other fundamental matters affecting the corporation and required by statute or charter."[202]

> "The public be damned. I am working for my stockholders." William Henry Vanderbilt (1821-85), American Industrialist

1. Typical Powers of Shareholders

- Vote in Elections of the Directors
- Right to Notice of, to Attend and Vote at, Shareholder Meetings (shareholder democracy)
  (Directors call the annual meeting – if 13 months have gone by and directors have not called the meeting, shareholders can obtain a court decree ordering the meeting.)
- Inspections of Corporate Books

To inspect the books, a shareholder must meet these 3 requirements:
(1) Ownership: 5% (or more) of the stock or at least 1 share for more than six months,
(2) Make a written demand, and
(3) Must have a proper purpose – to check one's investment, see how directors and officers are doing their job. (NOT to demand access to get secrets, or to dig up dirt, or perhaps to press political points)

- Amend Charter – via vote of the shareholders (Majority, often 2/3 required).[203]
- Preemptive rights – Allows shareholders to maintain their relative stock ownership strength (their proportion of the total equity) – May be granted to shareholders in the Articles of Incorporation or other corporate documents. So, the corporation cannot sell additional shares outside the corporation without the existing shareholders' permission (or, at least, his right to buy his proportion of the stock). The "right of first refusal" is a possible power for shareholders: If selling stock, the corporation must offer existing shareholders the stock before offering it to the public.

---

[201] While some accuse the union leaders of having a hidden agenda, some shareholders applaud the unions' actions as more representation and service as a watchdog over officers and directors. For example, unions have led drives to give stockowners a larger voice concerning the use of poison pills or golden parachutes and also the ability to kill them.
[202] Robert W. Emerson, *Business Law*. NY: Barron's Educational Series (6th ed., 2015), at 384.
[203] Increasingly, institutional investors (e.g., pension funds) seek bylaw changes (and, to a lesser extent, charter amendments) because management often ignores non-binding proxy resolutions. For example, figures compiled by the Investor Responsibility Center show that most companies do not heed non-binding resolutions in which a majority of the shareholders vote for measures restricting "poison pill" anti-takeover defenses.

Retaining Control, While Selling Equity

When a company issues shares of itself in an initial public offering (IPO), how do the people who have owned the company retain control? When a company "goes public" with an IPO it usually does not sell all of itself. For example, imagine Bergen Bell Co., owned entirely by a woman named Adrienne. Adrienne decides to sell 10% of the company to the public, via an IPO, in order to raise money for expansion. Adrienne, who currently owns all of the 90 million shares of the company, will sell 10 million new shares, so there will be 100 million shares after the offering. Investment bankers help her determine the valuation of the company and decide to price the offering at $20 per share. This means Adrienne will collect about $200 million for them when the shares are sold (less the investment bank's fee of about 7%).

She will retain ownership of 90% of the firm, or 90 million shares.

Lawsuits - The top reasons cited by shareholders/investors for suing companies: (a) overly optimistic reports; (b) failure to warn of bad news; (c) failure to correct wrong information; (e) taking too long to disclose bad news ("dragging it out"); (f) inconsistent statements; (g) refusal to comment.

2. Shareholder Suits Against the Corporation (see pg. 390; Emerson BL)

Shareholders can sue the corporation. Ordinarily, business owners cannot do that with a proprietorship or partnership; but shareholders can sue the corporation because they and the corporation are *legally different* persons.

In the United States and most common law nations, the ability and willingness to sue, as well as the potential damage awards, all tend to be relatively high compared to some other parts of the world. For example, in some Civil Law nations, such as Japan, costs and cultural barriers discourage even the most disgruntled shareholders from taking action. Another deterrent to suits, again in some Civil Law nations such as Japan, is that successful claims cause damage awards for the company (against its board), not the shareholders themselves. Indeed, in Japan many derivative actions "piggy back" on government enforcement actions, perhaps a necessary approach given (i) the lack of information available to Japanese shareholders and (ii) Japan's low white-collar crime enforcement rates.

In the United States, and throughout most of the world, inside directors can be held personally liable for damages in shareholder lawsuits. Outside directors in Australia, Canada, France, Germany, Japan, South Korea, and the United Kingdom – indeed, almost everywhere (with more limited success at protection in the United States) - enjoy near-immunity from out-of-pocket liability due to shareholder lawsuits.

3. Derivative Suits

Suits by shareholders on behalf of corporations. Power to sue "derives" from shareholders' ownership interests.

A derivative suit is a suit "brought by one or more shareholders on behalf of the corporation and for its benefit. Since these suits are not for the benefit of the suing party, any recovery belongs to the corporation."[204] It arises out of any owner's general power to oversee his/her business.

Usually, derivative suits concern alleged poor business judgment (in effect, often acts of negligence) or a breach of corporate opportunity (often some fraudulent behavior).[205] "There are certain strict requirements for such a suit. The shareholder must first demand that the directors bring the suit (demand may be excused if the shareholder can show that it would have been futile), and that demand must be refused. Some states and the Federal Rules of Civil Procedure also require that the shareholder notify other shareholders of his/her intent to bring a derivative suit in order to give them an opportunity to ratify or confirm the alleged wrongful action."[206]

As an owner, to sue in a derivative suit, a shareholder must have standing to sue: (1) Own stock

---

[204] Robert W. Emerson, *Business Law*. NY: Barron's Educational Series (6th ed., 2015), at 390.
[205] The Business Judgment Rule and the Corporate Opportunity Doctrine are discussed later in this section of the text.
[206] Robert W. Emerson, *Business Law*. NY: Barron's Educational Series (6th ed., 2015), at 390.

throughout the entire litigation, starting when the injury occurred throughout entire time period at issue: e.g., one cannot buy BP stock after the Gulf of Mexico oil spill and then sue about that spill; (2) Make the demand to the Board of Directors, unless it would be futile; and (3) If own < 5% of stock or < $50,000 of stock, post a bond for legal expenses.

A major risk is that if a judge throws the suit out, the suing shareholder must pay the other side's lawsuit coasts (most significant of all being the attorney fees). But if the shareholder wins, the loser pays the shareholder's attorney fees and other costs (because the corporation received a benefit).

In *Cuker v. Mikalauskas*, 692 A.2d 1042 (Pa. 1997), the Pennsylvania Supreme Court became the first state high court to adopt an American Law Institute (ALI) recommendation (made in 1994) that derivative suits could be barred by the board of directors, whose decision whether to pursue claims or drop them could not be challenged in court unless plaintiffs showed that the board failed to act in good faith. This ALI standard (7.03 of the American Law Institute Principles of Corporate Governance) is more restrictive than the standard presently found in Delaware and many other states, where courts have wide discretion to review a board's decision not to pursue a case (and where shareholders ordinarily can pursue a derivative action as long as they went to the board first - regardless of whether the board ultimately authorized the claim).

The ALI-Pennsylvania approach permits shareholder derivative suits to go forward, despite the board's decision against bringing the claim, only if the board's initial investigation (e.g., via a special litigation committee) of the claim was inadequate. Other state courts or legislatures may follow the Pennsylvania-ALI approach. Also, the American Bar Association (ABA) in its proposals on corporate law has – like the ALI - adopted a "universal demand" requirement. Under the ABA's proposal, plaintiffs in a derivative action must make a demand upon the corporation in all cases. The commencement of a derivative action is not permitted until 90 days after demand is made, unless the demand is rejected earlier. Model Business Corporation Act (MBCA) Annotated § 7.42. The MBCA demand rule, like the ALI Principles, excuses demand only if the shareholder can show irreparable harm. Over a dozen states, including Arizona, Connecticut, Florida, Georgia, Michigan, Mississippi, Montana, Nebraska, New Hampshire, North Carolina, Virginia, and Wisconsin, have adopted by statute some form of this "universal demand" mandate. Still, many states follow the approach found in Delaware: that a demand must always be made upon the corporation before filing a derivative suit unless making the demand would be "futile."

4. What Shareholders Cannot Do

As a shareholder, a corporate owner cannot carry out managerial functions for the corporation. *A person who is a shareholder can be a manager, but it is in that separate role (e.g., officer or employee) that he/she is a manager, not in his/her role as a shareholder.*

- No management duties of shareholders – cannot purchase stock for corporation, cannot make ordinary business decisions for corporation (hiring and firing of employees, dealing with suppliers, etc.), cannot require that dividends be declared because that is the board of directors' decision.
- No fiduciary duties of shareholders – directors and officers have those duties. Shareholders are not managers, nor are they trustees.

5. Shareholders' Agreements

Ordinarily, shareholders have no fiduciary duties.

Shareholders' Agreements are a method to impose duties on shareholders, by mutual agreement of all of the shareholders. These agreements are especially useful tools for small, closely held companies. Shareholders' agreements typically require, among other things, that each shareholder:
1. Vote to maintain all of the shareholders as Directors.
2. Favor close corporation status for this incorporated business and favor S corporation tax status.

3. Agree always to vote in favor of continuing S corporation status unless the shareholders unanimously choose to terminate it.

"Right of Refusal" means that a shareholder may not sell any of his/her shares unless the purchase of these shares is first offered to, and refused by, the corporation (through its board of directors). As with partnerships, no new owner is admitted to the business except with approval from other owners. One reason that shareholder voting rights may not be granted is the competing interests (e.g., profits vs. full employment) often at play between shareholders (ESOPs, Pension Plans, etc.) & employees (unions).

TOPICAL LECTURE: Directors and Boards, including the Corporate Opportunity Doctrine
Introduction to Topical Lecture:

Directors act collectively as a board. Officers are agents of the corporation; as do directors, they have fiduciary duties to the corporation, such as no conflicts, at a personal level, with corporate interests. Both directors and officers must attend meetings, remain apprised of corporate business, and have no self-dealing. Under the corporate opportunity doctrine, directors or officers violate their fiduciary duty if they personally avail themselves of a business opportunity that should have been reserved for the corporation.

6. Directors (see pgs. 391-397; Emerson BL) (Or employees or officers)

Directors often are, but do not have to be, shareholders.
"The board of directors is chosen by the shareholders to manage the corporation." [207] Corporations should have some outsiders (non-employees, non-officers) on the Board of Directors. These outsiders have a perspective insiders cannot have. There is some benefit to the corporation's having outside directors, who are unlikely to be held liable.

a. Powers of Directors

"The directors are neither employees nor agents of the shareholders; rather, they occupy a legal position of trust to the shareholders. This trust relation is legally described as that of a fiduciary – a position of loyalty to the corporate interest and well being, superior to the director's self-interest or desire for personal gain."[208] Directors act collectively, as a board. While American boards (and those in most other nations) are unitary – with just one board per company - some countries, such as Germany, actually have dual boards of directors for their corporations – a supervisory board like the American board of directors, as well as a lower board that has the officers who run the business **(see pg. 395; Emerson BL).**

"Co-determination" in Germany
For corporations in Germany and some other European nations, the corporation's purpose is not simply to maximize per-share-value (as American corporations emphasize). German businesses have a hybrid set of values. (As one example, Germans - and Europeans generally - often oppose the high pay packages commonly commanded by American executives, but somewhat rare in Europe.)

Under the German system known as co-determination, workers' councils are legally defined bodies that appoint half the members of a company's supervisory board. Workers' councils start at the shop-floor level, with divisional, group and European workers' councils representing workers at each level of a company's management. Otto von Bismarck created the co-determination system more than a century ago in order to limit the outbreak of crippling strikes. German unions can still strike, but only after exhausting all means of peaceful conflict resolution. Although it is sometimes ridiculed for an exaggerated sense of ritual, the system has given Germany some of the most peaceful labor relations in the world. (It also helps produce

---
[207] Id. at 374.
[208] Id.

labor peace that proxies (voting rights) normally given to management in the United States are usually controlled by the corporate creditors in Germany, where three large banks control 80% of all proxies.)

In exchange for restraint, the German system grants the workers' councils extensive power in running companies, including a say in hiring, firing, transfers, working conditions, and all major strategic decisions through representatives on companies' supervisory boards.

b. Directors' Powers: "BOARDSCAM"

The powers of the Board of Directors, through which it oversees/administers corporate affairs, can be understood with the mnemonic, BOARDSCAM:

- **B** ylaws - create, alter, or repeal
- **O** fficers - appoint, remove, and set their pay
- **A** ssets - lease, sell, or otherwise exchange corporate assets
- **R** ecords - each director has an absolute right to inspect the corporate records (the "books"), with no minimal time or minimal ownership amount, as for shareholders
- **D** ividends - decide whether to declare, and how much.

Fewer companies in the S & P (Standard & Poor's) pay dividends, down about 7% from 1995 to 1999 with the market value of companies that pay dividends (as a portion of the S & P) down about 22% in those four years. In addition, the average dividend yield has dropped by more than half, from the historical average of 4.5% (which companies exceeded in the early 1980s) to about 3.7% in the late 1980s, to about 3.0% in the early 1990s, to around 1.3% in 1999.

- **S** tock prices - determine how much to be charged for newly issued shares
- **C** ommittees - can designate a number of committees to perform a number of board activities (e.g., executive committee, audit committee, finance committee) under the general supervision of the whole board
- **A** cquisitions (and Mergers) - responsibility for approving or disapproving
- **M** eetings - power to call annual and special meetings

(That, along with officers' authority, constitutes a strong power to exercise and control "the bully pulpit")

Directors set the agenda for officers. Directors and officers owe duties but they control how their own duties are performed. They are more in control of how the corporation fares than the shareholders are.

c. Duties of Directors

Under the Clayton Antitrust Act (1914), no interlocking directorates are allowed

One cannot be a director or high-level officer for two competing corporations with more than $10 million in corporate surplus and undivided profits (**see pgs. 538-39; Emerson BL**). But even without the competition problem (thus no interlocking directorate problem), we still may worry about directors on different boards, while not being competitors, scratching each other's back on officer/director compensation.

Another restriction on directors is that *they cannot delegate responsibility.* For example, no proxies can be given, as shareholders can do (directors must make their own decisions, not pass it on to others). Also, no salary and no compensation (beyond reimbursement of expenses) is allowed for directors unless provided by bylaws (which, of course, they typically allow).

Directors (and Officers) are Fiduciaries

Some commentators, viewing profitability as only one mark of corporate success, would reform the board of directors and include in "success" sensitivity to ethical and environmental issues. The federal government already requires all corporations to have a special committee of the board of directors, independent of the officers, called the "audit committee," which scrutinizes fiscal actions for conflicts of interest.

7. Reports to the SEC

> There is much potential for fraud, for cooking the books. Perhaps even worse, there is much potential for stupidity, whether by businesses seeking investors, by investors or by their advisors. Even the so-called experts are often wrong. In 1929, an economist wrote, "Stocks have reached what looks like a permanently high plateau." Irving Fisher, Professor of Economics, Yale University 1929. (Note: A Harvard professor would never have made such a mistake! ☺)
>
> What happened in October 1929 – The Great Crash. Stock market prices plummeted and the nation fell into the Great Depression of the 1930s.

Every securities issuer with a registration under the Securities Act of 1933 (as amended), and every issuer on a national stock exchange, and every business with 500 or more equity shareholders and over $5 million in total assets, must file periodic reports with the Securities and Exchange Commission (SEC). Forms can be accessed at http://www.tenkwizard.com). Filings include:

- **10-Q** reports (quarterly reports) can be unsigned by a CPA.
- **10-K** reports (annual reports) must be signed (certified) by a CPA.
- **8-K** reports (monthly updates on significant corporate events) need be filed only for special situations.

The 10-Q and 10-K provide ongoing, continuous disclosures about the business and are a major source of information about business generally and specific businesses in particular.

8. The PSLRA, Insiders, and Tippees

The Private Securities Litigation Reform Act (PSLRA) is premised on the notion that lawsuits are interfering with efficient capital promotion. The counterview is that the stock market is just a giant corporation game, run by and for the powerful insiders (a cross between a giant casino and a pyramid scheme).

Who are **insiders**? Officers, directors, consultants, and experts of a company – all privy to information which is <u>not</u> available to the investing public. Many people can be insiders – and may disclose information in violation of employer's policies and even deterrent efforts.

Who are **tippees**? Spouses, relatives, friends, colleagues, and friends of friends, i.e., person who get private information regarding securities prospects from insiders. Just like insiders, tippees can be liable under Securities Section 10-b; they must not act on inside information or give it to others.

Comparative Law

There is a huge international market in securities, but no overarching treaty on the international securities market. Individual nations often have protections for investors, but exactly how extensive those protections are, and how a victim is to receive remedies for violations of another nation's domestic securities laws, is often unclear. "Caveat Emptor" (buyer beware) may be especially appropriate to any American investor in a foreign market.

9. The Sarbanes-Oxley Act (see pgs. 430-434; Emerson BL)

a. The Effects of Sarbanes-Oxley

The rules on internal controls were part of a larger effort to improve corporate governance in the wake of scandals such as at energy company Enron Corp. However, they have become a point of contention among small companies, investors and auditors. Small companies and even an SEC advisory committee have argued that the requirements add burdensome costs. Investors counter that the rules are especially needed at small companies, which are susceptible to accounting problems.

b. Reporting/Whistleblowing Under the Sarbanes-Oxley Act

Under SEC rules pursuant to the Act, 15,000 public companies must file annual certifications, in which chief executive and financial officers personally vouch for the accuracy of their corporations' financial statements. Those officers are expected to swear "to the best of my knowledge," that these financial reports are accurate. If the executives will not attest to the report's accuracy, they must file a statement explaining why.

Critics worry that the proposed rules could eliminate attorney-client privilege in a number of situations, leaving clients reluctant to seek advice. In addition, critics say, the rules are likely to lead to additional liability for lawyers, since violation of rules regulating professional conduct often is a basis for malpractice actions. But the response is that something had to be done to restore public confidence in the securities market after a stunning series of corporate problems, including the implosion of Enron and WorldCom in huge accounting scandals. That is what Sarbanes-Oxley was meant to do, by strengthening regulation of corporate boards and the professionals who work for them.

As a practical matter, the SEC rules may not make much of a difference to law-abiding companies and their lawyers. In general, the notion of going up the ladder with a problem (**see pg. 415; Emerson BL**) and taking it either to the general counsel or the CEO is something many corporate legal departments already expected their lawyers to do. The problem is what reporting is needed when an outside counsel's critical advice to inside counsel is not followed. The result could be a very difficult, strained relationship among the professionals, and an unclear conclusion of the corporation's difficulties.

10. Indemnification of Directors

Some corporations automatically provide it; and state laws often provide some protection, especially for outside directors.[209] Officers and directors have general fiduciary duties of honesty, fairness, and disclosure of information. Directors have duties to shareholders and the corporation. Officers have duties to the corporation.

11. The Corporate Opportunity Doctrine (see pg. 393; Emerson BL)

Directors or officers violate their fiduciary duty if they personally avail themselves of a business opportunity that should have been reserved for the corporation. For example, employees of corporations have a high duty to divulge what is going on.

> An officer, director or high-level employee must take opportunities first to the corporation before pursuing these opportunities for their own personal benefit (or to benefit others aligned with them – e.g., a family member, a friend, a personal creditor). Shareholders do NOT have that duty. For example, you can own 500 shares of Microsoft while often owning 500 shares of Apple.

While the Business Judgment Rule's focus usually is on extreme foolishness, with the Corporate Opportunity Doctrine the emphasis is often on alleged dishonesty.

If there is a conflict of interest between a director/officer's personal interests and the corporation's interests, the proper approach is disclosure to the corporation; give the corporation the first chance.[210]

---

[209] In the aftermath of *Smith v. Van Gorkom*, 488 A.2d 858 (Delaware 1985), discussed hereafter, the Delaware legislature and most other state legislatures enacted laws permitting corporations to limit or eliminate the monetary liability of directors for actions involving breach of the duty of care, as long as the directors acted in good faith. Seven states - Louisiana, Maine, Maryland, Nevada, New Hampshire, New Jersey, and Virginia - also provided this liability protection not just for directors, but also for officers.

[210] A fiduciary (director, officer, or controlling shareholder) cannot take advantage personally or through another company of a business opportunity that would serve a present of prospective corporate purpose. In such circumstances, the fiduciary must first disclose the opportunity to the corporation and give the disinterested directors or shareholders the chance to decide whether the corporation should act. The fiduciary's obligation to the corporation arises even if the fiduciary learned of the opportunity in a personal capacity, as the fiduciary cannot divorce himself/herself from the constant obligation to act in the best interests of the corporation.

Contracts between (1) directors/officers, or their friends, relatives, or associates, and (2) the corporation – these contracts must be fair, fully disclosed, and approved by disinterested directors. So, an officer, director, or other significant employee should try to do all that is reasonable to help the corporation.[211]

The touchstone of conflict of interest director transaction issues is fairness – i.e., was the transaction to which the corporation and the director were parties fair to the corporation. The main issue for corporate opportunity analysis is disclosure – was the transaction disclosed to the corporation, and then the corporation either declined to take the opportunity or was somehow unable to take the opportunity.

Plaintiffs, typically shareholders in a derivative action, have the initial burden to prove that a "corporate opportunity" existed. If that burden is met, the fiduciary that appropriated the opportunity must then prove that fiduciary standards were met. This can be done only by showing that the opportunity was offered to the corporation in a timely manner and with full disclosure, and that a majority of the disinterested directors or shareholders determined not to accept the opportunity for the corporation.

Corporate rejection does not necessarily free the fiduciary to take advantage of the business opportunity, as the fiduciary must also consider other aspects of the fiduciary obligation, such as the prohibition against directly competing with or engaging in activities that harm the corporation.[212]

If a fiduciary is found to have improperly taken a corporate opportunity, courts will generally impose a constructive trust or, if the opportunity has been re-sold by the fiduciary, assess damages in favor of the corporation. The corporation will thus be entitled to all profits or appreciation arising out of the particular venture. While this creates a windfall to the corporation that invested nothing and took no risk in the enterprise, the result is entirely consistent with agency theory that precludes an agent from keeping any profits gained at the expense or to the disadvantage of the principal.

A Corporate Opportunity Doctrine decision: *Ostrowski v. Avery* (Avery and Aesop Skit)

In *Ostrowski v. Avery*, 703 A.2d 117 (Connecticut Supreme Court 1997): The Connecticut Supreme Court first determined that (1) Avery and Passaro owed fiduciary duties to Avery Abrasives and its shareholders, and (2) the chance to develop small cutting wheels constituted a "corporate opportunity" for Avery Abrasives. The court then turned to the central question in its opinion: "What role does disclosure to the other directors and shareholders play in determining whether a corporate opportunity was in fact usurped?"

The court noted that the law of corporate opportunity contemplates the disclosure will be made to disinterested directors, who then are given an opportunity to accept or reject the opportunity. Adequate disclosure of a corporate opportunity will provide defendants with a safe harbor from liability for breach of fiduciary duty. But Avery and Passaro had apparently failed to give adequate notice. Their disclosure was to Avery's father who could not be considered disinterested. Moreover, the board as a whole (including its disinterested directors) was not informed of the opportunity until after Avery and Passaro had established ISW.

However, the court held that, under Connecticut law, failure to disclose would not give rise to automatic liability. A corporate fiduciary could avoid liability if he or she could prove by clear and convincing evidence that his/her exploitation of a corporate opportunity did not damage the corporation. The court remanded the case to the trial court and ordered the trial court to determine whether Avery and Passaro either: (1) made a disclosure sufficient to reach the safe harbor from liability, or (2) could establish by clear and convincing evidence that their conduct did not harm Avery Abrasives. If they could satisfy either of

---

[211] For example, suppose that a corporation might have pursued a particular opportunity, but it failed to do so, at least in part because of a lack of financing. If a corporate officer could have helped the corporation get financing, but failed to do so, and then that officer – as an individual – used his contacts and abilities to obtain financing for a separate venture (in which investors, including the officer, pursued the same opportunity the corporation declined), then the officer could be liable for violating his fiduciary duty to the corporation: for breach of corporate opportunity.

[212] If the venture is one that in others' hands could impact adversely on the corporation, it is no defense for the fiduciary that the corporation chose not to pursue it.

these affirmative defenses, the shareholders' claims would be dismissed. In effect, on remand, the second defense was met, as the company, it seems, would not have taken the opportunity, anyway.
YOU CAN SEE THE VIDEO INTERPRETATION OF THIS CASE, MODIFIED BY COMBINING IT WITH AN AESOP'S FABLE, IN THE **AVERY AND AESOP** VIDEO – YOUTUBE at RobertWEmerson – 4 different scenes (videos) as well as written discussion.

End of Topical Lecture on Directors and Boards, including the Corporate Opportunity Doctrine

12. Officers (see pgs. 397-398; Emerson BL)
a. Powers
Officers are *agents* of the Corporation. "They are named and hired by the board of directors. Designation of the various offices and the duties of each office are set forth in the bylaws. As a rule, the officers are the president, one or more vice presidents, the secretary, and the treasurer."[213]

b. Duties of Both Directors and Officers
Directors and officers must attend meetings, remain apprised of corporate business, and not engage in self-dealing or conflicts of interest. As fiduciaries, they should ensure that they have no conflicts, on a personal level, with the interests of the corporation.

c. Liability of Officers and Directors
Officers and directors can be successfully sued for all sorts of corporate activities in which they engaged or for which they otherwise have some responsibility, whereas shareholders, in their role as shareholders, have limited liability.

> How scary and amazing and likely to be a failure of judgment (negligence if not outright recklessness). A mistake that is obvious to everyone but the person making the mistake. These mistakes usually result from failing to appreciate value and to ask questions.

13. The Business Judgment Rule (see pg. 394; Emerson BL)
Officers' and directors' ordinary mistakes are not enough to make them liable. But they should try to do their best, including to seek information and expertise.

> *"There is one thing all boards have in common… they do not function!"*
> *(From Peter Drucker, Management: Tasks, Responsibilities, Practices 1989)*

"Both directors and officers must govern the corporation's affairs with reasonably good judgment…. Officers and directors cannot be held accountable just because they made a wrong decision."[214]

The Business Judgment Rule (BJR) generally means that as long as directors have made an informed decision and are not interested in the transaction being considered, a court will not question whether the directors' action was wise or whether they made an error of judgment or a business mistake. Not all decisions of directors will result in benefits to the corporation. As a result, directors will be personally liable for loss to the corporation only if the elements of the BJR defense are not satisfied.

In order *to use the BJR as a defense, directors must act in good faith and with reasonable belief that their conduct legally and legitimately assists in achieving the corporation's purposes*. They must also exercise their honest business judgment after due consideration of what they reasonably believe to be all the factors relevant to their decision.

Five commonly recognized elements of the BJR are:

---

[213] Robert W. Emerson, *Business Law*. NY: Barron's Educational Series (6th ed., 2015), at 397.
[214] Id. at 376.

- Business decision making. The BJR protects directors against claims for wrongful acts, but not against claims for failure to act.[215] Inaction by directors is protected by the BJR only if it is a result of a conscious decision to refrain from acting.
- Disinterestedness. The BJR protects directors who do not have a material, personal interest in the decision. A disinterested director does not appear on either side of the transaction, nor does he or she expect to derive any personal financial benefit from it (as opposed to a benefit which is advantageous to the corporation or all the stockholders generally).
- Due care. The BJR protects directors if they have informed themselves and considered all relevant information about the subject matter to the extent they reasonably believe to be appropriate prior to making a decision.

  Corporate managers generally owe a fiduciary duty exclusively to shareholders - a duty interpreted as requiring the managers to maximize shareholder value. When the firm is solvent, the duty to maximize shareholder value tends to give managers an incentive to act efficiently - that is, in a way that increases total value. Nevertheless, when the firm is insolvent, this duty might give managers an incentive to run the firm in a way that reduces the value of debt more than it increases the value of equity and, therefore, is inefficient. The leading view among corporate law scholars is that an insolvent firm's managers should maximize the sum of the values of all financial claims against the firm - both those held by shareholders and those held by creditors.

  An insolvent firm is likely to have two types of creditors: (1) "payment creditors" - parties owed cash, who hold financial claims against the firm; and (2) "performance creditors" - parties owed contractual performances, who have against the firm one or more claims for performance. The "financial value maximization" ("FVM") approach requires managers to take into account the effect of their actions on the first type of creditor - payment creditors - but not on the other - performance creditors. Opponents of the FVM approach contend that the FVM's failure to account for performance creditors might cause an insolvent firm's managers to act in a way that harms performance creditors more than it benefits those with financial claims against the firm and, thus, is inefficient. These opponents conclude that an insolvent firm's managers should be obliged to maximize the sum of the values of all claims against the firm, both claims for cash and claims for performance; that approach, they contend, would eliminate the distortions associated with the FVM approach and actually make shareholders better off.

- Good faith. The BJR protects directors if they rationally believed the decision was in the best interests of the company. The protection will not apply if the directors acted solely or primarily to preserve their positions or otherwise to benefit themselves.
- No abuse of discretion. The BJR protects directors against honest errors of judgment, but does not provide protection for decisions that cannot be supported by some rational basis.

> ### *Smith v. Van Gorkom*, 488 A.2d 858 (Delaware 1985)
> In *Van Gorkom*, the officers/directors agreed to sell the company without undertaking a good faith, thorough review and research of what the company was really worth. The officers'/directors' liability was not simply

---

[215] That runs counter to the contention that the higher up one is in an organization, the less one must do – that one can get by with little effort. The lesson for employees, apparently opposed by the BJR, is revealed in this parable:
An eagle was sitting on a tree resting, doing nothing. A small rabbit saw the eagle and asked him, "Can I also sit like you and do nothing?"
The eagle answered: "Sure, why not."
So, the rabbit sat on the ground below the eagle and rested. Suddenly, a fox appeared, jumped on the rabbit and ate it.
Moral of the story - To be sitting and doing nothing, you must be sitting very, very high up.

> for accepting a tender offer, but for their failure to get the information necessary to make an informed decision.

For some students, *Smith v. Van Gorkom* may be especially interesting because it shows businesspeople, too, may goof off and fail to do their homework! In this case, Trans Union's board was held personally liable, to the tune of $23 million, because it approved Trans Union's sale of its railcar-leasing business (for some nifty tax credits) to the Marmon Group (part of the Pritzker family).

The board members did not have need to have accounting expertise, but they should have known that they did not have it and that they needed to obtain it. They should have *known* that they did not *know* what they needed to *know*!

14. Criminal Liability

Sentencing guidelines provide hefty penalties for firms that do not have systems in place to assure that legal requirements are met. Corporate standards of conduct, properly formed and sincerely implemented, may serve as some protection for corporations when "rogue" company officers or other employees break the law. Those standards do not protect the actual officer/employee culprits. In fact, they tend to encourage corporations to help the authorities develop their evidence against those individuals.

If a corporation is convicted of a crime, the corporation's penalty could be a fine, to be paid from corporate coffers, or the corporation could lose its corporate charter, or a government license, or its right to contract with the government.

15. **TOPICAL LECTURE:** Piercing the Corporate Veil (see pgs. 360-361; Emerson BL)

Introduction to Topical Lecture:
The Sarbanes-Oxley (SOX) of 2002 provides for disclosures and certifications, auditor independence from firms, stricter controls by government (e.g., the Public Company Accounting Oversight Board, Section 404 ("Internal Control Systems")). Any number of legal violations could lead to an attempt to collect from beyond the corporate "monster": When third party creditors of the corporation collect directly from the shareholders on debts the corporation owes those creditors. To pierce the corporate veil, three elements usually must be proven: shareholders' control of the corporation for an improper purpose; the corporation's use as its owners' "alter ego"; and harm to the plaintiff.

> The Corporate Monster: Video
>
> YOUTUBE – Corporate_MonsterLaura1min27secs at RobertWEmerson
>
> Disclaimer: It will take you longer to read this summary than to watch the actual video, which lasts about ninety seconds.
>
> ### Summary
>
> Barbie is in a cool pink convertible enjoying a sunny day in Gainesville. Barbie and main squeeze GI Joe (what happened to Ken, anyway? Perhaps she is cheating? The horror!) Are driving along in what looks like a nice park, or perhaps the author's lawn. Never mind that Barbie is driving on the grass, which is surely a tort of some sort.
>
> On the plus side for GI Joe, he seems fine with Barbie's driving. Or maybe he just would not be caught dead behind the wheel of a hot pink convertible with what appears to be princess decals liberally sprinkling the paint job. (Maybe Barbie ditched Ken because he didn't let her drive?)
>
> Wait, here is a clue as to what might have happened to Ken! Out of nowhere, although it does (sort of) blend in with the grass, comes a horrible, hideous monster! Egad! Perhaps Ken was driving his own (pink?) convertible to pick Barbie up when he was attacked and mysteriously disappeared.

> The creature is remarkably strong and quite alarming-looking, lifting the car and its passengers for what must be the most surreal moment of their plastic lives. Wheeeeeeee – there goes Joe. He must have flown 10 feet! Impressive distance, but that landing had to hurt. Ouch… there goes Blondie, too. The creature looks really perturbed at this point, but do we know why?
>
> It seems that this creature is (drumroll……..) the "Corporate Monster," and it has sacrificed BarbiJo (like Brangelina, but smaller) to make us Business Law students think about an age-old question: if the corporate monster or company that "does you wrong" has no money and little assets, **who the heck do you sue?** Can you "pierce the corporate veil" and go after the owners when the beast is out of cash? (That seems to be a separate lecture—film at 11.)
>
> Ack! Sudden flashback to IBM circa 1993 – Blue Screen of Death! Whew, it went away… sorry about that. At this point, Joe seems to have had better days (he looks dead), and Barbie… well, she seems to have a dislocated head. (Wonder how much *that's* worth in punitive damages?) At least the car looks OK…unfortunately—that really is a hideous color.
>
> The moral of the story (very, very loosely interpreted): Do not drive on the grass unless you want your boyfriend/illicit lover to be savaged by a ravenous monster with no cash. (Maybe Ken wanted the car so he set them up!) More seriously, with a mangled or deceased Joe and an askew or paralyzed Barbie, the problem here is that often people are harmed by corporations; and, to recover damages from the people behind the monster outfit (the owners of the corporation), the victims must be able to pierce the corporate veil.
>
> The questions posed include:
>
> Q: If the Corporation has very little in the way of assets, what are the victims of the corporation supposed to do?
>
> Answer: Recovering damages in a situation where the corporation itself has little or no assets is very difficult. In order to recover damages, one must pierce the corporate veil. However, this feat is very rare - less than 180 cases in the last 12 years.
>
> Q: Do the victims have any sort of recourse against the corporate monster or perhaps the owners of that corporation?
>
> Answer: If the corporation is factually liable, then there is a possibility of recovering damages. If the corporation has any assets, then pursuing those assets is often the least painful route. Otherwise, the plaintiffs (Barbie and GI Joe, or their next of kin) will have to pierce the corporate veil to receive damages from the corporation's shareholders. To be successful, the victims must prove:
>
>   1. The shareholders were acting on behalf of the corporation to commit fraud
>   2. The corporation was merely an alter ego
>   3. The plaintiffs suffered actual harm
>
> Q: Can the plaintiffs pierce the corporate veil?
>
> Answer: For Barbie and GI Joe's case, it is hard to determine whether or not they would be able to collect damages from the shareholders, without more information regarding the corporation's shareholders and their role in this attack.

Piercing the corporate veil is: the unusual situation in which the third party creditors of a corporation can collect from the corporation's shareholders on the debts the corporation owes to those creditors "if the corporate name is used as a false front or 'stalking horse' behind which the owners or operators perpetuate fraud upon creditors or others dealing with them"[216]

Third parties > Corporate shield protecting shareholders (including, in some cases, subsidiary corporate shield protecting parent corporation from liability).

As practical matters, creditors or suppliers sometimes demand personal guarantees from small company's shareholders.

For the piercing of the corporate veil we must look for the first crack in the wall. A study of 232 state or federal lawsuits seeking the piercing of the corporate veil between 1995 and 2005 showed that not a single defendant was a publicly-traded corporation. Overall, the percentage of successful cases went down. Plaintiffs were most likely to succeed in piercing when the defendant corporations had three or fewer shareholders.[217]

The three most cited factors in piercing cases are:
1. Misrepresentation;
2. Intertwining (commingling) – personal and corporate transactions are mingled, with the shareholder treating the corporate assets as a "nest egg" or "shell," thereby not respecting the corporation as a separate entity ; and
3. Domination (control). - there is no "separate" will – no separate entity – between the corporation as an "alter ego" of owners – e.g., paying personal debts with corporate funds.

Failure to observe corporate formalities (e.g., no holding, and no recording, of stockholders' meetings) was also cited often, but it led to the lowest pierce rate, compared to other factors.[218]

Often the problem concerns subsidiary corporations or close corporations.

One cannot just let piercing the corporate veil occur simply because failure to do so would leave an injured party without a complete remedy.

> Courts do not just pierce the corporate veil because the defendant is a small company, or because it is an S Corporation, or because there is just one shareholder in the company, or because the corporate format was chosen solely to obtain limited liability of shareholders – e.g., in the corporate minutes one even has the statement from the incorporators, "Thank God for the corporate veil and the rules of limited liability!"

It is quite difficult for third parties to get through the corporate veil to hold shareholders liable. One important reason we have a very high standard for piercing is that business owners form corporations to obtain limited liability, and the corporate law is intended to encourage such incorporating.

Piercing the corporate veil involves a failure to follow corporate formalities (but also much more). It generally entails undercapitalization (severely below the "appropriate" level of corporate assets for that type of business), and plaintiffs almost always have to show fraud.

The first question to ask often is: Are the shareholders in fact also officers/employees and thus might be held liable for their misconduct in those roles? If so, trying to pierce the veil may not need to be attempted.

To pierce the corporate veil (and hold shareholders personally liable), these three elements usually must be shown: (1) Use of shareholders' control of the corporation for an Improper purpose, such as FRAUD (e.g., using a shell corporation; e.g., intentionally violating a statute, such as with a sham subsidiary to get around the requirement that a single business – in this case, the parent corporation – cannot have certain types of owners.

---

[216] Robert W. Emerson, *Business Law*. NY: Barron's Educational Series (6th ed., 2015), at 360.
[217] Richmond McPherson & Nader Raja, *Corporate Justice: An Empirical Study of Piercing Rates and Factors Courts Consider When Piercing the Corporate Veil*, 45 WAKE FOREST L. REV. 931 (2010).
[218] *Id.*

(2) Corporation as "Alter ego" of owner(s), such as paying personal debts with corporate funds (treating corporate assets as one's own individual assets); and (3) Harm to Plaintiff.

The classic shell corporation is one that is created for the sole purpose of insulating its owners from liability and is intentionally undercapitalized. Its owners intentionally put no assets into it so that there is nothing for creditors to go after. For example, suppose the 16 taxicabs owned by Shell Taxicab Inc. are all titled in the name of Shirley Shell, the firm's chief executive officer and chairperson of the board. When one of Shirley's cabs runs down Ida Infirm and Ida sues for $1.7 million, Shirley throws up her hands: "Oh, by golly," she says, "Too bad about that accident. You know, the corporation just has no assets - all these nice taxis are mine personally - and I am protected by the corporate entity." Wrong: Shirley might be liable personally, as this is a fraudulent corporation, an alter ego (just "another self") and is being used in a way that is unfair. Usually undercapitalization is not so much an issue in contract cases - where, after all, the creditor voluntarily dealt with the corporation - as it is in tort cases.

End of Topical Lecture on Piercing the Corporate Veil

16. **TOPICAL LECTURE:** The *Ultra Vires* Doctrine (see pgs. 375, 390; Emerson BL)
Introduction to Topical Lecture:
The Latin term *ultra vires* means "beyond the powers of the corporation," such as by violating the law. Usually an *ultra vires* claim centers on the corporate officers' or directors' failure to follow the procedures needed for proper corporate actions. Just two parties can obtain an injunction against *ultra vires* corporate activity: shareholders – in a suit against the corporation or via a derivative suit; and the government.

The term "ultra vires" means beyond the powers of the corporation, such as by violating the law. Usually an ultra vires claim centers on the corporate officers'/directors' failure to follow the procedures needed for proper corporate actions.

Only two parties can obtain an injunction against corporate activity:
(1) Shareholders – in a suit against the corporation or via a derivative suit; or
(2) The State – (the government)

Even if shareholders cannot get a rescission or injunction, they may still receive compensation from the corporation and/or from the directors/officers. When an injunction is not available (damages award may be possible): the party seeking to invoke *ultra vires* did not deal with the corporation (e.g., the party is simply a competitor).

The party involved in the *ultra vires* contract with the corporation is trying to use an ultra vires claim in order to get out of the contract. (What right does it have to complain? Ordinarily, none. It is the corporate owners and the state (which granted the charter) with an interest in corporate structure and powers.)

If a contracting party is seeking to keep the ultra vires contract intact (to not have ultra vires used to rescind or enjoin the enforcement of the contract), it often will succeed. Rescission or enjoinder on grounds of ultra vires is only granted if: (1) the contract is executory and there would be no harm to (detrimental reliance of) the contracting party due to a rescission; or (2) the contracting party knew that the contract was ultra vires.

Ultra vires was more of a problem in olden days (e.g., 60 or more years ago), when state law and the typical articles of incorporation were far more limiting on the powers - potential or actual - of a corporation.

> Some countries' corporate law is more constricted, with their rules and their governmental agencies more hesitant to let corporate entities do something without first getting express approval from directors and from the state regulatory agency.

End of Topical Lecture on *Ultra Vires*

Corporations, as persons, have many of the constitutional rights accorded to individuals. This includes rights of free speech. To conclude Part One, we consider the Constitution's First Amendment.

F. THE FIRST AMENDMENT AND FREEDOM OF SPEECH

YOUTUBE – Quil Brioche - Marie Antoinette.wmv, at http://www.youtube.com/watch?v=iiAKsiqOY3Q - 1 minutes and 38 seconds - at robertwemersonufl

I. THE FIRST AMENDMENT GENERALLY

All of our freedoms depend, for their continued existence, on other freedoms. Perhaps the most important underlying freedom is that of speech. Speech rights even extend to organizations and gatherings: freedom to protest and associate. A corollary First Amendment right is freedom of association.[219]

Some Learned Observations

"If there is any fixed star in our constitutional constellation, it is that no official, high or petty, can prescribe what shall be orthodox in politics, nationalism, religion, or other matters of opinion." *West Virginia Bd. of Educ. v. Barnette*, 319 U.S. 624, 642 (1943) (for the Supreme Court, Justice Robert H. Jackson's opinion).

A great American judge, Learned Hand, speaking to a group of newly naturalized Americans, said: "The spirit of liberty is the spirit that is not too sure that it is right; the spirit of liberty is the spirit which seeks to understand the minds of other men and women; the spirit of liberty is the spirit which weighs their interests alongside its own without bias."

"It is better to debate a question without settling it than to settle it without debating it." - Joseph Joubert

"Be who you are and say what you feel, for those who mind don't matter and those who matter don't mind." - Dr. Seuss

---

II. FREE SPEECH

YELLOW DOG CONTRACTS: FREEDOM TO PROTEST AND ASSOCIATE -[220]

Constitutionality Issues -

The Yellow Dog* YOUTUBE *video (3:22 long) (Emerson in a dark knit cap- a "working man").

In my home state of Maryland, there was a controller who was elected and then re-elected and re-elected many, many times. He was a Democrat, in fact a dyed-in-the-wool Democrat. At a particular fair or rally, a woman who was a big fan of his came up to him and said 'Sir, I really admire you but one thing that troubles me is you are such a democrat. I suspect you would vote for the devil himself if he were Democrat', to which the politician responded 'Not in the primary.' That is what we call a yellow dog democrat. What is a yellow dog democrat? I'll give you one other example from an historic figure that you

---

[219] Restrictions to foster English-language communications may not violate the freedom of association or free speech. In *Arizonans for Official English v. Arizona*, 520 U.S. 43 (1997), the U.S. Supreme Court unanimously ruled that a state could mandate an English-only policy for governmental matters (e.g., licensing).

After the Arizona law was thus upheld under the U.S. Constitution, a state court quickly ruled that the new law violated *Arizona's* constitution. The Arizona Supreme Court upheld that decision. That marks the only time that courts have found that an official English law violated a state's constitution, despite a number of similar court challenges.

[220] For articles on business associations having some analogy to employee unions – e.g., franchisee associations – see Robert W. Emerson & Uri Benoliel, 118 PENN. STATE L. REV. 99 (2013), available at http://ssrn.com/author=86449; Robert W. Emerson, *Franchising and the Collective Rights of Franchisees,* 43 VANDERBILT L. REV. 1503 (1990).

> probably have heard of. Theodore Roosevelt, one of our great presidents who was a Republican, progressive, but Republican, was addressing a crowd and there was apparently a drunken man in the back who shouted out 'My grandfather was a Democrat, my father was a Democrat, and I'm a Democrat' to which Teddy Roosevelt (remember, he's a Republican) gets out that little pinched glass of his and says 'Well, if your grandfather were a jackass, and your father were a jackass, what would you be?' to which the drunk man responded 'A Republican!'

[handwritten annotation: prohibit employees from joining unions]

- "Yellow Dog" contracts – Violate Freedom to Associate with whom one wants to associate
- "I'm not gonna join a labor union or talk to a union."
- "Only a yellow dog would join a union"
- Would you rather be a yellow dog, or associate with, play with, hang around with, a yellow dog than be with those "nasty" unions?
- Political Equivalent - Yellow-Dog Democrat
- Employer to fire employees- (1) Yellow dog contract clauses give employer cause to fire for breach of contract; (2) Statutes against yellow dog contracts

The courts usually overturned anti-yellow-dog provisions until the 1932 law — the Norris-LaGuardia Act finally effectively outlawed the yellow-dog contract.

> Now this is not to slight any political parties, some of my best friends are from either of the two major parties. The point, of course, is that that drunk, like the Maryland politician, was a yellow dog Democrat. He could not see beyond his political party. In the area of labor law, we had what were called yellow dog contracts, and those contracts provided that people could only work at a particular place of employment if they agreed that they would not join a union, that if they were a member of a union they would resign from that union, that they would not participate in any sort of unionization activities. In other words, they were to look at unions kind of like a yellow dog Democrat looked at Republicans. These laws that were passed in the early part of the 20th century in the unionization labor law reform movement were an attempt to get away from some of these restrictions that employers had imposed on employees, such as the yellow dog contracts. It took several decades for the labor reform movement to really stick in terms of the court's upholding the statutes and the statutes really having an impact, and that really hit during the Great Depression in the 1930s when we had significant laws such as the Wagner Act (also known as the National Labor Relations Act).

A. Constitution Just Restricts Governmental Actions

Because the First Amendment prohibits governmental restrictions on free speech, it does not ordinarily reach private employers who restrict their employees' speech. (Other laws may reach such restrictions, but not the Constitution itself.)

The free speech right does not always mean that you can keep your funds from being used for speech to which you object. But political organizations have some strong First Amendment rights to make political expenditures. In *Colorado Republican Federal Campaign Committee v. FEC*, 518 U.S. 604 (1996), the U.S. Supreme Court held that, as long as a political party's expenditures are made without coordination with any candidate, the party has a First Amendment free speech right to spend as much money as it wants to support candidates or attack opponents. Corporate rights of political speech are about as extensive as any individual rights, given the overturning of restrictions in political spending laws, per the highly controversial *Citizens United v. Federal Election Commission*, 558 U.S. 310 (a U.S. Supreme Court 5-to-4 decision on January 21, 2010). In other words, for speech as expressed through critical campaign expenditures independent of the candidates themselves, the Supreme Court held in *Citizens United* for federal laws and in *American Tradition Partnership v. Bullock* (2012) for state and local laws: "independent expenditures, including those made by corporations, do not give rise to corruption or the appearance of corruption."

Therefore, "[n]o sufficient governmental interest justifies limits on the political speech of non-profit or for-profit corporations."

B. Overall Free Speech Rights

The Constitutional right of free speech is broad and deep; beliefs can be strongly asserted, although perhaps in a distasteful or even highly offensive manner to many people. For example, there is a right to use the flag or religious symbols in ways that may deeply offend persons.

<u>Beliefs can be strongly asserted, perhaps in a distasteful or even highly offensive manner to many.</u>

Some speech is more effective than other speech. The Right of Free Speech is not necessarily a right to effective speech, to equality of access. It is a right to <u>not</u> be suppressed, but not a right to be helped (no right, generally, to government assistance in getting your speech before the public. No right to have a broadcast station, a magazine, a wonderful website governmentally provided for you.) In effect, the wealthier you are, the more speech you can afford and the more exposure you are given – your free speech rights are more effective. There is also a freedom not to speak.

C. Flag Burning

A particularly virulent debate has revolved around "speech" that includes burning the American flag.

In *Texas Johnson*, 491 U.S. 397 (1989), the Supreme Court, in a 5-4 decision, ruled unconstitutional a Texas statute forbidding "desecration of a venerated object." (Johnson had been convicted and sentenced to a year in jail for burning an American flag to protest the Reagan administration.) Congress then passed the Flag Protection Act of 1989, which provided for a fine and a maximum of one year in jail for anyone who "knowingly mutilates, defaces, physically defiles, burns, maintains on the floor or ground or tramples upon any flag of the United States" (excepting the disposal of soiled or worn flags).

In *United States v. Eichman*, 496 U.S. 310 (1990), the Supreme Court, by the same 5-4 vote as in the Texas case, struck down the Flag Protection Act as an unconstitutional infringement on First Amendment rights. Justice William Brennan, who served from 1956 to 1990, concluded one of his last opinions for the Court, "Punishing desecration of the flag dilutes the very freedom that makes this emblem so revered, and worth revering." *Id.* at 319. Subsequent efforts to enact a Flag Protection Constitutional Amendment have not gotten the necessary two-thirds vote of both Houses of Congress.

(In many countries, to burn or otherwise "desecrate" the national flag is a crime. For example, on December 15, 1999, bowing to pressure from the Chinese government, Hong Kong's highest court ruled that desecrating China's flag is a crime.)

The Supreme Court decision in *Brown v. Entertainment Merchants Association* (June 2011) ruled that "disgust is not a valid basis for restricting freedom of expression." In the 7-2 majority were justices Scalia, Kennedy, Sotomayor, Ginsburg, and Kagan (with Alito's concurrence joined by Roberts) - four conservatives and three liberals. The two dissenters were Breyer and Thomas. The ruling struck down a California law that prohibited the sale or rental of violent video games to minors and required packages to include an "18" warning label. This case followed *Snyder vs. Phelps* (2011), which by 8-1 (Alito dissenting) protected the anti-gay hate speech of the Westboro Baptist church, and *United States v. Stevens* (2010), striking down a federal law against the depicting of animal cruelty (only one dissent – Alito).

D. Commercial Free Speech

There are many different types of speech: political, artistic, scientific, and commercial. So, while political speech is at the core of protected speech, more than political speech is protected. For example, the arts are protected, as forms of expression. Artistic, cultural, social, and scientific speech all are protected, perhaps less than political speech, but generally more so than a rather recently recognized protected "area" of speech: commercial speech. Indeed, there are all sorts of artistic speech -

> Dance then, wherever you may be
> I am the Lord of the Dance, said he.
> And I'll lead you all, wherever you may be
> and I'll lead you all in the Dance, said he."
> -Sydney Carter (1915-2004)

Commercial speech was not recognized as protected under the First Amendment until a series of U.S. Supreme Court cases starting in 1975. For example, the *Va. State Board of Pharmacy* case (1976) was a challenge to rules setting a schedule of prices for pharmacists and not permitting individual pharmacists to do their own advertising of prices. The Supreme Court found that the pharmacists seeking to advertise their prices were seeking to engage in commercial speech, and such commercial speech is constitutionally protected. Thus, this was a case about 1) the need to disseminate commercial information, 2) how First Amendment rights are not just to say, but to receive information >>>Public information. The public's "Right to Know" justifies the media thrusting a microphone in front of someone whose entire life has gone up in smoke or otherwise been torn to shreds and asking that person, "How do you feel!?" and 3) – the reality, recognition that some citizens actually are more interested in whether there is a sale than in politics – more interested in a sale at Dillard's than in what happened at a City Council Meeting.

In *Bates v. State Bar of Arizona*, 433 U.S. 350 (1977), the high court considered attorney advertising. Because the court found it to be a type of commercial speech, governments cannot simply outlaw advertising for legal services. The *Bates* holding has been reiterated in other lawyer cases and extended to other professions.

State rules on the advertising of legal services typically have provisions governing: (1) what advertising and marketing materials may contain, including the content of disclosure statements; (2) how certain information may be presented, including methods for identifying areas of practice; and (3) the use of music, voice-overs, and other enhancements in television and radio commercials.

The Dying Opposition to Mass Advertising of Legal Services

Large corporate law firms and business lawyers generally have seen television ads as "sleazy soliciting" undertaken by personal-injury specialists looking for a high-volume business. But such an attitude – that it is inappropriate and/or ineffective for corporate business lawyers to advertise – seems to be dying. With a glut of lawyers and ever-sophisticated clients, more and more firms seek to set themselves apart from the herd. Internet ads, television commercials, fancy logos, and other advertising campaigns are catching on with more and more corporate firms.

Comparative Law and Culture: A Lawyer's "Costume" as Advertisement – India as an Example

Lawyers still must wear the British legal costume in India's high courts (Supreme Court and appeals courts), but not its lower courts: a layered coat, a black pleated gown, a white band worn around the neck, all worn over a white shirt and pants and weighing in total six pounds. Temperatures in most of India can exceed 100 degrees Fahrenheit, and few courtrooms have air conditioning. The costs of these gowns and of laundering are quite expensive, so most lawyers have only one "costume" and show up in court wearing coats and gowns that are torn, dirty, and malodorous. Still, many Indian lawyers favor the gown because it draws attention: lawyers in India cannot advertise their services, so they often stand in full regalia outside courtrooms and thus, via their satirical splendor, solicit potential clients.

E. Opinions versus Statements of Alleged Fact

Opinions cannot be false and cannot be regulated. Alleged facts can be false and can be regulated (as, for example, misleading). Facts can be proven/disproven. Government regulations (restrictions, even prohibitions) are permitted to prevent or correct false or misleading speech.

Unlike non-commercial, political speech, commercial speech can be regulated or restricted (in some cases even prohibited) if: (a) there is a substantial governmental interest, (b) the regulation accomplishes that interest, and (c) that regulation is the least burdensome means of accomplishing that interest. So, in 1971, Congress could, and did, prohibit cigarette advertising on television or radio. It met the above test and thus did not violate First Amendment rights: As opposed to what would be an unconstitutional restriction on RJ Reynolds Company's speaking out on political issues, even tobacco matters. Tobacco companies cannot advertise on radio or television because of the clear effects on public health (ads would encourage smoking). But tobacco companies do have the right to get on television or radio to speak about the lawsuits against them; the latter is protected political speech.

F. Protests Against a Business

> One has a right to protest as long as one is not defaming a business or preventing clients/customers from visiting that business.

Protests do not have to be about political or philosophical matters. They can stem from commercial disputes. For example, imagine a car purchaser who feels that the dealer has swindled her or otherwise horribly mistreated her. What if that customer shows up at the dealership, riding in the car she now despises? COMMERCIAL FREE SPEECH: VIDEO SKIT - "PROTESTING A LEMON" on the course website.

> **Lemon Laws**
>
> A lemon tends to be defined, in state lemon laws, as a purchased or leased new or used car that does not conform to the terms of the statutory warranty and the manufacturer (for a new car) or the auto dealer (for a used car) cannot repair it after a reasonable number of attempts (generally four attempts).
> Each year, tens of thousands of people return their cars because they qualify as "lemons." Many purchasers of these "re-acquired" cars do not know the car's former status as a "lemon" (even though laws require such notification).
> Throughout the United States, there have been some successful suits against car manufacturers and dealers for fraud or other claims. Of course, the best thing is to avoid buying a lemon in the first place. Here are some tips to follow when purchasing a used car:
> (1) Ask the dealer if you are buying a "re-acquired" vehicle or a car that was previously bought back by the manufacturer. If the answer is "yes," this might indicate you are buying someone else's "lemon."
> (2) Carefully review the stack of documents you sign when purchasing a car. Look for a disclosure notice listing past problems; this might indicate you are buying someone else's "lemon." Keep in mind - in most cases you will never see the word "lemon" on the documents.
> (3) If you suspect that you purchased a "lemon," you may wish to consult an attorney experienced in your state's "Lemon Laws." When dealerships are contacted by an attorney, they often realize that you are serious about protecting your rights as a consumer. An attorney may also be able to help you track your car's history.
> Car manufacturers try to avoid the pro-consumer impact of lemon laws by misleading people into thinking they do not qualify for lemon-law relief, by: (1) offering cheap financial incentives (extending a car's warranty, allowing $1,000 or $2,000 toward a trade-in) far less expensive than the rights the consumer in turn signs away, and (2) going to arbitration, instead of trial, with the arbitrator often an industry insider.

Some companies sue or threaten suits (for defamation and/or trademark/copyright infringement) and get sites removed. But new sites keep cropping up. For examples, there have been anti-McDonald's, anti-Microsoft, and anti-Ford Motor websites.

G. Limits on All Types of Speech

One social commentator has declared: "In some ways, we have become a numb society. Today almost anything seems endurable, inevitable, or unscotchable. … Nothing seems offensive any longer in a constitutional sense." LEONARD W. LEVY, BLASPHEMY: VERBAL OFFENSE AGAINST THE SACRED, FROM MOSES TO SALMAN RUSHDIE 569 (1993).

Despite Levy's concerns, in fact there are some limits on all types of speech, not just commercial, but also artistic, social, scientific, or any other form, including even political speech.

H. CAPDODFWEP: Five Exceptions to Free Speech

There are five exceptions to absolute free speech, which can be classified according to these labels: (1) Clear and Present Danger, (2) Obscenity, (3) Defamation, (4) Fighting Words, and (5) Expression-Plus.

1. Clear and Present Danger (CAPD)

Cases go back to right after World War I, with the seminal case of *Schenck v. United States*, 249 U.S. 47 (1919). For government to prohibit it, the advocacy must threaten public order in that it is (a) directed at producing imminent, unlawful action (e.g., a riot) and (b) is likely to bring about such unlawful action.

2. Obscenity (O) –

Obscenity is not the same as offensive language.

For legal purposes "obscenity" is to portray sex or another private bodily function in a highly offensive manner. How do you define obscenity? If you keep defining and refining, you could define away things that are NOT obscene; "I cannot define obscenity, but I know it when I see it!"[221]

a. Standard for Judging Obscenity:
Judged by Geography, Not by an Age Standard

In *Miller v. California*, 413 U.S. 15, 24 (1973) (judged by geography, not age standard), the Supreme Court held that, to prove that something is obscene, the government must demonstrate: (1) an average person, applying the contemporary community (i.e., LOCAL, not national) standards, would find that the challenged material, assessed as a whole, appeals to the prurient interest; (2) the challenged material depicts or describes, in a patently offensive way, sexual (or excretory) conduct specifically defined by state law; and (3) the challenged material, taken as a whole, lacks serious literary, artistic, political, or scientific value. (The prior standard had been that the work, to be obscene, must be "utterly without redeeming social value.")

b. Community Standards For Defining Obscenity Mean
Geographically Local Standards – on the Internet?

In *United States v. Thomas,* 74 F.3d 701 (6th Cir. 1996), cert. denied, 519 U.S. 820 (1996), the court held that the applicable standards were those of the community "where the material downloaded."

The Miller 1973 U.S. Supreme Court decision's "contemporary community standards" help define material that would be harmful to minors.

c.. Continuing Debate Over Obscenity and Social Policy

There are other questions of ethics, regardless of whether certain speech is allowed: Is it right, for example, to publish a book on how to commit suicide or on how to make a nuclear bomb?

Interesting alignments have developed: feminists joined with conservative Republicans in opposition to pornography. Even very liberal cultures, used to permitting almost any type of advertisement or performance, have sometimes reconsidered this approach. In France, for example, there has long been what one might call "porno chic" – ads regularly displaying nudity (usually of the female form) and

---

[221] Harvard Law Professor Laurence Tribe, as a young clerk for Justice Stewart, once asked his boss whether he had personally ever seen anything that qualified as obscenity. "Yes," Justice Stewart replied. "Just once, off the coast of Algiers." He refused to elaborate. Wall St. J., June 9, 1999, at A10.

involving strong sexual innuendo. Some ads have been seen as so overreaching (e.g., implying bestiality or sadomasochism) that some groups have called for more restrained advertising.

3. Defamation (D)

> *"Hurl your calumnies boldly; something is sure to stick."* Francis Bacon, 1561-1626 (English philosopher and statesman).

Just because you have freedom of speech does not mean that you are permitted to lie. Defamation is a false statement of fact that puts you in disrepute (causes damage).

N.Y. Times Co. v. Sullivan, 376 U.S. 254 (1964) is a Supreme Court case involving public officials. The court allowed libel judgments against media only for intended or grossly reckless (malicious) falsehoods; otherwise, allowing libel would "chill" free speech. Under this case and subsequent holdings, the defamation plaintiff MUST show actual malice, which is either (a) knowledge of falsity, or (b) reckless disregard as to whether something is true or false. Justice Brennan's opinion for the Court states, "The public official certainly has equal if not greater access than most private citizens to media of communication."

In 1967, two U.S. Supreme Court cases - *Curtis Publishing Co. v. Butts*, 388 U.S. 130, and *Associated Press v. Walker*, 388 U.S. 130 - extended the *N.Y. Times v. Sullivan* holding from public officials to cover, as well, public figures.

Finally, in *Gertz v. Robert Welch, Inc.*, 418 U.S. 323 (1974), the U.S. Supreme Court held that private individuals successfully suing for defamation could receive no punitive damages, only compensatory, unless there is actual malice.

> **Comparative Law: Defamation in England**
>
> In England, it is easier to sue and win regarding defamation. The defendant in England must show truth, and malice is not an element of the tort. That is why many American celebrities and other businesses file defamation actions in Britain that they abstain from filing against the media in the United States.

Free Speech Rights: Some Practical Concerns, on Wall Street or from Clients and Employers

Two issues are:
1. Wall Street analysts who dare to take the unusual step of criticizing companies in their research reports routinely risk being pilloried by their institutional investor clients, frozen out of company conference calls, or even fired, and they may even be sued for libel.
2. Web logs ("blogs") - online journals in which the authors can post their thoughts, rants, opinions, web links, etc.

Private" Speech: Employee Blog Examples

Employees writing about their work are increasingly running the risk that their employers will read and react to these blogs.

Several high-profile incidents have caught media attention. Mark Jen (Google), Ellen Simonetti (Delta Airlines), and Michael Hanscom (Microsoft) are three examples of employees fired for posting material on their respective blogs. Jen wrote about future Google products, Simonetti posted pictures of herself in her Delta airlines uniform, and Hanscom posted pictures of Apple computers being received at a Microsoft shipping and receiving department.

Perspectives on Blogs

Employees that set up blogs about their employer have a direct method of communicating with the public. Indeed, blogs posted on the Internet are not private - anyone can read them (and they tend to be easily found via Internet search engines).

Moreover, these blogs have potential business and legal consequences for the employer, not just the employee. Bloggers may wrongly use trademark or copyright material, they may post pictures of yet-to-be-released products, and they may defame another employee or a client. Just as employers promulgated policies to deal with employees' e-mail usage, many now have implemented policies for blogging, such as:

- Blogging employees must display prominent disclaimers that the views are their own and not their company's
- Employees are responsible for not disclosing confidential or proprietary company information or violating the privacy of others
- Employers are free to view and monitor employees' webpages at any time without the employees' consent
- Employees may not make statements about the company, coworkers, customers, competitors, agents, or partners that could be considered harassing, threatening, libelous, or defamatory in any way.
- Employees' webpages are subject to all other corporate policies, rules, regulations, and guidelines.
- Employees may not post any company logo, material, or trademarks without prior permission.
- Employees are subject to discipline, up to and including termination, for violating policies.

Privacy / Free Speech Issues

Does firing an employee for statements in his/her blog have First Amendment free speech implications? The First Amendment applies only to governmental entities and does not control how a private employer may discipline its employees. A private employer, therefore, may discipline or terminate an employee for public statements made about the employer, its operations, and/or the employee's coworkers without fear of violating the First Amendment.

Though employees may not intend for employers to read their blogs, the fact that many blogs are on public Internet sites does not give bloggers a reasonable expectation to privacy. Anyone with a search engine can find and read blogs on any topic. Employers may see blogs as no different than - indeed often more easily available than - what is printed in a magazine or newspaper.

Even under employment-at-will, employees can sue employers for wrongful termination under one or more of the following conditions:

- Discrimination – Employers cannot terminate an employee due to race, sex, creed, disability, or other protected classifications.
- Retaliation – Employers cannot terminate an employee for whistleblowing (reporting illegal activities to proper authorities). They also cannot fire a worker in retaliation for the worker's undertaking a legal action (e.g., claiming discrimination), or because the worker refused to do something contrary to public policy and sound morality.
- Defamation of Character – An employee can sue for wrongful termination if the employer defamed the employee's character while firing, or in order to fire, the employee.
- Breach of Express or Implied Contract – If an employee is working on contract and fulfilling its terms, the employer cannot fire without good cause before the contract ends. (Union workers, athletes, actors, upper management, and independent contractors usually work on such contracts.) Employers must specify the terms of employment at will and the requisite good causes for termination or some states may declare employee manuals/handbooks as binding, implied contracts of employment.
- Breach of Good Faith and Fair Dealing – In some states, "good faith and fair dealing" is an implied covenant that employees deserve to be treated fairly by their employers, especially dedicated, long-term employees. Examples of an employer's breach of this covenant include firing employees to avoid granting the rewards they have earned.
- Constructive Discharge – If an employee quits because the employer instituted or allowed a change that made working conditions intolerable, and if any reasonable employee would have quit under those circumstances, the quitting employee might have a case for constructive discharge,

a form of wrongful termination. In other words, the employer might have, in effect, wrongfully terminated the employee by making or allowing a change that forced the employee to quit. However, constructive discharge is not easy to prove.

Similar issues may present themselves in the business-to-business context, where one business challenges another business' exercise of "speech" that, for example, threatens the customer goodwill of the other business. One can see this in instances where a franchisor executive or another franchisee engages in political or religious speech – certainly protected against government control – but perhaps violative of the contract between these businesses.[222]

Employer Liability

Another issue of concern to employers with regard to employee blogs is one of employer liability. Under the doctrine of *respondeat superior*, the employer can be held liable for an employee's actions within the scope of employment, even if those actions are unauthorized. If an employee is blogging on company time with company computers, the employer could be held liable for the content, especially if the content concerns competitors, agents, and/or fellow employees. The employer could also face liability - either vicariously or for its own negligence - if it did not take steps (Internet use policies and/or controls) to prevent such actions from occurring.

The issue becomes murkier if blogging employees (such as former Delta Airlines' Flight Attendant Ellen Simonetti) post pictures of themselves in their work uniforms engaged in poses or activities that are unflattering to the company or that tarnish the company's image. Although she may have been on her own time when the pictures were taken, she was in her Delta uniform and on a Delta plane in several of them in which her attire and composure was less than professional. This can be seen as misrepresenting the company and its values, possibly even defamation of the company.

4. Fighting Words (FW)

In *Chaplinsky v. New Hampshire*, 315 U.S. 568 (1942), the Supreme Court, although very liberal at that time, unanimously sustained the defendant's conviction (for shouting curse words at an official; to whom he referred as the "g—damned fire marshal"). These were fighting words, which can be proscribed because they are expressions likely to provoke an immediate violent reaction from those to whom they were addressed; these "fighting words" serve *no useful purpose* in the exposition of ideas. In other words, fighting words are intended to get people upset without adding to public discourse.

> "There are certain well-defined and narrowly limited classes of speech, the prevention and punishment of which have never been thought to raise any constitutional problem. These include the lewd and obscene, the profane, the libelous, and the insulting or "fighting" words those which by their very utterance inflict injury or tend to incite an immediate breach of the peace. It has been well observed that such utterances are no essential part of any exposition of ideas, and are of such slight social value as a step to truth that any benefit that may be derived from them is clearly outweighed by the social interest in order and morality."

Still, just because something is extremely unpopular does not make it fighting words. "Fighting words" must not be restricted simply because of the message conveyed by those words. *R.S.V.P. v. St. Paul*, 505 U.S. 377 (1992).

5. Expression Plus (EP)

Expression-Plus Speech includes more than just "pure" speech: Conduct that also serves or relates to the expressions of views. So, "speech" can be more than just words (activities beyond just speech –

---

[222] *See* Robert W. Emerson & Jason R. Parnell, *Franchise Hostages: Fast Food, God, and Politics*, 19 J. LAW & POLITICS (U. VA.) 353 (2014), available at http://ssrn.com/author=86449.

conduct such as picketing, protesting, demonstrating, and parading). For this Expression-Plus Conduct, you do more than just speak/write, and thus can be restricted - e.g., required to get permits and to meet time or location restrictions. As long as the government regulates this expression-plus conduct in a narrow, nondiscriminatory way (e.g., to meet traffic concerns), and is not deciding based on the content of the speech, then denials of permits will be upheld. *See, e.g., Thomas v. Chicago Park District*, 534 U.S. 316 (2002) (Supreme Court decision unanimously upholding Chicago's process for deciding which groups could be granted a permit to hold demonstrations or other events in city parks, and thus denying a claim brought by the Windy City Hemp Development Board, which wanted to hold a rally supporting marijuana legalization).

Symbolic Speech

In a case featuring Vietnam War protests where draft cards were burned *(United States v. O'Brien*, 391 U.S. 367 (1968)), the U.S. Supreme Court found, in a 7:1 decision, a compelling government interest in maintaining proper administration of the selective service. The "speech" (burning draft cards) was beyond mere speech – it was "speech" accompanied by conduct interfering with selective services; therefore, it could be regulated.

Tinker v. Des Moines School District, 393 U.S. 503 (1969), had the U.S. Supreme Court find First Amendment protection for public school students wearing black armbands to protest the Vietnam War. (There was no proof of harm to school discipline or the learning environment; the protest was silent and peaceful, and other such silent "speech" (e.g., the wearing of campaign buttons) had been allowed.)

I. *Cohen v. California*: The "F the Draft" Case

The most prominent "F" word case is ***Cohen v. California***, 403 U.S. 15 (1971). In *Cohen*, the Court noted that "one man's vulgarity is another's lyric." It recognized that a word is "the skin of a living thought,"[223] so that forbidding words could lead to forbidding ideas.

On April 26, 1968, Paul Robert Cohen, a 19-year-old man opposed to the War in Vietnam, had gone to the L.A. Courthouse. On his jacket, plainly visible, was "F--- the draft ("FAD"). Women and children were present. Later he testified that he wore the jacket, knowing that the words were on the jacket, as a means of informing the public of the depth of his feelings against the Vietnam War and the draft.

In a courtroom, Cohen removed his jacket and stood with it folded over his arm. Meanwhile, a policeman sent the presiding judge a note suggesting that Cohen be held in contempt of court. The judge declined to do so, and Cohen was arrested by the officer only after he emerged from the courtroom into a court corridor.

Cohen was charged with violating the California statute against breach of the peace. He was convicted and sentenced to 30 days in jail. The question in court, after clarifying the statutory interpretation, was whether the California statute was constitutional, as enforced against Paul Robert Cohen.

Cohen's statement was speech. But was there an exception to Absolute Free Speech which permitted prosecution and conviction of Cohen?

In the California appellate court, Cohen had been convicted of violating part of California penal code §415 ("disturbing the peace"). By the time Cohen's appeals reached the U.S. Supreme Court, that statute read as follows: "Any of the following persons shall be punished by imprisonment in the county jail for a period of not more than 90 days, a fine of not more than four hundred dollars ($400), or both such imprisonment and fine: (1) Any person who unlawfully fights in a public place or challenges another person in a public place to fight. (2) Any person who maliciously and willfully disturbs another person by loud and

---

[223] This Famous phrase of Oliver Wendell Holmes, Jr., is even better understood if one reads the full sentence in which he uttered it. See Contract Wording, a few pages into the contracts section of this text, quoting Justice Holmes' opinion in *Towne v. Eisner*, 425 U.S. 418, 425 (1918).

unreasonable noise. (3) Any person who uses offensive words in a public place which are inherently likely to provoke an immediate violent reaction." §415(3) was the key.

The California Court of Appeals discussed several arguments. It held that this was not an obscenity case. To be considered obscene, the expression must be, in some significant way, erotic. "FAD" is not obscenity because the connotation is not sexual.

Another argument made by the majority of the Court was that Cohen did not use "fighting words." This is because there was no evidence that the he used the words with the intent to incite violence, nor were the words directed at any given person.

Thirdly, Cohen's attorney argued that Cohen's method of expressing his views could be classified as "expression-plus." Simply because his expression contained profanity did not mean that he could be deprived of the first amendment protection. The court agreed that Cohen had not invaded any major right of privacy of people by inflicting upon them unwanted and offensive views.

On Cohen's appeal to the U.S. Supreme Court, the high court held as follows:
- The conviction was solely based on the 'speech' of the defendant. The ability of the State of California to regulate speech is limited.

Let us look at the five limits to absolute free speech – possible excuses for conviction despite the First Amendment: CAPD – O - D – FW – EP.
Which could be valid excuses under court interpretation of free speech rights? The speech could not be considered obscene, as 'obscenity' is interpreted to be sexual in nature, and the message could not be construed as obscene.
- The speech could not be considered "fighting words." It was the U.S. Supreme Court's opinion that the message itself was not designed to incite violence.

- EP – Expression-Plus. This was a contested issue (as was the issue of Fighting Words). Here, Cohen was not just expressing his views but also putting on a jacket, wearing it in the courtroom (so, it was in some ways comparable to a parade). Cohen's actions were in a public forum, in this case a place (a courtroom) particularly concerned with expectations about appropriate dress and decorum.

Although the speech could be considered offensive to some, banning individual speech to "protect" against offensive speech would empower a majority to silence dissidents simply as a matter of personal predilections. "We are often 'captives' outside the sanctuary of the home and subject to questionable speech." (Indeed, context matters. The Court held in *Cohen* that there is more to speech than just intellect. One may be silly or even vulgar in his/her speech to show the depth of one's feelings. Defense lawyers argued that curse words simply are part of our language.)

- The US Supreme Court also found that California's Penal Code 415(3), as originally applied to Cohen (before it was amended and tightened in its language), indiscriminately swept within its prohibition all "offensive conduct" that disturbs "any neighborhood or person."

The Court's Opinion, as written by Justice Harlan for a 5-4 majority, was as follows:
[Can] California excise, as "offensive conduct," one particular scurrilous epithet from the public discourse, either upon the theory of the court below that its use is inherently likely to cause violent reaction or upon a more general assertion that the States, acting as guardians of public morality, may properly remove this offensive word from the public vocabulary?

The rationale of the California court is plainly untenable. At most it reflects an "undifferentiated fear or apprehension of disturbance which is not enough to overcome the right to freedom of expression. The argument amounts to little more than the self-defeating proposition that to avoid physical censorship of one

One may be vulgar to show the depths of one's feelings

who has not sought to provoke such a response by a hypothetical coterie of the violent and lawless, the States may more appropriately effectuate that censorship themselves.

Admittedly, it is not so obvious that the First and Fourteenth Amendments must be taken to disable the States from punishing public utterance of this unseemly expletive in order to maintain what they regard as a suitable level of discourse within the body politic. We think, however, that examination and reflection will reveal the shortcomings of a contrary viewpoint.

To many, the immediate consequence of this freedom may often appear to be only verbal tumult, discord, and even offensive utterance. These are, however, within established limits, in truth necessary side effects of the broader enduring values which the process of open debate permits us to achieve. That the air may at times seem filled with verbal cacophony is, in this sense not a sign of weakness but of strength. We cannot lose sight of the fact that, in what otherwise might seem a trifling and annoying instance of individual distasteful abuse of a privilege, these fundamental societal values are truly implicated.

Surely the State has no right to cleanse public debate to the point where it is grammatically palatable to the most squeamish among us. Yet no readily ascertainable general principle exists for stopping short of that result were we to affirm the judgment below. Indeed, we think it is largely because governmental officials cannot make principled distinctions in this area that the Constitution leaves matters of taste and style so largely to the individual.

Additionally, we cannot overlook the fact, because it is well illustrated by the episode involved here, that much linguistic expression serves a dual communicative function: it conveys not only ideas capable of relatively precise, detached explication, but otherwise inexpressible emotions as well. In fact, words are often chosen as much for their emotive as their cognitive force. We cannot sanction the view that the Constitution, while solicitous of the cognitive content of individual speech, has little or no regard for that emotive function which, practically speaking, may often be the more important element of the overall message sought to be communicated. Indeed, as Mr. Justice Frankfurter has said, "one of the prerogatives of American citizenship is the right to criticize public men and measures - and that means not only informed and responsible criticism but the freedom to speak foolishly and without moderation." *Baumgartner v. United States*, 322 U.S. 665, 673-674 (1944).

Finally, and in the same vein, we cannot indulge the facile assumption that one can forbid particular words without also running a substantial risk of suppressing ideas in the process. Indeed, governments might soon seize upon the censorship of particular words as a convenient guise for banning the expression of unpopular views. We have been able, as noted above, to discern little social benefit that might result from running the risk of opening the door to such grave results.

It is, in sum, our judgment that, absent a more particularized and compelling reason for its actions, the State may not, consistently with the First and Fourteenth Amendments, make the simple public display here involved of this single four-letter expletive a criminal offense. Because that is the only arguably sustainable rationale for the conviction here at issue, the judgment below must be Reversed.

The four Justices in dissent opined that if Cohen's appeal was not dismissed then the conviction should not be reversed, but the case remanded to the California courts for further review because there had recently been a new California supreme court decision about §415. Justice Blackmun, joined by two of the other three dissenters, also recommended affirming the conviction on these grounds:
"Cohen's absurd and immature antic, in my view, was mainly conduct and little speech. The California Court of Appeal appears so to have described it, and I cannot characterize it otherwise. Further, the case appears to me to be well within the sphere of *Chaplinsky v. New Hampshire*, 315 U.S. 568 (1942), where Mr. Justice Murphy, a known champion of First Amendment freedoms, wrote for a unanimous bench. As a consequence, this Court's agonizing over First Amendment values seems misplaced and unnecessary."

THE END OF PART ONE OF THE TEXT

ARTICLE II: MAKING DEALS

A. CONTRACTS: INTRODUCTION

I. BASIC CONTRACT LAW INFORMATION

Contract law is a foundation for learning about many subjects in the law (e.g., partnerships, employment law, agency, property, and corporations).

Contract law, as with most areas of the law, is a vocabulary–intense subject! Thus, a modern trend in law is to get away from some difficult language (so we now call parties by their names or other easily understood titles). However, one must know some terminology.

Contracts are very important to business. Surveys show that a plurality of business people find business law the most important subject in business school, and - of all the subjects in business law - contracts is considered the most significant.[1]

A. A Contract Law Dichotomy: Freedom of Contract and Freedom from Contract

Parties have freedom to make a contract and the freedom from making a contract (i.e., to not make a contract). But there are a few exceptions, such as discrimination law (public policy).

Self-imposed duties, in contract law, are distinct from torts and crimes, which have externally-imposed (nonconsensual) laws.[2]

Chapter One: I am Born - book from 1849-50
"Whether I shall turn out to be the hero of my own life, or whether that station will be held by anybody else, these pages must show. . . . To begin my life with the beginning of my life, I record that . . .

". . . . In consideration of the day and hour of my birth, it was declared by the nurse, and by some sage women in the neighborhood who had taken a lively interest in me several months before there was any possibility of our becoming personally acquainted, first, that I was destined to be unlucky in life, and secondly, that I was privileged to see ghosts and spirits; both these gifts inevitably attaching, as they believed, to all unlucky infants of either gender, born towards the small hours on a Friday night."

A Book a century later, published in 1951

"If you really want to hear about it, the first thing you'll probably want to know is where I was born, and what my lousy childhood was like, and how my parents were occupied and all before they had me, and . . .

In contracts, one can, and usually **should**, define terms. One can define things almost any way one wants.

---

[1] Perhaps some businesspersons like business law training because it gives them just enough legal insight to be dangerous and to harass their attorney friends!
[2] Torts include noncontractual claims for which a civil defendant may be held liable, such as negligence, fraud, battery, invasion of privacy, and numerous other claims, discussed later in this text. Crimes are public wrongs for which a defendant may be punished via fines and imprisonment. Examples are embezzlement, robbery, certain types of fraud, and arson. Again, this subject is discussed later in this text.

We can describe contracts as a type of private (consensual) law made by the parties themselves. A contract is a legally enforceable agreement: something that will be enforced by a court. The attorney's role often is to predict what a court would do if the agreement were challenged, if - down the road – things went awry.[3]

> The most important freedom, at least in American contract law, probably is not the freedom to have the general law changed, but the *freedom of parties to a contract to make their own "little" private contract laws* – for individual parties to change or avoid the effects of various contract law principles.

B. Expectations and Efficiencies

Contract law creates expectations that "grease the wheels of commerce." Expectations underlie the contract. And contract law is a framework to ensure that lawful expectations are met or that remedies are provided. "The social order rests upon the stability and predictability of conduct, of which keeping promises is a large item." Roscoe Pound, 1870-1964 (American jurist).

Contract law reduces transaction costs in at least three ways: (1) it encourages the performance of voluntary agreements by providing a sanction for breach; (2) it reduces negotiation costs by providing standard, or customary, terms for various types of transactions; and (3) it discourages misleading conduct in contract negotiations.

Besides the reduction of transaction costs, two other principles associated with an economic approach to contract law are: (1) deference to individual autonomy; and (2) maintaining or attaining a stable legal system.

Contract Law is necessary for business deals in that it ensures the other party will act as agreed. It furnishes Legal Clout - when the ethical restraints of carrying out one's word are not enough to outweigh a party's new perception that the contract is against his/her economic self-interest, then perhaps the fear of litigation will keep that party from acting on its temptation to breach.

However, some people dispute the efficiencies, in practice, of contracting. Because they seldom have complete and perfectly accurate information, and because they lack the perfect capacity to process that information, people are "intendedly rational, but only limitedly so."[4] Therefore, a number of scholars have used this "bounded [limited] rationality" notion to dispute the conventional law-and-economics claims that parties ordinarily negotiate the most efficient contract and that any governmental imposition of mandatory terms makes the parties worse off.[4]

---

[3] A second role of the attorney is to construct a contract intended to reflect the client's needs and desires while also avoiding litigation.

[4] HERBERT A. SIMON, ADMINISTRATIVE BEHAVIOR xxiv (2nd ed. 1957). Many scholars would agree that parties may be inexperienced and fail to realize the magnitude of the terms to which they are agreeing. That is a reason for government regulation and court intervention. See, e.g., Christine Jolls et al., A Behavioral Approach to Law and Economics, 50 STAN. L. REV. 1471, 1505 (1998). These scholars would agree that parties may be inexperienced and fail to realize the magnitude of the terms to which they are agreeing. That is a reason for government regulation and court intervention. See Robert W. Emerson, *Assessing Awuah v. Coverall North America, Inc.: The Franchisee as a Dependent Contractor*, 19 STAN. J. L. BUS. & FIN. 203, 209 (2014) ("potential franchisees are often novice business-people and may be affected by cognitive biases, which inhibit them from participating in a fair, arm's length transaction with a franchisor"); accord, Robert W. Emerson, *Fortune Favors the Franchisor: Survey and Analysis of the Franchisee's Decision Whether to Hire Counsel*, 51 SAN DIEGO L. REV. 709 (2014); Robert W. Emerson & Uri Benoliel, *Are Franchisees Well-Informed? Revisiting the Debate over Franchise Relationship Laws*, 76 ALB. L. REV. 193 (2012-2013). Those last three articles are at http://ssrn.com/author=86449.

> YOUTUBE – contracts_2mins6secs at robertwemersonufl
> "For many people, contracts law is viewed as a very difficult, terminology-laden subject and the role of lawyers is often to serve as just "captains" guiding people through a very difficult subject trying to steer them away from the eddies and shoals and sort of steer them through a navigable stream of understanding contract law (at least that's how I like to look at it!).
> Business surveys frequently indicate that the most important function lawyers serve is to advise on contracts. More alumni of business schools, undergraduate or graduate, say that, of all the subjects they took, business law was the most useful, with contracts the most useful area in terms of practicality.
> "When one hears of the rule of law at the international level, what we're usually really talking about is contract law. For instance, if a business here in America makes a contract with a business abroad, say in Russia or in China or in some other country, one of the fundamental questions is: Will that contract actually be honored abroad? Could you go to a court in another system, could you go to arbitrators and have that contract honored? So it's very important for people to understand the nature of what is a contract; and, at the very core, the questions become - is it an agreement, and is it an agreement a court will actually enforce?"
> Questions to Consider:
> 1. How do agreements and contracts differ?
> 2. Should a lawyer write or review the contracts you enter into? Explain.
> 3. Do you agree with the captain analogy?

C. Elements of a Contract

The law of contracts is a framework to ensure that lawful expectations are met or that remedies are provided.[5]

There are all sorts of contracts in everyday life. What contracts have you recently made? It is not just "Big Ticket" items, such as car purchases, apartment leases, and employment agreements, but also small items/services that can be the subject of a contract. The principles of contract are generally the same for <u>all</u> contracts, no matter the size.

1. A Basic Definition of Contract Is: a Legally Enforceable Agreement[6]

Three initial elements of a contract are: **Offer, Acceptance, and Consideration**.

"The simplest way to form an express contract begins with a **formal offer**. This offer is transmitted directly to the offeree by acts or by words, whether spoken or written, directly to the offeree, through any medium whatsoever."[7]

The offer must:
1. Indicate a clear *intent* to make a contract.
2. Be sufficiently *definite* so that a court can determine the actual intent of the parties.
3. Be *communicated* to the other party.[8]

Generally, Offer + Acceptance = Agreement. Then there must be some exchange of promises or property or services, or there must be some other mutual alteration of duties – a quid pro quo.[9]

---

[5] Robert W. Emerson, *Business Law* NY: Barron's Educational Series (2015, 6th ed.), at 93.
[6] An extensive definition of the term, "contract," is at the 'Lectric Law Library: http://www.lectlaw.com/def/c123.htm
[7] Robert W. Emerson, *Business Law* NY: Barron's Educational Series (2015, 6th ed.), a at 99.
[8] Id. at 99.
[9] A gift is not a contract (there is no consideration from the donee). The three elements of a gift are: (a) the donor's intent to give; (b) the donor's communication of that intent to the donee; and (c) acceptance by the donee, who takes delivery of the item. There are Ethical/Moral Problems concerning undelivered gifts, but there is no *legal* commitment. While an executory contract (one agreed to, but not yet carried out) is legally binding on the parties, an "executory" gift

> "Acceptance of the offer clinches the contract. However, the acceptance must meet certain standards. First, the acceptance must be *clear* and *unqualified*; an 'acceptance' that modifies the offer or attempts to get a better deal is treated in the law as a **counteroffer**, that is, a rejection of the original offer and the making of a new offer. . . . Second, the offeree *must accept in any manner required by the offer*."[10]

Other Contractual Elements/Defenses (besides Offer, Acceptance, and Consideration) include Capacity, Mutuality, and Legality (but not, generally, Form):

Recapitulation of Contract Requirements: **OACMCL**

Mnemonic for people who have a favorite doggie –
"**O**h, **A** **C**onsiderate **M**utt, **C**ute, and **L**egal"
       And transform that into:
Offer-Acceptance-Consideration-Mutuality-Capacity-Legality of Purpose. (There is nothing about form, since that is ordinarily not required.)

2. Capacity

Do the parties know what's going on?
Do the parties have mental capability?
Do the parties understand key concepts (e.g., money)?

Parties lacking capacity include minors (children), the mentally ill (sometimes), the mentally retarded, and the obviously inebriated. (This is arbitrary: No gradual period of binding for certain types or under a certain amount. Simply: are you bound or not?) German approach is different. More gradual for teenagers, as described later in this book.

Capacity is <u>not</u> a question for the court to answer by reviewing whether one side was more capable than the other. That one side had an A+ negotiator and the other side a D− negotiator does not raise capacity issues. As long as you meet the capacity definition generally (e.g., you are an adult, not drunk or mentally retarded, etc.), that is sufficient. The comparison of bargaining powers and ability arises more in cases involving issues such as undue influence and unconscionability.

(one promised, but not yet delivered) is only binding if it meets the definition of promissory estoppel (discussed later in this section of the text).

    While American law and the common law generally both require consideration, and thus the promise to make a gift does not bind the promisor absent other compelling circumstances (see promissory estoppel, discussed later), other countries do not follow this precept. For example, under Russian law a promise to make a gift is binding. There, consideration, or lack thereof, simply is not an issue.

    The author once represented a middle-aged man who had a falling out with his stepmother. The stepmother had, a year previously, given a deed to an Ocean City, Maryland condominium to the man's then 19-year-old daughter (her step-granddaughter). Now having regretted her generosity, the stepmother sued the man, his wife (the stepdaughter-in-law), and the step-granddaughter to have the deed returned. The defendants successfully defended the lawsuit by showing that there were no problems with the original tendering of the property to the daughter: no fraud, duress, mistake, undue influence, incapacity of the plaintiff, or the like. The three elements of a gift were present when the deed was given to the step-granddaughter, and she and her immediate family started using the property on occasion. As there had been the step-grandmother's intent to give, her communication of that intent to the step-granddaughter; and acceptance by the granddaughter, who took delivery of the property (the deed and the keys – even started using the property), the stepmother had no claim to have the property returned. The law does not countenance someone being an "Indian-giver" (regretting a gift and demanding its return).

[10] Robert W. Emerson, *Business Law* NY: Barron's Educational Series (2015, 6th ed.) at 103.

3. Mutuality
Did a party lie?
Was there a misunderstanding?
Was a party under duress or undue influence?
While the parties technically have "agreed," there is a problem of mistake, maybe even fraud.

4. Legality
A contract cannot violate criminal law or otherwise be against public policy.

5. Form
Rarely is any particular form required. There usually is no set format for contract formation. Most contracts need not be in complex language – in fact, most do not have to be written.[11]

LEGALESE - "THE SKY IS BLUE" EXAMPLE

"There are two things wrong with almost all legal writing. One is its style. The other is its content." Prof. Fred Codell's "Goodbye to Law Reviews."

What is legalese? *Why* is there legalese?
People who draft contracts want to cover all the bases. (The natural result of that approach is that the reader may have to look at it several times.)

A simple, perhaps implausible comment is expanded dramatically into an elegantly persuasive declaration to say, "The Sky is Blue." In some parts of the world, and possibly the universe, what is generally thought of as the sky (absent inclement weather) is likely, for a person of normal perceptive capacities . . . .

At least six reasons for all 49 of those words:
Our world – not some other dimension or planet
Good weather – not cloudy
What if the person cannot see? Or is color blind?
Outside- not looking at ceiling
Not at night
What do we call that color? May change – now, it is "blue"

D. Contract Wording

Words are so important, and their context is crucial. Justice Oliver Wendell Holmes, Jr. put it this way, in *Towne v. Eisner*, 425 U.S. 418, 425 (1918): "A word is not a crystal, transparent and unchanged; it is the skin of a living thought and may vary greatly in color and content according to the circumstances and the time in which it is used."

1. Comparative Law: Japanese Contract Negotiation and Wording

A typical U.S. view is that a contract defines all rights and responsibilities of the parties and seeks to cover every contingency. But even our legal cousins, the British, tend to consider our contracts in America as *too long*. We try to cover everything, and that is often unnecessary, they feel.

The traditional Japanese view is that a contract is secondary in a business transaction; the basis

---

[11] Some contracts are subject to the Statute of Frauds. As discussed later in this text, these contracts must have a writing (sufficient written evidence that they were agreed to) in order to be enforced (e.g., for a court to order the payment of damages for a breach).

upon which two parties do business is an ongoing relationship, with both parties committed to the pursuit of similar objectives. In transactions between themselves, Japanese tend to write generalized contracts that contain very little detail because the parties know each other well and are confident that the details can be worked out as and when they are necessary. Consequently, relationships, not contacts, are negotiated in Japan.

The specific details of a Japanese contract are seldom negotiated. Legal documents are usually brief and flexible. This is important to accommodate the evolving relationship between the parties. Contracts are often viewed as tentative agreements to be redefined as circumstances between the parties change. Long legal agreements drafted by one side, especially a foreign firm, are viewed with suspicion. The relationship should take precedence over formal rights and obligations. Practical problems can be resolved by compromise. Reflecting this belief, the Japanese include a good-faith clause in contracts with Westerners. This clause states that disputes are to be resolved through good-faith discussions among parties. This desire to establish and maintain mutual trust as a basis for a business relationship may account for the longer time it takes to negotiate and arrive at an agreement.

Japanese contract-negotiating teams are generally larger than American teams. Depending on the transaction, there may be ten or more people on the Japanese side, while commonly only a few people are on the U.S. side. Members of the Japanese group may excuse themselves during a session so they can caucus. By discussing an issue among themselves, they work for a consensus within the team and the company. As a rule, negotiations proceed slowly. The Japanese do not appear to operate with the urgency typical of Americans. The Japanese take the time they need until they are sure of a decision and have reached a consensus among themselves.

2. State Law Reform

Many states have enacted plain language legislation requiring, or at least setting guidelines for, the use of ordinary, understandable English words in legal forms such as residential leases and consumer contracts.

> YOUTUBE – Consumer_Protection_Law_2mins0secs at robertwemersonufl - An introduction from someone you may recognize, wearing a dinosaur hat and mask.
>
> "Not too long ago, certainly well after the age of the dinosaurs (let us say, a hundred years ago), it was customary to view almost any transaction between a business and a consumer as a "buyer beware" (caveat emptor) transaction. In the twentieth century, a lot of that fundamental principal that when you go into a contract you have to have your eyes and ears open has been undermined or bolstered (depending on your point of view) by consumer protection laws. These laws are found throughout our system, from the federal system through the states and even down to the local level.
>
> "Particularly at the federal level, one finds that these laws tend to be oriented not so much towards substantive protections but are more procedural in terms of a "right to know" (that information about warranties, for instance, has to be given to consumers in a number of transactions). And businesses that do not really keep up on developments in this area risk tremendous difficulties in terms of possibilities of legal action, perhaps even class actions against them. That is really the reason for the dinosaur prop and the dinosaur hat: the risk for a business that does not really keep abreast of the consumer protection laws is that it could be like the dinosaurs - a big, lumbering beast that ultimately ends up being driven extinct, probably by consumer activists and by lawyers.

3. For Practical Reasons, Important Contracts Ought to be in Writing

Most contracts can be oral or inferred from conduct. While oral agreements usually are okay at law, a basic problem with them is that they are difficult to prove in court. Thus, it is for practical reasons that important contracts ought to be put in writing:

(1) While writing, one often thinks of things that should be covered. The writing process helps to clarify terms, hence making the contract better.

(2) The written document serves as
    (a) Evidence that there was a contract, and
    (b) Evidence of what the parties agreed. Memories fade, but written evidence remains.

An Example:
The United Kingdom's National Lottery has a sample "syndicate" agreement for players who join together to play the lottery. Items include: names and addresses of players; which games, numbers, and draw days are being entered; each player's signature and his/her contribution per draw and his/her share of any winnings; whether the parties want to have publicity ("go public") if they win; and any special arrangements such as when payments will be collected, what happens if someone fails to contribute, and procedures when someone leaves the syndicate.

4. Writing and Signing an Agreement
Drafting the Agreement
Advantage: If you draft the contract (i.e., use your language), you have a lot of control.
Disadvantage: Ambiguity in the contract usually is resolved in favor of the party that did not draft the agreement.

NEVER SIGN A DOCUMENT WITHOUT READING IT FIRST. If you sign a document, the assumption is that you have read and understood it. Thus, you can be held accountable for any deviation by you from the terms of your deal. **If you don't understand the document, then you could hire a lawyer. That is what they are there for!**

If you have an ongoing electronic contract, check your e–mail regularly for notices and notify the company immediately if your e–mail address changes (since e–mail is not forwarded).

5. The Objective Theory of Contracts
In determining whether a contract has been formed, the element of intent is of prime importance. In contract law, intent is determined by the objective theory of contracts, *not* by the personal or subjective intent, or belief, of a party. The theory is that a party's intention to enter into a contract is judged by outward, objective facts as interpreted by a reasonable person, rather than by the party's own secret, subjective intentions. "In interpreting a contract, a court tries to determine the *intent* of the parties from words and actions considered in their entirety."[12] This is known as the "course of conduct."
Objective facts include (1) what the party wrote or said when entering into a contract, (2) how the party acted or appeared, and (3) the circumstances surrounding the transaction.

There is no formal wording requirement. Courts consider what the parties said and did - not what they thought - unless those thoughts were manifested to the other party. "Certain commonsense rules may be used to resolve contradictions and uncertainties. Fine print, obscurely placed, is given less weight than large, boldface type; handwritten interlineations, especially if initialed, are strong evidence of firm intention. Formal documents, diligently executed, may yield to conduct of the parties if that conduct clearly shows a mutual intent contrary to the written document."[13]

Ordinarily, contract law does not care to, nor could it, figure out what is inside someone's head – that information is invisible to the rest of us (and even, sometimes, to the very person with the head!). Instead, contract law looks for the objective viewpoint. It is almost as if the reasonable person were

---

[12] Robert W. Emerson, *Business Law*. NY: Barron's Educational Series (6th ed., 2015), at 95.
[13] Id. at 94.

watching a videotape of all that the parties had done and said, which included all the circumstances as well. It is as if one were all–knowing of the conduct and words that took place, but not the thoughts.[14]

> **Sometimes people contradict themselves. What should we conclude when a person keeps extending offers and then withdrawing them? Are acceptances possible? What is the BIG PICTURE?**

The following example may show how a judge would evaluate the entirety of a case, including the reasonable assumptions of the parties, not merely depend upon a narrow, technical reading of the evidence.

> ### A "CLEVER" STUDENT MESSES AROUND WITH CONTRACT LAW
> A male student wrote the following e-mail to the author.
>
> Hey Prof. Emerson (or Pimp Daddy Emerson, as I prefer)!
> Let me first say that I enjoy your class immensely - thanks for that. Sorry if you find this to be a waste of time, but I was curious about something and I thought you might find it amusing. Several months ago, I purchased a gift for a female friend's birthday. I wrapped said gift in fairly generic looking wrapping paper that depicted festive ribbons set against a dark background. However, upon closer examination, the words "Tearing this paper signifies consent to perform oral sex on the giver" can be seen in small but readable type on each ribbon graphic. My friend was careless enough not to read this text, so when she tore open the gift, I pointed it out victoriously and demanded my just compensation. Sadly, she has yet to fulfill her obligation. Would that, by any chance, constitute a legally enforceable contract? Do I have any recourse in collecting what is owed to me?
> Thanks in advance,
>
>   A Student
>   MY SHORT RESPONSE: NO!
>   NOW LET US WORK THROUGH IT ALL, WITH YOUR WORDS in regular lettering and MY COMMENTS IN ALL CAPITAL LETTERS.
> Let me first say that I enjoy your class immensely - thanks for that. A LITTLE BUTTERING-UP, PERHAPS?
> I purchased a gift for a female friend's birthday. WHAT GIFT? YOU NEVER SAY.
> Upon closer examination, the words "Tearing this paper signifies consent to perform oral sex on the giver" "PROVIDER" WOULD HAVE BEEN A BETTER WORD CHOICE THAN "GIVER," WHICH SEEMS TO CONCEDE THAT IT WAS A GIFT, NOT A CONTRACT OFFER.
> [The words] can be seen in small but readable type on each ribbon graphic. SMALL BUT READABLE PRINT – THAT SEEMS UNLIKELY TO BE READ. MORE IMPORTANT, IT SEEMS UNLIKELY SHE WOULD BE LOOKING FOR THAT PRINT ON WRAPPING PAPER. MANY, PROBABLY MOST, PEOPLE WHO RECEIVE A PRESENT EXCITEDLY RIP THRU THE WRAPPING PAPER TO GET TO THE PRESENT; THEY CANNOT BE EXPECTED TO SPEND TIME SEEING WHETHER THERE IS A CONTRACT "OFFER" ON THE WRAPPING PAPER.
> My friend was careless enough not to read this text. I DOUBT SHE WOULD BE CONSIDERED CARELESS, AS A REASONABLE PERSON WOULD NOT NECESSARILY REFRAIN FROM RIPPING OPEN THE WRAPPING PAPER AND INSTEAD STARE AT IT INTENTLY FOR ANY SMALL PRINT! ALSO, BECAUSE YOU WERE THERE TO SEE THIS, AS A MORAL MATTER

---

[14] The court ordinarily will look at the "four corners" of the document (the entirety of the document) to determine the intent of the parties. Depending on the integration of the contract, the court may not allow extrinsic evidence (testimony or documentation from outside the document itself) to determine the intent of the parties. The concept is the parol evidence rule, which is discussed later in this material on Contracts.

> YOU MAY HAVE HAD A DUTY – MORAL, IF NOT LEGAL – TO CALL THAT ""SMALL PRINT" LANGUAGE TO HER ATTENTION.
>
> So when she tore open the gift, AGAIN, AS STATED ELSEWHERE IN THE LETTER, THE WORDING IS "GIFT," NOT "ITEM" OR "GOODS" OR THE LIKE. YOUR WORDING EVEN SEEMS TO INDICATE THAT YOUR FRIEND DID NOT HAVE THE CHANCE TO EXAMINE THE GIFT AND SEE WHETHER SHE WANTED TO ACCEPT IT. INSTEAD, JUST TEARING THE PAPER TO GET AT THE ITEM IS SUPPOSEDLY BINDING, A HIGHLY DUBIOUS INTERPRETATION.
>
> I pointed it out victoriously and demanded my just compensation. NO DOUBT A JOKE, SO NOT MEANT TO BE A REAL "OFFER" FOR HER TO SOMEHOW ACCEPT.
>
> Sadly, she has yet to fulfill her obligation. BREACH? NO, SINCE THERE HAD BEEN NO ACCEPTANCE. EVEN IF THERE WERE AN AGREEMENT, IT WOULD BE AGAINST PUBLIC POLICY – WE HAVE LAWS AGAINST PROSTITUTION (PAYING FOR SEXUAL SERVICES).
>
> Would that, by any chance, constitute a legally enforceable contract? NO. NO! NO!!!
>
> Do I have any recourse in collecting what is owed to me? NO. YOU ARE NOT OWED ANYTHING. NOW THAT YOU ARE LEARNING THE LAW, I AM SURE YOU WILL USE YOUR BURGEONING KNOWLEDGE FOR NICENESS, NOT FOR EVIL!

A classic case, Lucy v. Zehmer, 84 S.E. 2d 516 (1954)
Selling Farmland in a Bar!
The sellers wanted out, but they were stuck, said the Virginia Supreme Court.

> A.H. and Ida S. Zehmer, husband and wife, contracted with the plaintiffs, brothers W.O. and J.C. Lucy, to sell their farm ("called "the Ferguson Farm") of 471.6 acres for $50,000, after forty minutes of negotiation. Both parties had been drinking that evening and before signing the contract, A.H. Zehmer disclosed to Ida Zehmer that the contract was being drafted in jest.
>
> Does the undisclosed intent of a party in an outwardly valid contract have any bearing on its enforceability?
>
> Holding: No, the contract can only be judged according to its outward manifestation.
>
> The Rule: Courts must follow the Objective Observer Test - if an objective observer would find that a valid contract had been established, then the court must enforce it.
>
> Rationale: Undisclosed intent cannot be proven in court. To subject contracts to such revelations would undermine the enforceability of contracts in all cases. Here, an offer to purchase property was made in a bar, and a contract was drawn up, changed to meet the buyers' objections, and then signed. The seller claimed the contract was written in jest, but the court disagreed. The Virginia Supreme Court stated that the law "imputes to a person an intention corresponding to the reasonable meaning of his words and acts," and it upheld the contract based on the seller's actions. *Id.* at 521.
>
> The Virginia Supreme Court held that the length of time the contract is under discussion, the parties' signatures, the terms of the contract, the revisions that were made, and the buyer's retention of the contract are all "persuasive evidence that the execution of [a] contract [is] a serious business transaction. . . . .The mental assent of the parties is not requisite for the formation of a contract." *Id.* at 521-522.
>
> The Opinion of the Court
>
> . . . The instrument sought to be enforced was written by A. H. Zehmer on December 20, 1952, in these words: "We hereby agree to sell to W. O. Lucy the Ferguson Farm complete for $50,000.00, title satisfactory to buyer," and signed by the defendants, A. H. Zehmer and Ida S. Zehmer.
>
> . . . A. H. Zehmer admitted that at the time mentioned W. O. Lucy offered him $50,000 cash for the farm, but that he, Zehmer, considered that the offer was made in jest; that so thinking, and both he and Lucy having had several drinks, he wrote out "the memorandum" quoted above and induced his wife to sign it; that he did not deliver the memorandum to Lucy, but that Lucy picked it up, read it, put it in his pocket, attempted to offer Zehmer $5 to bind the bargain, which Zehmer refused to accept, and realizing for

the first time that Lucy was serious, Zehmer assured him that he had no intention of selling the farm and that the whole matter was a joke. Lucy left the premises insisting that he had purchased the farm.

. . . .

The defendants insist that the evidence was ample to support their contention that the writing sought to be enforced was prepared as a bluff or dare to force Lucy to admit that he did not have $50,000; that the whole matter was a joke; that the writing was not delivered to Lucy and no binding contract was ever made between the parties.

It is an unusual, if not bizarre, defense. When made to the writing admittedly prepared by one of the defendants and signed by both, clear evidence is required to sustain it.

In his testimony Zehmer claimed that he "was high as a Georgia pine," and that the transaction "was just a bunch of two doggoned drunks bluffing to see who could talk the biggest and say the most." That claim is inconsistent with his attempt to testify in great detail as to what was said and what was done. It is contradicted by other evidence as to the condition of both parties, and rendered of no weight by the testimony of his wife that when Lucy left the restaurant she suggested that Zehmer drive him home. The record is convincing that Zehmer was not intoxicated to the extent of being unable to comprehend the nature and consequences of the instrument he executed, and hence that instrument is not to be invalidated on that ground. . . . .

The evidence is convincing also that Zehmer wrote two agreements, the first one beginning "I hereby agree to sell." Zehmer first said he could not remember about that, then that "I don't think I wrote but one out." Mrs. Zehmer said that what he wrote was "I hereby agree," but that the "I" was changed to "We" after that night. The agreement that was written and signed is in the record and indicates no such change. Neither are the mistakes in spelling that Zehmer sought to point out readily apparent.

The appearance of the contract, the fact that it was under discussion for forty minutes or more before it was signed; Lucy's objection to the first draft because it was written in the singular, and he wanted Mrs. Zehmer to sign it also; the rewriting to meet that objection and the signing by Mrs. Zehmer; the discussion of what was to be included in the sale, the provision for the examination of the title, the completeness of the instrument that was executed, the taking possession of it by Lucy with no request or suggestion by either of the defendants that he give it back, are facts which furnish persuasive evidence that the execution of the contract was a serious business transaction rather than a casual, jesting matter as defendants now contend.

On Sunday, the day after the instrument was signed on Saturday night, there was a social gathering in a home in the town of McKenney at which there were general comments that the sale had been made. Mrs. Zehmer testified that on that occasion as she passed by a group of people, including Lucy, who were talking about the transaction, $50,000 was mentioned, whereupon she stepped up and said, "Well, with the high-price whiskey you were drinking last night you should have paid more. That was cheap." Lucy testified that at that time Zehmer told him that he did not want to "stick" him or hold him to the agreement because he, Lucy, was too tight and didn't know what he was doing, to which Lucy replied that he was not too tight; that he had been stuck before and was going through with it. Zehmer's version was that he said to Lucy: "I am not trying to claim it wasn't a deal on account of the fact the price was too low. If I had wanted to sell $50,000.00 would be a good price, in fact I think you would get stuck at $50,000.00." A disinterested witness testified that what Zehmer said to Lucy was that "he was going to let him up off the deal, because he thought he was too tight, didn't know what he was doing. Lucy said something to the effect that 'I have been stuck before and I will go through with it.'"

If it be assumed, contrary to what we think the evidence shows, that Zehmer was jesting about selling his farm to Lucy and that the transaction was intended by him to be a joke, nevertheless the evidence shows that Lucy did not so understand it but considered it to be a serious business transaction and the contract to be binding on the Zehmers as well as on himself. The very next day he arranged with his brother to put up half the money and take a half interest in the land. The day after that he employed an attorney to examine the title. The next night, Tuesday, he was back at Zehmer's place and there Zehmer told him for the first time, Lucy said, that he wasn't going to sell and he told Zehmer, "You know you sold that place fair and square." After receiving the report from his attorney that the title was good he wrote to Zehmer that he was ready to close the deal.

. . . . If the words or other acts of one of the parties have but one reasonable meaning, his undisclosed intention is immaterial except when an unreasonable meaning which he attaches to his manifestations is known to the other party.

. . . . Whether the writing signed by the defendants and now sought to be enforced by the complainants was the result of a serious offer by Lucy and a serious acceptance by the defendants, or was a serious offer by Lucy and an acceptance in secret jest by the defendants, in either event it constituted a binding contract of sale between the parties.

Defendants contend further, however, that even though a contract was made, equity should decline to enforce it under the circumstances. These circumstances have been set forth in detail above. They disclose some drinking by the two parties but not to an extent that they were unable to understand fully what they were doing. There was no fraud, no misrepresentation, no sharp practice and no dealing between unequal parties. The farm had been bought for $11,000 and was assessed for taxation at $6,300. The purchase price was $50,000. Zehmer admitted that it was a good price. There is in fact present in this case none of the grounds usually urged against specific performance....

Comparative Law: *How Intent to Form a Contract Is Measured in Other Countries*

U.S. courts routinely adhere to the objective theory of contracts. Under the objective theory of contracts, the law considers what the parties said and did - not what the parties thought (unless those thoughts were manifested to the other party).

Courts in some nations, however, give more weight to subjective intentions. Under French law, for example, when there is a conflict between an objective interpretation and a subjective interpretation of a contract, the French civil law code prefers the subjective construction. Other nations that have civil law codes take this same approach. French courts, nonetheless, will look to writings and other objective evidence to determine a party's subjective intent. In operation, the difference between the French and U.S. approaches is therefore perhaps not as significant as it may seem at first blush.

6. Language Is Fundamental: Watch Your Wording

Ordinarily, in U.S. contract law there is no formal wording requirement.
Contractual definitions, or at least a dictionary, can be useful for interpreting terms in an agreement.

If one signs a document, the assumption is that you have read and understood it.
"Repairing the Driveway" Case: A gravel roadway went from the county street to the driveways connecting three houses. A covenant between the three homeowners stating that each will pay one-third of the costs to maintain and repair the roadway.

Two homeowners hired a contractor, who paved the roadway, and the homeowners demanded that the third homeowner (the author's client) pay them one-third of the contractor's bill.

What is the common understanding about maintenance and repairs? Definitions often matter. The author-lawyer bought in ordinary dictionaries and legal dictionaries. He referred to court decisions about the meaning of "to maintain, to keep in condition" – that is different from "to improve."

There was no quasi-contract result – enrichment, but not unjust enrichment. Just pay, under the contract, for one-third cost of what gravel would have been.

THE "CULPABLE" EXAMPLE - Blame or Guilt? A word's ordinary significance is different than any specific *legal* meaning it may have.[15]

> The Million-Dollar Comma: A Tale of High-Powered Businesspersons, Careless Contract Attorneys, Gross Foolishness, Lots of Money, and Schadenfreude – Thank Goodness for A Contract in Two Different Languages!
>
> A contract entered into between cable company Rogers Communications and telephone company Aliant Telecom Inc. (now Bell Aliant Regional Communications, LP) on May 31, 2002 allowed Rogers to use Aliant's telephone polls. In early 2005, Aliant sought to get out of the deal. To the Canadian Radiotelevision and Telecommunications Commission (CRTC), Canada's equivalent to the U.S. Federal Communications Commission, the case hinged on placement of the second comma in the 14-page agreement's Section 8.1: "This agreement shall be effective from the date it is made and shall continue in force for a period of five (5) years from the date it is made, and thereafter for successive five (5) year terms, unless and until terminated by one year prior notice in writing by either party."
>
> By a letter dated January 31, 2005, Aliant provided Rogers notice of the termination of the agreement, effective one year later, on February 1, 2006. Aliant contended that the second comma denoted that the deal could be terminated at five years, *or before*, as long as one year's notice was given. So Rogers became vulnerable to a steep rate hike - almost doubling the annual rate for poles from $9.60 to about $18 a pole: raising Rogers costs by over $1 million.
>
> However, Rogers insisted that the contract was good for at least five years. Rogers contended that if Aliant could terminate the contract at any time upon one year's notice to Rogers, then the express agreement by the parties to a five-year term was effectively meaningless, and all of the following words of the section would be superfluous: "for a period of five (5) years from the date it is made, and thereafter for successive five (5) year terms."[16] That the agreement had those words means that they must have some meaning.
>
> Aliant argued that section 8.1 allowed contractual termination at any time, by either party, after providing one year's prior notice. The argument focused on grammatical rules of punctuation - since the comma in section 8.1 closed the clause "and thereafter for successive five (5) year terms," the subsequent qualifier "unless and until terminated by one year prior notice in writing by either party" qualified all of the preceding section. To limit the right to terminate to the end of the five-year term, no comma would have been placed before the word "unless," and the date by which notice was required would have been specified.
>
> On July 28, 2006, the CRTC held that the comma should have been omitted if the contract was meant to last five years in its shortest term. On appeal, Rogers had two points in its favor: (1) the parol evidence rule exception allowing proof of mistake or ambiguity permitted evidence of what the parties really intended; (2) the language - with the second comma included - makes some of the rest of the language about an initial five year term and five -year renewal terms superfluous, which would seem to mean that the parties meant for five years to actually mean something. Rogers claimed that the French version's section 8.1 had a different statement clarifying the point:
>> Sous réserve des dispositions relatives à la résiliation du présent contrat, ce dernier prend effet à la date de signature. Il demeure en vigueur pour une période de cinq (5) ans, à partir de la date de la signature et il est subséquemment renouvelé pour des périodes successives de cinq (5) années, à moins d'un préavis écrit de résiliation à l'autre partie un an avant l'expiration du contrat.
>
> My translation of the French is:

---

[15] Clark D. Cunningham, *A Tale of Two Clients: Thinking About Law as Language*, 87 MICH. L. REV. 2459, 2464 (1989).

[16] The argument thus was that the agreement might as well have been worded more concisely, and directly, as follows: "This agreement shall be effective from the date it is made and shall continue in force, unless and until terminated by one year prior notice in writing by either party."

> Subject to the provisions concerning termination of this contract, the following takes effect from the date of signature. The contract remains in force for a period of five (5) years, from the date of signature and it is subsequently renewed for successive periods of five (5) years, unless a written notice of termination to the other party one year before the contract expires.
>
> On August 20, 2007, the CRTC overturned its decision. Rogers had successfully argued that the commas in the French version of the contract were in their proper position; the French version made clear that Aliant could not terminate before the contract's first five years ended. The CRTC agreed that this interpretation of section 8.1 was consistent with the parties' intentions. As both versions of the agreement (English and French) were official and binding, the CRTC turned to the French version as superior in this instance; for one thing, interpretation of the French language version did not even require grammatical analysis, but has only one possible interpretation, something consistent with one of the two possible interpretations of the English language version.
>
> The offending clause was boilerplate used by all Canadian cable telephone companies. So what about legal malpractice? Rogers and its attorneys should have detected the foolish second comma during the drafting stage. This case gives more ammunition for contract lawyers to tell their clients, "it's better to pay numerous lawyers to separately and fully review the language - many pairs of eyes are better than one! Ultimately, you'll still save money by paying for redundant proofreading compared to the costs of an avoidable lawsuit."

7. Boilerplate Language: Franchise Contracts as an Example

Courts rarely hold that the prefatory (introductory) language in an agreement has created legally enforceable obligations. Nonetheless, courts recognize that, under certain circumstances, such language may be used:

- ❖ If contract provisions are ambiguous.
- ❖ To ascertain the parties' intent when construing the contract.
- ❖ To explain the circumstances surrounding the execution of the contract.

Even if a plaintiff does not win with these arguments, it can be very costly for the other side to defend against them. So, parties should evaluate the introductory paragraphs and recitals in their agreements and revise or eliminate any boilerplate language that could be seen as creating significant expectations on the other side's part. That is especially called for when those expectations seem unlikely to be attained, which in turn could lead to hard feelings and perhaps even a legal dispute.

A good example of the potential problems associated with prefatory language is the franchise agreement. Many franchise agreements begin with an introductory paragraph, a "witnesseth" statement or various recitals that tout the virtues of the franchisor's business or systems. These introductory statements might state that the franchisor has "developed a proven system," "developed and perfected a system," or "developed a uniform system" for operating a particular type of business. The introductory statements also might highlight the success, reputation, or positive image of the franchisor's business systems.

Although these statements are not intended by the franchisor to have any binding legal consequences, a franchisee may seize upon this language if his/her business is less successful than the franchisee had hoped, or if a conflict develops between the parties. A number of franchisees have asked a court or an arbitrator to rule that, by including such statements in the franchise agreement's prefatory paragraphs of its franchise agreement, the franchisor has created an enforceable legal obligation to ensure the overall success of the franchisee's business. Courts that have addressed this issue generally have held that such introductory statements do not create any affirmative duties on the part of a franchisor.

Often because these prefatory "implications" are directly contradicted in the explicit language later in the agreement, it is not so much contract law but just the possibility of litigation and bad publicity that may still inhibit the use of overbroad prefatory statements favoring the franchisor. Despite the legal limitations on these prefaces, all franchisors and other businesses should examine very carefully the language in a contract document, even the nonbinding opening recital.

E. When Should a Promise Be Legally Enforceable?
(To call something a contract does not make it a contract)

When can a promise be enforced? Conversely, when should society permit a promisor to not keep his/her promise?

For example, Republicans running for office in the 1994 Congressional election put forth a "Contract with America." There were ten changes that the Republicans promised to enact if they were elected as the majority party. They were so elected, with the Republicans controlling both the U.S. Senate and the U.S. House of Representatives for the first time in forty years. The Republicans did ultimately enact, in effect, the ten promises. But, if they had not, could the electorate have successfully sued them for breach of contract? No, the remedy would simply be to defeat the promise–breakers when they ran for re–election.

Also, what about a parental "contract" with a teenager for the teenager's acting responsibly concerning the drinking of alcoholic beverages or the use of other substances? Putting their agreement in a written document, calling it a contract, and signing it simply reinforces the solemnity of that agreement. But what remedies are there for a breach? Is not this a social matter for families to deal with on their own, not in front of a court?[17]

What if there is a really insignificant matter? If Student Sally simply promises to lend another student, Milton, her notes, then there would be no consideration (no return promise from Milton). But what if, in return for Sally's promise, Milton promised to meet her at a local establishment and buy her a cup of coffee? Then there would be consideration from both parties; but a court might find the "contract" so trivial that Sally's or Milton's failure to perform would not matter, as the agreement was simply a social engagement not worthy of judicial enforcement.

In the common law, we presume that in "social and domestic agreements" there is no intention to be legally bound. This is a presumption that can be overcome from the evidence – the parties' words (oral or written) and their conduct, and any other pertinent circumstances. The parties' expectations, and what society thinks of these arrangements (whether one *should* go to court over a breach) are also important. For instance, a few, prominently reported suits have been brought over matters such as broken dates. Some have settled successfully for court costs of filing a claim, plus the jilted date's expenses, but the public reaction generally is very negative.

In Horsley v. Chesselet, a 1978 small claims case decided in the San Francisco Municipal Court, Mr. Horsley sued Miss Chesselet for $32 "that he expended … for gasoline and theater tickets in order to perform his promise to escort Defendant for an evening at the theater." She had breached the "contract."

A "Social" Contract? An Example from England

In January 2015, in Plymouth, England, a parent, Julie Lawrence, billed the parents of Alex Nash, age 5, because the boy was a no-show at a birthday party the previous month for Julie Lawrence's child. Julie had paid the party venue (a ski resort) a sum of money based on how many guests had accepted the party invitation. The reason for the no-show was that the invited boy's parents realized, after accepting the birthday party invitation, that their son had previously agreed to visit his grandparents that day. Derek Nash, Alex's father, said he understood that the parent arranging the party was upset about paying the ski resort for a child who was expected to attend but did not. But Derek said he did not appreciate the unusual way in which Julie notified him of the request for compensation (by drawing up an invoice for 16 pounds and asking the children's school to put the invoice in Alex's school bag, to give to his parents). So Derek refused to pay, and Julie sued Derek in small claims court for breach of contract. The ski resort denied any involvement in the dispute, and even said Julie engaged in fraud by naming the ski resort; no doubt the resort did not want any bad publicity, and its spokesperson said that in the rare cases when there is a no-show, the ski resort typically offers the parents who arranged the party other activities to compensate them for the money they lost because of the no-show.

---

[17] Of course, if the teenager is a minor, then any "contract" would be voidable due to incapacity.

1. Absent a specific statement in the invitation, would it normally be the invitee's understanding that it is the parents throwing a birthday party for their children who would be footing the bill. Parents have been known to rent sites for their children's birthday parties and pay the rental costs themselves. By contrast, for example, professors attending academic conferences understand that conference hosts usually do not pay for conference banquets or other social events out of the professional organization's own funds, since these events involve a commercial transaction between professors and the organization, as opposed to a purely "social engagement."

> An approach other than litigation: When people accept an invitation and then don't show up, never invite them again. These no-show examples in social settings seem like situations where social norms should dictate behavior, rather than invoices and threats to take the matters to court. Not all disputes are appropriate for court intervention. The operations of courts are generally funded by taxes of course, and money collected by taxes is obviously limited.

2. Invitations should perhaps say that each invitee who accepts the invitation will be asked to chip in, even if the accepting invitee ends up being a no-show. That might be enough to rebut our presumption of no intent to create contractual relations via a birthday party. Of course, it would have to be an agreement between the adults; a child's party invitation, even if deemed to be from someone with capacity (e.g., the child's parent), would not create legal relations with the child "guest."

3. *Not everything that sounds like a contract, and seems to have the elements of a contract, is really enforceable.* Do we really want contract law to cover some things? For example, can a precocious child somehow require that a parent sign the following: "I, the undersigned Dad, attest that I have never parented before, and – insofar as I have no experience – shall be accountable for my mistakes and liable, in perpetuity, for any counseling needed by my child as a result of my parental ineptitude." Why do we allow people to become parents (and keep their children) without signing something like that?!

Even though technically the elements of a contract may be present, some promises may not be enforced. E.g., family matters (chores, delineation of duties), highly personal areas – these are matters of morality and/or etiquette, but not necessarily law.

YOUTUBE – Moral Damages.wmv (12mins13secs) at robertwemersonufl

Some countries view contract rights and damages differently, and sometimes more broadly, than in the United States.

> **Comparative Law: Moral Damages**   (see pg. 477; Emerson BL)
> Is America lawsuit-happy? Does its legal system foster exorbitant damage awards? Many people think so. But most Civil Law nations permit breach-of-contract claims for moral damages and some even allow for emotional harm. All such claims American courts would deny.
> The Civil Law nations would argue that moral damages and psychological compensation – "bespokoistvo" in Russia – is really just a compensatory award for actual losses. If a hypothetical Russian beauty, Svetlana, not to be mean, but merely to cut her losses, intentionally breaks her contract with Vladimir, then that breach makes economic sense. It is an "efficient" breach, and American courts would restrict any damage awards to actual losses. On the other hand, Russian courts could award Vladimir a form of extra non-pecuniary damages to penalize Svetlana's intentional breach.
> In many Latin America nations, such as Brazil, Argentina, Bolivia, Peru, Ecuador, Venezuela, and Mexico, there are moral damages, sometimes called "agravio morat," that go beyond monetary loss. Following the old French Code, instead of the Spanish, these nations compensate for intangible injuries to feelings, honor, or moral principles. Some Latin American countries, such as Panama, Colombia, the Dominican Republic, and Chile, follow the Spanish Code and do NOT permit moral damages.

> Some other countries awarding moral damages include France, Belgium, Ukraine, the Philippines, Armenia, Georgia, and Malta. Also, within particular countries there are regions favoring moral damages, such as Quebec and Kurdistan. These countries' and Russia's comprehensive approach can funnel extra money to winning plaintiffs, both to punish horrendous breaches and to overcome annoyances.

F. Categories of Contracts

A modern trend in law is to get away from some difficult language. Contracts typically will now call parties by their names or other easily understood titles (e.g., "Jones" instead of "Third-Party Insurance Beneficiary"). Still, one must know some terminology. From the outset, knowing what some basic terms mean will assist in one's reading and understanding of concepts. If one can apply the legal nomenclature, one has the words to take notes easier, faster, and with the ability to survey and begin to understand major contract law concepts without cluttering up that overview with elaborations or tangential diversions describing what something is rather than just giving the one-word or short phrase term. For example, once the terms are understood, the sentence "Abraham extended a firm written offer open for one month, and, upon Benoud's e-mailed and FAXed acceptance 20 days later, the parties both began performing what they considered to be a valid, bilateral, enforceable, executory sale of goods." Knowing the meaning of each legally significant word – firm written offer, acceptance, performance, valid, bilateral, enforceable, executory, sale, and goods – makes this short, but dense statement much easier to follow than having to clarify some or all of those words.

Contract law is full of terminology. One can categorize contracts in numerous ways, such as by enforceability, degrees of completion, how contract offers are accepted, and how contracts (or comparable arrangements) are formed.

1. Enforceability (see pgs. 96-97; Emerson BL)
Categorizing Contracts by their enforceability: Valid/Void/Voidable/Unenforceable Contracts

Valid– a real contract, one that meets all requirements to be considered lawful and enforceable
Void– of no effect – as if there never were a contract (like an annulment)
Voidable – may be avoided (or to put it in legal terms, "voided"). This usually can be done by just one party, such as a minor or someone who has been defrauded (e.g., a defrauder cannot opt to get out). "Voidable" means able to be voided: Potential problems with a contract making it voidable – problems with mutuality of assent (e.g., mistake, undue influence, mental duress, fraud) or with capacity (e.g., a contract with a minor).
Unenforceable means a problem concerning an otherwise valid contract, such that courts will not enforce the contract. Three examples of Unenforceability are:
(1) Statute of Limitations – time period for bringing suit (the time period after a wrong in which you are able to sue) – in Florida, limitations usually are four years, unless a more specific law says otherwise;
(2) Statute of Frauds – written evidence requirement, discussed later; and
(3) Bankruptcy.

2. Degrees of Completion
Categorizing Contracts by *their degree of completion*: Executed and Executory Contracts.

> "Executed" means completed. "Executory" means not completed.

There is an important distinction for remedies.

[handwritten at top: promisor gives promise to promisee]

For executed but breached contracts, the remedy tends to be profit expectations (the difference between what you bargained for and what you got). For executory contracts, the remedy usually is to return the parties to the status quo ante – i.e., the parties' previous position, before the contract was reached – such as by paying back any deposits.

There are special rules for bankruptcy and probate concerning executory agreements.

When he/she takes over the estate, the Trustee or Executor can negate/deny/refute/refuse to carry out an executory contract (even though it is a real contract).[18]

Executory or Executed Contract?
You agree to pay Amir $300 for his cleaning and reorganizing your garage.
At the time you reach the agreement, the contract is an EXECUTORY contract.
Amir brings a dumpster over to the driveway next to your garage.
The contract is still an EXECUTORY contract.
Amir starts to move, dump and organize the "stuff" in your garage.
The contract remains an EXECUTORY contract.
Amir finishes his work.
The contract is an EXECUTED contract (at least on Amir's part).

3. Bilateral/Unilateral

[handwritten: article 2 of UCC]

Categorizing Contracts by *how they are accepted*: Bilateral and Unilateral Contracts

> "Promisor" means the person making the promise.
> "Promisee" means the person receiving the promise.

Under common law, there is no contract until performance occurs.
TWO EXAMPLES OF UNILATERAL CONTRACTS
 1. At a fair, climbing a greased flagpole in order to win a smoked ham;
 2. Swimming the English Channel in order to win a sporting goods endorsement deal.
Unilateral contracts involve offers to form a unilateral contract, with performance being the acceptance.

- Bilateral means two promises (a promise for a promise) – both sides make a promise ("bi"). Most written agreements, business deals, and typical executory contracts are bilateral contracts.
- Unilateral means one promise (action or forbearance – e.g., "I won't sue you" – for a promise): only one side makes a promise ("uni"). The offeree accepts only by doing what the promise calls for. As one example, reward scenarios tend to be unilateral contract offers.[19] In fact, any situation in which the promisor seeks a response other than simply a return promise falls under the "unilateral" label. If, after a snow flurry, Homeowner Harry declares to his neighbor, Strongman Steve, "Shovel My Walkway and I'll pay you twenty bucks," then Steve would only be able to accept by shoveling Harry's walkway. If Steve does that, then he has accepted the unilateral contract offer; Steve has thereby both accepted and performed, and he thus is entitled to Harry's payment of $20.

---

[18] Joke: "When you have told anyone that you have left him a legacy, the only decent thing is to die at once." Samuel Butler.

[19] Suppose that an anguished dog owner seeks to find his missing pet, Fido. Her flyers, posted throughout her neighborhood, inform readers that she will pay $500 to whoever finds Fido. Obviously, the recipients of this information cannot accept the pet owner's offer simply by promising to find Fido. And, because no one can accept the unilateral offer except through performance, no one can be bound to an executory contract – and therefore breach – by not finding Fido. Instead, the pet owner's unilateral offer only can be accepted by doing – by actually finding the dog.

There are significant problems with unilateral contracts:
(1) They are difficult to figure out, because usually not in writing.
(2) When does a contract occur? There are no contractual rights until performance occurs (so the offer can be revoked until the offeree has fully performed)

Here is a review of what seems to be the fine line between unilateral and bilateral agreements.

For purposes of contract law, actions and promises are distinct. For example, the unilateral contract involving lawn mowing has the <u>action</u> of mowing the lawn; if it were a bilateral contract, it would involve the <u>promise</u> of mowing the lawn. A bilateral contract involves two promises – each party has made a promise to the other party. In a unilateral contract, only one party has made a promise. The other party can accept only through action or forbearance from action: by doing or refraining from doing whatever the promisor asked the promisee to do (or refrain from doing).

Examples: Bilateral or Unilateral Contract?
• You offer $300 to your 25–year–old friend if the friend can drink an entire half–gallon of milk in under three minutes. UNILATERAL.
• You offer to give $20 to the first person who can name the composer of the classic work, "The Florida Suite." UNILATERAL. (The composer, by the way, was Sir Frederick Delius.)
• You promise your roommate that you will wash her car today if she promises to wash your dog tomorrow. BILATERAL.
• Eddie Nineteen, who is about to turn age 20, promises his proud parents, Mr. and Mrs. Twenty, that he will not smoke, drink, play billiards, gamble, booty–dance, or swear for the next two years, if they agree to buy Eddie a new car at the end of that two–year time frame. BILATERAL.

4. Express/Implied/Quasi–Contract (see pgs. 95-96; Emerson BL)
Categorizing Contracts by how they are formed: Express/Implied/Quasi–Contract

"Express" means mainly in words (oral, written, or both oral and written).
"Implied (in fact)" means based mainly on conduct (not just words).

Examples: Express or Implied Contracts?
• A customer and a car dealer sign a lease agreement. EXPRESS
• A man buys a snack from a vending machine. IMPLIED IN FACT

a. A Longer Example – Tad Taxpayer and Anyala Accountant
If Tad Taxpayer visits the office of Anyala Accountant, and he is seeking expert help with his income tax return, an implied contract may be formed. Suppose that Anyala explains what her services are, how much they will cost, and what forms and information she will need. No agreement is reached; it is clear that Tad may or may not hire Anyala, as he will "think about it."

The next day – February 13 – Tad returns to Anyala's office, with all of the documents Anyala said he would need to provide her. Anyala is out to lunch, but her secretary, Babu, is there. Tad says, "Oh, well, April 15th is not that far off, and here is all of my tax stuff." Babu says that he will give everything to Anyala when she returns. Tad says, "Good. She'll know what to do with it."

What if on March 30th Tad calls Anyala to find out the status of his return, and she says, "What return? I never promised to do your taxes. I'm too busy, buddy!"

Or, what if on March 30th Anyala calls Tad to tell him the tax return is complete. All he needs to do, she says, is just stop by the office to sign the return and to pay Anyala for her services. But Tad says, "Hey, I never promised to pay you for doing my taxes!"

In both cases, an implied-in-fact contract appears to have been formed. In the first case, Anyala has – or is about to – breach by not completing the tax return. In the second case, Tad has breached by refusing to pay for the return (presumably at the rate that Anyala had stated in their meeting on February 12th). Although no express agreement was reached on the 12th, an implied agreement was formed – or at least initiated – when Tad dropped off his documents and talked with Babu (Anyala's agent). Tad is bound to the arrangement as outlined on the 12th – he implicitly agrees to it by bringing the documents by and saying Anyala will know what to do with them.[20]

Anyala, too, is bound, if not on the 13th at least shortly thereafter. Her agent in her office took in the documents and promised to give them to her. Perhaps she could have called Tad right away (say, later on the 13th) and said that she just could not do his taxes, or that – now that she sees his documentation – the pay scale will have to be higher. But by holding onto the documents and not saying anything to Tad other than what Anyala said on the 12th and Babu said on the 13th, Anyala Accountant should be bound to the contract and pay for Tad's damages (e.g., additional costs in having to get a late replacement accountant to do Tad's taxes on time).

b. Quasi-Contract

"Quasi–Contract" (implied in law) means like a contract, but not a real contract; it is an obligation created by law > it is an equitable remedy to compensate for – and thus prevent - unjust enrichment (see pg. 740; Emerson BL).

QUASI-CONTRACT EXAMPLE OF A *COMATOSE PERSON ON THE SIDE OF THE ROAD*

The services provider could be entitled to reasonable compensation from the comatose person for the services he/she furnished. (This assumes there is no apparent mistake by the nurse in treating that comatose patient – e.g., presumably nothing on the comatose person's forehead, or elsewhere, stating, "Absolutely <u>Don't Treat Me!</u>")

In quasi–contract cases, the damages to be awarded are quantum meruit, meaning "as much as deserved" – reasonable value, not necessarily a contract or "asking" price. For example, regarding emergency medical services, quantum meruit is <u>not</u> the contract price generally charged (such as by a brain surgeon), but what the court determines the service provider deserves. Without paying anything, a person who benefits from services may be unjustly enriched and thus ordered to pay quantum meruit.

Central to quasi–contract claims is proof that Defendant D was enriched at the expense of Plaintiff P, that P actually conferred a benefit upon D. In summary, the underlying basis for awarding damages in a quasi–contract case is *unjust enrichment of the defendant and unjust detriment to the plaintiff*.

Example:
<u>Person who foolishly mows your lawn; he apparently thought he was mowing someone else's lawn – someone with whom he had a contract</u>

A man who mows lots of people's lawns in the neighborhood accidentally mows yours again the next week. Then, the next week, he again mows it. You are always gone each such weekend. *What duty do you have to figure out what is going on?*.

You think that having your lawn mowed for free is "swell," so you just sit back and let it happen. Is this acceptance? YES. Here, you could easily find out who was doing this – apparently he is a lawn-mowing idol well known throughout the neighborhood. Merely concluding that I'll never pay him, and that should cause him to stop, is probably insufficient. More active measures to contact him may be needed.

---

[20] Presumably, Anyala is not to tuck the documents away in a drawer (never to be seen again), or dip them in paste and turn them into a lovely papier–mâché, or just throw them in the trash! She is to do the taxes.

> **Different Equities:** Mistake of Service Provider about Mowing Lawn, but recipient observed and benefited, while the second the recipient did not know and, while benefiting, is unable to return the service.

> <u>Fired Hospital Doctor Example (taken from the author's practice)</u>
> For eight months after the doctor's termination, the hospital erroneously kept paying the doctor. When the hospital finally realized that it was continuing to pay the fired doctor, it stopped the payments and demanded that the doctor return the eight months' payments. She refused, so the hospital sued. The doctor then counterclaimed to the suit with a contention that she had been wrongly fired (alleged discrimination on account of her Indian ancestry). The court went ahead and granted the hospital a summary judgment for return of the money paid to her after her termination, while holding that the doctor's claim could be decided later. (The doctor later dropped her claim.)

In the <u>Balance of Equities</u> that matters under quasi-contract principles, it is not just enrichment to one side, but also a question of whether the other side was mistaken.

> <u>State Retiree Example</u>
> A pensioner gets much more than she is supposed to receive (enormous sums). A Massachusetts schoolteacher, Joan L. Phillips, retired in 1980 at the age of 55. Phillips correctly received $754 per month in benefits until 1990, when her monthly check bumped up, incorrectly, to $8,394. An audit in July-August 1999 revealed the error – for over nine years, she had been paid $905,486, nearly ten times the amount Phillips was due. The state then sued Phillips for the $814,950 she was overpaid, which Phillips wrongfully accepted and never offered to give back. Phillips' comment in late September 1999 was, "I'm just so confused." By December 1999, Phillips – through her attorney – paid back $72,000, but the state pressed for more; the state contended Phillips and her husband had placed $228,000 in 13 different bank accounts, were siphoning money from those accounts, and had spent hundreds of thousands of dollars on extensive travel. A court appointed attorney took over the Phillips' assets to prevent any more spending and to marshal the assets for repaying what could be paid to the state.
>
> The criminal charges against the Phillips would be theft or embezzlement. The civil claims would be the tort of conversion and/or a quasi-contract claim: unjust enrichment. Perhaps there was an express or implied contract – if Phillips was told something, given pamphlets, signed forms when she retired: so a Breach of Contract by her failure to report the overpayments. If there was no such express or implied contract, then a quasi-contract appears present: Phillips knew or should have known that she was being grossly overpaid, well beyond that to which she was entitled, yet said nothing and kept the money. So, to prevent the continued unjust enrichment at the state's expense, she and her husband should be ordered to return the money (to disgorge the funds).

    c. The Law Does Not Countenance Bootstrapping a Claim that Should be Interpreted Under "Regular" Contract Law, and Thus Found Insufficient, and Transforming that Claim into a Winning Quasi-Contract Claim

As with most contract law matters, this point may best be understood with an example.

> <u>Adam & Berthunia Example</u>
> Adam says to Berthunia, "I think we have a deal….Let's have it finalized by having it typed up." Is Adam's statement just meant to note that the contract has been reached, and the parties just have to put it in writing, or is the statement meant to take the contract development to the final stages of getting ready? No quasi-contract is available in the latter case: that would <u>not</u> be a fair interpretation, because what equity is there in bootstrapping around contract law? Equity only governs if contract law is ineffective and would not be proper for the situation.

G. The Uniform Commercial Code (UCC)

> *"Everyone lives by selling something."* Robert Louis Stevenson (1850-1894), Scottish author of *Treasure Island* and *Kidnapped*.

YOUTUBE – UCC-3mins36secs at robertwemersonufl
The Uniform Commercial Code – the author wrapped in the Maryland flag

> "There are numerous proposed and sometimes even adopted uniform laws here in the United States. These are laws put forth by scholars and practitioners and others (e.g., judges, business groups) in the legal field. But there really is only one that has truly become a uniform law, in the sense that all of the states (or almost all of the states) have adopted it; and it has been in full force for some time. And that law is the Uniform Commercial Code (UCC). It has been adopted by (totally in effect) 49 of the states, while the one remaining state (Louisiana) has adopted at least significant portions of the UCC. The reason this is significant is that most of our law is state law; there is state law for contracts, state law for torts, and so - if you really want to have uniform law - you can really only have it in one of two ways: (1) preempt the states through national regulation, or (2) have all of the states adopt the same law (that is what has happened, in effect, with the UCC).
>
> "The UCC has numerous articles. Three of the more important articles are Articles 3, 4 and 9. Articles 3 and 4 deal with negotiable instruments and the bank-customer relationship, while Article 9 deals with secured transactions. And what is so lovely about the UCC is, say, that you went to South Carolina and looked for the law covered in some area by a UCC article; you could assume with some certainty that the law is going to be the same or quite similar as the law that would be found in any of the other states, whether it is Illinois, Wyoming or the even the great state of Maryland. And that certainly is incredibly important for businesses to have some certainty that when they go from state to state they can have, in effect, the same law there.
>
> "Now, when we talk about secured transactions, what we are really talking about is the ability of lenders to be protected when they enter into some sort of relationship. The lenders acquire some ability to collect on that loan through a security interest if something goes awry, if the debt is not repaid.
>
> "The negotiable instrument - what is so important about that is the facility with which a document can go through commerce (can be passed from one person to another). You can take a check with some degree of certainty, that you can take it to a bank, you can get it cashed (can get the money), and that if something goes awry you have some sort of recourse under law because of Article 3 or Article 4 in the UCC. Again, there are numerous provisions. The best thing to do in this area is to do a little reading on your own to try and understand in practice how this works. Perhaps it's a sad prognosis, but, if necessary (if you are really in a squeeze), consult a lawyer who specializes in commercial transactions."

1. Introduction

By the early 1960s every state (including Louisiana, to some extent[21]) had enacted the Uniform Commercial Code, which has some basic sections, called Articles, on various commercial law topics. Many articles have since been revised, and the states have then enacted these reformed articles. Also, a few new articles have been added to the UCC. The UCC covers a wide range of business transactions, from

---

[21] Despite the fact that Louisiana is a "mixed jurisdictions," similar to Quebec, and follows both the common law and some Civil Law precepts.

negotiable instruments[22] to securities to the lease or sale of goods. For a website on each state's UCC financing forms and filings, see http://www.business.gov/business-law/ucc/

2. Sales Contracts (UCC Article 2)

What is a "sale"? It is a contract to transfer title to a good for a consideration (price).

UCC 2–106(1) states:
In this Article [UCC Article 2], unless the context otherwise requires, "contract" and "agreement" are limited to those relating to the present or future sale of goods. "Contract for sale" includes both a present sale of goods and a contract to sell goods at a future time. A "sale" consists in "the transfer of title [to goods] from a seller to a buyer for a consideration known as the price."[23] Under UCC Article 2 (Section 2–102), "Goods" are tangible, moveable, personal property (e.g., motor vehicles, ships, animals, mobile or modular homes, machinery, etc.). Services, real estate, and intellectual property are not under UCC Article 2.

The UCC adds to and sometimes explains the common law; occasionally, it contradicts the common law.[24]

The common law applies to sales under UCC 2–106 unless the UCC contradicts the common law. The UCC generally is there when the parties did not think of the common law or statutes about sales (such as the UCC) or did not care.

Altering or Voiding a UCC Provision

UCC 1–102 notes that parties to a sale can alter or avoid any UCC provisions that might apply to their contract – e.g., risk of loss, delivery terms – except for as provided in UCC 1–102(3) (good faith cannot be altered or excluded). Here is an example of such a "risk of loss" clause, between a company and its sales representatives (who receive goods from the company and then try to sell them):

"Every contract of duty within [the UCC] imposes an obligation of good faith in its performance and enforcement" UCC 1-203.

So, generally, every contract contains an implied covenant of good faith and fair dealing in its performance. This implied covenant imposes on each party a duty not to do anything that will deprive the other party of the benefits of the agreement.[25]

This is an example of a contract clause:

> "Shipping and Risk of Loss. Company shall sell all Products to Representative as such location as may be designated by Company. Upon delivery by Company to a carrier at the shipping point, Representative shall become responsible for all charges, expenses, losses or damages to Products so shipped. Company shall not be liable for shipping errors of the carrier, other than to correct orders incorrectly filled by Company."

---

[22] Negotiable instruments include notes (formal, written promises to pay a sum of money) and drafts (orders telling another party to pay someone a sum of money). The most prominent, widely used draft is the check – an order by an accountholder (the drawer) to his/her bank (the drawee) to pay a sum to the third person – the payee.

[23] Robert W. Emerson, *Business Law*. NY: Barron's Educational Series (6th ed., 2015), at 186.

[24] Likewise, the UCC can be supplemented by other non-contradictory sources of law, most notably the common law. UCC 1-102.

[25] For an interpretation of good faith and other standards in ordinary business-to-business relationships such as franchising, especially the cessation of the relationship, *see* Robert W. Emerson, *Franchise Terminations: "Good Cause" Decoded*, 50 WAKE FOREST L. REV. ___ (2016), to be available at http://ssrn.com/author=86449.

So, if goods are lost, burnt, stolen, moldy, nasty, or otherwise destroyed or nonfunctional, then who pays? Who is responsible, and who takes risks? Who pays insurance? Does one simply self-insure? Ordinarily, with a clause such as the one above, the person receiving the goods (here, the Representative) is the one taking those risks of loss.

* Good faith is the one part of Article 2 that the parties cannot agree to alter.

> **Comparative Law: Germany's Concern Over Relative Bargaining Power**
> Per the German Law on General Business Terms (**see pgs. 124-125; Emerson BL**), German judges may void all or part of a contract that favors the larger, more powerful party, especially when for a long period of obligation. With provisions thus stricken down, a party may discover that a desirable agreement has suddenly become unfavorable. Hence, as usual, American businesses cannot presume that foreign courts or arbitrators will sustain U.S. commercial practices and law, which ordinarily are strongly predisposed to upholding all unambiguous contract terms. The law that will govern a contract dispute can be crucial.

3. The UCC: All the Main Articles, Via the Example of Bobby & Bonita Boyyurdee

Assume that Bobby and Bonita Boyyurdee have developed a nifty new idea: fettuccine in a can. In order to obtain some financing, they may issue securities, which – at the state level (if not reaching federal regulation, because it is too small an amount or too few investors) – leads to regulation under state "Blue Sky Laws," including UCC Article 8 (Investment Securities). For greater flexibility, the Boyyurdees may obtain a letter of credit from a financial institution, such as a bank. (Letters of credit are even more common in international trade.) UCC Article 5 concerns letters of credit.

UCC Article 9 covers secured transactions, such as when one obtains a loan (e.g., to buy a car) and then gives a lien interest in the debtor's property to the creditor. As evidence of any loans to the Boyyurdee enterprise, besides giving security interests to the lender, Bobby and Bonita probably will have to sign promissory notes, covered in UCC Article 3, as evidence of the loans and as instruments facilitating enforcement of the loan payments (the promissory note would spell out terms of the loan, such as the interest rate, the duration, and collection costs in the event of a breach). In order to line up suppliers, employees, and others, and to make any further arrangements, the Boyyurdees presumably would need a checking account for the occasional, if not frequent, use of checks. Negotiable instruments, including promissory notes and drafts (the latter includes checks), are regulated under UCC Article 3. And the bank–customer relationship would be covered under UCC Article 4 (Bank Deposits and Collections) and, for electronic transfers, by the federal Electronic Funds Transfer Act of 1978 and by UCC Article 4A (deals with ATM machines, telephonic transfers, use of modems). UCC Article 2 (Sales of Goods) covers the Boyyurdees' sale or purchase of goods, including warranties thereunder. Leases of goods would be regulated under UCC Article 2A.

Now, let's assume that fettuccine is a seasonal product. That it grows out in the Midwest – vast fields of fettuccine, billowing in the wind (just like wheat, barley, and rye)! And that it is harvested in the summer, but ordinarily most of it is consumed in the late fall and early winter. (Health conscious, vegetarian folks are replacing the Thanksgiving turkey or ham or other meat product, and the Christmas/New Year Holiday Meats with fettuccine!) So, for a while, between harvesting and consumption, the fettuccine needs to be transported and stored. Warehouse receipts, bills of lading and other documents (e.g., for storage of inventory) are dealt with in UCC Article 7.

Alas! Fettuccine in a can is an idea ahead of its time – a difficult concept to stomach. The Boyyurdees have to sell off their business to Frannie and Franco American. But the Boyyurdee enterprise cannot simply sell off everything (beyond just inventory) – goodwill, customer accounts, equipment, spaghetti slicers, tomato dicers, cucumber cutters, fettuccine fryers - without first notifying creditors and giving them a chance to collect the money owed to them. Various laws cover such "bulk transfers," which go beyond the ordinary sales associated with an ongoing business and are, instead, related to the cessation of a business.

Lastly, having told you of Articles 2 through 9 (plus 2A & 4A), I note that UCC Article 1 is a comprehensive article containing definitions and general provisions that apply to all of the other UCC articles. Some important concepts, such as good faith, may be dealt with not just in particular Articles (e.g., Article 2), but also in introductory Article 1.[26]

H. Private Exchanges

Many companies (e.g., Hewlett–Packard Co., IBM, Wal–Mart Stores Inc.) have turned to "private exchanges" to link with a specially invited group of suppliers and "partners" over the Web. These are smaller than industry-wide Internet exchanges. These systems allow companies to automate their supply purchases and collaborate in real time with trusted suppliers – without having to open sensitive information to unwanted eyes. The businesses also do not have to give over control of their precious supply chains to third parties that are also serving their competitors.

It is important to test whether private exchanges – also called private marketplaces, e–trading hubs, or corporate marketplaces – can strike the balance between the cost efficiencies of electronic transactions and the personal relationships that have always been central to most company's buying practices. Even users of the "private exchanges" acknowledge that they still must rely on telephone calls and faxes for some transactions.

I. Thinking about International Contracts

When considering market conditions for establishing a foreign business outlet, one must understand product/service markets, know about operations and distribution, deal with personnel and management issues, and deal with matters of location, currency, competition, and achieving the "local touch." One should look for a favorable sociopolitical and economic climate of a host country: long-term economic stability, a positive (or at least neutral) attitude toward foreign investors, and a stable pro-market consensus. The substantive foreign law affecting international contracting matters includes:
1. import/export costs and controls;
2. foreign and domestic taxes;
3. laws for forming, governing, and dissolving foreign business entities;
4. securities, antitrust, and employment laws; and
5. exchange controls.

The legal norms of a foreign country – its application of the rule of law, its level of corruption, and the degree of judicial integrity – are very important.

CONTRACTS – RULE OF LAW: PROPERTY RIGHTS IN THE VIRTUAL WORLD

The original Star Trek television series' Episode 52 ("Return to Tomorrow," 1968) featured a species that became so smart it had evolved into a body-less form. The three remaining life forms of that species had their essence encased in glass bubbles, and the Starship Enterprise's Captain James T. Kirk allowed his body to be occupied by one of the three aliens. This alien, now in Kirk's body, met his beloved, now – conveniently enough - occupying the body of an attractive female crew member. Good things like that were always happening to Captain Kirk.

Now, a half-century after that episode first aired, perhaps humanity is headed to bubble-headedness. In virtual world sites (e.g., Second Life, World of Warcraft), you can be someone else and direct an "avatar" to interact with other fake people from whom you can buy and sell things. This faux

---

[26] A summary of the UCC coverage is in the first chapter of Robert W. Emerson, *Business Law*. NY: Barron's Educational Series (6th ed., 2015), at 18.

world has implications for the real world of property rights. And actual murder cases and divorces have been based on or arisen from the virtual world.

Virtual world participants expend substantial amounts of time, and sometime lots of money as well, creating items they claim to own. Applications or web platforms encourage such creation, as the software lets players make, use, transfer and exclude other players from the virtual items these players possess. Property rights expectations, with ancillary contract law, thereby arise. What are the terms of the service agreements? What is fair for applications or platform developers and players?[27]

J. International Sales and the CISG

1. Culture

Most judges, culture scholars, and legal practitioners would probably agree with University of Iowa Professor Gerhard Obenaus: "Legal documents have everything to do with culture. They are pregnant with it. This is especially true for documents from countries with different legal traditions."[28]

For international markets: know your customers, as culture does matter. There are numerous examples of foolish international marketing plans (e.g., the urban legend of the Chevrolet Nova's abysmal failure in Latin America, as "no va" in Spanish means "no go!").

In the international realm, one must consider the cultural factors connected with the country and people with whom Americans do business rather than just assume that everyone thinks and acts the way Americans do. Factors to be considered include a people's language, customs, and moral norms. Failure to consider such factors can have, and has had, disastrous results. Here are two classic stories of cultural screw-ups:

(1) When it tried in Africa to market its baby food with the famous Gerber baby on the jar label, the Gerber baby food company did not realize that, in many African countries, what is pictured on the front of the jar is what is inside. As one can imagine, there was no market for eating what appeared, to many Africans, pureed white babies!

(2) Dr. Pepper had a major surprise on its hands when it realized, only after marketing its soft drink in Europe, that in many European countries, "pepper" is a slang word for a prostitute.[29]

Indeed, business deals can be won or lost based on social gaffes. Although these mistakes may be innocent, they are often avoidable through a small but worthwhile investment in time and effort. Checking on the customs and mores of a country before entering into business relations with its people minimizes problems significantly. As always, contractual language is crucial.

**I would have just a two or three examples

For example, the Japanese have different concepts of personal physical space, and touching people without permission is unacceptable, although that intrusion on personal space (if not extreme and not of a sexual nature) usually presents no problem for most Americans. The Japanese reputedly have 17 different rules about the simple matter of exchanging business cards, including that a card should not be written upon by the receiver or put in the recipient's wallet, which is considered dirty. In some Middle Eastern countries, it is totally unacceptable to touch someone with one's right hand or to have the bottom of one's shoe face another person.[30] Finally, in some countries the "thumb up" symbol can be translated to mean "up yours."

---

[27] After tens of millions of years of evolution, maybe we will all be bubble-heads and step toward that final frontier where, just like Captain Kirk, we too can romance another bubble!

[28] Gerhard Obenaus, *The Legal Translator as Information Broker*, TRANSLATION AND THE LAW (Marshall Morris, gen. editor; Am. Translators Assn.) 247, 249 (1995).

[29] That gives a whole new meaning to the Dr. Pepper soft drink advertisement campaign, "I'm a Pepper, You're a Pepper, Wouldn't you like to be a Pepper, Too!"

[30] Of course, offers can be screwed up nationally/domestically as well.

In conclusion, an international sale of goods has all the commercial and legal problems inherent in any sale of goods. But the fact that the seller and the buyer are from different countries adds greatly to the transaction's complexity and risk. Here are four basic reasons:

(1) The seller and buyer are less likely to know anything about each other and will find it more difficult and costly to obtain information regarding, for instance, solvency or reputation.

(2) Ideally, the seller would prefer payment before handing over the goods (or any control over them) or incurring any expenses related to their transport. The buyer, on the other hand, would wish to receive and inspect the goods before making payment.

() Neither party wants to have capital tied up while the goods are in transit.

(4) Should anything go wrong with the transaction, obtaining a remedy is more complicated, more costly, and less certain.

2. The Convention on Contracts for the International Sale of Goods (CISG)

YOUTUBE – CISG_4mins1sec at robertwemersonufl

"The most important international convention on trade law is most likely the Convention on Contracts for the International Sale of Goods. Sometimes simply shortened to CISG, it is a convention which . . . the United States adopted in 1986 and became effective in the U.S. in 1987. Most of the major trading nations in the world have adopted the CISG. There are a few exceptions, such as the United Kingdom,[31] but most nations in the EU, most nations of East Asia, and most other important trading countries have adopted the CISG. It is, for want of a better term, the international equivalent of the Uniform Commercial Code (the UCC) in terms of the latter's operation at the domestic level.

"The CISG adopted some principles from the Anglo-American common law, developed some principles from what we have in the UCC, and took some principles from the Civil Law of Western Europe. It only applies to business-to-business transactions, and it only is applicable when two businesses are engaged in the sale of goods and each business is from a different country, both of which are signatories to the CISG. Like the Uniform Commercial Code, parties to an international sale of goods can opt out of the law framework and, in effect, preempt the CISG (just as you can domestically preempt the UCC and create your own law). But it is up to you to do that; if you don't do that, it is assumed that you are bound by the CISG. So it is a very, very important law.

"It (the CISG) has increasing importance internationally. In fact, there are even a few cases were the CISG may not directly have been applicable but courts have nonetheless turned to it for guidance as to general principles of international law affecting the sale of goods. I predict that probably, in the future, we will find that some of the principles found in the CISG will even be invoked in situations where the contract does not involve goods or perhaps doesn't even involve businesses. It (the CISG) won't be mandatory, but it will just be turned to for guidance in the same way that courts sometimes domestically turn to the UCC for guidance about applicable principles even though they don't have to do so.

"The CISG is just sort of a tool for the courts to figure out what the law should be. There are so many other conventions of significance, obviously at the international level, and some deal with trade. Part of what you should be doing in exploring the Internet is, of course, exploring websites such as those of the United Nations to find out what some of these other laws do and how they are applied."

Similar to the UCC for domestic transactions, the CISG – if it otherwise applies – only does so when the parties to an international transaction have failed to specify in writing the precise terms of the contract. As of December 2015, 83 nations[32] have adopted the CISG: Albania, Argentina, Armenia, Australia, Austria, Bahrain, Belarus, Belgium, Benin, Bosnia, Brazil, Bulgaria, Burundi, Canada, Chile,

---

[31] Since the taping of that video, Japan (and a number of other countries) ratified the CISG.
[32] http://cisgw3.law.pace.edu/cisg/countries/cntries.html; http://www.uncitral.org/uncitral/en/uncitral_texts/sale_goods/1980CISG_status.html. *See also* Robert W. Emerson, *Business Law*. NY: Barron's Educational Series (6th ed., 2015), which at page 183 states that the number of signatory nations is nearly ninety.

China, Colombia, Congo (Republic of), Croatia, Cuba, Cyprus, Czech Republic, Denmark, Dominican Republic, Ecuador, Egypt, El Salvador, Estonia, Finland, France, Gabon, Georgia, Germany, Greece, Guinea, Guyana, Honduras, Hungary, Iceland, Iraq, Israel, Italy, Japan, Kyrgyzstan, Latvia, Lebanon, Lesotho, Liberia, Lithuania, Luxembourg, Macedonia, Madagascar, Mauritania, Mexico, Moldova, Mongolia, Montenegro, Netherlands, New Zealand, Norway, Paraguay, Peru, Poland, Romania, Russia, Saint Vincent and the Grenadines, San Marino, Serbia, Singapore, Slovakia, Slovenia, South Korea, Spain, Sweden, Switzerland, Syria, Turkey, Uganda, Ukraine, United States, Uruguay, Uzbekistan, and Zambia.[33] As it has been adopted by most nations in Europe, North America, and East Asia, the CISG's rules can govern most of the world's trade. (These are the top 60 (in Gross Domestic Product) nations – 21 of them - that are non-signatories to the CISG: Algeria, Angola, Bangladesh, India, Indonesia, Iran, Ireland, Kazakhstan, Kuwait, Malaysia, Morocco, Nigeria, Pakistan, Philippines, Qatar, Saudi Arabia, South Africa, Thailand, United Arab Emirates, United Kingdom, and Vietnam.)

As a treaty, ratified by Congress, the CISG is the law of the land in all 50 American states, superseding the Uniform Commercial Code's Article 2 (Sales) when applicable. [Note: the CISG only applies to business contracts (contracts between merchants), not deals involving consumers.]

The CISG automatically applies when firms from two different signatory countries enter into a business sales contract with each other. The determinants are the contracting parties' places of business. The CISG recognizes multiple places of business. Therefore, the nationality (i.e., place of incorporation) of the company is not relevant (nor is the citizenship of the individual business owners or operators relevant). If Laura Lee, Inc. - a German corporation with Brazilian stockholders and its principle place of business in Lake City, Florida - buys (1) valves from Heidance, A.G., a business based in Stuttgart, Germany, and (2) toggle switches from Polk PLC, located in Manchester, U.K., only the valve contract will be ruled by the CISG. This is true because Germany and the United States are signatories to the CISG; the United Kingdom is not. The toggle switches purchase from Polk PLC will be governed by UCC or U.K. (English) law or, if a choice-of-law clause was placed in the contract, the law of the country chosen. Note that Laura Lee, Inc. is deemed an American business because its place of business is in the United States (Lake City, Florida); Laura Lee's German incorporation does not matter – if it were controlling, then the contract between it and Heidance would be a domestic contract (between two German firms), presumably controlled by German contract law. As for Laura Lee's Brazilian shareholders, again, that does not 'override" the American character of Laura Lee, Inc. – its American place of business; otherwise, if Laura Lee, Inc. were a Brazilian firm, then, as Brazil is not a CISG signatory nation, the contracts Laura Lee made would not be CISG contracts (*both* contracting parties are to be from a signatory nation).

Just as the drafters of the Uniform Commercial Code (the UCC) attempted to do for American transactions, the proponents of CISG undertook to bring some uniformity to the rules governing international sales transactions. The CISG is the product of their efforts, and it represents a compromise covering diverse rules, philosophies, and policies rooted in the legal systems of Europe and Latin America (Civil Law), the United Kingdom (the Uniform Sales Act, common law), and the United States (the UCC). The result is a mixed bag for Americans because certain basic UCC principles were rejected. Accordingly, some rules may surprise the American contractor. The good news, however, is that there are known rules – a much greater degree of certainty in international sales law than existed before the CISG was adopted. The CISG, as a compromise between the common law/UCC system and the Civil Law system, has been picked up on by courts and other authorities as evidence of international custom.

International business contracts can specifically adopt contract law other than the CISG (e.g., the UCC as adopted by the state of Florida). This avoidance of the CISG is similar to the process parties in the

---

[33] Two additional countries, Ghana and Venezuela, have signed the CISG (in 1980 and 1981, respectively), but they have not officially ratified it and the CISG does not apply to those two nations.

United States may take to choose contract law other than UCC Article 2. In other words, it must be an affirmative decision to follow some specified national or state law other than the CISG; the parties have to place in their agreement a contractual choice-of-law *and forum* clause: "This contract, its interpretation, performance, and other matters shall be governed by the law of Florida (or U.K., Germany, or whatever jurisdiction the parties choose) and not the CISG; any dispute hereunder shall be brought before courts (or arbitrators) in Florida (or U.K., Germany, etc.)." When applicable, CISG preempts the UCC or other national law unless the parties agree otherwise.

Finally, note that a party cannot win a petition to have national or international courts overturn the CISG. Instead, there must be something specific to which the parties agreed - an actual contract provision about the CISG (e.g., stating that some other law will govern the parties' contract).

K. Comparison of the Scope of the UCC, the Common Law, and the CISG

- The **UCC** covers Sales of Goods
- The **common law** reaches Contracts for Services, Loans, or the Sale of Land or Securities
- The **CISG** involves Sales of Goods by merchants in different signatory nations unless the parties opt out

L. A Sales Representative Contract

It is important and advantageous to draft your contract: you can cover things you really want, and you can make sure of the wording. The structure of an agreement can be controlling. Banks, insurance companies, landlords, etc. typically draft their contracts.

There is one main disadvantage in drafting the agreement: if you screw up and there are ambiguities, those ambiguities are construed against you, the drafter of the agreement.

So do a good job!

*The following are excerpts from A SAMPLE CONTRACT (*for illustrative purposes only)
<u>SALES REPRESENTATIVE AGREEMENT</u> **(EXCERPTS)**[34]   © <u>Robert W. Emerson, 2016</u>

THIS SALES REPRESENTATIVE AGREEMENT, made and entered into this _____ day of _____ 2012, by and between _____, with an office located at _____ ("Company"), and _____, with an office located at _____ ("Representative").

<u>Witnesseth</u>:

Company is engaged in the manufacture, sale, marketing and distribution of heat transfer, air handling, mechanical and electrical equipment, including parts thereof (the "Products"). Representative is capable of marketing and distributing the Products.

Company desires to appoint Representative, and Representative desires to accept appointment from Company as its sales representative in a limited geographical area (the "Territory") to sell, market and distribute the Products to the broadest number of purchasers possible, such appointment to be on the terms and subject to the conditions set forth hereafter.[35]

---

[34] The original contract included clauses about the agreement's duration, product changes, commissions, and sales and service.

[35] <u>Comparison to Japanese Law</u>: Such "recitals" (preambles) detailing the parties and the reasons for entering into the agreement are rare in Japanese contracts. That is largely because the existence of a contract under Japan's Civil Law system does not require absolute statements of offer, acceptance, and consideration, as the common law does. Rather, a declaration

[This preamble gives information about why the agreement was entered into, just as legislation often has preambles as well (or other legislative histories). It is not officially part of the written agreement, just background information. This information helps show underlying matters - what led to the contract, so courts may look at the Witnesseth section to get the "big picture." Courts generally are not inclined to find this prefatory language legally enforceable. However, under certain circumstances, such language may be used to flesh out a contract's terms: (1) if the contract's operative provisions are ambiguous, or (2) to ascertain the parties' intent when construing the contract, or (3) as an explanation of the circumstances surrounding the execution of the contract.]

[Even if a party does not win with these arguments calling for interpretation of the recitals, it can be very expensive for the other side to defend against them. So parties should evaluate the introductory paragraphs and recitals in their agreements and consider revising or eliminating any boilerplate language that could be seen as creating an expectation on the other side's part that ultimately may not be attained.]

NOW, THEREFORE, in consideration of the promises, agreements, and covenants herein, and intending to be legally bound hereby, the parties hereto mutually agree as follows:

Appointment and Territory. Subject to the terms and conditions of this Agreement, Company hereby appoints Representative, and Representative hereby accepts appointment by Company and agrees to act as Company's exclusive sales representative in the Territory specified in Exhibit "A" attached hereto [omitted from this text]

Duties. Representative will use its **best efforts [pacts elsewhere may clarify what that means; it could be an industry standard]** to promote, sell, market and distribute Products in the territory. Representative agrees to pursue vigorously and solicit the sales of Product in the Territory. Representative agrees not to sell or distribute the Products outside of the Territory without the prior written consent of Company. Representative agrees to file such reports with Company as Company may from time to time reasonably require so as to keep Company advised of Representative's sales activities and sales plans on behalf of Company.

Notice. Any notice required or permitted by this Agreement shall be in writing and shall be deemed given at the time it is sent, postage prepaid, certified or registered mail, return receipt requested, addressed to the other party at the address set forth above. Either party may change such address upon notice. **[puts burden on other side to tell of new address;** this is so that every future contact between parties, to be proven, need not be comparable to service of process.]

Waiver. Waiver by either party of a breach of any provision of this Agreement shall not be construed as a waiver of any subsequent breach of such provision or any other provision hereof.

[Just because one waives rights once does not mean one must waive that right thereafter.]

[handwritten: just cause being nice one time doesn't mean you'll be harmed from your generosity]

Severability. If any provision or clause of this Agreement or application thereof to any person or circumstance is held invalid or unlawful, such invalidity or unlawfulness shall not affect any other provisions or clause of this agreement, or the application thereof, which can be given effect without the invalid or unlawful provision, clause, or application.

---

of intention" - e.g., "Xio Corporation and Yoshi Company hereby enter into this manufacturing agreement as follows…" - seems to suffice under Japanese Law.

[Severability clause also found in most legislation - saying to courts that if there's a problem with one part of this statute or contract, don't throw out the whole thing; instead, treat the offending part, the bad section, as <u>severable</u>. Keep what <u>can be retained as lawful</u>! Please!]

[This provision instructs a judge interpreting the contract (the same as for language in a statute about the severability of legislation) to sever and void <u>only</u> the unlawful part of a contract, but to keep the rest.]

<u>Remedies</u>. All rights and remedies conferred herein upon or reserved to Company shall be cumulative and concurrent and shall be in addition to every other right or remedy given to Company herein or at law or in equity or otherwise. The Agreement's termination shall not deprive Company of its right to enforce against Representative any of the Company's rights or remedies at law or in equity.

[This is a provision dealing with what is to be done in the event of a breach.]

IN WITNESS WHEREOF, the parties hereto have caused this . . . .
Signatures of the Parties

II. OFFER

A. Introduction

An offer is from the offer<u>or</u> to the offer<u>ee</u>. It is a definite <u>objective</u> indication (communication) of present willingness to be bound – what parties objectively intended (what a reasonable person would think the parties intended). Ordinarily, there is no formal wording requirement.[36] What matters is what the parties said and did, not what they thought unless those thoughts were manifested to the other party.

If one signs a document, the assumption is that you have read and understood it. Imagine being a corporate officer who is handed a document and told to sign it because it is "something for the Securities and Exchange Commission" (or the Internal Revenue Service, or some other governmental authority). Your signing it without reading and understanding to what you are signifying your assent is like giving a three-year old child a pack of matches and saying, "This is something for you to play with." Who does that?!

Contrast offers, for example, clearly made in jest, strain, excitement, or anger. The problem is: what if the offeree does <u>not</u> recognize that the offeror was joking or mad. E.g., the offer was in writing, so the other side failed to see the emotional state of the "offeror" when the "offeror" was making the offer.

> <u>Example of an Offer NOT Clearly in Jest (at least according to the plaintiff)</u>   On October 12, 2001, a Panama City, Florida state judge denied a local Hooters restaurant's motion for summary judgment. A former waitress who claimed breach of contract had sued the restaurant, which had promised a Toyota for selling the most beer to customers in a month. Instead, the restaurant simply gave her a toy Yoda (a version of the little guy from Star Wars!).
> In May 2002, a settlement was reached for a confidential amount, reputedly $20,000. Hooters' attorney had by then been appointed as a judge, and Hooters claimed that getting a new attorney up to speed with all the facts and law of the case would have cost even more than the settlement. In the end, when one adds the settlement amount and the first attorney's fees, it is clear that it would have cost Hooters less to have just bought a Toyota for the waitress.

---

[36] The exception is when a writing is required because of the Statute of Frauds, discussed later in this text.

1. Three Elements of an Offer (see pg. 99; Emerson BL)

An offer must have <u>objective intent</u>, be sufficiently <u>definite</u>,[37] and be <u>communicated to the offeree.</u>

2. Non–offers

        a. Things Generally <u>Not Offers</u>

A mnemonic device for on-offers is ICE CAPS.

    ICE CAPS =   **I**nvitations
                        Circulars
                        Emotional Statements
                        Catalogues (generally, even if there are prices in them)
                        Advertisements (See Emerson,
                        Price Quotations
                        Social Invitations

Other Examples of Non–Offers are: Agreements to Agree, Opinions, Plans, Requests for Bids, Price Lists, Preliminary Negotiations, Statements of Future Intent ("I plan to sell my stock"), Brochures, and Announcements.[38]

> "[G]eneral advertisements, agreements to agree, catalogs, brochures, and announcements are usually *not* offers because:
> a) they are not sufficiently definite,
> b) they are not communicated to a specific person or persons, or
> c) the circumstances of publication indicate lack of contractual intent."[39]

        b. Advertisements

Ads typically are not offers. "Advertisements are usually considered 'invitations to deal,' that is, invitations to the public to make offers to the advertiser."[40]

        i. Example: "GREAT AMERICAN HOMES" ADVERTISEMENT

Ralph Waldo Emerson is spending a quiet day at home, leafing through a Sears catalog, when suddenly an advertisement catches his eye. "Sears Paints Great American Homes." Waldo (the name all of his friends call him) concludes that he is a great American and that Sears should paint his home. Waldo hurries down to accept the offer. The store manager, Henry Longfellow, informs Waldo that although Sears acknowledges that he is a great American, it is the company's belief that his home ("the Manse") is not a

---

[37] "so that the court can determine the actual intent of the parties." Robert W. Emerson, *Business Law*. NY: Barron's Educational Series (6th ed., 2015), at 99.

[38] Letters of Intent are a distinct arrangement. Assume that DJ's Delights has a plan for a new product. Some uncertainties remain regarding financing and marketing, yet to be settled internally by DJ's. However, certain components need to be fabricated by another firm. Natalie Nutrients Company (NNC) is approached. Lead-time in manufacturing the components will be important to NNC. DJ's would like NNC to gear up, buy raw materials, and await the "go" signal from DJ's. Sensibly, NNC wants a legal "go" signal now. Thus, the dilemma: how can DJ's induce NNC to prepare without DJ's being committed? This type of situation is a common setting for letters of intent. If at least one of the parties does not intend to be bound (e.g., DJ's), the legal, if not the business, answer is obvious. DJ's would demand that the document called a letter contract or letter of intent recite that "no legal agreement has been reached by reason of this document," or like language. Surely, such a lethal (to NNC) caveat is scant inducement for NNC to take preliminary expensive steps to perform. However, some other possible methods might be helpful. For example, an agreement to negotiate in good faith may be entertained. Or a binding promise could be made by one party to fund certain expenses of the other should final agreement not be reached.

[39] Robert W. Emerson, *Business Law*. NY: Barron's Educational Series (6th ed., 2015), at 100.

[40] Id. at 100.

great American home. Has Waldo any recourse? No! The advertisement was not an offer, but an invitation for Emerson to make a request. Its terms were not definite enough to constitute an offer.[41]

ii. *Mesaros v. United States*

The United States Mint sends out order forms soliciting random customers for commemorative $5 gold coins. You send in your order, but the Mint says that it is sold out. Has the Mint made an offer to you? NO, the court held in *Mesaros v. United States*, 845 F.2d 1576 (Fed. Cir. 1988). These mailings of forms were mere solicitations of offers from the customers; any offers by the recipient were subject to acceptance by the Mint before the Mint would be bound by a contract to deliver coins.

iii. Rewards: Calling for Specific Action

In ads, there is a key difference between ordinary non–offers and those that are offers: the latter sounds like a reward because it calls for specific conduct and is limited to certain numbers, such as the first ten people. (E.g., an ad calls for you to dress up like George Washington for Presidents' Day!) and thus pay half-price for five dozen cans of Mount Vernon cherry-juice "jubilee."

Advertisements that call for specific action

Lola sees an ad in the paper for Kelly Clarkson CDs, offered for $2 apiece on a "first–come, first–served" basis at a local music store. She is the first one there, but she is told that she cannot get the deal, because she is not an American Idol fan. Has the store made an offer? PROBABLY YES, because of the "first–come, first–served" statement asking for conduct.

This example is similar to *Lefkowitz v. Great Minneapolis Surplus Store, Inc.*, 86 N.W.2d 689 (Minn.1957). There, the Great Minneapolis Surplus Store published this advertisement in a Minneapolis newspaper: SATURDAY 9 AM. 2 BRAND NEW Pastel MINK 3–SKIN SCARFS Selling for $89.50 Out they go SATURDAY. Each .... $1.00 1 BLACK LAPIN STOLE . . . Beautiful, worth $139.50........$1.OO FIRST COME FIRST SERVED

Lefkowitz was the first to present himself at the store on Saturday, and he demanded the black Lapin stole for one dollar. The store refused to sell to him because of a "house rule" that the offer was intended for women only. Lefkowitz sued the store and was awarded $138.50 as damages. The court noted:

> "[T]he offer by the defendant of the sale of the Lapin fur was clear, definite, and explicit, and left nothing open for negotiation. ... The defendant contends that the offer was modified by a 'house rule' to the effect that only women were qualified to receive the bargains advertised. The advertisement contained no such restriction. This objection may be disposed of briefly by stating that, while an advertiser has the right at any time before acceptance to modify the offer, he does not have the right, after acceptance, to impose new or arbitrary conditions not contained in the published offer."

---

3. Essential Terms and Ambiguity of Terms

Offers should include essential terms: subject matter, quantity, price, and parties. Typically, for example, quantity needs to be designated: amount of property or service - is it an ear of corn or 500,000 bushels of corn?

Terms may be inferred by the court (Implied Terms) – e.g., time of performance, manner of performance, risk of loss, and where and when to deliver goods or services.

---

[41] The problem with some advertisements is not that they are non–offers (just invitations to deal), but that they are silly or otherwise do not say what the advertising party probably meant to say. Here are some actual advertisements for which the firm should fire the marketing manager:
Dog for sale: eats anything and is fond of children.
Tired of cleaning yourself? Let me do it.
Used cars. Why go elsewhere to be cheated? Come here first!

There is a trend in the courts to infer terms – that is, to find a contract if parties seem to have intended a contract, even though the parties did not specify every term. In essence, in these cases the courts find some terms (generally, though, not the basic provisions) for the parties.

The Offeror is the <u>Master of the Offer</u> – and <u>can put in it whatever lawful terms he/she wants</u>: how long offer is open, how offer is to be accepted, and to whom it is made. An offer is usually <u>person–specific</u>; it has a specific offeree.

Assignment of a Contract – when one already has a contract (not just an offer), then an assignment is usually okay. It is <u>not</u> ordinarily permitted for the offeree to assign an offer he/she has received but not accepted (there is no contract yet).

"Offer to Purchase Business" Example: The incorporated status was a figment of the real estate broker's mind! So how could the supposedly accepting corporation accept an offer when that corporation did not exist?

Corporation by Estoppel: Is There an Equitable (Fair) Case Against the Party Allegedly Dealing with a Business that Was in the Process of Incorporating

Most state courts probably would hold that a corporation not yet in existence when a contract was signed may nevertheless establish its status as a party to that contract under the doctrine of corporation by estoppel (if the other party contracted with something labeled a corporation, at least by name).[42] Thus, Party A to a contract may be estopped from denying the existence of Corporation B, and may not withdraw from a contract made before the B was incorporated, *when A knew that the B organization was in the process of incorporating, and where the individual who was forming the B Corporation had partially performed by the time A had repudiated the contract.*[43] Similarly, a supplier was barred from seeking damages from an individual who described a corporation as in the process of being formed, at the time the contractual relationship was discussed, notwithstanding statutes stating that corporate existence begins when articles of incorporation are filed with the secretary of state, where the supplier directed all communications to the corporation's name and address, and the corporation was eventually formed.[44]

On the other hand, courts have ruled that there is no estoppel when a person signed a contract before the corporation, on behalf of which the person was allegedly acting, was organized.[45] There also is no estoppel when the only representation made was that one party would form a corporation only if the transaction were completed; there, the rule is that when an individual purports to act for a nonexistent corporation, there is no corporation by estoppel, and the purported corporation has no standing to enforce the alleged contract.[46]

The different result for the last two cases arises from the fact that *the estoppel doctrine is based on there being a forming corporation, not a nonexistent corporation*. So there is no estoppel, and a party is not bound to an alleged deal with a corporation if there was no corporation being formed or otherwise *in vitro* (if it truly was simply a figment of someone's imagination).

---

4. Interpreting Terms

    a. Conflicting Terms

---

[42] Ross v. City of Berkeley, 655 F. Supp. 820 (N.D. Cal. 1987).
[43] P.D. 2000, L.L.C. v. First Financial Planners, Inc., 998 S.W.2d 108 (Mo. Ct. App. 1999) (concerning a contract with a forming limited liability company).
[44] Arbo Corp. v. Aidan Marketing/Distribution, Inc., 639 F. Supp. 1512 (D. Minn. 1986) (applying Minnesota law).
[45] Video Power, Inc. v. First Capital Income Properties, Inc., 373 S.E.2d 855 (Ga. App. 1988).
[46] Skipper Sams, Inc. v. Roswell-Holcomb Associates, Ltd., 543 S.E.2d 765 (Ga. App. 2000).

To determine the parties' intent, look at their conduct (what was done and said). *When basic terms conflict with one another, then - if it is unclear what meanings were intended - there is no contract.*

But what if specific language conflicts with more general language? The rule then is:
Handwriting > Type > Large Print > Small Print
For example, insurance policies must be in writing. State insurance statutes also typically require that significant terms not be hidden in lengthy paragraphs of verbiage or at least that they be highlighted by color or large print. Failure to follow such statutory requirements usually results in the voiding of the hidden terms by the courts. Another rule working in favor of the insured is that any ambiguity in the policy is construed against the drafting party (the insurance company).

An Inebriated Pedestrian
An insurance beneficiary argued that being drunk once does not constitute alcoholism.
The insured decedent was a run over, drunk pedestrian: Was she an alcoholic?
Contract ambiguity is interpreted against the drafting party.

Paula Pedestrian's life ended when she staggered home one night and fell into the path of an oncoming car. She was highly inebriated according to a test of her blood alcohol content. The life insurance company refused to pay on Paula's $200,000 policy because the policy specifically excluded payment when "death occurs as a result of alcoholism." The beneficiary of the policy sued and contended that one incident involving drunkenness did not constitute alcoholism. The court agreed and construed the ambiguous term against the drafter of the policy, the insurance company. The insurance company had to pay the beneficiary the $200,000 face value of the policy.

BUT THIS SEEMS TO BE URBAN LEGEND because of who the beneficiary allegedly was!
To: Professor Emerson
Issue: Inebriated Pedestrian
I spoke with a staff member at the General Service Office of __ about whether or not they will accept money left in a will, donated or in an insurance policy. She told me that they do accept money, but only in the sum of $1,000 a year. This is the maximum amount they will accept from one person, whether it is in a will, insurance policy or donation. [*My comment: The reason it apparently is against __ tradition to accept more than $1,000 per person, per year, is that in __ everyone is considered to be an equal. If someone left more money, and this bequest were accepted, that would make this person appear to have been of a higher statues than others.*] The only exception to this is if a person leaves money to a __ Club. This is a separate entity from __ because the club pays rent or has to buy a place to hold a __ meeting. The money can then go toward the payment of rent, etc. However, most __ clubs try to adhere to __ traditions and the woman told me that they may or may not have declined such a huge sum of money.
If the woman did leave __ as a beneficiary, __ would have had to decline the money. Tradition Seven of __ calls for every __ group to be fully self-supporting, declining outside contributions. There is an example in Tradition Seven of an incident, it reads, "One night in 1948, the trustees of __ were having their quarterly meeting. The agenda discussion included a very important question: a certain lady had died. When her will was read, it was discovered that she had left __ in trust with $10,000. The question was, should __ take the gift?" the group decided that although it needed the money, __ must always stay poor. "Difficult as it was, they officially declined that $10,000 and adopted a formal, airtight resolution that all such future gifts would be similarly declined."
No one that I spoke with had heard of the case you mentioned.
SO WHO ALLEGEDLY WAS THE BENEFICIARY?

The underlying idea is that courts try to determine what parties must have meant. So, handwritten terms, if conflicting with other terms, tend to control. Typed terms would supersede conflicting printed terms (but not handwritten terms), and large print would control over conflicting small print. So, if one does not like a contract form, one can seek to improve the proposed agreement by striking printed terms and/or adding handwritten wording. Although it may look messy, it is better to have this handwritten scribble (as long as it is legible), with signatures (or at least the signed initials) of the parties next to the handwritten terms, than to just sign the form as it is (or decide not to reach an agreement).

b. Examples
Examples of common conflicting terms in a lease are:
(1) No Pets, (2) Rental Amounts, and (3) Unstricken Alternative Language.

1. A printed statement says that there shall be no pets, but a typed or handwritten section states that the renter's dog – when outside – will always be on a leash, with the owner carrying (and, if necessary, using) a pooper scooper.
2. A handwritten statement provides a rental amount in numerals that is different from another handwritten provision with words indicating the rental amount.
3. A printed statement says that renewal can only occur in a particular manner, while a typed or written term provides another way to renew.

In all three situations, the latter provision controls. Note that in the second example, the latter provision is preferred because it is assumed that numerals are more likely to be misrecorded or misread, while words involve more writing and are thus less likely to be misrecorded or misread. For example, a "9" may be misread as a "4," but how likely is it that "nine" would be misread as "four?"

One can put definition clauses in the written agreement – otherwise, look at conduct, what parties said, what a reasonable person would believe – haul in dictionaries, perhaps.

B. Death of Offers

The death of an offer can occur in many ways:
- Offeror's <u>Revocation</u> – figuratively, the offeror's taking back his hand **before the offeree clasps that hand.**

  Offers ordinarily can be withdrawn until there is an acceptance. Unless an offer is a *firm written offer from a merchant* (described shortly), ordinarily even an offer expressly stated to remain open for a specified time may nonetheless be withdrawn.
- Offeree's <u>Rejection</u> – figuratively, the offeree slaps down the offeror's hand. Counteroffers cannot come back later and accept the initial offer after you have rejected it. Compare to "inquiries" preserve the other's offer.
- A party dies or becomes incompetent/incapacitated (e.g., insanity).
- The subject matter is destroyed.
- The contract's purpose becomes illegal. For example, a man who preaches the rights of people to assisted suicides may extend offers to ill persons: He offers to be "the last to let you down" (into the earth); and he promises that any contract you reach with him will be your last! But a statute is enacted making such assisted–suicide arrangements unlawful. Any outstanding offers (indeed, even existing contracts) are destroyed by that statute.
- Time lapses – the time stipulated in the offer expired, or a reasonable period, under the circumstances, has passed. The offeror does not have to go around "killing" every offer he/she has made. After a reasonable time lapse, the offer automatically dies. Of course, whenever it is important for the offeror to restrict the duration of the offer, it is always best to state the length of time that the offer is open. Otherwise, the other party may bring a lawsuit to determine whether his/her alleged acceptance occurred within a reasonable time. Once an offer lapses, a party wishing to accept may only make a new offer. In a

situation where no time is fixed and the offeror receives the acceptance after what is believed to be a reasonable time, the offeror must notify the offeree immediately that the acceptance is not valid or run the risk that his/her silent conduct will operate as an acceptance.

Example: William Penn owned a large oat farm. In June, Penn contacted Quaker, a food–processing concern, and offered to sell his oats. Quaker finally accepted Penn's offer in September, long after the oats had been harvested. By this time Penn had made other arrangements. Penn refused to ship the oats to Quaker, claiming that an unreasonable amount of time had passed. Does Quaker have any recourse? No! Because contracts are generally made before harvest, Penn is right: a reasonable time to accept the offer had elapsed.

> Comparative Law: German Law
>
> In German law, for a contract offer made during personal negotiations or on the telephone, that offer can only be effectively accepted if it is done immediately.

C. Irrevocable Offers (see pgs. 101-102; Emerson BL)

Usually an offer can be revoked at any time (until there is an acceptance). But there are four Situations in which offers cannot be revoked: (1) Firm written offers, (2) Options, (3) Unilateral contracts, and (sometimes) (4) Promissory estoppel.

Each is now discussed.

1. Firm written offers by Merchants – UCC 2–205

Direct marketers better know about this rule. They had better understand the possibility that they may be bound by their written signed offers.

UCC 2–205 requires that a merchant offeror keep his/her offer open for the period he/she stated or for 3 months, whichever is less; the merchant must keep it open even though there is no consideration to do so. UCC 2–205 states: "An offer by a merchant to buy or sell goods in a signed writing by which its terms give assurance that it will be held open is not revocable, for lack of consideration, during the time stated or if no time is stated for a reasonable time, but in no event may such period of irrevocability exceed three months; but any such term of assurance on a form supplied by the offeree must be separately signed by the offeror." [Remember: merchants are persons in the business of selling those goods or are otherwise experts regarding those goods.]

[The CISG's and French law's more relaxed, expansive approach to "firm offers" is discussed at **pgs. 183-184; Emerson BL**.]

2. Options

An option is a separate contract to keep an offer open for a specified period. The offeror cannot revoke the offer during the option period, as the option is itself a valid contract – one supported by consideration. That is, the offeror has made a contract to hold her offer open for a set period, with her promise to keep it open the consideration from the offeror and with the offeree's payment, or promise to pay, for that option being the offeree's consideration.

> Example of Option: Jewelry Store Example
>
> A newlywed couple could not afford nice wedding rings. On their honeymoon, one early afternoon walking along New York's Fifth Avenue, they entered a jewelry store and saw a beautiful, very reasonably priced ring that the bride adored. The price was $5,000, a "steal" given its incredible quality. The jewelry store owner even said, "I like you kids," and he offered to sell the ring to them for $4,000 if they bought it that very day. "I'll keep the offer open until the end of the day," the owner said. The owner told them that he closed his

> store at 6:00 p.m., and – as the bride and groom left, the groom sadly said that the price was still too much, but – without his bride seeing the signal, the groom slyly gave a wink to the owner.
>
> At 5:30 p.m., having managed to sneak away from his bride on some excuse, the groom re–entered the store alone. He was set to splurge and take the store owner up on his offer. But the store owner cut him off. "I'm so sorry, kid, but a lady came in about an hour after you and your honey left. The lady wanted that ring. And she was ready to pay the list price. I like you kids, but I don't like you enough to turn down $5,000. Heck, I didn't even know if you'd come back."
>
> "But I winked. I winked!" the groom groaned and then whined. "And you said you'd keep your offer open until you closed. Well, I'm here to accept!" But could the groom force a sale? Was the owner's offer a firm offer? It was a firm offer, by a merchant, but it was not in writing. And it was not an option, because neither the bride nor the groom had given anything in return (a wink, by itself, was not enough to bind the groom, and thus to bind the store owner). Without that consideration, no option existed.
>
> Sadly, the more the groom thought about it, the more he realized he had no legal right to enforce the merchant's offer. A few hours older, but seemingly years wiser, the groom now knew the need to put things in writing and/or to make a "too good to be true" offer into an option, by giving a little (say, $10) in return.

Employees' exercising of stock options, and employers' terminations of such employees just before they could be invoked, have led to many recent lawsuits, especially in California, the home of options–happy Silicon Valley. While most claims have settled before trial, the few courts that have addressed options so far have begun to signal that they are receptive to employees alleging that management acted unfairly in firing someone and forcing him/her to miss out on sizable option gains. Also, more and more discrimination claims and other more common employment suits now seek lost stock options as part of the damages.

3. Unilateral Contracts on Occasion

A Problem When There Has Been Significant Performance (or, at least, the offeree has started in response to the offer) – can the offer still be revoked at any time until the completion of the requested performance (the acceptance) by the offeree?

There are, in general, four different court approaches concerning Unilateral Contracts:
1. Common law – still revocable
2. UCC approach (involving sales) – treat the situation as if it were a bilateral contract. The problem with that approach is: Now the unilateral offeree is bound. Thus, by not performing the offeree breaches (instead of simply not accepting a contract).
3. Reasonable time for offeree to complete – how much performance so far? How much is substantial? When should it be done? (treating the offer as if the offeree holds an option).
4. Quasi–contract – offeror can revoke, but must provide compensation to the offeree for its reasonable expenses.
5. Promissory Estoppel **(see pg. 109; Emerson BL)**

Promissory estoppel is a consideration substitute (an equity concept), with no real contract and no real acceptance (the offer is not revocable, because of the offeree's justifiable reliance on the offer). It is a last resort used by the legal system to correct injustices that have slipped through the cracks of established contract laws.[47]

So, it is much more than simply a way for an offer to be viewed as irrevocable (but we might as well give it a fuller discussion here in the text!).

---

[47] In countries where consideration is not a necessary element of contracts, promissory estoppel is an unnecessary concept (there is no need to resort to promissory estoppel): it is not needed to assist adjudicators in getting around the lack of consideration to somehow still enforce a promise. In these "non–consideration" nations (e.g., Russia), the promise, by itself, is enforceable, whether supported by reciprocal consideration or not.

For there to be promissory estoppel, "It is not sufficient that the gratuitous promise be made carelessly or thoughtlessly."[48] It occurs when "the promise, relying upon the gratuitous promise, takes certain action, or fails to take action, to his detriment…Unjustified reliance on a promise does not give rise to promissory estoppel."[49]

a. Elements of Promissory Estoppel
- Promisor intended to induce reliance on his/her promise.
- Promisor can foresee that the promise will induce justifiable reliance.
- Promisee justifiably relies on the promise and thereby substantially changes his/her position.
- Promisee thereby harmed.
- It would be grossly unfair not to enforce the Promisor's promise.

So, the doctrine of promissory estoppels is a device for enforcing promises without reciprocal consideration, such as some promises to make a gift, when the failure to enforce those promises would be unjust.[50]

Promissory Estoppel Examples

PROMISSORY ESTOPPEL SKIT: Diamond Jane (a regionally renowned night-club entertainer) & Arty Slaw (night-club owner and theater producer)

People may foolishly rely on promises.

Because there was no reciprocal consideration, when a promisor breaks his/her word, there is no contract to support you against that nasty, promise-breaker. The promise – the person who relied on the promise - may hope for legal relief outside of contract law, but the path here is slippery. The hopes rest on the law of promissory estoppel.

Slaw offered Jane a six-month run at Slaw's night-club. Jane did not accept, but later quit her current job. She then told Arty Slaw she was ready to start at his club.

There had been no contract, but Arty Slaw must have known that Jane might end her current run to come to his club. When Arty refused to give Jane a job, would that leave Arty's happy ship susceptible to running aground on promissory estoppel?

A PLEDGE TO GIVE MONEY TO A CHARITY

Charities ranging from the Red Cross to Save the Seals depend on their donors for their very existence. Their annual budgets and special projects are based on reliable sources of funds.

Traditionally, charities have been forgiving of unpaid promises; these <u>charities fear bad public relations from suing people to make them "fork over" the money</u>. Lately, though, a number of colleges, hospitals, and other charities have sued contributors for reneging on promises to make a gift.

---

b. Duties of Employers?

Employers generally are not required to provide severance or outplacement for people to whom the employer extended a job offer, and then withdrew the offer. But such workers have sometimes successfully sued to recover their relocation expenses or other costs. The theory often is promissory estoppel rather than breach of contract. One needs to show justifiable, detrimental reliance on the promisee's part because proving a promisor's breach is so difficult; for an "at will" employee – one not covered by a contract specifying a set term of employment or otherwise granting some "tenure" – job–offer

---

[48] Robert W. Emerson, *Business Law*. NY: Barron's Educational Series (6th ed., 2015), at 109.
[49] Id. at 109.
[50] RESTATEMENT (SECOND) OF CONTRACTS § 90 (1979).

rescissions are legal unless they violate a clear public policy or are against a statutory mandate such as non–discrimination. (And job–offer withdrawals appear regularly during economic slowdowns.) [51]

c. The Classic Case of a Retiree Relying on a Promise: *Feinberg v. Pfeiffer Co.* [52]

In 1910, when she was 17 years old, Anna Feinberg started working for Pfeiffer (a pharmaceutical making predecessor of Warner-Lambert) as a secretary and rose, over the following four decades, to the position of assistant treasurer. At the suggestion of Pfeiffer's president, on December 27, 1947 the board of directors, in passing a laudatory resolution about Feinberg, concluded, "Resolved, that the salary of Anna Sacks Feinberg be increased from $350.00 to $400.00 per month and that she be afforded the privilege of retiring from active duty in the corporation at any time she may elect to see fit so to do upon retirement pay of $200.00 per month, for the remainder of her life." Feinberg testified that (1) the pension plan completely surprised her, and (2) she would have continued in her employment whether or not such a resolution had been adopted.

The court noted:

"[T]here was no contract, oral or written, as to plaintiff's length of employment. [S]he was free to quit, and the defendant to discharge her, at any time. . . .
Plaintiff did continue to work for the defendant through June 30, 1949, on which date she retired. In accordance with the foregoing resolution, the defendant began paying her the sum of $200 on the first of each month. Mr. Lippman [the President] died on November 18, 1949, and was succeeded as president of the company by his widow. Because of an illness, she retired from that office and was succeeded in October, 1953, by her son–in–law, Sidney M. Harris. Mr. Harris testified that while Mrs. Lippman had been president she signed the monthly pension check paid plaintiff, but fussed about doing so, and considered the payments as gifts. After his election, he stated, a new accounting firm employed by the defendant questioned the validity of the payments to plaintiff on several occasions, and in the Spring of 1956, upon its recommendation, he consulted the Company's then attorney, Mr. Ralph Kalish. Harris testified that both Ernst and Ernst, the accounting firm, and Kalish told him there was no need of giving plaintiff the money. He also stated that he had concurred in the view that the payments to plaintiff were mere gratuities rather than amounts due under a contractual obligation, and that following his discussion with the Company's attorney plaintiff was sent a check for $100 on April 1, 1956. Plaintiff declined to accept the reduced amount, and this action followed."

By the time of the subsequent trial Anna Feinberg was sick with cancer. But she apparently had been in good health until then. Instead, her age (63 in April 1956) had left her without any real prospects of finding new employment. [53]

The court found enforceable the company's promise of a pension, even though Feinberg gave no consideration for that promise, because promissory estoppel makes a promise enforceable if the promisee foreseeably and detrimentally relies on it, which Mrs. Feinberg had. She foreseeably relied on the promise by retiring before she otherwise would have; her reliance was detrimental because she gave up a much larger salary to take the pension. The application of the law of promissory estoppel to these facts is simple

---

[51] Federal or state laws may also protect employees who retire relying upon a promise related to their pensions. In Central Laborers' Pension Fund v. Heinz, 541 U.S. 739 (2004), the U.S. Supreme Court interpreted the federal law known as ERISA (Employee Retirement Income Security Act) and cutbacks in pension benefits promised to workers. The high court held that a multi–employer retirement plan cannot make changes to the plan that further restrict where employees taking early retirement may seek new work. The court ruled that the plan's adding restrictions is the same as taking away benefits, which is illegal under ERISA.
[52] 322 S.W.2d 163 (Mo. App. 1959).
[53] The appeals court took judicial notice of the fact (i.e., on its own declared to be self-evident) that Feinberg's age made "virtually impossible" any employment opportunities comparable to what she had before retiring at age 57.

and straightforward, and it could only have helped her equity case that Mrs. Feinberg appears to have been virtuous, the promise–giving late president a good and grateful man, and his cruel and selfish heirs to have been heartless number–crunchers.

III. ACCEPTANCE   (see pgs. 103-104; Emerson BL)

A. Again, an Objective Standard

Acceptances are evaluated by the same Objective Intent Standard as for Offers. Who and what is "reasonable," therefore, is an issue for determining the lawfulness of an alleged offer or acceptance. A "reasonable person," according to Oxford Professor P.S. Attiyah, comes in one of two definitions – (1) Descriptive: what parties knew or should have known at the time – this approach goes back at least to the time of Thomas Aquinas (1225-1274), a Natural Law philosopher who emphasized "the essence" of the contract; (2) Normative: to fill in the gaps, one may proceed from a personal (individual "reasonable person") standard to a "communal standard" (this is a more recent alternative "definition" of the "reasonable person" for purposes of contract law).

B. The UCC – Sales Contract Formation ("Get the Big Picture")

Uniform Commercial Code Section 2–204 articulates a fundamental public policy governing the law of sales:
> "A contract for the sale of goods may be made in any manner sufficient to show agreement, including conduct by both parties which recognizes the existence of such a contract.
> An agreement sufficient to constitute a contract for sale may be found even though the moment of its making is undetermined.
> Even though one or more of its terms are left open, a contract for sale does not fail for indefiniteness if the parties have intended to make a contract and there is a reasonably certain basis for giving an appropriate remedy."

OFFER AND ACCEPTANCE: TRAPEZE DRAWINGS
One trapeze artist (A) hangs from his legs and swings with his arms outstretched while the other trapeze artist (B) leaps, arms outstretched, toward A. Assume that A's outstretched arms are an offer, with the other person's arms clasping them being an acceptance. Would A's withdrawal of his arms be a revocation? If so, then, as B plunges downward (hopefully, to a net!), she cannot be consoled by contract law. There would then be no agreement, hence no breach. (Maybe she'd have a tort suit, but that is a different issue.)

C. Can Silence be Acceptance?

Example: You come home to find a huge piece of modern art in your front yard. A note attached to this sculpture reads, "An Original by Scilla Octavia Sculptrice ("SOS"). Price: $5,000." You don't want to pay five dollars, let alone $5,000, for this "art." And you wonder how many people and what kind of machinery would be needed to haul it away. As many have remarked when first seeing the sculpture, "that piece of ___ is ginormous!"

There is no acceptance simply because you have not somehow removed the sculpture from your property. If it were something you could easily return through reasonable, inexpensive methods, it would be wise for you to do so (and ask for reimbursement from SOS). Otherwise, simply contact SOS to get it removed. And be there to make sure no damage is done during the removal process!

1. The General Rule: Silence is *Not* Acceptance

Imagine that one day you walk out of your front door and nearly trip over a huge box on your welcome mat. You excitedly bring a shipment from Encyclopedia Fantastica (EF) into your happy home. You immediately commence reading volume A, starting with the entry for "Aardvark." Wow, you have the first five volumes of the multi, multi–volume set of the EF encyclopedia. You have always dreamed of having a set of EF encyclopedia, and at least you now have volumes A through E!

A week later, you are still reading your new encyclopedia volumes when a letter arrives in the mail thanking you for accepting the delivery of the EF encyclopedia and dunning you $1,499 for the lovely deluxe set, the first five volumes of which you have received and the rest of which will be arriving shortly upon your prompt payment of the amount due!

But you never ordered these books. You never had even communicated with someone from EF. Did your taking the EF shipment from your welcome mat into your cheery home constitute an acceptance of an EF offer to sell you the EF deluxe encyclopedia set for the standard price? The answer, much to your relief, is – absent a more compelling set of facts on EF's behalf – you are not obliged to pay EF. EF may send someone to retrieve the encyclopedia that were delivered to you, or work out other arrangements that are at EF's time and expense, not yours. But normally people cannot be forced to take action – utter some response or otherwise do something – or else be found to have accepted an offer by their silence.

So, for the basic question – "Can silence be acceptance?" – the answer, ordinarily, is "no."
The big question: How is it reasonable to put the duty on the other side to respond and/or return items?

2. The Post Office and Charities

The Postal Reorganization Act (1970) outlaws as an unfair trade practice the mailing of unordered merchandise. (Exceptions are free samples, mailings from charitable agencies, and mailings by mistake.) The Act states that unsolicited merchandise sent by U.S. mail may be reclaimed, used, discarded, or disposed of in any manner, without the individual incurring any obligation to the sender. 39 U.S.C. § 3009.

> **A Side Morals and Law Issue: Charities**
> Charities, hoping for a return contribution, sometimes send to potential donors certain items, such as address labels printed with the recipient's name and address. Under Federal Trade Commission rules, anyone who receives unordered merchandise in the mail typically can treat it as a gift. But is there a moral obligation to make a donation if you use the unsolicited item(s) a charity sends you?[54]

3. The Exceptions: When Silence Can Be Acceptance

There are only three situations in which, ordinarily, <u>silence may be acceptance</u>:

    i. Similar prior course of dealings/industry custom.

---

[54] Assume that the charity – in sending, on its own, the address labels – was upfront in asking for a contribution. While there is no legal duty to pay anything to the charity, perhaps there is a moral duty to also be "upstanding": make a contribution, at least if you <u>use</u> the address labels. No doubt the charity wants people to think about the charity and feel some guilt if, instead of simply tossing them away, the recipient uses the labels, but without making a donation.

When there has been such a pattern of dealings or an industry custom, then a party who wishes to change the customary practice or dealing must not remain silent but, in order to reject the offer (and not be bound by a silence-as-acceptance arrangement), must affirmatively present his rejection to the other party.

<u>Example: The Automatically Renewed Insurance Policy</u>

Suppose that Samuel Adams informed insurer John Hancock that he would like to purchase fire insurance on property Adams owned on Bunker Hill, near Boston. John Hancock accepted by issuing the policy. Because they are patriots, every year on July 4th the policy was automatically renewed, and a bill was mailed to Samuel Adams about two weeks later.

After several such years, on July 11th a fire totally destroys the property, and John Hancock refuses to pay the face value of the policy on the grounds that silence does not constitute acceptance.

However, Samuel Adams has recourse under contract law. John Hancock's conduct has reasonably led Samuel Adams to believe that the insurance has been granted for another year. If John Hancock wishes to cancel the policy, he must inform Adams in advance, thereby giving him a reasonable time to find insurance elsewhere. Of course, Adams will have to pay that year's premium to be entitled to the insurance coverage – and the payment on the damage – for the property.

ii. Offeree Accepted Benefits

As a matter of fairness, at some point a relatively minor effort may be called for on the part of the offeree if (1) there was a recurring pattern of benefits and/or if (2) and/or delay through silence would cause the subject matter to become unmarketable (or other damages would be sustained). For example, you discover that you are now receiving a newspaper or cable television subscription that you did not order. You are not contractually responsible for something to which you did not agree. On the other hand, since it would be so small an imposition on you to simply notify the newspaper or cable company, your failure to make such an effort could undermine any argument for allowing you to retain benefits without some compensatory payment on your part.

iii. <u>Parties</u> Agree to a "Silence as Acceptance" Arrangement

Example: A "Book of the Month" Club

Imagine that Gus Customer acquires twelve books for one dollar. Each month thereafter he is set to automatically receive another book, and must pay the "regular price" (a price some might call exorbitant!) – unless Gus affirmatively states (e.g., in writing) that the company should <u>not</u> send the book.

D. When Is Acceptance Effective?

1. The General Principle

Acceptance can turn the offer into a contract. When does acceptance occur?

<u>Unilateral contract</u> – when performance/forbearance is completed.

<u>Bilateral contract</u> – when offeree gives to the offeror the promise that the offeror requested from the offeree.

2. The Mailbox Rule

The Mailbox Rule is also called the "Deposit Acceptance Rule." It is a principle of contract law that, unless the offer states otherwise, an acceptance using the same method of transmission as the offer is effective when the acceptance is sent (when the offeree places it in the mailbox or otherwise relinquishes control over it).

E. Freedom–of–Contract Versus the Advantages of Standardized Forms

One very important freedom is our freedom, through our elected representatives, to establish difficult, hard–to–understand laws. (Two of those laws may be the Mailbox Rule, discussed above, and the Rule for Resolving the Battle of the Forms – which is discussed below.)

But the most important freedom, at least in American contract law, probably is not the freedom to have the general law changed, but the freedom of parties to a contract to make their own little contract laws – to change or avoid the effects of various contract law principles.

1. Standardized Forms

The freedom–of–contract doctrine originated when most contracts were individually negotiated by the parties. Much of modern contracting is different. Industrialization, mass marketing, and the rise of large corporations have led to the prevalence of contracting through standardized forms.

There are three advantages to standardized forms, as they: (1) Reduce transaction costs by relieving parties of the burden of individually negotiating and drafting contract provisions that regulate relatively routine exchanges; (2) Reduce agency costs by limiting the contractual discretion of subordinates within a corporate hierarchy; and (3) Facilitate centralized control by harmonizing contracts throughout a firm's national or international business activities.

However, there is a practical and legal problem with standardized forms. Since the forms may make negotiations unnecessary, the parties may never have really considered or understood the standardized terms. This problem continues in the digital age. An entire industry has sprung up around the use of eXtensible Markup Language (XML), adopted by a computer–industry standards body, as a way to identify data. Translation mechanisms (from ventures such as WebMethods Inc., Extricity Software Inc., and OnDisplay Inc.) allow companies to exchange key bits of data, such as inventory information, pricing and delivery status, and quantity, regardless of the different types of computer systems used by those companies. In effect, these mechanisms make it easier for companies, with differing forms – and even different digital "languages" (converted into XML and then back into the original computer language) – to reach contracts, or at least think they have!

There is a trend in the courts to infer and find a contract if parties seem to have implied one, even though the parties did not specify the terms. Courts thus try to find terms for the parties.

2. Battle of the Forms   (see pg. 184; Emerson BL)

There are lots of forms. For example, in one field (health insurance) there are over 30 different health insurers, with many, many affiliated entities, each with tens of thousands or hundreds of thousands of different terms.

> *A Sale of Goods: Some Introductory Information about the Battle of the Forms*
> In a typical battle of the forms scenario, the parties negotiated the essential terms of the contract (e.g., quantity, quality, and delivery date) but neglected to bargain over items that are less immediately important (for example, whether disputes will be subject to arbitration, for how long a period after delivery the buyer may assert complaints of defects, or on whom the risk of loss during shipment falls). The parties then exchanged standard printed forms, each of which was filled with fine print listing all kinds of terms advantageous to the party that drew up the form. Often goods have been shipped, received, and paid for before both parties have expressly accepted the same document as their contract. As a result of these exchanges, two questions arise: (1) Is there a contract? (2) If so, what are its terms?
> The UCC calls a truce in the battle of the forms by effectively abolishing the mirror image rule. It is not necessary for an offer and acceptance to match exactly in order for a contract for

> the sale of goods to exist. Adding to or modifying terms in the offer does not make the acceptance a counteroffer, as is true under common law.

The use of forms saves on transaction costs; there is no "reinventing the wheel." But, in the world of business, there are variations between forms – they are similar from business to business, but rarely are identical. So, there are legal problems with Standardized Forms. The main difficulty stems from the Mirror Image Rule, which is the legal principle that the offer and acceptance, in order to form a contract, must mirror each other exactly – the terms must all be the same. The mirror image rule produces practical problems for a modern society: if, for instance, an offer has 17 provisions and 229 subparts, then the acceptance must coincide exactly with the offer or else it is a counteroffer, not an acceptance.

The rule creates two perverse incentives: (1) it encourages parties to read closely their forms and to individually negotiate terms that do not match – this drastically erodes the cost savings associated with form contracts; (2) it rewards opportunistic behavior by allowing a party to repudiate a good faith, genuine agreement when the party's true motive is simply to "weasel out" of an arrangement that has become less profitable than originally predicted (i.e., the party seizes upon non–conforming forms as an excuse to renege on the agreement). [55]

a. UCC 2-207

i. UCC 2–207 (Additional Terms in Acceptance or Confirmation) states:
"A definite and seasonable expression of acceptance or a written confirmation which is sent within a reasonable time operates as an acceptance even though it states terms additional to or different from those offered or agreed upon, unless acceptance is expressly made conditional on assent to the additional or different terms.

"The additional terms are to be construed as proposals for addition to the contract. Between merchants such terms become part of the contract unless: (a) the offer expressly limits acceptance to the terms of the offer; (b) they materially alter it; or (c) notification of objection to them has already been given or is given within a reasonable time after notice of them is received.

"Conduct by both parties which recognizes the existence of a contract is sufficient to establish a contract for sale although the writings of the parties do not otherwise establish a contract. In such case the terms of the particular contract consist of those terms on which the writings of the parties agree, together with any supplementary terms incorporated under any other provisions of this Act."

ii. Resolution of Issues under UCC 2-207

In the United States, UCC § 2–207, for sales contracts, modifies the common law "mirror image" rule. This Uniform Commercial Code provision represents one of the major attempts to reduce the costs created by welshing, while simultaneously protecting the efficiency gains generated by using forms to make a contract. So, if there is a sale of goods (and thus 2–207 applies), these are the two questions to answer to resolve a "Battle of the Forms."

> 1. Is there a material (substantial, significant) difference between the offer and the supposed acceptance (differences such as on price, quantity,[56] or subject matter)?

---

[55] A Homer Simpsonism: "Marge, don't discourage the boy! Weaseling out of things is important to learn. It's what separates us from the animals! Except the Weasel."
[56] A difference in quantity typically would constitute a material difference. The amount of a property or service should be crucial. It is quite a difference to sell or buy 500,000 bushels of corn or just an ear of corn. There is a trend in the courts to infer and find a contract if parties seem to have implied one.

- Yes? (e.g., whether it is $9 or $10 for each widget) – Then there is no acceptance; the responding form is a counteroffer.
- No? (e.g., perhaps an arbitration provision, choice of law term, or a different color). Then proceed to the second question.

2. <u>Are one or more of the parties nonmerchants?</u>

Yes? The "offer" form (the initial proposal) is considered to be the contract. The "acceptance" form's differing provisions are just proposals (for the offeror to consider).

No? (Both parties are merchants) –the "acceptance" form becomes the contract unless (a) the offer expressly limits acceptance to the offer's terms, or (b) within a reasonable time, the offeror objects to the "acceptance" terms (then, in the event of a or b, the offer's terms become the contract)

So How to Avoid the "Battle?"

Merchants should limit acceptance to the terms of the offer (i.e., the offer states, "this is what you need to do; all else is a material difference"),

or

Merchants should closely monitor the form of all "acceptances"

(and nonmerchants, if they do not want to be stuck with an offer, should make sure that their "accepting" terms are conditional (in effect, a counteroffer)).

b. Criticism of UCC 2–207

Many critics, including numerous legal scholars, observe that UCC § 2–207 originally was drafted to deal with the "welsher" problem, but has been inappropriately applied to determine the very terms of the contract. An economic criticism of § 2–207 is that it does not economize on transaction costs. Under 2–207, either party that ignores the fine print faces the possibility that the other party will introduce surprising and uncustomary terms into the exchange.

It is probable that, whenever UCC Article 2 is revised, the new version will replace 2–207 with a less "technical" approach. (Note, though, such a change is still years in the future. I.e., you still need to know about § 2–207 for current Business Law courses!)

c. A Different, Less Formalistic Approach to the Battle of the Forms

Under the UCC, the CISG, and the national law of many nations (e.g., Germany), business customs may supply the contract terms when standardized forms conflict. When German law applies, the parties can rely on court provided terms to assure that the ultimate contract will be customary, reasonable, and presumably not overly harsh or oppressive. This approach is easy to administer, and it should bring stability and predictability to the law. This is different from a strict interpretation of UCC § 2–207, where either the offeror's form or the acceptor's form will control (and either side ignores the fine print at his/her own peril).

The customs approach gives the parties a strong incentive to master business customs (a duty to know the industry standard). Such mastery is essential to all market economies; shared customs forestall misunderstandings between parties and generally promote contractual endeavors. Thus this focus on customs may actually encourage and reflect deference to autonomy because it tells parties what "standard" terms to expect and how to avoid those terms (by express contract provisions).

Because most business customs reflect an economic logic, assigning the contractual duties and risks to the parties that can address such concerns in the most efficient manner, the customs approach should keep transaction costs to a minimum.

Some important legal matters are not subject to consideration requirements – these non-contracts include wills and gifts.

> **An area of law we will not explore, although clearly very important, is wills and estates. So there will be no testing on this, but – if you like –** *<u>read this at your leisure and (again, no testing on it)</u>* **you can also read Chapter 21 of the Barron's book.**
>
> *The YouTube video, Wills and Trusts* (see "Wills trusts" at robertwemersonufl), *talks briefly about these matters.*
>
> An old saying is that there are only two things assured of in life. One of them, of course, is taxes, and the other, of course, is the grim reaper, death. Because of that eventuality, it behooves us to at least consider the legal document which is most pressing in this area, and that is the will. For a number of people, a will would not really be necessary. If you are so young that you don't have any dependents and you really don't have much in the way of assets, you probably don't need a will. But once you've acquired assets, once you have a stream of income that you've decided you need to pass down to others, once you have people who depend upon you, particularly minor children, it really is important to consider having a will. The trend in the law has been to make wills a lot easier to understand and perhaps even execute without necessarily the assistance of lawyers. If you have a very typical allocation of what you want done with your assets and you don't have any complications such as a second or third marriage, stepchildren, and difficulty in terms of allocating business assets vs. personal assets, then you might be able to simply use a form that you get off the Internet or elsewhere. Once things become more complex, once one acquires a substantial amount of income or wealth, once one has complexities vis-à-vis family relations or business opportunities, then it probably is a good thing to get a lawyer involved, an expert, because the forms probably will not be sufficient and you really need someone in this area who can explain it much better than a form could.
>
> The interesting thing to me in this field, of course, is that because wills are executed ahead of when a death may actually occur, we are often talking about decades that pass before the execution of a will and the actual interpretation of it upon someone's demise. This makes this field much different from other areas of law where the time compression is much shorter, where you have maybe just a few years to decide 'are you going to sue over that alleged tort?', where you have a short period of time to decide 'are you going to enter into a contract?' or 'what are you going to do about an alleged breach of contract?' Wills and estates are not the same, they often take place and interpretation occurs over a stretch of decades, over a stretch of, perhaps, generations. This is why wills and estates lawyers, trust lawyers, may be more aligned with doctors in this field than are other lawyers. There's an old saying about doctors that goes they have an advantage over other professions because when they make a mistake, the doctors get to bury their mistakes. That doesn't apply for most lawyers but for wills and estates, if there are mistakes, what we're often talking about is interpreting what someone did or intended, perhaps decades ago. It opens up all sorts of interesting issues because of the expansion of time and the finality of death that you often do not have in other areas of law.

IV. CONSIDERATION   (see pgs. 105-110; Emerson BL)

A. Seals: A Vestige of Times Before Consideration Reigned Supreme

Before there was "consideration," there were seals - symbols of important, solemn vows such as for the transfer of real estate.

An "X" for a Kiss: Our custom of putting X's at the end of letters and notes to symbolize kisses grew out of medieval legal practices. In order <u>to indicate good faith and honesty in those days</u>, the sign of St. Andrew – a cross – was placed after the signature on all important documents. Thereafter, contracts and agreements were not considered binding until each signer added St. Andrew's cross after his name. <u>Then he was required to kiss the document to further guarantee faithful performance</u> of his obligations. The cross was drawn hurriedly, and often it was tilted and looked much like the letter "X". Over the centuries, the origin of the ceremony was forgotten. But people still associated the "X" with the kiss instead of the pledge of good faith, and the custom has continued into modern times.

In past centuries, s*eals* were used (consideration was not yet a requirement). Even after consideration arose as a contract law concept, the seal tended to be a substitute for consideration until the last several decades.

Now, the UCC and state law generally have abolished use of the seal as a substitute for consideration. However, <u>in a few special areas, seals may be required</u>: e.g., a notarized seal or corporate seal for some formal documents such as real estate deeds.

Some states still let the seal extend the limitations period for suing on an alleged breach of contract. The *practical effect of a seal* is that it may make the contract (and that there was a contract) even clearer.

Historically, consideration concepts can involve the exchange of symbols, illustrated by, for example, the symbols associated with the transfer of property (e.g., twigs for land, car keys for a vehicle, etc.). Property has always had a special, more formalistic approach. YOUTUBE – property_law_3mins50secs at robertwemersonufl

---

B. From Formalism to Consideration

In Roman times, the law did not care whether there was an agreement, but whether formalities had been met (the completion of formalities, such as sacred rituals). More recently, the law has looked to more indications or actual manifestations of consent (e.g., a seal; a writing; and certain operative words). That is referred to as "the legal alphabet" – just looking at the caption, wrote the 20th Century legal scholar, Lon Fuller. This modern approach is to not just have forms, but to channel the parties' intention through legally recognizable forms.

So, what is consideration, and when does consideration exist?

Consideration is "any lawful alteration of responsibilities that is given in exchange for the other person's consideration" ('his/her lawful alteration of responsibilities').[57] Consideration is based on the idea of *quid pro quo*... ([this for that]; 'something for something'): some action, forbearance, or promise. In almost all contracts, consideration is required for enforceability."[58]

Consideration entails a bargained for exchange: a "legal detriment" (or benefit), not necessarily an economic or material loss or benefit but any lawful alteration of responsibilities (e.g., giving up one's right to sue). Consideration involves changing one's duties: acting or forbearance (refraining from acting); or promising to do or refrain from doing. For example, agreeing not to sue someone is a form of consideration. Imagine that as a professor of business law walks past a note–taking student, the student's pen slips and slices into the professor! The professor acts rather nonchalant; he/she extracts the pen from his his/her thigh, returns it to the student, and then says, "That'll be $5,000, please!" In effect, the professor

---

[57] Robert W. Emerson, *Business Law* NY: Barron's Educational Series (2015, 6th ed.) , at 105.
[58] Id. at 105.

is asking for money in return for the professor's agreeing to release the student from any claim of liability.[59]

Traditionally, <u>consideration provides a symbolic function</u> (just as seals have done): evincing the parties' consent and providing a warning to each party that their agreement has a legal effect. This function means that the consideration concept does not primarily serve as a safeguard against opportunism. In keeping with the notion of consideration as being merely "symbolic" – a legal concept rather than an economic doctrine based upon the parties' exchange of goods/services/etc. of fairly equal value – courts recognize that nominal consideration is sufficient because it meets the purpose of showing the parties' consent and of warning the parties' about the binding, legal nature of an agreement.

Property

Property law is an ancient, venerable concept basic to the law [and *predating the concept of consideration*]. In fact, it was perhaps the most important reason for law in the Middle Ages - the recording of deeds and the noting of property. Land was the basis for wealth, it was the basis for power, and it was what political and social structure arose from. So, in honor of that I am decked out in my medieval garb, and I brought along a "No Trespassing" sign, which I assure you I did not have to trespass to acquire. In fact, if you go back to medieval England the most basic tort was to trespass, to go on someone's property without his or her permission or to stay there after the permission had been withdrawn.

Land was at the apex of all the structures in medieval England. Now, property includes a lot, lot more than land, but I think it helps you to understand property interests if you can at least understand (at a very basic level) this tangible property interest, the very land we stand upon. Contracts back then were so basic in this area of property interest that what we sometimes see is they would put all sorts of symbolism into their transactions. For instance, a sale of land from one medieval owner to another was not under-girded by consideration, it was not really under-girded by a concept of quid pro quo; it was represented through a symbolic transaction in which one person would literally give to the other person a stick, a rock, a piece of dirt, a clump of sod, or something else from the land to symbolize that you are now the owner of the land and it has now been entrusted to you.

To make this even more symbolic and even more significant, the documents that reflected this, the deeds, any mortgages if any loans were involved, any easements that were recorded and the like, were almost always recorded through a very formalized process of signatures, of notarization, and of seals. People would get out their wax and they would emboss these seals and this was the notion. This is so fundamental we have to make sure we have very good recording. So much of property law really deals with recording of interests and making sure that others are accorded notice, so that no one else can supersede your interests. There's no way they can take it from you because they know that it is your land and you are asserting an interest in this. This also occurs in other fields as well, far and apart from real estate, but that is the crux of it. All law in the field of property really emanates from and takes from this historic tradition which goes back to the Middle Ages, and real property estates.

Questions for Thought:

1. Why do courts, even today, care more about the "symbolism" of consideration than about the "adequacy of value" (consideration in economic terms)? Do you agree with that approach?

---

[59] Another example of consideration is that someone agrees to pay rent in order to have the opportunity to live in an apartment. This tenant is entitled to inhabit the premises and is not evicted so long as he/she makes payments.

> 2. Should real estate contracts continue to require greater formalism than other contracts, such as the requirement that there be a writing and a mandate that certain documents be filed with the government?

C. Adequacy of Consideration

Although not called by those terms (it was "laesio enormis"), adequacy of consideration was a major concept in earlier law. Nowadays, as long as there was some consideration, the adequacy of that consideration is NOT a legal issue.

A court will not strike down an agreement for lacking consideration simply because the court feels the consideration is inadequate or unequal.[60]

> ADEQUACY OF CONSIDERATION: Evan Longoria, Brett Gardner, and a Baseball Hat
> An example of perhaps a stupid agreement, but a contract (offer, acceptance, consideration, etc.), nonetheless: Evan Longoria of the Tampa Bay Rays is talking to Brett Gardner of the New York Yankees: "Try wearing this Tampa Bay Rays hat – at least an hour a day, for one week. I'll give you $10,000." Gardner responds: "OK. I could really use, I mean, I really need that money!"
> **Consideration does not have to be much. The same is true for goods or for services.**

"Adequacy of consideration is not an issue for the court *unless* (a) there was no consideration at all, or (b) in *equity* cases, there was grossly inadequate consideration."[61] There are gross examples (where there is insufficiency of consideration because things are so stark).

An Example: a liquidated sum is to be paid, and one party pays much less than the obvious, objective value (with little room for argument) – e.g., some Minitenders for Securities (where the fair market value, as established by the actual trading levels, are far higher than what the minitender offers were for).

Adequacy of consideration could well be an issue in non–contract law. For example, in tax law the IRS examines so–called overpayments — without adequate consideration — re: value of work (e.g., to child workers in a family corporation); those payments presumably are intended to avoid taxes at a higher rate (and thus the IRS challenges them as not being reflective of a fair market value, good faith exchange).

In equity cases, courts may not enforce a contract (order equitable relief – e.g., an injunction, specific performance) if the complaining party furnished grossly inadequate consideration (compared to what the other side provided).

In equity, courts are more likely to evaluate the alleged inadequacy of consideration than for common law cases. Combined with other evidence, that allegedly inadequate consideration may show that someone was defrauded, bamboozled, mistaken, insane, or under duress. (So courts may look at the adequacy of consideration in equity cases, but not common law cases.)

---

[60] "An agreement to pay a small amount of money in return for a larger amount of money is *not* enforceable; this is merely an agreement to make a gift of the difference." Robert W. Emerson, *Business Law*. NY: Barron's Educational Series (6th ed. 2015), at 106.

[61] Id. at 106.

Courts generally do not evaluate the adequacy of consideration unless it is grossly one–sided. The reason is that people attach different values to different things, depending upon such variables as tastes, interests, desires, and needs. Personal values are subjective. Whether a person has benefited from a contract depends on subjective values, on how the person feels. The law acknowledges people's freedom to contract, and it respects their judgment as to the legal value of the consideration they receive.[62]

> "COMPARATIVE" CONSIDERATION AND A BIBLE EXAMPLE: The Laborers in the Vineyard (adapted from the Bible, Book of Matthew, Chapter 20, verses 1-16).
>
> The kingdom of heaven is like a man that went out early in the morning to hire laborers for his vineyard. When he had agreed with the laborers for a shekel a day, he sent them into his vineyard. About the third hour, he saw others standing idle in the marketplace. And he said to them, "Go to the vineyard and labor, and I will pay you."
>
> Again he went to the marketplace about the sixth and ninth hour, and did likewise. And about the eleventh hour he went out, found others standing idle, and said to them, "Why stand here idle?" They replied, "Because no man has hired us." He responded, "Go to the vineyard; and whatever is right you shall receive from me."
>
> When night fell, the vineyard owner called the laborers and gave them their pay – all of them received a shekel.
>
> But those hired first in the morning supposed that they should have received more. They murmured, "these last workers labored for just one hour, yet you have made them equal to us, which bore the burden and heat of the entire day."
>
> The owner answered, "Friend, I do you no wrong. Didn't you agree with me to be paid a shekel? Take what is yours, and go on your way: Is it not lawful for me to do what I will with my money? How is my generosity a wrong to you? The last shall be first, and the first last: many are called, but few are chosen."
>
> The shekel was valuable consideration, and the men who started work early in the morning exercised their freedom to contract by agreeing to accept it for a day's work. The fact that someone else worked less and received the same ordinarily is of no significance in contract law (the only issue might be public policy – e.g., discrimination law).
>
> A blunder in bargaining – one side with a better deal > That is not inadequacy of consideration.

D. Love and Affection as Consideration?

There tends to be a continuum, with the more something has economic value the more likely courts are to treat it as consideration, while the more it is simply a moral obligation the harder it is for courts to speculate and hold that it is – for contract law purposes – consideration.

```
            "Moral" consideration?     Economic Obligation
            <————————————————————————>
            Moral Obligation           Economic Value
```

---

[62] For example, imagine that a dramatic professor on the legal environment of business has produced some exciting business law videos, known as "Emersons." A secondary market has developed for these "classic" videos. Here is the possible dialogue for the purchase of such types:
BUYER OF VIDEOS: "This is such a good deal. I am glad we agreed upon the right price. Five hundred dollars for even one Emerson video is such a bargain!"
SELLER OF VIDEOS: "I agree. And you get two! It is sad to part with them, but I know you will like them."
Have they reached a lawful contract? They have. One may doubt whether one side got a good deal ($500 for two "Emersons" seems awfully low!), but a court ordinarily will not second–guess what the parties have freely agreed upon.

There is *no* consideration in the following case.

> *Mills v. Wyman*: Moral Obligations
>
> In *Mills v. Wyman*, 20 Mass. (3 Pick.) 207 (Mass. 1825), the Supreme Judicial Court found that a moral duty did not compel the defendant to pay on a promise. Levi Wyman, age 25 and long living apart from and independent of his family, fell ill on his sea voyage return from abroad; poor and in distress, Levi was cared for by Daniel Mills for 15 days until he died. A few days later, after all Mills' expenses had been incurred, Seth Wyman, Levi's father, learned of what had transpired and wrote Mills promising to pay those expenses. Later, Seth Wyman decided not to pay, and Mills sued him.
>
> The Court held that the father's moral obligation was not adequate consideration for his promise to pay. As a general rule, a moral obligation may only form consideration for an express promise where good or valuable consideration once existed, that is, for (1) debts barred by the statute of limitations, (2) debts incurred by children, or (3) debts previously discharged by bankruptcy. In essence, for Wyman's type of promise, the common law leaves it up to the defendant's conscience whether to pay back a purely moral debt. And because the son was an adult and his own agent, the father had no legal duty to care for him; so a promise founded upon the debt of the man who cared for the son had no legally binding force on the father.[63]
>
> This case is analogous to the hypothetical case where a doctor treats an unconscious person who dies without regaining consciousness. The difference is that we do not know whether Levi Wyman, during his convalescence, expressed the intent, or lack of intent, to repay the plaintiff. Mills probably would have had a better shot at Levi Wyman's estate than at the father, who had nothing to do with the situation except the letter he sent after his son's death.

E. Not Consideration

We now consider three situations which do not constitute consideration.

1. Past Consideration

Because the Promisor gets nothing in the present for his promise, the Promisor can renege on his/her promise. The "Naming the Grandson 'August' Example"– an Iowa Supreme Court case, *Lanfier v. Lanfier*, 288 N.W. 104 (Iowa 1939) – and another Iowa "naming" case (naming the child "John"), *Daily v. Minnick*, 91 N.W. 913 (Iowa 1902), stand for the proposition that someone who promises money in return for having a newborn child named after him/her cannot be bound to that promise (assuming it is not already against public policy) if the promise came after the child had received that name. The parents need to negotiate with the rich relative who has the "funny name" before the child is named!

> An Ethical Problem: Is Altruism Its Own Reward?
>
> A person who performs the task necessary to obtain a reward, but who does not know about the reward while performing that task, ordinarily would not have a contractual right to receive the reward when he/she later finds out about that reward. As a matter of ethics, though, should he/she get the reward? Because he/she acted without being prodded by a reward, his/her motives are purer than those of others who performed the deed solely or mainly because of the reward offer. But only the latter persons may be legally entitled to the reward, if the altruistic persons latter are arguing, in effect, rights due to their past consideration.

---

[63] Just to Show that Cases Are NOT Always What They Appear To Be:
Some research indicates that the son had not died and had not even been at sea. Geoffrey R. Watson, *In the Tribunal of Conscience: Mills v. Wyman Reconsidered*, 71 Tulane L. Rev. 1749 (1997).

2. Illusory Promises

A *nudum pactum* is a "naked (illusory) promise," with the promisor not really bound as he/she gives the promisee no genuine assurances. Instead, the promisor is making statements such as "I'll reward you in the future," "You will receive all that I wish to provide!" and "I will pass onto you all that I decide you should get!"

Bonuses? Are they discretionary? ("Bonuses to be provided `if <u>our</u> profits are pretty darn good'"; "You'll get something some time or other.") The highly discretionary nature of the promisor's position undermines an alleged promisor's claim that he furnished consideration. Can the promisor postpone, cancel or not give a bonus in the first place? Again, that shows the promise is illusory.

Other Examples of Illusory promises
"All that I decide to buy,"
"Payable if we make a bundle!" or
"To be paid if we can afford it"
There is no way to pin down the promisor, and thus it is an illusory promise.

This is becoming much more an issue as employers move away from automatic or uniform pay raises to "merit pay" and performance–based bonuses. Lawsuits and arbitration of disputes, especially when an employee has quit or been fired and does not receive the bonus (e.g., for bringing in business) he/she expected, have been growing dramatically.

(These suits are particularly a problem for securities firms, telecommunications businesses, auto dealerships, clothing wholesalers/retailers, publishers, and software entities.)

3. Pre–existing duties

When there is a pre-existing duty, another contract already imposes that same duty.[64] For example, a police officer ordinarily already has a duty to try to capture criminals, so he/she would probably not be eligible for a reward offering money or some other prize for helping to capture criminals. And here are two more examples:
(a) A debtor owes $17,000. The debtor wants to settle this debt for $11,000. The creditor agrees to forgive the $6,000.
(b) A building contractor finds that it has bid poorly. It refuses to complete the job unless the owner agrees to add 20% to the contract price. The owner agrees.
The likely legal result for these two examples is that these promises, made without any new consideration, are unenforceable.

> *Alaska Packers Ass'n v. Domenico*, 117 F. 99 (9th Cir. 1902)
> A group of men were hired to work in Alaska. They left San Francisco, but – when nearing Alaska – refused to do any work unless they received a pay raise (from the $50 for the season they had each been promised to twice that much – $100 for the season). The superintendent agreed. Later, the company refused to pay more than the $50 per man.
> The court used the reasoning directly from a Minnesota Supreme Court Case (*King v. Railway Co.*, 61 Minn. 482): "No astute reasoning can change the plain fact that the party who refuses to perform, and thereby coerces a promise from the other party to the contract to pay him an increased compensation for doing that which he is legally bound to do, takes an unjustifiable advantage of the necessities of the

---

[64] The general principle, found in the common law and still usually good law, is that merely promising to do what one already has a legal duty to do furnishes no consideration.

> other party. Surely it would be a travesty of justice to hold that the party so making the promise for extra pay was estopped from asserting that the promise was without consideration."
> **What about the preexisting duty rule for the above case?**
> The agreement was to pay additional compensation for services which the to-be-paid party was already <u>legally bound</u> to render under the old contract; so the new agreement is void for lack of consideration.

Exceptions to the Pre–Existing Duties Rule are:

( )   Added duties (modified duties of both parties, and rescission and a new contract meant to cancel the old contract). Because consideration is anything of value, no matter how seemingly inadequate, an informed party can easily modify the behavior in the two examples, above, to make the new agreement enforceable. For example, the debtor furnishes not just $11,000, but also a hard–to–obtain theater ticket, or the building contractor promises to make a minor improvement in the plans to the desired benefit of the owner. In each case, the modification would upgrade the second promise to an enforceable one.[65]

(a)   Perhaps, unforeseeable difficulty or hardship (<u>not just inflation, other ordinary economic shifts</u>. This exception could only apply for extreme cases.[66]

F. When Consideration is Unnecessary

Here are six situations in which parties may be bound despite the absence of consideration:

a.   UCC 2–205 – A merchant's firm written offer to keep an offer open (discussed previously in this Article of the text, concerning irrevocable offers).

b.   Promises to pay past debts sometimes renew debts formerly barred by the statute of limitations or bankruptcy proceedings.[67]

c.   Commercial paper, such as checks (but consideration is needed re: the underlying contract)

d.   Composition with creditors agreements (e.g., a debtor just agreeing with its creditors to pay each 15 cents on the dollar)

e.   Promissory estoppel (a concept already discussed in this Article of the text).

f.   A modified sales contract (even if all changes are "one way" – just favoring one party – per UCC 2-209(1).

> An Example Involving UCC 2–209(1) Modification
> **The "it's okay to whine" rule (as long as it's in good faith)**
> **"I can't get this, I can't do that – you *must* modify . . . Please!"**
>
> Suppose that a computer wholesaler has agreed to sell 200 computer monitors to a retailer for $280 each, delivery in six to eight weeks. During this period the retail market price for these monitors drops to $295. The buyer says she cannot stay in business unless the wholesaler agrees to take less. The wholesaler agrees to a $10 price drop, down to $270. For this sale of goods, UCC 2–209 modifies the common law approach and provides that an agreement modifying a contract of sale needs no consideration to be binding (as long as the parties are acting in good faith).

---

[65] Of course, for both examples it is assumed that these are good–faith inducements, not merely shams or covers for some overreaching that may constitute fraud or duress.

[66] One cannot simply be excused from the new (additional) consideration requirement by saying, "the prices of my supplies went up, so I have to charge more"; or, "the prices other wholesaler are getting are less, so I will pay less to you, my wholesaler."

[67] For a past debt, which may have expired due to statute of limitations, the promise to pay can reinstate that debt – even though the promise is not supported by new consideration from the other side. Generally, the new promise must be in writing, and sometimes the promisor needs to have been represented by counsel at the time.

V. MUTUALITY (REALITY) OF ASSENT (see pg. 105; Emerson BL)

Apparent assent to the same terms should be <u>genuine</u>. Mutuality is lacking when there is mutual mistake, force, or trickery. And, without mutuality, there is no contract.

> A mistake outside the context of contract law: A divorce court judge looked at the weeping ex–wife and declared, "The court shall grant this woman $500 a week in alimony." The ex–husband's eyes brightened as he looked up and said, "That's very nice of you, Your Honor. Why, I'll even kick in a few bucks myself."

A. Mistake

> <u>Joke on mistake:</u>
> Do not let it be said that, in the end, the main purpose of your life was simply to serve as a warning to others!

Mistakes must be about a <u>material fact</u>, not just opinion.

1. Unilateral Mistake (see pgs. 116-118; Emerson BL)

For example: periodically, people have traded (bought or sold) stock that was inactive because of misinterpreting the stock symbol for a stock that was very well-known and active. Some people make money, and others lose money, depending on when the mistake is discovered and who is left holding the stock.

MISTAKE EXAMPLE: *Sale of apples or oranges.* Do the buyers and sellers know the difference? Do you know the fruits? Didn't your Mamma explain to you, when you were little, the differences between apples and oranges?! (like the birds and the bees!).

Do you know the language?
    E.g.,   Russian – Yablaka or Applesēn
              Dutch – Appelsien; German – Apfelsine; etc.

If the other side knew or should have known that the opposing party had made a mistake, then the contract is interpreted in favor of the mistaken party: it can enforce the contract or get out of it – generally a choice of the mistaken party.

<u>The basic philosophy underlying the law of unilateral mistake is that</u> <u>one should not benefit from</u> (be able to get out of a deal because of) <u>ignorance or carelessness</u> (e.g., failing to observe obvious defects, <u>failing to read what one signs</u>). Ignorance ordinarily does <u>not</u> give one contract rights.

The standard, ordinarily, is objective: How a reasonable person would see and respond to a situation. <u>For a unilaterally mistaken party</u>, the only main excuse arises if the other party knew or should have known about the mistake. A classic example is the mistake in international contracting made by Lockheed Martin Corporation. The U.S.–based aerospace firm's contract to sell its C–130J Hercules had the comma misplaced by one decimal point in the equation that adjusted the sales price for changes to the inflation rate. In Europe, commas are used instead of periods to mark decimal points. The net effect was that, in a contract worth billions of dollars, Lockheed lost $70 million from what it would have received with a properly placed comma. Even for a huge company and a huge contract, $70 million is nothing to sneeze at. This mistake, revealed in June 1999, was unilateral and apparently not obvious to the innocent, opposing party. So Lockheed had to swallow that loss (and probably fire the contract draftsmen, proofreaders, and anyone else who should have noticed that mistake!).

An Ethical Concern in this Consumer Protection Era

When a customer makes a unilateral mistake, but returns quickly to the business and asks to get out of his contract, many businesses – as a gesture of goodwill – grant the customer's request. Perhaps most people now expect this "gesture" as a matter of right (fairness > law). Should the law permit rescission based on that? Should, as a matter of ethics, businesses allow rescission? Should we require it? (Ordinarily, the law does not require such "gestures," but perhaps the practice will become so widespread and accepted that courts may, in the future, at least for some industries, make it a legal requirement.)

Some practical advice to the seller is: Treat your customer well, even if not legally required to do so.

Many businesses have the policy that "the customer is always right." That may make the most sense – money-wise. One needs to evaluate the statistics – how much does it cost the business(this generosity in taking returns and reimbursing customers) versus how much does it help bring in revenue via increased business, good will, etc.

We should never overlook customer relations, public relations, goodwill, leverage, and how tough people are – how much do they push? If you talk to any "Customer Service Department" at any major retailer, people there will tell you that only a small percentage of people actually complain about a product or service, and – of those complainers – only a relatively small proportion (probably predominantly lawyers!) really push matters to the limit. Even if someone has a legal right to do what he/she wants, he/she often does not; and sometimes one SHOULD NOT do what one has the right to do!

Customer service personnel learn to accommodate some of those folks or send them packing. But a lot of questions are *not* resolved so much legally but by huffing and puffing and determining what makes the most sense for your business.

[In extreme cases, retailers, manufacturers, and other businesses may face massive lawsuits involving allegations of fraud (an intentional tort), not just warranty (breach of contract) claims.]

---

2. Mutual Mistake

"In general, there is no binding contract if a material mistake or fallacy is mutual."[68] Either side can void (excuse from a contract), and thus either side can go back to the status quo ante.

Two classic cases are: (1) The cow, Rose of Aberlone; and (2) the "Peerless" ships.

The Cow, Rose 2nd of Aberlone

In *Sherwood v. Walker*, 33 N.W. 919 (Mich. 1887), Sherwood, an astute banker, invested in cows with "distinguished ancestry." He found a cow, Rose 2nd of Aberlone, residing with the Walkers, who were breeders of "royal cows." Rose was priced at $80. That is 5.5 cents per pound plus 50 pounds shrinkage. Rose's actual weight was 1,420 pounds. Certainly, Rose would have been mortified to know that her weight was published in the Northwest Reporter of Michigan Supreme Court cases. And that weight was, the parties presumed, a non-pregnant weight, as Rose was deemed to be barren (infertile). If Rose could have reproduced, she would have been worth a whole lot more – ten times more – than the agreed-upon price. But Rose was barren (or so everyone thought!).

After the contract for the $80 sale was negotiated, the Walkers discovered Rose was pregnant. Naturally, Sherwood still wanted Rose, but the Walkers wanted Rose even more. They all fought in court,

---

[68] Robert W. Emerson, *Business Law*. NY: Barron's Educational Series (6th ed. 2015), at 116.

and the court concluded there was a mutual mistake, set aside the contract, and allowed Rose to remain with the breeding Walkers.

Rose 2nd is just pregnant with opportunities for discussion! But for more mutual mistake we can also turn to an old British case with silly sounding names: *Raffles v. Wickelhaus.*

The Two "Peerless" Ships

Raffles v. Wickelhaus, 159 Eng. Rep. 375 (1864), is described and analyzed comprehensively in A. W. Brian Simpson, Contracts for Cotton to Arrive: The Case of the Two Ships Peerless, 11 CARDOZO L. REV. 287–333 (1989). The case involved sending cotton to England from Bombay, India. One ship was leaving Bombay in October and another ship was to leave Bombay in December. Both ships were named the "Peerless," and the parties did not know there were two such ships – one was thinking of the October "Peerless," the other of the December "Peerless."

This is another example of a mutual mistake, with either party able to have the contract voided.

Again, as with Rose 2nd, the Fertile "Barren" cow, and other cases of mistake, <u>if the other side knew or should have known that the opposing party had made a mistake, then the contract is interpreted in favor of the mistaken party</u>: it can enforce the contract or get out of it – generally a choice of the mistaken party. Here, in *Raffles v. Wickelhaus*, though, as with *Sherwood v. Walker,* both sides were mistaken, so either side could, in effect, opt to get out of the agreement.

UNILATERAL MISTAKE: FOOLS AND CHEATS: *THE CARD SHARK VIDEO*

Minors' contracts are <u>voidable at the option of the minor</u> (Laura); Shop owner (an adult--Daniel) cannot use Laura's lack of capacity as an excuse to avoid the contract.

Laura to Paul - "I don't know anything about baseball. I just know about dollies."
Laura to Paul - "Here's your ten dollars."
Daniel to Paul - "Where's the rest of the money?"
Paul to Daniel – "Oops. I thought I saw a decimal point."
Daniel to Paul – "I'll make you see decimal points!"
Laura to the Audience – "I am the great card shark!"

Not fraud.
Not undue influence.
Not duress.

Mistake may make a contract voidable. Mistake is by the shop (through employee Paul). Is the mistake merely of value or of identity? Does Laura know of the mistake? Is Laura an innocent or a crook? Is there an innocent third party?

- Legally, Fools beat Defrauders, but Innocents beat Fools.

A Postvideo Analysis of the Card Shark scenario is on YouTube:
card_shark_post_video_13mins40secs.wmv at robertwemersonufl.

PROVING KNOWLEDGE

Continuing with the facts of the Card Shark skit –

How do we determine Laura's knowledge of a card's value (or identity) when she bought it from Paul? — Using discovery. We question Laura under oath before any trial.

A Follow-up Video - **<u>A Deposition of Laura</u>** – "**LAURA IS SUED!**" - Proving bad faith conduct.

> This *video skit* **(6:11 long) is on the website in the Part Two resources.**
>
> Aha! So there we have it –
> A girl with lots of knowledge –An expert, if you will, on baseball cards – certainly, knowledgeable about a card of a superstar such as Babe Ruth!
> Now it appears Laura is not so innocent.
> 1. Laura has an extensive collection, including cards from the Ruth card's era (the 1930s),
> 2. Laura views the cards as an investment, and she keeps track of their worth on a monthly basis.
> 3. Laura knows the card is worth much more than $10 and is taking advantage of a unilateral mistake.
> 4. At worst, Laura overhears Daniel talking to Paul while standing in the shop, realizes Paul knows nothing about cards, and runs a scam by asking – all sweet and innocent - of the car marked $1,000, "is it really worth ten dollars?"
> The mistake here, about the correct price of the card, is unilateral mistake rather than mutual mistake. Sellers are responsible for knowing the worth of the item being sold.
> However, a unilateral mistake is actionable by the mistaken party (shop owner Daniel through his agent, Paul) **IF** the unmistaken party (Laura) is aware of the mistake and seeks to take advantage of it. **Between a fool and an innocent, the law favors the innocent. Between a fool and a crook, the law favors the fool.**
>
> Laura's title to the card is voidable if actionable unilateral mistake exists. The shop owner could recover the card from Laura on that basis. However, once Laura passes her voidable title to a good faith purchaser for value (someone who has no reason to know of how Laura behaved in getting the card, and who thus presumably paid Laura a reasonable amount for the card), that purchaser takes free of the rights of the shop owner. E.g., the purchaser pays a "reasonable" sum, such as $950, for a card with a retail value of about $1,000.
>
> Voidable title to a good faith purchaser for value is an exception to the general rule that a transferee gets no better title than his transferor had. (Note: while the shop owner could not get the card back from the good faith purchaser, he could collect damages from Laura.)

3. Another Example of Emerson's adage, "If you must make a mistake, make it huge!"

Imagine that you are typing an email message. You intend to offer your car (estimated retail value of $10,000) for sale at a price of $9,500. You erroneously type the offer as being for $9,000. What if a witness saw you typing your offer, and heard you simultaneously say, "Ah, 9,500 is just what I need." This would indicate a mistake about what was actually typed. But how would the offeree be expected to know that your offer was a mistake. It would be entirely different, of course, if you dropped a zero: Instead of just substituting a zero for a five, you mistakenly type one less zero? A $950 offer (instead of $9,500) - Now that is a big mistake! This means it is a mistake the offeree presumably recognizes. And thus you should be able to be excused from your offer, and perhaps even have the offeror held to what you intended. The offeree could have simply asked for clarification about the offer from you, because he knew or should have known that it was likely a mistake on your part – a price less than 10% of the car's estimated value.

4. What Type of Mistake May Courts Recognize?

Courts ordinarily do not recognize mistakes about value (ordinarily, no effect on an alleged contract) and thus do not let parties out of a contract for a mistake in value. But the courts do recognize mistakes about identity as they may indicate a lack of Mutuality of Assent. For example, if Seller Sid sells to Buyer Bub what Sid and Bub believe to be a diamond but in fact is quartz, is that a mistake about value or about identity? Sid likely will argue that it is simply a difference in value: Some rocks are worth a lot, and some are not. Both diamonds and quartz are simply differently valued stones. But Bub likely will contend that the difference between a diamond and a piece of quartz are so great that it is the difference between a precious gem and an ordinary pebble. It is a difference of identity; the two (diamond or quartz) are of a different order, not simply a different value. So that great difference between them should be treated as a difference recognized in the contract law of mistake, Bub would contend. (Because there are distinct terms for these types of "rocks" and because the difference between a diamond and quartz is so extreme, it seems Bub probably has the better argument.)

> MISTAKE OF VALUE OR IDENTITY? THE *STRADIVARIUS VIOLINS EXAMPLE*
> An Italian, Antonio Stradivari (1644-1737), made about 1,100 instruments, of which about 635 violins, 17 violas, and 60 cellos still exist.
> Is it simply that "A violin is a violin is a violin?" – just a difference in value?
> *Or,* is a Stradivarius of such a higher quality that it truly is of a different order?

If the mistakes are material (the type that really make a difference in deciding whether to enter a contract), then mutual mistakes (both parties are mistaken) take the parties out of the contract. A court would recognize that mistake, as was done in *Raffles v. Wickelhaus* and *Sherwood v. Walker*.

B. Undue Influence (see pgs. 122-123; Emerson BL)

An example of claims against cults: former members suing for return of money/property they gave; they want to undo a contract, but what about undoing gifts? In either case (gift or contract), was there undue influence? Does it depend on the cult, the circumstances?

Undue influence over the formation of a contract tends to involve the abuse of a position of trust, such as:
Parent–child
Spouse–spouse
Accountant–client
Doctor– patient
Attorney–client

> An Example of Foolish Reliance, Not Undue Influence
> A first-time car buyer visits a car lot, where the salesman says that she has the best cars in town, at the lowest prices. The buyer trusts her and agrees to buy a car at a price that's $3,000 higher than the price for the same make and model of car at the other dealerships in town. Could the purchaser successfully seek rescission on the grounds of undue influence? PROBABLY NOT. There was no pre-existing relationship between the buyer and seller, so it would be very difficult to convince a court that you rightfully gave up your free will in order to depend on the salesperson's best judgment.

The two basic elements of undue influence are (1) the use of excessive pressure by the dominating person, and (2) undue susceptibility in the subservient person. *Odorizzi v. Bloomfield School District*, 246 Cal. App. 2d 123 (1966). Odorizzi was a teacher exhausted from going without sleep for 40 hours while being questioned and booked on charges of homosexual activity. He was unduly susceptible to unfair persuasion by a dominant force: the principal of his school and the superintendent of the district had come to his house and insisted that Odorizzi sign a resignation notice.

Fiduciaries (persons who hold a position of trust, as in a guardianship) – another person is dependent on the fiduciary to look after the dependent person's best interests.

As educated, soon–to–be graduates of an august university, you are potential fiduciaries for "suspect" transactions (transactions with your own interests at stake).

> Practical advice to a potential fiduciary party: (1) Fully disclose your interests at the outset, (2) put disclosure in writing, in front of witnesses, (3) advise dependent person to get independent advice, (4) otherwise provide evidence that any contract reached is an "arm's length" transaction.

C. Duress – Physical, Mental, Economic? (see pgs. 123-124; Emerson BL)
Three examples of duress are:
1. Holding a gun to someone's head and demanding, "Sign the contract, or else!" Typically, duress makes a contract voidable. Duress is coercion, either physical or mental, that deprives a person of free will and leaves that person with no reasonable alternatives other than to accept the contract terms as imposed on him/her. However, physical duress such as the foregoing is so extreme that courts generally treat the resulting agreement as outright void.
2. Holding ice out in the summer sun until the owner/debtor agrees to sign a contract to pay a debt discharged in bankruptcy. *Chandler v. Sanger*, 114 Mass. 364 (1874).
3. Waiving your pension because your fire chief boss made you sign such a waiver (or else he would have told the world that you inhaled nitrous oxide (laughing gas) at work. And the workplace was not a dentist's office (there was no root canal taking place). *Enslen v. Village of Lombard*, 470 N.E.2d 1188 (Illinois 1984).

> Threats as Duress: *Haumont v. Security State Bank*
> Creditors threatened a farm couple with criminal prosecution of their adult son if they did not pay his debts. The parents mortgaged their property in order to get the money. Could the parents rescind the mortgage? Yes. That was the holding in *Haumont v. Security State Bank*, 374 N.W.2d 2 (Neb. 1985). "Duress" is application of such pressure or constraint as compels man to go against his will, and takes away his free agency, destroying power of refusing to comply with unjust demands of another.
> The instrument is a result of duress and contract may be avoided where parent or other relative is induced to execute the instrument by threats and fear of criminal punishment of child or relative.

1. Actual Harm from Certain Types of Threats
To constitute duress, threats must be of immediate physical harm, of criminal prosecution, of personal or family disgrace. Ordinarily, one is not allowed to threaten (thus, use as a club) criminal prosecution in order to obtain a civil remedy; any settlement contract arising from such a threat is subject to voiding for duress. [**My Bank Client's Vice-President cited a section of the state criminal law statutes, concerning bounced checks, in letters she sent to customers who bounced checks. We told her to stop. Threatening lawsuits is fine; threatening to have the police or prosecutors come after the debtor - that could be duress.**]

One can threaten to file a civil suit, if there is any basis for such a suit (a "colorable" claim). For example, sending a Demand Letter is okay (does not place the recipient under duress). But for crimes, one probably should just report it to the authorities. There is no mixing up the private remedy (contracts) with public recourse via criminal charges.

It is very difficult to show that threats of economic loss created duress. It is an inadequate defense to say, "I had less bargaining power."

> Prison Revolt, Leading to Negotiated Settlement: Is that Duress?

> All states, even the small ones, have penitentiaries. And, of course, there is the potential for prison riots. At such riots, one can see a gradation of demands. First, hostage–takers may demand one–way tickets out of the country to, say, some tropical "paradise" without an extradition treaty back to the United States (can you say, "Cuba?"). Then, when it becomes clear that the authorities will not cave on that demand, the rioting prisoners demand better conditions – more meaningful parole board hearings, better food, and better law library facilities. After the state's negotiators say they cannot even afford to provide more ice cream, let alone library books or parole officers, the hostage–takers finally pull back further and simply request that – in return for the release of the guards they are holding – no charges will be filed against them. Finally, the state authorities agree: if the prisoners will release the hostages and return to their cells, the state will overlook the crimes committed during the takeover. But it turns out the state was negotiating with its proverbial fingers crossed; once the state saw how many people were injured and/or property was damaged during the takeover, the amnesty promise was retracted and some prisoners were charged with crimes.
>
> In *State v. Rollins*, 359 A.2d 315 (R.I. 1976), the Supreme Court of Rhode Island upheld the conviction of two defendants tried before the Superior Court of Providence and Bristol Counties, Rhode Island. The convictions came in the aftermath of a prison uprising and were for assaults on the hostage correctional officer, assaults with dangerous weapons, as well as kidnapping and extortion. The Court held, among other things, that even if the state's Director of the Department of Corrections had power to make alleged promises of immunity to those inmates who participated in the uprising, these promises were unenforceable as a matter of public policy because they were secured by violence and coercion. The Court upheld the two defendants' sentences of 20 years' each, while a third defendant – who pleaded guilty – received an eight–year sentence.

2. Asserting Duress May Be Impractical

Just because the duress defense is legally viable does not always mean that it is practical. For example, the United States – Iran arbitration scheme established to resolve the Iranian hostage crisis of 1979–1981 depended upon the American government's abiding by that deal, even though it was reached under duress (i.e., in order to obtain the release of wrongfully held, in violation of all basic concepts of international law, U.S. diplomats). Pres. Jimmy Carter agreed to the deal, which placed $7 billion in frozen Iranian assets into the arbitration system, in return for the hostages' freedom. The U.S. government could have, under contract law, refused to honor the agreement after the hostages were released. But to assert duress at that point would have undermined the American government's ability to negotiate in future cases. By way of analogy, in a future prison riot, the hostage–takers would know to insist upon a trip to Cuba because anything less could later be revoked!

> **A DIFFERENT APPROACH TO THEFT THAN TO FRAUD OR MISTAKE: Three Examples**
>
> *After a theft, no strong title can pass.* With fraud, mistake, or other problems besides theft, a bona fide purchase can pass the title.
>
> Nazi Thievery
>
> A notable example where title cannot pass is the Nazis' theft of art during World War II. German records indicate that it took 29,984 railroad cars to move the Nazi-looted art to Germany.
>
> A Confederate Gun
>
> At the Museum of the Confederacy, in Richmond, Virginia, a .36-caliber Spiller & Burr revolver was stolen in 1975 when the museum collection was moved to a new building. As one of the first Confederate-manufactured handguns, the revolver was very valuable, with a current estimated value of $50,000.
>
> A woman in Knoxville, Tennessee discovered the gun in December 2010 in her late father's belongings. She tried to sell it to an Ohio antique dealer, who traced the gun to the museum. It was unknown how the woman's father, who collected Civil War items, came into possession of the gun. The woman was not charged with any crime, but the revolver was simply returned to the Museum.

> <u>Even Yale Sometimes Gets It Right!</u>
> The Machu Picchu ruins, perched in clouds on an 8,000 foot high mountaintop, are Peru's main tourist attraction. The Inca Empire built the complex of stone buildings in the 1400s, and Spanish conquistador Francisco Pizarro toppled the empire in 1532-1533.
> In 2008, the South American nation of Peru sued in U.S. District Court demanding that Yale University return artifacts that the famed scholar Hiram Bingham removed from the Machu Picchu citadel in 1912. The claim accused Yale of fraudulently retaining the relics, while Yale responded that it had returned dozens of boxes of artifacts in 1921 and that Peru knew it would retain other artifacts.
> In November 2010, Yale and Peru reached a settlement. Yale agreed to send back to Peru over 5,000 Incan artifacts (ceramic pieces, animal and human bones, and metal and stone objects). San Antonio Abad University in Cuzco, Peru will create a center (located in an Incan palace and operated by both universities) to house the artifacts. Yale's and San Antonio Abad's faculty and students will visit the other institution for training, research and field work. A small number of artifacts will remain on loan and displayed at the Yale Peabody Museum of Natural History.

D. Fraud (sometimes called deceit, false representation, or misrepresentation)
(see pgs. 118-120; Emerson BL)

It has been estimated that the typical organization loses about 6 percent of annual revenue to employee fraud, theft, and financial abuse. The average fraud scheme lasts 18 months before it is detected. Corporate insurance policies often provide reimbursement to the victims; if a credit card or checking account is abused, banks may cover some of the losses, too.

1. False Claims Act and SOX (see pg. 434; Emerson BL)

Since its inception, the Act has generated $12 billion for the federal treasury and more than $1 billion for hundreds of whistleblowers, who have been at the root of federal fraud cases against many well-known companies, including Tenet Healthcare, Columbia/HCA, Lockheed Martin, TAP Pharmaceutical Products Inc., and Boeing. Companies have been, among other things, caught selling defective parts for military aircraft, paying kickbacks to doctors for prescribing unneeded medicines and services, and overbilling Medicare and Medicaid.

Another whistleblower protection law, the Sarbanes–Oxley Act (2002) ("SOX"), covers fraud against publicly traded companies and is intended for those that destroy records, commit securities fraud or fail to report fraud to investors. Both Sarbanes–Oxley and the False Claims Act protect whistleblowers from being fired, but only the False Claims Act has triple damages and gives whistleblowers a reward.

2. MKIRDC

MKIRDC stands for all six elements which must be proven to demonstrate fraud: misrepresentation, knowledge, intent, reliance, damages, and causation.

> YOUTUBE – SixElementsofFraud1min40secs at robertwemersonufl -
> a quick offering (in video form) from a sartorially splendid salesman.
>
> "Imagine a man dresses as a car salesman, saying, 'Have I got a deal for you?'
> "When you see a person dressed like this (the proverbial, stereotypical, used-car salesman), you're supposed to run away! You're supposed to also recognize that this person may not be offering you a really good deal.
> The irony is that, because someone dressed in such a ridiculous fashion should be setting off all sorts of alarms or bells in your brain, you should <u>not</u> have justifiable reliance on anything this person says. The irony is that, if someone looked more presentable, then you would have a better case of fraud against

him based on his lies (because you more likely were reasonable to believe in him). But when someone is dressed like this [like the typical car salesman], where is the justifiable reliance?

"Reasonable reliance is one of the six elements in fraud. For fraud, you have to show (1) a material misrepresentation of fact, (2) that this misrepresentation was knowingly made, (3) that there was an intent to induce reliance, (4) that the reliance was justifiable (what I have just been talking about), (5) that there were damages, and (6) that there is a causal link between the misrepresentation of fact and those damages."

a. Misrepresentation of Material Fact
Material facts are significant, the type likely to induce assent.

> **Examples: material or non–material facts**
>
> If a party does not care about something – e.g., the precise color of a purchased item is unimportant (whether it is beige or mauve or black or blue – is an insignificant condition) – then it is immaterial and thus NOT something for which a successful claim of misrepresentation may be maintained.
>
> What about the statement that a car has only had one owner the past ten years (since it was purchased as a new car), when actually it has had ten different owners? For most purchasers that would probably be material. The fact that so many different people have sold or otherwise transferred the car may indicate it was not such a prize item!

i. Opinion is not a legally recognized misrepresentation (unless by an expert in his/her area of expertise – only then may it be treated as fact).

Puffing – sales talk – is neither a misrepresentation for Fraud purposes, nor for Unfair Competition purposes (e.g., deceptive advertising).

Exaggeration typically is allowed. It is often called "puffery" or "puffing": blustering and boasting upon which no reasonable buyer would rely, or a general claim of superiority over a comparative product that is so vague it would be understood as a mere expression of opinion. For example, to say one's product is "better" than that of competitors is puffing.

Eminent law professors have defined puffing as "a seller's privilege to lie his head off, so long as he says nothing [believably] specific, on the theory that no reasonable man would believe him, or that no reasonable man would be influenced by such talk." W. Page Keeton, et al., Prosser and Keeton on the Law of Torts, § 109, at 757 (5th ed. 1984).

ii. Puffing (Sales Talk)

> "It is customary for the seller to 'huff and puff' and to exaggerate the value of his/her goods, and many buyers, in turn, seek to diminish or deprecate the value of the goods in order to lower the price."[69]

Car dealers provide great examples of silly advertisements. They likely push the envelope because of all the marketing "noise" they face. Dealers need to do something to make their ads stand out.

It can be surprising how far businesses, such as auto dealers, are legally permitted to push the envelope with their promotional and marketing messages. They can go far without any liability for fraud or deceptive advertising. The Federal Trade Commission (FTC) and the courts hold that exaggerated claims are okay, if they are so far out or vague that a person would not reasonably rely on the statement as a basis for the bargain (i.e., "crazy prices"). Puffing determinations are not just restricted to consumer ads, but involve issues common also to Business–to–Business direct sales, too. More on fraud vs. puffing is at **pgs. 467-468; Emerson BL.**

---

[69] Id. at 119.

iii. By Actions, Not Just Words

A misrepresentation can be actions as well as words: painting rotten beams, putting silly putty on a cracked engine block, changing an odometer reading. The difference between an odometer reading of 10,000 miles and 110,000 miles certainly is great. Setting the odometer back is just as much a misrepresentation as if one had stated, in written or spoken language, that the car was nearly new (about 10,000 miles) rather than acknowledging that it was a car that had been around the block for many, many, many trips (about 110,000 miles worth!).

YOUTUBE – dancing_to_mazurka_fraud_5mina`8secs_skitandthenpostvideo at robertwemersonufl

Is it a material misrepresentation? False representations do not have to be in words. Misrepresentation can be through conduct, not necessarily by words. To win on fraud, the other elements must also be present (material fact, knowledge, intent to induce reliance, justifiable reliance, damages, and causation).

b. Knowledge (Scienter – pronounced, "see–enter")

A broad interpretation of knowledge – not just what you know, but what you should have known. Blinders will not protect. The fact that one literally does not know (because of blinding oneself to the truth) is not a sufficient defense (i.e., it does not mean one lacks scienter).

This all keeps people from just saying, "Can't prove it." A potential defendant cannot just dare the swindled party to even try to prove the defendant's knowledge.

"You can't prove that, when I sold my car to you, I knew the transmission was shot, the engine was dead, and the tires were all recalled Firestone threads! You may assume I knew all that, but that's not enough – you have to prove it, buddy!"

Scienter keeps defendants from insisting on such a high standard (proof of actual knowledge) when the facts indicate the defendant must have, or at least should have, had the requisite knowledge.

c. Intent to Induce Reliance

Ordinarily, a defrauding party will claim that she did not intend to deceive, but that any falsehood was "innocent." However, courts do not accept such subjective defenses. Indeed, this element of fraud is presumed present, if there is scienter. So, intent is usually easy to prove; it is inferred.

d. Reliance that is Justifiable (Reasonable)

Joke – Homer Simpsonism: "Marge, it takes two to lie. One to lie, and one to listen."

Reliance, or lack thereof, often is the most important issue in fraud cases. A key factor to resolve sometimes is: Was the source that the claimant allegedly relied upon the best source available to him/her?

Any time someone talks about how another person could make a bundle of money by doing something, there is an obvious question to ask: Is the speaker himself/herself engaged in that activity, or is he/she just seeking others to buy his/her book and pay for his/her tapes and seminars? If the speaker is not now doing what he/she urges others to do, why is that the case? The speaker perhaps has decided that his/her way to riches is to sell a plan, not to practice the plan. But with that overriding question – why is the speaker telling his/her listener to make money off of something that the speaker himself/herself does not do? – the listener may have no justifiable reliance on what he/she has heard.

The author had such a case involving a client who allegedly sold his home with the inducement that the purchaser would be able to subdivide the property and build a second home on the other half of the real estate. By halving the property, the purchaser could rent out or sell the existing home and use the proceeds to build his/her "dream house" on the rest of the lot. That, at any rate, was the plaintiff buyer's allegation in a lawsuit against the seller of the property. But would there be justifiable reliance on such a statement? The plaintiff had a heavy burden to overcome two common–sense assumptions: (1) based on the same reasoning as in the previous paragraph, how is it reasonable to depend on the seller's statement of how to make money off the property when the seller himself did not follow that course of conduct? (the seller did not subdivide the property); (2) Is it not the case that there are better sources of information subdividing the property than the seller (e.g., governmental zoning offices, real estate lawyers). Either point undermines the reasonableness of relying on the seller's alleged statement.

AN EXAMPLE FROM A CLASSIC CHILDREN'S STORY - "The Emperor's New Clothes."
Was the emperor's reliance reasonable? He was, as a child might say, "*butt naked.*" The irony: the outrageousness may mean no justifiable reliance. So a really big, outrageous lie may be less likely to lead to a successful fraud claim.

IS JUSTIFIABLE RELIANCE ABSENT? Two Songs about Love
    a. "How Could You Believe Me When I Said I Loved You, When . . ."
    b. "That's what you get for loving me!"
    ". . . And when your heart is on the mend, I just may come your way again!"
The problem here - for either song – is that there is no fraud because there is no reasonable reliance.

> Does fraud mean that there is no mutuality of assent and, thus, no contract in the following case?
>
> In early August, you visit a local dealership to buy a car. The salesperson tells you that the car has air conditioning, and – after you take the car on a test drive, you buy the car. Within a week, it dawns on you that the car has no air conditioning. You seek to rescind the contract on the grounds that the dealership and/or salesperson perpetrated a fraud. Will you win? No. *Williams v. Rank & Son Buick, Inc.*, 170 N.W.2d 807 (Wis. 1969). There was no reasonable reliance, because you should have turned on the air conditioner during the test drive.
>
> In the Williams case, the court refused to act for the relief of one claiming to have been misled by another person's statements when the relying party blindly acted (1) in disregard of knowledge about the statements' falsity or (2) with the opportunity to observe, not necessarily even search to discover, the likely falsity of the statements. A plaintiff may not close his/her eyes to what is obviously discoverable by him/her.
>
> The classic example involves a leaky, non-aligned Chevrolet Citation used-car purchase - Wendt v. Beardmore Suburban Chevrolet, Inc., 366 N.W. 2d 424 (Neb. 1985) – A Chevrolet Citation with 3,901 miles, but there were numerous signs of possible trouble (Tonya And Darrell Wendt sue the Dealer).

Even when lawsuits may not be feasible, administrative or collective action may succeed. For example, on June 26, 2001, Publishers Clearing House settled a suit brought by 26 states by agreeing to stop using such phrases as "You are a winner!" on mailings or the Internet. It also agreed to pay $34 million in refunds and other costs.

If warranties were provided, expressly or implicitly, the lack of reasonable reliance would not be an issue (would not be a defense) under UCC Article 2.

    e. Damages: So what if horrible things might have happened? What *did* happen? That is what matters.

    f. Causation: Causation is a link between the Lie and the Harm

3. Remedies and Standard of Proof

Remedies are generally, at the option of the defrauded party, to rescind the contract, to affirm the contract (revised to the way a defrauded party wants), and to sue for damages. One may even seek punitive damages (unlike ordinary contract breaches, fraud is a tort; an intended tort – it may arise out of a contract situation).

Standard of Proof: Because it is a blot on your character (a scurrilous accusation), there is a higher standard of proof (than the usual standard - preponderance of evidence - for civil cases): one must show the fraud by clear and convincing evidence. Fraud is thus often quite difficult to prove (e.g., scienter). It is not, though, a criminal standard, which is "beyond a reasonable doubt."

4. Silence as Fraud

Usually, that is much harder to prove than active misrepresentation. Is there a duty to speak? Silence usually is NOT grounds for a fraud claim. One way that such a duty might arise is if clarification or other information was sought.

What if a customer, upon seeing on a used–car a sign saying "one owner," asks the salesman: "Is that one owner since new or just one owner now?" (meaning, the car had many owners, but just has one now). Shouldn't the salesman be expected to respond? And a salesman's response, "how 'bout them Gators!" (trying to switch the subject rather than answer the question) would not be an appropriate approach.

So ask questions – e.g., if you are concerned about ghostly houses or bodies in the backyard!

A stockbroker who purchased a large home in Nyack, N.Y. discovered, only after moving in, that he would be living with poltergeists and spectral apparitions. The ghostly dwelling was commonly known to be spooked, but no one told the plaintiff!

Silence as misrepresentation?

Consider Professor Marianne Jennings' humorous article on the psychological questions for buyers concerned about prior property's use and history (13 J. Legal Studies Educ. 308):
Why do neighborhood children, with garlic around their necks, race by this house screaming?
Why have 17 families lived in this house in the past 18 months?
Why is this 4200 square foot Aspen, Colorado property selling for just $12,000?
Why do neighbors giggle each time we come to see the house?
Why are there potholes in the living room?
Is there anything significant about the large number of gun racks in the house?
Why do you keep referring to your, quote, "former" client? (Is he your late – I mean, dead – client?)
Why do you keep saying, "Talk to the neighbors?"
How often do uranium tailings float through the air, creating that radioactive pink haze?

Say "No Comment" (German – "Kommentar überflüssig"), Rather than Give Misleading Answers
UBERNAHMEGESPRACHE MEANS "TAKEOVER TALKS"

In *Buxbaum v. Deutsche Bank AG*, 196 F.Supp.2d 367 (S.D.N.Y. 2002), sellers of shares and call options of an American bank, Bankers Trust, acquired by the German bank, Deutsche Bank, brought a class action against Deutsche Bank claiming that a 1998 "Der Spiegel" magazine interview denial of merger discussions by Deutsche Bank's chief executive officer (CEO) depressed the value of Bankers Trust's securities.

The facts, briefly, were as follows: in Der Spiegel (Germany's largest circulation magazine), the CEO had denied Deutsche Bank was engaged in "Ubernahmegesprache'" with Bankers Trust. The word is roughly translated from German as "takeover talks." In reaction to his comments, and thinking no merger was in sight, some investors sold their Bankers Trust stock. Just over a month later, Deutsche Bank announced their takeover of Bankers Trust. Feeling that they were purposely misled in order to drive down the Bankers Trust stock price, the investors sued.

Deutsche Bank moved for summary judgment. The Deutsche Bank lawyers claimed that "ubernahmegesprache" had a more specific meaning than preliminary or generalized "takeover talks": formal and structured talks along with an exchange of confidential documents.

The U.S. District Court Judge denied Deutsche Bank's motion because: (1) fact issues as to whether there had been takeover discussions by the time of the interview precluded a summary judgment of liability for untrue statement under Securities Exchange Act §10(b); (2) fact issues concerning the CEO's knowledge of discussions precluded a summary judgment that the scienter requirement for a §10(b) action was not met; and (3) fact issues regarding materiality of any misrepresentation precluded summary judgment of §10(b) liability. 12 U.S.C. [U.S. Code] § 78(j)(b) (Statute 10(b)); 17 C.F.R. [Code of Federal Regulations] §240.10b-5 (SEC Rule 10(b)(5)).

When Deutsche Bank asked the judge to dismiss the case, the judge stated, "The plaintiff's interpretation of the phrase 'Ubernahmegesprache' is at least as plausible as the defendant's and is supported by sworn evidence." A jury will decide the case that literally hinges on a single word and its translation.

Then Deutsche Bank settled with the plaintiffs at approximately 90% of the difference in stock price, which was the claimed amount of damages.

Courts or regulators are more likely to find silence a problem if: a fiduciary relationship exists between the parties, or there was a serious defect – a potential problem knowable only to the seller. In those situations, as a reduction of transaction costs, one may put the burden on the person that could more easily know and transmit information. For example, there is a difference between (1) house appraisals for tax purposes – the buyer could easily contact the tax assessor's office to obtain that information (why must the seller disclose it?), and (2) pre–existing information about a termite infestation – something very costly to detect and which we may expect the seller to disclose to the buyer without having to be prompted.

A trend in some regulatory areas is to require disclosures. Examples of such required disclosures include: (1) Florida real estate forms – required disclosure to a potential buyer of any known latent defects or material facts which may not be readily visible; (2) Federal Rules – e.g., in franchising and in food labels.

5. When Better Sources Are Available and Opinions Are Not Guaranteed: The Sale of a Motel Example

Imagine that you are in the land of boiled peanut stands, a car jacked up onto a 40-foot high pole, and a big white metal horse – that is, you are in Waldo, Florida (or some other such rural "paradise"). You say to yourself: "Wow, this is the place for me! I would love to buy a business here." And then you notice the "For Sale" sign at a local motel.

You inquire at the motel, and the owner – Olga Orr - tells you how much revenue the motel netted last year. Olga also gives you the financial books, which cover everything related to the motel's expenses and revenue for the past five years. You ask for everything else filed with the state or local authorities in the past five years, plus all employment records and all correspondence for the past five years. Olga's accountant drops by the motel and provides you with all that you asked.

As you stroll throughout the motel and further discuss the situation with Olga, she tells you how much she predicts the motel will earn in the next 12 months.

You agree to buy the motel. The agreement is put in writing and finalized with the appropriate payment and exchange of documents, such as deeds, records, and licenses.

But the story does not stop there. And it has far from a happy ending. Poor you!
Here are the problems:
- A. The motel has not made anything close to what Olga had predicted; in fact, it is just half of what she had stated ($200,000 in net revenue rather than $400,000).
- B. Now, a year after the sale, you have determined that Olga misled you with her statement that the motel had made "over $330,000" in the year before the sale. In fact, motel netted about $220,000 during that time frame.
- C. A year after the sale, you are very troubled by how little traffic there is on the roadway in front of the motel. You ponder the motel's business downturn as you proceed for a long walk. After a few miles, you climb a big hill and as you descend on the other side notice a spanking new, busy highway! As you soon learn, the state transportation department approved the highway 15

months ago, with ground breaking for it shortly thereafter. The highway was completed three months ago, and you now recall that it was around then you saw a 15-25% diminution in the number of cars and trucks going on the roadway in front of your motel. A year ago, Olga mentioned nothing about this new highway.

Now you sue Olga. Your claim is based on the three points (A, B, and C), above. Alas, while you have lost money on your motel, you have no good claim that there were legally recognizable "mutuality of assent" problems. For A, the problem is that opinion about future earnings is merely an opinion, not a guarantee (and certainly not a statement of fact). For B, if one assumes that the books are, in fact, accurate, then you could not reasonably have relied on an offhand oral statement rather than the documented, expertly researched writings of the experts. You cannot have any reasonable reliance on oral statements without reading and understanding the actual books. Finally, for C, what duty did it have to overcome to defeat silence? The buyer could have called the Transportation Department and checked with the Zoning and Land Planning Offices.

6. Negligent Misrepresentation

A negligent misrepresentation may occur due to a statement by an expert. Negligent misrepresentation involves opinions/statements by a person who holds himself/herself out as having superior knowledge (far more than Plaintiff's own knowledge) – a professional.

For negligent misrepresentation, the element of Negligence substitutes for the MKIRDC element of Knowledge/<u>Scienter</u>.

Examples: (1) Accountant misrepresents accounting principles; (2) Lawyer misrepresents corporate law matters; and (3) Engineer misrepresents an engineering application of principles to a problem.

In *Tapia v. Banque Indosuez*, 1999 U.S. App. LEXIS 29260 (U.S. Ct. of Appeals, Second Circuit, decided Nov. 3. 1999), Spanish speaker Roberto Martinez Tapia signed an English–language document. The court found that the document (a contract) bound this Mexican businessman, a non–English speaker who informally depended upon the help of a translating friend from Banque Indosuez. The court held: "[W]here the contract involves a substantial sum and no emergency prevents access to a competent translator, <u>an individual who does not seek an independent translator is negligent</u>."

<u>*Vokes v. Arthur Murray*</u>, 212 So.2d 906 (Fla. Dist. Ct. App. 1968)

Audrey Vokes, a widow over fifty years old, had no family. She yearned to become "an accomplished dancer" and to develop a new interest in life. She was invited to a free "dance party" at Davenport's Dance School, a Clearwater, Florida franchise of the Arthur Murray School of Dancing. She took free lessons, dancing with the instructors while constantly being barraged with flattery and compliments about her dancing potential. She was baited with a trial offer of eight half–hour lessons for $14.50. The "baited come–on" worked over a period of time, for the dance school was able to induce her to buy fourteen dance courses, totaling over 2,300 hours of lessons. The cost was over $31,000. The fourteen course enrollments were evidenced by the Arthur Murray School of Dancing Enrollment Agreement.

The inducement used by the dance school included compliments concerning Mrs. Vokes' grace and poise as well as her rapidly improving and developing dancing skill. She was informed that the lessons would help her "find new interest in life" and "make her a beautiful dancer, capable of dancing with the most accomplished dancer" ("...a barrage of compliments [and] panegyric encomiums," the court noted). The plaintiff was even given dance aptitude tests to determine how many additional hours she needed.

At one stage, Mrs. Vokes was sold 545 additional hours, which qualified her for the "Bronze Medal." Thereafter, 926 hours were added for "Silver Medal," 347 hours for the "Gold Medal," and finally 481 hours for the classification "as a Gold Bar Member, the ultimate achievement of the dancing studio." The defendant also cajoled the widow into buying a life membership, which allowed her to take a trip at her own expense to Miami, where she was "given the opportunity to dance with members of the Miami Studio." She was also talked into buying still more hours to be eligible for trips to Trinidad and Mexico, again both at her own expense.

The truth, the court stated, was that Audrey Vokes was not improving in her abilities; her potential as a dancer was very limited, and she had difficulty actually hearing the beat in the music. Claims otherwise were "false and known to be false to all those claiming otherwise but withheld with intent to deceive and defraud." The court noted that the two parties were *not* on equal terms. Because of the defendant's superior knowledge and the plaintiff's situation, statements that might normally be considered mere statements of opinion could qualify as statements of fact.

There are lots of law cases involving Arthur Murray and other dance studios. Here the case would be against the Dance Company; agency law makes clear the company can be liable for its employee's actions.

In reality, Audrey Vokes had no "dance aptitude." Not only could she not dance to the musical beat, but she perhaps could not even hear the beat. She was told that she was entering into "the spring of her life," but actually there was no spring in her life or in her feet!

Would any of the following four claims work?

i. Undue influence
Claim: Vokes was an older person, very dependent on the instructor.
Defense: Vokes was an adult (willing & competent); Vokes met the instructor
   through a business relationship (not a fiduciary relationship)

ii. Negligent misrepresentation
Claim: The defendant held itself out as an expert in dance; its employee, the dance
instructor, lied about or negligently overstated Vokes' abilities and/or the usefulness of dance.
Defense: Vokes could & should have checked – it is a free world; she bargained for it.

iii. Fraud
Were the statements to the plaintiff much more than puffing?

iv. Unconscionability (gross unfairness)
Discussed later, concerning the contract law of legality and public policy

When Audrey Vokes was finally persuaded to take action, why did she not just sue for breach of contract? To get out of the contract, and get her money back, Vokes needed to argue that a problem existed with either the formation of the contract (e.g., fraud or procedural unconscionability) or that there was a problem with the contract itself – substantive unfairness. (She, therefore, sought a rescission; see the discussion of procedural and substantive unconscionability, including *Vokes* as well as other cases later in this part of the text.)

VI. ETHICS IN THE DEAL-MAKING PROCESS: A BRIEF DISCUSSION

Savvy Sales Ploy – A Wevbvideo on the Website
Unethical behavior is often driven by a compulsion to win, a fear and concern about maintaining self-esteem. "He who dies with the most toys wins!"

A. Introduction

What makes it difficult to be ethical in business? It is *not* just greed. It is also the compulsion to win, fear of others taking advantage of our honesty, and the desire to maintain self-esteem. Carnival Cruise Line used to have an ad campaign: "if your friends could see you now" – the point was that you should buy cruise tickets to make your friends envious.

What are acceptable methods for closing a deal? Are ethical questions distinct from legal questions? Fraud, or absence thereof, is *not* the entire issue. Even if the elements necessary to prove fraud – MKIRDC - are missing, an ethical question remains: Is the behavior acceptable?

If the misrepresentation, fib, puffing is not related to the value of the property itself, just to its availability, is such a lie different than a lie about the property itself? Examples include: (1) Salespeople stating about inventory, "There are no more in stock," (2) the classic statement, "The Sale will end – Another Will Never Occur Again." The attempt is simply to increase sales; actually, there will be more sales, and the salesperson knows it.

A legal defense may be: Act in haste, repent at leisure. It is not a problem if the representations are accurate – e.g., that there are very few in stock or otherwise available. It is not a salesperson's fault if the customer responds with a hasty decision to buy.

B. Using a Lie to Get in the Doorway

Is a lie to get people to listen to a sales pitch as serious a legal or ethical issue as a lie about the ultimate good or service itself (the subject one is "pitching")?

Surveys of salespeople indicate that usually the hardest part of obtaining a sale is not getting people to sign the bottom line, nor overcoming various objections the other side may raise, but simply getting one's foot in the doorway in the first place.

The fib could thus be:

(1) "we are here to inspect your furnace"; [Gee, I did not even know I had a furnace!]

(2) "we are here to give you some important information that the government may not have told you."

Thus, a salesman gets people to think he is from a public interest group or government safety agency or an insurance company, and that he is there to give advice about the homeowner's furnace. Then, before you know it, the salesman is inside the home, telling people that he actually represents a furnace manufacturer and is trying to sell a new furnace. A comparable action would be telemarketers hooking people (to listen to the full spiel) with an initial story that turns out to be misleading.

Here are seven key topics or questions:

1. Assuming that there are no other customers about to buy a property: Is it fraudulent to lie about the interest of others? Does it matter that any such "staging" deals more with matters other than literally the property itself – i.e., whether others want it? (But doesn't the latter still affect potential price, time to deal, etc.?)

2. The International Chamber of Commerce, an independent organization, has promoted self-regulation by developing voluntary codes of marketing practices for businesses.

3. Are there professional codes of ethics (realtors) that do or should say something about certain types of exaggerations or "indirect lies" to get interest in real property. (In the U.S., there are over

50 different professions with Codes.) For example, the "Code of Ethics and Standards of Practice" promulgated by the National Association of Realtors has:

      a. General language about treating everyone honestly.

      b. The statement that offers and counteroffers should be objectively, and as quickly as possible, transmitted to the other side.

      c. the admonition, "Realtors shall be careful at all times to present a true picture in their advertising and representations to the public."

There are numerous professional standards for different fields - www.uwaterloo.ca/society/standards.html Professionals, such as accountants, even if they do NOT engage in outright fraud, are bound to a code of ethics. Failure to meet the generally accepted standards for the profession could indicate that they are negligent or worse in treating someone.

---

4. For certain consumer transactions (particularly those that the business party initiated), the law may allow customers to change their minds and get out of a deal within a certain time period - e.g., three to ten days after the deal was reached. The FTC Door-to-Door Sales Rule of 1973 **(see pg. 263; Emerson BL**) has a three-day post-sale period of protection. Do such consumer protection rules reduce or eliminate a customer's right to complain about a pushy salesperson's clever approach? A year or two later, a defendant could contend, "the consumer had time to think it over afterwards. So there was no real causation. The consumer <u>could have</u> gotten out of the deal (he had three days to change his mind)."

There are sometimes unintended consequences of a law. Just as a mandatory-wearing-of-seatbelts law intended to bolster safety and diminish the number and severity of auto accident injuries may, in some states and for some cases, be used to diminish the compensation to which an injured person is entitled (because he/she failed to wear a seatbelt and thus committed negligence contributing to his injuries),[70] the same approach may stem from a consumer-protection law: Since it lets people get off the hook for several days after they reach a deal, that extra time affords the consumer enough time to evaluate appropriately the entire deal and to reduce or eliminate the value of a defense or claim based on the haste in which one first entered the deal. It turns out the consumer had time, after all, and so may be bound because of the consumer protection law? That may well be an unintended consequence.

5. Suppose that a sales representative "knew" that the buyer would eventually buy the property anyway, or "knew" that the purchase truly was in the buyer's best interest. Does that affect your assessment of the ethics of a clever, pushy sales technique? (But isn't it too easy to assert - too self-serving, yet ultimately hard to prove - the two above suppositions about what a salesperson "knew"?). **Do the ends justify the means?** It is really a tricky, difficult argument to make: "Okay, we were unscrupulous, but, in the end, you got a good deal!" We had the buyer's best interests at heart when we, in effect, lied to her to get her to make the deal!

6. How much weight should an employee give to his/her own self-interest (keeping his/her job, getting a raise, a promotion) in deciding whether to adopt an ethically dubious, "winning" approach? How should the employee's interests be balanced with those of customers? If an ethically problematic approach seems to be endorsed by the employer, (say, through the words or conduct of its Senior Vice-President), that means (a) the employer itself, not just the particular salesperson, can be liable for the use of that approach, and (b) an employee has more reason to use the approach - her employer endorses it - than if it is simply the tactic of a renegade sales representative. Still, **Does Behaving Unethically, Per Orders of the Boss, Actually Protect Your Job** (If Not Your Self-respect)? The irony is

---

[70] Some laws have been passed to prevent such a legal impact (reducing damages awards or liability), which would otherwise seem to be a logical extension of legal principles from the statute calling for certain conduct.

that employees sometimes discover that doing everything the supervisor wanted was not only unethical but didn't even serve the employees' own interests. <u>When people higher up in the company find fault with a supervisors' actions, they may simply "clean house": throw out everyone in the department who behaved unethically</u> (or otherwise in a suspect manner); people thus are terminated <u>no matter who actually gave the unethical orders.</u>

When asked to participate in something ethically dubious, you may better deal with that situation if you have already evaluated such a scenario, and thus have developed ideas and goals <u>before</u> you were placed in such a crisis.

7. Sometimes criminal sentencing guidelines or other outside pressures induce employers to fire allegedly malfeasant employees, provide the authorities with evidence against those ex-employees, and otherwise distance the employer from the alleged wrongdoing of its employees. The employer thereby hopes to reduce any criminal charges or bad publicity it may suffer, but does so at the expense of the ex-employees.

C. Ethics and Fraud and Capacity

Ethics and fraud clearly matter in contract law. There are moral issues in contract law. For example, how should we deal with overreaching bargaining? With fishy behavior?

As for the next subject – capacity – there may be: (1) so-called fishy uses of capacity – to raise the lack of capacity as a defense to thwart what seem fair contracts; (2) on the other hand, the possible abuse/taking advantage of people who lack capacity.

> Because of a child's limited view of his/her relationship to others, society must protect the child, who clearly has little or no understanding of contracts.
> See, for example, *The Toddler's Creed*, BURTON L. WHITE, RAISING A HAPPY, UNSPOILED CHILD (1995), and various anonymous versions.

VII. <u>TOPICAL LECTURE</u>: CAPACITY (see pg. 129; Emerson BL)

Introduction to Topical Lecture:
A key contractual issue often is capacity: whether the party to a contract knows what is happening – has mental capability (understands key concepts). For children, the standard is an arbitrary one in which the person proceeds from infancy to adulthood (no middle ground) and is measured generally by the legal age of majority, not by a subjective standard of the child's experience. Important issues include practical concerns such as alleged fraud by the incapacitated, the leverage of who owes what, and the responsibility for necessaries.

> *Some Historical and Cultural Context*
> An Old-fashioned concept – certainly present in most societies until the past couple centuries, was that - even if physically and chronologically a child – a minor was viewed as being a little adult - once a child reached a still fairly young age, he/she was put to work. A newer concept that started to take hold in the mid-to-late 1800s was that children really are completely different from adults, that they need to be protected for a very long time (until say, age 18 or 21).

"[O]nly a person who is legally competent has the power to make a binding contract and can be held to any promises contained therein."[71]

Children's sensibilities are always suspect.
The Toddler's Creed,
"If I want it, it's mine.
If I give it to you and change my mind later, it's mine.
If I can take it away from you, it's mine.
If I had it a little while ago, it's mine.
If it's mine, it will never belong to anybody else, no matter what.
If we are building something together, all the pieces are mine.
If it looks just like mine, it is mine."
BURTON L. WHITE, RAISING A HAPPY, UNSPOILED CHILD (1995).

A. An Absolute Bar to Contract Responsibility, or a Limited Capacity: The Common Law Compared to the German Civil Code

In the common law, until the child attains the age of majority, the child simply cannot be bound to a contract. The child is a legal "infant."[72] While the approach in the United States thus tends to be absolute (you either can enter a contract or you cannot), other societies may follow a more nuanced approach, not just as a cultural matter[73] but as a matter of law. For example, a minor's limited capacity to contract is anchored in Germany's Civil Code (the *Bürgerliches Gesetzbuch* – the "BGB"). The relevant articles are BGB Articles §§106-113, which indicate that children under the age of 7 are completely incapable of making a binding agreement, but that children have limited capacity from age 7 until they attain full capacity at age 18. This means, for instance, that a person in that eleven-year time span (from age 7 until 18) can enter a contract without written permission when his/her legal representative (usually, a parent) "provided the means to do so"; therefore, everything that child buys with his/her pocket money creates a valid contract [BGB §110]. Furthermore, once the parents and a family court allow a minor to run his/her own business, the minor has the full capacity to enter any contract (BGB §112). (The latter provision is not really comparable to the emancipation process followed in American law, although there are special types of contracts – e.g., educational loans, health and life insurance policies, transportation contracts (e.g., airline tickets), and court-approved employment contracts – which US state law often prevents minors from disaffirming (**see pg. 130; Emerson BL**).)

Examples: Daisy and Teenage Web Designers
Daisy is four years old; she appears at her neighbor's house and says "Oh, look, Mr. Clod! See, I got a new tricycle!" Mr. Clod says, "Yes, my niece would like a trike like that one. Say, I have four shiny new quarters. I'll buy your trike from you!" And the deal is done. Shortly thereafter, Daisy comes back to Mr. Clod: "Well, my mom says I have to give you your four quarters back, and I want my trike, please." Mr. Clod: "No way, kid; we had a contract. Get lost!"

---

[71] Id. at 129.
[72] This is that rare area where the law preceded cultural changes, not vice-versa. Childhood as a distinct and protected phase of life is, culturally and socially, a relatively recent notion.
[73] Even when the law says a child cannot be bound, custom or family dictates may impress upon the child his/her moral duty to honor his/her word.

> Daisy can disaffirm (get out of) the contract. Her mother or someone else acting on Daisy's behalf can disaffirm because Daisy <u>lacks capacity</u>. On this matter, the law is the same in the United States and in Germany.
>
> Teenage Web designers often are technologically adept but inexperienced financially and in negotiations (e.g., agreeing to do work for far less than adults would charge). Companies have paid teens far less to handle Cyber–projects than they would full–time, adult employees or consultants. Is that fair? Should it be illegal? The ethics here should not matter regardless of whether it is in the United States or Germany.

B. The Basic Principles and Law of Capacity

Many businesses must sell to minors or people buying for minors. It is a huge market! A toy store, to deal with capacity issues, cannot, as a practical matter, say: "No children allowed!" Instead, a store should *also* deal with the parents: get them to sign in addition to, or instead of, the minor.

<u>Is a party able to understand the nature of his/her actions</u> – the subject and nature of a contract – and can the person comprehend its probable consequences <u>at the time of making the contract?</u> We are looking at a <u>party</u> – not at the meeting of minds between parties.

Minors and insane persons generally are protected. (In Florida and other states, children attain capacity at 18 years of age). So, the practical advice for dealing with minors is: Have adults (e.g., parents) also involved, as parties or guarantors.

Ordinarily, a contract with an incapacitated person is voidable – so there are three alternatives:

(1) Could sue to have contract rescinded
(2) Could use lack of capacity as a defense if others sue to enforce the contract
(3) Disaffirmance (avoidance) - the cancellation or rejection of a contract made during one's incapacity.
  (a) Infant, or parent on his/her behalf, can disaffirm during minority and for a reasonable time after becoming an adult;
  (b) Duty of restoration (generally less of a duty for children than for others lacking capacity) - To return what one can, when one disaffirms, such as:
    i. Giving me back the part of the cake that the child who bought the cake did not yet eat (how is that for "having your cake and eating it, too!"); or
    ii. 13-year-old Billy Bob's returning the bicycle he bought, and being entitled to full reimbursement of his contract price without paying for any depreciation.

> <u>The Restoration Duty: An Example Featuring Jack, Jill and Humpty Dumpty</u>
> Jack and Jill were sweethearts. They were both sixteen. As a surprise for Easter, Jack bought Jill a large ceramic Easter egg—let's call it "Humpty Dumpty"—from a gift shop. Jill's apartment had a beautiful terrace up on a hill that Jack and Jill always went up, to fetch water from Fairy Tale Lake. Jill sat the egg on the terrace wall. A blustery wind developed and blew the egg off the wall. It crashed into a thousand pieces. Jack and Jill fetched a pail and picked up all the pieces. They tried to put the egg back together again, but their attempt was unsuccessful. Jack returned the pieces to the gift shop, but the shop refused to reimburse him. Has Jack any recourse? Yes!
> In most states, Jack would be entitled to a return of his "consideration" because he is a minor. The fact that the gift shop's "consideration" is returned in pieces is part of the risk the shop must accept in dealing with minors. The trend in some states, albeit still a minority of states, is to account for depreciation while the good (the "consideration") was in the minor's possession. Under such a scheme, Jack would receive very little, if anything, in return for a cracked egg.

C. Ratification (the opposite of disaffirmance)

Ratification is defined as "a person's explicit or implicit approval or adoption of a prior act that did not bind him/her." **See pg. 740; Emerson BL** ("Once a minor reaches the age of 18, he/she may accept the contract, and thus ratify it **ab initio** (from the beginning). *Such ratification may be express or implied – an understanding of the kind required to have made a contract in the first place.*") **see pg. 132; Emerson BL.**

The ratification comes in two forms:

a. Express (e.g., upon attaining capacity, declaring "That was a great contract I entered into while a drunk/child/lunatic; certainly I'll honor it!")

b. Implied (e.g., after attaining capacity, continuing to live in an apartment and paying rent for several more months)

> Courts sometimes differ on what actions constitute implied ratification. In general, however, making payments when due, continuing to enjoy the benefits of the agreement, or other clear, unambiguous action within the scope of the contract usually implies acceptance."[74]

YOUTUBE - CapacityEmersonKidsInterview1min48secs.wmv at robertwemersonufl and then CapacityEmersonKids_postInterview_discussion.wmv (17mins30secs) at robertwemersonufl

1. Three Problems Involving Capacity:
Alleged Misrepresentation of Capacity, Necessaries, and Leverage

a. Alleged Misrepresentation of capacity by the party lacking capacity

Trend –> such misconduct may estop the minor. However, courts still worry about the other side's raising this claim of misrepresentation to excuse its duping the minor – e.g., demanding of the minor that he/she misrepresent his/her age. If a child is too young to understand contracts, he/she may also be too young to understand Fraud, let alone resist the words of an adult.

In Florida, when there is a case of intentional, egregious fraud by a minor misrepresenting his age, the minor loses his right to disaffirm.

Practices

Suppose that businesses have a practice that employees make the purchaser (the child) "put down his crayons," stand up and sign the name to say he was an adult! That is then followed by a squeaky voice from a 4-foot-two-inch boy - "My name is Billy Bob and I'm 18 years old."

But what if there is justifiable reliance - that it really seems as if the kid is over 18? My childhood friend started ordering stuff through the mail; when asked for the money his reply, "I don't have to pay; I am only 13. Let that be a lesson to you!"

What can the store do? It may be very hard for it to win a case and enforce a judgment.

My friend certainly was precocious and had quite a collection. He learned some law, both the principles and the practicalities, at an early age.[75]

b. Necessaries

---

[74] Id. at 132.
[75] In fact, he is now a very successful lawyer in Washington, DC!

Example: Goldilocks, age 10, while hiking through the backwoods of Vermont, decides to stop at the Three Bears Inn. She enjoys a nice dish of cereal and a warm bed. The next morning she refuses to pay for the room and board, asserting infancy as a defense. Is the defense applicable? No! Food and shelter are necessities, and a minor is liable for the reasonable value of necessities.

What are necessaries? Food, clothing, shelter, education, etc. (things that the parents should be providing, or that an emancipated child should be getting for himself/herself).

What effect do necessaries have on a contract? A minor can still get out of the contract, but must pay the reasonable value of what the minor got. This is not necessarily the contract price. The minor is liable on a quasi–contract.

Example: 6 months into a one–year lease. Now the minor, who is the tenant, wants out of the lease. The landlord only is entitled to payment of the reasonable value of what the tenant received, not necessarily the rental amount. The tenant is not responsible for the rest of the lease

Why shouldn't a business simply go ahead with any business–minor contract, if the contract involves necessaries?
(a) It may not be a necessary, at least in the eyes of the court. (What does it matter if the parties to the contract believe that it concerns a necessity? What does matter is what a court thinks.)

(b) Even if it is a necessary, the business only gets reasonable value, not necessarily a contract price.
(c) The business only gets paid for what the minor actually received or used (and cannot return).

c. Practicality – A Problem of Leverage
Who has the money? Who holds the goods?

Did the party allegedly lacking capacity furnish consideration (e.g., for goods, the sales price)? If so, that party is not – as a practical matter – in as good a position as if it had not performed.

Even though legally obliged to return money and receive back the goods, many businesses: "sue me" or "let's split the difference" or "take store credit" (rather than automatically allowing rescission). Leverage exists because, perhaps ironically, the amounts are too small and it is thus not worth going to court.

An executive of one large chain stated that five percent of sales are rescinded because of the company's liberal return policy, but he sees no substantial element of disaffirmance by reason of minority in such returns:

> "If there are large–scale (numerous) sales, then the risk is spread in dealing with minors. Obviously, the hazard in dealing with minors is potentially severe, but if the issue is the sale of a large number of small–ticket items to a large number of minors, the business risk is considerably diminished."

D. Others (Besides Children) Perhaps Lacking Capacity

Others (besides children) perhaps lacking capacity are drunks, insane persons, enemy aliens, illegal aliens, and convicts.

Drunks are so intoxicated that they do not comprehend the legal consequences of entering into a contract.

In Florida, and many other states, there is less ability to disaffirm for most drunkards than there is for legal infants. An intoxicated person only can disaffirm if, in effect, he/she did not understand the nature of the transaction – that it was a contract.

Disaffirmance can occur while the person is intoxicated or within a reasonable time after he/she becomes sober. <u>The Voiding Party must make restitution.</u> He/she <u>must pay reasonable value for what was consumed</u>.

The intoxicated person cannot disaffirm if an innocent third–party (e.g., assignees) would be harmed. **[One cannot just hang around in bars and come back later with the ones you want or don't want. Cannot simply disaffirm some, keeping the ones you like- "I ought to get drunk more often!" you think. That is foolish thinking.]**

E. Habitual Drunkard Statutes

A habitual drunkard is a person who exhibits an involuntary tendency to become intoxicated as often as the temptation to do so is presented. The person may be more often drunk than sober. However, once the court has been shown that the person lacks the willpower needed to control his or her appetite for alcohol or drugs, it will permanently relieve the person of his or her capacity to contract.

As with the permanently insane, a guardian will be appointed to handle the estate of the habitual drunkard. All contracts, checks, notes, wills, deeds, and other legal actions taken by the incompetent will thereafter be considered void. Liquor stores and bars would soon realize that they could not expect payment for his/her drinks.

F. Insane Persons

> In an episode of "The Simpsons," the television character Homer Simpson was declared sane and given a certificate which he could proudly display. In reality, it is extremely rare for anyone to have such a certificate; also uncommon, albeit not as rare, is to have the opposite "certificate": one that says you are <u>insane.</u>

So, are you "certified"?

1. Yes - judicially declared incompetent (very rare)- then the contract is *void*; it is wiped out from the face of contract law- there is a similar status for incapacitated persons under Habitual Drunkard Statutes. It is as if you have an "I" stamped on your head (like Nathaniel Hawthorne's Scarlet Letter with the "A" stamped on adulteress Hester Prynne's cloak).

2. No - then the contract is *voidable* until a reasonable time after lucidity; one still must pay for necessaries.

Ordinarily, a contract that an insane person enters into is voidable (by that person or someone acting on his/her behalf) until a reasonable time after the person acquires lucidity. Insane persons still must pay for necessaries.

Determining whether someone was insane when he/she made an agreement is generally a question for the factfinder. For example, suppose that a business law professor dresses strangely for public performances, such as in staged readings from court opinions and in an annual "classic" dance spoofing the "Nutcracker" ballet. If he enters into contracts while in his "best" tutu, does that render those contracts voidable? The answer is "no," unless he is more than eccentric, but is in fact incapacitated. The wearing of the tutu does provide some notice to other parties that the professor is certainly a bit different, but more would be needed to show incapacity.

What is the approach for those who are certified insane? These people have been judicially declared incompetent (a very rare procedure). The contracts the certified insane try to make are void. So, these insane persons' status is similar to the status of incapacitated persons under Habitual Drunkard Statutes.

G. Others Perhaps Lacking Capacity

Other groups, such as enemy aliens,[76] may have limited contractual capacity. In some states, convicts may lack capacity. Unless specified in a statute, a person convicted of a crime generally has the capacity to enter into contracts. Some statutes rendering a person civilly dead may render him/her entirely, or to a limited extent, unable to contract. Thus, under statutes imposing a deprivation or suspension of civil rights in general terms, it has been held that a convict's contract is void, unless for necessaries.[77]

End of Topical Lecture on "Capacity"

VIII. LEGALITY (PUBLIC POLICY) (see pg. 133; Emerson BL)

A. Public Policy

"There are two reasons why a contract's subject matter may be illegal: statute and public policy. Statutes are legislative acts; **public policy** is a judicial determination of prevailing morality."[78]

For this element of contracts, there are two key questions. What is the contract's purpose? What is the court's opinion about prevailing morality?

With Contracts, there are competing concerns: balancing freedom of contract versus upholding the public interest (e.g., protecting "small fry"). The underlying question thus may be: Even if there is a genuine agreement between parties that have capacity, do we as a society want such contracts to stand?

Small Examples of Problems with Legality!
Florida

On November 28, 2001, 3–foot–2–inch Dave Flood (a Tampa radio show host known as "Dave the Dwarf") sued in federal court to have overturned a 1989 Florida statute that permits the Florida Department of Business and Professional Regulation to fine or revoke the liquor license of a bar that allows dwarf tossing (an activity popular in some Florida bars in the late 1980s). Only Florida and New York have state laws banning dwarf tossing in bars.

Flood sought no monetary damages, but wanted to wear a harness with handles so that patrons at bars can pay to toss him into an air mattress or other padded area. The lawsuit contended that the dwarf–tossing ban violates Flood's 14th Amendment equal protection rights.

The federal judge dismissed Flood's case.

France

France is a land of *haute couture,* but it is no more immune than the United States, Ireland, Australia, Canada, and many other "civilized" places to the apparent allure – and scourge - of having

---

[76] These would be persons who, during wartime, are the citizens of a belligerent nation. For example, during World War II enemy aliens included the people and businesses of Germany and Japan. Generally, all contracts involving those persons were put on hold and unenforceable while the war continued.

[77] Until 1882 in the United Kingdom and the late 19th century in the United States, married women were without contractual capacity. That was because at common law they were considered the creatures of their husbands and without wills of their own. This disability has been removed by statute throughout all common law nations. These Married Women's Acts of over 100 years ago may seem quaint, by today's standards, but they made sure that women did not lose their full contractual capacity just because they got married.

[78] Robert W. Emerson, *Business Law*. NY: Barron's Educational Series (6th ed., 2015), at 133.

into bars or discos and pay to toss tiny people. After proceeding through French courts, the case Wackenheim v. France (2002) was brought to the UN Human Rights Committee in Geneva, and. The legal grounds for a French law permitting local authorities to ban dwarf tossing was of the European Convention on Human Rights, which states, "No one shall be subjected to torture or inhuman or degrading treatment or punishment." The committee observed that prohibiting dwarf-tossing was not unlawful discrimination against dwarfs but was a justifiable decision to prevent an affront to human dignity.[79] It thus denied the dwarf's claim that his being deprived of the right to employment was the same as being deprived of the right to dignity. The committee observed that the Convention's Article 26 labels differentiation as discrimination "when it is not based on objective and reasonable grounds." The committee noted that the state had illustrated that dwarf tossing was "necessary to protect public order" and did not amount to "abusive measures."

Overall

In these and other cases, the absolute freedom of the parties may be trumped by society's desire to prevent exploitation and potential harm to these "little people." More importantly, regardless of whether the dwarfs could either take measures to protect themselves or simply agree to assume the risks, society may set boundaries on what people can agree to do.

Note that the same rationale applies to bans on other activities such as prostitution.

B. Good Faith

If something is illegal or otherwise against public policy, then a contract intending, supporting, or otherwise contemplating such wrongfulness is void. A fundamental notion is that to allow a person to profit from his/her own wrongdoing is bad public policy.

Good Faith is a core concept associated with legality (it encompasses moral or ethical issues). In the Uniform Commercial Code, there are numerous provisions directly concerning good faith, such as UCC 1–102(3), 1–201(19), 1–203 & 2–103(1)(b). The principles are clear:

"Every contract or duty within the UCC imposes on the parties an obligation of good faith." UCC 2–103(1)(b). Good faith means honesty in fact and – for merchants – it also means "observance of reasonable commercial standards of fair dealing." Id.

Under the CISG, from the very beginning of sales negotiations onward, parties must have good faith. But there is no express good faith provision (except to try to promote good faith transactions).

For example, if showing pornographic movies is illegal, then making and financing it may also be illegal – and the contracts about that would be rendered void. A family financing such ventures gone bad is the subject of a New York case, *Braunstein v. Jason Tarantella, Inc.*, 450 N.Y.S.2d 682 (1982). In Braunstein, parents sued the son to get their money back, but courts held the contract void against public policy.

As courts' contract interpretation becomes the law of contracts, so public policy, at its most basic level, simply is the courts' opinion about prevailing morality.

Good Faith and Fair Dealing principles mean, among other things, that one should:
1. Refrain from imposing improper conditions on the negotiations.
2. Disclose enough about parallel negotiations to allow the other party to make a counterproposal.
3. Keep negotiating until an impasse or an agreement has been reached.

C. Changing Public Policy in a Changing Social and Moral Climate

Social policy and Public policy are often linked to concern about family matters and morality.

---

[79] The principles of international human rights dictate that all human beings are born free and equal in dignity and rights. They also all are endowed with reason and conscience, which may argue for the dwarf's right to be employed in any way he/she chooses.

Technological change inevitably leads to entirely new types of contracts as well as changes in the subjects and terms of current contracts. There are thus corresponding legal issues associated with this transformation. For example, surrogate motherhood agreements were difficult to imagine, and impossible as a matter of actual obstetrics, until the last quarter of the 20th Century. In this way, technological advances lead to new contracts and thus to judicial consideration of public policy. Along these lines, changes in social norms and practices lead to legal turmoil and transformation.

1. An Example: Contracts and Cohabitation (Folks Livin' Together)

A Changing Social and Moral Climate May Lead to Court Decisions Reflecting a Change in Public Policy. Cases involving nonmarital cohabitation furnish some excellent examples. A representative case is *Marvin v. Marvin*, 557 P.2d 106 (California Supreme Court, 1976).

Marvin involved a couple's alleged agreement about living together. It did not involve a possible common–law marriage. Common–law marriage can only arise in 13 states. (California and Florida are among the large majority that do NOT have common–law marriage.)[80] Before the Marvin decision, agreements about living together were considered "meretricious" (lustful, licentious) agreements and were not allowed. In Marvin, though, the court held, such agreements could be allowed, and thus "palimony" could be awarded.[81]

Times have changed, the court noted; it observed that many unmarried couples now live together, with little (if any) social stigma. The court's decision is a precedent for California courts and is guidance for other courts (e.g., in other states). The *Marvin* view (that an express agreement between cohabitants is enforceable except to the extent that it is explicitly founded on consideration of sexual services) is followed in, most states, including Florida. But a few states may still cling to the view that an agreement is invalid if illicit sexual relations constitute any part of the consideration for the agreement. And all states still look carefully at agreements between cohabiting nonmarital parties; and agreements tending to dissolve a marriage or to facilitate adultery are closely scrutinized to determine whether the agreement's main objective is to produce that result.

2. More on Marriage as an Example: Contracts Undermining Existing Marriages

More generally, the law declares void any contract restricting people (e.g., adults) who otherwise have a right to marry, except for laws reinforcing monogamy. So agreements generally should not restrict or prohibit marriage, nor should they foster divorce.[82] If Jane takes $5,000 in return for agreeing never to marry, or not to marry for the next three years, or not to marry a particular individual, she may do so anyway, as such contracts are void. Similarly, if Jane is paid $5,000 in return for promising to divorce her

---

[80] Common law marriage generally occurs when two single adults of the opposite sex live together, for a minimal time period (several years, the number depending on the state), agreeing or intending to be married (entering into a type of marital relationship), and publicly holding themselves out as being married. But such a common law marriage can only occur in the District of Columbia and these 13 states: Alabama, Colorado, Iowa, Kansas, Kentucky (only for workers' compensation death benefits), Montana, New Hampshire (only for inheritance purposes), Oklahoma, Pennsylvania, Rhode Island, South Carolina, Texas, and Utah (but in Utah a judge must determine its existence within one year of the common–law marriage's termination).

[81] Palimony is a term for support that might be awarded when unmarried couples separate, and it is somewhat comparable to alimony for divorcing couples.

[82] In *McCall v. Frampton*, 439 N.Y.S.2d 11 (New York Appeals Division, 1980), Peter Frampton, the rock singer, was sued by his former live–in girlfriend. Both had been married to other people when they started to cohabit; therefore, the ex–girlfriend's claim was denied. Adultery was still a crime in New York. While this prohibition may not have been enforced as a matter of criminal law, it still represented a public policy that cannot be overcome by a private contract.

As a more recent example, one may also think of Craigslist ads supposedly for something else (e.g., a roommate), but really about sex.

husband, she may keep the money and her husband if she so desires, as that contract is also void. However, property settlement agreements between divorcing spouses are valid.

3. Proposed Changes

On November 29, 2002, the American Law Institute (ALI)[83] recommended that the states adopt a number of changes in family law. One proposed change concerns domestic partners, who are defined as "two persons of the same or opposite sex, not married to one another, who for a significant period of time share a primary residence and live together as a couple." At the end of an intimate relationship, the ALI recommends that a domestic partner be entitled to compensatory payments similar to alimony "on the same basis as a spouse." Also – here it becomes like *Marvin v. Marvin* – when domestic partners split up, their property should be divided in the same way a divorces court would divide the property of a husband and wife.

D. Specific Types of Problems

Specific Types of Problems involving Illegality/Public policy include usury, insurance matters, licensing issues, *in pari delicto*, unconscionability, exculpatory clauses, and adhesion clauses (which we now will deal with, one by one).

1. Usury (see pg. 134; Emerson BL)

What is usury? It is unlawful interest charges (e.g., loan sharking). It is not simply what you might consider "excessive" interest or other charges. For example, every time a big spender reviews her Visa bill she might find the finance charges "excessive," indeed "outrageous!" But that is simply in the eyes of the beholder. What matters is the law and whether the charges are in compliance with the usury and other lending laws.

Generally, any interest rate can be charged against loans for a business purpose. If there is a consumer purpose, then the interest rate is limited by law. And, therefore, crooked lenders sometimes inaccurately label a consumer loan as one for business purposes.[84] For example, in June 2000 two Gainesville business owners were arrested for illegal lending practices. They allegedly charged their customers as much as 500% interest on loans. Customers wrote checks for $120, not to be cashed for 15 days, and just received $100 in cash. Each two–week extension in paying the loan would cost another $20. The business owners were arrested on charges of usury, racketeering, and making illegal consumer loans.[85]

Usury laws are complex, but if a creditor knowingly breaks that law, then ordinarily the creditor gets nothing, not even the principal. If the violation is unintentional, then there generally are three court alternatives, depending on the state and the overall circumstances. The creditor gets: (i) Nothing, as if the violation were intentional; (ii) Just the Principal (no interest at all); or (iii) Principal, plus the lawful maximum of interest (or some other judicially–determined amount of interest).

---

[83] The ALI is an influential group of lawyers, judges, and academics that study laws, issues reports, and sometimes recommends legal reforms.

[84] Normally, a franchisor does not finance directly its franchisees. If the latter need some financing, it usually comes through third-party sources. The issue of franchisee financing, though, contains issues perhaps as easily likened to consumer financing as business financing, and – as such – leads to public policy issues under both state and federal law. Robert W. Emerson, *Franchisees in a Fringe Banking World: Striking the Balance Between Entrepreneurial Autonomy and Consumer Protection*, 46 AKRON L. REV. 1 (2013), available at http://ssrn.com/author=86449. The analysis applies across the business law spectrum generally.

[85] Under Florida law, charging more than 45% annual interest on a consumer loan is usury, a felony. Also, to make check–advance loans, a business must have a state license.

> Joke – Homer Simpsonism: "If you really want something in life, you have to work for it. Now quiet; they're about to announce the lottery numbers."
> (That would be gambling, something typically unlawful unless a state sanctioned system. Private gambling is thus distinct from insurance, which is lawful if concerning an insurable interest.)

2. Insurance (see pg. 527-530; Emerson BL)

Insurance is a special contract intended to transfer and allocate risks from the insured (person taking out the policy) to an insurance company (insurer). The insurer issues an insurance policy covering a possible loss. For the insurance agreement to be enforced, it must meet the usual requirements of a contract and the insured person must have an insurable interest in the subject matter (e.g., property, health, life) that is being insured. No "wagering" on the life/health/property of another person.

An insurable interest is a legal or equitable interest in the subject matter. For property (real or personal) insurance, the insurable interest is usually ownership; for life insurance, it may be the insured's own life, or that of his/her spouse, children, parents, business partners, debtors and other shareholders or key personnel.

An insurable interest (an economic interest) is: a property interest – owning of property, or lending money so somebody else can buy it. **One must have an insurable interest; one cannot just insure someone or something and hope for the worst.**

Which of these are insurable interests?
a. Mortgagee of a house (the lender)
b. Employer of a Key Worker
c. Spouses (or minor children)
d. "You don't look so well!"

En viager example – involving an approach common in France and many other countries: paying a property holder's rent/mortgage/payments/utilities until a person dies, and then that property becomes the payor's property. By paying the mortgage and perhaps also the utilities, the payor helps the old person living in that home have some extra spending money. These "en viager" (meaning, "for life") deals to purchase apartments, while not as common in the United States as France or many other Civil Law countries, are far from rare in the United States (e.g., reverse mortgages have some similarity to an *en viager* arrangement).

In all such arrangements, whether in France, the United States, the homeowner gets a monthly income and - upon the owner's death - the buyer inherits the apartment, regardless of how much or little was paid. In effect, the buyer gambles on getting a real estate bargain- provided that the owner drops dead in due time.

In 1965, 47-year-old notary, Andre-François Raffray thought he had a great deal. He would pay his client, 90-year-old Jeanne Calment, $500 a month until she died, then move into her grand multiple-room apartment in the southern French town of Arles, which is northwest of Marseille in Provence. The ultimate outcome was quite unforeseen, but certainly lawful. *[handwritten: She lived for 30+ yrs, Andre died before Calment. The wife keeps paying. Calment died at 122]*

Insurable interests can be for a close relationship – e.g., family (even if the interest is not an economic interest), or for a key employee or partner.

Reasons for key–employee insurance are that it (1) helps in recruiting a replacement employee, (2) bridges revenue gaps when important people are lost, and (3) sends a positive message to investors, customers, and suppliers.

Could you just get insurance on a person and try to bump him off? Of course not, as that is murder (or at least attempted murder or conspiracy to commit murder). It is still unethical and illegal even if one simply gets insurance on someone because you think he is going to die soon (even though you don't try to speed him on his way!). If he dies, ordinarily the insurance company can refuse to pay you on the policy because there was no insurable interest. But the scenario can be altered what may appear to be only slightly and result in an insurable interest. There was, for example, an investor who wished that his former accountant would die. Why? The accountant had stolen funds from the investor and others; the accountant was convicted in criminal court, but did not have money to repay the investor. Therefore, the investor took out life insurance on the accountant. Here there is an insurable interest – an unpaid civil judgment against the accountant and in favor of the investor. Like all insurance, it may not "pay off" if the insured lives long enough (more premiums paid than justified given any final payout to the beneficiary).

Gambling (against public policy) or Insurance (generally acceptably)?

Some skill? (versus luck and/or vicarious interest); i.e., some skill versus pure luck!

What connection do you have to it? If just a vicarious interest, then it is gambling – a void contract. (void when it is just an emotional interest – who's gonna win this season? Bet on it?) UNLESS specifically state-authorized (e.g., the lottery)

The Golfing Hole-In-One Example:
Dhyana put $10 into the jar, then walked out to the tee, with three balls to try for the $5000 hole-in-one prize. The flag was only 200 meters away, but on a dogleg turn. Dhyana teed up the three balls, made three or four practice swings, then smacked one ball into the woods, the second alongside the rough, and the third onto the green and into the hole. Several people saw that. When she went into the office to claim her prize, the manager refused to pay, even with the witnesses. Dhyana sued, but the golf course's lawyer said that the game involved chance (<u>no</u> consideration), and therefore was against public policy. The court should therefore declare the contract void and not compel the golf course to pay, the lawyer argued.

The judge ruled in favor of Dhyana: "There was consideration - $10 from Dhyana - and that hole-in-one involved skill. The defendant owes Dhyana that prize."

---

3. Licensing
Licensing can raise issues of legality. There are two types of licensing: (1) regulatory licensing, for fields such as law, medicine, dentistry, accounting, plumbing, engineering, and numerous other areas; and (2) revenue licensing.

a. Regulatory Licenses
In regulatory licensing fields, the prime concern of the state is the competence and integrity of professionals. The primary purpose is to protect the consumer/client/patient (i.e., protect the public). The result is the voiding of contracts regarding services by unlicensed surgeons, lawyers, dentists, accountants, and other professionals.

Her Clients Were Swayed by Her Credentials

Arline Ek of California, age 59, advertised $300 "one-day divorces" available directly from the Dominican Republic, where "the rich and famous obtain divorces" without any residence requirements.

Stephen Taylor, deputy district attorney in San Joaquin County, California, filed a civil complaint against Ek seeking to fine her $50,000 for false advertising. Taylor found other things about Ek, manager of a legal typing service, to be incredible. A letter to potential customers, signed "Arline Ek, H.S.G.," falsely asserted that she was a "certified paralegal." Taylor further complained, "And those letters after her name. I don't know what the hell they mean."

Ek was barred from continuing to advertise or do any such work.

Unlicensed "Service" provider – gets nothing under the contract; it does not matter how good a job was actually done, because he did <u>not</u> have a REGULATORY license.

b. Revenue Licenses

In revenue licensing, the purpose is mainly to raise money – through taxes, fees, or other charges. The idea behind the licensing is to use it to keep tabs on numbers – Demographics!

Many contract issues are distinct from license issues (e.g., fraud, consumer protection generally)

4. *In Pari Delicto*: a Latin phrase, means "at equal fault."

> **Some Amateur Psychology**
> From the outset, children may blame others for any difficulty. Often there are mutual recriminations; the situation appears to be *in pari delicto*: "You bit me first!" "Well, you pushed me first." So, we learn early on, and we may continue throughout adulthood, taking any blameworthy act and saying someone else is also to blame!

Sometimes both parties to an alleged contract have behaved wrongly. Courts may choose to wash their hands of the matter. To do so, the courts invoke the legal concept, *in pari delicto*.

Suppose that a man charged with a crime bribed a judge to avoid a conviction. If the judge nonetheless convicted him, could the man (who now has plenty of time sitting in a jail cell!) successfully sue the judge for breaching their bribery "contract." Of course, the agreement is void as against public policy. The parties are *in pari delicto*. The man is not entitled to have a court order his money returned. Conversely, suppose the judge was promised money if he acquitted the man, and the judge then acquitted him, but that man refused to pay the bribe he "owed" to the judge, the judge's lawsuit to receive his bribe would be denied.[86]

5. Mergers and Takeovers

Just as the "Ubernahmegesprache" case discussed above (*Buxbaum v. Deutsche Bank AG*, 196 F.Supp.2d 367 (S.D.N.Y. 2002)) illustrates that fraud can occur from a failure to provide information (remaining silent, particularly after some incomplete information has been provided), so the case dealt with corporate takeovers. The legality of such takeovers and the related behavior is sometimes an issue in contract law (and was discussed in LSB Part One concerning corporate law).

6. Unconscionability - sometimes referred to as "Outrage" (see pg. 124-125; Emerson BL)

a. The Basics

A basic, catch–all concept for many areas of possible illegality or violations of public policy is unconscionability. For something to be unconscionable, it must be more than just "merely" unlawful; it must be grossly unfair.

Unconscionability "describes special situations in which an overbearing party in a superior position imposes outrageously unfair terms on some other party."[87]

An equation for unconscionability would be:

$$(\neq BP \text{ and/or} \neq Info \text{ or unfair surprise}) + GUT \approx U$$

KEY: GUT means "grossly unfair terms" and BP means "bargaining power"

---

[86] In either case, the authorities would certainly investigate what the judge had done. No judge in his right mind would sue to receive a bribe!
[87] Robert W. Emerson, Business Law. NY: Barron's Educational Series (6th ed., 2015), at 124.

Some states (e.g., California, New York, and Texas) require that a party claiming unconscionability must show both procedural and substantive unconscionability.

Procedural unconscionability concerns assent and focuses on the bargaining process (the formation of the contract): Did the parties actually bargain over the terms of the contract claimed to be unconscionable? Was there a very high degree of inequality in bargaining power or unfair surprise due to "hidden" terms in a contract that is lengthy, confusing, or both.

Substantive unconscionability concerns the fairness of the agreement. It may be present when there is an overly harsh allocation of risks or costs or a great price disparity (e.g., three to four times higher than or below the fair market value). The question may simply be: Was the contract unfairly burdensome to the complaining party?

b. *Henningsen v. Bloomfield Motors, Inc.*

One of the most notable and cited cases pertaining to unconscionability in contract law is *Henningsen v. Bloomfield Motors, Inc.*, 161 A.2d 69 (N.J. 1960). There, plaintiff Claus Henningsen purchased from a dealership, Bloomfield Moors, Inc., a Plymouth automobile manufactured by Chrysler Corporation. Ten days after Claus received the car, and presented it to his wife, plaintiff Helen Henningsen, as a Mother's Day present, Helen was driving the car when it unexpectedly swerved into a wall and was totaled. Mechanical failure was determined to be the sole cause for the collision.

The claimed damages in the suit against the dealer and Chrysler included Helen's injuries from the crash. However, the vehicle's sales contract disclaimed all liability for the manufacturer except for replacement of factory parts within 90 days after delivery or 4,000 miles of driving the car, whichever came first. This disclaimer was printed in small text, but was not so small that it would be difficult for the average person to read. Still, it was on the back side of the sales contract and was different from the front side, which had head notes and margin notes and thereby simplified for the reader that part of the agreement. The dealer did not point this clause out to Claus when he purchased the car, and Claus admitted later that he did not read it when he bought the car.

The court dismissed the negligence claim due to insufficient evidence. The court ruled in the Henningsens' favor on their other claim - that there was an implied warranty of merchantability. It found the liability disclaimer to be unconscionable. The New Jersey Supreme Court's unanimous opinion affirming the trial court's holding delineated many of the aspects which led to the ruling for the plaintiffs:

(1) that the ordinary consumer "cannot be expected to have the knowledge or capacity or even the opportunity to adequately inspect automobiles to decide whether they are reasonably fit for their designed purpose";
(2) that absolutely no bargaining took place over the terms of the contract;
(3) that the disclaimer was used not just by Chrysler, but by other large automobile manufacturers, which adopted it directly from the Automobile Manufacturer's Association (AMA) as a standard "warranty" provision;
(4) that, in an *entirely* 'take it or leave it' manner, consumers needing automobiles were forced to accept these terms in order to purchase a car automobile;
(5) that the AMA clause would in no way signal to an ordinary reasonable person that he/she is giving up the right to receive damages for personal injuries resulting from a defective car, and to hold otherwise would be an "abandonment of justice";
(6) that because personal injuries from a defective automobile could be severe, the right to receive compensation for such injuries is "the most important and fundamental one";
(7) that the bargaining position "was so grossly unequal, that the inexorable conclusion which follows is that [the purchaser] is not permitted to bargain at all"; and
(8) that the AMA clause, which would disclaim the implied warranty of merchantability as "violative of public policy" and it is therefore void.

c. The *Lesion*

In France, a concept similar to unconscionability is called lesion, which in a narrow sense refers to the loss caused to a party by the disproportion between the two sides of a contract (e.g., far too high a price paid for property sold); and which in a wider sense refers to any substantive unfairness in a contract's provision.

d. UCC § 2-302

The Uniform Commercial Code § 2–302 (Unconscionable Contract or Clause) sets forth the law on unconscionable sales:

"1. If the court as a matter of law finds the contract or any clause of the contract to have been unconscionable at the time it was made,

    a. the court may refuse to enforce the contract, or

    b. it may enforce the remainder of the contract without the unconscionable clause, or

    c. it may so limit the application of any unconscionable clause as to avoid any unconscionable result. **Make it "conscionable!"** (fair).

2. When it is claimed or appears to the court that the contract or any clause thereof may be unconscionable, the parties shall be afforded a reasonable opportunity to present evidence as to its commercial setting, purpose and effect to aid the court in making the determination."

e. Cases

The following cases involve unconscionability.

1. *Vokes v. Arthur Murray* (previously discussed) and *Parker v. Arthur Murray*

The Florida court ordered the rescission of the Vokes – Arthur Murray dancing lessons contract. Parties were not of equal bargaining strength. Arthur Murray Dance Studio used its superior bargaining position to take advantage of Vokes (e.g., to induce her to enter into an unfair contract, one premised on Vokes' belief in the dance studio's exaggerations about her dancing ability and her capacity for improvement via lots of lessons).

Because of the influence of "constant and continuous barrage of flattery and false praise…it would be *not only inequitable, but unconscionable* for a Court to allow such contracts to stand," the court held [emphasis added].

However, to show how facts can be crucial, consider *Parker v. Arthur Murray*, 295 N.E.2d 487 (Ill. App. 1973). Other than the plaintiffs' situations, the facts of *Vokes* and of *Parker* were similar.

Ryland Parker was 37-years-old when he contracted for dance lessons. He lived alone at the time and was college educated. In November 1959, Parker visited the Arthur Murray Studio in Oak Park, Illinois to redeem three free dance lessons. Similar to Audrey Vokes, he was excessively complimented and told of his bright future and "exceptional potential" as a dancer. He then enrolled for 75 hours' worth of lessons for one thousand dollars. Parker made little, if any, dancing progress but was continually praised for his skills as he agreed to pay for more lessons totaling over 2,700 hours at a price of almost $25,000. Then, in September 1961, Parker was severely injured in a car accident before he could attend all of the lessons for which he had paid.

Parker's injuries left him unable to use the lessons, and - despite the contract's saying that no refunds would be granted - the court ordered the dance studio to refund Parker's payment for the remaining hours due to impossibility of performance. Parker claimed fraud and also sought rescission of all the contracts he had made with Arthur Murray. The court refused because of Parker's educational background and the relationship between him and the studio. What Parker contended was fraud, the trial judge described as "a matter of pumping salesmanship" (Parker had been told he had "exceptional potential," that he was "a natural born dancer" and a "terrific dancer"). Although the studio acted unethically, the circumstances failed to satisfy the high requirement necessary for the resulting contract to be considered unconscionable, that is, unlawful (not just *morally* problematic).

      2. *Piehl v. Norwegian Old People's Home Society of Chicago*, 469 N.E.2d 705 (Ill. 1984)

The plaintiff was the administrator for the estate of Finn. He sued to set aside a contract Finn had made with the Defendant for lifelong care in Defendant's nursing home. The contract required Finn to relinquish all of her assets, present and future, in exchange for the lifelong care. Because Finn died about 5 1/2 months into the contract, the plaintiff alleged that the contract was unconscionable. The court disagreed. Although the contract was more favorable to the nursing home than to Finn, the court found that it did not shock the conscience of society. Therefore, the contract was upheld. Was not this, in a sense, simply the opposite case – on the facts – than the *en viager* case involving Jeanne Calment? (In the former, the person lives such a short period of time, and in the latter the person far outlasts that which actuarial tables predict.

Business-to-Business Contracts and Unconscionability – Two Different Cases, with Different Outcomes

     Gianni Sport Ltd. v. Gantos, Inc., 391 N.W.2d 760 (Mich. App. 1986), *Cardinal Stone Co. v. Rival Mfg. Co.*, 669 F.2d 395 (6th Cir. 1982), and *Three D Depts., Inc. v. K Mart Corp.*, 940 F.2d 666 (7th Cir. 1991), show the high standard necessary for a court to find an agreement unconscionable.

     In *Gianni*, defendant Gantos purchased women's clothing from plaintiff Gianni. The purchase order, drafted by Gantos, included a clause that stated Gantos could, upon notice to the seller, terminate the entire order if any goods were not delivered for any reason. After Gantos gave such notice and cancelled the entire order, Gianni agreed to a 50% reduction in price if Gantos would accept the original order.

     At trial, Gianni argued that the purchase order's cancellation clause was unconscionable and the trial court and later an appellate court agreed. The Michigan appeals court concluded that "a last minute cancellation places the seller in the untenable position of absorbing the loss or negotiating with the buyer to accept the goods at a reduced price." As the Gianni-Gantos contract formed about 20% of Gianni's annual sales and about only 1% of Gantos's business. The goods to be delivered from Gianni to Gantos were made specifically by Gianni for Gantos, so it was extremely unlikely that these goods could be sold at all if not to Gantos.

     The court found no evidence that the cancellation clause was negotiable. It found one witness's testimony that "the buyer in our industry is in the driver's seat" and the description of those buyers as "big sharks" particularly telling: the buyers' unequal bargaining power let them impose such clauses. So, the second agreement (the one at half price) was invalid because the cancellation clause was *unconscionable*. Gianni was held to be entitled to the full price under the original contract.

     The contract in *Cardinal Stone Co. v. Rival Mfg. Co.* included a similar unilateral cancellation clause, but the court ruled differently because of the parties' respective situations: (1) the contracting companies were of similar size; (2) the plaintiff knew that demand for the product the defendant produced was volatile, which was sound reasoning for having a cancellation clause; and (3) finding that the plaintiff "expressly relinquished" so, right in agreeing to that clause, the court ruled in favor of the defendant.

     The contract in *Three D* concerned non-apparel merchandise stores that K Mart had established; the plaintiff, a K-Mart licensee for such stores, was terminated when K-Mart decided to close the entire chain. A clause in the contract between Three D and K-Mart expressly stated that K Mart could close "any stores." Three D argued that the contract was "unconscionable" because K Mart was much larger than Three D, the cancellation left Three D in a difficult spot, and contracts that allow one side to terminate without cause are unconscionable under Michigan law. But the federal appeals court claimed the argument "bordered on the frivolous" because, when the contract was signed, Three D was a publicly traded corporation with more than $50 million in annual sales from 28 free-standing stores and 53 licensed departments in four national chains. The court noted that the contract was negotiated over a six-month period by Three D's president, who was a lawyer with experience negotiating similar agreements and who had his staff counsel and three outside attorneys read the agreement and pronounce it fair before he signed it. Indeed, the plaintiff's president negotiated a number of changes from the contract form that K Mart had proposed. Thus, the court found no procedural unconscionability in the negotiations leading to this contract, nor any substantive unconscionability, which "will rarely be found" in business contracts like this one, with "experienced businessmen" knowingly accepting risks and a commercial relationship between business parties that is "not so one-sided as to give one party the bargaining power to impose unconscionable terms on the other party."

7. Exculpatory Clauses (see pgs. 136-138; Emerson BL)

a. What Are these Clauses?

"Many agreements contain exculpatory clauses, that is, provisions that disclaim liability for negligence or other actions."[88] An exculpatory clause is thus meant to hold someone harmless (i.e., to relieve someone of liability). In effect, one is "Not responsible for this," or "you can't sue me for that," or "damages are limited to this." Key questions are: Who are the parties to the clause? How far does the clause go?

Usually, contracting parties can exculpate negligent acts or omissions if the parties have roughly equal bargaining power (but they cannot exculpate gross negligence or intentional misconduct).[89] The legal concept of unconscionability may release the "little guy" from an exculpatory clause; i.e., the law leaves the "little guy" still able to pursue the other party – generally, a business – for liability under the contract (liability that might otherwise be exculpated).

b. Superior Risk Bearer?

When excusing contract duties, one may consider: who is the superior risk bearer? Law and economics principles argue that an obligor's excuse for not performing its contractual duties should be granted when the obligee is the "superior risk bearer" and denied when the obligor itself is the superior risk bearer. A party is defined as a "superior risk bearer" if it is relatively more efficient in preventing an event from occurring or in insuring against the risk of its occurrence. Thus, for example, unforeseen problems in constructing a building are more likely to be the builder's "superior risk" than that of the less knowledgeable party that hired the builder; so the builder is not excused from the contract because of heightened costs it had to incur in stabilizing the ground before starting to lay the building's foundations. As another example, if a buyer of goods could insure against disaster by diversifying its portfolio of supply contracts, but an individual supplier of those goods to the buyer has no such ability to diversify (i.e., a disaster affects its entire line of goods), then the obligor supplier would be excused from the contract because the obligee buyer is the superior risk bearer.

The "superior risk bearer" approach has been criticized; in most jurisdictions it is still generally *not* the law.

c. Indemnity

The exculpatory clause (Indemnity, below) often is combined with an insurance requirement, as in the following example from a contract between a sales representative and the manufacturing company for which he/she works.

---

[88] Robert W. Emerson, *Business Law*. NY: Barron's Educational Series (6th ed., 2015), at 136.
[89] Likewise, Germany's Law on General Business Terms (AGBG), its commercial code most like the UCC, prohibits clauses that disclaim liability for acts of gross negligence.

Insurance and Indemnity Clauses: An Example from a Sales Representative Agreement
"(i) <u>Insurance</u>. Representative agrees to procure and maintain general liability, automobile liability and products liability insurance in such amounts and written by such insurers as shall be approved by Company and to submit annually to Company certificates showing such insurance. Representative shall require any insurer providing coverage hereunder to notify Company ten (10) days before the termination, modification or expiration of any such policy or policies.

"(ii) <u>Indemnity</u>. Representative hereby indemnifies and holds Company harmless from and against any and all liability, losses, damages, claims or causes of action and expenses connected therewith (including, without limitation, reasonable attorneys' fees and costs) which are caused or asserted to have been caused, directly or indirectly, by or as a result of any action of Representative in connection with its duties hereunder, specifically including, but without being limited to, incorrect engineering, measuring or ordering by Representative or for which Representative is responsible."[90]

d. Three Exculpatory Clause Examples

<u>Landlord–Tenant Example</u>

Suppose that Tenant is injured while in the commons area, because of the collapse of rotten wooden steps up to the second floor apartments. That area is under the landlord's control, and the landlord should know about, and act to rectify, the problem. A clause in a residential lease agreement absolving the landlord of responsibility for such harm is probably unconscionable. But a clause exculpating the landlord from personal injury claims arising within the tenant's own "zone of control" (within his/her own apartment), depending on the circumstances, is much more likely to be legally acceptable (e.g., the tenant slips on a bar of soap while using his apartment's shower). The public policy concern about overreaching landlords forcing tenants to hold them blameless is much clearer in the former rather than the latter case.

<u>Armored Courier Misdelivery of Securities Example</u>

Assume that Brink's Armored Courier has a standard contract clause, for its agreements with large business customers who regularly use Brink's services. The clause absolves Brink's of liability for ordinary acts of negligence. That clause will almost certainly be upheld in court because the parties have relatively equal bargaining power. Both are businesses and the public policy concerns over disproportionate power or information are much greater when it is a business–to–consumer relationship than a business–to–business agreement.[91] Of course, the clause can only excuse ordinary negligence. The other side always may seek to show that the supposedly excused party behaved so poorly as to constitute <u>gross</u> negligence or recklessness. If shown, then the exculpatory clause would not apply.

---

[90] Indemnification clauses are standard provisions in many commercial contracts. For example, they are found in most net leases (in which the lessee pays rent plus property expenses such as taxes and insurance) – that the lessee will indemnify the lessor for property, use, sales and other miscellaneous taxes that may be imposed on the transaction.

Lease indemnification clauses also may protect the lessor from loss of its tax depreciation deductions for leased equipment. An "all events" indemnity may state that the lessee protects the lessor from this tax depreciation risk in all events. A lessee may at least try to have the indemnity only apply if the lessee is actually responsible for the lessor's loss of depreciation deductions (due to the lessee's own breach or misrepresentation).

[91] For example, most franchisees have found it difficult to obtain as strong protections vis-à-vis the franchisor as they likely would have if the franchisee were considered a consumer. South Africa's franchise law is unique in explicitly treating franchisees as consumers. Robert W. Emerson, *Franchisees as Consumers: The South African Example*, 37 FORDHAM INT'L L.J. 455 (2014), available at http://ssrn.com/author=86449 (considering South Africa's system and other leading franchise regulatory regimes in Australia, China, France, and the United States).

AN EXCULPATORY CLAUSE SKIT: "Watch that Bumper! (*Don't* Park Your Car in the Harvard Yard)" - This <u>webskit</u> is 5:32 long, immediately followed by Emerson's discussion, which is 8:56 long and is also on the website in the Part Two resources.

    a. We already know from Part One of the course (agency law principles) that this employee's behavior binds the garage.

    b. Consider the inherently contradictory nature of Wilbur's admission that he moved the car but then asking for proof that Lola parked the car in the garage!

    c. Bailments (bailor's entrusting of property to the bailee): different levels of entrustment – and thus different levels of rights for the person (the bailor) entrusting the property.

    d. Although the garage would argue that Lola agreed, by buying a parking ticket, not to hold the garage company liable for damages to her car, she might be able to sue successfully the garage company and still be awarded some money for the garage company's misconduct. Consider the length and the incredibly fine print (literally!) of the Cram 'Em In parking garage written agreement. The customer would be better served, and the garage might be better protected from customer lawsuits, with large print warnings.

    e. As in many areas of law, resolutions of bailment issues very much depend on the facts. If a court finds that Lola could not reasonably be expected to read/understand the exculpatory clause in the contract she had with the parking garage, then she could get the court to find it unconscionable (against public policy). Factors to be considered would include: (1) were there "exculpatory" signs, and how prominent were they? (2) did Lola have a clear opportunity to leave the premises, with her car, and not have to pay for any parking, once she learned of the garage's "no blame" clause? (3) the garage people were responsible for parking/re-parking the car, not Lola.

    f. was the damage to the car the result merely of negligence (which can be exculpated) or of gross negligence bordering on recklessness, which ordinarily cannot be exculpated.
In evaluating the facts presented in the brief skit, you need not decide, definitively, whether Lola would win a case against the garage. It <u>is</u> important to know the types of issues that could arise.

    g. As in all cases, one must consider: Is it worth pursuing as a practical matter?

8. Adhesion Clauses

For an adhesion clause to exist, the party with superior bargaining power in effect says, concerning a contract provision, "no bargaining allowed!" This is an important problem arising with the advent of standardized forms (e.g., very lengthy documents), with very little bargaining over terms except for a few basic terms such as, perhaps, price, quantity, or other buyer requirements.

    Courts (finding, "Hey, <u>contracts are supposed to be a bargained for exchange!</u>") may protect consumers and employees (persons otherwise seen as without power, with no meaningful bargaining, and no leverage because of little, if any competition). These people have no ability to go elsewhere.

    Thus, if Party P is presented with a "Take it or leave it" proposition, the question is: Could Party P have "left it" and found elsewhere a deal more to his/her liking?

    If a consumer could easily have obtained the same goods or services from another provider without being subjected to a similar adhesion contract, and if the consumer knew or should have known of that option, then most courts will find no unconscionability. In effect, the consumer had some bargaining leverage, even if he/she did not use it. We thus see that unconscionability is not an "easy out" from contract obligations. The burden of proof is high, and the law imposes a duty to resist high–handed, aggressive tactics before entering a contract, if that is at all practical.

    The concept of unconscionability has been the focus of most courts when they hold an adhesion contract to be unenforceable.

Remedies for unconscionable adhesion clauses are to: "Enforce the rest of the contract," or to enforce the unconscionable clause, but limit its application so as to avoid an unconscionable result."[92]

An Exculpatory Clause Issue: Click wrap Licenses

In click wrap licenses purchased over the Internet, the buyer may not realistically have the opportunity to read the entire license agreement prior to purchase. While click and buy contracts do appear in "boxes" on a computer screen that prevents further negotiation without the consent of the buyer, the terms are so long and crammed into a small box that scrolling down the page makes comprehensive and detailed reading difficult. Second, many of the click–to–agree statements or contracts do not offer the viewer a print option. The buyer must either read the entire agreement in a small box on the computer screen or be dropped out of the transaction. However, assuming that the buyer ultimately has the right of return of the software, service or product if he/she objects to the terms of the agreement, and that the company includes a written copy of the licensing agreement inside the package of the software or product, that click–to–agree type contract is probably enforceable even if it is an adhesion clause.

B. SPECIAL RULES ABOUT WRITTEN AGREEMENTS

I. WHY DO WE LIKE WRITTEN AGREEMENTS?

Imagine that a man has dozens of ugly blue ties. You can probably picture what these ties might look like. But, even after you see a tie, and are then asked – once that tie is no longer in view – to describe the tie, your description will be an *interpretation*. Without a photograph (or the tie itself!) to memorialize what a particular tie looks like, there probably would be – for twenty people - about twenty different "pictures" (memories, in different minds) of the tie: there would be some similarities from interpretation to interpretation, but also differences, e.g., in pattern or size.

With implied or oral agreements, there are possible different interpretations. So, even if it is not required that a contract have some written evidence, ordinarily – for any important contract – one wants a contract to be in writing. The problem, if the contract is purely oral, is that – like any witnessing – everyone sees things differently. These different *witnesses* are not necessarily lying; they just do not see or remember things exactly the same. This problem with an oral contract may be analogized to the story of a committee of five blind men that undertook the task of examining an elephant and reporting what they found. One man has the trunk, one the tusks, one the tail, one a leg, and one the ears – their account of what an elephant is like will differ drastically (just like different accounts of what was in an oral contract).

II. THE STATUTE OF FRAUDS (see pgs. 141-147; Emerson BL)

The Statute of Frauds is the requirement of written evidence (for some contracts). The writing does not have to be the full agreement, just sufficient evidence that there was a contract. If the Statute is not met, that renders the contract unenforceable – not void (illegal) or voidable.

---

[92] Robert W. Emerson, *Business Law*. NY: Barron's Educational Series (6th ed., 2015), at 124.

Will several documents suffice instead of just one? Yes, unless the Parol Evidence Rule says otherwise, one can gather proof from several documents – e.g., a series of letters collectively may show a contract.

Courts just need some evidence of the contract - quantity, price, signatures (i.e., enough to go on, enough to assume there was a contract). For example, the evidence could just be a napkin with writing on it, especially if initiated and signed by the other side and if it has sufficient information on it.

A. Origins of the Statute of Frauds

To prevent fraud on alleged oral contracts, the English Parliament established the first Statute of Frauds in 1677. (France had a similar rule, the Royal Edict of Moulins of 1566 applying to contracts generally.) The Statute of Frauds is, in a sense, an evidence rule because rather than going directly after the fraud problem it indirectly approaches the matter: unless there is an exception to the statute, it bars the use of oral evidence (testimony) to try to prove the existence and alleged terms of a contract.

We say, "I want to look at the contract," but the contract is actually the meeting of the minds - what the parties actually agreed upon, not the document.

B. The Document Is Just Evidence

Assume that a man, Mark, makes a deal with a real "devil." Mark's best friend, Jonathan, has a devil of a time getting Mark out of the contract. Ultimately, through sleight of hand, Jonathan obtained and destroyed the contract form, which Mark had signed.

Taking the document away from the other party does not make a contract legally unenforceable. As a practical matter, getting rid of the evidence probably helps the party who denies there is a contract. But if both sides admit there is a contract (or the fact there was/is a contract is otherwise incontestable), then the disappearance of the underlying document does not transform a lawful contract into something less "legal." Making the paper disappear does not legally "undo" the contract.

C. MYLEGS

YOUTUBE – Statute_of_Frauds_Six_Elements_MYLEGS at robertwemersonufl (an introductory video (2:46 long)

"In the area of writing a contract, there are a couple of things to note: first of all, most contracts do not have to be in writing. Those that do have to be in writing (or have a form of the contract in writing - some evidence in writing) are because of something referred to as the statute of frauds, which goes all the way back to the late 1600s in England. It was a law passed to counter the effects of presumed perjury in court, fraud on the court by people contending that there were oral contracts when in fact there were not.

"The statute of frauds, which has been adopted by all of the states, requires that some evidence be provided for certain forms of contracts. And for those contracts the easy way to remember them, I believe, is a mnemonic device: MYLEGS. You don't have to think of my legs; you can think of the legs of your choice, but it goes "MYLEGS" as in: (1) M for marriage - contracts in consideration of marriage; (2) Y – for year-long-plus contracts that will take longer than a year after the contract has been brought into existence; (3) L for land - the contracts involving the purchase, sale, or lease of land; (4) E for executors - concerning any special arrangement they make to pay off personally on a particular contract; (5) G for goods - if a sale of goods is for over $500, you need some written evidence; and (6) S for securities - sales of securities for over $5000.

"The statute of frauds is an important rule. It is one not to be overlooked, but the main reason you want things in writing is more the practical element: If you have a long term relationship, if you've got a contract that really matters in terms of meaningful money or services, you probably want to put it in writing. That is not necessarily because you don't trust the other person, but simply because memories fade. Moreover, the process of actually putting something in writing often also improves the contract; by putting it down ("writing it up"), people think about other things and often end up forming a better deal for both sides than they would have if they had kept it purely oral.

"The six types of contracts covered are the ones that "fall under" the Statute of Frauds – meaning that these types must comply with that statute. These six types may be remembered with the mnemonic device: <u>MYLEGS</u> (standing for marriage, years, land, executor, goods, and securities)."

1. <u>M</u>arriage, contracts in contemplation of (e.g., prenuptial agreements).

Prenuptial Agreements

About 5% of all marriages are preceded by a prenuptial agreement.

Prenuptial agreements detail how assets will be divided if a marriage ends in divorce or the death of one of the spouses. The agreements also can cover alimony, child support, and inheritances. Prenuptial agreements have the best chance of being enforceable if three conditions are met: (1) full disclosure is present;(2) the bride and groom each had his/her own lawyer; and (3) the agreement was not signed under duress.

A "PAROL EVIDENCE RULE" MUSIC VIDEO
"The Business Law Blues," with John Stevens & Eric Anderson

Since my baby left me, my heart's been feeling blue.
 Now she wants a divorce. I don't know what to do.
She's taking all the money, and heading out the door.
 She's taking all the credit cards; I'm sleeping on the floor.
She knows her rights, she knows the law,
 She's suing me again.
She took that class from Emerson: BUL Forty-Three-Ten.
 (Man, I used to drop her off at that class!)

She made me sign a "pre-nup." I didn't like what it said.
 Her daddy had a shotgun, pointed at my head.
And, you know, I ain't a lawyer, but I think it's called duress.
 If I hadn't signed the dotted line, my face would've been a mess.
She knows her rights, she knows the law,
 She's suing me again.
She took that class from Emerson – BUL Forty-Three-Ten.
 (Come to think of it, she did do a lot of "extra credit!")

I pleaded for demurrer, sealed it with a kiss.
 Judge fried it, denied it and threw it away/ No Motion to Dismiss
I guess we're separated. We're calling our marriage quits.
 She took the beamer, she stole the kids; I'm really in a fix!
She knows her rights, she knows the law,
 She's suing me again.
She took that class from Emerson – BUL Forty-Three-Ten.
BUL 4310 Blues, Y'all!

A prenuptial must be in writing; PER usually applies through integration clauses in such agreements. But here, in this example (from the song), there is duress. One can claim all of that to the judge – One can sing the song to the judge!

2. <u>Y</u>ears – contracts that, by their terms, must take more than one year to complete after the contract was entered into.

The Statute of Frauds and Contracts that Must Take More Than One Year to Complete: Three Examples

1. A lecturer alleges that in February 2010 she entered into an oral agreement with a university to teach the next academic year (from August 2010 to May 2011). She goes to court seeking to enforce the alleged contract. Even though the performance (and payment) period is for less than a year (August 2010 to May 2011), the Statute of Frauds test is for a different time frame: from when the contract was entered into until when it can first be completed, and in this case that is more than a year (from February 2010 until May 2011); so the alleged agreement falls under the Statute of Frauds, and the university successfully can raise the lack of written evidence as grounds for a court to dismiss the lecturer's claim. (*Same result under Florida law*).

2. A university doctoral candidate alleges that she was promised certain benefits under an oral contract with the university. She sues to enforce the alleged contract. The university denies her claim and asserts the Statute of Frauds as grounds to dismiss her claim. The university notes that it is almost unheard of for a doctoral candidate to complete his/her work within a year after being accepted by a university. However, if it is not impossible for the candidate to complete the work in less than a year (i.e., there is no requirement that the candidate must be at the university for over a year), even though such fast completion is incredibly rare, then the possibility of completion is sufficient to keep the alleged contract from falling under the Statute of Frauds. The doctoral candidate can proceed with her claim and not have it dismissed due to a lack of written evidence. (*Probably a different result under Florida law*, as the Florida courts would look at the purpose and surrounding circumstances of the alleged agreement and probably conclude that written evidence is required because doctoral candidates almost always take more than a year of work and the parties must have intended a contractual performance period of more than one year).

3. Little Lordie ("LL") Fauntleroy's parents allegedly hired a nanny to take care of LL indefinitely. The nanny sues to collect damages for the parents' breach of the alleged agreement. The parents deny that there was an agreement and seek to have the case dismissed, due to the Statute of Frauds, because there is no written evidence of the alleged agreement. The parents contend that LL is only 7–years–old and surely would require "nannying" for many years (thus the alleged agreement contemplated services for more than a year). But the alleged time period was not specified, and apparently it could have terminated before a year after the alleged agreement was formed; so a court should deny the parents' Statute of Frauds defense and allow the case to proceed. (*Probably the same result in Florida*, although here it may be a closer call. Under the ordinary, "possibility" test, as long as the plaintiff does not acknowledge any specified time period extending over more than a year after when the contract supposedly was formed, written evidence simply is not required. But in Florida the courts could go beyond that to examine what, given the circumstances and purposes of the alleged agreement, the parties must have intended; if the court finds that the parents and the nanny surely would have meant for the contract period to extend for over one year, then a writing would be a Florida legal requirement)

---

3. <u>L</u>and – contracts (leases, mortgages, sales, etc.) involving land or interests in land.[93]

4. <u>E</u>xecutor (or Guarantor) contracting to pay, personally, debts of the estate – no writing required if the contract's main purpose is the guarantor's (executor's) own interests

---

[93] However, most states, allow an oral real estate lease for one year or less to be valid. Robert W. Emerson, *Business Law*. NY: Barron's Educational Series (6th ed., 2015), at 142.

5. <u>G</u>oods – contracts to sell goods for a price of $500 or more (UCC 2–201(1)) – It has been proposed to raise that amount to $5,000 – so far, though, the amount remains $500. (By way of comparison, Germany and the Netherlands have no statute of frauds and the French do. Under the French Civil Code, a sales contract must be memorialized in a writing signed by the party against whom it is being asserted if that party is a <u>non–merchant</u> and the contract is for more than about 800 Euros.)

> <u>Uniform Commercial Code Provision</u> 2–201(1) (Formal Requirements; Statute of Frauds) states:
> "Except as otherwise provided in this section, a contract for the sale of goods for the price of $500 or more is not enforceable by way of action or defense unless there is some writing sufficient to indicate that a contract for sale has been made between the parties and signed by the party against whom enforcement is sought or by his authorized agent or broker. A writing is not insufficient because it omits or incorrectly states a term agreed upon, but the contract is not enforceable under this paragraph beyond the quantity of goods shown in such writing."

6. <u>S</u>ecurities (or certain other personal property besides goods) – contracts for their sale if the price is $5,000 or more.

Generally, courts try to find a way to enforce contracts (find a way around the Statute of Frauds).

D. Ethical Ramifications re: Statute of Frauds

Lawyers, Courts, Business people – most recognize the ethical dilemma. One has a legal right to assert the Statute of Frauds, but what if you raise that defense although you know there <u>was</u> a contract? Is that right?

E. Exceptions to the Statute of Frauds

Just because there is <u>an exception to the Statute of Frauds does not mean that the party claiming a contract automatically wins. The application of an exception simply signifies that the other side cannot use the Statute of Frauds as a defense.</u>

There are five exceptions to the Statute of Frauds:
1. <u>Admissions</u> (that there was/is a contract) – under UCC Article 2 and sometimes other non–sales scenarios.
2. <u>Promissory Estoppel</u> (because there never really was a contract)
3. <u>Partial Performance</u> (if one has already started to pay or perform, one has admitted that the contract exists)
4. <u>Specially–made goods</u>

> Uniform Commercial Code Provision 2–201(3) states: "A contract which does not satisfy the requirements of subsection (1) but which is valid in other respects is enforceable
> (a) if the goods are to be specially manufactured for the buyer and are not suitable for sale to others in the ordinary course of the seller's business and the seller, before notice of repudiation is received and under circumstances which reasonably indicate that the goods are for the buyer, has made either a substantial beginning of their manufacture or commitments for their procurement; or
> (b) if the party against whom enforcement is sought admits in his pleading, testimony or otherwise in court that a contract for sale was made, but the contract is not enforceable under this provision beyond the quantity of goods admitted; or
> (c) with respect to goods for which payment has been made and accepted or which have been received and accepted."

Imagine that the Chicago Bulls' basketball star Joakim Noah has refused to pay for some specially–made boots that he allegedly agreed to buy from shoemaker Sherry. Sherry claims that Noah agreed to pay $2,000 for a pair of custom–made size–20 boots with the English letters N, O, A, and H on one boot and the letters P, A, I, and X (French for "peace") on the other boot. Because the good was to be sold for more than $500, the contract fell under the Statute of Frauds. But because these shoes were specially prepared goods, they fell under the exception to the statute. Noah could bring in teammates to testify that Sherry has pulled this act (making "special" shoes) for them too!

The assumption is that people would not normally make a special set of goods unless they had a basis for thinking there was a contract. It does not mean that the factfinders must find there was a contract, but at least the parties do not have to have a writing.[94]

5. Oral contract between merchants, as confirmed later in writing – (UCC 2–201(2))– no more than ten days to refute the information in the confirming letter.

> Uniform Commercial Code Provision 2–201(2) states:
> "Between merchants if within a reasonable time a writing in confirmation of the contract and sufficient against the sender is received and the party receiving it has reason to know its contents, it satisfies the requirements of subsection (1) [meets the statute of frauds] against such party unless written notice of objection to its contents is given within ten days after it is received."
> **SO, after receiving a Confirming letter, the merchant has ten days to object in writing (or loses any statute of frauds defense).**

F. Comparative Law on Written Requirements for Contracts

England abolished its Statute of Frauds in 1954. Other common law nations such as New Zealand have followed suit. Few countries in the world have the formal requirements that still exist in the United States, most Canadian provinces (exceptions being British Columbia, Manitoba, and Quebec), the Bahamas, Ireland (contracts of guarantee, for sale of lands or land interests, and contracts not to be completed within one year), and some Australian states; these common law countries, or at least parts thereof, continue to follow the Statute of Frauds. Other common law countries have no statute of frauds, but do require a writing in very limited cases. For example, South Africa only requires a writing for land sales, leases exceeding ten years, transfer deeds, mortgage bonds, and some credit agreements.

The Soviet Union and its satellite states constituted the only other legal regime with more rigid adherence to a writing requirement for contracts generally. When centralized planning dominated the economies of Eastern European countries controlled by the Soviet Union, these highly bureaucratic states often required a writing for most contracts, especially any of important business transactions. These writing requirements tend to have diminished considerably, throughout Eastern Europe (including Russia), once Soviet hegemony collapsed in the late 1980s.

Even the relatively few European countries that presently seem to have requirements of a writing, such as France, Italy, and Belgium, have exceedingly easy ways to get around it (e.g., oral testimony that while no written evidence now exists there was, at some point, the start of a writing related to the alleged contract). When a writing does seem to be necessary, Civil Law judges typically can and do exercise wide discretion to

---

[94] The example is not as far–fetched as you might think. In February 2004, Daytona Harley–Davidson sued former pro basketball star Shaquille O'Neal for breach of contract because he allegedly reneged on the purchase of a custom–made motorcycle. And the dealer was unable to resell the one-of-a-kind motorcycle.
The case filed in Florida circuit court alleged that O'Neal, at 7–foot–1, 340 pounds, agreed to pay for a custom motorcycle. After delays in production, the plaintiff delivered to O'Neal the motorcycle, but he refused to pay for it. Daytona Harley–Davidson contended that it took O'Neal at his word because O'Neal previously paid for another custom motorcycle. The case did not go to trial. As there are no further reports about it, the suit likely was settled.

let in evidence that may demonstrate the parties in fact had a contract. Still, from country to country the issues are very complex in terms of the types of contracts possibly needing written proof and the methods for meeting that proof.

International contractual proposals or restatements of law, as well as conventions, all in effect call for the abolition of the Statute of Frauds – the Principles of European Contract Law Article 2:101, UNIDROIT Principles of International Commercial Contracts Article 1.2 (2004), a proposed revision of UCC Article 2 (this proposal was abandoned in the past decade), and the UN's Convention on Contracts for the International Sale of Goods (the CISG) Article 11 all declare, expressly or implicitly, the absence of a writing requirement to be the best approach. (That is a far cry from saying parties should not, as a matter of good business sense, put their deals in writing – just that there should not be a legal requirement of a writing.)

Under CISG Articles 12 and 96, the countries that have adopted the CISG may override the CISG's permission for oral contracts and instead require a written format for international sales contracts; but only eleven nations have done so, and none are the common law countries most associated with the statute of frauds in their own domestic laws (Australia, Canada, and the United States).

The CISG and the Statute of Frauds: An American/Argentine/Spanish Dancing Example about Oral International Sales Agreements

If an Argentine woman had a business and I owned an American business and we were dancing around each other trying to reach a possible contract, then any arrangement we reach would be an executory arrangement – unexecuted, no performance yet. There would be NO enforceable contract.

But what of a contract with the other businesswoman? Let us say that she is a businesswoman from Spain, which is a CISG signatory nation that has not opted out of requiring a writing (as Argentina and seven other CISG countries have).[95] Then any oral, executory contract we reach, albeit unwritten and perhaps difficult to prove, is nonetheless enforceable.

Interestingly, while the U.S. has a fairly strong Statute of Frauds requirement under the UCC, we did not opt for such a provision when we adopted the CISG. So, internationally, many contractual arrangements involving American businesses do not require the written evidence that a domestic contract would. (I can be bound to the Spanish woman's business, even just based on dancing and nothing in writing!)

> Joke –
> Client: Good contract you drew up, Lawyer.
> Attorney: Okay, what's your first question?
> Client: No questions.
> Attorney: Not even one?
> Client: Nary a one.
> Attorney (getting increasingly agitated): You understand everything?
> Client: Yep. It's clear as a bell.
> Attorney (grabbing client and pleading for his/her silence): Do you realize if this gets out I could be disbarred!

---

[95] Robert W. Emerson, *Business Law* NY: Barron's Educational Series (2015, 6th ed.), at 185.

III. TOPICAL LECTURE: THE PAROL EVIDENCE RULE (PER) (see pgs. 147-149; Emerson BL)

Introduction to Topical Lecture:
When a written agreement is meant to be the complete contract, the words (parol evidence) in prior or contemporaneous communications cannot alter the terms of the contract, unless the language is ambiguous or some other exception is present. In business dealings particularly, an exception to the parol evidence rule (e.g., for fraud) often is difficult to obtain.

> Unlike Statute of Frauds, PER does not require writing; it just deals with interpretation of contracts. What about trying to get around a written form of contract?

A. An Introductory Example: The Parol Evidence Rule and the "% Interest to be Earned" on a Settlement

Susanna left a meeting with one of her disgruntled customers after signing a writing agreeing to a settlement of the customer's claim for $20,000 plus a credit on all returns after November 1st. During the negotiations, the parties had discussed the interest rate the settlement amount would earn pending payment.

The customer believes that ten percent was agreed to, but the signed writing recites six percent. Whether the customer is permitted to testify about his memory of the oral agreement will depend on whether the court rules the writing is the final and complete understanding of the parties. If the writing was final and complete, the Parol Evidence Rule bars the testimony (unless there is an exception, e.g., fraud, to the Parol Evidence Rule).

> **PROFESSOR-STUDENT EXAMPLE**
> Professor Lee Galese used his car, a Fiat convertible, as a subject matter for examples of how contracts work. He would lecture, then make an offer to sell the car to a class member. "I'll sell you my 1985 Chevy Chevette for $3,000" became a joke among many students.
>
> During one lecture, however, a student named Eva Dents surprised Galese by making a serious counteroffer of $2,500. Just as the period ended, Galese agreed to the deal in front of the whole class. The classroom emptied quickly. As the last three students filtered out, they overheard Galese's and Dents's oral contract fall apart when Dents said he could not pay Galese for thirty days. Galese then said that he would take $2,600, the additional $100 being his payment for waiting thirty days. Dents agreed.
>
> The three students then left as the classroom door closed behind them, Galese remembered that the alternator light had been coming on as he drove in that morning. "I just remembered," Galese said, downcast, "the car probably needs a new alternator. It will cost $200." Dents thought a moment, then replied, "tell you what, I'll pay you $2,300 for it as is. That's the $2,600 less the $200 for the part and $100 for my labor in installing it." "Fine" said Galese. "Let's put it in writing." Galese wrote out the contract, then they photocopied it. And each signed the other's copy.
>
> Thirty days went by and Galese refused to take $2,300 for the car, saying he had a classroom with some witnesses who would say the deal was for $2,600. Which contract would the courts enforce?
> In this case, the final agreement reached was the contract, *but many witnesses saw and heard earlier "agreements."* **In this situation there is evidence of 3 different contracts:**
>   1.) What all students heard & saw – $2,500
>   2.) What some students heard & saw - $2,600 within 30 days
>   3.) What no one heard & saw but the prof and student - $2,300 as is.
>   **If put in writing, with an** *integration clause*, **PER should resolve it. PER should make the written form the controlling evidence.**

The parol evidence rule (PER) prohibits the use of evidence of prior or contemporaneous words (written or oral) that contradict an integrated written agreement. It is an efficiency idea – if the document is meant to cover it all, we want people to be assured that that document truly is it. (We want the parties, after all of their negotiating, to make sure that all important terms (concepts) are reflected in the written agreement.)

Analysis of PER

The PER may apply to contracts, if the contract's terms are in writing. The parol evidence rule prohibits either of the parties from contradicting or invalidating a fully written contract by means of evidence prior or contemporaneous to the contract and external to the contract. The policy behind the PER is that if parties have put their agreement in writing why should they be permitted to introduce other evidence contrary to their own written understanding?

Here is a *four–part test* for deciding whether to apply the PER:
1. Have parties reduced their contract to a writing? (put it in writing?)
   if yes, then
2. Is the contract "integrated"? (a final expression of all contract terms). This is sometimes also referred to as "merging" the terms into a writing. An example of such an integration or merger clause (which makes the contract "integrated" or "merged") is the following:
"Entire Agreement. This Agreement contains and constitutes the entire agreement of the parties hereto and supersedes all prior agreements, contracts and understandings, whether written or otherwise, between the parties relating to the subject matter hereof."
   if yes, then
3. Is the proposed evidence to be introduced at court as evidence of a prior or contemporaneous agreement?
   if yes, then
4. Does the evidence conflict with or substantially add to the terms of the integrated contract?

*If the answer is "yes" to all four questions, then the PER bars the introduction of that evidence. If there is a "no" to any of the questions, the inquiry stops and the determination is that the PER does not apply.

C. Exceptions to the Parol Evidence Rule

> "Great care should be used, however, in attempting to apply this broadly stated rule, because the exceptions are also broad and the courts are reluctant to withhold evidence of clear understandings freely assented to by both parties."[96]

One can, despite PER, get evidence of allegedly fraudulent promises not put in the contract. But the safer action to take, rather than rely on PER exceptions, is to put the matter in writing. Cross out contrary wording and add into the written document what is intended to be in the document.

Five exceptions to the PER, or circumstances for which the PER simply is not applicable (the effect is the same either way – parol evidence is allowed) are as follows:
1. Clarification of ambiguity (or clerical error) – seeking explanations, definitions – what words or concepts are all about. That is why contracts often have definitions set forth.

---

[96] Robert W. Emerson, *Business Law*. NY: Barron's Educational Series (6th ed., 2015), at 147.

2. Later modification, "particularly if there was mutual consideration, or reliance by either party, with respect to such dealings."[97]
Subsequent to (after) the contract, even oral changes are permitted (not barred by PER) as long as both sides agreed to those changes. That is true even if the writing says that changes must be in writing, unless the Statutes of Frauds would require a writing. Why? Parties are masters of the contract, not vice–versa. (It may, though, be hard to convince a judge or jury that both sides agreed to an oral change, if one side denies it and there's a contractual provision attempting to require that all changes be in writing.)
3. Evidence of contract's voidability or voidness (showing mistake, duress, undue influence, fraud, incapacity, illegality, unconscionability, or no real intent to have the writing be a contract)
Example: there is an exculpatory clause in the writing, but the sales representative allegedly said to the other party (the buyer) that this clause was just a formality and that nobody cared about it.
4. Evidence of a condition precedent – evidence of something that must occur before the parties become obligated
5. Incomplete agreement – evidence to show that the agreement was incomplete, that a necessary or agreed upon part was omitted from the written evidence.

D. Comparative Law

Under the French Civil Code, for contracts involving lower monetary amounts, there is no parol evidence rule except to protect non– merchants who did not draft or sign what was, in effect, an "integrated" writing. For larger amounts (disputes involving amounts over approximately 800 euros), Article 1341 of the French Civil Code adopts a interpretative approach comparable to the parol evidence rule, regardless of whether the contract is "integrated": for those consumer contracts of over 5,000 francs (800 euros) the parties must have notarial acts or signed documents, and the parties are forbidden to introduce evidence about what negotiators said to one another.
The CISG has no parol evidence rule (parol evidence is admissible).

E. A Final Question Related to Protections from the Parol Evidence Rule

Non–negotiated, "Buried" Provisions are a major problem, and are considered at **pgs. 148-149; Emerson BL.**

Consumers' Need to Know about the Parol Evidence Rule: An Ethics Question

Since many people enter into written contracts believing that oral representations made during the negotiation process are part of the bargain, even though not in writing, should merchants be required to advise buyers of the Parol Evidence Rule and, at the very least, place the Integration Clause in bold print and in plain English (at least as to "big ticket" items, such as real estate and automobiles?). That is one of the author's contentions – concerning franchise negotiations, franchise contracts, and the duty of franchisors toward potential franchisees – in a recent law review article.[98]

End of Topical Lecture on "Parol Evidence Rule"

---

[97] Id. at 148.
[98] Robert W. Emerson, *Franchising and the Parol Evidence Rule*, 50 AMERICAN BUSINESS LAW JOURNAL 659-728 (2013), available at http://ssrn.com/author=86449.

> A Review Example involving the Parole Evidence Rule and a Possible Exception:
> THE BASKETBALL SUMMER CAMP - An Incomplete Agreement – or Ambiguity in Terms
>
> Rodney Rimshot, former UF star and NBA and CBA has-been, opens a basketball camp in Gainesville. Over the years, attendance starts to go down, and so Rimshot contracts with a P.R. firm to "publish" 40,000 leaflets.
> – following was the worst attendance ever!
> In August, Rimshot is at an ice cream shop; it turns out there was no mailing, only handouts at just about ten locations, 4,000 at each.
>
> a. What did the camp owner/operator expect?   Something far more thorough (reaching many people via many means) than what was done.
> b. Why did the camp owner expect that? The conversations between the parties and the brochures of the PR firms, as discussed or examined shortly before the written agreement was signed.
> c. So what does "publish" mean?
> What did Rimshot think it meant?
> **If the term "publish" was not defined in the written agreement, it does not matter that there was an integration clause, because there is a PER exception to define the term and to complete an incomplete contract.**
> THE LESSON: *If a term matters, then define it.*

C. THIRD PARTIES AND CONDITIONS

I. THIRD PARTIES

A. Privity of Contract

Privity of contract relates to notions of privacy in contracting.
Privity refers to a private relationship between the parties themselves – privity creates reciprocal rights and duties. Generally, others (people not party to the contract) lack privity – thus they lack contract rights (or duties) a court will enforce.
Three instances in which a non–contracting party may have rights under a contract: Third–Party Beneficiary Contracts, Assignments, and Novations.

B. Third–Party Beneficiary Contracts

1. Creditor Beneficiaries and Intended Donee Beneficiaries

"A third party beneficiary is a person for whose benefit a contract is made but who is not an actual party to the contract."[99] There are two types of third–party beneficiary contracts with recognized rights for a third–party. The two groups of beneficiaries are:

(a) Creditor beneficiaries (intended recipients of contractual benefits who are creditors of one of the two consenting parties and intended, by those two other parties to thus benefit).

---

[99] Robert W. Emerson, *Business Law*. NY: Barron's Educational Series (6th ed., 2015), at 152.

Example One – A owes money to creditor C. In a contract between A and B, A performs services for B and B in return is to pay money directly to C to help satisfy A's debt to C. (The consideration from B to A is B's payment to A's creditor or B's promise to pay A's creditors.)

Example Two - Holly owes Lawrence $300. When Fox asks Holly to borrow $300, Holly agrees, if in return Fox agrees to pay Lawrence $300 the next day. Fox never pays Lawrence the money. Lawrence sues Fox for the $300, but Fox argues that Lawrence should lose because there was no privity of contract between Fox and Lawrence. However, Lawrence was an intended beneficiary and can recover a judgment against Fox for the money Fox had agreed (with Holly) to pay Lawrence.

When Holly and Fox contracted, they had the <u>intent</u> that Lawrence would be the third party beneficiary. Fox received consideration from Holly, and Fox was obligated to pay Lawrence, as if the purpose of the contract was for the benefit of the plaintiff. Fox was a trustee of the property ($300) that would be transferred to Lawrence the next day. Therefore, Lawrence had the legal right to collect the $300 from Fox.[100]

(b) Intended donee beneficiaries (recipients, by gift, of a contractual performance agreed to by two other parties).

Example: Let us imagine you have rich parents who want to give you a Lamborghini. There was no contract between you and your parents. If there is a contract between parents and a dealer for the dealer to send a car to you, and - once you learn of the deal – you rely upon it, then your rights exist. You can sue for breach. (You are a *donee beneficiary*).

2. Incidental Beneficiaries

Incidental (unintended) beneficiaries have no legal protections (no vesting of benefits).[101]

a. Example: Your Roommate's Car: Unlike the previous example, it is your roommate who is the one with the rich, giving parents. You may have all sorts of emotional connections to the deal. You would like to have double dates, and you say to the roommate that if he goes away, "I'll keep it revved up for you." But if there is a breach of the contract between the roommate's parents and the dealer, your roommate is the one with a possible claim (as an intended beneficiary); you, as a mere incidental beneficiary, have no legal claim.

b. The Marilyn Monroe and Joe DiMaggio Example

Joltin' Joe DiMaggio and Marilyn Monroe were married for nine months from January 14, 1954 to October 6, 1954. After Marilyn's death in 1962, Joe arranged for a half–dozen long–stemmed red roses to be placed at his ex–wife's crypt in L.A.'s Westwood Memorial Park each Tuesday, Thursday, and Saturday. Parisian Florists delivered over 180,000 roses for 20 years (never raising the price on him). Joe stopped having the flowers delivered in late August 1982 (perhaps at that point Joe decided to give the money to charity instead).

Suppose that somehow Joe and the deceased Marilyn reached an agreement for him to have flowers left on her grave three times a week[102] in exchange for her giving him continuing fame.[103] If Joe stopped

---

[100] *Lawrence v. Fox*, 20 N.Y. 268 (N.Y. Ct. App. 1859).
[101] "Beneficiaries of contracts other than creditor or done beneficiaries cannot sue on the contracts of other parties. Although [an incidental beneficiary] may show a benefit under the contract, the contract was not made expressly for him/her or for his/her benefit." Robert W. Emerson, *Business Law*. NY: Barron's Educational Series (6th ed., 2015), at 153.
[102] I.e., imagine that Marilyn has capacity (even though she is dead) and that she can communicate with DiMaggio. Perhaps it was reached via a Medium, via a Ouija Board, or through the National Enquirer Magazine.
[103] While Joe's incredible Hall of Fame career was magnificent, the former New York Yankee's brief marriage to the sex goddess, Marilyn Monroe, over time may have given him almost as much fame as had his baseball career. While he

carrying out his end of the bargain (because he heard that Marilyn, in the hereafter, was carrying on with JFK, and RFK, and Elvis!), Marilyn's estate could sue him for breach. But the florist could not. The florist simply was an incidental beneficiary. In effect, the florist probably benefited the most – certainly tremendously – from the contract, but he was not an intended beneficiary just an incidental one (so there are no rights under the contract – parties not caring who the florist was).

c. *Anderson v. Regents f University of California*

In *Anderson v. Regents of University of California*, 203 Wis.2d 469 (1996), tourists had contracted with tour operators and ticket agencies for tour packages to the Rose Bowl game in Pasadena. Upon arriving in Pasadena, these fans learned that tickets to the game were unavailable, and they sued for breach of contract the Board of Regents, whose football team was competing in the Bowl. The case was brought in Wisconsin (by these Wisconsin Badger fans–tourists), but the substantive law was California law of contracts. Under California law (but likely to be the same throughout the United States and other common law jurisdictions), the tourists were not intended third–party beneficiaries of any agreement controlling Rose Bowl attendance.

3. Vesting of the Third Party's Rights

When rights have vested, they generally cannot be taken away. Rights vest when known and relied upon. Once vesting occurs, the contracting parties cannot rescind or change the contract without the third party's consent – the third party can file suit to protect its rights.

C. Assignments

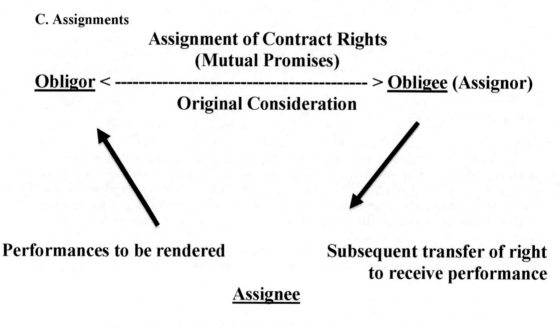

Once a contract is entered into, assignments may be possible.

A Preliminary Matter: Comparing Contracts to Offers

---

aged, Joe's ex–wife did not; Marilyn Monroe's movie and modeling life – forever young and beautiful on the screen – remained so current!

> Only after an offer is accepted may one be able to assign the contract. There is no right, simply as an offeree, to assign an offer. But one can assign <u>options</u>. Those <u>are contracts</u> to keep an offer open.

1. Introduction

Assignments concern rights, duties, and issues of delegability. "Whenever rights are assigned, the party to whom they are assigned (called the assignee) is simply substituted for the person making the assignment (called the assignor.)"[104] The assignment is from the Assignor to the Assignee. The Assignor is * not "out" of the original contract if the Assignee breaches that contract. An example is the typical lease and sublease, with sublessors still liable on the original lease (e.g., if the sublessee breaches).[105]

In effect, delegated duties are now to be carried out by the Assignee, but the Assignor is still accountable as well in the event something is not done or is performed poorly: The delegation does not relieve the delegating party of the underlying obligation, at least until the delegated tasks are successfully completed. If Slim has a business contract with Bill, and Slim delegates these non–personal contract duties to Tina, who fails to carry out those duties, then ordinarily Bill can successfully sue Slim for failing to carry out those duties. That Slim may seek recovery from Tina, for a breach of duty to him, does not relieve Slim of duties to Bill.

> Example: Delegations (No Significant Personal Skill involved)
> Tom agrees to feed Jerry's fish and pick up Jerry's mail for three weeks while Jerry is away, in exchange for ten dollars. Tom delegates his duties to Felix. If Felix does not feed Jerry's fish and does not pick up Jerry's mail, Jerry can sue Tom.

It is easier to assign rights than to delegate duties. Almost all contract rights can be assigned (e.g., the right to receive money). Most non–personal duties, such as administrative, clerical, or mechanical tasks, can be delegated. But if a party was chosen because of his/her own talent, skill, reputation, standing, or credit, that party cannot delegate to someone else the duty to perform the contract. Also, even if a duty normally could be delegated, the contract can prohibit or limit any delegation. Here is a sample contract clause in an agreement between a sales representative and a manufacturing company, providing that the representative has <u>no</u> assignment rights:

> "<u>Non–assignment</u>. The Representative's rights and duties under this Agreement shall not be assignable by Representative without the prior written consent of Company. Subject to the foregoing, all rights and obligations under this Agreement shall inure to the benefit of and shall be binding upon the parties hereto and upon their executors, successors and assigns."

> Assignability of Rights and Duties
> Is a right or duty assignable? The answer generally is "yes." Assignability is present for a sale unless prohibited by statute (e.g., ordinarily no assigning of a worker's compensation award) or prohibited in the contract (e.g., first–refusal or non–assignment clauses, such as in many leases) or the assignment materially alters parties' duties.

---

[104] Robert W. Emerson, *Business Law*. NY: Barron's Educational Series (6th ed., 2015), at 150.
[105] If A leases to B, who subleases to C, then – ordinarily – if C violates the lease, <u>B</u> can still be liable to A under the lease.

2. Specific Instances of Non–assignability

For these types of contracts, assignments are not permitted:
a. Credit – no assignability regarding your rating
b. Insurance – no assignability regarding you as an insured (e.g., you cannot transfer your car insurance to Karen Krash – a driver with a history of accidents; nor can you transfer your life insurance to insuring the life of Grandma, who is 80 years old).
c. Usually no assignments allowed for personal matters (e.g., covenants against competition, contract <u>duties personal in nature</u> – such as writing a novel or acting in a movie)

For example, Baltimore Oriole pitcher Chris Tillman can assign you his right to receive money (salary), but not his duty to play baseball. Some assignments simply are not permitted because they are too personal in nature. While one typically can assign something relatively liquid, fungible, and impersonal – the <u>right</u> to receive money – drawing upon a source of funds, there are activities which are too personal to the performer of that activity so that he or she cannot assign his <u>duty</u> to perform. So if Tillman would like to change positions with Prof. Emerson (and who wouldn't?! Who wouldn't want to teach Business Law rather than be a professional ballplayer!), there should be no problem with his assigning his salary to me. What does it matter to the Orioles to whom the check is sent: future Cy Young Award winner Tillman, or Professor Robert Emerson? But Tillman cannot assign his personal duty of performance – to pitch – to Emerson or anyone else. Emerson can show up at the Orioles' training camp – glove and ball in hand, Orioles hat on bald head, and singing, "Put me in, Coach, I'm ready to play!" But the Orioles surely do <u>Not</u> have to let Emerson play. So he cannot simply have the contract assigned to me.

D. Novations

Novations are distinct from assignments: "A <—> B" becomes "C <—> B"
That is, the A-B agreement is now completely replaced by the C-B agreement.

A novation is a complete substitution of another party – both original parties agree to it. <u>It is a new contract.</u> To the contrary, in assignments, the assignor would still be in the contract, still responsible for a breach, e.g., by the assignee.

II. CONDITIONS (see pgs. 158-160; Emerson BL)

Conditions are events that take you into or out of a contract.

A Condition Example: Reputedly, a jail in Jacksonville, Florida was built without outer locks on the cells. Clearly such locks are a necessity for these types of structures: jails. [106] That likely breached the contract. At the very least, the failure to install functional locks to keep people in jail would be a condition – a situation taking people out of what would otherwise be a contract (that would be a condition subsequent taking the parties out of a contract) or a situation keeping that contract from ever existing (that would be the absence of a condition precedent to there being a contract).

Conditions are distinguished from promises. Broken promises generally constitute breaches of contract; the occurrence of conditions takes the parties into or out of a contract (i.e., conditions bring a contract into existence or negate the contract). Conditions change, limit, preclude, give rise to, or terminate

---

[106] One guard to another: Gee, each morning, all the prisoners are gone. Is there something we're missing here, besides the people we jailed?!

a contractual duty; there is no contract breach – and the parties just cannot enforce the other party's promise because the condition bars that.

Conditions can be classified by formation:
Express - actually stated in the contract, either orally or in writing. Express conditions require strict compliance. Phrasing could even be "on condition that. . ."

For express contracts, when "making a contract, either party should carefully state as essentials or conditions the things that must be done in order to call forth his/her obligation to perform."[107]

Implied - needs substantial compliance –
For example, imagine someone is hired as a Bar Mitzvah singer is hired for a personal services contract, with the implied condition that the singer physically able to perform (no laryngitis).
    1. The hiring party cannot demand the performance. That is, a singer cannot be compelled to sing; and, on the other hand,
    2. The singer cannot show up and demand to be paid, saying "I can still croak out Hava Nagila (song in Hebrew meaning, 'Let Us Rejoice')."
In this situation, the laryngitis takes either party out of the contract. IT is a subsequent condition which removes either party's obligations. So neither party's failure to perform is a breach.

Constructive (requires substantial compliance) - put into the contract by a court - imposed by the court in order to achieve justice, fairness (custom, tradition may guide the court in reaching its determination).

Conditions can be classified by timing. This classification is in relation to when the contractual duty was/is to be performed. These timing conditions are:

Concurrent (e.g., implied condition that payment for and delivery of goods at a store is to occur simultaneously) each party's performance is conditioned on performance by the other party.
Most conditions are concurrent.

Precedent – may be implied or constructive– the usual rule is "doing before paying" (e.g., the painter must paint the house before the other side pays him/her, unless it is otherwise stated in the contract). Until the condition's occurrence, there is no right to receive performance (e.g., a unilateral offeree must perform the requested performance before a contract arises).

Subsequent – a contract has been formed, but the occurrence of the condition extinguishes a contractual duty – no breach; the subsequent condition just takes the parties out of a contract.
    (1) e.g., zoning – if a nonconforming use is desired and the purchased land is not brought within conformity (via a zoning change) by a certain time after the land's purchase.
    (2) e.g., insurance – an example: the policyholder must make any claims (report losses under the insurance policy) within 6 months after a loss; if the policyholder does not file a timely claim, there is no breach, just a condition subsequent taking the parties out from the contract.
    (3) e.g., governmental approval – a clause may excuse contract duties or place particular duties on a specified party. Here is an example of such a Governmental Approval Clause:
> "Any approval of this agreement by [foreign government] that is required to
> enable [foreign party] to enter into it, perform it, do business with, or pay [U.S.
> party] shall be secured by [foreign government]. Any approval of this agreement

---

[107] Robert W. Emerson, *Business Law*. NY: Barron's Educational Series (6th ed., 2015), at 158.

required by the government of the United States, or one of its states, territories, or local governments, shall be secured by [U.S. party]."

In effect, the clause sets forth a subsequent condition that could take the parties out of the contract if there was a good faith, but unsuccessful, attempt to obtain governmental approval.

<u>Another Conditions example: Good Faith in Exercising Rights - both express and implied conditions</u>
Seller and Buyer enter into a real estate purchase contract "contingent upon Buyer obtaining a mortgage loan" (financing). That language constitutes an express condition precedent, but there is also an implied condition because the buyer implicitly promises to <u>use reasonable efforts to obtain the loan</u>. Two other examples regarding a home purchase are: (1) an inspection condition, and (2) sale of present home contingencies. Again, both must be exercised in good faith.

AN EXAMPLE ON CONDITIONS – TESTING THE BLOOD OF MORTGAGE OR LIFE INSURANCE APPLICANTS – see the "VAMPIRE" MORTGAGE SKIT VIDEO (6:05 long) - MOUTHPIECE MOVIES & BOB E., BARRISTER SUBMITS: *The Case of the Vampire Mortgage*

Before accepting a mortgage application, mortgage companies usually require that a borrower furnish financial and credit records, evidence of insurance and employment, and tax documents. Regulators and courts routinely approve mandatory documentation as a condition precedent to a mortgage. **But what of a contract formed through *BLOOD*?** How could it be a legitimate condition precedent to getting or keeping a mortgage that the borrower provide blood samples? Is there something in blood – evidence of illness, of a genetic predisposition, of anemia – that mortgage companies have a right to know? Even if there is a right to know, what about the intrusiveness of extracting blood? Does a poking needle invade a borrower's privacy more than does a review of the borrower's insurance, credit, and tax records?

Two key questions arise: What kind of person would be so foolish as to give out blood samples in her own home? What kind of business would request such samples? Just because information <u>might</u> be useful does not mean that a business always can demand it. There is a balance of interests. Indeed, privacy may win out, with mortgage decisions - and any resulting mortgages - rendered <u>bloodless</u>.

Most states have laws with extensive protections from health insurers' or employers' requiring genetic testing or discriminating based on the results of such tests. For protection from health insurers' or employers' discriminating based on DNA differences, Congress enacted the Genetic Information Nondiscrimination Act (2008) **(see pg. 528; Emerson BL)**.

In applications for insurance or a mortgage, may a third party that really wants the information obtain a blood sample from the applicant? It is now quick and relatively inexpensive for a business to perform its own genetic testing. Nonetheless, the regulatory and statutory trend is to eliminate or at least restrict the use of such tests. No poking, prying, or prodding needles allowed!

Perhaps less emphasis should be placed on regulating the procedures for disclosure of information by physicians and other holders of medical records and more detailed focus placed on the circumstances surrounding the acquisition of information by third parties. Who are these third parties, and how do they plan to use the information? What substantive rights of the individual are implicated by a third party's use of genetic information? A third party's needs and rights will vary tremendously depending on whether it is a life insurance company, a school, a mortgage company, a law enforcement agency, a court, or some other interested party (e.g., the media reporting about a politician). Protecting genetic privacy requires multiple approaches, with a variance that depends on the industry and on the prospective information usage.

D. DISCHARGE OF CONTRACTS AND REMEDIES FOR BREACH (see pgs. 157-166; Emerson BL)

There are four main ways to discharge a contract: By Performance, Breach, Agreement of Parties, or Law.

I. PERFORMANCE

Presumably, this is the most common form of discharge.

A. Tender of Performance

A tender of performance is one party's promise to perform unconditionally (and this party – the one that made the promise – is fully, ready, able, and willing to perform). If the tender is rejected, it is still as if the party that made the promise had actually performed.

Assume that there is a contract between A and B, with A to perform work at B's house. Further assume that A truthfully tells B, "I've got everything I need and I'm ready to come over and start working at your house whenever you want me to do so." Further assume that B rejects this tender of performance. So A, by offering a valid tender of performance, has discharged his/her duty of performance because B refuses to accept the performance itself or because B has simply breached.

1. The Perfect Tender Rule

At common law, the "perfect tender rule" requires that the seller of goods must deliver goods (or at least tender delivery of goods) conforming exactly to the contract terms. Any deviation from the promised performance of the sales contract is a material breach. If the goods do not exactly comply – whether as to quality, quantity, or method of delivery – the buyer can reject the goods and rescind the contract.

The rule is adopted in UCC 2–601(2). However, other UCC provisions – e.g., the seller's right to cure (correct) nonconforming goods after the buyer rejects them – have eased the rule's impact. Now, instead of automatically favoring buyers, this modified principle permits a breaching seller, even one whose breach was serious and purposeful, to within a short, reasonable time correct , most problems with his/her performance.

2. Examples of Performance and Perfect Tender Issues

Does the less-than-perfect performance in the following two examples allow Jamison to reject and discharge the contract?

1. Wilhelm has an agreement to send 1,000 purple widgets to Jamison on or before October 31, 2015. Because this is a case involving the sale of goods, assume that the perfect tender rule applies.
o Cameron ships 999 purple widgets on time.
o Cameron ships 1,000 red widgets on time.
o Cameron ships 999 purple, and 1 red widget on time.
o Cameron ships 1,000 purple widgets, but not until November 5, 2015.
ANSWER: YES to each of the four answers. Jamison can reject any and thus discharge the contract.

2. Rosa agrees to conduct extensive rebuilding of Jamison's city townhouse residence for $1.5 Million. The written agreement states, "Rosa will use only grade A wood and UL-Approved Nails." However, Rosa cuts her costs by using only average-quality wood and nails.
ANSWER: Whether Jamison has to pay depends on how significant the difference is between what the contract called for and what Rosa actually used. If it is a minor discrepancy in building materials, then

Jamison can receive damages (or just deduct from what she would owe the difference in value received), but she is still bound to honor the contract. On the other hand, under the substantial performance test, if the difference in wood or nails is important, then the breach was material and Jamison need not pay – she has been discharged from her contractual obligation.

> What is a failure to meet a condition?
> What is a breach?
> How significant is a failure to meet what was apparently promised?
>
> Judging conditions/guarantees by Reasonableness and circumstances – A Range . . .

B. Substantial Performance or Material Breach

Suppose that you contract to buy, for $10,000, a car, including the changing of a flat tire (or having whitewall tires). What if the car is delivered, but without the tire provision being carried out? If that nonetheless constitutes substantive performance in good faith, there is no discharge of the other side. (That is a breach, but not a material breach. It is just enough to subtract the difference between complete and substantial performance. The car seller gets $10,000 minus the costs of changing the tires.)

If you and I contract for me to pay you $2,500 to paint the outside of my house, and you do a good job except that you fail to get under the eaves on the north side of the house; it may be appropriate for me to deduct an amount, say $100, from the $2500 I owe to cover my costs in painting that one area you missed. Again, only if the breach is material should I not have to pay you the contract price (minus any difference between complete and substantial performance).

If something is a material breach, then that constitutes a discharge of the other side.

C. Satisfaction Performance Standards:
Time Is "of the Essence" and Some General Examples

> "Satisfaction" – a Song seemingly tied to contracts: performance or lack thereof.
>   Some lyrics and, in ALL CAPITAL LETTERS, some comments from this text's author
>
> I can't get no satisfaction
> DOUBLE NEGATIVES GALORE – BUT ACCEPTABLE IN POPULAR CULTURE, AND EASIER TO SING THAN "I CAN'T GET ANY SATISFACTION."
>
> Cause I try, and I try, and . . .
> When I'm driving in my car and a man comes on the radio he's telling me . . . 'bout some useless information [for] my imagination
> MICK JAGGER ATTENDED THE LONDON SCHOOL OF ECONOMICS, SO EVEN BEFORE HE BECAME "FILTHY RICH" PRESUMABLY HE WAS FAMILIAR WITH MARKETING PRINCIPLES!
>
> When I'm watching my TV and a man comes on to tell me how white my shirts could be
> AN OFFER? UNLIKELY – IT'S AN ADVERTISEMENT;
> ANYWAY, NO ACCEPTANCE, SO NO CONTRACT.
>
> But he can't be a man cause he doesn't smoke the same cigarettes as me
> GRAMMAR POINT (AGAIN) – SHOULD END WITH "AS I," NOT AS ME."

> BUT THAT MAY BE OUTWEIGHED BY ARGUMENTS OF COMMON USAGE, PRECEDENT, UNDERSTANDABILITY, AND – MOST IMPORTANTLY FOR A SONG (NOT A CONTRACT!) – THE NEED TO RHYME).
> SECONDLY, WHAT ABOUT FRAUD? THERE IS NO RELIANCE, BECAUSE THEY SMOKE DIFFERENT CIGARETTES!
>
> I can't get no satisfaction
> I can't get no girl reaction
> OFFER, BUT NO ACCEPTANCE!
>
> When I'm riding 'round the world and I'm doing this and I'm signing that . . .
> AH, FINALLY, CONTRACTS ! ! ! ! ! MAYBE.

1. "Time Is of the Essence"

For performance, is time *of the essence*? If time is crucial, ordinarily one must put that expressly in the contract. Otherwise time is <u>not</u> critical. The usual contract clause on this matter simply says, "Time is of the essence."

There are, though, some circumstances indicating the necessity that deadlines be met. These particular circumstances permit courts to find time as material <u>by implication</u>. For example, during a presidential election campaign, the candidate's manager contracted with a badge company that promised to make and deliver a certain number of <u>campaign buttons</u> on or before July 1st. Because of a breakdown in plant machinery, the buttons were not offered for delivery until months later.

The manager refused them and was sued for the invoice price. The court ruled that time was of the essence by implication and denied recovery to the badge company. Similarly, a specific date by which a stationery printer agrees to deliver <u>wedding announcements</u> to the bride's parents is likely a material term (time is of the essence) without being expressly mentioned in the agreement.

The significance of deadlines is clear. If time is so material that the entire bargain is at risk, one should state it, always remembering that inconsistent behavior during the contract might unravel what was originally formed.

2. Satisfaction Standards

Here are three examples:
1. A sculptor promises a corporate officer that she will create a sculpture for the corporate headquarters lobby.
2. A computer networking contractor agrees to install a complete system.
3. A seller of land promises to deliver a good marketable title to a buyer.

In each of these agreements, these words may have been added: "to your personal satisfaction," "fully satisfactory cooling," "satisfactory to the buyer's attorney" or the like. A court may have to determine the meaning of such language as it applies to the issue of contractual performance.

The sculptor and the computer networking contractor may have had to offer that additional promise to obtain the contract. And land contracts, by custom, frequently contain such language as the sale will not "close" or "settle" unless the attorney or title company for the buyer is "satisfied" that the state of the record title is sound.

For the sculptor example, satisfaction ordinarily will be judged by a subjective standard. A brief illustration of that is SubjectiveSatisfactioninContractLaw_BigHeadDrawings_1min42secs.wmv – a YOUTUBE video at robertwemersonufl

a. <u>Subjective Standard</u> - *Example of Portrait Drawn at the Beach*

i. Subjective standard: if to X's satisfaction and - if in a personal area - taste, <u>esthetics</u>, comfort.

ii. Even a subjective satisfaction standard must be exercised in good faith; one cannot reject the painting just because one changed his mind and no longer wants his picture painted (or wants the painter to lower his price, even though you had agreed to a higher price).

iii. How do photographers, artists, others survive? They are confident that most people will like their work and pay for it.[108]

b. <u>Objective standard:</u> <u>the usual standard for satisfaction</u> -- e.g., concerning mechanical, technical, expert areas, operative fitness, and merchantability. Here, one usually cannot avert contract duties merely by declaring, "I don't like it."

The computer networking contractor's work probably will be judged by an objective standard, although the contract could be phrased to require a customer's subjective satisfaction.

As for the land sale example, satisfaction there will be judged by an objective standard. Often, a building contractor will promise to build something (e.g., a house) "according to the attached plans." The builder has thereby agreed to an objective standard of satisfaction. If the builder complies with the plans, this objective standard of satisfaction is satisfied. The other party (e.g., the homeowner) cannot unreasonably claim to be unsatisfied. For this type of case, satisfaction is not a matter of taste.

II. BREACH

A. A Breach and Its Consequences

A material breach discharges the non–breaching party. "If one party to a contract *fails* in a material way to *perform*, the other party has no obligation on the contract."[109]

> **The Three Medieval Merchant Partners and Their Bundle of Entrusted Gold**
> There are many versions of this story, going back to Ancient Greece. Here is one by French writer Alain-René Lesage (1668-1747), in his novel, <u>The History of Vanillo Gonzales, surnamed the Merry Bachelor</u> (1734), at chapter XVI:
> "About six months ago, Charles Azarini, Peter Scannati, and Jerom Avellino, three merchants, came to me, accompanied by a public notary, and, bringing with them the sum of ten thousand crowns in gold, informed me that they had agreed to make me the depositary of this money, which they intended to export whenever an advantageous opportunity happened. Delivering it into my possession, they desired me to give them an undertaking in writing, that I would not deliver it, or any part of it, to any one of them except in the presence of the other two; and I accordingly entered into this engagement by executing a document which the notary

---

[108] There is a psychological element at play: While the customer may understand that he/she has a right to disapprove the work, he/she usually is psychologically predisposed to approve it. And a marketing tool of the sellers is to anticipate the natural, emotional reaction of others. For example, a customer asks a photographer, "what do you do with the photos that we don't buy?" The Studio responds, "We rip 'em up and toss 'em out!" Perhaps the customer cries out "Oh NO!!!!" and buys them all (takes, and thus pays for, far more than the basic, "bargain package."
[109] Robert W. Emerson, *Business Law*. NY: Barron's Educational Series (6th ed., 2015), at 160.

> prepared for this purpose. We carefully preserved the money thus deposited for the parties concerned whenever its delivery should be required. But a few nights ago, Jerom Avellino knocked loudly at my door, and, on its being opened, hastily entered my room in great agitation. 'Signor,' said he, 'if I break in upon the hours of repose, you must excuse the interruption from the importance of the business which occasions it. Azarini, Scannati, and myself have learnt that a Genoese vessel richly laden is just arrived at Messina, from which, if speedily employed, we have an opportunity of deriving great advantage, and have therefore resolved to employ the ten thousand crowns which are in your hands. Make haste, if you please, and deliver them to me; my horse is waiting at the door; and I burn with impatience to reach Messina.'
>
> 'Signor Avellino,' said I, 'you seem to have forgotten that I cannot part with them unless the . . .'
>
> 'Oh! no, no,' interrupted he, 'I very well recollect that it is expressed in the agreement, that you are not to deliver them unless the three parties be present; but Azarini and Scannati are ill, and could not accompany me to your house; they however absolve you from that condition, and desire that you will deliver me the money immediately: every moment is of consequence; come, you have nothing to fear; you have long known me; I have always maintained the character of an honest man, and I hope you will not, by any unjust suspicion of my integrity, disturb the friendship which has subsisted between us, and be the cause of our losing the present advantageous opportunity. Do, do make haste,' continued he; 'deliver me the money instantly, or I am fearful I shall be too late at Messina.'"
>
> ---
> If the narrator relents and gives the gold to Avellino, has he breached the contract? If Avellino then absconds with the booty (the gold), do the other two merchants then have a claim? What obligations, if any, would the other two merchants have toward the narrator? Does the narrator have a good defense?

B. Anticipatory Breach

[handwritten note: don't declare breach too soon]

How long must one wait when a breach appears imminent? "If one of the parties to a contract clearly states or implies that he/she cannot or will not perform as agreed, the other party does not have to sit idly by and await the due date of performance before declaring the contract breached and therefore discharged. Such a statement of nonperformance creates an anticipatory breach."[110]

Anticipatory Breach (Repudiation) must be definite, not just probable, that the other side is going to breach. You can treat the contract as breached and start to mitigate.

1. Two Anticipatory Breach Examples

a. Construction contract for building an office building within one year

If a builder has agreed to construct a large building on a site within 365 days after the contract signing, and it is now 333 days after the signing, and no work has started – not even the bulldozing and leveling of the ground to prepare it for the building process – THEN the landowner does not have to wait another 33 days (until past the 365th day) to see if a breach will occur. If it is absolutely clear that the building cannot be completed within 33 days, the landowner ought to be able to start making arrangements to have someone else construct the building. The landowner can anticipate the builder's breach.

b. Purchase of a car

For example, suppose that Pam and Sheila had executed an agreement on a Friday afternoon, with the understanding that the following Tuesday Pam would deliver to Sheila a cashier's check for the full sales price

---
[110] Id. at 161.

and with Sheila then tendering the car to Pam. But there would be an implicit repudiation of Pam's contract to purchase the car from Sheila if Pam, on Saturday morning, found someone else (Ella) driving "Pam's" car, and – when stopped by an incredulous Pam – that someone else insisting that she (Ella) had paid Sheila for the car. The most definite proof would be Ella's producing for Pam's inspection the new car registration (in Ella's name) and a copy of the written agreement reached between Ella and Sheila. That very day Pam could look for a different car and otherwise treat her agreement with Sheila as already breached. Pam does not have to wait until Tuesday because the proof is so definite that Sheila cannot perform the contract, as agreed: Sheila no longer even has the car in her possession!

2. What If You Anticipate a Breach Too Soon? *Goldman v. Allyn & Bacon, Inc.*

Watch out about invoking anticipatory breach too quickly. An example of that problem was the case of the authors and their "troubled" publisher. The authors believed that their publisher was not doing what it was supposed to be doing to carry out its contractual obligations, so the authors did not complete their work in assembling and submitting the manuscript to the publisher. Ultimately, the authors discovered that they lost any claims against the publisher because the authors had "jumped the gun." They had not done enough to verify that the publisher definitely was going to breach. So the authors were not yet discharged from their contractual obligations to the publisher (e.g., their duty to submit the manuscript). Thus, it was the authors who were in breach.[111]

What can the other side do about a possible, future breach?
(1) Put on spot or demand a confirming letter.
(2) Make the allegedly about–to–breach party admit that it was going to breach or demonstrate that it could and would perform. For example, it should post a bond, or let the other side review its books.

Until one is sure, one should not stop performing. The soon–to–be breaching party should inform the other party about what it is or is not doing, so that the non–breaching party would have a better chance to mitigate damages.[112]

III. DISCHARGE BY AGREEMENT OF THE PARTIES (pgs. 161-163; Emerson BL)

The following are five ways in which an agreement may be discharged.

a. mutual rescission – a contract to end a contract; each party gives up its rights under the original contract in return for the other party's also giving up its rights under that same contract. E.g., in a bilateral, executory agreement, both parties give up their existing right to receive the other side's performance of its contractual duties.

b. novation – substituting a new party for one of the original two parties to a contract.

c. substituted agreement – the original, two parties each agree to a new performance by each of those two parties (in substitution for the performance called for by the old contract).

d. release and/or waiver – knowingly give up rights

---
[111] *Goldman v. Allyn & Bacon, Inc.*, 482 F. Supp. 963 (D. Mass. 1979) (finding that the authors had mistakenly anticipated a breach and – by not upholding their own duties – were the ones that actually breached).
[112] While traditionally in England the party who files a lawsuit can get only damages (equity matters are still distinct), in the United States the lawsuit plaintiff not only can ask for assurances of performance (to deal with anticipatory breach), but also, in appropriate cases, can get specific performance (generally in lieu of a damages award).

> A release or a waiver may result in acceptance of defective or incomplete performance.

e. accord and satisfaction
What is the accord? It is the new agreement.
What is the satisfaction? It is the carrying out of the new agreement.

Is there a real dispute? For example, is there a dispute over whether an obligation is due yet, and is there a raised issue, one not yet resolved, such as contractual obligations, defenses, etc.? Finally, is there uncertainty about amounts owed? As defined it at **pg. 162 - Emerson BL** - this would be an unliquidated debt – thus something potentially subject to accord and satisfaction.

On the other hand, if there is no real dispute, it will not do for someone to say, for example, "I'll take my $10,000 Visa bill and pay it with $40 check marked "payment in full!!!" Also, there is No Accord if the other person writes "without prejudice" or "under protest" or if he takes payment while striking out "payment in full." UCC 1-207.

IV. DISCHARGE BY OPERATION OF LAW

Bankruptcy, statute of limitations, material nonconsensual alteration of written agreement, and impossibility and commercial impracticability are methods by which contracts can be discharged through the operation of law.

Impossibility is probably the method of discharge most often an issue in court cases; that is perhaps because impossibility is the one method most full of issues and most difficult to understand.

A. Comparison of Impossibility with Commercial Impracticability

Impossibility definitely excuses performance when a contractual duty cannot physically be performed. This is Objective Impossibility ("It cannot be done"), a core defense. It is distinguishable from the much less convincing defense, at least for the courts, Subjective Impossibility ("Sorry, but I just cannot / will not do that"). For Subjective Impossibility, Party X's performance is physically possible but would be extremely burdensome for X to carry out.

As a legal term, therefore, "impossible" means, literally, impossible, not just very, very difficult. If something was foreseeable, that is not the same as probable. Something that was foreseeable – thus could have been covered in a contract (could have had a Force Majeure Clause)[113] – thus is not deemed to have rendered a contract impossible.

Five examples of impossibility are:
1. **the subject matter is destroyed** (e.g., a necessary component – say, wombats - disappear from the face of the earth; with no more wombats, then no more contract!)
2. **the supply disappears entirely;**

---

[113] The following example of a clause excusing contract duties or placing particular duties on a specified party is a Force Majeure Clause:
"The parties hereto are excused from nonperformance in case of war, declared or undeclared; riots; fire; flood; interruption of transportation; inflation beyond the expected rate; embargo; accident; explosion; shortage of supply materials, equipment, or production facilities; governmental orders, regulations, or restrictions; rationing priorities by strike, lockout, or other labor troubles interfering with the production, transportation, or manufacturing of the goods."
In effect, the clause sets forth subsequent conditions which could take the parties out of a contract.

3. **there is subsequent illegality** – the contract, or its purpose, becomes illegal;
(unless the general legislation making certain acts or conditions illegal contains a grandfather clause, an exemption for conditions or circumstances (including contracts) existing before the legislation was enacted – e.g., the nonconforming uses exception for already existing uses that is usually found in zoning statutes)

Although it is not always treated as impossibility, courts usually treat "subsequent illegality" as a form of impossibility. Imagine you are quite ill; so you enter into an assisted suicide contract with a man known as "Dr. Death." It'll be your last contract! But then, before Dr. Death is to be the last to see you off to the Great Beyond, the legislature enacts a law declaring such arrangements unlawful. Dr. Death may be coming after you with a syringe of poison, saying "you've still got yourself a deal!" But he is wrong; you are out from any contractual obligation due to the legal principle of *subsequent illegality*.

4. **a party in a personal services contract dies or becomes incapacitated** (covers both parties who were to perform the services and those who were to receive the services)

5. **unforeseen event makes completion of the contract impossible** – For this situation, insofar as a contracting party is a corporation or other business entity, one must have something more than an officer of the contracting corporation dying or becoming disabled; that is because a corporation is distinct from the natural persons who constitute its officers and directors.

   a. Suez Canal Example of alleged Impossibility - the Year 1967

Due to the closing of the Suez Canal, which the parties to intend to use for the shipping, in one case there were $45,000 more in costs on a contract price of $305,000. This was found to *Not* be Commercial frustration, although it greatly increased costs to obtain oil from Iran, Iraq, etc. and bring to the USA. The increased costs, by themselves, were not enough to discharge the parties from the contract. Foreseeable difficulties are not the same as "probable," but should be covered in a contract, such as through a *force majeure* clause (see below).

   b. Orange Grove Example of Impossibility
      A contract just for "Grade A oranges," or "Grade A oranges from Emerson's grove": Imagine that a hailstorm hovers over exclusively Emerson's property and destroys the grove. Acts of God must be unforeseeable, so the seller can cover (get the goods elsewhere). In this example, it is only impossible IF the contract says the oranges must be "Emerson Oranges."

   If there is nothing in the Contract about where the oranges must come from, then likely it is not impossible just because one has problems with (will lose money from) covering for a loss by getting other oranges.

   The lesson is: Draft contracts carefully! Courts are reluctant to let parties out (to find "impossibility"); most courts find that the circumstances were not an impossibility, that the parties stuck with higher shipping costs were not discharged from their contracts.

6. **Commercial impracticability** may be considered a somewhat watered down version of impossibility. There, relief from contractual obligations may be granted when an unforeseen contingency has rendered performance – while not impossible - extremely difficult, harmful, or expensive. Under UCC 2–615, the impracticability arises "by the occurrence of a contingency the non–occurrence of which was a basic assumption on which the contract was made." Some jurisdictions state that commercial impracticability can only be found if there is no provision within the contract that allocates risk between the parties.

7. Force Majeure Clauses

The purpose of contract law is to reduce transaction costs, clarify agreements, ensure parties act as agreed. But what happens when performance is impeded by forces outside the parties' control? The doctrine has changed from simply "physical impossibility" to also cover "commercial impracticability" due to unexpected circumstances: If the contract can be performed, but doing so is economically senseless, the contracting party can claim force majeure. *natural forces*

a. A rose by any other name?

Force Majeure is a French term meaning "superior, irresistible or greater force."

The French Civil Code long recognized how unfair it is to penalize a contracting party who fails to perform a duty because of an unforeseeable, unexpected event.

Force majeure is a broader phrase than "vis major" (Acts of God), which tend to be interpreted more strictly as natural disasters and those things that were not caused by humans in one way or another. That is because force majeure can apply to situations ranging from natural disasters (Acts of God that no one can prevent, such as floods, earthquakes, volcanoes, hurricanes, tsunamis, wildfires, lightning strikes, and tornados)) to human actions (acts of third parties, including wars, riots, labor strikes or lockouts, terrorist attacks, air raid sirens, and laser strikes).

b. A common clause, especially in business transactions

Force Majeure is a common clause releasing both parties from a contract duty when an extraordinary event beyond the parties' control prevents them from fulfilling that duty. While the clause use to only apply to contracts that were "impossible" to complete, it is now often used as a risk allocating mechanism between two contracting parties. For example, if the parties consider a risk to be uninsurable or unacceptable, they might decide that rendering the performance would be too inconvenient or impractical.

So the clause serves two purposes: (1) it allocates risk; and (2) it provides notice to the parties of events that may suspend or excuse performance.

c. Requirements

Requirements for Force Majeure are:
1. A triggering event has occurred;
2. The triggering event was unexpected & unforeseeable - not regular or frequent;
3. The event made performance under the contract impossible/impractical; and
4. The triggering event's effects could not be mitigated through the exercise of reasonable skill.

A hurricane directly hitting a coast is foreseeable during hurricane season; but the devastating effects of Hurricane Katrina may not have been foreseeable.

d. Court Approaches

Courts tend to interpret force majeure clauses narrowly; that is, only listed events and events similar to those listed will be covered. For example, while acts of terrorism might be a specified force majeure event, it does not necessarily follow that a court would also excuse a party's performance based on "threats" of terrorism.

e. What force majeure does not cover

The force majeure clause is NOT intended to excuse negligence or other malfeasance of a party. The usual, natural consequences of external forces such as a rainstorm preventing an outdoor event is not covered under the force majeure clause. Rain in Florida (or most other locations) would not be covered; rain in the Sahara Desert could be!

Courts will generally deny force majeure claims if the triggering event was caused by the party's poor business planning.

f. DuPont and Huntsman: An Example

An example of a domestic force majeure cases is the distinction in the court's treatment, in the aftermath of Hurricane Katrina (2005), of the DuPont and Huntsman corporations.

i. DuPont

Floods damaged the physical structure of a Mississippi plant halting operations for months. DuPont spent over $150 million to rebuild and clean up after Katrina. It invoked force majeure due to the "acts of God" from the hurricanes. All electrical and electronic system in the plant needed replacement. The force majeure declaration was lifted less than one year after Katrina, once the facility was stable. Supply was at first limited, but production was again reliable.

ii. Huntsman

There was no structural damage to manufacturing facilities, but the company lost access to supplies for butane and feedstock. That limited its ability to deliver on contracts - Huntsman was only able to deliver on 50% of its allocations. Huntsman raised prices on many products. In effect, the force majeure clauses of the other companies (for Huntsman's supplies) drove market prices up.

B. Court Doctrine

Courts look at contractual parties' intent, at overall circumstances, not just increased costs. Simply because circumstances put someone in a tough financial situation does not get him/her out of his/her contract. **Impossibility is to be narrowly construed. If unlikely, but possible, it is not to be termed "impossible."**

A long line of Florida cases indicates that Florida courts will not follow the commercial impracticability doctrine, but will instead, as in many states, adhere to the stricter Impossibility Test. The only exception, for all the states, is that Article 2 of the UCC codifies a commercial impracticability test for some sales of goods.

The Civil Law tradition often is more receptive to reformation of contracts unsuited to the parties' needs than in the common law tradition, which might simply find a breach or impossibility.[114] In Germany, for example, unlike the United States, courts can revise (rewrite) a contract based on the impossibility of that contract.

ESSENTIAL ELEMENTS OF THE PLAINTIFF'S CASE IN A CONTRACT SUIT

Three practical, necessary elements in a contract suit are:
   a. Proof of the <u>existence of a contract</u>.
   b. Proof that the <u>defendant breached</u> the contract.
   c. Proof that, as a result of defendant's breach, the plaintiff has been harmed (<u>damages</u>).

Let us consider remedies for breach: damages awards and equitable remedies.

REMEDIES FOR BREACH: OUR CONTRACTS SKIT
 - THE TALE OF <u>THE PIED PIPER</u> - at http://www.youtube.com/watch?v=-fiv0B6JPNI at Robert Emerson ("The Pied Piper: A Lesson in Contracts" by Robert Emerson)

A. Was There <u>a Contract</u> Between the Village and the Piper? Yes.

B. What <u>Defenses</u> to a Contract Claim Could the Village assert? Would the Village Win?

Risky defenses or claims? The type of claim or defense that causes skepticism about the party's entire case.

---

[114] There is more on reformation in a section hereafter on equitable remedies.

> So the shotgun approach may be overdoing it. Risking too much.
> **Do not risk a bolt of lightning for saying such a thing, do not cause such a stink that people check their shoes. If your claim or defense stinks to high heaven, that could "infect" the opinion of the judge, jury, and public.**
>
> (1) Over $500, under the Statute of Frauds?
> (a) Was it a service?
> (b) Are rats goods? **NOT in this case. Not buying rats as goods, but actually buying a service (removal of the rats).**
> (c) A UCC in Medieval Europe? **Of course not! No UCC not until the 1950s in America.**
> (2) Duress? **No.**
> -Who created the problem? **A key question. The Pied Piper did not impose the crisis on the village. This was NOT comparable to a fireman creating some business for himself (digging up some work) by committing arson.**
> (3) Unconscionability? Were the contract terms grossly unfair?
> (4) Is it against public policy? Cruelty to Animals?
> A society that likes rats or life generally may value that life so strongly that it extends rights to those living things. May one go beyond small gnawing rodents to other living things, such as trees? Do they have rights?
> (5) Impossibility? "A mighty fiscal deficit lay over the land."
> **Poor economic condition is insufficient excuse.**
>
> C. Shotgun Approach: Make all arguments that don't cause you to turn "beet-red." Shoot lots of pellets in hopes something hits the target.
> But do too many seemingly spurious claims sully the claimant's other better claims?
> D. Assuming that there was a lawful agreement, what are the Piper's Remedies for a breach? (The law recognizes human nature)
> (1) Sue. You should win.
> But often lawsuits are costly and <u>un</u>satisfying (e.g., besides possibly losing the suit, one can lose reputation-suffer a poor image); it is better to get money upfront.
> (2) Self-Help (Cover, Set-Off) **Buying/trying elsewhere for what you need.** Set-off is deducting the amount the other side owes to you from what you owe it.
> (3) But cannot go overboard re: remedies - was the Piper's solution a lawful response to the town's breach? It can even be risky to sue: A possible opening of a can of worms. And then maybe even countersuits!

> E. Just as matters of heart are not generally matters for contract law, so, when there is a breach of contract, it is <u>not</u> viewed as a moral concern. Not bad, Not wrong: Businesses make choices. Sometimes they choose to breach. But they must then "Pay the Piper."[115]

V. DAMAGES AWARDS (see pgs. 166-171; Emerson BL)

A damages award, whatever its kind (e.g., punitive damages, compensatory damages, a combination of different types of damages) is a court order that the defendant pay the plaintiff a particular amount of money. In the event of a breach, a damages award is the most common type of remedy. But that

---

[115] There is a saying: "It's time to pay the piper!" It is derived from the Tale of the Pied Piper, and it means to face the consequences of one's actions.

is it. Normally, there is no penalty for breaching a contract beyond restoring the non–breacher to the status quo ante or giving the non–breacher his/her contract expectations (making the non–breacher "whole"). Contract damages almost always mean nothing more than compensating for actual losses. Even though a contract breach may cause considerable "mental anguish" to the breach's victim, courts generally do not compensate for this anguish.

A. Punitive (Exemplary) Damages? (see pgs. 170-171; Emerson BL)

The common law heritage, such as in the United States, India, and the Philippines, permits punitive damages in some non–contractual (tort) lawsuits.[116] The punitive damages (to punish), sometimes called exemplary damages (to serve as an example), constitute a damages award meant to punish and make an example of the defendant's outrageous, malicious, and oppressive conduct.

The Civil Law (Code law) approach, such as is found in France, Germany, and other European countries, is more simply to never (or almost never) award punitive damages in any type of case.

On contract matters, though, both legal systems – common law and Civil Law – coincide in not viewing punitive damages as an acceptable remedy. Courts almost never allow punitive damages for breach of contract. But a tort corollary to the breach may lead to punitive damages.[117]

The Restatement of Contracts on Punitive Damages
RESTATEMENT (SECOND) OF CONTRACTS § 335 (1981) provides that "punitive damages are not recoverable for breach of contract unless the conduct constituting the breach is also a tort for which punitive damages is recoverable." Many courts, therefore, have awarded punitive damages for breach of a contract to marry because the plaintiff's injuries are seen as uniquely personal, with his/her harmed interests (in the olden days, often the loss of a woman's chastity) having more in common with a typical tort action than with a contract action. Special types of cases, for which punitive damages might be awarded, have involved public service companies that failed to discharge obligations to the public (e.g., a railroad toward its passengers) and fiduciaries with duties toward clients (e.g., a real-estate broker toward his customer).

B. Compensatory, Including Consequential, Damages (see pgs. 167-168; Emerson BL)

1. Different Standards in Different Countries

YOUTUBE – Bespokoistvo.wmv at robertwemersonufl (8mins37secs)

While in America breach of contract damages are only for actual monetary losses, Russian contract law (and that of a number of other Civil Law nations) permits a much broader form of compensation, based on Bespokoistvo, a term that translates literally as bother or annoyance. But it means far more than that – far beyond what is typically compensable under United States law. Bespokoistvo includes even psychological damage. **See pg. 478; Emerson BL.**

---

[116] Torts are discussed in Part III of this text.
[117] Consider a breach of contract accompanied by a tort (e.g., fraud). In *Boise Dodge, Inc. v. Clark*, 453 P.2d 551 (Idaho 1969), the plaintiff was told that he was purchasing a new car, but the automobile was, in fact, a well–used demonstrator model with its odometer turned back. The plaintiff received, in tort, punitive damages due to the defendant's fraud.

de minimis non curat lex
reformatum — Germany)

2. The Terms "Compensatory" and "Consequential"

In successful breach of contract cases, the most typical remedy is for the court to award compensatory damages to the plaintiff. The award is the amount of money the court decides that the plaintiff needs to compensate him/her by making him/her "whole." As for consequential damages, they are a type of compensatory award, again to remedy the plaintiff's harms resulting from the defendant's faulty performance or other such breach; the consequential damages is a monetary amount meant to cover indirect injuries that the plaintiff suffered, such as lost profits. Because they are indirect and thus more remote in time and effect from the breach, consequential damages must meet legal tests for fairness, namely that they were foreseeable and that a fair, quantifiable amount really can be determined.

> "Limitations on the Ability to Be Legally Compensated for Damages **(see pg. 168; Emerson BL)**:
> 1. Damages must be proved to a reasonable certainty.
> 2. Defendant is liable only for damages that were reasonably foreseeable at the time the contract was made or at the time the breach occurred.
> 3. Plaintiff must use every reasonable effort to mitigate, that is, avoid or minimize, the damages."

3. Damages Concerning Executed and Executory Contracts

For breaches of executed contracts, courts should give parties their reasonable expectations. For breaches of executory contracts, courts should return the parties to the *status quo ante*.

4. Lost Profits as a Consequential Damage

Lost profits can be a basis for a damages award if the damages were <u>foreseeable</u> when the contract was made and are <u>ascertainable</u> now that the contract has been breached. But what if the person claiming damages is a <u>new business</u>? Lost profits are difficult to prove, because there is a <u>problem of speculation, of no historic record</u> upon which to calculate losses.[118]

> AMERICAN LAW, BRAZILIAN LAW, AND FORESEEABILITY **(see pg. 170; Emerson BL**
> In the Brazilian system, the foreseeability rule distinguishes non–performance (*inadimplemento contratual* - total breach for which one can recover for even unforeseeable losses) from mere tardiness (*mora* - not an absolute breach but mere delay for which one recovers only foreseeable losses).
> For moral damages, **see pg. 477; Emerson BL.**

To illustrate this concept of speculation and limited or nonexistent records, consider the Christmas cards example. Suppose that Hallmark fails to deliver cards to a stationery shop until December 20th. The failure to deliver those cards until then certainly led to foreseeable damages – lost profits because too late for most shop customers who wanted to buy Christmas cards; these customers would have already obtained cards long earlier. The shop simply needs to be able to show the level of sales that were lost.

5. Measuring Damages: Two Examples

a. Widgets Went Away (as illustrated in YOUTUBE -
The Paul/Daniel/Laura "Emerson Contract Players" Video (5:45 long): ContractDamageCalculations_5mins45secs.wmv at robertwemersonufl - https://www.youtube.com/watch?v=dyXGh41b26o) – also the post-skit review of the

---

[118] Almost all areas of law involve <u>practicality</u>: not just trial as to guilt/liability, but also the practical problems of preventing and/or detecting crimes/torts. It is not just the legal question of was there a breach and, if so, the amount of damages, but also the practical issue of dealing with human nature – the tendency to be self-serving, to exaggerate one's damages. So public officials and the law must take that into account; at contract law, for example, judges hold people accountable for proving their damages – not just speculating/guessing.

skit (10:02 long) – how to calculate damages – is at
https://www.youtube.com/watch?v=ToQCoZv2V_U

Imagine that Paul agreed with Robert, a store owner, to deliver X grade WWW widgets to Robert at $8 per widget. The store stocks and sells a number of items, including grade WWW widgets.

Paul breaches the contract by failing to deliver any widgets. Daniel comes to the store and leaves in a huff, because there were no WWW widgets to buy.

Robert moves promptly to cover the WWW widget deficit in his store. He arranges with Laura to buy X grade WWW widgets for the best terms he can find, which is delivery within three weeks and at $11 per widget.

The example leaves it simple: keeping out interest, depreciation, inventory, stocking and other factors.

Robert's Direct Losses will be Compensatory Damages. Assuming that he had not prepaid Paul for the widgets, Robert is not out the $8 per widget price), his direct compensatory damages, per widget, are X times the difference between what he must pay Laura and what he would have paid Paul: $11 (market replacement price), minus the contract price of $8, and then multiplied by X. That is, $3 in damages per item, times X (the number of items).

Robert's Indirect Losses are Consequential Damages, a special type of compensatory damages). These are more difficult to prove. They are easier to exclude or limit in a contract if the parties had relatively equivalent bargaining power. In this example, consequential damages would be the lost sales of grade WWW widgets at Robert's store when he should have had the widgets in stock from Paul) and had not yet received the widgets from Laura. Lost sales presumably would have been to customers such as Daniel. As Robert would have sold each widget for $16, each lost sale would be $5 an item more in consequential damages (Robert's lost profit of $5; that is, $16 minus $11). We already have accounted for the amount up to $11 on each widget, in that Robert did not receive that money from a customer but he also was not out of pocket for it (did not prepay the $8 per widget to Paul, and receives the $3 in compensatory damages for the difference between Paul at $8 and Laura at $11).

To show how many lost sales of WWW widgets Robert would have had, we must not just talk about individuals who actually came to the store and we vividly remember (the outraged Daniels of the world), all such person we may be able to surmise would have bought such widgets if they were available. To have evidence of lost sales, we must look at past sales, demographics, store traffic, even information concerning competitors' sales.
One cannot just say, "we think we would have sold more."

b. The Three Ships

Assume that Columbus has contracts with three shipbuilders. Either Columbus breaches, or the builders breach. What are the damages? Assume neither side has yet paid the other. What remedy is available to the non–breaching party? In other words, what is the measure of damages?

(a) Fully Built Santa Maria
1. Columbus alleges and proves the Builder breached – Columbus must pay the Builder the contract price minus the cost for repairing defects.
2. Builder alleges and proves Columbus breached – Columbus must pay the Builder the full contract price.

(b) Ship Not Built (No Nina)
1. Columbus alleges and proves the Builder breached – Columbus recovers from the Builder his foreseeable, reasonable, nontransferable expenses (e.g., Builder must return any deposits), and also gets

from the Builder the difference between the contract price and the market price (assuming the latter is higher) (as with $8 to $11 difference in Paul–Daniel–Laura example, above)

2. Builder alleges and proves Columbus breached – Columbus must pay to the Builder the profits that the Builder lost because of the breach.

(c) Partly Built Ship (a Pinta)
1. Columbus alleges and proves the Builder breached – Columbus owes the Builder the contract price minus the cost of completing the ship (e.g., minus the cost of getting another shipbuilder to finish the job).
2. Builder alleges and proves Columbus breached – Columbus must pay to the Builder the costs which the Builder has incurred plus the profits that the Builder lost because of the breach.

6. *Hadley v. Baxendale*, http://www.bailii.org/ew/cases/EWHC/Exch/1854/J70.html

Hadley v. Baxendale, 9 Exch. 341, 156 Eng. Rep 145 (English Court of Exchequer 1854) is the leading early common law case on consequential damages due to the defendant's failure or delay in performance. There, the engine shaft in the plaintiff's corn mill had broken. The plaintiff hired the defendant, a common carrier, to take the shaft to the manufacturer, who would make a new one based on the broken shaft as a model. The defendant failed to deliver the shaft within the time promised, and thus – with no new shaft available – the plaintiff's mill remained shut down. The plaintiff sought a damages award for the lost profits incurred after the mill should have been able to re–open, but could not, because the new shaft was late. The court held that the defendant need not pay these consequential damages because most mill operators have a spare shaft and would not have needed to shut down; since the plaintiff did not tell the defendant about its special circumstances – that the mill would be shut down until a new shaft was delivered – the defendant could not be held liable for these indirect (consequential) damages from the defendant's breach.

7. Comparative Law: Moral Damages in the Civil Law, and Emotional Distress for Some Common Law Contract Breaches

As mentioned near the start of this Part of the text, the YouTube video – Moral Damages.wmv at robertwemersonufl (12mins13secs) - covers some of what is now discussed.

Some countries may go beyond what the United States typically makes available in breach of contract cases. A notable example is moral damages. Moral damage, in its broadest sense, encompasses every harm, contractual or in tort, that does not have an economic value. It involves contracts where a personal interest is involved or where the defendant's activity concerns the public. It includes pain, hurt, and suffering that a party unjustly causes to another. It includes harm to one's feelings, honor, or moral principles. Moral damages are similar to emotional distress damages and also, in effect, function in much the same deterrent effect as do punitive damages.

Moral damages and awards for pain and suffering are allowed in many Civil Law nations (e.g., in some Latin American countries such as Argentina, where it is termed "agravio morat," as well as in Bolivia, Ecuador, Mexico, Peru, and Venezuela). Generally, such damages are never available in common law jurisdictions' breach–of–contract cases.

In the United States and other common law nations, damages for emotional distress may be awarded for a breach of contract if, but only if, serious emotional disturbance was a particularly likely result of the breach.[119] Examples have included misdelivered telegraph messages and mortuaries mishandling corpses.[120] In effect, these contracts, where the emotional distress claim is at least a

---

[119] RESTATEMENT (SECOND) OF CONTRACTS § 353 (1981)
[120] See *Lamm v. Shingleton*, 55 S.E.2d 810 (N.C. 1949) (water and mud entered what the funeral home promised to be an airtight vault for the plaintiff's deceased husband).

possibility, concern personal matters (e.g., hotel accommodations, promises of marriage, and personal transportation), not commercial concerns, or where the plaintiff incurred bodily harm.[121]

Breaching conduct so willful, wanton, reckless, or insulting as to also be tortious may permit a plaintiff in a breach–of–contract case to also receive damages in tort for emotional distress (as is also the case for punitive damages, discussed hereafter in this text). In *Chung v. Kaonobi*, 618 P.2d 283 (Hawaii 1980), the Supreme Court of Hawaii in effect found the defendants' breach of contract to also be behavior constituting a tort: the defendants had surreptitiously negotiated with a third party, made numerous statements to the plaintiffs that the defendants would comply with their lease agreement, and falsely denied that they were negotiating with another party, all while knowing that the plaintiffs had expended money and effort in reliance on the defendants' promise of a lease for a restaurant in a shopping center, so the plaintiffs' deserved emotional distress damages.

8. The Intersection Between Malpractice and Breach of Contract

While a surgeon may so seriously breach a contract to perform cosmetic surgery as to possibly lead to emotional distress damages,[122] the other claim for damages besides from the contract is for the tort of malpractice. In the *Sullivan* case, the Massachusetts high court found that "psychological as well as physical injury may be expected to figure somewhere in [the plaintiff's] recovery," whether for contract breach or for a tort. Id. at 189.

C. Mitigation

Breaches are not necessarily bad, because – in fact – a breach sometimes may even be an economically efficient choice. We do not punish breaches, but simply require the breacher to "make whole" the non–breaching party. Since breaching is not, by itself, a moral wrong, the law still imposes a duty on the non–breaching party: to try to mitigate its damages.

"Mitigation means reduction to a minimum. It is the requirement that the injured party use reasonable efforts to minimize his/her loss."[123] The duty of mitigation is to reduce, alleviate, help out, and try to cure. There should be no gouging, even by otherwise innocent parties who have been wronged because someone else breached. (One cannot simply sock it to the defendant and sit on one's bottom, collecting damages.)

If the non–breacher does not mitigate his/her losses, and – in a breach of contract case (or other such cases, e.g., for alleged employment discrimination) – the court finds that the non–breacher could have mitigated, then the court will reduce the amount owed to the non–breacher in a damages award by the amount of mitigation that the court decides the non–breacher could have gotten in mitigation. (So, since a court will treat you as if you had mitigated, anyway, you had better do so! That is, undertake "self-help.")

> Self–help is encouraged in contract law and in the legal system generally. Indeed, law typically is implemented through a combination of public and private mechanisms. Burglars, for example, are deterred from unauthorized entry in part by the threat of jail time and police intervention, and in part by the knowledge that many homeowners have guns, security systems, and other private measures by which to defend their property. Similarly, while entrepreneurs use patent, copyright, and trade secret law to protect proprietary information, they also routinely take matters into their own hands by, for example, dividing sensitive information across employees such that no single employee knows enough to betray the firm

---

[121] See also Douglas J. Whaley, Paying for the Agony: The Recovery of Emotional Distress Damages in Contract Actions, 26 SUFFOLK U. L. REV. 936, 940 (1992).
[122] *Sullivan v. O'Connor*, 296 N.E.2d 183 (Mass. 1973) (a "nose job" that failed to achieve the promised improvement in appearance but actually resulted in disfigurement and deformity).
[123] Robert W. Emerson, *Business Law*. NY: Barron's Educational Series (6th ed., 2015), at 168.

completely. Every area of law can to some degree be characterized in this manner, framed in a way that emphasizes substitutability between public responses and their private alternatives.

When a buyer of land breaches a contract, common law generally as well as various state law principles of real estate and equity require that the seller must mitigate and hold a public sale (presumably to insure fairness and the best obtainable price). Under the UCC, however, a seller may resell goods privately when a buyer breaches.

Incidental damages are awarded to pay for costs incurred in mitigating damages. The court awards incidental damages to reimburse an innocent party for expenses caused by a breach of contract in connection with inspection, storage, and transportation. The expenses that the innocent party incurs in attempting to locate substituted performance may also be recovered from the party in breach. For instance, if a landlord spends $150 to advertise to locate a new tenant to replace a breaching tenant, the cost of that advertising, if reasonable, is part of the landlord's damages (along with, for example, the diminution in rent payments that he ultimately will get – e.g., a month with no rent at all, remaining rent payments from the new tenant that are $75 a month less than the monthly payments contracted for with the breaching tenant).

Duty of Mitigation: Three Examples

1. You contract with a roofer to repair your leaky roof. The roofer supposedly repairs the roof, and you pay him the contractual amount. But the next big rainstorm reveals that the roof still leaks! Even though you are the nonbreaching party, and the roofer appears to have breached his contractual duty by not effectuating adequate repairs, you still have a duty to try to keep your damages to a minimum. For example, you should put plastic buckets or other receptacles underneath leaks to keep the water from landing on, and ruining, say, expensive flooring. And, if you can, you should move items that would be damaged by the leaks – e.g., furniture, important papers, and other personal items. But you are not expected to take extraordinary measures; so, for example, courts would not expect you to go up onto the roof yourself (particularly during a storm!) and try to put pitch and tar up there to plug the leaks yourself!

2. A tenant breaches his lease by no longer paying the rent, with several months remaining on a yearlong lease. The tenant has vacated the premises. While it is the tenant who has breached the lease, the landlord must try to get a new tenant. The landlord must try to reduce his/her damages by getting someone else to rent the place and pay at least part of the now–absent rent.
In Florida, though, the duty of mitigation may not be imposed, depending in what a landlord does. Fla. Stat. 83.595 (choice of landlord remedies upon breach by tenant).

3. An employer wrongfully fires an employee, in breach of the employment contract. The employee nonetheless has a duty to try to get a new job (i.e., some replacement income) and thus mitigate his/her damages in terms of lost compensation.

D. Breach of Contract and International Law: The Nachfrist Notice

Some CISG provisions should please American contractors. For example, one CISG provision (Article 49(1)) makes available the German Nachfrist notice. A Nachfrist notice occurs when the non-breaching party notifies the breaching party that it has been given an additional specific period of time to comply with their contract.

The CISG permits the Nachfrist notice to assist non–breaching parties, both buyers and sellers, when their contractor appears to be committing a minor breach. Both in American law (except in instances where the UCC "perfect tender rule" is literally applied) and the Civil Law, a minor breach does not permit the innocent party to avoid the contract and be relieved from further performance. Instead, the injured party may only sue for damages. Only material breach, or under Civil Law a "fundamental breach," permits avoidance or establishes the right to cancel the contract.

For more about the Nachfrist Notice, **see pgs. 160-161; Emerson BL.** A Nachfrist Notice example is at **pg. 161; Emerson BL.**

E. What if There Is a Breach, But the Other Party Was Not Really Injured?

Can you sue? Yes.
Will you win? Maybe.
Is it worth it? Almost certainly No!

Ordinarily, then it is not worth suing. Nominal (in name only) damages usually are just a pyrrhic victory. There even is the Equitable concept of *de minimis non curat lex* (trivial, minimal) – the law does not "care about" (cure) little things.

F. What About Externalities?

The common law of contracts typically does not contemplate how a breach may lead to third party harms or public harms. The individualism of the common law may countenance breaches that are "okay for the parties, but not so good for others," while the Civil Law would likely view such contract breaches with more skepticism.

Economists frequently talk about positive and negative "externalities." A negative externality occurs when the private costs of engaging in behavior are less than the true costs to society. For example, the private cost to Blast Furnace Factory Company (BFFC) due to its polluting is less than the true cost: the external world (outside the factory) is paying part of the price by bearing the cost of pollution – stinging eyes, respiratory illnesses, deteriorating car finishes, crumbling bricks, dead plants, sooty house exteriors, etc. If BFFC must install gas scrubbers or electrostatic precipitators, or use other devices to reduce the pollution, then its production costs will rise and these costs may then be passed along to the consumer; the consumer, in turn, will purchase less of the product or have less money to buy some other product, and the standard of living thus decreases. Of course, this standard of living is measured from the standpoint of humans in economic – *materialistic* - terms. The "standard of living" for trees, wildlife, nature lovers, businesses associated with nature tours, and others may increase greatly when pollution is reduced.

G. Liquidated Damages

"Liquidated" means a readily obtainable, definite, certain amount. A liquidated damages clause serves as a kind of notice to each side about the risks of breach. Liquidated damages: (a) are specified in the contract itself; and (b) are a substitute for compensatory damages – one does NOT get both; and (c) to be enforceable, must, when the contract was made, be a good faith, reasonable estimate – not a penalty. To be safe, parties should not term any such provision a "penalty" or a "punishment," although comparable contractual stipulations in other countries may have a punitive–sounding name yet be upheld as serving the same breach–deterring and time–efficient functions (no need for lengthy damages inquiries and calculations) as American liquidated damages.[124]

A liquidated damages clause should be "preceded by a statement that the parties understand and agree that profits in certain amounts are expected and are dependent on timely completion of

---

[124] E.g., in Brazil these contract terms are called cláusula penal (penal clauses), but function essentially the same as American liquidated damage clauses.

performance."[125] Such a clause makes it difficult to challenge the liquidated damages provision, or for a court to not award the amount specified, as long as the amount was not, as stated above, a penalty.

> Penalty Example
> A lease states that there is a $200 per day damages clause for late payment of rent. That is not reasonable: (A clause of $5 a day may well be lawful: Is it a reasonable estimate of the increased costs incurred due to the tardiness of rent payments?). In 1999, Cox Communications – having been pursued in a class action on behalf of its customers in Gainesville, Ocala, and Pensacola – agreed to stop charging a minimal late charge of five dollars for any payment received even just a day late. Cox agreed to reduce the initial late charge to two dollars and also to expand the billing period (so that customers have more time to pay a bill before it is late). If the case had proceeded to trial, the high fee for late payments, with no connection to the overall size of a bill or to the actual costs of servicing late accounts, almost certainly would have been ruled an unlawful penalty because it far exceeded the contemplated or actual damages arising from the tardiness.[126]

Liquidated damages in contracts can exclude or limit consequential damages, e.g., lost profits, lost wages, medical bills, and other indirect costs. Many states have established statutory liquidated damages ceilings for certain types of contracts. For example, Wisconsin places a 5% (of purchase price) ceiling on liquidated damages for a buyer's breach of an automobile purchase contract. In 1997, there were two state–court judgments totaling $11.6 million against cable companies for charging excessive late fees on monthly cable–TV bills; the fees were unreasonably disproportionate to any losses actually incurred, and were thus an unlawful penalty.

VI. EQUITABLE REMEDIES (see pg. 172; Emerson BL)

A. An Introduction to Equity

Common law is heavily procedural, with restricted remedies – e.g., money (a damages award). So Equity was created. Equity was a separate body of law and a separate set of courts; technically, in an equity case you were going to the King directly for relief. But the King was a busy guy, so a chancellor in equity (a type of judge, appointed by the King) heard the case.

American law has adopted other nations' concepts, especially from England, which in turn took ideas from medieval France. And certainly other nations have adopted American terms for their laws. So a key question in a shrinking world is how to translate equity and other Anglo-American concepts into a global business and legal environment.

Juries are available at common law, but not in equity - those cases decided by a *chancellor* sitting without a jury. And, as canon law (church law) merged into equity (before equity and common law courts were combined), that means that those matters historically covered by canon law (e.g., divorce) remain free of juries. (The canon law of the Catholic Church, the oldest legal system in Western Europe after the fall of Rome (476 A.D.), nurtured respect for law, including concepts of humanity and of inviolable and inalienable rights, long before the rise of Europe's nation-states toward the end of the Middle Ages.) Church law (canon law) included family law (divorces and annulments), real property, personal property, trusts, wills, guardianships. So, depending on how a case is framed, these matters may be viewed as

---

[125] Robert W. Emerson, *Business Law*. NY: Barron's Educational Series (6th ed., 2015), at 170.
[126] Cox also agreed to give coupons for free movies and/or monetary reimbursement to its customers. The $175,000 legal fee that Cox would pay the class' two lawyers was challenged in court.

equitable in nature and thus with no jury available. Certainly, one could have a jury for a separate lawsuit between spouses concerning a breach of contract, or abuse - but not the divorce itself.

Equity remedies are distinct from common law remedies. Because an equity claimant seeks a type of equity as "high-grade," "high octane" relief, the claimant must himself be high-grade, that is, acting fairly.

Some equitable maxims are:
- "Come into court with `clean hands'"
- "Whoever seeks equity must do equity (behave fairly)"
- "Do not sleep on your rights" (delay that results in prejudicial changes defeats equity - leaves the delaying party without an equitable remedy)
- "Equity suffers no wrong without a remedy"
- "Equity considers substance, not form"
- "Equality is equity"
- "Equity regards as done that which should be done"

Equity remedies are generally anything other than money:

In the 20th Century, Equity and Common Law claims have combined: They are now heard and decided by the same court, but (1) the remedies still are distinct and (2) a jury still is only for common law claims, **not equity issues** (no jury in equity cases).

B. The Remedies

In essence, equitable remedies are any correction of, or at least treatment of, a contract breach other than the award of monetary damages.

When are these equitable remedies to be awarded? Courts prefer to just award money, so equitable remedies are available only if:
1. no remedy at law (money) is adequate, determinable & available;
2. the aggrieved party's behavior was fair/equitable (no bad faith, fraud, laches)[127]; and
3. the court will not have to supervise the remedy too much.

Types of Equitable Remedies

The various forms of equitable remedies may be remembered as "Triple R–rated, for high IQs (mnemonic device – RRRIQS) – Rescission, Restitution, Reformation, Injunction, Quasi–contract, Specific Performance

1. Rescission

Rescission is a cancellation of the contract, with *restitution* usually also awarded (i.e., a return of the consideration).

2. Reformation

Reformation is a relatively unusual remedy. The Court corrects a contract to meet the parties' intent (only if the courts have very strong beliefs regarding what the parties truly intended). So a reformation is meant to state the parties' actual agreement.

Reformation usually involves restructuring of the contract's technical terminology/phrasing to make it reflect what the parties really meant. Normally, if there is a mistake, there is no reformation:

---

[127] As discussed earlier in the text concerning the topic of Consideration, it is in equity, rather than ordinary common law cases, that courts often look at the adequacy of consideration.

Courts throw out a contract when the mistake is mutual or the courts enforce the contract as it was objectively reached if the mistake is unilateral.

When reformation is impractical or the law of mistake otherwise prevents the "rewriting" of a contract, the judge may order a rescission."[128]

a. Comparative law

Germany, unlike the United States, permits courts to revise (reform) a contract based upon impossibility of performance of the existing contract.

b. Reasons for Opposing Reformation

Four arguments against letting courts redraft contract terms because of unforeseen events are:

(i) that violates the principle of respect for private autonomy; it subjects parties to contractual terms to which they did not consent;

(ii) if strict contract enforcement using the parties' own contractual language, or rescission and restitution, or a finding of impossibility and voiding of the contract, do not suit the parties, they can redraft the contract themselves; this preferred solution allows the parties to use individual information usually unavailable to courts, and thus the agreement is more tailored to the parties' particular needs; this solution also saves administration costs;

(iii) judicial willingness to redraft may introduce uncertainties into the private negotiations of the parties, and thus actually makes it harder for the parties to settle their differences and redraft the contract or otherwise bring their relationship to an amicable close;

(iv) a proclivity for judicial redrafting will muddle the law and thus reduce its predictability (that poses problems both generally for all of contract law and, again, for the parties themselves in their attempts to reach a settlement).

3. Injunction

Injunction is a court order to stop doing something (the restrained person is "enjoined"). A typical example is that of a lawful non–compete covenant: if it is violated, courts can issue an injunction to stop such competition. So, if a party, Paulo, violates an injunction, now he is not just breaching a contract, but also a court's order. The court then could hold Paulo to be in contempt of court, and could send Paulo to jail (presumably something far more serious than just holding a party liable for breach of contract).[129]

To help bolster the claim that an injunction is necessary (that a damages award would be insufficient), some written agreements anticipate a possible breach and state that the parties recognize that, in the event of a breach, "damages will not suffice, and thus an injunction is the appropriate remedy."

4. Quasi–Contract

Examples:

(1) Previous story about Bill Bob mowing the wrong lawn, and you are watching without intervening;

(2) A nurse treats a comatose person. This assumes the nurse has made no mistake by treating the comatose person (presumably there is nothing on that person's forehead, or elsewhere(!), stating, "Absolutely don't treat me!")

Quasi-contract involves *quantum meruit* (Latin for "as much as you earned"). It constitutes, in effect, a contract-like remedy for a noncontractual wrong, such as unjust enrichment. It is an equitable

---

[128] Robert W. Emerson, *Business Law*. NY: Barron's Educational Series (6th ed., 2015), at 173.
[129] Moreover, sending someone to jail for contempt of court is not something issued in lieu of a civil judgment; the civil case could still lead to a finding that there was a breach of contract, with a judicial order requiring the payment of a damages award as well as or in addition to an injunction or other equity remedies.

remedy for something that is a real wrong, although not a "real" contract (just an implied-in-law contract). The concept is discussed earlier in this Article of the text and also at **pg. 95; Emerson BL**.

5. Specific Performance (see pgs. 171-172; Emerson BL)

Land is special. A 5th Amendment clause, permitting eminent domain,[130] concerns a highly controversial power of the national, state, or local government: "nor shall private property be taken for public use, without just compensation."

An example of the controversy is *Kelo v. City of New London,* 545 U.S. 469 (2005), described at pg. 35; Emerson BL. While eminent domain generally has been limited to government projects (e.g., roads or public buildings) or slum clearance, New London's plans were for the 90-acre neighborhood of small homes include a waterfront hotel and conference center, office space for high technology research and development, retail space, and 80 new homes. This private development was held to be a public use.

Another example is *Hawaii Housing Authority v. Midkiff*, 467 U.S. 229 (1984). There, a Hawaii statue gave lessees of single-family homes the right to invoke the government's power of eminent domain to purchase the property they leased, even if the landowner objected. The state then condemned the property, paid Fair Market Value, and then resold the land to the lessee. (The idea was land redistribution – to many small, new landowners.) The Supreme Court held: It is the purpose of the taking, not the use of property, that is important. The legislature just needs some "reasonable foundation" for its use of eminent domain.

> YOUTUBE – Lake Tahoe 1stScene 4mins49secs , Lake Tahoe 2ndScene 2mins45secs, Lake Tahoe 3rdFinalScene 1min14secs (three different scenes (three videos) – at robertwemersonufl (a field trip to Lake Tahoe, about another Supreme Court case - *Sierra Preservation Council, Inc. v. Tahoe Regional Planning Agency*, 535 U.S. 302 (2002).
>
> The defendant was the Tahoe Regional Planning Agency ("the TRPA"), established under an interstate compact between California and Nevada, which share the coastline of Lake Tahoe and its famously deep-blue, crystalline water. The plaintiffs in the Tahoe case originally were about 700 people who had bought undeveloped residential lots, some 400 altogether, in the expectation of building houses on the shore of scenic Lake Tahoe. [These 700 in 1984, when the lawsuit commenced, were down to 449 by 2002 – fifty-five had died, and the rest had simply withdrawn over the years.]
>
> The plaintiffs sought millions of dollars in compensation for two TRPA regulations that had blocked virtually all land development on those 400 residential lots for 32 months from August 24, 1981 to April 25, 1984. The TRPA used the development moratorium to study the impact of development and then to create a long-term land-use plan for combating lake water degradation traced to run-off from developed areas above the shore. The plaintiffs argued that a restriction that even temporarily deprives property owners of all "economically viable" use of their land is a taking for which the Constitution requires compensation.
>
> Writing for the court, Justice John Paul Stevens said, "A rule that required compensation for every delay in the use of property would render routine government processes prohibitively expensive or encourage hasty decision-making. [Such hasty actions could foster] inefficient and ill-conceived growth. . . . Such an important change in the law should be the product of legislative rule making rather than adjudication." The majority thus rejected an expansive ruling of one of Justice Antonin Scalia's most important opinions, the *Lucas v. South Carolina Coastal Council* holding. In Lucas, the Court first held that a land-use regulation which, while leaving property in the owner's hands, permanently deprived it of all economic use was a "categorical taking" requiring compensation; therefore, Lucas breached what had been a doctrinal wall between a physical taking (with government actually taking possession of private property), for which compensation has always been required, and a "regulatory taking" (e.g., zoning), in

---

[130] Under the 5th Amendment, private property may only be taken for a public use, and the owner must receive just compensation. (Fair Market Value is required, the courts have held.)

> which the government restricts the owner's use of the property. The Tahoe holding was that no categorical taking had occurred. It also restated the key difference between a governmental body actually taking property for a public purpose and simply regulating property in a way that limits its use. When the government acquires property, Justice Stevens wrote, the Constitution "in plain language requires the payment of compensation. [But] the Constitution contains no comparable reference to regulations that prohibit a property owner from making certain uses of her private property."
>
> The Supreme Court reaffirmed a doctrine, disputed by property rights advocates, known as "the parcel as a whole" rule. Under this rule, when a regulation affects only part of a piece of land, typically a wetlands or wildlife habitat, the analysis of that regulation still must take into account the impact on the property as a whole, not just on the regulated portion. Without the protection of the "parcel as a whole" rule, much environmental land use regulation would be considered a taking and would be prohibitively expensive.
>
> Before Lucas, regulatory takings were subject to a case-by-case balancing test that weighed the government's interests against the owner's legitimate expectations. Because Lucas involved a regulatory taking - an environmental ban on coastal development - Lucas raised the prospect that even temporary restrictions might be subject to the "categorical taking" rule. But Tahoe indicates that the distinction between physical and regulatory takings remains vital. The majority opinion relegated Lucas to "the extraordinary case in which a regulation permanently deprives property of all value," a rule with no application to a temporary even if prolonged moratorium. As Justice Stevens explained the reason for treating the two categories of takings differently: "Land-use regulations are ubiquitous and most of them impact property values in some tangential way - often in completely unanticipated ways. Treating them all as per se takings would transform government regulation into a luxury few governments could afford. By contrast, physical appropriations are relatively rare, easily identified, and usually represent a greater affront to individual property rights."

So, having discussed constitutional principles and land, let us return to Equity to consider how land has always been special – one of the very few areas deserving of *specific performance*.

Specific performance orders (the opposite of injunctions) are available for certain types of contracts (when money will not do) – due to uniqueness. Under law, all real estate, for example, is unique.

The court issues a writ of mandamus – an order that a party must perform the contract

Specific performance orders are available for certain types of contracts (when money will not do), due to the contract subject's uniqueness (e.g., real estate).

What about services? If the contracted–for services have not yet been performed, courts are extremely reluctant to order performance; instead, they just order a damages award. If services have been performed and produced a tangible result, courts may order delivery of that result (the already finished product).

CISG Article 28 states: "If, in accordance with the provisions of this Convention [the CISG], one party is entitled to require performance of any obligation by the other party, a court is not bound to enter a judgment for specific performance unless the court would do so under its own law in respect of similar contracts of sale not governed by this convention." So an American court need not order specific performance no matter how clear the CISG breach is.

Comparative law

Under the French Civil Code and Code of Commerce (with rules followed in many nations), specific performance is a far less likely remedy than in the United States. Under the CISG, specific performance is left up to the rules of the court hearing/deciding the case.

E. EMPLOYMENT DISCRIMINATION LAW

Studies by the Society for Human Resources Management have found that more than half of employers say their companies have been sued over employment-related issues.

TOPICAL LECTURE: Employment at Will
Introduction to Topical Lecture:
In employment law, competing philosophies include the right to market freedom such as making contracts and the need for level playing fields, such as through protection of inalienable rights, even in the economic sphere. The employer's right to terminate an employee without cause may be restricted due to an express contract provision or an implied contract, such as a covenant of good faith and fair dealing. The firing may violate whistleblower statutes. More broadly, if the termination is against public policy it can constitute an abusive (wrongful) discharge.

I. COMPETING THEMES AND COMPETING PHILOSOPHIES

A. Themes: Market Freedom vs. Level Playing Field

Employment issues involve general, competing themes: freedom to contract, to let parties resolve matters on their own, versus having the government intervene to rectify perceived marketplace problems and difficulties of business and society (e.g., discrimination).
  1. Freedom of contract (opportunity - "Maybe I am a wage slave now, but some day I may be a wage master") - so, I have the freedom to enter into whatever deal that I want to reach).
  2. Imbalance of power between employer and employee (we should look beyond "opportunity" to who holds power and to actual results); sometimes a contract simply is not in the best interest of the weaker party and, in more extreme cases, society needs to protect the weaker party, even if that means overturning what he/she agreed to.

B. Philosophies: Inalienable Rights vs. Rights of Contract

Not as a matter of just law, but also as a matter of ethics, a business decision maker may worry about bad publicity and may have concerns about retaining his/her workforce's loyalty and morale. So, employers may need to treat their employees better. Also, social policy, as expressed in the law, clearly establishes that some classifications are viewed more strictly than others – for example, categorization by race, religion, or sex are viewed with great suspicion, more so than some other classifications, such as by levels of education.
On the other hand, freedom of contract – the freedom to choose – argues against "outside interference," such as from the government.
Often, an empirical question is simply: Has there been, or is there likely to be, an abuse of power?

> Sign on an employer's door: "The beatings will continue until morale improves."

A general conflict is between those arguing the utility of market forces and those espousing the need for governmental intervention. There are competing notions of workers (a) as part of the economy, as agents of an enterprise, or (b) as individuals, endowed with fundamental rights. Again, the conflict is between freedom of contract versus the need to protect individuals (even from themselves) - e.g., working for too little pay, unsafe conditions, no pension, etc.

> A key issue sometimes is a very basic one: Was the plaintiff an employee? For example, in *Ernst & Young L.L.P. v. Simpson*, 100 F.3d 436 (6th Circuit Court of Appeals, 1996), cert. denied., 520 U.S. 1248 (1997), the federal appeals court in Cincinnati upheld a jury verdict of more than $4 Million for an Ernst & Young accounting firm partner (age 52) who claimed he was fired in violation of the Age Discrimination in Employment Act. The circuit court (and also some state courts) held that the partner was an employee, thus protected under anti-discrimination laws.[131]

II. THE EMPLOYMENT AT-WILL DOCTRINE

Employment at will is far more likely to be present in the United States than in most European countries. With employment at will, there is no set term. The employee can be fired or quit whenever; it is still a common form of employment (still lawful). Generally, there is no remedy if one is fired or laid off, whether for a good reason or for no reason at all.

There are still no restrictions on the at-will employee's freedom to quit. But in the United States there are two recent exceptions to the employer's freedom to fire the employee: implied contract and abusive discharge.

A. Implied Contractual Restraints

The personnel manual (or a pamphlet, sometimes even an employment application) becomes a kind of contract between the employer and the employee. The lawyers' approach (restrictive or non-existent manuals; promise nothing to protect employer's rights) versus the managerial approach ("Be Nice," "We're all part of a Corporate Family"). The latter approach is meant to give the employees rights and to instill in them trust in and loyalty to the employer; that will, it is hoped, establish good working conditions, improved employee morale, and higher productivity. The January 1998 Harvard Business Review described a study of 800 Sears stores that found if employee attitudes on ten essential counts improve by just 5%, then customer satisfaction jumps 1.3% and in turn drives a 0.5% rise in revenue.

B. Abusive Discharge (also sometimes called "Wrongful Discharge")

The "Nurses Go Camping" example - *Wagenseller v. Scottsdale Memorial. Hospital,* 710 P.2d 1025 (Ariz. 1985). After a camping weekend of work bonding, nurse Wagenseller returned to the hospital. And she felt a chill in the air (not on her backside, but back at work). The hospital ultimately terminated nurse Wagenseller. The case involved indecent exposure, a firing, and public policy.

- **It is no wrongful discharge/firing to fire "at will" employees for good or even no reason: the only thing that is abusive discharge is a firing that conflict with public policy (Not just a personal conflict or a layoff, but a public wrong).**

---

[131] If the partner were viewed as simply an "owner," not an employee, he would be considered exempt from the protections of most anti-discrimination laws, discussed shortly hereafter in this text. (For much on discrimination claims in a non-employment context, franchising, see Robert W. Emerson, *Franchise Termination: Legal Rights and Practical Effects When Franchisees Claim the Franchisor Discriminates,* 35 AM. BUS. L.J. 559-645 (1998), available at http://ssrn.com/author=86449; Robert W. Emerson, *Discriminating Between Members of the Same Network: American Statutes and Cases,* INT'L DISTRIB. (2011) (European-based journal); Robert W. Emerson, *Franchise Discrimination and Goodwill: An American and Comparative Law Perspective*, in COMMERCIAL DISTRIBUTION (Groupe Larcier, 2016).

The tort of abusive discharge involves a termination against public policy. For example, an employer may not be permitted to fire the employee for reporting, or refusing to engage in, inappropriate behavior (e.g., an accountant refusing to violate tax laws; a comptroller refusing to break bankruptcy or securities laws; a corporate employee failing to make corporate-ordered, but unlawful political contributions; a truck driver refraining from illegally dumping toxic wastes). But the employer's wrongful firing of the employee must be tied to a public policy, which the firing flouts.

So abusive discharge is generally connected to the refusal to break a law (and that law represents an important public policy). For instance, Plaintiff alleges: "It's not just my rights that are involved. I was trying to comply with tax/environmental/etc. laws and that is why I was fired. The Court should protect me in order to support those laws I was trying to uphold."

Even if not in an area typically associated with significant commercial activity, the employment impact must be upon something of substantial public importance. A stupid firing (e.g., the employer's decision is counterproductive to the company's bottom line, the supervisor fired a worker whose present skills, potential for improvement, and actual output far exceeded many other workers that were retained) is, without anything more, NOT an abusive firing (a wrongful discharge); there must be a public policy concern. Any number of employer actions could lead to public policy concerns that constitute a possible wrongful discharge. Consider something as ubiquitous yet seemingly personal as the naming of a newborn child. In France, parents traditionally were required to give their child a name from the official list. A child without a name from the list did not officially exist. In Spain, one must spell names correctly.[132])

What if an employer in the United States said that henceforth he would fire any worker who gave a child a name not on his "official" list? His list contains hundreds, perhaps thousands, of acceptable names, but it invariably omits some possible names. Would such a "company rule" violate a statute? Probably not (unless the list adversely impacts people from a race, a religion, an ethnic group, or one sex; then it may well violate Title VII). Would the mandated list contravene public policy? Probably so, as most courts would likely find that a family's right to decide names is something personal, fundamental, and not typically something about which employers need to be concerned and possibly interfere.

---

1. Statistics indicate that former executives are more likely to win wrongful termination lawsuits than other classes of workers. They also win larger awards. These people made more money in their jobs (and thus lost more), but there are other reasons for these trends. Ex-executives make better spoken and perhaps more credible witnesses. They are familiar with the inner-workings and policies of the company. And, last but not least, they have the means to hire better lawyers to fight for them. A study conducted by Jury Verdict Research showed that "executive managers" [and "paraprofessionals"] won 64% of the time, with victory occurring 42% of the time for "general laborers," 48% for "professionals" and 58% for "middle managers and salespeople." These type of cases won the following median awards for wrongful termination: (1) age discrimination – $219,000, (2) race-discrimination - $147,799-$106,728, (3) disability-discrimination - $100,345, (4) pregnancy-discrimination - $87,500, and (5) sexual-harassment - $38,500.
2. Men won twice as often as women. Altogether, workers won more times than they lost.

---

[132] The author's brother and sister-in-law had an extremely difficult time trying to get a birth certificate for their newborn daughter, who had just been born in Madrid. This difficulty arose because the parents wanted to spell the girl's name, Susanna, with two "n"s, a nontraditional spelling for the Spanish (who evidently believe that name should always be spelled with just one "n" – "Susana"). Were it not for the fact that the parents and their baby were all Americans, residing in Spain only because the father was then a diplomat in Spain, who knows if they could have gotten the authorities to relent on their unorthodox spelling of the tot's *nombre*!

III. WHISTLEBLOWING OR RETALIATION CLAIMS

A. Whistleblowing

The whistleblower laws protect a whole range of things that are not just retaliation for exercising rights. They can also protect an employee who assists others in exercising their rights; and they can protect an employee who opposes violations not just of one's own rights, but also the rights of other people. The protected conduct can be disclosing employer misconduct, such as the classic whistleblower situation, where an employee discloses misconduct by the employer to someone within or outside the company, such as law enforcement authorities.[133] Or the preceding behavior can be simply exercising legal rights (e.g., voting in a political or union election) or undertaking legal obligations (e.g., jury service or military duties).

B. Retaliation

> Remember: when you post your resume online (as about 6 million people do every month), your employer can access it and take measures based on this indication that you are looking to go elsewhere. In most cases, such retaliation would be lawful.

1. Retaliation Cases: the Path of Least Resistance for Plaintiffs

Many lawyers who defend employers accused of discrimination (e.g., under Title VII, the ADA, the ADEA) say that they would rather defend almost any other case than a retaliation case. Judges or juries hearing the case may tend to simply assume that the employer is going to want to get even. Easily, an employer may get caught in the heat of the moment. After learning about a discrimination charge, a supervisor may barge into the office of the complaining employee and say, "How dare you make that complaint! I'll get you!" or "I'll teach you!" That itself may be enough to get the plaintiff summary judgment.

2. Statutes, the EEOC, and Federal Appeals Courts

Retaliation claims are relatively "easy" because many federal statutes, such as Title VII of the Civil Rights Act of 1964, the Age Discrimination in Employment Act, and the American with Disabilities Act ("the ADA"), explicitly provide for lawsuit claims if there is retaliation for someone's exercising rights or pursuing remedies under that statute.[134] This has been expansively interpreted. For example, in *Gomez v. Potter* (2008), the Supreme Court held, 6-3 (Roberts, Scalia, and Thomas dissenting), that not just private workers, but even federal government workers, may sue for the reprisals they allegedly faced after filing an ADA discrimination claim.

Even a federal act that says nothing about retaliation – the Civil Rights Act of 1866[135] – has been interpreted as granting persons who file a race discrimination claim, and then face retaliation, a right to sue to remedy such retaliation.[136] Also, many state and local laws have specific anti-retaliation provisions, and many states have comprehensive whistleblower protection statutes.

> Alleged retaliation accounts for a large and increasing number of complaints. In 2009, unlawful retaliation was a basis for 36.0% of all the discrimination claims brought before the federal Equal Employment Opportunity Commission (EEOC) or a state agency. About 86% of these retaliation claims (31.0% of the

---

[133] In a common law suit still relevant today, the *qui tam* action, if the misconduct is fraud, the employee may be able to sue and receive part of the penalty imposed (the rest going to the government on behalf of whom the plaintiff is suing)!

[134] Retaliation claims also may succeed in workers' compensation and many other administrative hearings. Employers must not fire or otherwise retaliate against employees for filing costly claims for job-related injuries. In September 1997, for example, a Texas jury awarded five Levi Strauss workers $10.6 Million due to such wrongful retaliations.

[135] This Act is described below under the heading, "Discrimination Statutes."

[136] *CBOCS West, Inc. v. Humphries* (2008), a 7-2 decision, with Scalia and Thomas dissenting.

36.0%) – stemmed from Title VII complaints. The percentage that was for retaliation has risen steadily from 15.3% (14.5% for Title VII claims) in 1992 to 20.6% (18.5% for Title VII claims) in 1996, to 27.1% (24.7% for Title VII claims) in 2000 to 28.6% (25.5% for Title VII claims) in 2004 to 36.0% (31.0 for Title VII claims) in 2009 to the above figures (41.1%; 33.6%) for 2013.

So what constitutes the type of retaliation that gives rise to an employer's liability? What exactly is retaliation depends on the statute and the court interpreting it. Most federal appeals courts broadly define the "adverse employment action" required to establish a retaliation claim. And the EEOC's compliance manual prohibits any adverse treatment that is "based on a retaliatory motive and is reasonably likely to deter individuals from engaging in protected activity." Actionable retaliation claims, according to the EEOC, thus may be based on "threats, reprimands, negative evaluations, harassment, job transfers, or other conduct that has a negative effect on an individual's employment." But a federal appeals court, such as the Fifth Circuit (based in New Orleans), generally requires "ultimate employment actions," such as termination, suspension, or demotion.

3. *Burlington Northern*

The Supreme Court helped to clarify the legal meaning of "retaliation" in *Burlington Northern & Santa Fe Railway Co. v. White*, 548 U.S. 53 (2006). There, the court found that illegal retaliation can take place on or off the job and that it applies to situations in which the employer's actions are "harmful to the point that they could well dissuade a reasonable worker from making or supporting a charge of discrimination."

The case involved Sheila White, a forklift operator and the only woman working in the "maintenance of way" department at Burlington Northern & Santa Fe Railway's Tennessee Yard in Memphis. White complained to officials that her immediate supervisor had repeatedly told her that women shouldn't be working in the department and had made insulting and inappropriate remarks to her. While the supervisor was disciplined, White was transferred from forklift duty to the more onerous task of track laborer. In the course of a dispute over her new duties, White was suspended without pay for 37 days for insubordination. The company ultimately overturned the suspension and awarded Ms. White back pay for that period.

Writing for the eight-justice majority (the decision was unanimous, but Justice Samuel A. Alito, Jr. wrote his own concurrence), Justice Stephen G. Breyer emphasized that "petty slights or minor annoyances" would not rise to the level of retaliation, and that the conduct had to be objectively problematic – enough to dissuade a "reasonable" employee. Justice Breyer noted, "Context matters. . . . A change in an employee's work schedule may make little difference to many workers, but may matter enormously to a young mother with school age children."

Thus, while both White's forklift driving and her track-clearing duties fell within the same job description, "Common sense suggests that one good way to discourage an employee such as White from bringing discrimination charges would be to insist that she spend more time performing the more arduous duties and less time performing those that are easier or more agreeable."

Similarly, Ms. White's suspension without pay could have been unlawful retaliation even if she was eventually compensated for the time off. "Many reasonable employees would find a month without a paycheck to be a serious hardship," and take that into account before filing a complaint, Justice Breyer noted.

Frequently, a plaintiff has a better retaliation claim than discrimination claim, and thus, may win a retaliation claim and recover substantial damages for that retaliation, despite the loss of the discrimination case.[137] That is because retaliation cases are generally somewhat easier to prove, for several reasons:
(1) the elements of proof are simpler (one just needs to show that the plaintiff engaged in some protected activity; that an adverse employment action occurred; and that there's a causal link

---

[137] The EEOC's statistics show that nearly two-thirds of all claims case found to have no reasonable cause.

between those two events) – this is simpler than proving discriminatory intent, the basic standard under Title VII.
(2) Juries and judges are more receptive to retaliation claims. It is much easier for jurors to understand the basic motive of people who retaliate against somebody who has made a complaint, whether about discrimination or something else. People can more easily accept the notion that the defendant's witnesses engaged in retaliatory conduct than to conclude that these same persons engaged in discriminatory conduct (with a motive to discriminate based on, for example, race, religion, or sex).

> Here is an example of a losing case for the plaintiff where the defendant employer's own response turned the plaintiff into a "winner!" On March 30, 2004, in *Romero v. Allstate Ins. Co.*, 2004 WL 692231 (E.D. Pa. 2004), a federal trial court in Philadelphia ruled that Allstate Insurance Company unlawfully retaliated against about 6,200 of its employees by requiring them to give up their workplace discrimination claims in order to continue to work as agents with the Northbrook, Ill.-based insurance giant. EEOC's suit alleged that Allstate implemented a mandatory policy at all of its U.S. facilities requiring employees to sign a release waiving all workplace discrimination charges against the company in order to be retained as independent-contractor agents. The effect of the policy, the EEOC said, was to deprive Allstate employees of equal employment opportunities by attempting to prevent their participation in activity protected under federal anti-discrimination laws. The court found no basis for underlying age-discrimination claims; it was the retaliation (threats of retaliation) which undermined Allstate's defense.

Of course, employers can be tricky! A way for employers to avoid retaliation claims in discrimination cases (which more than tripled in number from 1992 to 2007 – to 26,663) is for the employer to just bide its time. For example, in the U.S. Court of Appeals for the Eight Circuit, in St. Louis, the judges tend to assume that any adverse employment action taken more than six months after a discrimination claim is not causally connected to the complaint. It is still possible to prove retaliation, but more evidence is required.

End of Topical Lecture on Employment at Will

IV. DISCRIMINATION STATUTES AND REGULATIONS

> EMPLOYMENT DISCRIMINATION LAW: YOUTUBE video (1:32) (the author in a Monet shirt)
> There has been a tremendous revolution in employment law, particularly in the field of discrimination or alleged discrimination. That is the reason for the shirt I am wearing; just as Monet helped to orchestrate a revolution in art in the late 19th century, so we had a revolution in employment law in the 1930s with employee welfare protections, and in the 1960s, in particular, in the area of discrimination law, with the most important law still being Title VII of the 1964 Civil Rights Act. What has emanated from that has been case law in numerous areas, particularly in the areas involving racial discrimination, sexual discrimination, and religious discrimination, and other statutes which cover other classifications of protected peoples. Discrimination based on age, for instance, is unlawful under the Age Discrimination Employment Act. Discrimination against the disabled is unlawful under the Americans with Disabilities Act. We have numerous other laws, but they have all tended to model themselves, and courts have tended to interpret them, based on Title VII.

These laws – found at federal, state, and local levels - are extremely important for all aspects of business, not just employment.[138] More specifically, one of the great trends of the late 20th Century and early 21st Century American and other legal systems is the growth of employment law protections related to certain employee characteristics that are immutable or highly personal and that raise important public policy concerns (e.g., race, nationality, sex, religion, age, physical or mental disability). <u>More so than abusive discharge claims, lawsuits under the various discrimination statutes have been, and remain, the main method for employees seeking vindication of their rights.</u>

Comparing Discrimination Law with Abusive Discharge Claims

As discussed previously, abusive discharge claims, although typically rooted in a private dispute (between a private employer and its former employee), must involve matters that courts recognize as fraught with public policy – a judicial task not necessarily as clear-cut as when discrimination is alleged and judges or regulators turn to what are usually very broadly worded statutes, often incredibly comprehensive interpretative regulations, and a panoply of case holdings. This is the first factor no doubt inhibiting the use of abusive discharge claims when a discrimination claim could be asserted: the complex, often unpredictable adjudicative task in which common law courts deciding an abusive discharge claim must find the facts and delineate the law insofar as they are linked to public policy. (To put it simply, the law on discrimination may be more discernible.)

The second major reason for the comparatively limited number of abusive discharge cases is that there must be *an actual termination*, which, in turn, must stem from the employer's decision in violation of the aforesaid public policy. This obviously means that the only plaintiff with standing to sue for abusive discharge is a fired employee, not an unsuccessful job applicant, or a current employee, or any former employee whose claim is about how he/she was treated on the job, not the circumstances of his/her termination.

As an example, note how hard it might be for the following recruited "employee" in Hell.

- Beware of the Difference between Recruitment and the Actual Working Environment

While walking down the street, Eleanor, a highly successful executive, was hit by a bus and died. Her soul arrived in heaven, where she was met at the Pearly Gates by St. Peter himself.

- Welcome to Heaven, said St. Peter. "Before you get settled in though, it seems we have a problem. You see, strangely enough, we've never once had an executive make it this far and we're not really sure what to do with you"

- "No problem, just let me in" said Eleanor.

- "Well, I'd like to, but I have higher orders. What we're going to do is let you have a day in Hell and a day in Heaven and then you can choose whichever one you want to spend an eternity in."

- "Actually, I think I've made up my mind… I prefer to stay in Heaven", said Eleanor.

- "Sorry we have rules…"

- And with that St. Peter put the executive in an elevator and it went down to Hell. The doors opened and Eleanor found herself stepping out onto the putting green of a beautiful golf course. In the distance was a country club and standing in front of her were all her friends – fellow executives that she had worked with and they were all dressed in evening gowns cheering for her.

- They ran up and kissed Eleanor on both cheeks and they talked about old times. They played an excellent round of gold and at night went to the country club where Eleanor enjoyed an excellent steak and lobster dinner. She met the Devil, who was actually a really nice guy, and Eleanor had a great time telling jokes and dancing. She lost track of time, and soon Eleanor had to leave.

---

[138] These laws tend to be, at their core, statutory – e.g., legislation by Congress – but then they are further developed by judicial interpretation (court decisions) and by regulatory (e.g., Equal Employment Opportunity Commission) rulings and guidelines.

> - Everybody shook Eleanor's hand and waved goodbye as she got on the elevator. The elevator went up and opened again at the Pearly Gates, with St. Peter waiting for her. "Now it's time to spend a day in heaven," he said.
> - So Eleanor spent the next 24 hours lounging around clouds, playing the harp and singing. She had a good time and before she knew it her 24 hours were up and St. Peter came and got her.
> - "So, you've spent a day in hell and you've spent a day in heaven. Now you must choose your eternity," he said.
> - Eleanor paused for a second and then replied, "Well, I never thought I'd say this, I mean, Heaven has been really great and all, but I think I had a better time in Hell."
> - So St. Peter escorted Eleanor to the elevator, and again she went down to Hell. When the elevator doors opened she found herself standing in a desolate wasteland covered in garbage and filth.
> - Eleanor saw her friends were dressed in rags and were picking up the garbage and putting it in sacks. The Devil came up to her and put his arm around her. "I don't understand," stammered Eleanor, "yesterday I was here, and there was a golf course and country club and we ate lobster and danced and had a great time. Now this is a wasteland of garbage, and all my friends look miserable."
> - The Devil looked at her and smiled, "Yesterday we were recruiting you; today you're staff."
>
> ---
>
> Certainly, Eleanor has no claim for abusive discharge – she was not fired. Was she defrauded? Was there a breach of contract?[139] Unless Eleanor is in a class of discriminated against persons (e.g., recruited women become "staff" while hired men, simply because they are men, are given better positions), she will have little chance of winning a statutory claim (under Title VII, discussed below).

In the United States, the most important national law on employment discrimination, Title VII of the 1964 Civil Rights Act (amended many times since), provides protections from employment discrimination in all areas of employment (hiring, termination, compensation, promotion, demotion, and everything else related to the job). It applies to these categories (My mnemonic for you – ROPRAHS), with the percentages for each of these claims being out of the total number of claims:

R ace (includes color; this category has the most complaints, **35.3%**)[140]
O rigin[141] (i.e., National Origin; **11.4%**)
P regnancy[142] (**5.8%**)

---

[139] Let's assume she could sue (presumably, there are a lot of lawyers in Hell!). But it would be a difficult case to win.
[140] All of these figures are based upon: Equal Opportunity Commission, Charge Statistics FY 1997 Through FY 2013, http://www.eeoc.gov/eeoc/statistics/enforcement/charges.cfm.
[141] Title VII's prohibition of discrimination based on national origin covers both discrimination based on (1) a person's (or his ancestors') country of origin, or (2) a person's possession of physical, cultural, or linguistic characteristics shared by people of a certain national origin. For example. If Employer Edie discriminates against Worker Joe because the employer thinks Joe looks like, acts like, or sounds like, someone from Mexico, then - regardless of whether Joe's nationality is, in fact, Mexican-American - the employer's conduct may violate Title VII.
[142] Pregnancy Discrimination Charges EEOC & FEPAs Combined: FY 1997 - FY 2011, http://www.eeoc.gov/eeoc/statistics/enforcement/pregnancy.cfm (2011 figures). Discrimination on the basis of pregnancy is a form of Title VII discrimination, per a 1978 amendment (the Pregnancy Discrimination Act) to the civil rights laws. The German system treats mothers as a category distinct from simply male or female and does accord them special attention in the form of leave and subsidies; that approach is distinct from the U.S. law, which simply treats discrimination against pregnant women or those who have given birth as a type of sex discrimination. **So, unlike Germany, no special protection; but treat pregnancy the same as another, similar in impact health condition (although there really is nothing like pregnancy!). E.g., if time off for a hernia, a broken leg, etc, then same for pregnancy.**

R eligion (**4.0%**)
A ge[143] (**22.8%**)
H andicap[144] (Disability – **27.7%**)
S ex (the 2nd most complaints – **29.5%**).[145]

NOTE: the percentages total more than 100% because some claims involve more than one alleged type of discrimination.

V. SPECIAL TOPICS: RELIGION, THE WORLD, AND SEXUAL ORIENTATION

> - Here is an old saying: Regardless of what courts say, there will always be prayer in public schools as long as there are algebra tests.

A. Religious Discrimination

1. Introduction

For Title VII purposes, the term "religion" encompasses almost all beliefs that are sincerely held and that acknowledge a Supreme Being, that include rituals, or that otherwise have a set of ethical values with an effect on the believer's life similar to that produced by "traditional" religions. Title VII bars not just discrimination against a person because of his/her religion, but also because of a person's religious observances or practices (e.g., apparel, Sabbath observances).

Religious discrimination charges, while far fewer than for racial or sex discrimination, have increased greatly in the past 15 years, far faster than other, more typical claims. Alleged examples of religious discrimination leading to lawsuits have included: discussing religious topics at work; organizing Bible study groups with other employees; and employers talking about religion to workers.

2. An Example of Religious Discrimination

A bank teller's employer had a 100% record of having every employee give to the United Way. One of its tellers decided not to contribute. So, to keep the perfect record(!), the bank's president terminated her. The teller claimed that her Christian Fundamentalist beliefs kept her from donating because some of the United Way money, she understood, supported abortion. The bank knew that was why she would not donate. Very soon she was offered reinstatement. What impact should that have had on her claims for compensatory damages and punitive damages? The bank's argument was that, even though the firing was violative of Title VII's prohibition of religious discrimination, the teller had almost no damages. She had been offered reinstatement only one day after being fired; the very evening after her termination

---

[143] Age discrimination is outlawed not under Title VII, but under the Age Discrimination in Employment Act (1967), but many of the rules and principles are the same as for Title VII.

[144] Discrimination on account of disability is prohibited by the Americans with Disabilities Act (1990). As with age discrimination, many of the rules and principles follow the approach taken under Title VII.

[145] Principally a Title VII protection (with nearly 30% of all claims concerning sexual harassment – Equal Employment Opportunity Commission, Sexual Harassment Charges FY 2010 - FY 2013, http://www.eeoc.gov/eeoc/statistics/enforcement/sexual_harassment_new.cfm), the laws against sex discrimination in employment are also found in the Equal Pay Act (1963), a very narrowly drawn and construed law outlawing lower pay for a woman doing exactly the same job as a man. Equal Pay Act claims annually number about 1,000, which is just 1.1% of the total number of federal discrimination claims. Equal Employment Opportunity Commission, Charge Statistics FY 1997 Through FY 2013, http://www.eeoc.gov/eeoc/statistics/enforcement/charges.cfm (for all figures).

made news nationwide, a very embarrassed bank board of directors reprimanded the bank president who had fired the teller and offered the employee her job back, with the president's apology. What kind of damages could she have had when the firing lasted only one day, and that was her day off?

> Title VII is meant for remedies, not punishment.

3. Reasonable Accommodation of an Employee's Religious Beliefs and Practices

To be accommodated, an employee's beliefs must be sincere, within some reasonable standard. The employer must try reasonable accommodations up until it imposes "undue hardship" on an employer's business; then it is unreasonable (and thus an employer need not do that). E.g., the employer should try to arrange work schedules to meet an employee's religious needs, if that is not too great a burden on the employer and other employees.

B. Employment Discrimination: International Comparison

Many countries do not protect minorities or women to nearly the extent that the United States does. For example, many countries have no laws against sexual harassment. Also, in many cultures men (and sometimes women, too) frown upon multinational companies that have hired a woman for a managerial position rather than hired a man. Finally, not only do most cultures not have laws against discrimination based on sexual orientation, but many nations actually have laws and social norms absolutely opposed to the granting of such protections.

C. Discrimination Based on Sexual Orientation

There are no recognized rights under Title VII or other federal statutes that specifically protect homosexuals. Four times since 1994, Congress has rejected a bill to amend Title VII to protect homosexuals. In 1998, though, Pres. Clinton issued an executive order banning sexual orientation discrimination in the federal civilian work force. Pres. Obama has also issued executive orders to protect anyone who works for a company with federal contracts.

Twenty-two states (California, Colorado, Connecticut, Delaware, Hawaii, Illinois, Iowa, Maine, Maryland, Massachusetts, Minnesota, Nevada, New Hampshire, New Jersey, New Mexico, New York, Oregon, Rhode Island, Utah, Vermont, Washington, and Wisconsin), the District of Columbia, and well over 100 municipalities (cities and counties) in the remaining 28 states have laws barring employment discrimination based on sexual orientation. Also, many employers (particularly large employers) have voluntarily adopted policies prohibiting discrimination based on sexual orientation.[146] Furthermore, gays or others may be protected under the Constitution.

Even in states or municipalities without any statutory protections based on sexual orientation, people still can file common law claims. Depending on the facts, an employee mistreated on account of his/her sexual orientation may be able to sue his/her employer or co workers on a number of legal theories that apply to everyone, including gay men and lesbians:

- intentional or negligent infliction of emotional distress
- harassment
- assault
- battery
- invasion of privacy
- defamation
- interference with an employment contract, and
- abusive discharge (wrongful termination)

---

[146] About 90% of Fortune 500 companies prohibit, within their companies, discrimination based on employees' sexual orientation.

Some courts have adopted innovative approaches. In effect, they have found protections for people whose dress or behavior violated "gender norms." Is not an unintended consequence of such holdings, though, protection for men who adopt a feminine persona, but none for guys who are not so "noticeable?"

The vast majority of larger American companies offer their employees' domestic partners the same job benefits (most notably, health insurance) as afforded other employees' spouses. As for the public sector, some states, the District of Columbia, and about 300 municipalities provide domestic partnership benefits to their employees.

VI. TITLE VII PRELIMINARY INFORMATION

A. Title VII'S Comprehensive Coverage

Title VII covers all aspects of employment: hiring, recruiting, and job advertising; firing; layoffs, recalls, demotions, promotions, and transfers; wages, compensation, and fringe benefits; training and apprenticeship programs; disciplinary actions; testing; retirement plans and disability leave; and all other terms, privileges, conditions, and benefits of employment. While employers are liable for Title VII violations, federal courts have held that supervisors are not personally liable for such discrimination if they are simply implementing a company policy.

Varying compensation standards - As stated in the Barron's text (6th ed., 2015) at page 576: "An employer can lawfully apply different compensation standard or terms or condition of employment pursuant to a bona fide *seniority* or *merit system*. However, there must be no intentional discrimination in establishing or continuing that system." However, a key point to add is the following: **An unlawful perpetuation of past discrimination is *not* protected because it is the result of an arrangement with a labor union."** *Id.*

There are far more discrimination suits brought concerning compensation, other employment conditions (e.g., nonpromotion), or termination than about alleged discrimination in hiring. *Failure-to-hire claims often involve nebulous matters such as job criteria, interviews, and "subjective" factors.* It is usually much easier for an existing employee to find evidence of discrimination than for a prospective employee to ferret it out. For example, how would a job-applicant who did not even get an interview suspect that the following was taking place?

Discrimination Based on Job Applicants' Names

Resumes with white-sounding first names elicited 50 percent more responses than ones with black-sounding names, according to a study by professors at the University of Chicago Graduate School of Business and the Massachusetts Institute of Technology. The professors sent about 5,000 resumes in response to want ads in the Boston Globe and Chicago Tribune. They found that the "white" applicants they created received one response – a call, letter or e-mail – for every 10 resumes mailed, while "black" applicants with equal credentials received one response for every 15 resumes sent. The professors analyzed birth certificates in coming up with what names to use. The white names included Neil, Brett, Greg, Emily, Anne and Jill. Some of the black names used were Tamika, Ebony, Aisha, Rasheed, Kareem and Tyrone. Firms that purported to be equal opportunity employers were no more likely to respond to black resumes than other businesses, the study found.[147]

---

[147] Marianne Bertrand & Sendhil Mullainathan, *Are Emily and Greg More Employable than Lakisha and Jamal? A Field Experiment on Labor Market Discrimination*, 94 American Econ. Rev. 991-1013 (2004).

B. Developing The Title VII Case

In *Swierkiewicz v. Sorema N.A.*, 534 U.S. 506 (2002), the US. Supreme Court unanimously held that a plaintiff does not need to present direct evidence of discrimination (in this case, discrimination against national origin) when the lawsuit is filed (e.g., to fight a motion to dismiss). Such direct evidence can be developed later, during the discovery stage of the case. All that federal procedural rules require, in Title VII and most cases generally (discrimination or otherwise), is that the defendant - in reviewing the complaint - receive "fair notice" of the plaintiff's allegations; the rules require only that a complaint must include a "short and plain statement of the claim showing that the pleader is entitled to relief."

C. Employer Actions and Job Applicant Behavior

1. What Should Businesses Do?

First and foremost, employers should be fair. But they should also:
a. Communicate with the Employees.

> "Next to doing the right thing, the most important thing is to let people know you are doing the right thing." John D. Rockefeller, 1839-97 (Industrialist and Philanthropist).

a. Keep Good Records.
(1) Contemporaneous, comprehensive personnel documentation ("you were fired/demoted/not hired because of this well-established set of facts, not due to discrimination.")
(2) Unfortunately, when employers examine flaws in their workplace practices, they open themselves to legal attack. For federal agencies (e.g., the EEOC) to use a company's own audits may cramp the audits' effectiveness.

b. (Perhaps) Buy Insurance. Increasingly, employers can, and do, obtain insurance to cover and defend themselves from discrimination suits.

2. What Should Job Applicants Do?

A job applicant, before being interviewed, should prepare for the questions he/she may be asked. The goal is to show that one is a thinking, caring, interesting person. For example, if asked to describe a strength and a weakness, an applicant probably needs to be able to say something other than, "I have no discernible weakness," or – at the other extreme – blubber out an enormous list of stupid behaviors and habits!

Employment interview experts say that the most important thing to do while interviewed is simply to smile. At this early point in employment matters, psychology likely matters even more than law, with the mistakes by job candidates being in areas outside the legal realm. If a job applicant says some things which make it easy for the interviewing employer to decide against hiring that applicant, the employer's subjective choice tends to be quite difficult to challenge (no really *practical* legal rights).[148] Ordinarily, non-hired applicants need to show discrimination or a violation of public policy, not simply an employer's reluctance to take on what seems to be a risky job candidate.[149]

---

[148] For example, while a job applicant certainly has a right to know about any job benefits, including any severance packages, a lot of questions about severance pay may lead employers to wonder, "why the keen interest? Is this person planning on being here long? Does he expect to be fired?"

Two questions from applicants that no doubt fostered concerns, and perhaps laughs, were: (1) What are the zodiac signs of all board members and their spouses? (2) Will the company move my two-ton rock garden from California to Maryland?

[149] The following is some truly stupid behavior, in actual interviews, reported by personnel officers:
- Challenged the interviewer to arm-wrestle ("sure my resume may be skimpy, but look at these biceps!")

EMPLOYMENT INTERVIEWS AND THE LAW – A VIDEO SKIT AND POST-SKIT DISCUSSION

At http://www.youtube.com/watch?v=dmWn9HKm-D4 -
(employment_interviewsskit9mins32secsandpostskitcommentary10mins0secs.wmv)

Employer Beware: Interviewing Do's and Don'ts - what Employers Legally Can or Cannot Ask their job applicants.

a. Asking for an applicant's full name is fine. But for the interviewer or the application to use the term "Miss" "Mrs." or similar terms may be considered an inquiry about marital status. And that is NOT allowed. Of course, the employer could ask, "Are your spouse or other relatives employed by this employer." Obviously, the answer might reveal an applicant's marital status, but the question is okay in order to comply with a company's policy against nepotism - the hiring of relatives.

b. Asking where an applicant was born is problematic because it may cause distinctions (illegal discrimination) based on the applicant's national origin.

c. It is okay to ask whether an applicant is a U.S. citizen. However, to avoid possible charges of discrimination based on national origin, it would be better to ask this question not during the job interview but after an individual has been hired. The question on citizenship is necessary under immigration laws and for visa and work permit purposes.

d. It is permitted to ask someone how long he/she has lived in a particular state or city.

e. One should not simply ask when the applicant was born (potential problems with age discrimination). But one can ask an applicant if he/she is of the legal age for employment, such as age 18.

f. Asking for the applicant's height or weight (even though visually an employer could form an estimate, anyway) is a problem in that it could evince a pattern of using inappropriate criteria - it could lead to Title VII Adverse Impact Claims or to Americans with Disabilities Act Claims. (Employers should ask no questions to elicit information on disabilities unless a job applicant asks for a reasonable accommodation in the hiring process.) When interviewing a candidate with disabilities, don't ask the person how the disability occurred, even in informal conversation, and don't ask questions you wouldn't ask any other candidate. However, you may ask the candidate questions about the person's qualifications and job experience the same way you would for any applicant.

g. Asking what languages an applicant is fluent in is okay. But do not ask how the applicant learned those foreign languages - Potential discrimination based on national origin.

- Said that if he were hired, he would demonstrate his loyalty by having the corporate logo tattooed on his forearm (how is that for brown-nosing?)
- Interrupted to phone his therapist for advice on answering specific interview questions (when you don't know the answer, you typically cannot refuse to answer and call your lawyer, friend, mother, whomever!)
- Brought her large dog to the interview (winning the job through intimidation!)
- A balding applicant abruptly excused himself, then returned to office a few minutes later wearing a toupee (however you look when you enter the interview, you should stick with that look)
- Chewed bubble gum and blew bubbles (applicants shouldn't chew gum, but – if they do – at the very least they shouldn't blow bubbles to make it even more obvious!)
- Stretched out on the floor to fill out the job application (if the interviewer asks the job candidate to relax, that doesn't mean to lie on the floor; maybe ask for some coffee or water, but act within reason!)

h. There is nothing wrong with asking an applicant about his/her schooling and his/her previous jobs (as long as that information is relevant to the position). That is often essential information in hiring someone.

i. For most jobs, one cannot ask about an arrest record, while one can inquire about felony convictions. It is typically only for law enforcement positions that an arrest - even without a conviction - is deemed relevant.

   (An ongoing controversy is: what convictions, and for how long, are job-related? Civil rights groups and some federal or state government agencies seek to limit the employers' right to *not* hire ex-convicts, while employers oppose them. Ironically, if employers hire an ex-convict who then harms or kills a customer or fellow employee, the employer may be sued for failing to protect the victim. Personal-injury attorneys and feminists who normally side with civil rights proponents often oppose them on this topic and argue that employers need discretion to not hire ex-cons.)

j. One can ask an applicant about the organizations to which he/she belongs, whether as an officer or a member. A possible problem, though, is to leave open the inquiry to include organizations whose names might indicate the race (e.g., NAACP), color, nationality, or religion (e.g., B'nai B'rith) of their members. It is better to tell the applicant that he/she may omit from his/her answer any organization which indicates one of those protected classes.

   k. Some questions an applicant may want to ask the employer: What are the employer's immediate and long-term plans? With whom would I be working? May I have a copy of the job description? Do you have a performance appraisal system? What training programs does the employer offer? What are the opportunities for advancement?

   Questions for your consideration:

1. Is there a particular limit on questioning that you find an unfair restriction on employers? Why?
2. Are there other restrictions on questions that you believe should be imposed upon employers? Why?
3. If the employer cannot ask a question in a particular form, is it fair for the employee applicant to bring up these areas on his/her own? In what position does that leave applicants who do not volunteer such information?
4. Have you had interviews where the employer prepared no better than Prof. Emerson had?

Subjective evaluations of interviewees are more common for higher level jobs. They are likely harder for these interviewees to challenge as discriminatory: court and administrators tend to be reluctant to "over-manage," particularly if any assessments of job characteristics and candidate qualifications do seem to be, on their face, a fair construction of what the job entails and what the candidates should bring to that job.

VII. THREE THEORIES FOR PROVING A TITLE VII VIOLATION
   (see pgs. 573-578; Emerson BL)

The three theories for proving a Title VII violation are: (a) disparate treatment, (b) adverse impact, (c) pattern or practice. Of the three, only disparate treatment requires proof of intent.

The treatment must be *different:*

In *Hardin v. S.C. Johnson & Son, Inc.*, 167 F.3d 340 (7th Cir. 1999), the 7th Circuit U.S. Court of Appeals upheld a trial court's dismissal of a black female worker's claims of sexual and racial harassment. The worker had sued her employer – S.C. Johnson & Co., a home-cleaning-products manufacturer, because a male co-worker allegedly berated her and others, using expletives, some with racial overtones. The man also allegedly touched her, let a door slam in her face, and cut her off in the parking lot. The co-worker "treated all of his co-workers poorly," and – courts have held – in racial-bias cases, "equal-opportunity harassers" are not discriminating. While courts have not accepted equal mistreatment as a defense against sexual harassment, it seems quite possible – The co-worker abused everybody, so there was NO illegal discrimination. (i.e. *"I hate everyone regardless of race, religion, nationality, gender, etc.*). It isn't discrimination unless there is differential treatment; plaintiffs claim must be for differential treatment (i.e., treated differently from other groups because of race).

"Hardin [the plaintiff] testified in her deposition that Anderson [the male co-worker] cursed at all employees on the line, white and black, male and female. This is supported by the depositions of nearly everyone who testified; it is undisputed that Anderson was a crude individual who treated all of his coworkers poorly. Thus, it would not be rational for a trier of fact to conclude that Anderson made the workplace less congenial for women or blacks than he did for men or whites."

<u>*Discrimination Need Not Be "Mean";*</u> One Might be Discriminatory by Being Too *Nice*. Thus, it could be the opposite of being too harsh – acting too nice, failing to correct, to tell an employee that what he/she was doing was inadequate. This may insulate the employee from criticism, so he/she could not improve and, ultimately, ends up fired or demoted. For example, in *Vaughn v. Edel*, 918 F.2d 517 (1990), the U.S. Court of Appeals for the Fifth Circuit (based in New Orleans) held that an employer's failure to disclose a black employee's faults, due to her race, effectively denied that worker the chance to improve. It was thus discriminatory.

A. Disparate Treatment

1. Elements

Disparate treatment is the theory of employment discrimination which all members of Congress - both those for the Civil Rights Act of 1964 and those opposed – knew courts would use in evaluating employment discrimination (Title VII) claims.

With a disparate treatment claim, one person allegedly is treated worse than another person on account of the mistreated person's race, religion, color, national origin, or sex. The following is a prima facie case, under the disparate treatment theory, proving discrimination in hiring:

    (i) Plaintiff belongs to a protected group
    (ii) Plaintiff applies for a job with the defendant
    (iii) Plaintiff is qualified for the job
    (iv) Plaintiff is rejected for the job
    (v) Defendant continues to seek job applicants

Intent to discriminate is an element. Without it, a defendant is <u>not</u> liable for Disparate Treatment. Once the plaintiff's prima facie case has been established, it is up to the defendant to state legitimate, nondiscriminatory reasons for the challenged employment decision (or else the defendant loses the case).

> Ordinarily, employers cannot treat people differently (on account of race, sex, etc.), even if only provisionally.

2. Comparable Worth

Comparable worth is a concept not accepted at the federal level (e.g., under Title VII or the Equal Pay Act) or in most state or local laws. The idea is that if two different jobs – one held mainly by men and the other by women – are essentially worth the same, then there should not be a wage disparity or other difference in treatment between such comparably worthwhile jobs.

So, are different job categories (e.g., a university's clerical staff and groundskeepers) worth about the same: "comparable?" Do we trust judges, administrators, management consultants, and the like to decide the relative worth of various jobs? Or do we just let the marketplace (supported by more limited, anti-discrimination laws such as Title VII and the Equal Pay Act) determine wage scales?

Some state governments (e.g., Washington State) and some local governments have comparable worth, but it is only for those governments' own workers. Also, corporations may, on their own, as a matter of fairness, employee morale, greater efficiency and competition with others, try to set up wage scales premised on comparable worth. But there is no legal requirement that they do so. (In Ontario, Canada, though, employers who implement equity-pay reforms gain immunity from litigation.)

> Subtle(?) Discrimination
> *Boss to Worker:* "That's an excellent suggestion, Ms. Smith. Perhaps one of the men here would like to make it"
> *Job description:* use of "he/she" may not be enough – e.g., "The secretarial applicant must be able to type 75 words per minute and use various software packages, and he/she must have great legs!"

B. Adverse (or Disparate) Impact

1. Unintentional Discrimination

Have we achieved a color-blind society? Courts tend to recognize that we have not.

Intent to discriminate is not required in order to prove Adverse Impact.

2. Employment Tests and Other Hiring Requirements

A key question, under the adverse impact approach, is: Do the tests for a job create a narrower pool of "qualified" applicants than the job actually necessitates?

Employment tests and other requirements must be a reasonable measure of prospective job performance - any test should be professionally developed – relevant to the job requirements.
i.e. -- Strength and agility tests tend to be important in law enforcement, so these tests are okay.
The EEOC has promulgated detailed guidelines on making and using "ability tests" in order to select or promote employees

- Height and weight requirements - employers must evaluate for adverse impact - if such an impact is present, there must truly be a business necessity for the employer to use such requirements. In *Dothard v. Rawlinson*, 433 U.S. 321 (1977), the U.S. Supreme Court looked with disfavor at job requirements for prison guards (e.g., height and weight minimums) that adversely impacted women. - In the *Dothard* case, the high court held that for correctional officers and related professions (e.g., cops, fireman), a true test would simply measure strength, speed, whatever really matters - not just height/weight minimums.
- Advertisements must not expressly or implicitly encourage only some job applicants and discourage others based on protected classifications – e.g., ads featuring female swimwear models, might be seen as only seeking young female applicants, or perhaps only males, whose eyes are drawn to the advertisement for, implicitly, male "help wanted."
- Tests must be job related – hiring and promotional criteria (e.g. high school graduation) must be job related

> Job Tests – Math and jewelry? (A true story, based on an actual client)
> A large jewelry store in a major metropolitan area of the United States conducted testing, including math tests, for all job applicants. However, such tests were irrelevant to the job requirements for some of the store's jobs. Must a person who stocks shelves or drives trucks possess good math skills? Passing the test

is not a valid qualifying factor, and the employer's adherence to that standard could help to establish a job discrimination case (adverse impact and/or pattern or practice of discrimination) against the employer.

C. Pattern or Practice of Discrimination

Intent to discriminate is Not required in order to prove Pattern or Practice of Discriminating. This theory depends on proof through statistics - a protected class' underrepresentation in the work force, as compared to its percentage of the job applicant pool (e.g., the Teamsters were forced to take remedial measures about the underrepresentation of African-Americans and Latinos); these statistics indicating underrepresentation may indicate a possible problem.

Of course, statistics - indicating that groups are not evenly represented in occupations or institutions - do not automatically evidence discrimination. For example, men suffer more than 90% of all deaths on the job, although men are only 54% of the labor force. There is no evidence that disparity results from discrimination, but mainly from the hazardous types of occupations in which men are much more likely to be engaged than are women. (Outside of employment, here are two more comparisons – (1) Asian Americans' applications for mortgage loans are approved a higher percentage of the time than whites, and whites are approved a higher percentage of the time than are blacks; (2) American men are struck by lightning six times as often as American women. Clearly, the latter is not "discrimination," but is the former?) Some critics contend that businesses accused of discrimination – with statistics touted against them – may feel that they are expected to prove their innocence in the court of public opinion. If these businesses cannot prove a negative (that they do not discriminate), they may feel compelled to settle out of court rather than let the bad publicity continue.

> Merit pay or seniority systems **(see pg. 582; Emerson BL)**, even if part of a collective bargaining agreement, must not serve to perpetuate unlawful discrimination. Merit pay, such as a piecework system, must be precise, communicated to the workers, and neutrally applied.

VIII. TITLE VII DEFENSES

Two types of defenses are business necessity and bona fide occupational qualification (BFOQ).

A. Business Necessity

This defense is that a challenged practice is job-related because it accurately predicts employees' ability to perform tasks that are important for their jobs. To counter this defense, plaintiffs may argue that there is a less discriminatory alternative to the challenged practice.

Business necessity focuses on the employer's needs, while Bone Fide Occupational Qualification (BFOQ), discussed below, focuses on the legitimacy of a worker's particular characteristics/qualifications. This difference may be more semantic than substantive, with the judicial or regulatory decision being the same (upholding or outlawing an employment practice), whether it is an alleged BFOQ or an alleged business necessity.

> **Private Clubs and Single-Sex Health Clubs?**
> Some states, such as New York and California, have anti-discrimination laws that apply to business clubs. But six states have statutes specifically allowing single-sex health clubs. A court has upheld the constitutionality of single-sex health clubs because of the privacy rights of members. Other courts, however, have found that exercise is not an inherently private event, and thus it should not be protected from public policy concerns requiring access to both sexes.

> Depending on what you see at a health club, many would argue that – for most people – exercise *ought to* be a private matter!

B. BFOQ (Bona Fide Occupational Qualification) (see pg. 575; Emerson BL)

As stated in the Barron's text (6th ed.) at page 575: "BFOQ defenses are generally construed very narrowly and unfavorably."

Examples: A Baptist church may interview only Baptist members for the job of parish pastor; a seminary may consider the religion of its teaching applicants; a theater company may interview only women to play the role of a woman. A BFOQ cannot lawfully be based on assumptions about the comparative employment characteristics of a group (e.g., that women have a higher turnover rate). A BFOQ also cannot be based on stereotyped characterizations of groups (e.g., that men are less capable of assembling intricate equipment than are women). Finally, it may not be affected by the supposed preferences of customers, employers, or coworkers for one group (e.g., women) over another. Gender *may be* a BFOQ if physical attributes are needed for a position (e.g., a wet nurse) or to protect others' right to privacy (e.g., sauna room attendants - same-sex requirements for passing out towels seem legitimate in order to not have some gawking male handing towels to naked women!).

Although employers are required to try to accommodate an employee's religious beliefs, that accommodation need only be reasonable; the employer can fire an employee rather than significantly disrupt workplace productivity."

Consider a significant Supreme Court case, *Hosanna-Tabor Evangelical Lutheran Church v. EEOC* (decided Jan. 11, 2012). The Court unanimously endorsed the "ministerial exception" to discrimination protections: the First Amendment requires civil courts "to defer to a religious organization's good faith understanding of who qualifies as its minister" regardless of the employee's actual work duties. The Court thus held that the employer can terminate such ministers (who have religious duties) without the employer being subject to the Americans with Disabilities Act; presumably the Court's reasoning would apply to cases involving other anti-discrimination laws.

The BFOQ defense applies only to hiring, job classification, and referral decisions. The convenience of the employer generally is *not* okay, if that is all it is.

If insurance companies hire only Indians as Gujarati speakers (to service a growing market of potential policy purchasers from the Indian subcontinent), that would not be discriminatory if, in fact, the only people able to speak Gujarati are from India.[150] That would not be the case for a language that is widely known among the general populace. For Gujarati, the assumption goes, the ethnicity and language skills are tied in a way that is not true for, say, Spanish or French.

Another example: A synagogue has a right to hire only a Jew as a Rabbi.
But what about a custodian or a secretary? No, that would not be a BFOQ. A custodian or secretary clearly can work well without being of the same faith as the members of the congregation.

Generally, a BFOQ may be based on sex, religion, national origin, age, or physical ability, but not race or color.[151] Of course, some employers may still hire or assign people based on race or other physical characteristics, regardless of law and morality against such a practice.

A toothless maid at a ski resort sued after she was fired for being toothless. The maid, Mary Hodgdon, did not wear her false teeth because they hurt. Hodgdon decided to buck the system(!) and won her suit; her appearance generally, and her teeth specifically, were not a BFOQ for the job of maid at a

---

[150] The assumption is that this language of Western India — with 50 million Gujarati speakers (one of the 22 official languages and fourteen regional languages of India (and the first language of both Mohandas Gandhi and of Muhammad Ali Jinnah, the founder of Pakistan) – simply is very unlikely to be learned by people outside of India.

[151] As a practical matter, of course, in the performing arts, the actors, dancers, and others may be chosen, at least in part, based on their race or ethnicity. George Gershwin's musical, "Porgy and Bess," generally features African-American leads, "Fiddler on the Roof" usually has actors that could pass for Russian Jews, and theme park performers tend to look like the cartoon characters they portray (e.g., Disney's Snow White.)

four-star resort.[152] Further, Hodgdon was fired while a male maintenance worker who also had no teeth, was allowed to roam the ski resort premises freely smiling toothlessly at the posh resort's guests.[153]

But what about as a dental hygienist or a toothpaste model? What about as an actor or model generally? There it seems logical to find teeth to be a business necessity and/or BFOQ.[154]

A BFOQ for Hiring Only Male or Female Servers at a Restaurant?

Some restaurants have (or, at least, used to have) a single-gender waiter or waitress staff, with only male or female servers. But that is clearly illegal; there is no bona fide occupational qualification (BFOQ), according to almost all legal experts. For example, in August 1998, U.S. District Judge Daniel T. K. Hurley found "the Old World notion that it is 'classier' to have only male food servers is, at best, a quaint anachronism. It is not a defense to the charge of sex discrimination." So Judge Hurley ruled that the landmark Joe's Stone Crab restaurant of Miami Beach must pay more than $150,000 altogether to four women not hired by Joe's, with new hiring to be cleared by the court for three years. Between 1986 and 1991, a total of 108 men - and no women - were hired to wear Joe's tuxedo uniforms. After the EEOC filed its complaint in 1991, Joe's began to hire women (by August 1998, of the 79 servers eighteen were women). Judge Hurley ordered an elaborate series of methods to monitor Joe's hiring practices, including mandated comprehensive recordkeeping.

Some employers will fight strenuously and pay large settlements to maintain their single-gender practices. For example, in October 1997, the Hooters restaurant chain paid $3.75 million to settle a class-action suit on behalf of men who were denied jobs; under the settlement, Hooters continues to employ scantily clad women as servers, although men are eligible for other positions.

Customer Preference

While Title VII forbids employers from using customer preference as a defense to illegal discrimination, the preference for one sex or the other may succeed as a BFOQ in three situations:

1. At a health care facility or a prison, when a patient or inmate has a fundamental right to personal privacy or when safety is at stake.

2. If the central mission of the employer's business is to sell sex or sexual entertainment, if the sex-differentiated job qualification relates to the "essence" or the "central mission" of the employer's business, and if the qualification is objectively and verifiably necessary to the employee's performance of his/her job.[155]

3. To guarantee authenticity for a dramatic production. 29 C.F.R. §1604.2 (an EEOC ruling).

These exceptions are to be interpreted narrowly. Ordinarily, employers could be treading on legal quicksand when they allow presumed customer preference (often just a nicer sounding word for prejudice) to justify a discriminatory practice.

For example, the author had a client who owned a store. The store customers supposedly preferred white (or almost exclusively white) women as sales clerks because the customers themselves were almost exclusively white, elderly women. The author had to convince the client to abandon this

---

[152] *Hodgdon v. Mt. Mansfield, Inc.*, 624 A.2d 1122 (Vt. 1992).

[153] Now, the puns in this case nearly overwhelm me (!):
Mt. Mansfield needed to get a grip.
This form of indenture is barbaric.
This case represents the roots of discrimination under the Americans with Disabilities Act.

[154] Courts may hold, for example, that a hotel maid is distinct from a store manager, for purposes of physical appearance and hiring, firing, or promotion decisions. In *Chico Dairy Co. v. Human Rights Commission*, 382 S.E. 2d 75 (W. Va. 1989), the West Virginia Supreme Court upheld the employer's right to not promote an employee to store manager because of the ugly appearance of the employee's sunken eye socket, which made the employee seem "unsavory" according to management.

[155] *Automobile Workers v. Johnson Controls, Inc.*, 499 U.S. 187, 201 (1991).

policy of preferring white women as sales clerks. The customers might not actually have preferred white female clerks; anyway, employers should not argue that they do not want to discriminate, but have to do so, because their customers are prejudiced. This is often an empirically unsupported allegation, and it is almost always a morally repugnant contention that is an easy excuse for the employer to make. Most important, though, as a matter of law the customers' preferences in this area – real or imagined – simply cannot be the basis for a store's employment hiring or promotion policy.

IX. SEX DISCRIMINATION, ESPECIALLY SEXUAL HARASSMENT

A. Introduction

Under Title VII, sex discrimination deals with treatment based on gender, not sexual orientation.[156] About half of the 40 to 50 "glass ceiling" reviews that the U.S. Labor Department performs annually show patterns of wage and job discrimination by federal contractors (pay and promotion).

Because the EEOC is said to have little effectiveness, many believe that most workplace discrimination cases are better left to private attorneys.

B. Sexual Harassment (see pgs. 578-580; Emerson BL)

Perhaps the most common form of discrimination, especially against women, is sexual harassment. It can have a devastating impact on a person's career advancement, with many persons still reluctant to complain. On the other hand, employers that do not do everything possible to detect and deter sexual harassment can suffer severe consequences in terms of lawsuits and damages awards, poor public relations, low workforce morale, and reduced productivity. As a moral as well as legal matter, sexual harassment should not be tolerated.

YOUTUBE – sexual_harassment_5mins24secslecturewith_woodentoupee is at robertwemersonufl

Teresa Harris was sexually harassed, and this led to a very important case that went all the way to the U.S. Supreme Court in 1993, and the Supreme Court agreed that she had been sexually harassed.[157] It also agreed that she did not have to prove that she had suffered incredible humiliation, it just had to show that, in effect, given the circumstances, the conduct that was oppressing her was unlawful, illegitimate. What exactly took place? For one thing, her boss at the trucking company at which she worked was constantly making remarks about her appearance. Also, her boss was constantly making sarcastic comments about her alleged behavior. For instance, when she managed to snag a new client for the business, he opined that she basically must have slept with the boss of that company in order to get the business. When she asked for a raise, he said 'Why don't we go to a motel?' and negotiated. When he wanted some coffee one time, he said 'Come get some coffee, honey, you can fish the change out of my pocket', and he did all sorts of other things which were just kind of stupid, obnoxious or worse.

The thing that's so interesting to me, I suppose maybe it's because of my legal learning, is I look at his behavior and I say 'How could he not have known that what he was doing was boorish and possibly unlawful?' The irony is in a lot of these sexual harassment cases one sees that the only person, in

---

[156] State and municipal laws extending employment protection and benefits to homosexuals were discussed earlier in this text.
[157] *Harris v. Forklift Sys.*, 510 U.S. 17 (1993).

retrospect, who seems to have not known that what was taking place was unlawful was the idiot who was engaged in the behavior himself. Everyone else knew that it was wrong. It's kind of like a bald man who puts on a toupee and somehow thinks that he's fooled everyone. Everyone else in the world can see that this is a $5 toupee that I'm wearing, and the only one who doesn't know seems to be me. That's the same thing in these sexual harassment cases, that's why it becomes very important for businesses to make sure that their supervisors and their employees and everyone else who deals with their business understands at least the basics of sexual harassment law, and understands what to do if they fell aggrieved that they are being harassed so that one sexual harassment is far less likely to take place at that employment area, and secondly that if it does begin to develop, the people that feel they are being harassed have some outlet, some way to go through the chain of command in the company and get some sort of recourse.

What gets businesses in big, big trouble is not just a pattern and practice of discrimination or a pattern and practice, in particular, of harassment, it is the failure to have systems in place to try to prevent it, to try to detect it, or to try to weed it out and prevent it from happening in the future. That's when businesses end up facing spectacular judgments against them, because they've, in effect, condoned (even though they may not have directly supported) some sort of discriminatory behavior.

Sexual harassment is just one of many, many, many types of discrimination in the workplace, and there are numerous laws covering this. The idea for you, I suppose, is to search the Internet, to search books, to find what you can about the basics of the law in this area. There's so much out there that there is really no excuse for not learning at least the basics in this area.

You could not really find sexual harassment law until approximately 1980, when it started to blossom tremendously. Is it because sexual harassment has suddenly just grown out of all proportions in the last 20-25 years? I don't think so. I think it's because the interpretation of the law has progressed and moved much farther than it was back in the 1960s or 1970s. It's the same statutes, but the regulations, the case law and other developments have added much more to it. Yes, Congress has sometimes gotten in the act, but it's much more the courts, the administrators, and, frankly, the private litigants and employers themselves that have furthered the law in this area.

Questions to Explore:

1. Do you have an example of sexual harassment you can briefly mention?

2. Do you believe that sexual harassment is more of a problem of abuse of power, of employers ineffectively overseeing obnoxious employees, or simply a poor corporate "culture?" Explain your answer.

3. Have any older people related to you accounts of sexual harassment that occurred before the concept of sexual harassment was a distinctly recognized legal concept (i.e., before about 1980)? Please briefly outline what was told to you.

4. Some commentators maintain that the law of sexual harassment – or, at least, worries about it – unduly inhibit behavior and make the workplace more rigid than it ought to be. Do you agree? Why or why not?

1. Two Types of Sexual Harassment: *Quid pro quo* and Workplace Environment

Quid pro quo means "this for that." But sexual harassment also goes beyond that – As far back as 1980, EEOC Guidelines stated that there is no need for a plaintiff to show physical contact or involuntary sex. The harasser can be one or more co-workers, although it is easier to show intimidation if the alleged harasser is the boss or otherwise in a superior position.

Workplace environment (the Human Resources term is "hostile work environment harassment") is a less obvious, but a growing basis for claims. A claim of workplace environment sexual harassment depends upon this definition: Sexual behavior and atmosphere so severe and pervasive that it creates an intimidating, hostile, or offensive work environment. Evidence would include the following: (1) members of one sex are exposed to disadvantageous terms or conditions of employment to which members of the other sex are not exposed; and (2) the "exposed" employee did not solicit or initiate the act, and he/she finds it undesirable or offensive.

Workplace harassment may be created if:
(1) any individual is actually offended; and (2) a reasonable person could find the material offensive; and (3) the conduct is severe or pervasive.

To determine if the conduct was objectionably sexual in nature, most courts use the test of whether a reasonable person of the same gender would find the conduct objectionable.

> Consider a news magazine's manager (we'll call him Dennis Artman) makes "dirty" pictures for a story about pornographic websites. But Artman's boss, Gordon, says that Artman should take the layouts down. Some might disagree with Gordon because, they contend, the layouts are appropriate for the work assignment. It is about X-rated Web Sites and the design is only reflecting the content of the article.
> **WRONG!** The layouts should come down. A reasonable person was offended and the layouts and graphics are too sexual in nature; displaying them was far from necessary.
> Although the cybersex story is sexual in nature, even Dennis Artman knew that some of the material he posted was too explicit for the magazine his employer produced. Posting the photos and graphics just for the staff "to experience" was insensitive and showed poor judgment.
> In certain situations, it may be necessary to work with potentially offensive materials, like Jessica's experience with the cybersex article. However, displaying the potentially offensive materials for the general interest of co-workers is inappropriate and may violate the law and/or an employer's own anti-harassment policies.
> It does not necessarily absolve the company that Gordon was the only person at the editorial meeting who complained about the pictures – the only person evidently offended. The key question is not how many people found the conduct offensive. One offended person may be sufficient.

To constitute sexual harassment, the harassment generally must be more than just offensive speech (harassment is more than breach of a "code of civility").[158] Speech without offensive *sexual* connotations is very unlikely to somehow violate title VII and may in fact be constitutionally protected speech (if government, and therefore the First Amendment, is implicated). One gauche remark, by itself, typically is insufficient.

In *Clark County School District v. Breeden*, 532 U.S. 268 (2001), the U.S. Supreme Court unanimously held that a supervisor's off-color remark was not sexual harassment. Shirley Breeden was reviewing job applications at the Clark County, Nevada school district where she was an administrator when her supervisor and another worker had an exchange involving a joke that Breeden found offensive. The supervisor read aloud a statement that one job applicant admitted saying to a co-worker at a previous job: "Making love to you is like making love to the Grand Canyon." The supervisor then allegedly looked at Breeden, shrugged his shoulders, and said that he did not know what that meant; the other worker responded, "Well, I'll tell you later," and both men laughed.

Breeden complained. A month later her job was downgraded. Breeden sued because of the alleged retaliation. The U.S. Supreme Court upheld a trial court's dismissal of Breeden's claim: "No reasonable person could have believed that the single incident recounted" violated federal anti-discrimination law. The Court relied upon prior holdings and noted that to violate the sexual harassment

---

[158] The U.S. Supreme Court held in *Harris v. Forklift Systems, Inc.*, 510 U.S. 17 (1993), that the acts complained of must be "pervasive" and "continuous." Isolated instances are not unlawful. Under both bodies of law, the plaintiff must prove that his victimization was injurious not only subjectively, but also objectively. The *Harris* court imposed this requirement on Title VII sex harassment claims by adopting the "reasonable person," rather than a "reasonable woman," standard regarding whether the defendant's conduct was "pervasive." "Reasonable woman" presumably is an easier burden of proof for the plaintiff.

guidelines under Title VII the alleged harassment must be "so severe or pervasive as to alter the conditions of the victim's employment and create an abusive working environment."

Still, while a pattern of harassment usually is an element of sexual harassment, the EEOC has stated, in its guidelines, "a single, unusually severe incident of harassment may be sufficient to constitute a Title VII violation." In *Brennan v. Bally Total Fitness*, 198 F.Supp.2d 377 (Federal District Court in New York City Manhattan-2002), Brennan was employed by Bally for some two years prior to filing a complaint for sexual harassment by her manager with the company officer responsible for such complaints. The officer took the complaint but took neither remedial action nor any steps to prevent further harassment. Brennan transferred to another location accepting a demotion to avoid the harassment. Brennan received a communication requiring her to attend an educational meeting. She and about twenty other employees were shown a video on sexual harassment by the officer that had received her complaint. As soon as the video ended they were given a 16-page document that he described as containing procedures for bringing discrimination claims. The employees were told to review, sign, and return the document. They were given about 5 minutes. He did not explain that it contained an arbitration provision. They were told that anyone not signing would not be promoted. Brennan signed believing that her failure to sign would lead to her termination. The officer checked each employee's form to see it was signed and gave them no chance to turn it in later after reviewing it personally or with an attorney. Brennan quit her job and filed this cause after filing a complaint with the EEOC, receiving a right-to-sue letter for a pattern of harassment, related to the sexual complaint and her pregnancy. The court found that in order to compel arbitration it first had to determine if the arbitration agreement was unconscionable. The court stated that the test for procedural inadequacy in forming the contract is whether in light of all the facts the party lacked "a meaningful choice" in deciding whether to sign the contract. And, the court said, a contract is substantively unconscionable when its terms are unreasonably favorable to the party against whom unconscionability is claimed. The court found that this agreement was procedurally unconscionable because the circumstances at its making denied Brennan the time or opportunity to understand it and coerced her agreement to its terms. The court further held that the agreement was substantively unconscionable because the circumstances at its making unfairly favored Bally. The court recognized that arbitration clauses can be reasonable even if they favor the stronger party (e.g., the terms limiting the time and damages were not unconscionable); but Bally's retaining the right to unilaterally modify the agreement, and Brennan's having no right to proceed in court against Bally, were unreasonable terms found to be unconscionable and unenforceable.

2. Supreme Court Cases: *Oncale v. Sundowner Offshore Services, Inc.*

The net effect of several 1998 U.S. Supreme Court decisions on sexual harassment makes it easier for sexual harassment plaintiffs to win cases and collect damages.

Oncale v. Sundowner Offshore Services, Inc., 523 U.S. 75 (1998) (discussed **(see pgs. 579-580; Emerson BL)** is a landmark case. It illustrates a trend of men making sexual harassment claims. Sexual harassment claims filed by men with the EEOC have grown from 9% of all charges in 1992 to 12% in 1999 to 15% in 2004 and 16% in 2009 and 17% in 2013. Claims usually are male-on-male; harassment of men by women is rarer.

Joseph Oncale, a worker on an offshore oilrig, filed the Oncale case. He claimed that his male supervisors restrained him several times while another worker harassed him and that he ultimately had to quit out of fear of being raped. Justice Scalia found the allegations so distasteful that – as he put it – "in the interest of both brevity and dignity," the Justice in his written opinion described the allegations only vaguely. For the Court, Justice Scalia wrote that while "Male-on-male sexual harassment was assuredly not the principal evil Congress was concerned with when it enacted Title VII," it was a "reasonably comparable" evil that ought to be covered.

> In a strikingly direct and short (seven-page) opinion, Justice Scalia tried to distinguish between harassing acts not covered by Title VII and those that are. "We have never held that workplace harassment, even harassment between men and women, is automatically discrimination." The law does not cover "ordinary socializing in the workplace – such as male-on-male horseplay or intersexual flirtation – for discriminatory conditions of employment." Nor does the law apply to "genuine but innocuous differences in the ways men and women routinely interact." Courts, Scalia wrote, must carefully distinguish between "simple teasing" and truly abusive behavior. For example, Scalia noted, it is not harassment when a pro football player's coach "smacks him on the buttocks as he heads onto the field." By contrast, Scalia wrote, it might be illegal for the coach to do the same thing to the secretary back at the office. Courts must consider "the social context in which particular behavior occurs."

3. Management Attempts to Prevent Sexual Harassment
As stated at **pgs. 578-580; Emerson BL:**

> "Employers need not immediately discipline the accused harasser. But employers must thoroughly investigate complaints. Employers can be liable for inaction either way: insufficiently investigating, and thus retaining, what proves to have been a harassing worker; or inadequately investigating, and thus firing, a worker who turns out not to have been harassing others. In either case, the employer can be held liable for damages - either to the Title VII harassment victim, or to the innocent fired employee for his/her wrongful dismissal (grounds might be abusive discharge, breach of contract, reverse discrimination, or even perhaps defamation)."

Romance on the Job? The Hamburger Rule

The rule may sound funny, but draconian measure to prevent sexual harassment claims can be morale-suppressing and even counterproductive legally.

In the name of preventing sexual harassment, some employers prohibit potentially benign forms of sexual conduct, without examining the larger structures of sex segregation and inequality in which genuine sex harassment flourishes. Employers may impose strict disciplinary measures, costing many people their jobs or reputations and threatening employees' ability to form their own work cultures.

Employers also may ban or discourage employee romance, chilling intimacy and solidarity among workers of both a sexual and nonsexual variety. In more extreme cases, employers may even use sexual harassment charges as a pretext for punishing employees for discriminatory or other suspect reasons. That managers can justify their actions with reference to a feminist-inspired body of law is not just ironic, but has sometimes facilitated a firm's ability to implement zealous policies that extend the law far beyond its actual requirements.

While employers certainly should have educational programs to inform employees what sexual harassment is, and to deter such harassment, and to tell employees what to do (e.g., who to contact) if they are being bothered,[159] companies may go overboard in fighting harassment. Employers often choose to fire an alleged harasser – and thereby risk a wrongful termination suit – rather than to do nothing and get sued by the alleged victim. Such a choice may make some economic sense, in that most wrongful-termination

---

[159] Without such programs, employers may be held liable for an employees' harassing conduct. *Meritor Savings Bank v. Vinson*, 477 U.S. 57 (1986).

cases cost less to settle than to harassment claims, with the latter more likely to bring punitive damages (and of a higher amount, if awarded).

But employers can protect themselves with thorough investigations of harassment claims. Once an employer is satisfied that harassment occurred, it should be able to successfully defend against a wrongful-discharge allegation. Absent such an investigation, an employer may risk liability. For example, in 1997 Miller Brewing Company was ordered to pay $24 million to an alleged harasser who was found to have been wrongly fired.

Companies should:
1. Tailor a sexual-harassment policy to their businesses and fill it with real-life (i.e., realistic) examples;
2. Require every employee, even the Chief Executive Officer (CEO), to periodically take customized training on sexual harassment awareness;
3. Spell out what internal recourse victims have;
4. Promise victims that the employer will use an outside investigator whenever that is needed;
5. Assess employees' familiarity with corporate sexual harassment policies and complaint procedures;
6. If the CEO is accused of harassing conduct, provide for reporting to others with authority - e.g., the company's General Counsel; and
7. Emphasize in their anti-harassment policies and other communication to employees that workers who complain of harassment will not be punished and that they can complain to an authority other than their supervisor.

Such procedures may protect the employer from legal liability.

---

4. Sexual Harassment by Customers: A Pizza Hut Franchise and Safeway, Inc.

An employer can be held liable for the harassment of employees by people who are not supervisors or coworkers. One example is of a successful lawsuit, and the other was a problem resolved without litigation.

a. *Lockard v. Pizza Hut, Inc.*

The facts and law in *Lockard v. Pizza Hut, Inc.*, 162 F.3d 1062 (10th Cir. 1998) (discussed at **pg. 580; Emerson BL**), were as follows:

Micky Jack, the shift manager of the Pizza Hut restaurant in Atoka, Oklahoma knew that two "crude and rowdy" male customers were the same men that Lockard had complained about previously. The customers had subjected Lockard to sexually suggestive comments, such as "I would like to get into your pants." Lockard did not tell Jack the particulars, but she had said that she did not want to serve the men.

Apparently, no one in the restaurant wanted to wait on these two nasty men. Even male servers tried to avoid them.

When the two men arrived at the Atoka Pizza Hut on November 6, 1993, Lockard – who had been working at the restaurant since September 1993 and had served those men several times - again told Jack that she did not want to wait on them. Jack, nonetheless, instructed her to wait on them. He continued to instruct Lockard to serve them even after she reported that they were harassing her by pulling her hair. Lockard testified that Jack responded, "You wait on them. You were hired to be a waitress. You waitress."

Lockard returned to their table with a pitcher of beer. As she reached to put the beer on the table, the customer pulled her to him by the hair, grabbed her breast, pulled her toward him, and put his mouth on her breast. Lockard now told Jack that she was quitting and wanted to go home. She called her husband who picked her up.

Pizza Hut's policy manual on sexual harassment instructed managers to take steps once they become aware of customers who harass employees. Managers are specifically authorized to ask customers to refrain from the harassing conduct and, if the customers persist, to ask the customers to leave the restaurant. Instead of following the guidelines set forth in Pizza Hut's policy manual, the manager ordered Lockard to continue waiting on the two customers. By doing so, he placed her in an abusive and potentially dangerous situation although he had the authority to avoid doing so by directing a waiter (a male) to serve the men, waiting on them himself, or asking the men to leave the restaurant. Because of the manger's notice of the customers' harassing conduct and his failure to remedy or prevent the hostile work environment, the franchisee employer of the manager was held liable for the manager's conduct. The appeals court upheld the compensatory damages award of $200,000 to Lockard, who, among other things, could no longer work and had suffered much anguish requiring two years of therapy and a totally different career.[160]

b. Safeway Grocery Stores' Policy Mandating "Friendly" Service

A large grocery store chain, Safeway, had allegedly led some customers to harass cashiers because required business "friendliness" was misread as flirtatious come-ons. Under Safeway's "Superior Service" policy, phased into operation in the mid-to-late 1990s, employees were expected to anticipate customers' needs, take them to items they could not find, make selling suggestions, thank customers by name when they paid by check or credit card, and offer to carry out their groceries.

After four years of a voluntary phase-in, Safeway began enforcing the "Superior Service" policy by using undercover shoppers and warning that negative evaluations can lead to remedial training, disciplinary letters, and termination. But trouble developed. Women workers complained about being propositioned daily by men who mistook their company-mandated friendliness as flirtatiousness. Twelve female Safeway employees and one male Safeway employee aired their grievances with Safeway executives. And their union filed charges with the National Labor Relations Board contending that the policy was illegally imposed.[161] The union lawyer, Matthew Ross, stated that Safeway has "battalions of MBAs who are coming up with these policies who don't take into account the real-life implications."

The union wanted workers, especially women, to have more freedom to choose not to make eye contact with a potentially threatening customer or to refuse to carry groceries out to a man's car at night.

In the face of these criticisms, Safeway revised its program. Workers were given the discretion to not be "friendly" when, in their judgment, a customer might misunderstand. The program, and the degree to which workers followed it, was no longer a basis for evaluating employees for possible promotions, pay raises, demotions, firing, or other treatment.

X. TOPICAL LECTURE: THE AMERICANS WITH DISABILITIES ACT – THE "ADA"
(see pgs. 583-586; Emerson BL)

Introduction to Topical Lecture:
The ADA prohibits discrimination against disabled persons in a number of areas – e.g., access to buildings, education, and employment. The key focus is often the reasonableness of an accommodation that an employer should provide for the disabled worker.

Besides Title VII of the Civil Rights Act of 1964, there are many other federal anti-discrimination statutes. There also are numerous such laws at the state level. The Americans with Disabilities Act (1990) (ADA) is one such very important <u>federal</u> law.[162]

---

[160] Earlier in the text, we address issues of agency law and of an employer's liability for its employee's wrongful acts.
[161] One female produce worker said that she often hid in a back room to avoid customers who had harassed her, propositioned her, and even followed her to her car.
[162] Another important law is the Age Discrimination in Employment Act (1967), alluded to throughout these materials on Employment Discrimination Law. More information is provided in Robert W. Emerson, *Business Law*. NY: Barron's Educational Series (6th ed., 2015), at 583.

The ADA prohibits discrimination against various disabled persons by businesses with 15 or more employees. Protected disabled persons are those with a physical or mental impairment[163] that substantially limits "one or more life activities" (e.g., learning, thinking, concentrating, caring for oneself, interacting with others, speaking, performing manual tasks, working, and - by a 5-to-4 decision of the Supreme Court (*Bragdon v. Abbott*, 524 U.S. 624 (1998) - reproduction), those with a record of such an impairment, or those regarded as having such an impairment.[164]

Mental Impairments

About 13% of ADA cases are brought by individuals suffering from emotional or psychiatric impairment, including anxiety disorders, depression, bipolar disorder (manic depression), and schizophrenia. A worker receives ADA protection if the mental impairment kept him from a major life activity or if he/she had a history of mental impairment. People are not covered for temporary moodiness – e.g., because of a romantic break-up – or for the misuse of prescription drugs or illegal drugs, or for bisexuality, homosexuality, sexual behavior disorders, compulsive gambling, kleptomania (compulsive theft), or pyromania (compulsive setting of fires).

Workers with mental impairment may request reasonable accommodations, such as:
1. Partitions to provide a more secluded work station for a worker who has trouble concentrating.
2. A modified work schedule so that a worker can keep counseling appointments.

Serious misconduct – such as making threats, destroying property or stealing – can subject to discipline (e.g., demotion or termination) any worker, even one with a mental or physical impairment. The ADA is not meant to compel employers to tolerate problems interfering with normal business activity.

After determining whether someone is disabled, the next step is to verify that he/she otherwise is qualified for the job: someone with the requisite skill, education, and expertise. If so, then the employer must seek reasonable accommodations of the disabled employee's needs. If cost-effective measures are available, then the employer should adopt them to give disabled employees and potential employees more access to jobs.[165]

The ADA provides not just employment protection (**employers should, if they reasonably can, accommodate the disabled applicant or employee**); but the ADA also protects access to stores, restaurants, hotels, government buildings, banks, theaters, *and* places of employment. The ADA requires program accessibility, *not* necessarily building accessibility.[166] In other words, the ADA encourages low-cost ways to solve a problem.[167] Still, in tandem with the recommendations and guidelines of national organizations (e.g., the American Institute of Architects), the ADA effectively has created something likened to a national building code.

---

[163] Depression accounts for about 2% of all ADA claims. The problem is that for this and other mental illnesses, it is more difficult to recognize the illness and often much harder to fashion remedies than it is for a physical disability (e.g., for the disabled why not just install a wheelchair ramp?). For a professional job, how much could the need for mental stress reduction be accommodated? Could an attorney at a law firm, because he/she suffers from stress, be accommodated with fewer hours of work?

[164] E.g., HIV. Indeed, states also have laws against discrimination based on some conditions or illnesses. For example, discrimination based on an HIV-related condition is illegal in two-thirds of the states.

[165] Employers do not have to accommodate personality quirks that fail to rise to the level of mental illness. But, say, employee Joe may get a note from a psychiatrist or psychologist – "Joe shouldn't have to do more work"; "Joe should have a new supervisor." Whether an employer would accept the note, or a court would order employer compliance, depends on a reading of all the facts.

[166] Restaurants may, for example, simply have servers read menus to blind customers, not provide menus in Braille; and a business located on the second floor of an old building need not install an elevator if it can, and does, offer curbside service to disabled customers.

[167] The mean average spent (based on a survey of 448 businesses) is less than a few thousand dollars.

<u>We don't have to treat the disabled and the able-bodied the same, but there is an element of fairness in trying to accommodate the disabled.</u>

Effective disability-management programs might avoid much ADA litigation. Employers using such programs would perhaps avoid inadvertent discrimination against the disabled; and employers would explore other options for productive employment before failing to hire someone or - even worse - firing an employee. From the vantage point of disability-management programs, keeping a worker in a job he/she performs satisfactorily probably is more cost-effective than hiring someone new.

To avoid problems with the ADA, Employers should:

(i) Have good job descriptions – so there is no reason not to hire. Problems arise if the job description is inadequate and only later is it discovered that the employee cannot do the job (e.g., waiters/waitresses need to be able to remember/recite the new specials), so it is better to exclude potential employees from the outset.

3. (ii) Have "fitness for duty" (aka "strength tests") exams even after hiring workers that builds employer expertise regarding why a person would need to be fired. (Just because a person's firing or non-hiring somehow relates to a health problem does not mean his firing/non-hiring violates the ADA. For example, in 2004, the U.S. Supreme Court held that an employer's refusal to rehire a worker fired for illegal drug use does not amount to "disparate treatment," which would have violated the ADA.)

(iii) Have well-trained, knowledgeable supervisors. For example, there are numerous rules and principles concerning pre-employment testing, qualification standards, tests and selection criteria:

(a) Before the ADA, often people needed a driver's license to get things like a bank account. A blind man cannot get a driver's license, but he should still be able to get a bank account. Obviously, the ADA changed that.

(b) Under the ADA, an employer can give a drug test medical examination only after making an offer.

(c) ADA-compliant employers must give the same examination to everyone who applies for a job, not just specifically certain people.

(d) As usual for employment discrimination law, examinations have to be based on the qualifications needed for a job.

But a change of supervisors may not be a reasonable accommodation for a worker who claims that a supervisor's taunts gave her depression. For example, in late 1999 a case involved a nurse at Dresser-Rand Company who handled workers compensation cases; her boss was the plant's comp expert, so the

EEOC and a federal appeals court agreed that a change in bosses would not be a <u>reasonable accommodation.</u>

A permissible exclusion from the ADA is that one cannot perform essential functions of the job or that employment would pose a significant risk to the health or safety of others.

Cost of accommodations – how "reasonable" are they?

THE COMPOSERS EXAMPLE

The hypothetical example of blind composer George Friedrich Handel, one-handed pianist Paul Wittgenstein, and deaf Ludwig van Beethoven

---

YOUTUBE - employee_welfare_law (4mins30secs) is at robertwemersonufl

End of Topical Lecture on the Americans with Disabilities Act (ADA)

THE END OF PART TWO OF THE TEXT

ARTICLE III: RIGHTS AND WRONGS

A. LEGAL PLAYERS: LAWYERS AND JUDGES

> *"No brilliance is needed in the law. Nothing but common sense, and relatively clean fingernails."*
> *John Mortimer*

I. LAWYERS

We may prefer not to look at lawyers. However, we must study them and their ways. Lawyers are very important, especially in the United States; common law and the adversarial system both use a lot of lawyers. Add to that - individualism - which creates even more legal strife. Surveys of business executives have ranked knowing when to consult an attorney and how to communicate and work most effectively with counsel, the highest and second highest in importance of instruction in business law courses. Indeed, studies indicate (1) that the most useful course in business school is law,[1] and (2) that knowing about the role of lawyers may be the most practical "take-away" a layperson gets from almost any course on law.

> YOUTUBE – Lawyers 5mins40secs - www.youtube.com/watch?v=DcivmtYMREQ at robertwemersonufl - Anecdotes, Adversaries, and Advertising (with a shark shirt and hat!)

A. The Reputations of Lawyers

There have always, historically, been problems with and criticism of lawyers. For lawyers, their poor reputation (selfish, too clever, etc.) may precede them! *"The first thing we do, let's kill all the lawyers."* William Shakespeare, Henry VI, Part 2. *"May your life be full of lawyers."* Mexican curse.
The portrayal of lawyers in entertainment programs (e.g., lawyers with wacky personalities; lawyers who are extremely good-looking; lawyers who are genuinely evil or almost saint-like) often misrepresents reality. Only interesting cases (e.g., with funny, pretty, outrageous, or unusual persons or causes) tend to be picked for "reality" courtroom shows. In so-called documentaries or dramas "based on" real events, if information is tedious or does not develop the plot, it is often left out. If a program – even a plainly fictitious one - can be both accurate and entertaining, then most producers will do both. But when the two conflict, entertainment always triumphs over accuracy.

B. Training of Lawyers

Training of lawyers involves, in the United States, law schools (three-year post-bachelor's degree programs) and bar exams. Successful completion of both, as required by the state to which the

---

[1] At least two reasons immediately spring to mind: (1) law is incredibly important, affecting almost every aspect of our lives; and (2) most people know little about the law, and many of them fail to realize how little they actually know.

applicant seeks entry, is required for someone to become an attorney in the United States.[2] Such schooling and testing often is not mandatory elsewhere. In a large majority of other countries there is no more (often less) law school training than for American lawyers. And there is definitely more post-bachelor's degree law training in the United States: while U.S. law schools are all, in effect, graduate school programs, other nations often tend to have their professional schooling as part of the undergraduate experience. Finally, board certification of legal specialties is increasingly used in the United States whereas, again, it is found less in other countries.

Board Certification of Lawyers

This is a state bar process of bestowing a law specialty credential based on post-law school work experience and further course work, generally with some testing. It is increasingly used in the United States to market the expertise of some lawyers in numerous fields. Such fields often include Civil Trial and Appellate; Bankruptcy; Consumer and Commercial; Criminal Trial and Appellate; Estate Planning and Probate; Family; Health; Immigration; Juvenile; Labor and Employment; Personal Injury; Real Estate; Tax; and Workers' Compensation. Even after board certification is obtained, it normally requires an ongoing involvement in the specialty area, including annual professional "refreshment" through continuing legal education courses to stay abreast of current trends in the law. The percentage of attorneys who are board-certified is relatively small (perhaps 10% to 15%), although it is rising and may vary greatly depending on the state and the particular specialty. Ordinarily, it is *not* required, although the certification is often touted by specialists who have it and can be a basis for attracting clients.

Masters of Law

The Masters of Law (the LL.M.) is a supplemental degree, after the juris doctorate (J.D.). To practice law in the United States and almost all other countries, only the JD, or its equivalent in that country, is required. Most practitioners do not have an LL.M., and many law schools do not even grant masters in law. The majority of the masters in laws programs are designed to expose foreign legal graduates to the American legal system. Other programs involve specialized studies in areas such as Tax Law, Securities, Banking and Financial Law, Elder Law, Intellectual Property, Environmental Law, Admiralty, and International Law. The most popular of these specialized LL.M.s, and the one that, for a particular field, may actually help graduates' job prospects, is in tax.

Note that the programs for foreign legal graduates to get an LL.M. degree from an accredited American law school are often spurred by foreign lawyers' desire not just to learn but to become eligible to apply for admission to the bar (get a license to practice law) in certain states. Each state has different rules relating to the admission of foreign-educated lawyers. Some states, including Florida, require a JD from an accredited American law school; however, a few states – Alabama, California, New Hampshire, New York, and Virginia – provide that an LL.M. degree from an accredited American law school qualifies a foreign legal graduate to take the bar exam and, if successful, gain admission to that state's bar.

An exception to that is Germany, where a law program (the equivalent of college and law school) takes about eight years (the American "program" is seven years – four for college and three for

---

[2] The passage rate for the bar exam varies from states to state, but average passage rates are about 75%-80%. The state with the lowest passage rate is, consistently, California – at 49% from 2005 through 2011. Florida's pass rate at the same time was about 66.7%.

Those who fail the bar exam get at least one more time (usually more) to take the test again and pass this time. And they usually do succeed, ultimately. Much information about bar admissions and examinations is at http://www.ncbex.org/, the National Conference of Bar Examiners.

law school). After that, the German students take a state-run examination, then serve in a series of traineeships with courts and firms and then complete a second state exam.[3]

Thus, the United Kingdom graduate – with the more traditional (outside of the U.S. and Germany) shorter program - is on average almost five years younger than the German lawyer when entering the legal profession. Two criticisms of German law training are that it is exclusively government-run, focused on educating students for a job – being a judge – that most people will never have, and that it is short on dealing with recent legal developments. In fact, major German firms prefer their lawyers to have an additional law degree (three more years) from a U.S. law school!

C. Employment of, and Numbers of, Lawyers

Lawyers' principal areas of employment are law firms, corporations, government, and academia. We certainly have far more use of lawyers than people long ago probably imagined.

> *"That one hundred and fifty lawyers should do business together ought not to be expected."* Thomas Jefferson

Still, are there more lawyers per capita in the United States than in other developed nations? The numbers depend on how you count or define lawyers. In the United States, we count all members of the state bar.

In many other countries, only trial lawyers - those who represent clients in court - are counted as lawyers. Still, when counting all professionals performing legal services, data from five of the six largest economies in the world (excluding only China) indicate that the United States has the most such professionals per capita, followed by its fellow common law nation, the United Kingdom (63% the U.S. level), Germany then close behind (57% the U.S. level), France far below that (24% the U.S. level), and Japan the lowest by far (at 7% the U.S. level).

D. The Titles for and Roles of Lawyers

What do people call lawyers, besides various curse words(!)? Titles and roles vary from country to country.

In Great Britain and most of Canada, there are solicitors and barristers. Solicitors prepare legal documents, give legal advice, and represent clients in some of the lesser courts. Barristers are the only "lawyers" who can practice before higher courts and administrative agencies.

In Quebec and France, there are three types of lawyers: the avocat, who can practice before the higher courts and give legal advice; the notaire, who can handle real property transactions and estates and can prepare some legal documents; and the juriste (legal counselor), who can give advice and prepare legal documents.

In Germany, a lawyer who litigates is called Rechtsanwalt, and a lawyer who advises clients but does not appear in court is called Rechtsbeistand.

Japan has but one class of lawyers, called bengoshi. "Bengo" means defense, and "Shi" represents a person. A bengoshi delivers, on behalf of a client, an argument or testimony before the courts. The bengoshi, who is licensed, also prepares the paperwork related to various legal proceedings.[4]

---

[3] In October 2000, a new law school – Bucerius Law School (the first private law school in Germany) - opened to 100 students in Hamburg. Its ten-term curriculum focuses on international corporate law. The overall aim has been to reform and redirect the antiquated German, state-run system of legal training. See http://www.law-school.de/home.html?&L=1

[4] The *shihoh-shoshi* is a "judicial scrivener." "Shi-hoh" means the administration of justice, with "Sho" meaning writing, and "Shi" representing a person. The laws for Shihoh shoshi changed in 2005 drastically. Shihoh shoshi

In Italy, the two types of lawyers, similar to the dual British system, are avocati and procuratori. What we call lawyers ultimately matters far less than how they function. For example, although coming from quite distinct systems and traditions, German and American lawyers often function similarly. Lawyers in both Germany and the United States advance partisan positions from first pleadings to final arguments. German litigators suggest legal theories and lines of factual inquiry, superintend and supplement judicial examination of witnesses, urge inferences from fact, discuss and distinguish precedent, interpret statutes, and formulate views of law that further the interests of their clients.

E. Too Many Lawyers Working for Too Narrow a Class of Interests?

In 1978, speaking to lawyers, President Jimmy Carter voiced criticism of the legal profession.[5] He stated that a very high proportion of America's lawyers are working for a small percentage of its citizens.

> *"We have more litigation, but I am not sure that we have more justice. No resources of talent and training in our own society, even including medical care, are more wastefully or unfairly distributed than legal skills. Ninety percent of our lawyers serve 10 percent of our people. We are over-lawyered and under-represented."*
>
> Jimmy Carter, Remarks at 100th Anniversary Banquet of the Los Angeles County Bar Ass'n, May 4, 1978, in Public Papers of the Presidents: Jimmy Carter, 1978, at 1:834, 836 (1979).

Is that a criticism of law, lawyers, or simply the marketplace (the labor economy)? Lawyers were offended, but where lawyers work tends to reflect which people and institutions (possible clients) have the money and the need for legal services. Change the marketplace incentives, and then where and for whom lawyers work should change.[6]

Topical Lecture: Legal Fees
Introduction to Topical Lecture:
The basis for attorney fees should be disclosed to clients at the outset of an attorney-client relationship. Fee arrangements include (1) the set fee (sometimes arising through a competitive bids process), (2) the contingency fee (allegedly a reason for American litigiousness), and, (3) still the most common fee, one based on an hourly rate.

F. Fees

Legal ethics and consumer protection concerns generally require professional clarity about legal fees. For example, the fee arrangement should be put in writing & explained in-depth - e.g., for a client to sign (a requirement in Florida and in many other states).

---

now can attend a summary court on behalf of a client for the following duties: to plead cases, deal with arbitration, and enter into out-of-court settlements (source: the Japan Federation of Shiho-shoshi Lawyer's Association). So, a shihoh-shoshi is a person who prepares the documents and/or registrations to present to courts, prosecutors, and the central or regional affairs bureau on behalf of a client.

[5] Carter was among the minority of Presidents who were not lawyers. In chronological order, these are the U.S. Presidents who were lawyers: John Adams, Thomas Jefferson, James Madison, James Monroe, John Quincy Adams, Martin Van Buren, John Tyler, James K. Polk, Millard Fillmore, Franklin Pierce, James Buchanan, Abraham Lincoln, Andrew Johnson, Rutherford B. Hayes, Chester Alan Arthur, Grover Cleveland, Benjamin Harrison, William McKinley, William Howard Taft, Woodrow Wilson, Calvin Coolidge, Franklin Delano Roosevelt, Richard M. Nixon, Gerald R. Ford, William Jefferson Clinton, and Barack H. Obama – 26 of the 43 men who have held the office.

[6] An amusing, but unsettling book by a former lawyer is: Cameron Stracher, DOUBLE BILLING: A YOUNG LAWYER'S TALE OF GREED, SEX, LIES, AND THE PURSUIT OF A SWIVEL CHAIR (1998).

1. Hourly Fees

As with most professionals, a lawyer's time is his/her "stock in trade" - the ticker is running all the time. It has long been complained that some lawyers thus feign work or inflate their hours.

> "A sergeant of the laws . . . Discreet he was and of great reverence . . . Nowher so bisy a man as he ther was: And yet he seemed bisier than he was."   Geoffrey Chaucer (1340?-1400).

A common complaint, throughout the ages, has been that lawyers charge for everything.

> "It is the trade of lawyers to question everything, yield nothing, and to talk by the hour."
> Thomas Jefferson
>
> "A shell for thee - And a shell for thee - But the oyster is the lawyer's fee."
> Thomas Lewis Ingram
>
> Prospective Client: What's your least expensive fee?
> Lawyer: $300 for three questions
> Isn't that a lot of money for just three questions?
> Lawyer: Yes. What's your third question?!
>
> A lawyer's bill for services rendered: To my client for crossing the street to greet you, and, on discovering that it was not you, crossing the street again. Fifty Dollars ($50.00).

2. Who Pays?

Ordinarily, unless a statute is clearly on point, or a claim or defense was outrageously wrong, the parties pay their own attorney's fees. So it is still somewhat unusual that a loser must pay the winner's attorney's fees. But in Britain and many other countries the loser customarily must pay the winner's attorney's fees. (That is another discouragement of "risky" litigation.)

3. A Lawyer's Duty to Disclose Information About Fees

Lawyers have an ethical duty, often also found explicitly in court rules, to disclose fully, at the start of the attorney-client relationship, the basis for their charges and fees. In Florida, for example, the disclosure must be in writing, with the client's signed approval.

> **Retainers**
> Retainers may merely assure a client that if work is needed, the firm or lawyer will be available. They may be used to neutralize an attorney - leave him unavailable to work for the opposition. But a retainer is usually just advance payment; it, or part thereof, should be returned to the client for any unused "lawyer's time." **See generally pg. 16; Emerson BL**

4. Set Fees

Alternatives (e.g., the set fee) to the hourly fee arrangement started to grow quickly in the late 1980s. Studies show that these alternatives continue to be increasingly used. However, even now, the alternatives to hourly fees are used for less than a third of all civil matters.

Set Fees are fees per a particular service - per "job." Set fees are increasingly popular with large corporations where specifications are set forth and legal service providers make bids.

Set fees are a type of cost-management procedure. Clients can comparison-shop, particularly for "shelf items" - standard types of legal work, such as handling collection cases, bringing or defending commonplace lawsuits, drafting contracts, preparing wills, forming a corporation, partnership, limited liability company, or other business entity, and conducting real estate transactions.

Legal Service Plans often have set-fee arrangements. Such plans are often union plans, association plans (e.g., through the American Association of Retired Persons (AARP)), and individually-purchased legal "insurance."

It has been difficult, even for in-house general counsel perpetually under pressure to trim and better manage expenses, to move away from the familiar billable-hour system and a value-based billing. Traditionally, neither companies nor law firms could accurately predict what a complex piece of legal work would cost. But increased use of sophisticated "matter-management" software programs helps counter this problem. Studies show the percentage of large companies occasionally using fixed fees rose from 54% in 2002 to 62% in 2007 to even higher since.

5. Contingency Fees

> A Sad Example of Personal Injuries and Lawsuit Costs
>
> Imagine that a lawyer's ad on the back of a coupon book - says, "PERSONAL INJURY LAWYER — NO FEE UNLESS YOU WIN!"
>
> Sadly, Veronica Victim is smacked by a copy of that book as it falls from the coupon book company's delivery vehicle. The ad is imprinted on Veronica's face. She looks in her mirror, sees the ad, deciphers it, and calls the lawyer, who represents Victim against the company.
>
> To add insult to her injuries, the company successfully defends Veronica's case. A few weeks later, she gets a bill for several thousands of dollars, none of which is to pay for the lawyer's time or effort. Is that permitted, given the advertisement? Yes, even if a lawyer states that his/her fee is contingent upon winning, the client may still be responsible for the expenses that the lawyer incurred. Who is responsible for these expenses (photocopying, travel costs, filing fees, expert witness fees, telephone charges, etc.) is covered in the written fee arrangement.
>
> A client should always read carefully his/her lawyer-client fee arrangement and clarify with the lawyer any remaining questions. Furthermore, the lawyer has an ethical duty to ensure that these matters are discussed and pertinent information is imparted to the client at the outset of the attorney-client relationship.

A contingency fee is only charged if the case is won. The amount then charged is a percentage (e.g., 25%, 33%, 40%) of the plaintiff's monetary recovery.

Many states impose limits on contingency fees in malpractice cases or workers' compensation cases. Some states limit contingent fee rates more generally, such as in personal injury cases. For example, New Jersey Court Rule 1:21-7(c) sets a schedule of maximum limits on the contingency fees that attorneys can collect in tort litigation: (1) 33% on the first $250,000 recovered for the client; (2) 25% on the next $250,000 recovered; (3) 20% on the next $500,000 recovered; and (4) on all amounts recovered above a million dollars, a reasonable fee in accordance with other rules requiring the lawyer to apply to the court.

A good contingency-fee practice often followed by lawyers is to charge the client a contingency fee only on that portion of the ultimate monetary recovery which is above the amount the defendant offered the plaintiff before the lawyer got involved. The premise of this fee arrangement is that lawyers should only be rewarded for the additional amount their efforts brought to the client.

Unless otherwise provided, the losing party still owes costs besides the attorney's fee - e.g., experts' charges, photocopying, travel reimbursement, filing fees, telephone bills, court reporters' charges, etc.

The two most basic criticisms of contingency fees are: (1) That they encourage too many lawsuits;[7] (2) That sometimes lawyers charge even when they were taking no real risks.[8] Reform proposals include limits on the amount of contingency fees, at least considering the hours worked. Some lawyers sometimes do that on their own. E.g., if a client already has an offer, then a lawyer that he/she hires may only take a contingency fee for the amount the client receives above that offer.

An argument favoring contingency fees is that they allow lower and middle class people to bring suit and to have the more knowledgeable person, the lawyer, bear the risk.

International Comparison re: contingency fees

The vast majority of countries still do not permit contingency fees. But a number of countries do have forms of contingency fees (in which plaintiffs only pay legal fees to their lawyer if the plaintiffs themselves win money. For example, all Canadian provinces (Ontario only for class actions) permit contingency fees, including – for some provinces – outright percentage-of-recovery fees.

In England and Wales, ordinarily the loser pays the winning side's attorney fees, and that still applies to cases where a losing plaintiff had something similar to a contingency fee arrangement (what the British call a *conditional fee* arrangement - more commonly called "no win, no fee"). For a winning plaintiff with a "no win, no fee" agreement, the lawyer bills the loser not just for his/her regular fees, but also charges the loser a "success fee." The latter is based on a percentage of the damages won for the client, but it is to be no more than 100% (and usually far less than that – say 25-50%) of the lawyer's regular fee. Typically, the losing defendant also must pay the plaintiff's "disbursements," such as court costs and medical report fees.

Other nations in which lawyers are permitted to represent clients on a "speculative basis," whereby the lawyer's failure to meet the goal (victory in the lawsuit) means the plaintiff pays no fee to the lawyer, include: (1) the entire British Isles (England, Wales, the Irish Republic, Northern Ireland, and Scotland), (2) the common law nations of Australia and New Zealand, and (3) several Civil Law countries.

Here is more concerning those Civil Law countries:

a. While few Japanese auto accident cases go to trial, Japan sees its bengoshi (lawyers) normally charge for trying such cases on a "no win, no fee" basis;

b. Among the other Civil Law nations, sometimes lawyers may charge fees conditional on victory; they actually even allow some sort of percentage-of-recovery payment to victorious plaintiffs' attorneys:

c. In France, major Paris law firms often use contingency fees, with fees based in part on results achieved.

d. The Dominican Republic permits percentage fees (*cuota litis*) up to 30% of the plaintiff's recovery.

e. Italy allows supplementary fees (*palamario*) - percentage-of-recovery payments to the plaintiff's attorney.

---

[7] However, studies indicate that contingency fee lawyers turn down at least as many cases as they accept, usually because potential clients do not appear to have a basis for their case. Herbert M. Kritzer, *Contingency Fee Lawyers as Gatekeepers in the Civil Justice System,* in JUDICIAL POLITICS: READINGS FROM JUDICATURE (ed. Elliot E. Slotnick, 2005), at 157-165.

[8] The most prominent academic advocate of contingency fees has examined the frequently voiced criticisms. He determines them to be factually unsound. Herbert M. Kritzer, *Seven Dogged Myths Concerning Contingency Fees,* 80 WASHINGTON U. LAW Q. 739 (2002) (disputing the following assertions – (1) Contingency fees are peculiarly American, (2) There is in reality little risk to the attorneys in most contingency fee cases because most cases result in some recovery for the client, (3) The use of modern advertising techniques by contingency fee lawyers has produced a flood of clients seeking compensation, (4) Contingency fee lawyers accept most cases that potential clients bring to them, (5) Contingency fee lawyers charge a "standard" fee of one-third of the recovery, (6) Lawyers routinely obtain windfalls from contingency fee cases, and (7) The interests of contingency fee lawyers and their clients are routinely in conflict).

> f. Luxembourg and Portugal permit a percentage-of-recovery payment to winning plaintiffs' lawyers.
> g. Brazil allows fees that include a contingency/percentage element up to 20% of any award.

a. When Contingency Fees Are Rare or Outright Prohibited

Contingency fees are quite rare, even in America, in most corporate or other business activities. Contingency fees are not allowed, even in the United States, in cases of family law (e.g., divorce) or in criminal law.

> Suppose that an Internet Pop-Up Ad says, "ACCUSED OF A CRIME? I CAN HANDLE IT! $2,500 FLAT FEE, BUT YOU PAY ZIP IF WE DON'T WIN!" (EXCLUSION: OFFER DOES NOT APPLY TO ANY FIRST-DEGREE FELONY CHARGES.) Because this proposed contingency-fee arrangement concerns criminal cases, it is unethical. Even to advertise such a fee, let alone to charge it, violates the lawyers' Model Rules of Professional Conduct adopted in almost all states, including Florida. The offending attorney could be disbarred or otherwise punished.

b. Reform Based on Early Settlements

Many reforms of contingency fee practices have been proposed, including an early settlement approach: say, in the first 60 days after a lawyer has been hired – and notice of that fact is given to the defendant – no contingency fee could be charged (just an hourly rate worth, say, no more than 10% of the ultimate recovery). After the 60 days' lapse, a customary contingency fee could, instead of the hourly rate, be charged. This approach, whether voluntarily undertaken or required by a state statute, would, the reformers contend, induce many defendants (and insurers) to settle early, when parties might be more receptive and their lawyers could not yet take as large a chunk of the recovery.

6. *Pro Bono*

Most lawyers engage in some *pro bono* work, for which the lawyer receives no pay from the client. *Pro bono* is short for *pro bono publico*, which is Latin meaning, "for the public good." The clients may be individuals who cannot afford to hire a lawyer, or they may be nonprofit organizations in need of counseling or other legal assistance.

American Bar Association (ABA) Model Rule of Ethics 6.1 calls for lawyers to contribute at least fifty hours of pro bono service annually. Some state bar associations, however, recommend fewer hours. For example, the New York State Bar Association recommends twenty hours of pro bono service per year. The Florida Rules of Professional Conduct, at Rule 4-6.1(b), are typical:

> "The professional responsibility to provide pro bono legal services as established under this rule is aspirational rather than mandatory in nature. The failure to fulfill one's professional responsibility under this rule will not subject a lawyer to discipline. The professional responsibility to provide pro bono legal service to the poor may be discharged by:
> (1) annually providing at least 20 hours of pro bono legal service to the poor; or
> (2) making an annual contribution of at least $350 to a legal aid organization."

G. Financing of Lawsuits

As legal costs have soared, a growing number of states have relaxed the centuries-old, common law ban on outsiders (non-lawyers, non-parties) investing in lawsuits (financing the costs in return for a percentage of the winnings, if there is a victory). Now only a few states ban it entirely.

<u>End of Topical Lecture: Legal Fees</u>

H. "Mere" Businesspersons vs. Professionals

1. Legal Minimums versus Ethical Standards

Is the legal minimum really a sufficient ethical minimum? It has been argued that considering ethics is an "ivory tower" approach, that hindering business competitiveness is foolhardy, or even that profitability and ethics are antipodal concepts. Yet considering ethics can be pragmatic in the long term. For example, the United States Federal Organizational Sentencing Guidelines offer businesses compelling reasons to formalize ethics training. By instituting a code of conduct and a compliance program that reduces the likelihood of criminal conduct, a corporation reduces the possible penalty in the event of a corporate crime.

2. The Lawyer

A professional, such as a lawyer, should have goals beyond just making money. These ethical duties go beyond just legal requirements. The professional's first priority is to the client.

But what is the reality of the legal marketplace? The market may not reflect the so-called ethics, the supposed duties. Some lawyers (and others) do not rise to these values.

That is why it is especially important to have rules for lawyer-to-client business transactions, especially contracts.

Compare the law with the other ancient professions: medicine, the ministry, and teaching. Have the techniques changed much? Is there an adversarial method? The problems of ethics in law and the legal system are not simply the problems of lawyers, but also of their clients. Pathological behavior is not unique to lawyers.

Are clients themselves partly to blame for the wrongful behavior of their overreaching lawyers?

3. The Businessperson

What if one is not a professional, but "merely" a businessperson? Is Business Competition the same as War? In 1958, in the Harvard Business Review, Theodore Levitt, warned against social responsibility in the Business Context. He wrote: "[b]usiness must fight as if it were at war. And, like a good war, it should be fought gallantly, daringly, and above all not morally."

But does not even the horror of war operate under rules of law and the concepts of a "just" versus an "unjust" war? And should not business operate within some moral boundaries in addition to legal ones? *See* MICHAEL WALZER, JUST AND UNJUST WARS (1992).

Are we not expecting enough from the client?

> YOUTUBE – two videos – **lawyer & potential business client 3mins35secs.wmv**
> (http://www.youtube.com/watch?v=-ZZyrvzWrsw&feature=related) and
> **lawyer_potentialbusinesspostvid_17mins57secs.wmv**
> (http://www.youtube.com/watch?v=1JrPoIZF8Tg) – **both at RobertWEmerson**

The Relationship Between a Lawyer's Ethics and a Client's Expectations and Ethics

The problem of ethics in law and the legal system are not simply the problems of lawyers, but also of their clients. Pathological behavior is not unique to clients.

Assuming that two attorneys have comparable educations, experience and expertise, which attorney would you hire? (1) The First Attorney, who said, "I could do all sorts of things for you, but I won't, because those things would be wrong." OR (2) The Second Attorney, who said, "I can do all sorts of things to help you - who gives a darn whether they're unethical?! I'll do 'em and I'll be effective!" (Note how different are the concepts that each attorney has about their role as an attorney!)

> When we criticize professionals, it's a two-way street. We expect professionals to maintain certain standards, but it is easier for them to maintain certain standards if their clients/patients agree- if the client understands that he/she should <u>not</u> ask or expect a lawyer to do something unethical, or to do <u>whatever it takes</u>.
>
> Lawyers' ethics and behavior do <u>not</u> occur in a vacuum. A lot of us, in an individual setting, want something different than what we say we want for society as a whole. But, do people want from their lawyer behavior they deplore generally in other lawyers?
>
> ### Comparison to Attitudes Toward Congress
>
> Most people view Congress very poorly, but representatives tend to be re-elected easily. What we feel on a macro level may not match our behavior on a micro level.
>
> ### Comparison to Economics' Thrift-Paradox
>
> For people to advance economically, they may have to behave differently than others. Again, micro behaviors must differ from macro.
>
> ### Gamesmanship
>
> When evaluating the effectiveness and morality of Gamesmanship, does it matter whether it is in civil law as opposed to criminal law? Surveys show the vast majority of people think criminal defense attorneys should not use so-called technicalities to help acquit a client if that client is in fact guilty. But when we turn to civil law, whether small-claims court squabbles or grand disputes between large multi-million dollar businesses, usually far more people see the role of the attorney in a gray area. Yes, justice is an issue, but people also recognize a Gamesmanship Theory: Hire the best lawyer and whoever fights the best - you may win even though your case is not that good.
>
> How easy is it for your lawyer (or another professional you hire) to skirt the edges of propriety toward others, but then do no such thing towards you?

Professor Grace M. Giesel writes in this area of attorney-client relations. She notes that many court opinions state that attorneys are the agents of their clients. Traditional agency law allows principals to be responsible for actually and apparently authorized acts of an agent. Thus, one would expect courts to apply traditional agency bases of principal liability and hold client principals responsible for the authorized acts of agent attorneys. However, some judges have shied away from issuing such a holding, whether in court cases, in overseeing settlements, or concerning attorney-client privilege and the waiver thereof. For instance, while holding lawyers responsible for torts such as abuse of process, some courts refuse to recognize traditional agency bases of principal liability, and thus fail to hold responsible the lawyer's client (the principal). In these situations – cases, settlements, and the attorney-client privilege - the courts deviate from traditional law to protect the client principal from liability that might otherwise occur as a result of the agency relationship. Courts appear troubled by viewing the relationship of lawyers and clients as a run-of-the-mill agency relationship, one in which a client would be responsible for his/her attorney's actions. But are such paternalistic, additional protections for clients necessary, given how empowered clients already are? Although the lawyer-client relationship is a unique agency relationship, it need not require special rules mandating better treatment of the client-principal than of other principals. That is at least the case, Prof. Giesel or others would argue, when a user of legal services is sophisticated about the services attorneys provide and/or is intimately involved in making decisions about the legal representation.[9]

4. Lawyers: Procrastination, Preparation, and Professionalism

a. A Reason for Procrastination –
The lawyer's trying not to have too many hours of work until necessary.

---

[9] Grace M. Giesel, Client Responsibility for Lawyer Conduct: Examining the Agency Nature of the Lawyer-Client Relationship, 86 NEBRASKA L. REV. 346 (2007).

b. A NEED FOR PREPARATION MORE THAN INNATE SKILLS –
Former Supreme Court Justice (and world-class lawyer) Abe Fortas vs. A Government Lawyer at the U.S. Court of Customs and Patent Appeals (now the U.S. Court of Appeals for the Federal Circuit) See Robert W. Emerson, *Editor's Corner: Preparation, Procrastination, Production, and Perfection*, 52 AM. BUS. L.J. *v* (Winter 2015).

> "Unauthorized practice of law" is practice of law by a person, typically a nonlawyer, not licensed or admitted to practice law in a particular jurisdiction. BLACK'S LAW DICTIONARY 1362 (10th ed. 2014).

c. Allegedly Unethical Behavior - Does it "Smell?"

Being a "professional" means more than just competence. It requires ethics and integrity. Without specific examples or rules, this standard can be rather broad and vague. Moreover, surveys by industry and by academics have proven unscientific, with the documenting of actual behavior being quite expensive and difficult. Often researchers, reporters, and regulators get anecdotes, not statistics. Evidence seems to indicate that, for instance, banks, utilities, and drug companies operate in fairly ethical industries. Even if this is true, this may be just because they are so strongly regulated. In the international sphere, surveys seem to indicate businesses in the U.S., Canada, Britain, Switzerland, and Germany are - on average - upholding high ethical standards as compared to other nation's businesses. Also, some research has shown that lawyers in large corporate firms are actually more honest than those in smaller private firms. This is likely because of the strong hierarchical structure of the large firms.

> Professions have at least four key elements: (1) an accepted body of knowledge, (2) a system for certifying that individuals have mastered that body of knowledge before they are permitted to practice, (3) a commitment to the public good, and (4) an enforceable code of ethics.
> Professions thus are oriented toward practice and focused on client needs.

5. Duties of Lawyers

There are legal duties for businesses, but often unclear ethical duties. A leading ethicist, Michael Hoffman of Bentley College, poses six basic questions in business ethics training classes intended to help managers evaluate an action: (a) Is it right? (b) Is it fair? (c) Who gets hurt? (d) Would you want to read about it in the newspaper? (e) What would you tell your child to do?

a. Lawyers: Professionals and "Friends"
Businessperson's Duties Versus Duties of Professionals:
YOUTUBE – two videos - **Car_Repair_Fiasco50secs.wmv and Car_Repair_Fiasco POST VIDEO discussion6mins32secs.wmv – both at RobertWEmerson** (The links are http://www.youtube.com/watch?v=NTl65jNRzKw and http://www.youtube.com/watch?v=AHC6kwPZHuY, respectively).

Professor Charles Fried's analogy of lawyers to friends is limited to the standard view of lawyers zealously pursuing clients' interests within the law's formal limits. Fried conceived of the lawyer as a "limited purpose friend."[10] Fried continued with the analogy, "A lawyer is a friend in regard to the legal system... [L]ike a friend [t]he [lawyer] acts in your interests, not his own; or rather he adopts your interests as his own." *Id.* While not referring to Aristotle, Prof. Fried tapped into the Western

---

[10] Charles Fried, *The Lawyer as Friend: The Moral Foundations of the Lawyer-Client Relationship*, 85 Yale Law Journal 1060, 1071 (1976).

thinking on friendship originating from Aristotle's definition that a friend is one who selflessly acts for another.[11]

b. Not a Question of Popularity

But the lawyer's job is not to be popular but to be proficient and principled – that is, professional. Consider the story of the little bird and the pile of poop into which the fowl fell:

The Story of the Little Lone Loon Flying South

A little bird was flying south for the winter. It was so cold the bird froze and fell to the ground into a large field. While he was lying there, a cow came by and dropped some dung on him.

As the frozen bird lay there in the pile of cow dung, he began to realize how warm he was. The dung was actually thawing him out! He lay there all warm and happy, and soon began to sing for joy.

A passing cat . . . .

The three morals of the story

(1) Not everyone who . . . is your enemy.

(2) Not everyone who . . . is your friend.

(3) And when you're in deep doo-doo, . . .

> *We should hire lawyers for their perception and for their honesty, not necessarily to tell you what you want to hear (and in a corporate sphere- watch what you say even to the corporate attorney – he/she is not, in most cases, YOUR attorney).*

c. Business Transactions, Especially Contracts, Between Lawyers and Clients

These transactions are subject to special rules because of the fiduciary nature of the attorney-client relationship and the supposed dominant powers of persuasion of attorneys. As one court opined: "Attorneys wear different hats when they perform legal services on behalf of their clients and when they conduct business with them. As to the latter, the law presumes the hat they wear is a black one."[12]

The constraints on business transactions with clients take two forms. First, the Rules of Professional Conduct contains specific requirements for any such transaction. Second, the law of contracts supplements the professional conduct standards by applying a presumption of undue influence to any contract between attorney and client other than the initial fee agreement.[13]

I. Effectiveness of Counsel

THE *CORPUS DELICTI* (BODY OF HARM) CLOSING ARGUMENT

Scene: A courtroom where a person is on trial for murder. There is strong circumstantial evidence indicating guilt; however, there is no corpse (no body was recovered).

---

[11] Kieran Tranter and Lillian Corbin, Lawyers, Clients and Friends: A Case Study of the Vexed Nature of Friendship and Lawyering 2, at http://www98.griffith.edu.au/dspace/bitstream/handle/10072/23214/52615_1.pdf;jsessionid=B4229D5625CC751BED4DB94E0E5359FB?sequence=1 (quoting Aristotle, The Nichomachean Ethics, Book 9, 1169a2-b11 (translation by J.A.K. Thomson, revised trans. H. Tredennick, Harmondsworth, Penguin, 1976)).
[12] *Mayhew v. Benninghoff*, 62 Cal. Rptr. 2d 27 (Cal. App. 1997).
[13] Grace M Giesel, *Business Transactions with Clients*, Bar Briefs, May 2006, at 1, Univ. of Louisville Legal Studies Research Paper Series Paper No. 2008-31.

Consider the Ethics and Ineffectiveness of the Argument that there was no murder

- "Members of the jury, I have some astounding news to tell you!" It is about the alleged victim.

- That's why we have a jury

- Can't introduce evidence in argument

- Have to have some basis for the argument

- What are the ethics of making such an argument?

- Maybe the argument was so bad—so nonsensical—the convicted defendant argues, "it ruined my case; no competent lawyer would have made such an argument."

Still, this was a Matlock Episode! Here is an email letter from a student one semester after I told the story: "The example you used in class about not being able to prove there was a body and the lawyer saying at the count of five the ex-girlfriend would walk in the door--- that was used for an episode of the wonderful law drama of Matlock. However, minus the behavior of that one juror, or Matlock would have lost."

J. Bar Exam *and* Character Checks

Qualifying for professional service is a continuing process - whether in law, medicine, accounting, or other professions - even after one is admitted and licensed. So, for example, one of the worst things a person can do is to lie on the bar application.[14] That can come back to haunt the lawyer even years later; it is far worse, usually, than just losing cases, charging a lot of money (more than usual) to clients, or other problems with one's legal practice. So lawyers must not only be competent (graduate from an accredited law school and pass the bar exam), but also be of good character.

What, then, is "lack of character" or other evidence of unfitness to practice law?

DENYING A RACIST ADMISSION TO THE ILLINOIS BAR –
The Case of a White Power Leader, Matthew Hale
In 1998, Matthew Hale graduated from Southern Illinois University law school, an accredited law school, and he passed the bar exam. He also was hired by a Champaign, Illinois law firm that says it knew nothing about Hale's work as head of the World Church of the Creator, a "white power" organization.

---

[14] Of course, another extremely bad act is to try to cheat, especially on the bar exam. For example, in California a bar applicant, who had already failed the bar exam once, enlisted the help of his wife, a licensed California attorney. She took the bar exam while pretending to be the applicant. There were several problems: (1) most important, the immorality of her action; (2) the foolishness of her behavior, in that she – once again – did very well on the exam (thus bringing her exam into focus, and causing the authorities to marvel at how much better the applicant apparently had done the second time); and (3) the tremendous blind faith in remaining anonymous, when this "man" actually had taken a bar exam while seven months' pregnant. Once uncovered, the plotters lost everything: she was disbarred, he never became a lawyer, and – to top it all off – they got a divorce.

Every state bar (including Illinois') requires law license applicants (1) to demonstrate proficiency in the law on a written bar examination, and (2) to pass a character and fitness exam by appearing before a judge or attorney (usually in a committee) working for the state Supreme Court. Typically, the committee looks for problems: dishonesty, criminal activity, academic misconduct, or financial irresponsibility.

Matthew Hale had succeeded in satisfying the first hurdle (the bar exam), but not the second (the character/fitness to practice law test). The Committee on Character and Fitness that the Illinois Supreme Court appointed found Hale unfit to practice law, as Hale publicly advocated white supremacy and led an organization dedicated to racism and anti-Semitism.

All but 25 of more than 3,000 applicants in 1998 were approved at the initial stage. Hale was not, and then a three-member inquiry panel voted 2-1 in December 1998 not to give him a license. (Meantime, in November 1998, the Champaign law firm fired Hale because he had not obtained a license.)

"The balance of values . . . leaves Matthew Hale free, as the First Amendment allows, to incite as much racial hatred as he desires and to attempt to carry out his life's mission of depriving those he dislikes of their legal rights," panel members wrote. "But in our view he cannot do this as an officer of the court."   On June 30, 1999, the full Character and Fitness Committee voted to deny Hale's admission. Illinois officials said the last case similar to Hale's was in the late 1950s, when a law student refused to take an anti-Communist loyalty oath, and was denied bar admission. In re Anastaplo, 121 N.E. 2d 826, cert. denied, 348 U.S. 946 (1954); and 163 N.E. 2d 429, aff'd, 366 U.S. 82 (1959). The U.S. Supreme Court last considered a similar case in 1971, when two applicants for law licenses in other states would not reveal their political beliefs. The court ruled in their favor.

On July 2, 1999, one of Hale's former church members, Ben Smith, went on a shooting spree that targeted minorities. Smith killed two people and injured several others before committing suicide. Hale has been sued by one of the injured persons. (Smith had in his car World Church of the Creator racist tracts.) And Hale mourned Smith as a martyr. Certainly this tragic turn-of-events, and Hale's reaction to it, could not have helped Hale's appeal.

On November 17, 1999, in In re Matter of Matthew F. Hale, 723 N.E. 2d 206, the Illinois Supreme Court upheld the Character and Fitness Committee's findings and denied Hale's bar admission. Illinois Supreme Court Associate Justice James D. Heiple dissented from the majority's refusal to hear the case:

"The crux of the Committee's decision to deny [Hale's] application to practice law is [his] open advocacy of racially obnoxious beliefs. The Hearing Panel found that [Hale]'s 'publicly displayed views are diametrically opposed to the letter and spirit of the Rules of Professional Conduct.' The Inquiry Panel found that, in regulating [attorney] conduct, certain 'fundamental truths' of equality and nondiscrimination 'must be preferred over the values found in the First Amendment.' [Hale] contends that the Committee's use of his expressed views to justify the denial of his [bar] admission violates his constitutional rights to free speech. That constitutional question deserves [this court's] explicit, reasoned resolution . . . . [Is it] appropriate for the Committee to … assess an applicant's character and fitness on speculative predictions of future actionable misconduct. If all of petitioner's statements identified by the Committee had been made after obtaining a license to practice law, would he then be subject to disbarment? [I]s there one standard for admission to practice and a different standard for continuing to practice?"

On June 26, 2000, the U.S. Supreme Court denied Hale's petition for a writ of certiorari. *Hale v. Committee on Character and Fitness of the Illinois Bar*, 530 U.S. 1261.

Hale claimed - "If you are a racist, as am I, then they're saying you don't have the right to say what you believe and be a lawyer. That's a denial of free speech." The Committee responded by stating that, "Hale cannot wrap himself in the First Amendment and avoid any inquiry into his character and

> fitness. He is absolutely entitled to hold these beliefs, but at the same time the public and the bar are entitled to be treated fairly and decently by attorneys."
> Some commentators argue that denying Hale the opportunity to practice law . . . could lead to a "slippery slope" allowing prejudice into the licensing of professionals. The actual rationale for denying Hale a law license is:
> a. Hale opposes the Bill of Rights as applied to the States through the 13th, 14th and 15th amendments. Therefore, he cannot, in good faith, swear to support and uphold the US Constitution.
> b. Hale's petition for admission omitted reference to his felony conviction. Although the conviction was reversed on appeal, the fact of the conviction was an application requirement. Hale's failure to disclose the conviction was not an oversight. His own website bragged about it before he applied to the Bar.
>
> *Drawing a Line – Finding a Balance*
> Can Matthew Hale dedicate his life to hatred and be an officer of the court? The license to practice law is not a constitutional right, but, one could argue, simply a privilege that should be granted solely to those possessing the highest ethical standards. Licensing officials need to set the bar high!
>
> **Update**
> Hale's First Amendment problems with the Committee are now moot. In April 2004, Hale was convicted of three counts of obstruction of justice and one count of soliciting the murder of a federal judge. He is serving a 40-year sentence at the Supermax federal prison in Florence, Colorado.

Some experts predict many changes in the coming decade for the licensing and admission of lawyers, with a system of specialty examination and licensing. For example, lawyers practicing in certain fields may no longer simply opt to seek certification through classes and examinations (which they may then market as evidence of their greater skills); instead, they may have to take tests to prove their fitness for particular specialties.

Enforcement of professional ethics will likely become more nationalized - a more uniform system of professional regulation and a greater degree of negotiation among the states and federal government concerning the types of regulation that are appropriate. Redefinition of the practice of law will result in a decrease in some forms of licensing. Since the 1960s, numerous academics, judges, and even lawyers have noted, for example, that some legal practice specialties, such as auto accident work, entail skill sets that might be met by non-lawyer "representatives" and a more protective regulatory framework. The lawyers could use their much greater training and abilities in more complex work where lawyering work is essential.

Greater recognition of the interrelationship between legal and non-legal work has already occurred in Europe and other parts of the world and probably will come, ultimately, to the American legal profession. That means more negotiation among the professions (accounting, law, real estate, insurance, etc.) concerning who may provide services tangential to law.

K. Lawyers' Roles

Lawyers are (1) advocates, (2) counselors, (3) guild members, and (4) officers of the court. They thus often have many hats to wear.

1. Advocate

As advocates, attorneys must zealously represent the client. That might even be to the point of obfuscation![15] The same problem occurs elsewhere. E.g., Anthony Trollope (1815-1882), in Orley

---

[15] Joke: Lawyer to Prospective New Client – "Just explain things clearly – I'll confuse them later [for the judge or jury]."

Farm, wrote, "No amount of eloquence will make an English lawyer think that loyalty to truth should come before loyalty to his client."

Nearly all lawyers' behavior is directly or indirectly fueled by clients' desires or needs, as the lawyers perceive those needs. But extreme advocacy leaves lawyers as simply "hired guns" whose behavior may violate ethical, if not legal, norms.

One example of an ethical limit is the rule restricting attorneys' contact with laypersons. Ordinarily, lawyers are not permitted to contact directly those people who are already represented by an attorney. Instead, the legal ethics rules require that a lawyer in such cases must deal with the other attorneys (*not* directly with other parties). In February 2002, the American Bar Association (ABA) removed language in Model Rule of Professional Conduct 4.2, which some companies had used to keep outside lawyers from speaking with many current employees. In effect, the ABA restricted the above rule – barring lawyers from contacting represented laypersons – so that fewer corporate employees are insulated from outside lawyers' contacts. (Fewer employees are deemed "off-limits" because they have a corporate lawyer who represents them) This new approach comports with the existing approach toward corporate attorney-client privilege.

2. Counselor

As counselors, lawyers advise clients and practice "preventative law": trying to keep, or get, a client out of trouble. Most professional dictates for American lawyers tend to revolve around the attorney's role as a counselor and/or advocate, not as someone working for systemic improvement. For example, in 1994 the American Bar Association's Commission on Partnership Programs prepared, "My Declaration of Commitment to Clients." The declaration pledges to every client: (1) courtesy, respect, competence, independent professional judgment, and diligence, in accordance with the highest standards of the profession; (2) reasonable fees; (3) prompt return of telephone calls; (4) copies of important papers and otherwise keeping clients informed; (5) respecting a client's case objectives, as permitted by law and the rules of professional conduct, including whether to settle; (6) working with others to make the legal system more accessible and responsive [the only commitment oriented toward the system as a whole]; (7) preserving confidential information disclosed during the lawyer-client relationship; and (8) maintaining the highest degree of ethical conduct in accordance with the Model Rules of Professional Conduct. Of course, an indirect benefit of almost all lawyers' following this Declaration might be an improved public image for the legal profession. But the focus is *micro*, not *macro* (better dealings with individuals, not overall reforms).

Almost all the commitments above (1 to 8) are oriented toward good counseling. Only one is about the system as a whole (which is most related to the "officer of the court" role than other roles).

3. Guild Member

As guild members, lawyers have duties related to their position as a part of a profession. They have duties to each other and to the profession - as colleagues, to uphold the profession. This notion goes back to the Middle Ages (e.g., guilds of weavers, candle makers, haberdashers, and fishmongers). And people worried about lawyers' behavior raise the fear that, as in the Middle Ages, these guilds (here, of lawyers) will, in upholding certain standards, operate anti-competitively (and thus force upon clients an increase in fees and other costs).[16]

But the guild model also seems to have induced many lawyers, or at least their bar authorities, to review carefully the behavior of their fellow professionals. In almost any state, there are far more disbarments, suspensions, or censures - often because of ethics (not just law) - than there are actual criminal violations (lawyers going to jail). So the guild seems to go after some ethical miscreants who

---

[16] In MEDIEVAL CALLINGS (edited by Jacques LeGoff & translated by Lydia G. Cochrane, 1990), eleven medievalists present essays considering the major social and professional groups – the callings – of the Middle Ages.

otherwise would have escaped any judgment (who were not going to be punished outside of their roles as professionals).

Commentators believe that attorney disciplinary systems will become more transparent, particularly with respect to policy-making in the disciplinary process and enforcement. Opening the process will enhance respect for the rules and improve enforcement techniques. Local bar associations will reevaluate the functions they perform and acknowledge the multiplicity, and occasional inconsistency, of the goals they seek to achieve; they may then rely more on other regulators to restrain lawyer misconduct. Instead, bar associations may shift their priorities toward functions, such as lawyer assistance (continuing education), that bar associations are uniquely suited to fulfilling.

Self-regulation is the notion that members of a profession know best about how to develop and apply appropriate standards for that profession and about how to evaluate the conduct of a member of the profession. There are State Discipline Boards - Lawyer-dominated; but the lawyers' self-regulation is overseen by the state's Supreme Court.

We hope that the self-regulation is not so parochial, so protective of members - that the incompetent or malfeasant professional's colleagues fail to "go after" him. (Such problems with Florida's Medical Board have been reported since the late 1990s.) We also worry about anticompetitive behavior - e.g., the U.S. Supreme Court unanimously held, in *California Dental Association v. FTC*, 526 U.S. 756 (1999), that the Federal Trade Commission can regulate some nonprofit professional groups to protect competition.

4. Officer of the Court

Finally, lawyers act as officers of the court. Another duty, besides ones to the client or to the profession, is a Duty to Society>>> lawyers are licensed by the state, and thus have some duties because of that role ("lawyers [as] the soldiers of justice").

Harvard Law School Professor Charles Fried, former Solicitor General and Massachusetts Supreme Judicial Court Justice, gave the following ADVICE TO NEW LAWYERS –

> "As lawyers you are the servants of truth. . . . This is the first and simplest lesson of the rest of your professional lives.
>
> "As lawyers you are the soldiers of justice. Justice is your profession. Justice is your goal. Justice is your subject. Justice is your specific virtue. And of all the parts of justice none is more fundamental than fidelity to truth."

"There may be great problems, and complexities in knowing what is ultimately just. . . . but the beginning of justice is always a scrupulous regard for truth. And the beginning of injustice is a lie. So do not listen to those who like Lenin tell you that truth is relative to what you want to accomplish, a story that you choose to tell in your way for your purposes. If you shrug truth away, then there can be no justice." Commencement address, by *Professor Charles Fried, at Pepperdine U. Law School. Fall 1994 Harvard Law Bulletin, p. 42.*

If lawyers were just zealous advocates, then they would not need to worry about being officers of the court; instead, they would just have their witnesses "lie often, and lie well!" Obviously, the officer of the court model – with its emphasis on seeking fairness and justice from a societal perspective - may conflict with the advocate role. For example, one cannot fabricate or hide evidence, or lie, or help others to do so, even though that might help one's side tremendously.

Comparison with Lawyers' Roles in Other Countries

A lawyer is the client's representative. In the courtroom, the lawyer "re-presents" the client's story. The lawyer translates and thus transforms the story a person has lived into a story that an audience – the judge or jury - hopefully identifies with and finds compelling. The lawyer translates or shapes her client's experiences into claims, arguments, and remedies. But many societies have had trouble recognizing a role for lawyers. For example, the tradition in China, until quite recently, was to discount the need for lawyers and to disparage their use.

Different nations may emphasize certain roles more than others do. In the highly individualistic society of the United States, with our adversarial approach in the law, we probably emphasize the zealous advocacy model (even when posed against the government itself) more than do most other nations, where the emphasis is on the officer of the court role. A criticism is that our system may lead to the assertion of rights without accepting responsibilities.

Perhaps the Civil Law/Inquisitorial Approach emphasizes the Officer of the Court role more so than does the Common Law/Adversarial system. But there is no evidence that one system or approach emphasizes more the counselor or guild roles than does the other system or approach. U.S. Supreme Court Justice Robert Jackson (1892-1954), Chief U.S. Prosecutor in the International Military Tribunal at Nuremberg, drew these conclusions - American lawyers are more oriented toward fighting "the system" (being advocates, not just "officers" for the government).

American Lawyers in History

American lawyers, because of their overall society and due to their legal culture and norms, were and are more inclined to preserve freedom than were German lawyers in the 1930s and 1940s, as the latter were indoctrinated to think of themselves as simply part of the system.[17] There are many examples of American lawyers fighting the government on behalf of unpopular persons or causes. One can go back to colonial times, when John Adams defended British soldiers charged with the death of Americans in the Boston Massacre. Another example is the lawyers defending Copperheads (Northerners sympathetic to the Confederacy during the Civil War), often at great personal cost. Again, lawyers have fought the authorities to defend anarchists, unionizers, civil rights advocates, war protesters (e.g., during and after World War I and during the Vietnam War), militia groups, religious "cult" leaders, and others often despised by government officials and most of the public. The lawyers presently defending alleged terrorists or other Patriot Act detainees often invoke American lawyers of prior generations, such as those fighting the Red Scare of the 1920s or the McCarthyism of the 1950s, as their inspiration.

CONCLUSION

The American system is an adversarial, individualistic system, but better, more inclined to preserve freedom, than regimes where attorneys see themselves as a part of the system. It is a matter of emphasis: liberty or order, individuality or society.

L. Internet Legal Information and Documents

Most of the one million or so lawyers in the United States can be found online. There are over 150,000 law-related websites. Increasingly, people use the Internet to obtain legal advice, such as from ALM's law.com or from LegalZoom.com. For example, Nolo.com of Berkeley, California touts an online legal advice columnist named "Auntie Nolo." Nolo.com also offers numerous legal documents customers can customize to their computers for a small fee. Users can download complaints and demand

---

[17] For more, see Kenneth C.H. Willig, "The Bar in the Third Reich," 20 American Journal of Legal History (1976) (noting that the Nazis made the German lawyers into bureaucrats – no longer "servants of justice," but just servants of the National Socialist State); ROBERT H. JACKSON, THE CASE AGAINST THE NAZI WAR CRIMINALS (1946); ROBERT H. JACKSON, THE NUREMBERG CASE (1947). In MICHAEL STOELLEIS's THE LAW UNDER THE SWASTIKA: STUDIES ON LEGAL HISTORY IN NAZI GERMANY (translated by Thomas Dunlap, 1998), the author bases his work on a rich investigation of academic essays written by legal scholars during the Nazi period as well as through analysis of the secondary literature from the entire postwar period. The book demonstrates that the Nazi legal system period did impact the German law and legal profession in times since.

letters. Just three examples of Nolo.com online aid involve state landlord-tenant laws, sexual harassment complaints (including citations to Supreme Court cases), and links to relevant state traffic laws in order to fight a ticket.

The Internet can be a fantastic, albeit general and always potentially erroneous or misleading legal learning resource. FindLaw Inc. and Cornell Law School are among the leading online law libraries. Also, person-specific learning is available. For example, LRN Inc., a Los Angeles research firm, has signed up companies to receive a web-based product that educates employees about antitrust, discrimination, securities, trade secrets, and other laws. The service includes online quizzes and seeks to teach basics, point out legal pitfalls, and link workers to in-house counsel. LRN markets this this product/service as a cost-effective way to limit liability.

State bar regulators say there are several reasons for concern - including questions about who is responsible for the advice and whether it is dispensed by lawyers. In Texas, the state supreme court's committee on the unauthorized practice of law shut down several websites for practicing law (e.g., processing divorce petitions for a fee) without a license. Indeed, many suspended attorneys apparently have used the Web to maintain a virtual office. Bar authorities would have shut down their practices if it were in a physical location, but lack the resources to monitor the Internet. Some states, though (e.g., California, at http://www.calsb.org), have implemented online systems whereby consumers can find out whether a lawyer has been publicly sanctioned for violating professional ethics rules.

The American Bar Association says that websites may be useful for giving consumers much-needed information about their rights, but potential problems remain inasmuch as lawyers are involved. Bar regulations vary from state to state, so a lawyer in Florida giving information over the Web to a consumer in Wyoming may unwittingly violate that state's rules on marketing and advertising. Some experts worry that a lawyer providing advice over the Internet could be deemed to be practicing law in another state.

M. **TOPICAL LECTURE**: Attorney-Client Privilege
Introduction to Topical Lecture:
The attorney-client privilege arises when the parties have a professional relationship and a reasonable expectation of confidentiality. It is the best protected of all privileges (i.e., compared to spousal, accountant-client, and doctor-patient privileges), but there are limits on its scope, such as the crime-fraud exception, statutory restrictions, and the corporate question: for whom does the business entity's lawyer work?

The attorney-client privilege permits clients to keep confidential matters discussed by or with their attorneys.[18] The privilege extends to agents of either the client or the lawyer who facilitate the communication (e.g., paralegals or secretaries) **(see generally pgs. 13-14, 16-17; Emerson BL).**

The privilege protects both communications from the client and any advice or other response given by the attorney. The confidential communication covered by this privilege may be written or oral. But it must occur under the existence of legal counsel being sought by the client. This also covers the initial consultation a client seeks from a potential attorney. Even if further counsel is not sought, the privilege remains.

---

[18] In order for an attorney to do his/her work, he/she must be able to work with a certain degree of privacy. Only if extreme necessity is shown, such as hardship and injustice towards the other party, may work-related material be obtained. The work-product doctrine is broader than the attorney-client privilege. For example, in *National Education Training Group, Inc. v. Skillsoft Corp.*, 1999 WL 378337 (S.D.N.Y. June 9,1999), the attorney-client privilege was waived because the assistant to one of the directors was attending the meetings. However, the assistant's notes were protected under the work-product doctrine.

To whom does the privilege extend? A client holds the privilege. Also, there must be a professional relationship and a reasonable expectation of confidentiality. That means there is no protection for statements made in the presence of, or letters sent to, persons other than or in addition to the attorney and the client. These statements/letters are non-confidential (hence, unprotected via the attorney-client privilege).

So key questions are: Was there a confidential relationship? What were reasonable expectations given the circumstances? (e.g., where and when were the statements made? Who, if anyone, was present besides the lawyer and client/potential client?)

Who can waive the privilege? As the attorney-client privilege is solely the client's right, only the client can waive the right. The client's intent with respect to confidentiality determines the applicability of the privilege. The intent of any other recipient, including the lawyer, is irrelevant. A lawyer may waive the right, but only acting on behalf of the client. In the end, the lawyer's decision to waive it must be based on authority from, and the consent of, his/her client.

Attorney-client privilege even extends beyond the death of a client and will only be waived under those circumstances in very rare cases. A 6:3 decision of the U.S. Supreme Court - *Swidler & Berlin v. United States*, 524 U.S. 399 (1998), held that the attorney-client privilege continues even after the client has died.

For disputes among a dead person's heirs, many courts and legislatures, though, deny the attorney-client privilege concerning the decedent's communications with his/her lawyer. The three dissenters (O'Connor, Scalia, and Thomas) argued that the privilege must sometimes be waived when testimony is needed for law enforcement.

Clients cannot use the right of confidentiality as both a shield and a sword, such as in a fee dispute between client and lawyer. Also, lawyers can talk about their services contracts generally, in order to collect a fee.

> A post-September 11, 2001 rule promulgated in October 2001 gives government authorities the right to monitor communications (both conversations and mail) between people in federal custody and their lawyers if the U.S. Attorney General deems it "reasonably necessary in order to deter future acts of violence or terrorism." Lawyers and clients generally are to be notified if the government intends to monitor their conversations or correspondence. The monitoring is to be done by a special "privilege team" and a "firewall" will be established between that team and prosecutors. Only "disclosures necessary to thwart an imminent act of violence or terrorism" will be made to investigators or prosecutors, with any other disclosures first needing a federal judge's approval.

N. Other Privileges

1. Statutory Confidentiality Privileges

There are many statutory confidentiality privileges: (Fla. Stats. 90.502 et seq.)
1. Lawyer + Client[19]
2. Psychotherapist + Patient[20]
3. Sexual assault counselor + Victim

---

[19] Until enactment of the Sarbanes-Oxley Act in 2002, there was no strong whistleblowing requirement for the legal profession, while others (e.g., accountants) had at least a moderate whistleblowing mandate.

[20] Psychologist/ social worker-patient discussions are privileged as discussed in the U.S. Supreme Court case, *Jaffa v. Redmonds*, 518 U.S. 1 (1996).

4. Domestic violence advocate + Victim
5. Husband + Wife
6. Communications to Clergy
7. Accountant + Client[21]
8. Trade Secrets

None of the other privileges tend to be as strongly protected as the attorney-client privilege. Certainly the three reasons for that are: (1) the rich common-law heritage of strong lawyers protecting their clients from everyone and everything, including even a powerful state, employer, or other institution; (2) the belief that attorney-client privilege is a fundamental counterweight to the government's powers in criminal cases, where the privilege is often most subject to countervailing claims, yet is most needed to uphold the individual's rights; (3) the judiciary's strong understanding of the context in which the attorney-client privilege arises (after all, almost all judges themselves practiced law), while there is no such easy familiarity with any other profession and the needs of its clients or patients.

Doctor/patient confidentiality is less extensive than attorney/client confidentiality. Discussions with a physician are privileged except for any information that is related to a claim made in court. For example, anything related to an injury that a patient is suing somebody for is not privileged, as the other party should be able to verify that the injury was not preexisting.

2. Marital Privilege[22]

Husband/wife privileges are not as well protected as are attorney/client privileges.

In *Hawkins v. United States*, 358 U.S. 74 (1958), the U.S. Supreme Court reaffirmed common-law doctrine and held that for federal cases the testimony of one spouse against the other is barred unless both consent.

Hawkins was overturned 32 years later in *Trammel v. United States*, 445 U.S. 40 (1980). There, the U.S. Supreme Court held that, for federal cases, the privilege against adverse spousal testimony vests in the witness spouse alone, and that the witness may be neither compelled to testify nor foreclosed from testifying. The Court further held that because a spouse's testimony in a criminal prosecution comes after a grant of immunity and assurances of lenient treatment, such immunity and assurances do not render the spouse's testimony involuntary.

A slight majority of states continue to follow the *Hawkins* approach and give the privilege to the party (i.e., the criminal law approach). The rest of the states follow the federal *Trammel* approach giving the privilege only to the witness-spouse. So, for most states, if criminal defendant D worries about his girlfriend's being required to disclose something she has heard or seen, D may marry her the night before the trial, and thereby keep her off the stand by using the adverse testimony privilege.

Most jurisdictions (including federal courts) grant the above adverse testimony privilege (whether for just the spouse-witness or for the party) only in criminal cases.

---

[21] An American Institute of Certified Public Accountants (AICPA) requires in-house accountants to report materially misstated financial statements to their superiors and, if no action is taken, to strongly consider reporting the situation to auditors and regulators (e.g., the Securities and Exchange Commission). Accountants who fail to whistle blow could suffer sanctions (fines, reprimands, temporary suspensions) and, in extreme cases, even lose their licenses. Also, they could be sued by shareholders claiming damages due to a cover-up of corporate wrongdoing. On the other hand, whistleblowing can cost in-house accountants their jobs and cost independent accountants many of their clients.

[22] There is a distinction (in Florida at least) between Spousal Privilege and Marital Privilege. Spousal relates to communications generally and marital relates specifically to testifying in court. The latter is what we discuss here.

O. The Crime-Fraud Exception to Attorney-Client Privilege

Communications that further a crime or other illegal act are excluded from the attorney-client privilege. A party trying to compel a lawyer's testimony in spite of the attorney-client privilege may allege this crime-fraud exception to the attorney-client privilege. To meet that exception, the party invoking it must show: (1) the client was engaged in or was planning criminal or fraudulent activity when the attorney-client communications took place; and (2) the communications were intended by the client to facilitate or conceal the criminal or fraudulent activity.

The tobacco companies ran aground of this limitation when their attorneys tried to shield from evidence the eight confidential documents related to the tobacco attorneys' participation in an industry-wide conspiracy to defraud the public about the dangers of smoking. The Florida District Court of Appeals applied well-established legal principles to rule that communications furthering the commission of a crime are excluded from the attorney-client privilege.[23]

P. Corporations and the Attorney-Client Privilege

1. Court Tests for the Privilege

There have been problems with the attorney-client privilege in the context of corporate or other matters involving a business' attorney. Beware what you - an individual employee - tell the corporation's attorney. Courts do not want to have corporations broadly cast a net over – and thus protect - all activities dealing with the corporate attorney. The corporate attorney is not the individual's attorney (just as the White House attorneys are not the President's own, individual, personal lawyers) **(see generally pgs. 13-14; Emerson BL)**.

Originally, courts used a "control group" test to determine the scope of the attorney-client privilege. The "control group" basically protected two tiers of management. The first tier consisted of top management. The second tier consisted of staff that advised top management. Therefore, the attorney-client privilege only protected communications between an attorney and senior management.[24]

In 1981, the United States Supreme Court recognized the weaknesses of the "control group" test in *Upjohn Co. v. United States*, 449 U.S. 383 (1981). The Court developed a test, deemed the "Upjohn Test" to determine if the attorney-client privilege applies for a corporate client. Under the test, the following communications are protected by the attorney-client privilege:

1. Communications between employees
2. At the direction of corporate superiors
3. For the purpose of obtaining legal advice from counsel
4. Communications concerned matters within the scope of the employees' corporate duties
5. Communications were treated and kept confidential
6. Communications were to counsel

---

[23] *American Tobacco Company v. State*, 697 So.2d 1249 (Fla. Dist. Ct. App. 1997). *See also* Michael V. Ciresi et al., *Decades of Deceit: Document Discovery in the Minnesota Tobacco Litigation*, 25 WM. MITCHELL L. REV. 477 (1999) (tobacco companies unsuccessfully asserted attorney-client privilege as grounds for shielding research on addiction and tobacco-related illness from litigation disclosure). Simply put, attorneys are not immunity machines.

[24] Under the Model Rules of Professional Conduct, Rule 1.13(d), the corporate lawyer should remind employees, who might be misled into thinking that the corporate lawyer represents the employees, that that is not the case. As stated in *W.T. Gant Co. v. Haines*, 531 F.2d 671, 674, (2d Cir. 1976), the lawyer must avoid confusion as to whom the lawyer represents. The Restatement (Third) of the Law Governing Lawyers §103 comment e notes that an employee expressing "a belief that the lawyer will keep the conversation confidential from others with decision making authority in the organization … would normally require a warning by the lawyer." If that wrong belief was induced by the lawyer's statements, the bar could discipline (e.g., fine, censures, disbar) the lawyer. The corporate lawyer must avoid providing any legal advice to the employees other than the advice to get separate legal representation. Model Rules 4.3 ("Dealing with Unrepresented Person" and 1.13 ("Organization as Client").

7. Information was not available from upper echelon management
8. Employees knew they were being questioned so the company could obtain legal advice.

Recently, there has been movement to modify the rules of the attorney-client privilege to require lawyers to report on corporate clients' activities. Under current ethics laws, lawyers would not be obligated to blow the whistle on their business clients. However, under the Sarbanes-Oxley Act (2002), lawyers would be obligated to alert the SEC about problems companies refuse to fix **(see generally pgs. 430-434; Emerson BL).**

2. Guidelines

To keep communications within the boundary of attorney-client privilege the Supreme Court's decision in the Upjohn case suggests that attorneys and corporations follow the following guidelines.

1. Communication between an attorney and a corporation is protected only when the client is seeking or receiving legal advice, not business advice. Corporations should request legal advice in writing and assign communications with an attorney to a specific employee.
2. Corporations should make sure that senior management directs all communication between employees and corporate counsel and that the employees know they must keep all communications confidential.[25]
3. Corporations should deal directly with counsel and maintain confidential files and documentation.
4. When a corporation gives a governmental agency access to its communications or files, the corporation should negotiate a written agreement of confidentiality with the agency or an agreement that the agency will not take physical possession of the documents. The corporation should also investigate the possibility of statutory protection in this situation.

Q. Limits on the Attorney-Client Privilege

Attorney client privilege is limited to communication between a practicing attorney and his/her current or prospective client regarding legal matters. The following are two limitations to that privilege:

1. Parties peripheral to the attorney-client relationship are not protected. For example, if a conversation between attorney and client takes place in the presence of the client's friend or relative who is not also an agent of the client, the privilege will not keep the friend from being subjected to a subpoena and compelled to disclose what he/she heard.

2. Information irrelevant to the attorney's legal responsibilities is not protected. What if, for instance, a conversation sails off into matters unrelated to the legal representation? Client C, represented in a tax fraud case, tells the lawyer completely unrelated, embarrassing details of a sexual affair between the lawyer's spouse and someone the client happens to know. That conversation is unlikely to be privileged and the lawyer could pursue that information in his/her own action for a divorce.

Communication regarding future illegal acts is excluded. There is a tremendous difference between a client saying to his criminal defense lawyer, "I killed her, and I'm glad I did it," and "I'm glad in my heart because I've decided how and when to do her in." The lawyer likely has not just a moral, but even a legal duty to take some action to try to prevent a murder.

---

[25] Corporate self-critical analyses have been deemed privileged by some courts. The idea here is to protect corporations that are conducting their own investigations of their operations in order to improve safety or anything else that can be deemed beneficial to society. Without this protection a corporation might not conduct these analyses for fear that the analyses later will be used against that corporation. An example is *Tice v. American Airlines, Inc.*, 192 F.R.D. 270 (N.D. Ill. 2000).

The purpose of the privilege is "to encourage clients to make full disclosure to their attorneys."[26] The privilege protects communications between a client and an attorney, not communications that prove important to an attorney's legal advice to a client (e.g., a language translation of a lawyer's advice would be privileged). The privilege extends to a situation where the attorney uses an expert to improve comprehension of the attorney client communications (e.g., uses a CPA or an engineer[27] or a microbiologist to "translate" information). However, the privilege does not extend to individuals used by the attorney as information providers for the purposes of simply better advising the client (e.g., having a co-worker of the client present to help explain and give further information). As decided in *Hickman v. Taylor*, 329 U.S. 495 (1947), "the protective cloak of this privilege does not extend to information which an attorney secures from a witness while acting for his client in anticipation of litigation. Nor does this privilege concern the memoranda, briefs, communications and other writings prepared by counsel for his own use in prosecuting his client's case."[28]

In *United States v. Frederick*, 835 F.2d 1211 (7th Cir. 1987), cert. denied, 486 U.S. 1013 (1988), the US Court of Appeals for the Seventh Circuit held that "legal matters" are limited to a lawyer's legal representation function. Specifically, an attorney who also prepares taxes cannot invoke the attorney-client privilege over a client's supporting tax documents. Furthermore, a dual-purpose document (a document used in preparing tax returns and in litigation) is not privileged.

For an account of a September 2010 EU decision about attorney-client privilege, see http://www.abanet.org/buslaw/blt/content/departments/2010/09/keepingcurrent-privilege.shtml. There, the European Union confirmed in *Akzo Nobel v. Commission* that documents prepared by in-house lawyers are not privileged under EU rules; the decision was consistent with the approach adopted by most European continental legal systems, but it contradicts the principles applied in several EU Member States (Greece, Ireland, the Netherlands, Poland, Portugal, and the United Kingdom) as well as in the United States, where legal professional privilege extends to communications with all lawyers, including in-house lawyers admitted to a national bar or law society.

End of Topical Lecture on "Attorney-Client Privilege"

II. JUDGES

"The Judicial Department comes home in its effects to every man's fireside: it passes on his property, his reputation, his life, his all." John Marshall, 1755-1835 (Chief Justice, 1801-35).

The roles (particularly the decision making process) of Judges and Juries are, to laypeople, often cloaked in mystery. Usually, we just see their finished product: the actual decision. Judges or juries are expected to turn messy facts (a goulash of mixed facts) into law (a legal pronouncement - a verdict). And judges are often expected to explain their decision, in writing. That is not necessarily required of legislatures or the executive branch of government. Yet, because the latter two groups (legislature and executive) are filled with regularly-elected individuals who respond directly to citizens' concerns (e.g., lobbying) and to news developments, etc., the third branch – the judiciary – is the one perhaps least understood.

In the United States, the judges' background tends to involve not much special training, just on-the-job training. (Almost all judges, until their elevation to the bench, were lawyers, usually in practice

---

[26] *Fisher v. United States*, 425 U.S. 391, 403 (1976).
[27] *United States v. Kovel*, 296 F.2d 918 (2d Cir.1961).
[28] *Id. at* 508.

for many years.) In other nations, such as France, judges often have specialized training and a distinct career path from lawyers.

In the United States and most federal systems, the judiciary is derived from two distinct sources: nationally chosen judges and state (provincial) appointed or elected judges.

A. Comparison to Other Federal Systems, Such as Canada and Germany

Even other federal republics may *not* have two distinct court systems, such as the state and national courts found in the United States. For example, Canada, although it has a federal system of government, has only one court system - all of its judges are picked by Canadian federal authorities, none by the provincial governments. Likewise, Germany has a single court system, with courts divided according to subject (general matters – civil and criminal; administrative; tax; social; labor relations; and constitution) and vertically, the courts going up from municipal, to regional, to higher regional and to federal courts. (But, just as in the United States, Germany has state courts (here, specific state constitutional courts) that exclusively decide state constitutional law.)

B. The United States Federal Courts

Besides the U.S. Supreme Court, the two main levels of federal courts are:
(1) The U.S. District Courts – these are the trial courts; there are 94 districts, with 665 District judgeships altogether, dozens of which are vacant. There may be more than one district in a state (e.g., New York and Florida each have four; Pennsylvania has three; New Jersey and Maryland each have just one). However, no district crosses state lines.
(2) The U.S. Court of Appeals – these are the lower appeals courts, with a total of 179 judgeships; there are 13 Circuits, 11 of which cover regions comprised of a few to several states (e.g., the Eleventh Circuit encompasses Alabama, Florida, and Georgia and has 12 authorized active judges), with one appeals court being simply for the District of Columbia (with 12 active judges) and another – the U.S. Court of Appeals for the Federal Circuit (again, with 12 active judges), hearing cases involving customs, patents, certain contract claims concerning the federal government, and other special claims.[29] No matter how many judges serve on a particular circuit, the decisions tend to be by three-judge panels, with cases occasionally reviewed *en banc* (with all of the circuit's judges reviewing the matter).
Federal court websites include http://www.fjc.gov and http://www.uscourts.gov.

---

[29] Besides the 11th Circuit Court of Appeals based in Atlanta (covering Florida, Georgia, and Alabama) and the D.C. Circuit, the other regional circuits are: First (based in Boston, with 6 authorized active – not senior status, i.e., semi-retired - judges) – Maine, New Hampshire, Massachusetts, Rhode Island, and Puerto Rico; Second (New York City, 13 authorized active judges) – Vermont, New York, and Connecticut; Third (Philadelphia, 14) – New Jersey, Pennsylvania, Delaware, and Virgin Islands; Fourth (Richmond, 15) – Maryland, West Virginia, Virginia, North Carolina, and South Carolina; Fifth (New Orleans, 17) – Mississippi, Louisiana, and Texas; Sixth (Cincinnati, 16) – Tennessee, Kentucky, Ohio, and Michigan; Seventh (Chicago, 11) – Indiana, Illinois, and Wisconsin; Eighth (St. Louis, 11) – Minnesota, Iowa, North Dakota, South Dakota, Nebraska, Missouri, and Arkansas; Ninth (San Francisco, 28) – Montana, Idaho, Nevada, Arizona, California, Oregon, Washington, Alaska, Hawaii, and Guam; Tenth (Denver, 12) – New Mexico, Utah, Wyoming, Colorado, Oklahoma and Kansas. At any particular time, there may be a vacancy or two or even three among the judges in a circuit.

There are recurring proposals to split the Ninth Circuit into two circuits. The last split was in 1980, when the Fifth Circuit split into what are now the Fifth and Eleventh Circuits.

C. America's State Courts

State trial courts have many different names, but their functions tend to be the same.[30] States have lower trial courts which hear minor matters (e.g., small claims) and for which no juries are available).[31] For more serious matters, or cases in which a jury has been demanded, the general trial jurisdiction courts hear the cases.[32] These trial courts typically cover a particular region (e.g., a county or cluster of counties) in a state.[33] There is little or no discovery, no jury, ordinarily no motions for summary judgment, and no pretrial conference in small claims court cases.

Above the trial courts are lower appeals courts (in 40 states), and then – at the top - a state supreme court.[34] Florida, for example, has five regionally based District Courts of Appeal above its 20 circuit courts.[35]

The Florida Courts

Florida's Supreme Court

The Florida Supreme Court has seven Justices, including the Chief Justice. Each Justice is selected by the governor from a list of nominees chosen by a panel that includes representatives from the Florida Bar and the governor. Thereafter, the justice must stand for a retention election ("Yes" or "No" on keeping that justice on the court) every six years. All of Florida's state judges, including its Supreme Court Justices, must retire at the age of 70. At least five Justices must participate in every case and at least four must agree for a decision to be reached.

Supreme Court's workload is substantial. Each year there are about 2,500 cases added to the Florida high court's docket, several times more than the few hundred a year that the national Supreme Court handles in some way.

Florida's Courts: What They Handle

---

[30] Of the 50 states' general trial courts (for more important trials, including with juries), thirteen are termed circuit courts, twelve are called superior courts, fifteen (as well as the federal trial courts) are labeled district courts, and ten have other names – often combining various terms such as circuit, chancery, and superior.

[31] In Florida, these lower, limited jurisdiction trial courts are the county courts (one for each of Florida's 67 counties). These county courts have original jurisdiction in all criminal misdemeanor cases where there is not a concurrent felony, and in all violations of municipal and county ordinances, and for traffic offenses. In civil matters, county courts have original jurisdiction in all actions of law in which the matter in controversy does not exceed the sum of $15,000, exclusive of interest and costs, and which is not within the exclusive jurisdiction of the circuit courts. County court judges also serve as committing magistrates (e.g., at the initial stage of some criminal matters).

[32] The circuit court is Florida's trial court of general jurisdiction. Each of the state's 20 judicial circuits incorporates one or more counties. Circuit courts have exclusive original jurisdiction in all of the following: actions in which the matter in controversy exceeds $15,000, exclusive of interest and costs; proceedings relating to the settlement of estates; guardianship; involuntary hospitalization; determination of incapacity; and other matters concerning court of probate; in all cases in equity including all cases relating to juveniles except traffic offenses. In criminal matters, the circuit courts have original jurisdiction in all felonies (in Florida, defined as crimes punishable by a year or more in jail) and in all misdemeanors arising out of the same circumstances as a felony that is concurrently charged. Also, circuit courts preside over all cases involving the legality of tax assessment, in the actions of ejectment, in all actions involving the titles or boundaries or rights of possession of real property, and in other actions not heard by county court. Family cases such as dissolution of marriage, child custody, visitation, domestic violence, and juvenile dependency cases are all heard in the Circuit Court.

[33] The sixty-seven counties in Florida are combined to form 20 circuit courts, and five district courts of appeal. A map of the trial court (circuit court) distribution is at http://www.flcourts.org/courts/circuit/cir_dist.shtml

[34] The official website for information about the Florida Supreme Court is at http://www.floridasupremecourt.org/

[35] The map of the Florida district courts of appeal is at http://www.flcourts.org/courts/dca/dca_dist.shtml

> Appeals to Florida's Supreme Court
> **Mandatory Jurisdiction:** "Mandatory" jurisdiction defines those cases that, under the constitutional and statutory framework of a state, must be considered and decided by the court as a matter of right if properly appealed.
> The Florida Supreme Court **must** review:
> - final orders imposing death sentences,
> - district court of appeals decisions declaring a state statute or provision of the state constitution invalid,
> - bond validations,
> - certain orders of the Public Service Commission on utility rates and services.
>
> **Discretionary Jurisdiction**: If discretionary review is sought by a party, the Court at its discretion **may** review any decision of a district court of appeal that:
> - expressly declares valid a state statute,
> - construes a provision of the state or federal constitution,
> - affects a class of constitutional or state officers,
> - directly conflicts with a decision of another district court or of the Supreme Court on the same question of law,
> - is certified as of great public importance,
> - is a certified direct conflict,
> - is a certified judgment of the trial courts,
> - is a certified question from federal courts.
>
> Appeals to Florida's District Courts of Appeal (five intermediate courts of appeal) (courts of last resort)
> o   All matters not directly appealable to the Supreme Court
>
> Circuit Courts (20 courts, with general trial jurisdiction and also appellate court jurisdiction over appeals from county court decisions: Thus, circuit courts are simultaneously the highest trial courts and the lowest appellate courts in Florida's judicial system)
> o   Felonies
> o   Family law matters
> o   Civil cases (over $15,000)
> o   Probate/Guardianship/Mental health
> o   Juvenile Dependency & Delinquency
> o   Appeals from county court
> o   Some Certified questions
>
> County Courts (courts of limited jurisdiction in Florida's 67 counties)
> o   Misdemeanors
> o   Small claims (under $5,000)
> o   Civil (under $15,000)
> o   Traffic

D. Appointed Federal Judges and, Mostly, Elected State Judges

Federal judges have lifetime appointments. Other federal, common law systems may not. For example, Canadian Supreme Court Justices must retire when they turn age 75. As for American state judges, they almost always have a mandatory retirement age (e.g., age 70), they sometimes have term limits, and they usually have set terms (e.g., 10 years) with possible reappointment.

The President nominates the federal judges. To be confirmed and serve as a judge, these nominees must be approved by a majority vote of the U.S. Senate. President Reagan, in 8 years, named

375 lower-court federal judges (83 being appeals court judges); the first Pres. Bush, in 4 years, named 191 (43 being appeals court judges); President Clinton appointed, in 8 years, 372 (66 being appeals court judges); and the second Pres. Bush appointed 324 in 8 years (63 being appeals court judges).

> **Overt Political Input in American Judicial Appointments**
>
> "[T]he United States is somewhat exceptional in terms of the degree of overt political input and competition that goes into its judicial selection process. Western European democracies with civil law systems provide a stark contrast to U.S. selection systems: many have competitive exams for entry into the judiciary, with promotions influenced considerably by senior members of the judiciary or judicial councils. In France, for example, the Conseil Supérieur de la Magistrature (CSM) plays a significant role in the appointment and promotion of judges. Initial appointments to the civil and criminal courts (following training at the Ecole Nationale de la Magistrature) and lower-level promotions are subject to review by the CSM whose decisions are binding on the Minister of Justice. The CSM also nominates individuals for senior posts in the judiciary. The Spanish system goes farther by having a constitutionalized judicial agency that both makes appointments — primarily based on seniority — and runs the judicial system. In both models, a majority of the members of these bodies are from the judiciary. These systems encourage technical expertise and appear to increase appointments of women and of those with less traditional professional backgrounds (owing to the participation of some lower-ranking judges on the judicial councils, who may be open to less traditional choices for appointment). Such systems also reduce executive influence on appointment and promotion. Despite the potential benefits of these civil law systems of appointment, they can place extensive power in the hands of the senior judiciary, move the locus of political struggles to the judicial councils themselves, or insulate the judiciary from accountability (as in Italy, where reforms to make the court system more efficient have been stymied by the judges themselves)."[36]

Judges are appointed based on academic background, experience, ideology, contacts, age, and luck. Some attorneys may even scan obituaries, looking for openings![37]

Voters in 40 states elect at least some of their state-court judges. Nationwide, 82% of state appeals court judges (including state supreme court judges) and 88% of state trial court judges face some form of election.

This percentage has changed little in the past century. In 1910, only about 14% of all state trial judges were initially appointed, with some then subject to retention elections. Now, that percentage is about 22%, but, once again, of those state trial judges that come to office via an appointment, many ultimately must face a retention election.

The entire legal establishment – the national bar association, nearly all state bars, and almost all academics and other interested observers – has pushed to get rid of judicial elections. However, whenever these matters come up for a popular vote, the people themselves tend to overwhelmingly favor

---

[36] Troy Riddell et al., *Federal Judicial Appointments: A Look at Patronage in Federal Appointments Since 1988*, 58 U. Toronto L.J. 39, 65-66 (2008).

[37] One time, almost immediately after a prominent judge (let's call her "Judge Jones") had died, many lawyers called the governor to tell him that they were available to serve as the new judge (i.e., to be appointed by the governor). The governor was so annoyed by the sheer volume and the gall of all these calls that when one lawyer said, "I want to take Judge Jones' place," the governor responded, "Well, it's all right with me, if it's all right with the undertaker!"

retaining that "control" over the judicial selection process. For example, in 2000, the majority of voters in every Florida county voted to keep nonpartisan judicial elections and not replace them with an appointment process.

A state's high court justices are elected in 38 states. In the other 12 states, the justices are: (1) chosen by the state legislature in South Carolina (ten-year terms) and Virginia (twelve-year terms); (2) appointed by the governor for a lifetime appointment (in Rhode Island) or until mandatory retirement at age 70 (in Massachusetts and New Hampshire); or (3) appointed by the governor, with possible reappointment, in seven states.[38] Note that all six New England states, as well as New York and New Jersey – in essence, the Northeastern United States - comprise eight of the 12 states without judicial elections for high court office. With Delaware, Virginia, and South Carolina – three more of the original colonies – also being non-election states, there is only one other state (Hawaii) that does not have some form of election for its highest court's judges.[39]

Electing Judges in Other Countries: Very Rare and Limited Even There

The only other nations that elect even a small number of judges are France, Japan, and Switzerland, and these countries narrowly limit the scope of the elections.

France has specialized commercial and labor courts that, while very different from the American model, have elected judges; these specialized trial judges lack formal judicial (and usually even legal) training and are elected mid-career to serve temporary terms of office. Decisions can be appealed to "regular" courts of appeal (with appointed, legally-trained judges), but these commercial or labor court judges have tremendous powers, comparable to arbitrators, over the cases involving the particular professional and social groups whose disputes they resolve – the very groups responsible for electing them. These judges are merchants, human relations professionals, or others with real life experience in their field and thus should have the substantive expertise (and social and political legitimacy) necessary for effective resolution of disputes among group members.

In Japan, the emperor appoints the chief judge, and the cabinet initially appoints other high court judges, who eventually have to face a one-time retention reelection but often retire before facing such an election.

In Switzerland, some lay judges of canton courts (the provincial courts) are elected.

For most courts, there are some good basic introductions on the internet.

For British courts, *see* http://www.ilex.org.uk/about_legal_executives/the_uk_legal_system.aspx

For some general information about the German legal system, *see* http://ec.europa.eu/civiljustice/org_justice/org_justice_ger_en.pdf

For French courts, *see* http://www.justice.gouv.fr/organisation-de-la-justice-10031/lordre-judiciaire-10033/ From there you can click on more information, such as about France's Supreme Court, the Cour de cassation.[40]

For information about the EU's courts, see http://europa.eu/institutions/inst/justice/index_en.htm

Many of the principles involving evaluation of evidence and the role of judges apply even to legal systems much different than the American system.

Of the remaining 38 states, in 17 states a high court justice is initially selected via a nominating commission and/or gubernatorial appointment, but then subsequently must either run for

---

[38] The appointments may be after a nominating commission suggests names, with the governor picking from among those names. The terms are for six years (Vermont, with reappointment via a General Assembly vote), seven years (Maine, New Jersey), eight years (Connecticut), 10 years (Hawaii), 12 years (Delaware), and 14 years (New York).

[39] New York's lower court judges are elected, but not the judges on its highest court, the Court of Appeals.

[40] It's all in French! http://www.justice.gouv.fr/multilinguisme-12198/english-12200/ is the link for English articles, but it does not seem to do the website justice (pun intended).

election in either a contested or a retention election.[41] For the remaining 21 states, the justice only gets to serve, for an initial term and any subsequent term, via elections.[42]

In Florida, state supreme court justices and lower appeals court judges are nominated via a commission, with the governor picking one of the nominated choices to a one-year term. Then, he/she faces retention elections for six-year terms. On the other hand, the circuit court trial judges are chosen for six-year terms via contested, nonpartisan elections. None of Florida's Supreme Court Justices has ever been denied a new term by the voters, which would happen if more people voted "No" on retaining that judge than voted "Yes."

E. Judicial Campaigning: *Republican Party of Minnesota v. White*

In *Republican Party of Minnesota v. White*, 536 U.S. 765 (2002), the U.S. Supreme Court voted 5-4 (with the more conservative Justices then – Rehnquist, O'Connor, Scalia, Kennedy, and Thomas – in the majority) that the limits in Minnesota and nine other states barring some judicial candidates from giving voters their views on "disputed legal or political issues" were unconstitutional violations of free speech. (A separate state prohibition on specific campaign "pledges or promises" was not challenged in that case.)

Many other states have similar statutes which presumably are likewise constitutionally suspect. While these statutes protect judges from being pressured into taking sides on issues that may come before them (and thus would, at the very least, hurt the image – if not reality - of the courts' independence and impartiality), these laws do restrain speech, and that is what – as in the Minnesota case – could easily render them unconstitutional. On the other hand, restrictions on (even outright banning of) a judicial candidate's soliciting contributions for their elections were upheld in *Williams-Yulee v. Florida Bar* (U.S. Supreme Court, decided April 29, 2015).[43]

Attorneys' Contributions to Judicial Campaigns

Three studies in 1998 (by the Association of the Bar of the City of New York, by the American Bar Association, and by a nonprofit advocacy group, Texans for Public Justice) suggest what you would imagine: lawyers making campaign contributions get favorable treatment in receiving lucrative court appointments (such as guardianship) and in court opinions for their clients. Finally, in 2000, the influential New York State Bar voted to ban such "Pay-to-play" campaign contribution arrangements.

In 2002, fifty-five percent of surveyed state judges said that they believe the conduct and tone of state judicial electoral contests have worsened since 1997. And 26% said that campaign contributions

---

[41] Most have nominating commissions which suggest names, with the governor picking a judge from among the small panel of names chosen (usually about three to five names). Then, after a fairly short term of one to three years, or at the next general election, or – in some states - only after the completion of an initial term of office of about six to twelve years, the justice sits in a retention election for a full term of office (from about six to twelve years long). These 17 states are Alaska, Arizona, California, Colorado, Florida, Indiana, Iowa, Kansas, Maryland, Missouri, Nebraska, New Mexico (initial election is a partisan contested race; thereafter, a retention election),Oklahoma, South Dakota, Tennessee, Utah, and Wyoming.

[42] Fifteen states have nonpartisan elections for six-year terms (Georgia, Idaho, Minnesota, Nevada, Ohio (which has a partisan primary nomination process), Oregon, and Washington), eight-year terms (Arkansas, Kentucky, Michigan (which does have party nominating conventions), Mississippi, Montana, and North Carolina), or ten-year terms (North Dakota and Wisconsin). Six states have partisan elections for six year terms (Alabama and Texas), ten-year terms (Illinois, Louisiana and Pennsylvania – with Illinois and Pennsylvania having retention elections after the first term is completed), and twelve-year terms (West Virginia). See http://www.ajs.org/selection/sel_state-select-map.asp (produced by the American Judicature Society).

[43] The upheld Florida legislation allows candidates for judgeships to raise money through campaign committees, but prohibits the candidates from soliciting the funds themselves.

have too much influence on judges' decisions. Source: Justice at Stake (a nonpartisan watchdog group in Washington, D.C.), 2002.[44] (Query: Isn't *any* such influence *too much* influence?)

In 2004, North Carolina became the first state to fund fully its judicial campaigns. Other states are trying to make private contributions more transparent. And several state bar associations have created bipartisan watchdog panels that chastise candidates who cross the line with misleading advertisements, overly partisan rhetoric, or positions casting doubt on their ability to rule impartially.

F. Overview, Removal, and Retirement of Judges

1. Censure of Judges

Behavior that garners applause in the television "courtroom" of Judge Judy and others (e.g., screaming at or otherwise treating litigants disrespectfully) could well result in official censure or worse of a judge acting that way in a real courtroom. For example, an Atlanta judge repeatedly brow-beat litigants and once barked, "You are an able-bodied person, OK? There are lots of jobs out there. I suggest you go find one." The judge was censured in 2000 for improper behavior.

2. Federal Judicial Oversight of Fellow Judges

In *McBryde v. Committee to Review Circuit Council Conduct*, 537 U.S. 821 (2002), the U.S. Supreme Court denied certiorari for a constitutional challenge to the Judicial Councils Reform and Judicial Conduct and Disability Act of 1980. That law authorizes the federal judiciary to discipline its own misbehaving members short of removal from the bench. A panel of his fellow judges - the Judicial Council of the Fifth Judicial Circuit – had reprimanded U.S. District Judge John H. McBryde of Fort Worth, Texas and suspended him from hearing new cases for a year. The panel found a pattern of "intemperate, abusive and intimidating" treatment of lawyers and other judges.

3. Impeachment and Removal of Judges

Impeachment is not a practical tool for removal of a physically and mentally declining judge. Indeed, impeachment – generally reserved for persons convicted of crimes - is extremely rare.

4. Retirement

Mandatory retirement is found in most state courts (including Florida), usually affecting judges once they have reached the age of 70 to 75. That avoids the problem of unimpeachable but impaired old judges. But that process removes some brilliant people.

In the federal system, most notably for the U.S. Supreme Court, judges can serve for a lifetime and can still hear cases and rule on them well into their seventies, or eighties, or – possibly – beyond! U.S. District and Circuit Court judges take senior status at age seventy; if they have served for ten years, they receive retirement pay at the same level as active judges earn, and these senior-status judges can still hear cases (in effect, on a part-time basis).

For the U.S. Supreme Court, the method by which most Justices leave is voluntary retirement, although in some instances it is retirement by persuasion (colleagues, friends, and relatives telling the Justice that he/she really needs to go).

---

[44] Justice at Stake's 2002 poll of 894 elected judges found that 48% felt a "great deal" of pressure to raise more money during election years. Asked how much influence contributions had on their decisions, 4% said "a great deal of influence," 22% said "some influence," and 20% said "just a little influence." So, collectively, 46% concluded that campaign contributions influence their decisions.

G. How Judges Decide a Case

Typically, a Judge follows a process of <u>Legal Analysis and Reasoning</u> whereby matters are addressed in this order:

1. Allegations
2. Issues of Fact and Law
3. Rules
4. Remedies
5. The Decision
6. Public Policy

<u>Facts are crucial in most cases</u>. As stated by Justice Louis Brandeis (on the Supreme Court from 1916 to 1939), "Facts, Facts, Facts. Give me Facts!"

Common law systems, whether using juries or judges, directly incorporate unstable cultural concepts by means of what Edward Levi called a "moving system of classifying concepts." This system of classifying concepts focuses largely on discerning and evaluating "facts." [In Islamic law, the emphasis seems to be on a person's connections, the customs used to form them, and the consequences that actions have within the interlocked webs of negotiated obligations by which the person operates.]

Law may be described as a set of generalizations. In applying these generalizations, one may fit (bend?) the law to the facts. <u>One cannot simply change the facts</u>. A judge is like a tailor fitting the law (clothes) to the facts (the body) of the case: Balancing social needs with legal requirements.

<u>When studying case law (court decisions), (1) do not argue with the facts as they are given to you, and (2) do not confuse the legal rule with the facts that prove the case</u>. First, if you argue, for example, that Anne should or must have understood the contract although the case decision requires that Anne did not (e.g., because she was uneducated), then you will fail to understand the relevant legal principle - that sometimes people who cannot understand the nature of the agreements they enter may be relieved of their contractual obligations if the agreement is extremely one-sided. Second, when, for example, the law does not require that there be written evidence of a contract, and thus a purely oral contract can be enforced against the parties, do not simply say, "Well, without written evidence how can one prove that there was a contract?" That is an excellent question going toward proof of one's case. But it is irrelevant to the law. (Hypothetical examples of contracts, whether oral or in writing, can be good illustrations of contract law principles, even though the facts in some examples, particularly for the oral agreements, may be hard to prove in court.)

Knowing half the facts in a case is often even worse than knowing none of the facts at all. It makes one more likely to go off on wrong tangents and make wrong assumptions, sometimes because one does not know how little one knows.

Concerning the conflicting social, economic, and political interests balanced by judges – that conflicts with democratic ideals; judges may be benevolent, presumably are well-intentioned, and generally are intelligent and experienced in the law, but they are an elite (unrepresentative of the people).

As a descriptive matter, we can agree that the judge's role is very important, that judges balance all sorts of interests and therefore are extremely powerful. But, as a normative matter, the question remains: Is it appropriate/right for judges to do all this balancing? That is controversial. (For example, that was a core concern in the debate over the roles of judges, especially the Florida Supreme Court and the U.S. Supreme Court, in the 2000 Presidential election controversy.)

<u>Judges Are People, Too</u>

At a hearing in Washington state, Federal Communications Commission (FCC) administrative law judge ordered a private lawyer's removal for making statements similar to, and certainly no more disrespectful, than what the lawyer read at the hearing when he showed up the next day. The lawyer, Ben Cottone, then made this final declaration, directed at the administrative law judge:

> "Your mind, sir - and this is a written statement - is a cesspool of filth, venom, venality, bias, and prejudice. To call you a savage would cast aspersion on innocent savages. If I believed you had any semblance or vestige of rationality [sic], I would call you a very, very evil man."
>
> This example of "contemptible behavior" is from an article by Robert W. Emerson in 9 THE JOURNAL OF THE LEGAL PROFESSION 43, 60-61: *Ethics Overseer for the Private Bar: The Federal Communications Commission and its Disciplinary Practices*.

H. THE ROLES OF APPELLATE AND TRIAL COURTS

Judges balance rights and duties –
1. balance the law with individual circumstances crying out for a "bending" of the law;
2. balance society's interests and those of individuals;
3. balance long-term and short-term interests;
4. balance the ideal versus the practical.

Distinctions between the two types of courts involve, among other things, a difference in Style and Approach. There is a profound difference in orientation revolving around factual analysis versus legal analysis. Trial courts focus on factual analysis, on – for example - hearing the testimony of witnesses (looking at and hearing the people in the case). Appeals courts focus on issues of law and on publishing opinions (guidance) for posterity.

It depends on the state, the type of case, whether there is a jury, whether there are lawyers on both sides, and the temperament of the judge as to how involved the trial judge becomes in the actual presentation of the case. Sometimes lawyers have found trial judges' participation to be too much, and these lawyers have responded with sarcasm - for example, after questioning the witness, the lawyer says, *"Your witness, Your Honor!"* or the lawyer lectures the judge (a dangerous practice!), *"Judge, I don't mind your trying my case, but for God's sake don't lose it!"*

The appeals court's role is not to second-guess on the facts but to concentrate on the proper interpretation of the law. Appellate courts are not as oriented toward individual parties. Some great law cases have been brought by, or on behalf of, some people who behaved irresponsibly or even maliciously. A classic example is that of Ernesto Miranda, who brought us the great Supreme Court decision of *Miranda v. Arizona*, 384 U.S. 436 (1966), but was, to say the least, not a very nice man.[45] But the Supreme Court's review of his 1963 arrest on a rape-kidnapping charge and his confession, while in custody, brought him to national attention. The high court issued its famous ruling in 1966, finding that suspects are entitled to know their rights because "custodial interrogation is inherently coercive." Miranda rights became law. The man, Ernesto Miranda, ultimately died, but his last name, Miranda, became an adjective describing a type of constitutionally prescribed admonitions: *Miranda* warning

I. U.S. CIRCUIT COURTS OF APPEAL

The lower federal appeals courts (known as the Circuit Courts of Appeal) are very important, especially as, in recent years, the Supreme Court has reviewed fewer of their decisions. In effect, these courts tend to be the last ones who actually may hear and decide a case.[46] Normally, these courts sit as panels of three judges. In rare cases, the entire court may hear a case *en banc* (meaning that the entire court hears the case rather than just a panel of three of the court's judges).

---

[45] Miranda spent most of his short adult life in facing criminal charges or in prison for various crimes, such as rape, kidnapping, and robbery.

[46] Someone with a legal claim files a lawsuit in a trial court, such as a U.S. District Court, which receives evidence, and decides the facts and law. Parties dissatisfied with a trial court's legal decision can appeal. In the federal system, this appeal usually is to the U.S. Court of Appeals, which must consider and rule on all properly presented appeals. Someone dissatisfied with the Court of Appeals' ruling can request that the U.S. Supreme Court review the

While all circuits have some judges appointed by Democratic Presidents and, even more so, some appointed by Republican Presidents, some circuits are more likely to have three-judge panels that are conservative – Fourth (Richmond), Fifth (New Orleans), Seventh (Chicago), and Eighth (St. Louis) – and some are more likely to have liberal panels - Second (New York City) & Ninth (San Francisco).

J. THE U.S. SUPREME COURT (http://www.supremecourtus.gov)

The U.S. Supreme Court not only is the highest court in the United States, but also is the only court specifically required by the U.S. Constitution.

Article III of the Constitution confers original jurisdiction[47] on the U.S. Supreme Court over cases involving ambassadors and suits involving states as parties. This grant, however, does not preclude Congress from granting concurrent original jurisdiction to other courts. Recognizing that the Supreme Court is better suited to exercise appellate review than to conduct trials, Congress has granted concurrent original jurisdiction to the federal district courts in all controversies except where the Constitution clearly supports placing the dispute outside the federal trial courts' purview. Consequently, the Supreme Court hears very few original jurisdiction cases, with most involving a state suing another state over contested borders. When such state-versus-state cases are filed, the justices normally appoint a special master (frequently a former judge) to determine the facts and recommend the outcome. The Court then treats the reports of the special master in much the same way as the appealed lower court ruling and issues a final opinion accepting, modifying, or rejecting the recommendations

In effect, the Supreme Court is almost exclusively an appeals court. The Court's only trial jurisdiction involves, as stated above, either diplomats or disputes between states. Nonetheless, the Constitutional right of appeal to the Supreme Court is very rare; the Court, in essence, controls its own docket. Indeed, the President or Congress cannot require the Supreme Court to resolve a particular issue. (Many states have a process whereby certain issues are referred from the legislature or governor to the state supreme court; there is no such process at the federal level.)

On the Supreme Court there are nine Justices (eight are Associate Justices and one is the Chief Justice). There must be a Chief Justice, a separate appointment, as required by the Constitution; but the exact number of Associate Justices is specified by an Act of Congress, not the Constitution itself. So Congress can change the number of Associate Justices simply by amending the statute (that has not been done since 1868).

The President nominates all federal judges, including Supreme Court Justices, for lifetime appointments.[48] The Senate votes whether to confirm a nominee, which requires a simple majority.

There is no formal requirement that a Justice be a lawyer, but every Justice has been. In practical terms, all appellate court judges (state or federal), to be appointed, must be attorneys. That is also true for trial judges, except in a few states for very minor courts.

Court of Appeals' holding, but the Supreme Court rarely agrees to do so. See "writ of certiorari," discussed shortly below in this text.

[47] *Original Jurisdiction* is the jurisdiction exercised by the court that initially hears a lawsuit. As a court of first instance, this tribunal must conduct a trial or similar proceeding in order to determine the facts in the dispute and then settle the case by applying the law to those factual findings. Congress created the U.S. Districts Courts as the primary courts of original jurisdiction for the federal judiciary. *See* Robert W. Emerson, *Business Law*. NY: Barron's Educational Series (6th ed., 2015), at 42-43.

[48] As the Constitution says it, Justice "shall hold their Offices during good Behaviour" (i.e., they can only be involuntarily removed from office by impeachment).

The Constitution does not specify qualifications for Justices, such as age, education, profession, or native-born citizenship. A Justice does not have to be a lawyer or a law school graduate. However, all Justices have been trained in the law. As with most judges and lawyers for the first 100-plus years of the United States, many earlier Justices studied law under a mentor but did not attend a law school. There were few law schools, and it was not until the modern era that law school attendance became, in effect, the universal method for becoming a lawyer.

The Chief Justice is first among relative equals. All nine Justices have one vote, but the Chief Justice is the Chief Administrator of the United States (federal) court system. In this role, he/she has several functions. For example, he/she petitions/reports to Congress, re: funding and other administrative issues. The Chief Justice assigns who will write the court's opinion in a case if he/she is in the majority. If the Chief Justice is opposed to the majority view, then the most senior Justice (the one who has been on the Supreme Court the longest and who supports the majority view) assigns the opinion-writing. Dissenting and concurring opinions are entirely up to individual Justices: whether to write them and/or to "join" (agree with) another Justice's dissent or concurrence.

1. Some History of the Court

Article III of the U.S. Constitution establishes the US Supreme Court and describes the Court's powers: "The judicial power shall extend to all cases in law and equity arising under this Constitution, the laws of the United States, and treaties made, or which shall be made under their authority."

Throughout U.S. history the Supreme Court has been called upon to interpret the Constitution in one of two ways: (1) a "strict construction" of national law, which holds that the principal governmental authority remains with the states and that the federal government should have only secondary authority; or (2) a less strict, more nationalist position, which asserts that the Constitution, through a broad interpretation of its phrasing, allows for implied, more expansive powers in the central government.

We have had 16 nominees confirmed as Chief Justice; with an average term of about 14 years. One hundred (100) people have been Associate Justice. Since there is some overlap (4 men have been both Associate Justices and Chief Justices), only 112 persons altogether have ever served on the court. The high court – really, most courts throughout the world – is more about process than substance. John Hart Ely (1938-2003), author of "Democracy and Distrust: A Theory of Judicial Review" (1980) (the most cited American law book of the past 30 years), argued that the primary purpose of the Supreme Court is to ensure that the processes of democratic government remain open and fair, not to serve as an independent source of moral and political values.

Justices Leaving the Court

John Marshall Harlan had a problem. His fellow Supreme Court justices had asked him to approach Justice Stephen Field, now in mental decline, and somehow persuade him to retire.

Justice Harlan remembered a useful nugget: Two decades earlier, in 1869, Field himself had been part of a group that met with a justice to urge retirement. So when Harlan approached Field in the robing room behind the bench, Harlan began by reminding Field of that occasion. Did he remember it, Harlan asked gingerly?

"Yes," spat out Field, "And a dirtier day's work I never did in my life!"

Nonetheless, a president who wants to pry open a Supreme Court slot has some tools at hand. President Lyndon B. Johnson (LBJ) was able to dupe Justice Albert Goldberg into stepping down for the United Nations ambassadorship, which Johnson had led him to believe would be a position of great influence on Vietnam peacemaking. In doing so, LBJ opened the seat for his pal, Abe Fortas. Two years later, Johnson prompted the departure of Justice Tom Clark by appointing his son, Ramsey Clark, as attorney general. The elder Clark resigned to avoid a conflict of interest, giving Johnson the chance to put Thurgood Marshall on the court.

David N. Atkinson, <u>Leaving the Bench</u> (2000) identifies law clerks as a key cause of justices staying too long without attracting public notice. Most justices rely on their clerks to draft opinions, with the justices serving as editors. There also is a creed of omerta (code of silence) that generally succeeds at keeping the court's internal business closed off to the press. So, perhaps, a justice can stay on even if he has slipped to the point of near-senility.

Atkinson concludes that a Justice rarely retires because he/she thinks the current president is like-minded and will replace him with an ideologically compatible appointee. But Justices do hang onto office to keep from being replaced by ideological opponents.

"I am older and slower and less acute and more confused," Chief Justice William Howard Taft conceded in a private letter a year before his death in 1930. He then added, "I must stay on the court in order to keep the Bolsheviki from gaining control" - referring to his more liberal colleagues. Likewise, on the left end of the spectrum, Justice William O. Douglas, seeing himself as an indispensable progressive, stayed on the court into his late 70s despite a badly deteriorating body and mind. "I won't resign while there's a breath in my body - until we get a Democratic president," he told a friend. (This didn't work. Douglas had a stroke and _ after nearly a year of imploring from his wife and friends - Douglas ultimately resigned, which left Republican President Gerald Ford able to pick his replacement.)

In the end, though, most justices simply leave when physical and mental health compels it. Atkinson's book thus is a compendium of heart attacks, strokes, and cancer (poor physical health, mental deterioration, and visits from the Grim Reaper!). It is a list of every malady of old age. As Justice Thurgood Marshall said when he retired in 1991: "I'm getting old and I'm coming apart!" (He would be dead within 18 months.)

2. Legal Experts Propose Limiting Justices' Powers and Terms

In 2009, a group of prominent law professors and jurists led by Duke law professor Paul D. Carrington proposed in a letter to congressional leaders four reforms, none of which go directly to the substance of the Supreme Court's work, but each of which would directly affect the court's functions. The group said Congress has every right to address how the court *operates*, "a subject it appears not to have seriously considered for at least seventy years." The four proposals were taken from various studies, commissions, and previous reform efforts.

a. Term Limits of 18 Years

Justices would take "senior status" after 18 years on the court. Justices in office so long that may not "reflect the moral and political values of the contemporary citizens they govern." No other countries have lifetime appointments for their judges, perhaps because that is very undemocratic. To get around the Constitution's prescription that justices serve for life, the group would let justices stay on the court in a senior role -- filling in on a case, perhaps, or dispatched to lower courts -- or lure them into retirement with promises of hefty bonuses. This would have the added benefit of setting up a regular rotation on the court reflecting in effect the popular will in that it would provide for the President's nomination of a new justice each new two-year term of Congress. If that resulted in more than the current nine justices, only the nine most junior would hear cases.

b. Chief Justices Limited to Seven Years in that Job

This service involves many "political, administrative and non-judicial roles calling for a measure of special accountability" and thus any one Justice should not have the job indefinitely.

c. A Process for Removal of Justices in Failing Health

The chief justice would have the duty to advise such a justice to resign and promptly report that fact to the Judicial Conference of the United States. If the Chief Justice is the one in question, the duty would fall to other justices to report him/her.

d. A Separate Court for Deciding the Cases that the Court Hears

Other than perhaps term limits, this proposed reform would have the most impact. The idea is to deprive the justices of one of their greatest powers: choosing which cases they decide. The Supreme Court annually reviews thousands of petitions for certiorari and typically grants (and thus rules on the

merits) of about 80 cases (starting in the 1980s the annual number accepted for review declined from an average of about 140). A proposed "Certiorari Division" made up of senior justices and appellate judges would review the petitions for certiorari and send 80 to 100 each year to the Supreme Court to decide, whether the court wanted to review them or not. While the most important power of the Court is how it rules on the cases it decides, and it seems likely there would be an overlap between what a Certiorari Division would select and what the Supreme Court itself has accepted for review, the separation of those two powers (what cases to hear and what actually to rule on those cases) means the removal of Court control over its docket. It would signal a dramatic diminution of Court power, and service on the Division would need to be refined in terms of how judges are selected, how long they serve (e.g., temporarily, for just one court term), and their process for review.

3. The Supreme Court's Current Justices
a. Generally

All current Justices but one (Elena Kagan) were federal appeals court judges before being appointed to the U.S. Supreme Court. Presidents hope that their past judicial rulings make their future work on the Supreme Court more predictable (hopefully compatible with the President's ideology). Secondly, lower federal appellate court judges tend to score high on confirmability: for their prior appointment as a federal judge, each of these judges earlier was reviewed by the American Bar Association and confirmed by the Senate.

On the predictability factor, though, note: while judicial writings give some idea of how judges would behave as a Supreme Court Justice, appeals court opinions often are narrow and technical and bound by precedent. So these writings may give less of an indication than one might suppose. Then again, the narrow nature of these lower court opinions may provide a far smaller target for a nominee's critics than do the more "visionary" writings by a nominee who is an academic or politician.

Knowing something about the background and ideology of individual Justices may help us to see trends in the law. Knowing their orientations and voting patterns can help us discern greater meaning in their present opinions and votes. On a divided court, the Justices in the middle, such as Lewis Powell in the 1970s and 1980s, and then Sandra Day O'Connor until her retirement in 2006, probably have more influence for their votes deciding cases than simply for the power of their words.

The following columns indicate the Liberal and Conservative factions of the Supreme Court (four members each), and the one "moderate" most likely to be in the middle.[49] The more seniority a Justice has (Chief Justice status, or the longer that any of the 8 Associate Justices has been on the Supreme Court), the higher up he/she is in that column. Thus, for example, Ginsburg is a senior, liberal Justice, while Alito is a junior, conservative Justice.

---

[49] While politics are important to understanding the Court, there is such a thing as "legal" analysis that exists separately from the political will of the Justice. Loyalty to *stare decisis* (precedent) as well as court awareness of legislative and executive policy preferences is part of a decision-making process guiding judges' actions "and sometimes prohibits [judges] from acting consistent with their ideological preferences." MICHAEL A. BAILEY & FORREST MALTZMAN, "THE CONSTRAINED COURT: LAW, POLITICS AND THE DECISIONS JUSTICES MAKE." As Chief Justice John Roberts noted in his concurrence in *Citizens United v. Federal Election Commission*, 558 U.S. 310 (2010) concurrence, precedent should only be overturned when - according to Maltzman - "(1) validity is so hotly contested that it cannot reliably function as a basis for decision in future cases,(2) its rationale threatens to upend our settled jurisprudence in related areas of law, and (3) the precedent's underlying reasoning has become so discredited that the Court cannot keep the precedent alive without jury-rigging new and different justifications to shore up the original mistake."

For each Justice is listed the year of birth, year starting on the Court (and the President who appointed him/her), the state residence in his/her youth, the law school attended, and any court service immediately before coming to the Supreme Court.

LIBERAL	**"MODERATE"**	**CONSERVATIVE**
Ruth Bader Ginsburg		John G. Roberts, Jr. -Chief Justice [50]
1933, 1993-Clinton		1955, 2005 – Bush II
N.Y., Harvard & Columbia		Indiana, Harvard
D.C. Circuit		D.C. Circuit
Stephen G. Breyer	Anthony M. Kennedy	Antonin Scalia
1938, 1994-Clinton	1936, 1988-Reagan	1936, 1986-Reagan
Calif., Harvard	Calif., Harvard	N.Y., Harvard
1st Circuit	9th Circuit	D.C. Circuit
Sonia Sotomayor		Clarence Thomas
1954, 2009-Obama		1948, 1991-Bush I
N.Y., Yale		Georgia, Yale
2nd Circuit		D.C. Circuit
Elena Kagan		Samuel A. Alito, Jr.
1960, 2010-Obama		1950, 2006-Bush II
N.Y., Harvard		New Jersey, Yale
No Court Service (was Solicitor General)		3rd Circuit

In each Presidential term of four years there has almost always been at least one vacancy on the Court to fill. Indeed, only one President who was elected to and served out a full four year term never had the opportunity to appoint at least one Supreme court Justice: Jimmy Carter (1977-81).[51] Of the five Presidents since Carter, each has two appointees now on the Court, except George H.W. Bush (1989-93), who has just one.

With Justice John Paul Stevens' retirement in August 2010, there are, for the first time ever, no Protestants on the Court. Three of the four "liberal" Justices are Jewish. Justice Sotomayor, Justice Kennedy, and the four "conservative" Justices are all Roman Catholic. Also for the first time ever, there are three women on the Court (indeed, only four women – Ginsburg, Sotomayor, Kagan, and former Justice O'Connor – have ever served on the Court).

b. Individual Justices, from Left to Right

Ruth Bader Ginsburg was a leading women's rights attorney in the 1970s. President Carter appointed her a federal circuit court judge in 1980. As a justice, Ginsburg has become increasingly outspoken for her positions, which often lose because she is left-of-center on a conservative court.

---

[50] Kennedy is most likely to be the fifth vote in a 5-4 decision (generally aligned with the four "liberals" or the four "conservatives." Chief Justice Roberts is the most likely of the four most conservative Justices to vote with the liberals. He was, for example, the fifth vote (not Kennedy), upholding Obamacare in the 2012 Supreme Court decision.

[51] The only other Presidents who never got to appoint a Justice were three 19th Century Presidents: William Henry Harrison (who served just one month, in 1841), Zachary Taylor (who served just 16 months, 1849-50), and Andrew Johnson (1865-69).

A former Harvard Law School Professor, Stephen Breyer is a more Junior Justice than Justice Thomas, who actually is a younger man, because Breyer was appointed to the Court after Thomas was.[52] Breyer tends to be liberal on social polices and civil liberties, but is also a leading jurist on governmental marketplace regulation. He is an influential Justice and is quite willing to spar intellectually with Scalia.

President Reagan chose Anthony Kennedy to the Court in early 1988 after Robert Bork and then Douglas Ginsburg proved to be unsuccessful nominees. Kennedy is the key "swing vote" (most likely to be the fifth vote) in the Court's 5:4 Court decisions. Kennedy loves Shakespeare, and some unkind souls have compared him to an equivocating Hamlet. With former Justices Sandra Day O'Connor (appointed by Reagan) and David Souter (appointed by George H. W, Bush), Kennedy cast the decisive votes in upholding *Roe v. Wade*, 410 U.S. 113 (1973), by a 5:4 majority in a 1992 case. Kennedy is a moderate-conservative, over the years more likely to line up with the conservative Justices than with the liberal Justices. However, Kennedy has voted enough with the liberals that the Court's holdings are difficult to predict. He, for example, was the fifth vote (with the four liberals) in the 5-to-4 June 2015 decision declaring same-sex marriage to be a constitutional right.[53]

Antonin Scalia is a very conservative, bright, and acerbic man. The first Italian-American on the Court, "Nino" Scalia often cuts off other Justices during oral arguments and may not be liked by many of his fellow Justices. Personal relations matter, as they may affect Justices' ability to agree on reasoning and form alliances to write majority opinions, rather than write fiery dissents and quarrelsome concurrences.

Clarence Thomas was approved by the second closest Senate confirmation vote margin in Supreme Court history, 52-48, in the aftermath of Anita Hill's charge that Thomas had sexually harassed her while Thomas was Equal Employment Opportunity Commission Chairman in the 1980s. Thomas is the one African-American on the Court; he replaced the first African-American Justice, the extremely liberal Thurgood Marshall. Thomas is very conservative and aligns with Scalia on over 80% of split decisions. Because Thomas was only 43 when elevated to the Supreme Court, he has a realistic chance of breaking Justice William O. Douglas's record of 36 years' service (1939-1975).

As for the four most recent appointees to the Court – Roberts, Alito, Sotomayor, and Kagan - all had stellar careers before their nominations and confirmations. Both Roberts and Alito have proven to be, for the most part, quite conservative (as expected). They have tended to be "pro-business" with their support of limits on legal liability, on employee rights, and on federal regulation. Sotomayor and Kagan, on the other hand, have been reliably liberal votes when the Court is divided.

4. Writs of *Certiorari*

Certiorari is a Latin word meaning "to be informed of, or to be made certain in regard to." It is also the term for certain appellate proceedings to re-examine the actions of a trial court or lower appeals court. The U.S. Supreme Court still uses the term certiorari in the context of appeals.

Losing parties may file with the Supreme Court a petition for writ of certiorari (informally called a "cert. petition" - "cert." is the abbreviation for certiorari). This document asks the court to review a lower court's decision. The petition lists the parties, states the facts of the case, sets forth the legal questions presented for review, and contends why the court should grant the writ.

Rule 10 of the Rules of the U.S. Supreme Court provides, "Review on writ of certiorari is not a matter of right, but a judicial discretion. A petition for writ of certiorari will be granted only for compelling reasons."

---

[52] Also, as Chief Justice, John Roberts has the most "seniority" simply because of that status as Chief Justice, even though Roberts is the second youngest Justice and has been on the Court for less time than five of the Justices.

[53] *Obergefell v. Hodges*, 576 U.S. __ (2015) (a fundamental right to marry is guaranteed to same-sex couples by both the Due Process Clause and the Equal Protection Clause of the Fourteenth Amendment).

> **Statistics on the U.S. Supreme Court and the Grant of Certiorari**
> In a typical year, some 6,500 to 7,500 petitions for writ of certiorari are decided, with only about 100 to 120 (less than 2%) granted and the rest denied or otherwise dismissed. About half of the cert. requests are in criminal cases, with only 20-30 (0.5%) granted, while the other half of the requests are in civil cases, with maybe 80-95 of these (about 3.0%) granted. (A little over 1% of the petitions are in administrative matters, with only 3 or 4 (about 5%) granted.
>
> So, "cert. denied" is the most common phrase the Supreme Court utters, since about 98% of requests for certiorari are turned down. This abbreviation - "cert. denied" - is used in legal citations (immediately after the citation of the opinion(s) by the lower courts) to indicate that the Supreme Court denied a petition for writ of certiorari.

When the Supreme Court denies certiorari (refuses to take the case), the decision court from which the cert. was sought (usually, Court of Appeals) is unaffected. However, the Supreme Court's refusal to grant certiorari does not necessarily reflect agreement with the lower court decision. All it means is that fewer than four Justices wanted to grant certiorari. The denial of certiorari, by itself, is not a precedent. Indeed, it is very rare for a Justice to write anything about the denial of certiorari (e.g., in a "dissent" from the Court's refusal to issue the writ).

When cert. is granted, an order (a **writ of certiorari - pg. 51; Emerson BL**) is issued to the lower court to send up the records from the case. Cert. is granted if four Justices vote for it. Grounds are: (1) the matter is a crucial constitutional or statutory question, or (2) different lower courts have ruled differently.

5. Special Constitutional Courts Elsewhere

In the United States, it may be harder to bring a complaint about constitutional matters than under new national constitutions with special tribunals for resolving those issues (and, of course, exercising powers of judicial review). Consider, for example, some European Union nations with these special reviewing bodies. Austria, Germany, and Italy have constitutional courts, Spain has a constitutional tribunal, and France has a constitutional council. Outside Europe, there also are such special courts, such as South Africa's 11-judge Constitutional Court. On the other hand, in Latin America and Japan – influenced by the United States – national supreme courts tend to be like the U.S. Supreme Court, without a special subject-specific agenda; nonetheless, these courts have long been at least theoretically capable of judicial review and may be as likely, or more, to exercise it as any special court.

6. Judicial Review: *Marbury v. Madison*

President John Adams appointed John Marshall chief justice in early 1801, right before Adams left office. Marshall held his position for over 34 years, until his death on July 6, 1835. He served longer than any other Chief Justice, and longer than almost every other Justice. Marshall is so revered that when lawyers, judges, and legal scholars mention him he is usually called not just "Chief Justice Marshall," but also "the great Chief Justice Marshall."

Marshall ended the practice of seriatim opinions - a British tradition in which appeals courts judges wrote and presented orally their individual opinions on each case. Instead, the Supreme Court under Marshall issued a single majority opinion. Indeed, dissents were much rarer than for the more recent Court. Marshall reasoned that the opinion of the Supreme Court would be more supported if all the judges were to support one opinion; a sign of its importance is that all American high courts (state and federal) tend to follow Marshall's approach of having a single majority opinion.

Still, the most important thing Marshall did was to write so many important opinions – the substance of those opinions is even more important than that there rarely were dissents or concurrences. And of all these incredibly significant opinions the first and most important of Marshall's great cases was *Marbury v. Madison*, 5 U.S. (1 Cranch) 137 (1803). The decision upheld the Court's power to review legislation and to overrule acts of Congress and of state legislatures that it considered unconstitutional. Chief Justice Marshall "crowned himself," that is, the Court (a la Napoleon crowing himself). Even though nothing in the Constitution says that the Supreme Court can declare governmental laws or actions unconstitutional - hence, throw them out – Marshall declared the Court's power of judicial review.

The only real power of the Court is the power of persuasion, and there are a few, now antiquated, examples of the President simply not being "persuaded" to follow what the Court clearly has ruled:

(1) Andrew Jackson and the Cherokees- In two separate Supreme Court Rulings, *Cherokee Nation v. Georgia*, 30 U.S. 1 (1831), and *Worcester v. Georgia*, 31 U.S. 515 (1832), the U.S. Supreme Court ruled that the people of the Cherokee Nation had a right to their land and the State of Georgia could not force them from it; but by 1835 President Jackson's army was marching the Cherokees and other Native American tribes from Georgia to Indian territory in Oklahoma; Jackson reputedly said, "John Marshall [Chief Justice of the Supreme Court] has made his decision; Now let him enforce it!"[54]

(2) Lincoln and Chief Justice Roger B. Taney - Taney's court, during the Civil War, ruled against the Lincoln Administration's use of imprisonment without promptly stating the charges and holding a hearing, but Lincoln and his officials tended to ignore what the Court said. (Fighting the Confederates, and their sympathizers, took precedence for Pres. Lincoln).

Despite these cases, over time there has been general acceptance (by other federal branches, by the states) of the *judicial review* concept announced in Marbury: the Supreme Court (and other courts') has power to rule on the constitutionality of other branches' actions.

Comparative Law on Judicial Review

Most of the countries in the world - even England - have no Supreme Court judicial review power. The few countries that do, such as Canada, Germany, India, Israel, and South Africa, model their systems, at least to some extent, on America's approach. Indeed, Canada and India are two examples of aggressively active Supreme Courts, and all of the above nations, as well as a few others (and some super-national bodies such as EU commissions) have engaged in profound judicial review – striking down executive or legislative actions as violative of the highest law for that jurisdiction.

---

7. What Does *Marbury* Mean Today?

Although *Marbury v. Madison* is viewed as fundamental to the American constitutional enterprise, there have been widely differing views as to precisely what *Marbury* means. Some commentators have identified *Marbury* with the "judicial veto" principle, under which anyone disappointed by a statute or executive decision is entitled to a judicial determination of that law's constitutionality. Others have suggested judicial *supremacy*: that the current Supreme Court believes that *Marbury* and its progeny mean that in most cases, there is no room even for constitutional interpretation by other branches of government: legislative and executive acts have no constitutional status until the judiciary passes on them (i.e., takes a pass, and thus lets the other branches interpret the law or act). Still others treat *Marbury* as standing for the far more limited proposition that judicial review only permits courts to engage in constitutional interpretation within a limited sphere of "cases and controversies" in which they are authorized to do so, and outside that sphere there is a vast realm where constitutional issues are delegated to the political branches. Under this limited "cases and controversies" approach, there is a wide scope for activity by other governmental branches - activity that amounts to constitutional interpretation. While the judiciary may review these implicit constitutional judgments by others (e.g.,

---

[54] As Josef Stalin once said of the Pope, "Who is this Pope? How many army divisions does he have?!" Actually, many historians opine that Jackson (a former lawyer and territorial judge) did not say that and was not as disrespectful of the actual decision as the quotation would indicate.

legislatures, the executive branch), that power includes the freedom to decline to do so. So, our understanding of *Marbury* does not depend on the legitimacy of "judicial supremacy" (which, in at least some context, almost everyone accepts), but on the *scope* of judicial supremacy: on the extent to which the courts, especially the U.S. Supreme Court, have allowed other branches to carve out some space for their own constitutional interpretations.

B. LITIGATION (see generally pgs. 59-78; Emerson BL)

This section of the text discusses lawsuit chronology, from initial pleadings to appeals.

I. SUING AND SETTLEMENTS

A. Perceived Injury

Once a person believes that someone else's misconduct (e.g., a breach of contract or a tort) has harmed him, litigation may commence.

B. Potential Settlement

1. The Rules

Judges usually encourage settlement; the rules specifically support the settling of disputes. For example, Rule One (the very first rule!) of the Federal Rules of Civil Procedure states that judges are expected to promote "the just, speedy, and inexpensive determination of every action

2. *Abraham Lincoln on the Need to Compromise*

Abraham Lincoln's cases were typical of his times - boundary disputes, commercial claims, divorce cases, damages by wandering cattle, and common brawls. Most of his cases were in common law and less than 10 percent were in criminal law. Lincoln encouraged all lawyers to really try to settle disputes. He considered it the right thing to do. There will "still be plenty of work," Lincoln told other attorneys.

3. Negotiation

Settlement can come at any point in the process, from the moment one is aware of a possible case through to the trials themselves and even post-trial appeals. Many potential cases are not filed. Of those filed, only 6% or 7% of American lawsuits go to trial.

The Story of the Genie

Two workers and their boss were walking to lunch when they find an antique oil lamp. They rub it and a Genie comes out.
The Genie says, "I'll give each of you just one wish."

Moral of the story: In negotiating, it may be best to let others . . .

4. Litigation Etiquette

A civil action (the lawsuit process) should proceed in order.
There is an analogy between "proceeding precipitously" in litigation and "going fast" in dating.

> **Sample Settlement Agreement**
> AGREEMENT made this 25th Day of March, 2016, between ATLANTIC COURIER CO., a Maryland Corporation ("ACC"), and the SELMA EQUITABLE CORPORATION ("SEC"), an Alabama corporation.
> WITNESSETH: WHEREAS, a dispute has arisen between the parties concerning the loss of certain athletic equipment which, on or about October 30, 2015, in Richmond, Virginia, SEC entrusted to ACC for delivery to the Greater Gator Hootenanny, in Gainesville, Florida; and, WHEREAS, both parties want to continue their business association; and WHEREAS, both parties desire to settle all controversies between them arising from the aforesaid loss; 1. SEC hereby renounces any direct claim against ACC for the aforesaid loss and agrees not to file suit against ACC. 2. Nothing in this Agreement shall be construed as a relinquishment of SEC's rights against any party other than ACC. 3. SEC specifically reserves the right to seek and obtain relief from Bad News Air, Inc., a Delaware corporation ("Bad News"), and from any insurers, including those of ACC. 4. ACC hereby agrees to cooperate with efforts by SEC to obtain relief from Bad News, from ACC's insurer(s), and from any other party besides ACC itself.
> IN WITNESS WHEREOF, the parties have executed this Agreement the day and year written above.
>
> ATLANTIC COURIER COMPANY, INC.   SELMA EQUITABLE CORPORATION
> By: _____   By: _____

C. Secret "Side Deals"

There is a brewing debate over the ethics of allowing certain "side deals" in civil court cases. Side deals can involve a defendant settling a case and then helping the plaintiffs against co-defendants. There are pacts where plaintiffs who win their case ask the judge to erase the ruling from court records (often in exchange for the defendant agreeing not to appeal and writing a quick settlement check). Another settlement arrangement, called Mary Carter agreements, allow defendants who settle a case to get some of the settlement money back if the plaintiff wins in court.

Those who support the idea of secret accords say that it helps to speed up the court system and lower legal fees. Those who oppose these side deals argue that they hide important information from juries and erase records that would be helpful to other lawyers and plaintiffs in the future.

> **The "McLibel" Case**
> Settlement – Compromise, or even just letting things slide, seems to be the best approach to most disputes. As a practical matter, suing simply to make a point is unwise. A classic exposition of this principle is the ENGLISH "MCLIBEL" CASE, *McDonald's Corp. v. Steel & Morris* – an English case of foolishly suing for principles' sake. In the mid-1980s, environmentalists had picketed McDonald's in England and claimed that McDonald's was destroying ozone and the Amazon Rainforest. The environmentalists' pamphlet issued in 1984 and entitled "What's Wrong with McDonald's" accused McDonald's of starving the Third World and selling unhealthy food. As English defamation law is more favorable to plaintiffs than American defamation law (American free speech protections serve to constrain its defamation law), McDonald's thought this to be a great opportunity; it sued for defamation. What ensued was the longest trial in English history.
> The McLibel case also evidences that sometimes there is little leverage over a "little guy," who therefore has the ability to avoid the usual pressures exerted during litigation.[55] While other environmentalists quickly settled with McDonald's, two poor, fearless ones did not. The trial itself lasted

---

[55] If one has little, then one has little to lose. What leverage, then, is derived from threats of fines or damage awards?

for two years. It became a media circus. The two defendants, Helen Steel (an unemployed gardener) and David Morris (a postman), represented themselves and, especially the glib Morris, became heroes to many. While McDonald's ultimately won a judgment, it spent inordinate time and money to do so and – worse yet – lost the public relations campaign. Instead of proving it was an ecologically friendly business, it came across as a bully.

Ironically, even the legal judgment was, years later, overturned. On February 15, 2005, the two British activists found to have libeled McDonald's won a reversal of the English court's decision at the European Court of Human Rights, in Strasbourg, France. The court ruled that Steel and Morris did not receive a fair trial and their freedom of expression was violated by the 1997 judgment ordering them to pay 60,000 pounds (then about $113,200) in damages.

D. The Demand Letter –

A RIGHT TO SUE versus IS IT RIGHT TO SUE? See a video example: "Woman vs. Truck" - the case of the late Gertie Witherspoon. An optional YouTube *video*, *Woman_v_TruckCartoon_BoxingAnalogyandAnalysis_4mins19secs*, reviews the Gertie Witherspoon scenario, with some cartoon boxing to add some zest.

DEMAND LETTER – AN EXAMPLE

DEWEY, CHEATHAM & HOWE
100 Attorney Boulevard
Miami, Florida

Mr. Iggy Renaldo
4835 Kenilworth Avenue
Ft Lauderdale, FL
Dear Mr. Renaldo:

This letter is to inform you that my client, Mr. Michael Von Bismarck, sustained damages of $1,051.43 due to the negligent installation of an oil filter at your Ft. Lauderdale Texaco station. As the independent operator of said service station, you are liable for the negligent work of your employees. If satisfactory reimbursement of the $1,051.43 is not tendered to my client within 15 days, you will be sued. In order for you to see more clearly how my client has had to pay the aforementioned amount solely because of faulty servicing at your Texaco station, the following paragraphs state the facts in more detail.

On July 8th of this year, in response to an advertisement about a sale on oil filters and lube jobs, Michael Von Bismarck came to the Texaco station located at 4835 Kenilworth Avenue, Ft. Lauderdale, Florida. He paid $17.50 to get an oil change, lubrication, and a new oil filter for his '2003 Taurus. (A copy of the bill is enclosed. It is titled, "A1's Sunoco"; apparently, you used invoices from your former Sunoco Station for work performed at the Texaco Station.) The services performed at the Ft. Lauderdale Texaco station were matters of routine maintenance. Mr. Von Bismarck's Taurus was in excellent condition when it arrived at the station.

Shortly thereafter, while Mr. Von Bismarck was driving on I-95 South, his Taurus's oil indicator lit up. He immediately pulled to the side of the road and discovered that no oil registered on the car's dipstick. Mr. Von Bismarck added three quarts of oil and then attempted to re-start the engine.

The engine was dead.

Mr. Von Bismarck again got out of the car. He noticed oil dripping underneath the engine. Even more ominous, the oil filter was completely off, lying at the bottom of the engine block.
Trying to capture some of the leaking oil, Mr. Von Bismarck put the filter back on. However, the engine still failed to turn over. The car had to be towed to a repair station.

> As you can see from the enclosed bill of Fox Ford, the repairs called for many hours of labor and many new parts. With the exception of one minor repair (a $49.00 labor charge which we have not included in the $1,551.43), all of the work at Fox Ford was necessitated by the severe engine problems which followed the displacement of the oil filter. It is only logical to assume, as we are sure a judge and jury would, that the oil filter came loose because of faulty installation at your Ft. Lauderdale Texaco station.
>
> Mr. Renaldo, we expect a prompt reply. While we would prefer to settle this matter amicably, we will, if need be, seek relief in court. It is quite clear that Mr. Von Bismarck has a very good case against you and your station. It is, we suggest, to your advantage to send forthwith reimbursement of the $1,551.43. Otherwise, besides just reimbursement, further expenses (interest on any judgment awarded, legal fees, court costs, etc.) probably await you.
>
> Please make the reimbursement check payable to the order of Michael P. Von Bismarck. The check should be sent to Sue Yerpantzoff, Dewey, Cheatham & Howe, 100 Attorney Blvd., Miami, Florida.
>
> I may be reached at (305) 999-0000. If I am not available, you may contact Ms. Dunnem Dewey at the same number.
>
> Thank you for your cooperation in this matter.
>
>   Sincerely,
>   Sue Yerpantzoff

Try never to bring a lawsuit just for principles' sake, especially in business. There are too many variables and expenses. Court cases are much better suited to award money, or not, than to pronounce meaningful, soul-quenching, vindication.

Another problem is that the other side may not be susceptible to ordinary pressure points. Some plaintiffs or defendants are: (1) so-called professional "suers"; (2) non-payers who routinely say, "So sue me"; and (3) prisoners suing the state. Although states and the national government have tried to deter frivolous civil suits by prisoners (the Prison Litigation Reform Act of 1995 provides for applicable countermeasures to discourage frivolous and abusive lawsuits, such as causing these prisoners to lose some "early release" or "gain" time they had earned as punishment for filing silly civil suits), they have not taken such measures for criminal motions or appeals. For example, in upholding a 1996 Florida statute, the Florida Supreme Court ruled in *Hall v. State* (2000), that prisoners can be punished for filing frivolous civil suits.

The overall principle in America is that claims or defenses, if generally lawful, are permitted even though the actual motives for them are bad. The legal problem arises only if the claim or defense itself (not the motive) is frivolous or malicious. And concerns about frivolous, malicious, or unending litigation have existed throughout the ages. An excellent literary examination of these longstanding troubles - costly, overly long and oft-delayed litigation - is the Charles Dickens novel, *Bleak House*. The book centers on one such horrible case. In writing of the dispute, *Jarndyce v. Jarndyce*, Dickens states, "the lawyers have twisted [the case] into such a state of bedevilment that the original merits of the case have long disappeared from the face of the earth. It's about a Will, and the trust under a Will - or it was once. It's about nothing but costs [e.g., attorneys' fees] now."[56]

E. The Complaint (see pgs. 60-61; Emerson BL)

The complaint is the initial pleading in a lawsuit (sometimes called a declaration, petition, or bill of complaint). It includes a statement of facts, the legal basis of the suit (cause of action), and a request for one or more remedies. So, besides the Allegations of Fact, there are Statements of Legal Causes of

---

[56] CHARLES DICKENS, BLEAK HOUSE (1852), at chapter 8.

Action - which assert the law allegedly leading to a possible remedy and endeavor to show how the so-called wrong is unlawful.

In essence, a complaint says, "I've been wronged, and these are the remedies I seek." It must state sufficient facts to show a legal wrong (e.g., that the conduct constitutes a breach of contract; that the facts of this auto "accident" constitute the tort of negligence).

> **Comparison to Other Litigation Systems**
>
> Individualism, greed, legal advertising, access to juries, less governmental compensation for the sick or injured, and presumably more favorable substantive laws and procedures (e.g., pretrial discovery) may explain why more suits are filed in the United States than elsewhere. However, there are more basic reasons for the large number of lawsuit filings in America.
>
> In the United States, it is cheap to file a lawsuit; the plaintiff's start-up costs are minimal. Court fees are very low, service of process generally can be achieved easily with very little expense (e.g., by mail), and lawyers typically take personal injury cases on a contingency fee basis, i.e., usually without an up-front retainer.
>
> In most other countries, to initiate a lawsuit costs much more. For a case seeking a significant amount in damages (say, the equivalent of $1 million), the filing fees in Germany or Japan usually are about 20 to 30 times greater than in the United States (several thousand dollars, perhaps much more) and the up-front retainer fee for hiring a lawyer will be perhaps the equivalent of $5,000 in Germany and $50,000 in Japan, while the American personal injury lawyer will not be paid a fee ahead of time (because it is a contingency). In many countries, including Germany or Japan, it is less likely than in America that litigation expenses later will race upward at a phenomenal rate, the financial entry-barrier in the other nations is so much more significant.
>
> Higher financial entry barriers lower the number of suits filed in two ways:
>
> 1. Many plaintiffs will not be able to advance the necessary funds, or at least not be willing to risk losing these funds if their case is dismissed (and in most countries, they would also be liable for the defendant's costs and attorney's fees under the prevalent loser-pays-all rule);
>
> 2. Differences in start-up costs lead to differences in strategic behavior, as American "victims" tend to sue quickly and then settle most of their claims; but "victims" elsewhere often seek to avoid the high cost of lawsuits. Only suing if no compromise can be reached, they instead first try to reach a settlement.

1. Electronic Filing

All federal courts and most state courts permit electronic case filing (receiving some documents from lawyers electronically and making entire court files available on the Internet). Some courts even require it for certain cases, especially complex civil litigation. Moreover, many courts will scan paper files onto their webpages. *See* PUBLIC ACCESS TO COURT ELECTRONIC RECORDS, http://www.pacer.gov/.

2. Notice

Notice is crucial. It is a fundamental concept in the application of law for many legal subjects. For example, regulatory laws such as workers' compensation and the Occupational Safety and Health Act require that employers furnish notice to their employees about the law in that field.

Many employers conduct seminars and issue bulletins intended to reduce the number and severity of incidents - not just to stay on the Occupational Safety and Health Administration's (http://www.osha.gov/) good side, but also to keep workers' compensation insurance premiums lower.

F. Service Of Process

Comparison of a Summons to a Subpoena

Subpoenaing of Witnesses

In Latin, the term *subpoena* means, "under penalty."

A subpoena is a court order. Do <u>not</u> ignore it! Whenever a person fails to obey a court order (e.g., a subpoena to be a witness at a trial or a deposition, or a summons to appear for jury duty), he/she can be held in contempt of court - possibly go to jail.[57]

Persons may specialize as private entrepreneurs serving subpoenas to difficult-to-reach, evasive witnesses, just as they do to serve processes on "difficult" defendants.

A defendant cannot just shove the process back (or throw it out) and then run away. If service of process papers are handed to you, you cannot just shove them back under the door. Judges tend to believe "unbiased" sheriffs or private process servers; it is hard to challenge their claims that process was served.

To have a case assured of proceeding, there must be **service of process** upon the defendant. To serve process is to deliver to the defendant a copy of the complaint and the **summons,** which indicates the time period for the defendant to respond.

Service of process is a technical requirement, but it must be met: One cannot simply say, "I know the defendant knows he/she has been sued," or "I mailed something to the defendant," or "I talked to the defendant and told him about the lawsuit," or "I told the defendant's lawyer." If a plaintiff never obtains service of process, then the lawsuit does not proceed to the next step.[58]

A defendant can waive service of process - e.g., to avoid embarrassment, to save on time and costs. For example, after two businesses have negotiated and ended up going to a lawsuit, their lawyers ordinarily will just agree that the complaint will go directly from one lawyer to the other, and that the other will respond without requiring formal service of process.

1. Terminology: Due Process and Types of Service

Rules of Civil Procedure (http://www.law.cornell.edu/rules/frcp/) determine the proper form of legal process and how it should be served. The rules vary among federal and state courts, but they are meant to give the defendant notice of the proceedings and to command him to either respond to the allegations or to appear at a specified time and answer the claim. The concept of NOTICE is critical to the integrity of legal proceedings. Due process forbids legal action against a person unless the person has been given notice and an opportunity to be heard.

Process must be properly served on all parties in an action. Anyone who is not served is not bound by the decision in the case. A defendant can challenge the alleged service of process at a pretrial hearing. There, the defendant (or his/her attorney) makes a "special appearance" before the court for the limited purpose of challenging the service or other matters of personal jurisdiction.

---

[57] Joke about contempt of court –
Judge: Are you showing contempt for this court?
Response: I hope not, your honor. I'm doing my best to hide it."

[58] That is what happened in the case where we sent the demand letter for the Sue Yerpantzoff, of the law firm, Dewey, Cheatham & Howe, example above (names changed, of course!). We ended up filing a lawsuit, but we never could locate the defendant, who had left the country.

There are three main methods for service of process: (1) personal service, (2) substituted service, and (3) service by publication. Of these methods, personal service is preferred because it most effectively ensures actual notice and is thus most difficult for the defendant to challenge successfully. Traditionally (at common law), personal service was the only lawful method of service. Although some states require strict compliance with substitute and constructive service statutes mainly because they are in derogation of common law, other states require strict compliance explicitly on due process grounds.

Personal service requires in-hand delivery of the complaint and summons to the defendant himself/herself. The following are three forms of personal service: certified mail, by court personnel, or via private process servers.

Certified mail is inexpensive, but a problem is that, despite the requirement that it be signed by the addressee, sometimes another person (e.g., a spouse, a colleague, a fellow employee, a secretary) will sign it, instead. Then there is no clear proof that the defendant actually received the complaint and summons.

Use of sheriffs or other court personnel is still fairly inexpensive, but there can be bureaucratic problems. Sheriffs are busy people, and they have more pressing duties. (Ordinarily, there are no "commissions" or other financial rewards for public officials serving summons on defendants.)

Private Process Server is most assured of succeeding, but can be quite expensive. In some states, such as Florida, private process servers must obtain certification from the local sheriff. Fla. Stat. 48.021. Servers fill out affidavits and explain circumstances. http://www.serve-now.com/resources/process-serving-laws/Florida (Florida Rules of Civil Procedure).

For the most part, courts have allowed process servers to use any means necessary to serve papers on reluctant defendants as long as no law is broken. For example, a process server can knock on the defendant's door and state that he has a package for the defendant. If the defendant opens the door, the resulting service of process is valid. Indeed, some process servers (e.g., Irving Botwinick, whose New York process serving firm is called "Serving by Irving"[59]) acknowledge that "creativity is in their blood" and even advertise for employees in theatrical trade publications. Therefore, most courts have permitted process servers to "lie" to some people (e.g., submit to a full medical examination in order to serve papers on an elusive physician; pose as an autograph seeker to bestow papers on a professional ballplayer) to obtain access to the person that needs to be served. Private process servers may make much more than the standard fee (instead, often charging by the hour) for the small minority of cases where the defendant is an "avoider."

Substituted service is any method other than personal service, which may include but is not limited to the following mechanisms of delivery: leaving the documents with an adult resident of the home of the person to be served, with an employee with management duties at the office of an individual, or in some cases by posting in a central location followed by mailing copies by certified mail to the person to be served.[60]

With service by publication the legal notice must be published in at least one newspaper of general circulation where the court is located and/or where the defendant is likely to be found. This is typically a method of last resort.

---

[59] Serving by Irving's motto is: "If they're alive, we'll serve them. If they're dead, we'll tell you where they're buried."

[60] See http://legal-dictionary.thefreedictionary.com/Substituted+Service; http://law.jrank.org/pages/10165/Service-Process-Methods-Service.html

2. Avoiding Service

A defendant cannot avoid the service of process by refusing to accept delivery of the papers.[61] Many cases have upheld service where the process server dropped the papers at the defendant's feet, hit the defendant in the chest with them, or even laid them on the defendant's car when she refused to get out or open the door.

3. The Federal Approach

In federal cases and also in a few states (e.g., New York) which follow the federal approach, a plaintiff can follow a simplified or expedited procedure for service of process: sending to the defendant a copy of the complaint and a "notice of commencement of action" via the U.S. mail. When the plaintiff includes a request that the defendant waive a formal service of process, and the defendant refuses to do so, the plaintiff can later collect from the defendant the costs incurred in having to serve process.

Defendants who waive service effectively have 60 days to respond to a complaint, rather than the normal 20 to 30 day period. (A defendant's refusal to waive the service of process requirement is NOT justified by a belief that the plaintiff's claim is unjust or that the court lacks jurisdiction or venue. The defendant can still raise all those defenses in responding to the lawsuit.)

The U.S. mail "notice of commencement of action" cannot be used against government entities, legal infants (children) or incompetent persons. Ordinary service of process must be used against them.

4. International Law on Service of Process (see pgs. 61-62; Emerson BL)

The Convention on the Service Abroad of Judicial and Extrajudicial Documents in Civil or Commercial Matters, more commonly called the Hague Service Convention (1965), provides procedures for serving process in another country. The United States is one of the 69 signatory nations. In the landmark case, *Volkswagen Aktiengesellschaft v. Schlunk* (Schlunk), 486 U.S. 694 (1988), the U.S. Supreme Court held that service of process pursuant to this Convention applies exclusively when parties must sCerve process abroad, but that it does not apply when parties could serve process in the United States.

As of December 2015, the Convention's "main" signatory nations include these 50 countries: Albania, Antigua and Barbuda, Australia, Bahamas, Barbados, Belarus, Belgium, Belize, Bosnia, Botswana, Canada, Croatia, Cyprus, Denmark, Estonia, Fiji, Finland, France, Hungary, Iceland, India, Ireland, Israel, Italy, Japan, Kiribati, Kuwait, Luxembourg, Macedonia, Malawi, Mexico, Monaco, Morocco, Netherlands, Nevis, Pakistan, Portugal, Romania, Russia, San Marino, Serbia, Seychelles, Slovenia, Spain, St. Kitts, St. Lucia, St. Vincent and the Grenadines, Sweden, the United Kingdom, and the United States. In addition, 19 other nations - Argentina, Bulgaria, China, the Czech Republic, Egypt, Germany, Greece, Latvia, Lithuania, Malta, Norway, Poland, Slovakia, South Korea, Sri Lanka, Switzerland, Turkey, Ukraine, and Venezuela - are signatories, but they do not permit service of process under the Hague Service Convention via mail (the "postal channels").

---

[61] That runs counter to notions sometimes found in popular culture. For example, the classic jazz tune, "Comes Love" (1939 - Sam H. Stept, with lyrics by Lew Brown and Charles Tobias) includes many lyrics about how you can overcome almost anything except falling in love. Two of the stanzas are:

"Comes a headache, you can lose it in a day/ Comes a toothache, see your dentist right away/ Comes love, nothing can be done.

Comes a heat wave, you can hurry to the shore/ ***Comes a summons, you can hide behind the door***/ Comes love, nothing can be done."

It is a wonderful song, but it is just plain wrong about the law of service of process!

II. PLEADINGS

After the Complaint, the plaintiff and defendant may file a number of pleadings.

A. Request for Jury Trial

At the beginning of a case, either the plaintiff or the defendant can ask for a jury trial (a right guaranteed by the Seventh Amendment). Jury trials are complex, time-consuming, and costly; they take much longer and involve more expense than do judge only trials (called "bench trials"), because they require the selection of jurors, the instructing of them, and sometimes isolating/sequestering them.

If not requested at the outset, then jury trial is waived.

Sequestering the Jury

Sequestering a jury means keeping all the jurors together in a location separate from their normal abodes, under the care of court authorities, throughout some or all of the trial. No matter what type of case it is, most jurisdictions do not require sequestration during either the trial or deliberation stages, but give the trial judge discretion to order sequestration in any case.

Some states require sequestration in certain kinds of cases (typically, death penalty cases), but give discretion to the trial judge in all other kinds of cases. A few states require sequestration for deliberations but give discretion to the judge concerning whether to order sequestration before deliberations. And two states require sequestration in certain cases for either the whole trial, or for deliberations, if either litigant requests it.

Four reasons to sequester are to keep jurors from being exposed to prejudicial, out-of-court information, to minimize pressure on jurors from outsiders seeking a particular verdict, to ensure jurors' safety from harassment, threats, or outright violence, and to promote the public perception that a trial was fair because of sequestration's assurances against out-of-court influences.

Arguments against sequestration include:
(1) its cost to taxpayers;
(2) its potential harm – psychological and otherwise – to long-isolated jurors; and
(3) its adverse impact on the jury's role as truth-seeker in that
    (a) it may create non-representative juries if only limited categories of people (e.g., people with little, if any personal, family, or job responsibilities) are available to serve,
    (b) it can lead jurors to identify with the government (the jury's caretaker) or against the government (the jury's "jailer"),
    (c) it can lead lawyers and judges to rush cases along to avoid having a jury blame them for prolonging the case, and
    (d) sequestered juries may rush to reach a verdict merely to escape sequestration.

Prof. Strauss concludes that the costs of sequestration outweigh its benefits, and that the practice should be abolished.

B. Demurrer (Motion to Dismiss) (see pg. 62; Emerson BL)

Demurrers are based solely on the pleadings - the defendant is not disputing the acts as alleged by the plaintiff. For purposes of the Motion to Dismiss the defendant is admitting the facts, but saying there is no legal case based on those allegations. Grounds for the motion could be (1) problems with something such as venue or jurisdiction, or (2) that the Complaint's allegations do not indicate a legal wrong (no remedy available based on the alleged problem).

Problems with the pleadings themselves are subject to dismissal motions. But the defendant has to go to court, or file additional pleadings, if the problem with the Complaint is that it is a "pack of lies."

Usually, one may sue. One can have a legal claim even though an underlying reason for suing is "improper." When a complaint is deemed "non-frivolous" (i.e., there is some basis for its filing), then only in extremely rare cases have courts thrown out the complaint or imposed fines on lawyers. In these extreme situations, the courts found, in effect, that the only purposes for bringing the complaint were inappropriate purposes (e.g., to harass, to cause needless delay, to force needless litigation expenses upon the defendant).

But there is a problem with a motion to dismiss: even if it is granted, the dismissal usually just delays the case if the plaintiff is persistent. Dismissals usually are without prejudice, meaning that the plaintiff can file a claim again. For example, if dismissal is because of jurisdictional or venue problems, the plaintiff usually can just re-file, but in the right place or with modified claims.

TWO EXAMPLES ABOUT DEMURRER (MOTIONS TO DISMISS)

1. One Ugly Defendant

2. Failure to Lend Hedge Clippers

The grant of the demurrer is like, in baseball, strike one on a batter; it is not a strikeout. So problems that led to the granting of a demurrer can usually be corrected. For example, in the Hedge Clippers example, suppose the neighbor re-files his claim; in his amended complaint the neighbor states that you earlier borrowed his lawnmower and agreed at that time to lend him a gardening tool whenever he asked for it.

C. The Answer (see pgs. 62-63; Emerson BL)

1. The Answer's Format

An **answer** generally admits or denies each of the various allegations set forth in the complaint. The defendant, therefore, responds to each claim made in the complaint. His/her answer may include affirmative defenses - e.g., statute of limitations, contributory negligence, assumption of risk (plaintiff consciously exposed himself to the danger), or estoppel (plaintiff's actions inhibit him from seeking a legal remedy) (http://www.jurisdictionary.com/Sidepages/Samples/pForms.pdf). *If not raised early in the case, then these defenses are waived (given up).*

Once the answer is filed, the case is "joined." That is, the whole case joins together the plaintiff and the defendant. Now, many steps in the process remain.

2. Default Judgment

The defendant cannot simply refuse to respond because he thinks the complaint is a "pack of lies." Failure to make any response (either an answer or a motion to dismiss) can easily lead to a default judgment. As is the case with your bank statements, which you should promptly examine and reconcile with your own records, do not just stuff the lawsuit papers in a drawer and forget about them. It is a real hellish, expensive mess if you do not respond. Even more analogous would be, say, a termination notice for utility services (e.g. electricity) - ignore it, and it will not go away. Instead, it is your utility service that is destined to expire!

D. Counterclaims (see pg. 64; Emerson BL)

A counterclaim is, in effect, a "reverse" complaint – one by the defendant against the plaintiff.

E. The Cross-Claim and Third-Party Claim (see pg. 64; Emerson BL)

For a cross-claim, one defendant files the claim against another defendant (the claim is that another defendant is really responsible). For third-party claims, a party (almost always a defendant) brings in an outside party and makes it another defendant.

Cross-claims and third-party claims often raise the plaintiff's hope that defendants will fight among themselves (focus more on who has to pay the plaintiff, not whether anyone has to pay the plaintiff).

F. A Liberal Right to Amend Pleadings

There are *few legal problems with changing claims or defenses,* as long as it is done early enough so that other parties can deal with these changes (by conducting additional discovery, filing a response, etc.). So changes are allowed unless they unfairly prejudice the other side's case preparation, such as by changing one's contentions/pleadings just a few days before trial.

However, even if done in a timely and procedurally fair fashion, significant changes in pleadings can create practical problems for the party making the changes. For example, suppose that Demetrius Defendant initially defends a car accident case by claiming that he could not have been driving the car in question because he was out-of-state on the day in question, then subsequently amends his answer and acknowledges that he had his dates wrong and was in town when the accident occurred (but was still not driving the car in question), and then – in a third pleading – admits to driving the car and being in the accident (but contends that he was driving responsibly and did not cause the accident). Demetrius usually has the legal right to make such changes in his defense, but he had better have some convincing evidence as to why he has put forth such radically different factual contentions. Otherwise, the plaintiff is probably more than happy to have Demetrius keep amending his pleadings and leaving himself more and more open to some very tough questions and some strong opposing arguments challenging his credibility.

G. Alternative Pleadings and Class Actions

Alternative pleadings are permitted, but can present a practical problem. At some point, generally before trial, the defendant or plaintiff (whoever is asserting contradictory claims/defenses) will have to choose a theory and stick to it. Otherwise, a judge may require the defendant to do so, or the jury may not listen to a defendant who seems to be contradicting himself.

Here is an example of four different contentions a defendant might make in defending a breach of contract case. Each contention, by itself, suffices as a defense IF the factfinder – the judge or jury - believes the defendant. But each of these four defenses is an alternate contention. No two of them can be true. These alternate defenses to the plaintiff's breach-of-contract case are:

(1) I don't even know the plaintiff;
(2) I know the plaintiff, but we had no contract;
(3) I know the plaintiff and we had a contract, but the contract was not what the plaintiff contends it was (the contract read differently); and

(4) I know the plaintiff, we had a contract, the contract was what the plaintiff contends, but I did not breach the contract (often, defendants in that situation also say that, in fact, the plaintiff was the one who breached).

Well before trial, the defendant will doubtless have to choose which of these alternate theories to adopt as its ultimate position.

Class actions are an important tool, increasingly used in some countries (e.g., China), not just the United States **(see pgs. 64-66; Emerson BL).**

III. DISCOVERY (see pgs. 68-72; Emerson BL)

Discovery is a set of pretrial procedures. Discovery may informally take place from the moment an injury is perceived.[62]

In the formal sense of the word, *discovery* is a procedure for parties to get information about a case from the other parties and from others who have access to information.

Discovery generally is done just by, in front of, attorneys; the judge usually is not there. Court reporters will be there, for example, for a deposition.

Discovery is the key to many, probably most, larger cases - cases can turn on the discovery itself (the development of evidence) or on the rising costs associated with pretrial discovery.

To win at trial, one must gear up ahead of time with discovery: Marshaling facts/documents, getting witnesses prepared, avoiding disasters in testimony or other evidence, looking toward how people and their evidence will perform at trial.

> In *Intel Corp. v. Advanced Micro Devices, Inc.*, 542 U.S. 241 (2004), the U.S. Supreme Court held that Advanced Micro Devices can seek to require its bigger rival, Intel, to turn over documents that are in a U.S. court for use in a European antitrust investigation. The decision's effect is that many companies involved in overseas litigation may seek information in the United States, where discovery rules are more liberal, for use in the overseas lawsuit.

A. Preparation versus the Surprise Approach

The rules of litigation generally permit parties to spend the time and money to know a great deal about the case, including the other parties' evidence. However, sometimes – as a practical matter of having too little time or of saving money – parties will not fully exercise their discovery rights. Also, less frequently, a lawyer may determine that he/she would rather leave some things up to the trial process itself; the lawyer fears that, in some instances, discovery may benefit the other side as much or more than it will assist his/her client. For example, a deposition may give a witness advance warning – before the trial itself - of some avenues of attack; hence, the decision to avoid some discovery and adopt a *surprise approach*. (The hope may be to surprise the witness, or – at least – leave him/her less prepared than he/she might have been.)

The risk in not undertaking the discovery (i.e., not subpoenaing the witness for a pretrial deposition) is that the witness, at trial, may not be as limited in his answers ("pinned down" by a deposition transcript) as he could have been if the witness had previously provided answers during a deposition. Also, by not deposing the witness, the lawyer himself/herself may have less sense of how the witness will come across to the judge or jury. In effect, to not carry out this discovery, the lawyer must decide that such fears and uncertainties do not justify his/her time and expense, and/or the preparation of the other side or of witnesses that the discovery would potentially foster.

---

[62] Robert W. Emerson, *Business Law*. NY: Barron's Educational Series (6th ed., 2015), at 68.

B. The Scope of Discovery

The range of discovery is very broad. Is a "fishing expedition" permitted? That probably depends on the circumstances and on your perspective.

The scope of discovery is far broader than what is permitted at trial.[63] That can also lead to mass tedium, and massive expense.[64]

Discovery occurs under rules that allow for more flexibility in (1) questioning and in (2) other requests for information than is usually allowed in the courtroom: the discovery of all evidence that is admissible in court and all other information that could lead to other, admissible evidence.[65] Depositions often feature objections, just like in trial. However, unlike a trial, where the judge rules on the objection and decides whether and how a witness shall answer a question, the deposed witness goes ahead and answers the questions, with the objections recorded in case of the need for a judge's ruling later.[66]

C. Criminal Law Comparison: The Criminal Defendant's Right to Information (and a Hearing)

A 6th Amendment provision – "In all criminal prosecutions, the accused shall . . . be informed of the nature and cause of the accusation." That is the right to know for what you are standing trial; there should be no Franz Kafka's "The Trial" (1925, in German; English translation, 1937).[67] In *Zadvydas v. Davis*, 533 U.S. 678 (2001), the U.S. Supreme Court ruled 5-4 that immigrants who commit crimes in the U.S. cannot be held in jail indefinitely just because the federal government can't find a country to

---

[63] Most judges and lawyers in a case reflexively favor obtaining everything that might conceivably have some bearing on a case. Privacy usually is a lost concern. While that may be fair to parties in a case, what about nonparty "witnesses"? Does the scope of discovery lead to inappropriate intrusions upon privacy rights? During litigation, everything from medical and employment documents to telephone and mail records to credit card charges, are regularly converted from private material to public knowledge. Incompetent or overworked personnel offices, banks, and other institutions may be "too" helpful in furnishing information about employees or customers. While individuals can fight to have a subpoena *duces tecum* quashed, or at least reduced in scope, few witnesses do that.

[64] Lawyers may suffer as follows: (1) the mind-numbing tedium of "document production" in big cases (e.g., product-liability, securities fraud); (2) in the last twenty-five years, lower percentages - under 10% - of big-firm associates have made partner; and (3) the average number of minimum billable hours expected of big-firms associates has risen since 1990 over 10%, to more than 2,000 hours per year. It is thus harder to get associates to do this type of dreary work, when the long-term payoff (making partner) seems unlikely. Paralegals help, but lawyers must decide crucial questions such as whether a document can be classified as "privileged" attorney-client communication. Corporate clients increasingly use their own in-house legal departments - at lower rates - to handle document production in *all* cases, even huge product liability class-actions. While most people have little sympathy for the lawyers, the costs are, in turn, passed on to clients and to society.

[65] Even items in "the trash" (thought to be deleted or otherwise "private") usually are not protected from discovery. For example, old e-mail letters to and/or from Microsoft insiders dogged Microsoft as it unsuccessfully fought various antitrust suits in 1998-1999.

[66] On rare occasions, the judge is asked to rule on objections during the discovery stage itself (with perhaps a deposition even interrupted while a ruling is sought). Usually, though, the deposition proceeds, and the objection only matters if the very same matter comes up at the trial.

[67] Franz Kafka (1883-1924) was a lawyer in Prague. Born into a middle class, German-speaking Jewish family, Kafka achieved fame as a writer only with the posthumous publication of many of his works, all of which he wrote in German. *The Trial* [*Der Prozess*] deals with a man persecuted and put to death by the inscrutable agencies of an unfathomable court of law. The imprisoned man never even knows who his accusers are, or what indeed the charges against him are!

Highly influential, Kafka is one of the few authors to have an adjective derived from his name. This word, "Kafkaesque," means "marked by a senseless, disorienting, often menacing complexity" or "marked by surreal distortion and often a sense of impending doom."

which to deport them. In *Boumediene v. Bush*, 553 U.S. 723 (2008), the high court, by a 5-4 vote (the four most liberal Justices, plus swing Justice Anthony Kennedy), affirmed *Rasul v. Bush*, 542 U.S. 466 (2004) that the foreign prisoners in Guantanamo had a constitutional right to challenge their detention in U.S. courts.[68] In *Hamdi v. Rumsfeld*, 544 U.S. 507 (2004), the U.S. Supreme Court held 8-1 (Thomas dissenting) that a U.S. citizen, Yasser Hamdi, seized with a Taliban military unit in northern Afghanistan in late 2001, could not be indefinitely detained and was entitled to a hearing.

D. Limits on Discovery

While the scope of discovery is much broader than the actual evidence at trial, there are limits. For example, plaintiffs cannot simply seek the deposition of a corporate CEO because they would like to "ask him/her some questions" (i.e., make his/her life miserable!).

In discovery, one cannot get privileged information, trial strategy, or work product (evidence prepared for litigation). Discovery disputes are brought, via motions, to a judge or magistrate in the court where the trial is to take place. Almost anything can lead to a dispute. For example, in a libel suit Phillip Morris Companies fitted about Capital Cities/ABC Inc., ABC lawyers complained that Phillip Morris produced stinky, sickening (literally) documents that were on difficult to read on red paper. Richmond, Virginia state Circuit Court judge Theodore J. Markow ruled in May 1995 that the red paper was okay and that he did not smell anything.

Here is a general limit on discovery found in the Federal Rules of Civil Procedure (FRCP) applying to federal litigation: FRCP Rule 1 states that the FRCP "shall be construed and administered to secure the just, speedy, and inexpensive determination of every action." And under the federal rules, one side – no matter how many parties there are (whether co-plaintiffs or co-defendants) on that side – may call only 10 oral depositions. For more, or to depose someone a second time, one needs court permission.

E. Two Ways How Discovery May Lead to a Settlement

Discovery can lead to rapidly rising costs: attorneys' fees, court reporters' charges, travel expenses, photocopying, experts' fees, etc. A party with more resources may seek to "paper to death" the other side, as it asks for everything, or gives the side everything (makes the other party go through enormous piles of materials)!

Discovery can cause a party to see the other side's case better: one may better realize one's risks, and the other side's advantages, so that one is left more willing to compromise.

F. The Four Major Types of Discovery

The four major types of discovery are depositions, interrogatories, requests for admissions, and requests for production of documents.

1. Depositions (see pgs. 68-69; Emerson BL)

Depositions put witnesses on the spot (testimony, under oath, transcribed by a court reporter). Via a deposition, one can question people besides just parties.

The deposition process can be very expensive- court reporter fees, transcript costs, attorney fees, lots of lost time for personnel, etc. It is often the most crucial pretrial part of a case. So emphasis must

---

[68] In *Munaf v. Geren*, 553 U.S. 674 (2008), the Court considered that overseas an American-led international force had detained American citizens. The Court unanimously held that these citizens can challenge the constitutionality of their detention, but it also ruled that U.S. judges lack the power to order the release of criminal suspects whose detention is at the request of the country where they are held. So, these Americans may have a so-called right without a genuine remedy.

be on performing well. Important concepts include getting a good transcript, using correct video techniques, obtaining proper documentation for the evidence often accompanying depositions (documents), and making sure that an expert witness' deposition was indeed effective.

Preparing for and conducting a good deposition is like producing a show: writing the script, preparing lines and knowing one's part. To deal with conflicts in credibility, parties may attend an adverse party's deposition. Good attorneys understand the need to pay attention to and follow-up on a witness's non-verbal reactions, facial expressions and hesitations, which may suggest a qualification of the witness' answer; lawyers know to try to get witnesses to exaggerate or adopt an incredible position.

Courts now sometimes must consider whether depositions can be posted on the Internet; usually, they *can*. While full depositions usually are not found in court files, and parties frequently stipulate that depositions cannot be posted, excerpts are often cited in court papers or introduced as evidence at trial.

Some Foolish Lawyer Questions

Q: Doctor, how many of your autopsies have been performed on dead people?

Q: This myasthenia gravis, does it affect your memory at all?
A: Yes.
A: I forget.
Q: You forget.
A: Can you give us an example of something you've forgotten?

Q: Doctor, isn't it true that when a person dies in his sleep, he doesn't know about it until the next morning?
A: Would you repeat the question, please?

Q: The youngest son, the 20-year-old, how old is he?

Q: Do you recall the time that you examined the body?
A: The autopsy started around 8:30 p.m.
Q; And Mr. Dennington was dead at the time?
A: No, he was sitting on the table wondering why I was doing an autopsy on him.

Q: Were you present when your picture was taken?

Q: She had three children right?
A: Yes
Q: How many were boys?
A: None
Q: Were there any girls?

Q: You say the stairs went down to the basement?
A: Yes
Q: And these stairs, did they go up also?

Q: Are you qualified to give a urine sample?

Q: How was the first marriage terminated?
A: By Death
Q: And by whose death was it terminated?

Q: Doctor, before you performed the autopsy, did you check or pulse
A: No
Did you check for blood pressure?
A: No
Q: Did you check for breathing?
A: No
Q; So, then it is possible that the patient that was alive when you began the autopsy?
A: No
Q: How can you be so sure, doctor?
A: Because his brain was sitting on my desk in a jar.
Q: But could the patient have been alive nevertheless?
A: Yes, it is possible that he could have been alive and practicing law somewhere.

Q: So the date of the conception of (the baby) was August 8th?
A: Yes.
Q: And what were you doing at the time?
A: I resent the question.

And these are things people actually said in court or depositions, word for word, taken down and now published by court reporters. How did they keep from laughing while these were all taking place?

Judge: "Sir, I have reviewed this case and I've decided to give your wife $775 a week,"
Husband: "That's fair, your honor. I'll try to send her a few bucks myself."

Q: What is your date of birth?
A: July fifteenth
Q: What year?
A: Every year.

Q: What gear were you in at moment of the impact?
A: Gucci Sweats and Reeboks.

Q: How old is your son, the one living with you?
A: Thirty-eight or thirty-five, I can't remember which.
Q: How long has he lived with you?
A: Forty-five years.

Q: What was the first thing your husband said to you when he woke up that morning?
A: He said, "Where am I, Cathy?"
Q: And why did that upset you?
A: My name is Susan.

Where was the location of the accident?
A: Approximately milepost 499.
Q: And where is milepost 499?
A: Probably between milepost 498 and 500.

Q: Sir, what is your IQ?
A: Well, I can see pretty well, I think.

> Q: Did you blow your horn or anything?
> A: After the accident?
> Q: Before the accident
> A: Sure, I played for 10 years. I even went to school for it.
>
> Q: Is your <u>appearance</u> here this morning pursuant to a deposition that I sent to your attorney?
> A: No, this is how I dress when I go to work.
>
> Q: All your responses must be Oral, Ok?
> A: Ok
> Q: And what school did you go to?
> A: Oral.

2. Interrogatories (see pg. 69; Emerson BL)

Interrogatories (written questions[69]) are only directed toward parties. So if one wants to question a non-party, a deposition is the only way to require such persons to give information.[70] Interrogatories are fairly good for less expensive (boilerplate) questions about plain facts, such as naming potential witnesses, listing documents, and other basic matters. If one wants theory, justification, or explanation, one probably needs a deposition.

But who really prepares the answers to interrogatories? Lawyers do. Parties must sign <u>under oath</u>, with the possible penalty of perjury. But lawyers have <u>lots of time to prepare</u> and mull over a truthful, <u>but useless</u> answer.[71] On the other hand, one must answer direct questions, and one must look up some information if one has access.

3. Requests for Admissions (see pg. 69; Emerson BL)

Requests for Admissions are about the genuineness of documents; about the truth of certain allegations. These requests may also lead to stipulations at pretrial conferences.[72]

4. Requests for Documents (see pg. 69; Emerson BL)

The request for documents is an important discovery tool in many cases, especially those involving business entities. Businesses ordinarily have a duty to keep records, not just for good management and for taxes, but for potential lawsuits.

Document requests can be a hassle for both sides. One side may have to turn over, or at least evaluate, all sorts of documents; and the other side may have far more documents to review than it would like to have – sifting through documents day after day after day!

---

[69] "Interrogatory" is the word used for this form of discovery, rather than the simple word "question." The word "interrogatory" may be preferred by lawyers and judges because it is more specific and (here comes the joke about lawyers and verbosity!) because "interrogatory" is six syllables rather than just two ("question").

[70] A subpoena can be for a witness to show up to testify at a deposition *or* it can be for the witness to come to a trial.

[71] E.g., assume that an interrogatory asks a party accused of driving negligently, "Are there any restrictions on your driver's license?" The response, based on a literal perusal of the license, may be "Do not fold, spindle, or laminate." Here is another example of an interrogatory for an auto accident case: "Please state the location of your right foot immediately prior to impact." The interrogatory almost certainly was intended to determine whether the foot was pressing the brake, the accelerator, a clutch, or whatever. But a literal answer (albeit one that could, in extreme cases, lead to judicial sanctions) might be: "Immediately before the impact, my right foot was located at the immediate end of my right leg!"

[72] See samples at http://www.millerandzois.com/Sample_Request_for_Admissions.html

The discovered documents may prove useful in other suits as well. That is partly because open courts and open records customarily are available to all people. After all, our taxes pay for the litigation system.

Plaintiffs in different suits involving the same defendant(s) or industry may seek to share information (e.g., in tobacco cases and defective product cases).

5. A Side Issue: Court Records in the Internet Age

Making court documents public has taken on a new meaning in the Internet age. Until recently, court documents tended to remain in "practical obscurity": Public, but with few people bothering to sift through files buried in courthouses to find the information they seek. However, now many courts and individuals post rulings and related documents on the Internet. Also, court files can contain medical and psychiatric records, tax returns, unproven allegations, bankruptcy or divorce files (including Social Security, telephone, and credit-card numbers, salaries, bonuses, stock-option data, home addresses, account balances, and names and ages of children), and other matters.

Privacy advocates warn that the data could be used by businesses to build customer databases, by neighbors to embarrass one another, and by criminals to engage in fraudulent schemes. While they urge the automatic removal of sensitive data from both paper and electronic files, media groups urge an individual approach and state that if something is sensitive then a person can ask a judge to seal that information. When business parties exchange evidence during pretrial discovery, lawyers often seek the sealing of that evidence (so outsiders cannot access certain sensitive evidence).

Besides privacy concerns, some hot topics in modern discovery are due process, outsourcing, and electronic databases. For more on e-discovery (seeking or providing information in an electronic format), **see pgs. 69-70; Emerson BL.**

G. Two Less Used Types of Discovery

There are <u>two less used types of discovery</u> (they are less used because these means of discovery often simply are irrelevant to the case). These two types are: (1) Viewing (inspection) of Premises; and (2) Physical/Mental Examinations.

Parties cannot ordinarily get a physical or mental examination, say, for a breach of contract case. The opposing party cannot just say, "The other side is crazy! Let's have a psychiatrist examine him!" A physical examination could be ordered for a party claiming that he was injured in an accident; or a mental examination could be ordered to probe the alleged psychological harm from defamation or mental anguish.

As for a viewing of the premises, that form of discovery, too, cannot take place unless there is cause to do so. If one has been sued, one cannot simply say, "Oh yeah, I'd like to see the inside of the plaintiff's house." However, if one is being sued over alleged problems on the plaintiff's property, then – of course – one has the right to inspect that property.

H. Comparative Law on Discovery

Most other nations, including even other common law countries (e.g., England and Ireland), allow far less discovery than does the United States. Parties may seek to use these systemic differences strategically (e.g., use heightened discovery rights in America, but file a suit in Europe because of some advantages to using that forum).

IV. MOTIONS AND OTHER MATTERS

A. Motion for Summary Judgment (SJ) (see pg. 66; Emerson BL)

A "motion" is a request for court action. The motion for Summary Judgment (SJ) is often the most important pretrial motion that a plaintiff or defendant may file. That is because SJ is <u>**a pretrial decision**</u> <u>on the merits of a case</u> (so, it is more than just a demurrer).

Either side can seek SJ - from the start of the case until shortly before trial. Unlike the motion to dismiss (demurrer), a motion for SJ can go beyond the pleadings themselves (e.g., beyond just the complaint). Thus, while a demurrer cannot introduce outside information, the SJ motion can use, for example, the facts gathered so far in the case to convince the judge that a trial is unnecessary (that a judgment can now be granted on some or all of the case). Parties seeking or opposing SJ can use affidavits, deposition transcripts, answers to interrogatories, authenticated documents, or other evidence.

The Standard for Granting SJ is: (1) No genuine issue as to material facts, and (2) Law, as applied to these facts, clearly entitles one party to a verdict.

There is a high standard or burden to meet to win summary judgment. It is *not* just that the judge thinks your side would win at trial. But a motion for SJ can serve to "educate" the judge, if that same judge for the motion would be the judge at trial.

A motion for SJ can be used to obtain a partial SJ - e.g., by a defendant to eliminate the plaintiff's punitive damages claim. Example: to reduce a $20 million claim (including punitive damages) to a $100,000 claim (just for compensatory damages).

The motion for summary judgment is based on the pleadings, the discovery, the disclosure materials on file, and any affidavits.

In the federal courts, there is a little more leeway for courts to reduce caseloads by entering a summary judgment than is the case in state courts. The U.S. Supreme Court has elaborated on the summary judgment standard found in Federal Rule of Civil Procedure 56(c)(2) by noting that summary judgment must be granted if there can be only one reasonable conclusion as to the verdict. So, for example, an opposing party cannot simply deny the facts or assert uncorroborated inadmissible hearsay statements. That is because a judge, before he/she denies a properly asserted, factually and legally supported summary judgment motion, must find sufficient evidence that a jury could reasonably rely upon in reaching a verdict for the party opposing summary judgment.

> Both the directed verdict (taking a case away from the jury - Barron's page 73) and the JNOV (overturning a jury verdict - Barron's page 76) have the same high standard as the summary judgment motion. Federal Rule of Civil Procedure 50 calls both motions - for a directed verdict or a judgment notwithstanding the verdict (JNOV – judgment *non obstante veredicto*) a judgment as a matter of law.

B. The Pretrial Conference (see pgs. 71-72; Emerson BL)
The pretrial conference usually is not held in small cases, such as in small-claims court.

Two goals of the pretrial conference tend to be: (1) to foster settlement talks; and – usually most important – (2) to try to narrow the trial's scope. The latter may be accomplished by having parties agree on which witnesses will be called, what documents will be introduced, and what issues will be tried (thus making, via stipulations, a simpler, shorter case - say, two days long instead of two weeks).

C. A Very Brief Review of Major Discovery/Pretrial Devices
Discovery/pretrial devices are numerous, and failure to use them wisely can kill your chances in litigation. To summarize a number of these devices, one can refer to this mnemonic Device - "DIM? DIE, ASS!" (If you are dim in litigation, you're likely to die – at least figuratively - from the process.) The nine letters in DIM-DIE-ASS stand for:

Depositions, **I**nterrogatories, **M**otions (such as summary judgment),
Documents, **I**nspections (viewing of property), **E**xaminations (Mental/Physical),
Admissions, **S**ubpoena, **S**tipulations.

A Talk on Discovery, by Litigator Tim Hardwicke (6:53 long), is in Part Three of the Resources section of the course website.

V. PROCEDURAL FAIRNESS

> *Greatness - "[T]he American Constitution is the most wonderful work ever struck off at a given time by the brain and purpose of man."*
> WILLIAM F. GLADSTONE, late 19th Century British Prime Minister.

The first order of concern when a lawsuit is filed is the proper notice and protections for the defendant. There are fewer such concerns for the plaintiff, who – after all- chose to bring the case. But the plaintiff, too, has rights: He/she has the right to ask the courts to identify, and then remedy for the plaintiff, the wrongs done to him/her. Furthermore, the public has a fundamental interest in the fairness and efficiency of its civil justice system.

A. Procedural Due Process

A key underlying theme of all court cases – civil or criminal – is: "I got rights." No matter who I am or what I am accused of, or who I am opposing, I have certain inherent rights. I may not win a substantive claim or defense, but I have certain procedural protections. To recognize these rights is, in fact, not just to my benefit, but for the well-being of a democratic system and a value of humanity, of individual worth.

Procedural due process involves notice, an opportunity to be heard, having a competent and unbiased tribunal, and other basic rights in bringing or defending a claim. It is essentially a guarantee of fairness. *Fuentes v. Shevin*, 407 U.S. 67 (1972) is an example of a procedural due process case. It concerned a creditor's pre-judgment repossession of the debtor's property, in which the creditor had a lien interest. YOUTUBE at robertwemersonufl (includes the author's Description of the Video and some Comments) - The Sad, Sad Case of Margarita Fuentes (5:00). A YOUTUBE skit followed immediately with discussion by an MBA team about *Fuentes v. Shevin* and due process issues (about 13:30 long) is at https://www.youtube.com/watch?v=IuVzxGOJLTU

Fuentes v. Shevin, 407 U.S. 67 (1972)

Background

Margarita Fuentes was a resident of Florida. She purchased a gas stove and service policy from the Firestone Tire and Rubber Co. (Firestone) under a conditional sales contract calling for monthly payments over a period of time. A few months later, she purchased a stereophonic phonograph from the same company under the same sort of contract. The total cost of the stove and stereo was about $500, plus an additional financing charge of over $100. Under the contracts, Firestone retained title to the merchandise, but Mrs. Fuentes was entitled to possession unless and until she defaulted on her installment payments.

For more than a year Mrs. Fuentes made her installment payments (almost $400 altogether). But then, with only $204.05 remaining to be paid, a dispute developed between Firestone and Mrs. Fuentes over the servicing of the stove. Firestone instituted an action in a small-claims court for repossession of both the stove and the stereo, claiming that Mrs. Fuentes had refused to make her remaining payments. Simultaneously with the filing of that action and before Mrs. Fuentes had even received a summons to answer its complaint, Firestone obtained a writ of replevin ordering a sheriff to seize the disputed goods at once.

To comply with Florida procedure, Firestone had only to fill in the blanks on the appropriate form documents and submit them to the clerk of the small-claims court. The clerk signed and stamped the documents and issued a writ of replevin. Later the same day, a local deputy sheriff and an agent of Firestone went to Mrs. Fuentes' home and seized the stove and stereo.

The deputy sheriff had a communications problem with Mrs. Fuentes since Mrs. Fuentes spoke little or no English. Gradually, however, he was able to communicate his purpose and the effect of the writ. At this point, the plaintiff's daughter-in-law, who lived in the same house with plaintiff, became 'upset and emotional' and protested the repossession. She sent for Mr. Leon, the plaintiff's son-in-law, to assist her and the deputy agreed to wait. When Mr. Leon arrived, he explained to the deputy in English that his attorney had advised him that a court proceeding as necessary before the merchandise could be repossessed and that, on his advice, he was not going to give up the property. The deputy 'explained the effect of the write to Mr. Leon, that he was obliged to repossess the stove and stereo in accordance with its terms.' Mr. Leon then agreed to the repossession and let the deputy, who until then had been standing outside on the front porch, and the two men from Firestone, who had been waiting outside in their truck, into the house and showed them where the merchandise was located.

Fuentes, represented by Legal Services of Miami (government-paid legal services for the poor), filed an action in federal court. Her lawyers argued that the seizure had denied her due process of law by allowing Firestone to obtain her property without adequate notice or an opportunity to challenge issuance of the writ.

The Supreme Court rejected Firestone's argument that, even assuming that Florida's replevin statute did not comport with the Due Process Clause of the Fourteenth Amendment, Fuentes waived her procedural rights by signing the conditional sales agreement. The Court emphasized that "[t]he facts of the present cases are a far cry from those of *Overmyer*," a case where attorneys for two corporations with presumably equal bargaining power negotiated, specifically bargained for, and then drafted a waiver. *Overmyer* was not a contract of adhesion, but the Fuentes situation was quite different: The purported waiver provision was a printed part of the form sales contract and a necessary condition of the sale. Fuentes was not made aware of the significance of the fine print (the waiver).

The Court found that the state's replevin statue, allowing creditors to repossess collateral goods through a writ issued by a state official, involved state action and violated the Fourteenth Amendment's Due Process Clause.

The Supreme Court Opinion
"[Under the Florida pre-judgment attachment statute, and a similar Pennsylvania statute,] at the same moment that the defendant receives the complaint seeking repossession of property through court action, the property is seized from him. He is provided no prior notice and allowed no opportunity whatever to challenge the issuance of writ. After the property has been seized, he will eventually have an opportunity for a hearing, as the defendant in the trial of the court action for repossession, which the plaintiff is required to pursue. And he is also not wholly without recourse in the meantime. For under the Florida statute, the officer who seizes the property must keep it for three days, and during that period the defendant may reclaim possession of the property by posting his own security bond in double its value. But if he does not post a bond, the property is transferred to the party who sought the writ, pending a final judgment in the underlying action for repossession.

... To be sure, the requirements that a party seeking a writ must first post a bond, allege conclusorily that he is entitled to specific goods, and open himself to possible liability in damages if he is wrong, serve to deter wholly unfounded applications for a writ. But those requirements are hardly a substitute for a prior hearing, for they test no more than the strength of the applicant's own belief in his rights. Since his private gain is at stake, the danger is all too great that his confidence in his cause will be misplaced. Lawyers and judges are familiar with the phenomenon of a party mistakenly but firmly convinced that his view of the facts and law will prevail, and therefore quite willing to risk the costs of litigation. Because of the understandable, self-interested fallibility of litigants, a court does not decide a dispute until it has had an opportunity to hear both sides–and does not generally take even tentative action until it has itself examined the support for the plaintiff's position. The Florida and Pennsylvania statutes do not even require the official issuing a writ of replevin to do that much.

> ... There are 'extraordinary situations' that justify postponing notice and opportunity for a hearing. These situations, however, must be truly unusual [emergency situations -e.g., summary seizure of misbranded drugs and contaminated food], with showings of immediate danger that debtor will destroy, conceal, or abscond with the disputed goods]. [Then due process may be satisfied by a post-seizure hearing shortly after the seizure.]
>
> ... We hold that the Florida and Pennsylvania prejudgment replevin provisions work a deprivation of property without due process of law insofar as they deny the right to a prior opportunity to be heard before chattels are taken from their possessor. Our holding, however, is a narrow one. We order to protect the security interests of creditors so long as those creditors have tested their claim to the goods through the process of a fair prior hearing. The nature and form of such prior hearings, moreover, are legitimately open to many potential variations and are a subject, at this point, for legislation – not adjudication."
>
> **Aftermath: The Rules Remain Unsettled**
> *Fuentes* was a four-to-three decision issued by a seven-member court as the justices awaited the confirmation of new appointees Lewis Powell and William Rehnquist. With the arrival of the two new justices, the court decided another case concerning the respective rights of debtors and creditors. Just two years after *Fuentes*, the two new justices joined the three *Fuentes* dissenters to issue a decision upholding Louisiana's statutory seizure of debtors' property without notice to the debtor and prior to a hearing. Justice Potter Stewart was so disturbed by what he perceived to be a sudden doctrinal reversal that he issued a sharp dissent in which he noted that "[t]he only perceivable change that has occurred since Fuentes is in the makeup of the Court." Stewart warned his colleagues that:
>
> "A basic change in the law upon a ground no firmer than a change in our membership invites the popular misconception that this institution is little different from the two political branches of the Government. No misconception could do more lasting injury to this Court and to the system of law which it is our abiding mission to serve."[73]
>
> What Stewart characterized as "misperception" is actually the political reality that as the Court's composition changes, so too does the definition of the rights that citizens enjoy under the Bill of Rights.

U.S. Government Actions Abroad: No Constitutional Rights for Non-Citizens

Due process rights do not necessarily protect Americans while they are abroad. Certainly, U.S. constitutional rights do not protect American citizens if they are subject to legal action in another nation. Similarly, U.S. constitutional rights do not always extend to non-citizens not in the United States. The Supreme Court, in *United States v. Verdugo-Urquidez*, 495 U.S. 259 (1990), held that the Fourth Amendment does not apply to the search and seizure by US agents of property located outside the United States that is owned by a non-U.S. citizen. The Amendment protects people in the United States against arbitrary action by the government; it does not restrain the federal government's actions against aliens outside American territory.

VI. THE TRIAL (see pgs. 72-74; Emerson BL)

A **trial** is a proceeding before a competent tribunal, in which a civil or criminal case is heard and adjudicated. A trial is not a search; it is more like a test.

---

[73] *Fuentes v. Shevin*, 407 U.S. 67 (1972).

The Trial as Test: Meeting (Or Not) their Burdens of Persuasion

"The methodologies of a test and a search are fundamentally different. A search is investigative, exploratory, and expansive. A search involves a protagonist who wanders, imaginatively tracking leads, following intuitions and suspicions, rummaging in hidden places, making often fruitless inquiries, and foraging for the undiscovered.

"A test is different. It is not a quest. It is a neutral assessment, an evaluation. It analyzes, measures, and weighs. A test limits itself to a closed universe of variables. It does not wander. It compares. It follows an orderly protocol and applies a predetermined standard of measurement.

"Trials involve disputes in this latter way. A neutral trier-of-fact evaluates the credibility of evidence that contesting parties present within strictly defined rules to support their conflicting claims and defenses. The trier-of-fact analyzes and compares what evidence the parties have chosen to offer and then, applying a predetermined standard of proof, weighs the evidence to decide whether the burden of proof has been satisfied.

"The modern American trial, like its common law model, is simply a dispute resolution system. When one of the disputing parties asks for judicial intervention, the law requires one of them – usually the person seeking to change the status quo - to prove facts that demonstrate the party's entitlement to relief. The party must persuade the trier-of-fact to a degree of satisfaction that the law prescribes. . . .

"In the end, the duty of a petit jury is to decide not what the truth is but whether the party with the risk of nonpersuasion has satisfied its burden of proof.

". . . . If the jury is confused about the evidence it heard, if it did not fully understand the evidence presented, if the lawyers were unsuccessful in presenting evidence clearly or in persuading the jury of their clients' version of the facts, the jury in every case is told exactly how to deal with the failings: Decide against the party that had the burden of persuasion on the point of confusion [i.e., against the party that failed the test]. . . . The trier-of-fact doesn't rummage around, independently searching on its own for additional evidence either to aid or to frustrate the burdened party."[74]

A. Evidence

> *Objection - "the cry of a lawyer who sees truth about to creep into the courtroom!"*

Evidence is both testimony and authenticated documents. There are many rules of evidence, so if you represent yourself (appear in court *pro se*), you may have a fool for a client. Why? Because of your: (1) lack of objectivity (inability to see the big picture, to view issues fairly, to see one's own flaws, to compromise); and (2) lack of expertise.

1. Hearsay

Rules of Evidence can be extremely complex. One example is *Hearsay* what someone else said or wrote - an out-of-court statement, written or oral, offered to prove the truth of that statement.[75] Hearsay, thus, is evidence heard or otherwise learned from someone other than the person testifying in court, and its veracity rests on the credibility of someone who is not a witness.

---

[74] Richard S. Walinski, "The ABA's New Vision of the Jury's Function: An Opposing View," 32 LITIGATION (Spring 2006), at 5, 6.

[75] Traditionally, hearsay is testimony that is given by a witness who relates not what he/she knows personally, but what others have said, and that is therefore dependent on the credibility of someone other than the witness.
 In federal law, the Federal Rule of Evidence 801(c), is a statement, other than one made by the declarant while testifying at a trial or hearing, offered in evidence to prove the truth of the matter asserted. Federal Rule of Evidence 801(c). The Federal Rule of Evidence 802 defines the hearsay rule as "the rule that no assertion offered as testimony can be received unless it is or has been open to test by cross-examination or an opportunity for cross-examination, except as provided otherwise by the rules of evidence, by court rules, or by statute." The main two reasons for the hearsay rule are that out-of-court statements amounting to hearsay are not made under oath and are not subject to cross-examination.

a. Problems with Hearsay

A problem with hearsay is: How can you cross-examine the person really responsible for the evidence? You cannot, because he/she is not a witness at trial (or through discovery).

"I know Ms. Smith is a liar."
"How do you know?"
"Because that's what Ms. Jones told me."
"Well, how does she know?"
"Beats me. Ask her!"

Another problem is, simply, that interpreting hearsay and the rules for hearsay can be quite complex. Consider that there is a special type of hearsay called **double hearsay** (also termed **multiple hearsay** or **hearsay within hearsay**). It is a hearsay statement containing further hearsay statements within it, none of which are admissible unless exceptions to the rule against hearsay can be applied to each level.[76] An example would be an investigation's report (the report being one level of hearsay) stating that Amy admitted to running the red light (that alleged statement of Amy being another level of hearsay).

b. Approaches to Hearsay

One approach to hearsay is to just do the best you can: let the hearsay evidence in (as long as it is probative – relevant to the case), but recognize that it may be problematic. That is the approach still typically followed in small-claims court, in arbitration and mediation, and in administrative hearings. That also was the approach typically followed in the courts until the 1800s; although the term "hearsay" has been around for several centuries, it really came to prominence in the law only in the 19th Century American and, to a lesser extent, British courts developed the procedural complexity for dealing with alleged hearsay and possibly excluding it from testimony. By the 20th Century some jurists thought the hearsay rules had gone too far – too complex, with too much evidence barred.[77]

Modern courts' usual approach to hearsay is: Keep hearsay out, unless there is an exception to this rule. However, there are lots of exceptions to the hearsay rule. These include: statements made under the belief of impending death, statements of a deceased person, excited utterances, business records, and statements of family history, among others.[78] For federal trials, for example, Federal Rule of Evidence 803 provides 23 explicit exceptions to the hearsay rule, regardless of whether the out-of-court declarant is available to testify, and Federal Rule of Evidence 804 provides five more exceptions for situations in which the declarant is unavailable to testify.

c. Non-Hearsay, or Exceptions to the Hearsay Rule (thus, for either, they are admissible as evidence)

Three examples:
NOT HEARSAY
(1) Admissions against interest (if by a party)

> ***Admission by party-opponent*** – An opposing party's admission, if it is offered against that party and is (1) the party's own statement, in either an individual or a representative capacity; (2) a statement of which the party has manifested an adoption or belief in its truth; (3) a statement by one authorized by the party to

---

[76] Federal Rule of Evidence 805.

[77] "The great hearsay rule… is a fundamental rule of safety, but one over-enforced and abused—the spoiled child of the family—proudest scion of our jury trial rules of evidence, but so petted and indulged that is has become a nuisance and an obstruction to speedy and efficient trials." John H. Wigmore, *A Student's Textbook of the Law of Evidence* 238 (1935).

[78] *See* http://www.courts.state.nh.us/rules/evid/evid-804.htm.

make such a statement; (4) a statement by the party's agent concerning a matter within the scope of the agency or employment and made during the existence of the relationship; or (5) a statement by a co-conspirator of the party.

HEARSAY EXCEPTION
(2) Excited utterances ("Oh, my God! He has a . . ."; presumably not enough time to construct a lie)

An excited utterance, under Federal Rule of Evidence 803(2) is:
A statement about a startling event made under the stress and excitement of the event.

Likewise, under Federal Rule of Evidence 803(1), "a statement containing a *present sense impression* is admissible even if it is hearsay." A *sense impression* is one's perception of an event or condition, formed during or immediately after the fact.

HEARSAY EXCEPTION
(3) Dying declarations (also called "deathbed declarations")

These are statements by a person who believes that death is imminent, relating to the cause or circumstances of the person's impending death.

Comparative Law on Hearsay

Many Civil Law nations (e.g., Germany) generally accept hearsay in <u>all</u> proceedings (including even civil and criminal trials), while American and other common law judges usually only accept its admission at trial if it falls under one of the many hearsay exceptions. (Even in American legal proceedings, when one is before less formal bodies, such as small claims courts or administrative agencies, the rules of hearsay are relaxed or even abolished altogether. In other words, hearsay is admitted.)

---

2. Evidentiary Mistakes

Occasional minor mistakes about evidence - whether by lawyers or judges - are viewed as perhaps unavoidable. Thus, if the errors were relatively small, they are *unlikely to indicate* (1) malpractice by the lawyers or (2) grounds for a successful appeal (against a trial judge's actions). Indeed, the appellate courts ordinarily refer to such small mistakes, which are insufficient for a successful appeal, as "harmless error."

B. Witnesses

Two Jokes about Witnesses

The judge solemnly stated to the defendant, "Due to the seriousness of this case, I'm going to give you three lawyers."
"Never mind the three lawyers," said the defendant. "Just get me one good witness."

"Are these your witnesses?" asked the defense counsel. "They are," replied the plaintiff's lawyer. "Then you win," said the defense counsel. "I've had those witnesses twice myself."

---

1. Sequestration of Witnesses

A BIBLICAL ACCOUNT OF SEQUESTRATION AND CROSS-EXAMINATION –

A TRIAL FROM THE APOCRYPHA: "*SUSANNA AND THE ELDERS*"

There dwelt a man in Babylon, called Joacim, and he took a wife, whose name was Susanna, the daughter of Chelcias, a very fair [beautiful] woman, and one that feared the Lord. Her parents also were righteous, and taught their daughter according to the law of Moses.

Joacim was a great rich man, and had a fair garden joining unto his house; and to him gathered [his fellow] Jews, because Joacim was more honorable than all others.

The same year were appointed two of the ancients of the [Jewish] people to be [their] judges. The Lord had warned that Babylon had wicked judges who wrongly governed the people; and these two men, indeed, were evil. They stayed much at Joacim's house; and all that had any suits in law came unto them.

When the people departed away at noon, Susanna went into her husband's garden to walk. And the two elders saw her going in every day, and walking; so that their lust was inflamed toward her. And they perverted their own mind, and turned away their eyes, that they might not look into heaven, nor remember just judgments.

They both were wounded with her love, yet dared not one show the other his grief. For they were ashamed to declare their lust, that they desired to lie [have sex] with her. Still, they watched diligently from day to day to see her. And the one said to the other, "Let us now go home: for it is dinner time."

So when they were gone out, they parted the one from the other, and turning back again they came to the same place; and after that they had asked one another the cause, they acknowledged their lust; then appointed they a time both together, when they might find her alone.

And it fell out, as they watched a fit time, she went in as before with two maids only, and she was desirous to wash herself in the garden; for it was hot. And there was nobody there save the two elders, that had hid themselves, and watched her.

Then she said to her maids, "Bring me oil and washing balls, and shut the garden doors, that I may wash myself." They did as she bade them; they shut the garden doors, and went to fetch the things that she had commanded them. But they saw not the elders, because they were hid.

Now when the maids were gone forth, the two elders rose up, and ran unto Susanna, saying, "Behold, the garden doors are shut, that no man can see us, and we are in love with thee; therefore consent unto us, and lie with us. If thou wilt not, we will bear witness against thee, that a young man was with thee: and therefore thou didst send away thy maids from thee."

Then Susanna sighed, and said, "I am straitened on every side: for if I do this thing, it is death unto me: and if I do it not, I cannot escape your hands. It is better for me to fall into your hands, and not do it, than to sin in the sight of the Lord."

With that, Susanna cried with a loud voice, and the two elders cried out against her. Then ran the one, and opened the garden door.

So when the servants of the house heard the cry in the garden, they rushed there. But when the elders declared their lies, the servants were greatly ashamed, for there never had been such a report about Susanna.

The next day, when the people were assembled, the two elders came full of mischievous imagination against Susanna to put her to death. They declared, "Send for Susanna, the daughter of Chelcias, Joacim's wife."

So Susanna came with her father and mother, her children and all her kin. Now Susanna was a very delicate woman, and beauteous to behold. And these wicked men commanded to uncover her face (for she was covered), that they might be filled with her beauty. Therefore her friends and all that saw her wept. The two elders stood up in the midst of the people and laid their hands upon Susanna's head. She wept, yet looked up toward heaven, for her heart trusted in the Lord. And the elders said, "As we walked in the garden alone, this woman came in with two maids, and shut the garden doors, and sent the maids away.

> Then a young man, who there was hid, came unto her, and lay with her. Then we that stood in a corner of the garden, seeing this wickedness, ran unto them. But the man we could not hold, for he was stronger than we. He opened the door and leaped out. Having taken this woman, we asked who the young man was, but she would not tell us. These things do we testify."
>
> The assembly believed them, as those two men were the elders and judges of the people. So the assembly condemned Susanna to death.
>
> Susanna cried out with a loud voice, "O everlasting God, that knowest the secrets, and knowest all things before they be: thou knowest that they have borne false witness against me, and behold, I must die: whereas I never did such things as these men have maliciously invented against me."
>
> The Lord heard her voice. When Susanna was led to be put to death, the Lord raised up the holy spirit of a youth, whose name was Daniel. This youth cried with a loud voice, "I am clear from [not responsible for] the blood [the death] of this woman."
>
> All the people turned toward Daniel and said, "What mean these words that thou has spoken?" Standing in their midst, he said, "Are ye such fools, ye sons of Israel, that without examination or knowledge of the truth ye have condemned a daughter of Israel? Return again to the place of judgment, for these two men have borne false witness against her."
>
> The people knew that God had given Daniel the honor of an elder, and Daniel commanded, "Put these two aside one far from another, and I will examine them."
>
> When they were put asunder one from another, Daniel called one, and said unto him, "O thou that art waxed old in wickedness, now thy sins which thou has committed aforetime are come to light: for thou hast pronounced false judgment, and has condemned the innocent, and has let the guilty go free: albeit the Lord saith, `The innocent and righteous shalt thou not slay.' Now then, tell me under what tree sawest thou this woman and thy supposed young man?"
>
> He answered, "Under the mastic tree."
>
> And Daniel said, "Very well; thou has lied against thine own head; for even now the angels of God hath received the sentence of God to cut thee in two."
>
> So Daniel put that man aside, and he commanded the other to be brought henceforth. Daniel said unto him, "O thou seed of Chanaan, and not of Judah, beauty hath deceived thee, and lust hath perverted thine heart. Thus have ye dealt with the daughters of Israel, and they for fear companied [had sex] with you. But this daughter of Judah, Susanna, would not abide your wickedness. Tell me under what tree didst thou see them [Susanna and the young man] companying together [having sex]?"
>
> He answered, "Under a holm tree."
>
> Daniel proclaimed, "Well; thou has also lied against thine own head: for the angel of God waiteth with the sword to cut thee in two."
>
> All the assembly cried out with a loud voice, and praised God, who saves those that trust in Him. And they arose against the two elders, for Daniel had convicted them of false witness by their own mouth. According to the Law of Moses, the assembled of Israel did unto them as they maliciously had intended to do to their neighbor; and they put them to death. Thus the innocent blood was saved that same day.
>
> Therefore, Chelcias and his wife praised God for their daughter Susanna, with Joacim her husband, and all their kin, because there was no dishonesty found in her.

Two Modern Examples:

 a. *The author's case - the woman who allegedly recklessly endangered the neighborhood children!*

- Each witness I cross-examined and asked the same questions; I elicited different answers from the five different witnesses. Thus, inconsistencies were shown.

 b. *Testing Scenario- a chemistry test, a road trip, and a flat tire*

2. A Fundamental Principle about Being a Witness: Not Remembering or Lying

When testifying, if you do not recall, say that you do not recall. On the other hand, if you do recall, you must not say that you don't.

Lying about what you recall constitutes perjury. Nonetheless, until authorities prosecute people who actually remember but claim they "don't recall," then a lawyer's more demanding clients will want to know why they should not just take the easy way out and use that defense ("I don't recall"). A client may thereby succeed, but justice fails.

3. Comparison to Criminal Law: Jury Instructions about Taking the Stand

a. A Constitutional Right to Decline to Testify

There is a 5th Amendment right not to take the stand, but there also is a practical matter of jury instructions. The jury in a criminal case is not to hold it against the defendant if he/she decides to exercise his/her Fifth Amendment right against self-incrimination. However, prison rehabilitation programs that require inmates to reveal undisclosed crimes do not necessarily violate the constitutional right against compelled self-incrimination even if inmates lose privileges[79] for refusing to participate, a sharply divided Supreme Court ruled in *McKune v. Lile*, 536 U.S. 24 (2002).

> A prosecutor must not offer any adverse commentary when a criminal defendant exercises his/her right not to testify – *Griffin v. California*, 380 U.S. 609 (1965).
>
> The defendant is not required to make his refusal to testify in open court (for the jury to hear), and he/she can demand (but need not do so) a jury instruction that the defendant's failure to testify may not be held against him. *Castor v. Kentucky*, 450 U.S. 288 (1981).
>
> On the other hand, though, the defendant may not prevent the court from giving such an instruction should the court so desire. *Lakeside v. Oregon*, 435 U.S. 333 (1978).
>
> For a Comparative Law view, see **pg. 449; Emerson BL.**

b. Civil Lawsuit Comparison

In a civil case, the defendant is forced to submit to questioning under oath or waive his defense and accept any judgment that the trial judge imposes. The U.S. Supreme Court has never undertaken to explain the difference.

> **International Military Comparison**
> "No physical or mental torture, nor any form of coercion, may be inflicted on prisoners of war to secure from them information of any kind whatever. Prisoners of war who refuse to answer may not be threatened, insulted or exposed to unpleasant or disadvantageous treatment of any kind." Article 17 of the Third Geneva Convention on the treatment of prisoners of war. Article 17 also provides, "The questioning of prisoners of war shall be carried out in a language which they understand."

c. Polygraphs

The Supreme Court in *United States v. Scheffer*, 523 U.S. 303 (1998), 8 to 1 (Stevens dissenting), upheld a categorical rule that barred any use of polygraph evidence at trial; in effect, it held that a legislature or court could determine that only a jury can be the "lie detector:" The Court noted, "By its very nature, polygraph evidence may diminish the jury's role in making credibility determinations. . . . The aura of infallibility attending polygraph evidence can lead jurors to abandon their duty to assess credibility and guilt."

---

[79] E.g., to earn money, have visitors, or engage in recreation.

Thus defeated by the high court in criminal trials, and with businesses restrained by Congress from using the intimidating device to screen employees, the "polygraph community" nonetheless claims the ability of its testers to root out spies or perform other valuable services.

Opponents argue that the tests are unreliable – that clever people can use dodges like a sphincter-muscle trick and a Valium pill to defeat polygraph operators.

In October 2002, after 19 months of study, experts convened by the National Research Council (an arm of the prestigious National Academy of Sciences) concluded that "national security is too important to be left to such a blunt instrument," and noted pointedly that "no spy has ever been caught [by] using the polygraph."

4. The Three Types of Witnesses

There are three main types of witnesses - Character, Expert, and Eye.

Character witnesses are much more common for criminal cases, such as the sentencing stage.[80]

Expert witnesses testify about not so much what the facts are, but *what the facts mean.* There are many different types of experts, such as economists, architects, accountants, plumbers, medical doctors, accident reconstruction specialists, and even lawyers.

Eyewitnesses must be someone with something relevant to say and here (from top to bottom, with a-c much higher than d-f) is how judges have ranked six characteristics for evaluating testimony[81]:

a) Ability to be a witness (powers of observation)
b) Consistency (internal – with himself; external – with others)
c) Motivation (e.g., to lie)
d) Known integrity/wisdom of the witness (his/her reputation)
e) Verisimilitude (appears to be true)
f) Demeanor of the witness

<u>Some more on two of the characteristics</u>

Ability to be a witness

We do not generally let people testify about a negative: the fact that they did not see something. For example, if someone is accused of driving erratically and causing an accident, witnesses can testify about what they claim to have seen, but not what they missed seeing. It will not do for the defendant's lawyer to argue, "Yes, there are five people who say they saw my client drive negligently, but I can

---

[80] *"How long have you known the defendant?"*
"Fifteen years."
"Please tell the court, Ms. Johnson, whether you think she is the sort of woman who would steal."
"How much was it again?"
Obviously, this testimony is not very helpful to the defendant!
Here is another example - Kathleen Rae Price, then an Ingham County, Michigan prosecutor, once prosecuted a woman on bad check charges. Because the defendant had a long list of prior convictions, Price was surprised when the defense lawyer brought in a character witness. Price asked for a hearing outside the jury's presence, and the examination went this way.
"Do you know the defendant's reputation in the community for truth and veracity?" Price asked.
The witness looked up and said, "Yes, but I like her anyway."
The judge decided the witness was not qualified to testify.

[81] The ranking/level may vary from case to case. Moreover, in court decisions, judges rarely articulate any such ranking. However, an overall review of judicial decisions and of statements by judges makes clear that this order of importance is both observed and practiced in most cases.

produce a thousand people who will testify that they did not see my client drive at all!" The latter witnesses have nothing to add to the trial proceedings. Their testimony would be irrelevant.

Verisimilitude

The term means "an appearance of truth." A derogatory connotation of the word is that it is "something having *merely* the appearance of truth." As Charles Lamb wrote, "They are, in truth, but shadows of facts, verisimilitudes, not verities." Just because something seems connected to the truth may actually cloud the issue.[82]

A Story of Verisimilitudes

In 1866, some former slaves were talking in a sleepy Georgia town when one of them, perhaps just to break the monotony or to build herself up, said that she had just seen Abraham Lincoln.

The other freedmen were astounded. She had seen the Great Emancipator! They were thrilled as the ex-slave excitedly told how she had seen a tall, gaunt man with a stove-pipe hat came wearily down the town's main dusty lane. As he came closer she realized it was Mr. Lincoln! She asked how he was and if there was anything he needed. Father Abraham simply noted how hot that Georgia sun was and asked if he might have some water. The ex-slave gladly scurried to a nearby well and filled a pitcher of cool water for the President.

Everyone in her audience was overjoyed and sought more news about this, the most wonderful event in any of their lives. Apparently, Abe Lincoln had drunk long and hard from the pitcher, wiped his mouth with his sleeve, smiled in gratitude, tipped his hat, and bid "good day" to the woman as he ambled out of town.

However, one of the many gathered persons was not so entertained by the woman's story. He told her that this tale was preposterous, that President Lincoln had been murdered a year ago, up in Washington. "I don't know what you saw, and I don't rightly care, but it sure wasn't Abraham Lincoln," he snorted.

The storyteller was adamant. "How dare you doubt my word? It's the Gospel truth," she declared. And, she produced the pitcher AS PROOF! "Here's the very pitcher he drank from!"

The pitcher was a *verisimilitude* – an extraneous, irrelevant item thrown in to somehow support the woman's story. This story may seem silly, and the likelihood that people would respond, "Oh, okay, now you've definitely proved it," may seem remote, but if one sees enough small claims trials, enough daytime talk shows, and enough other matters of popular culture, one will see plenty of such irrelevancies masked as somehow connected to the truth.

C. Interpreting the Evidence

"The law's truth never ends strictly with the evidence. It depends as well on what attorneys call 'inference' and what less-restricted souls refer to as imagination." SCOTT TUROW, PERSONAL INJURIES (2000).

Various states now provide for instruction in the applicable law at the start, rather than conclusion, of trials. Also, many states now permit civil juries to discuss the case among themselves during breaks in the proceedings.

1. Experts versus Eyewitnesses

---

[82] Comedian Stephen Colbert, on his television show, thus referred to something perhaps appearing to have an air of truth about it, but having no genuine connection to reality. When demagogues use feel-good, emotional platitudes that are, in fact, demonstrably false, Colbert maintained that they are engaging in "truthiness."

Until the last ten years or so, most states simply would not let an expert testify about supposed weaknesses in an eyewitness' account. The courts agreed with the party that called the witness: any weaknesses could be revealed through cross-examination. Now, though, almost every state (two exceptions are Kansas and Tennessee) allow parties to call experts to explain the potential flaws of eyewitness testimony.

Such experts' testimony generally involves discussing studies that show, for instance, that strong witness confidence has little to do with accuracy; and that identifications are even less reliable when a witness and the person he/she identifies are from a different race or ethnicity. According to the Center on Wrongful Convictions at Northwestern University School of Law, eyewitnesses played a role in convicting half of the 86 people sentenced to death since 1972 but later exonerated. A study by the Innocence Project at New York's Benjamin Cardozo School of Law found that mistaken identifications contributed to 81% of the 74 convictions that DNA testing later proved wrong. Of the 43 DNA exonerations in Texas, the most in any state, more than 80 percent of the initial convictions were due to faulty eyewitness identification. Furthermore according to the Mid-Atlantic Innocence project (D.C., Maryland, and Virginia), in the first 239 DNA exonerations, mistaken eyewitness identifications were a factor in more than 70% of the cases, making it the leading cause of wrongful convictions in DNA cases.

Ultimately, the expert witness must tie the studies to an eyewitness's testimony and why it may be faulty (e.g., if someone robbed at gunpoint can accurately describe the weapon perhaps that shows the witness was so focused on the gun that he/she did not get a good look at the perpetrator).

D. Direct Examination and Coaching

Most attorneys believe coaching happens a lot (even though it is <u>not</u> supposed to). Should a lawyer help a client use more vivid language? E.g., recommend that a client-witness not merely say "My head hurt," but jazz it up with "the pain felt like my head was being split with a chainsaw!" A lawyer goes over the line into unethical behavior if his/her advice sounds like a command – "say this." There is a slippery slope from discussing testimony, to suggesting approaches, to recommending particular words, to <u>strongly</u> recommending a line of testimony, to outright commanding the words the client-witness must say.

So, in direct examination, <u>no coaching of specific answers</u> is allowed. The lawyer's role is not to put words in the client's or another witness's mouth. However, there is a fine line between preparing a witness (okay) and suborning perjury (illegal). It is plainly unlawful for anyone to suborn (persuade a witness to commit) perjury or obstruct justice.

Presumably, coaching is less a problem in England, where the Barristers ordinarily do not meet witnesses in advance of trial.

> More on Coaching of Witnesses
>
> Ethical rules for lawyers mandate that they "shall not . . . counsel or assist a witness to testify falsely."[83] Nor may they "knowingly use perjured testimony or false evidence."[84] But as a practical matter, bringing a successful subornation case or ethics charge against lawyers is almost impossible, experts say. When a lawyer is advising a client, the attorney-client privilege keeps most coaching conversations hidden. Courts will not breach the privilege without very strong evidence of crime or fraud.
>
> The line where legitimate witness preparation crosses into unethical coaching is fuzzy. And whether the offender is a lawyer or sophisticated layperson, there's almost always a scarcity of corroborating evidence and much ambiguity about exactly what was said and meant. So proving the suborning of

---

[83] Model Rules of Professional Conduct 3.4(b).
[84] Model Code of Professional Responsibility DR 7-102(A)(4).

perjury - unethical witness coaching - is extraordinarily difficult. But many attorneys say, "It is a very easy thing to coach your witnesses. And if you have unscrupulous witnesses to begin with, that's the only nudge they need . . . It really is unfortunate." So it happens frequently.

EEOC Advice to Women Who May Have Been Sexually Harassed

Is it coaching for the Equal Employment Opportunity Commission (EEOC) (http://www.eeoc.gov/) to advise women who worked for an employer accused of sexual harassment to try to remember whether or not they had experienced or observed various incidents, such as sexual jokes, unwelcome touching, and circulation of pornographic photographs? Here are two arguments that it is proper: (1) The EEOC's advice is in writing, disclosed to the other side, and in good faith; and (2) women who have suffered sexual harassment often feel shame and humiliation, so they may require lots of prodding before opening up and offering information (even to their own attorneys).

Still, without some coaching, a client uneducated in the law may leave out facts that could help his/her case. And just because someone may be tempted to lie does not mean that he will, or that it will succeed. Still, one can see that information and preparation can facilitate not just a better, more accurate case presentation but also prevarication.

Direct examinations involve open-ended questions of the witness by the party that called him to the stand - let the witness testify using his/her own words.

There is a special approach for Hostile Witnesses: witnesses averse to the interests of the party that called them to the stand. The party calling a hostile witness is allowed to treat that witness as if he/she were under cross-examination. For instance, one can ask this witness leading questions.

Why might a party call a hostile witness? Sometimes, the only way to prove one's case is to depend on the statements of people who would be predisposed against your position. For example, a plaintiff alleging employment discrimination might have to prove certain facts about the defendant employer's hiring and firing practices, and to do that the plaintiff would call to the stand, among others, a witness from the defendant's own personnel department. Or, in responding to a claim of negligence arising from a car accident, the defendant might have to call a family member or friend of the plaintiff, who was in the plaintiff's car, to try to undermine the plaintiff's contentions and show possible contributory negligence on the plaintiff's part.

Criminal Law Comparison

A 5th Amendment clause proscribes self-incriminating testimony: "Nor shall [any person] be compelled in any criminal case to be a witness against himself. . ."

The reasons for this policy against compelled, possibly self-incriminating testimony are many, including: (1) Concern about the trustworthiness of evidence thus produced, and (2) The concept that society's standards for the treatment of defendants, even those who appear (or in fact, are) guilty, should be of the highest level - Not stooping to unfair behavior, even in order to obtain convictions that may be "correct."

This "testimonial" privilege is personal, so it cannot be used by your agents. Therefore, your tax accountant has no privilege for your tax records; and the privilege cannot be used by corporations (e.g., concerning corporate records). The courts may force a corporation, through its agents, to turn over incriminating documents. That was the holding in *United States v. White*, 322 U.S. 694, 699 (1944). The ruling was based on the theory that since a corporation cannot be coerced physically into a confession, the privilege against self-incrimination is "personal";[85] so corporations or other organizations have no such 5th Amendment protection. Similarly, the sole owner of a corporation cannot claim the privilege to prevent production of records *belonging to the corporation*; the corporation is a separate entity. Evidence adduced (brought forward as proof) in such a case may be used against the corporation, but it cannot be used against the sole owner personally. *United States v. Doe*, 465 U.S. 605 (1984)

In a 5-4 June 28, 2004 decision, *United States v. Patane*, 542 U.S. 630 (2004), the Supreme Court even upheld the use of physical evidence, such as a gun, which was obtained by questioning a suspect without fully warning him of his rights. "Reliable" physical evidence should not be thrown out simply because it came from a suspect who had not waived his rights.

Comparative Law: Biblical Reference

According to some legal historians, Jesus was an early proponent of the right to not answer questions in a legal proceeding.

"And Jesus stood before the governor, and the governor asked him, saying, Art thou the King of the Jews? And Jesus said unto him, Thou sayest.

And when he was accused of the chief priests and elders, he answered nothing.

Then said Pilate unto him, Hearest thou not how many things they witness against thee?

And [Jesus] answered him to never a word; insomuch that the governor marveled greatly."[86]

E. Possible Perjury

While it is easy to tell one lie, it is hard to tell only one! Witnesses usually have to elaborate and explain and may thus be tripped up. They thus may be hung upon their own prevarication. Lawyers realize that; and – if simply for practical reasons (regardless of morality) – lawyers, therefore, probably persuade more people to not lie than to lie.

F. Cross-Examination

Quintilian (Roman rhetorician, 1st Cent. A.D.): "A liar should have a good memory"

The lawyer can lead the witness in cross-examination. Cross-examination covers the witness' direct testimony and his/her truthfulness generally.

Leading questions are questions that so suggest to the witness the specific tenor of the reply desired by counsel that such a reply is likely to be given regardless of an actual memory.

A desired reply can be suggested by: (1) the emphasis on certain words, (2) the questioner's tone, (3) the questioner's nonverbal conduct, (4) the questioner's inclusion of facts still in controversy, and (5) the question's form.

Leading questions are only allowed:
(1) when questioning witnesses are called by the other side, or

---

[85] "The constitutional privilege against self-incrimination is essentially a personal one, applying only to natural individuals. It grows out of the high sentiment and regard of our jurisprudence for conducting criminal trials and investigatory proceedings upon a plane of dignity, humanity and impartiality. It is designed to prevent the use of legal process to force from the lips of the accused individual the evidence necessary to convict him or to force him to produce and authenticate any personal documents or effects that might incriminate him. Physical torture and other less violent but equally reprehensible modes of compelling the production of incriminating evidence are thereby avoided. The prosecutors are forced to search for independent evidence instead of relying upon proof extracted from individuals by force of law. The immediate and potential evils of compulsory self-disclosure transcend any difficulties that the exercise of the privilege may impose on society in the detection and prosecution of crime. While the privilege is subject to abuse and miss-use, it is firmly embedded in our constitutional and legal frameworks as a bulwark against iniquitous methods of prosecution." *United States v. White*, 322 U.S. 694, 698-699 (1944) (Justice Murphy for a unanimous Court).

[86] THE BIBLE (New Testament), BOOK OF MATTHEW, CHAPTER 27, VERSES 11-14.

(2) when calling and questioning
  (a) an adverse party (e.g., the defendant calls the plaintiff to testify),
  (b) a witness identified with an adverse party (e.g., a plaintiff suing his former employer for discrimination may have to call his former employer's workers to prove his case), or
  (c) a hostile witness ("hostile" does not have to mean "hateful, full of venom or ready to bite!" just adverse to your interest).

On direct examination, leading questions actually are considered appropriate for these limited situations: (1) the witness is young, reluctant, nervous, and upset; (2) the testimony presents preliminary information such as name, age, residence, and relationships to parties; (3) the witness' impaired physical or mental condition necessitates that he/she be spared having to make long, narrative answers; (4) to incorporate a witness' prior sworn statement; and (5) to refresh the witness' recollection.

Even in cross-examination there are limits on the questioning. Lawyers, for example, cannot ask argumentative or otherwise unfair questions. Sometimes a lawyer – let alone a layperson representing himself – is incapable of such a restrained approach. Here is an example involving a *pro se* plaintiff (someone who represented himself), P, asking questions of the defendant, D, in a small-claims case involving a car accident that P alleged D had caused.

P: [shouting at D] "You're a horrible driver! You know you hit my car! You'll be punished for lying!
  Objection from D's lawyer – no badgering.
  Judge tells plaintiff just to ask questions.
P: [shouting] "You're a devil! They should take away your license! It's criminal that they let you drive!
  D's lawyer rises to object again, and the judge waves him down and tells the plaintiff – "Sir, you have to limit yourself to asking questions. I'll give you one last chance."
P: [nods, walks directly to the witness stand, opens his mouth, closes it, pauses, and asks] "Have you always driven like a damn-fool maniac?!"[87]

Three Examples
  a. A Pool Room Shooting and Circumstantial Evidence
  b. Lorena Bobbitt: What if she had been stopped a minute earlier? (What kind of evidence was found in her hand?)
  c. Bar Room Assault

Bit off a man's ear – cross-examination of a witness
  Foolish, foolish. Never ask an open-ended cross question (e.g., "Why?") and very rarely ask one to which you do not know the answer.

  It is "only" circumstantial evidence, but still very good evidence.

Comparative Law: Cross Examination
Some nations, particularly those with Inquisitorial/Civil Law traditions, generally do not permit leading questions and/or cross-examinations. Germany is one such nation.

G. Circumstantial Evidence Compared with Direct Evidence

<u>An Example: Drunk or Just Ready to Boogie?</u>
How strong is this circumstantial evidence against a woman charged with driving while intoxicated? This is from actual testimony in court.
Q: Trooper, when you stopped the defendant, were your red and blue lights flashing?

---

[87] "War Stories," March 1984 ABA J., p. 164.

A: Yes
Q: Did the defendant say anything when she got out of her car?
A: Yes, sir.
Q: What did she say?
A: What disco am I at?

Circumstantial evidence can be just as compelling as direct. In criminal law, there clearly are far more <u>gross</u> miscarriages of justice due to erroneous eyewitness testimony (direct evidence) getting the wrong guy than there are because of circumstantial evidence.

1. Re-Direct Examination and Re-Cross Examination

Each line of examination after direct (cross, re-direct, re-cross, etc.) is restricted to areas of the preceding testimonial phase (e.g., direct) and to impeaching the witness. So there is a *narrowing of scope* for each line of examination: no more than (no area beyond that which) was in the prior series of questions.

2. Civil Lawsuit Burden of Proof

There are two different meanings for the term, "burden of proof."

a. Burden of Persuasion

In many cases, a crucial element is the *burden of proof* that a judge or jury applies when deciding a case (*the burden of persuasion*) is the necessity for one party (almost always the plaintiff) to persuade the trier of fact (judge or jury) that a preponderance of the evidence supports his/her contentions - that his/her version of the facts is, at the very least, slightly more credible than the opposing party's contentions.[88] If dead-even, the opposing party (generally the defendant) wins.

b. Burden of Coming Forward

The burden of "coming forward" is a less common usage of the term, "burden of proof." It applies to a party's need to put forth evidence (say, to support a particular claim or defense), not the ultimate question of how credible that evidence is (this latter, credibility issue involves the burden of persuasion).

H. The End of the Trial

The following actions are, in chronological order, at the conclusion of a case: Motions for Directed Verdict; Closing Arguments; Jury Instructions; and the Verdict.

1. The Directed Verdict (see pg. 73; Emerson BL)

A directed verdict is a judge's ruling, typically made after the plaintiff has presented all his/her evidence, and before the defendant puts on his/her case. The directed verdict awards a judgment to the defendant, usually because the judge concludes that the plaintiff failed to offer the minimum amount of evidence to prove his/her case. As a matter of law, no reasonable jury could decide in the plaintiff's favor, the judge is ruling.[89]

Judges are reluctant to grant motions for a directed verdict because the effect is to take the case away from a jury (not let it decide the case, despite having heard the evidence).

---

[88] In a criminal trial, the burden of proof that a prosecutor must meet to prove guilt is "beyond a reasonable doubt." Anything less than that level (even though it may be well above "preponderance of evidence) should result in a "not guilty" verdict.

[89] For criminal cases, a directed verdict is a judgment of acquittal for the defendant.

2. Appeal (see pgs. 76-77; Emerson BL)

Briefs and Oral Arguments generally are not polished speeches. The lawyer has a few talking points and should be prepared to be peppered by questions from the appeals court.

In criminal law, *pro se* briefs to judges, attorneys, or anyone else who will read them often detail how the appellant's rights have been trampled, how life for the defendant (who was convicted and now is incarcerated) has been a real "jungle." Here's an excerpt from one such appeal, in the Bronx: (Count the animal allusions!)

"I feel I am not getting a fair shake. My pelican lawyer[90] has sold me up the creek, but I will not weasel on the toad that ratted me at this time. I know I am the target of lots of allegations, but you should know by now that the alligator[91] is a liar."

---

a. The Appellant Usually Loses

Most appeals fail, and thus the lower court judgment is affirmed. To win an appeal, the appellant must do more than seek to have appellate judges say, "We'd have seen the evidence differently." That is because appeals courts ordinarily have no basis for intervening and upsetting a lower, trial court's verdict simply because the appeals court disagrees with the trial court's fact findings. Instead, to win, an appeal needs to point to significant issues of law upon which the trial court made an important error quite possibly affecting the trial's outcome. Indeed, appeals are to be decided solely based upon the law and not facts.

The Devil may be in the details, but courts of appeal rarely desire to be bogged down in details; instead, they seek to see the big picture – overall, despite some problems, was the trial fair?

Usually it is very difficult to overturn on appeal a decision supposedly based upon mistakes at the trial, including even translations.[92] Therefore, it is not just judges who may be insulated, but other court personnel such as court-authorized translators.

For a court to take action on appeal, <u>Errors</u> must be <u>material</u> (significant) legal errors - not simply disagreeing with the judge or with the jury's fact finding. The grounds could be problematic judicial rulings about the law, faulty instructions to the jury, and errors in trial procedures.

<u>Avoiding Inconsistent Jury Verdicts:</u>
<u>The Jury and the Defendant on Trial for Allegedly Stealing a Horse</u>

Stealing a horse in the Old West was a very serious offense. A person could be hanged if found guilty of such a deed. A man whose horse was stolen had always made it a point to get the best of any person with whom he had any dealings. He had never tried to do anything good for anyone other than himself. Consequently, the man whose horse had been stolen had no friends in the entire town or among the people who formed the jury.

The evidence against the accused man was pretty strong. After about thirty minutes of deliberation, the jury returned to the court chambers. "Gentlemen of the jury, have you reached a verdict?" The judge asked. The jury foreman stood up. "Yes we have, your honor," he replied. "We find the defendant not guilty, although we would like to know: What became of the horse?

The judge upbraided the jury: "You cannot do that; don't ask questions in your verdict – just tell us your conclusion."

So the jury went back for more deliberation and then returned with its verdict: "We find the defendant not guilty, . . . as long as he returns the horse."

---

[90] "Pelican lawyer" is a term used by some criminal defendants for "*appellate* division attorneys."
[91] Here, the "alligator" is *not* the renowned Gainesville, Florida newspaper, but a person who makes allegations.
[92] See the *State v. New Chue Her* criminal case discussed shortly hereafter and represented in a YOUTUBE video.

> Now the judge said: "OK, I'll admit, there are no questions asked in your verdict. You put forth two statements, but it still is no good. That's completely inconsistent – You cannot have a verdict like that; come back with a verdict that makes sense, a consistent verdict."
>
> For a third time, the jury went back to the jury chambers for more deliberation. No member of the jury had any particular liking for the man whose horse had been stolen. At one time or another he had gotten the best of each of them. About an hour passed before the jury could reach another verdict. They re-entered the courtroom. They took their place in the jury box and the courtroom grew silent. "Ladies and gentlemen of the jury," began the judge, "have you reached a verdict?"
>
> The foreman stood up. "Yes we have, your honor," he replied. "What is your verdict?" asked the judge.
>
> The courtroom was totally silent. You could have heard a pin drop. Everyone eagerly awaited the verdict. The foreman read the decision reached by the twelve good jurors, tried and true: "Your honor, we again find the defendant *not* guilty, and he can *keep* the horse!"
>
> ---------------------------------
>
> **Moral of the story: If you spend your life trying to take advantage of others, never caring about them in any way except what you can get from them or what they can do for you, you will end up a loser, like the man who lost his horse.**
>
> **If you desire a friend, then be a friend. If you desire for other people to help you, then help other people. If you desire justice at the hands of others, then practice justice toward them. The Biblical admonition is true: We reap what we sow.**

Courts have reversed convictions because of judges' inappropriate behavior. For example, in criminal cases, courts have reversed convictions when the running commentary of the trial judge mimicked that of a talkative, mean televised courtroom "judge."[93]

b. What Appeals Courts Do

In deciding how to treat the lower court's decision, the appellate court has three choices:
(1) Affirm (most likely by far),
(2) Reverse (least likely), or
(3) Vacate and Remand - to return a case to the trial court for further action, usually accompanied by the appellate court's directions and/or judicial opinion (e.g., a liability verdict is upheld, but a new trial is ordered (a remand back to the trial court) on the issue of damages).

YOUTUBE – Hmong Sex Assault Case Skit 7mins41secs at robertwemersonufl

> **Overturning on Appeal: Difficult to Do**
> Appeals courts almost never reverse a trial judge's or jury's fact-findings. Indeed, appeals courts rarely even review non-legal issues. So, if a trial judge accepts a witness' testimony, appeals

---

[93] In *People v. DeJesus*, 42 N.Y. 2d 519, 520 (1977), a reversed trial judge had remarked at trial:
"Let's not be playing any games…"
"And I don't need any help from you…"
"Oh, come on…"
"It is not good enough…and you know better" (in response to questioning of an alibi witness).
"You had better learn about conduct of a lawyer at trial, and I'm . . . tired of trying to teach you.'"

courts usually refrain from any second-guessing. Trial judges are given great leeway in how they control court proceedings, including the use of translators.

For example, consider the Hmong (pronounced *mung*), a people from Southeast Asia. There are estimated to be about 12 million Hmong worldwide. Of the more than 165,000 Hmong in the United States, most came to America in the mid-1970s as refugees of the Vietnam War and the civil war in Laos. The American city with the largest number of Hmong (over 25,000) is St. Paul, Minnesota, with significant clusters sprinkled throughout California, Michigan, Colorado, Wisconsin and North Carolina. The Hmong have elected a state senator in Minnesota, and St. Paul police have learned to speak Hmong.

Hmong culture is rooted in an oral tradition, and they had no written language until about 50 years ago, when Christian missionaries in Laos used the Roman alphabet to translate the Bible into Hmong.

Naturally, some court cases have involved people who mainly or exclusively speak Hmong, not English. The Minnesota case, *State v. New Chue Her*, concerned the translation of certain foreign words used by a non-English speaking criminal complainant.

To properly translate legal documents or courtroom testimony from one nation's language to another's, translators must know not just the two languages involved, but also all relevant legal terminology. Cultural knowledge also is crucial, especially for fundamental matters such as family, religion, and sexuality. In the New Chue Her case, a recent Hmong immigrant, an 18-year-old woman in Minneapolis, reported to police that a Hmong employment counselor sexually assaulted her.

The alleged victim, while talking about what happened, used <u>three</u> important Hmong words, each of which has a different translation, depending on whether your interpretation is pro-defendant. What were the words used? What did they mean? The prosecutor and defendant had a major difference in perspective.

The words in contention were:
a. Mos (pronounced "maw") – wrestle or rape
b. Kuav (pronounced "ku-ah") - shi_ or _____
c. Txiag (pronounced "See-uh") - fu_____ or sexual violation

Minnesota's appeals courts denied the defendant's appeal of his conviction. This failure in the criminal context, with the burdens of proof so strong in the defendant's favor, shows how much harder it must be for the loser of a <u>civil</u> case, trying to contest what happened at trial!

In *State v. New Chue Her*, no judge would second-guess the two courtroom translators. They had, apparently, given the jury the essential gist, in English, of what the woman had said in Hmong. The defendant, a speaker of both English and Hmong, had failed to object to the translations at trial, even though he was specifically given the opportunity.

In an appeals court argument, just like in a good research paper or law journal article, one must provide support for everything. The opposition has time to check your sources, as do the judges (or, much more likely, their law clerks).

There is a difference between what works in an appeals court argument and what might work in a "street" argument – the type of debate you might have with a friend or in a social situation (e.g., at a party), but probably should not try on professionals in the field, such as trial lawyers and judges.[94] These

---

[94] An excellent example of how to argue effectively, although not fairly, is from a column by the humorist Dave Barry, entitled "How to win an argument." http://www.digitalroom.net/index2.html (you can look at it for some tips, or at least laughs). Among other suggestions, Barry recommends that you do what is so often done on talk shows and in politics: compare your opponent to Adolf Hitler. Generally, that is an *ad hominem* ("on the man" – that is, personal) attack of the most odious kind.

Among Barry's many other pearls of wisdom are that you use a lot of Latin phrases, especially abbreviations of those phrases. I tell you that three of his recommended abbreviations have these meanings:

tactics especially should *not* work in an appeals court proceeding, assuming that the judges and your opponent are well prepared. Instead, you will have to furnish support for your statements - the facts and the law that you cite. The judge, the judge's law clerks, and your opponents can all look up what you argue and – most important – the alleged support that you cite.

3. Res Judicata ("the thing decided")

After a decision on the merits, there will be no other trial on the same matter (res judicata is, in a sense, the civil lawsuit equivalent of the Constitution's "no double jeopardy" provision).

Some purposes for res judicata are: (1) to have complete lawsuits - parties know that there is no second chance except for those fairly rare cases in which a judgment is overturned on appeal; (2) to save judicial time and expense; and (3) to prevent harassment of the winning side.

States must honor orders and decrees from other states (including judgments) under the U.S. Constitution's Full Faith and Credit clause. Analogous principles also may arise under international law. For example, through a web of treaties, such as the World Trade Organization (WTO) framework or the North American Free Trade Agreement (NAFTA), a U.S. business – or a business from another signatory nation – may seek redress from a national government because of alleged improprieties in that nation's courts (depriving the business of the rights it would have received if it were a domestic business). So, under NAFTA, any Canadian or Mexican business claiming that it has been treated unjustly by the U.S. judicial system can file a claim.[95] The government whose court system is challenged is responsible for awards by NAFTA arbitration tribunals. That is a fundamental reorientation of our constitutional system, with an international tribunal essentially reviewing American court judgments. In practice, though, NAFTA has not threatened national powers; to date, only two such claims against the United States have been decided, and both ultimately failed.[96]

4. Comparison to "Double Jeopardy" in Criminal Law

A 5th Amendment provision, the double jeopardy provision, prohibits a second trial for a person who has been acquitted: "nor shall any person be subject for the same offence to be twice put in jeopardy of life or limb" (this is a common law concept dating back 800 years)

Many European countries also follow the double-jeopardy principle, which can be traced back to Roman Law principles: The Code of Justinian – "the governor must not allow a man to be charged with the same offense of which he has already been acquitted." (*Nemo bis in idem debet vexori*, meaning – "No one should be troubled/vexed twice for the same matter.")

But many nations allow exceptions to the rule. Altogether, many countries, including Canada, do not have a double jeopardy provision. In Canada, while judges no longer have the right to overturn a jury's decision and order a conviction, either a trial judge or, on appeal, a higher court, can order a new

---

Q.E.D. - *Quod Erat Demonstrandum*, Latin meaning "which is what had to be proven";
e.g. – *exempli gratia*, Latin meaning, "for example."
i.e. – *id est*, Latin meaning, "that is (to say)" or "in other words."
Barry tells you that those phrases are "all short for 'I speak Latin, and you do not.'"
[95] U.S. businesses with similar complaints about Canadian or Mexican court judgments can do the same: file against the Mexican or Canadian governments.
[96] The claims were by a Canadian businessman, Raymond Loewen, who was an investor in the Loewen Group, Inc. (stung to the tune of $175 million in a Mississippi state case), and by a Canadian company, Mondev International (challenging a Massachusetts' court holding).

trial for someone acquitted at his first trial. In the United States, an acquittal is the final word for those particular criminal charges resolved in the defendant's favor.[97]

Other than Canada, most common law systems, but only a few Civil Law nations (mainly in Europe), do not allow prosecutors to appeal an acquittal. A few of the many nations allowing prosecutors to appeal acquittals include Argentina, China, Denmark, Finland, France, Germany,[98] Israel, Italy, the Netherlands, and Russia. And the Australian states of New South Wales and Queensland have taken away double jeopardy protections for very serious crimes.[99]

Popular Culture and the Public's Knowledge of, or Ignorance about, Constitutional Concepts? The "Double Jeopardy" Movie

Double Jeopardy is a 1999 movie starring Ashley Judd and Tommy Lee Jones. It is about a woman (Libby Parsons, played by Judd) whose husband frames her for his murder, when in fact he simply disappeared. In prison, a former lawyer, also convicted of murder, advises Libby that when Libby gets out she can kill her husband in the middle of Times Square and the police would be powerless to do anything about it because of double jeopardy (the constitutional provision - "nor shall any person be subject, for the same offence, to be twice put in jeopardy of life or limb"). At the end of the movie, Jones' character, also a lawyer, later confirms this radical interpretation. In effect, the movie's writers and director would have us believe that Libby, having been convicted of a crime which never actually took place, is now at liberty to commit that same crime in reality - in other words, she has a license to seek her husband and kill him.

There are two problems with the ex-lawyer/present-con's counsel to Libby: (1) why would Libby trust the legal mind of an ex-lawyer who managed to get herself convicted of murder? (2) the interpretation of the Constitution's Fifth Amendment double jeopardy provision is just plain wrong!

"Double jeopardy" means that a defendant must not be tried for the same crime twice. Furthermore, while you cannot be convicted of the same crime twice in the same jurisdiction, you can be charged with the same crime in a different jurisdiction. For example, you can be tried both in state court and in federal court for the same crime because they are different sovereign entities. Or you can be charged with manslaughter in one state and second degree murder in another state. Examples abound, such as the April 19, 1995 bombing of Oklahoma City's Alfred P. Murrah Federal Building. In a U.S. District Court, Terry Nichols was convicted of eight counts of manslaughter; the state of Oklahoma then charged Nichols with capital murder, and he was convicted on 161 counts of first-degree murder. Another example involves the Rodney King beating trials. First, in state court four Los Angeles cops were prosecuted for beating King, and two who were not found guilty were nonetheless charged, in federal court, for violating King's civil rights (again, by beating him), for which they were found guilty. So, even though they were not guilty of beating King (the state charge), they were guilty of violating his

---

[97] For more, see Howard Schneider, "Conviction of Innocent Man Spurs Questions About Double Jeopardy in Canada," WASH. POST, June 22, 1997, at A24; see also the book describing a horrific Kentucky case - Bob Hill, Double Jeopardy: Obsession, Murder, and Justice Denied (1995).

[98] For example, on November 16, 2006, Germany's Federal Court of Justice, an appeals court, ruled that the evidence showed a Moroccan man, Mourir el Motassadeq, knew that the plotters of the 9-11 terrorist attacks planned to hijack and crash airplanes; therefore, the appeals court found el Motassadeq "guilty not only of membership in a terrorist organization [of which he had been convicted at trial], but also as an accessory to murder" reversing the acquittal on that charge of direct involvement in the attacks.

[99] In April 2005, the new Criminal Justice Act for England and Wales enacted an exception to the double-jeopardy rule for 30 serious crimes – including murder, rape, some illegal drug sales, and war crimes – so that an appeals court could order a retrial if "compelling" new evidence of guilt emerged after the acquittal (evidence such as DNA, new witnesses, or a confession). One concern is that once a senior judge finds evidence compelling enough to order a retrial, the presumption of innocence would be undermined as juries likely would assume that indicates the defendant is guilty. But there could only be one such re-trial, and only a "handful" of such second trials are expected.

federal civil rights while beating him. And please note that double jeopardy only applies to "jeopardy of life or limb," not money. So civil trials can follow criminal ones, such as in the O.J. Simpson cases involving the killing of Nicole Brown Simpson and Ron Goldman (O.J. found not guilty of the crime, but later found liable for the wrongful deaths).[100]

The double jeopardy concept normally relates to situations where a defendant has already been acquitted of a crime, so that the defendant cannot be tried again for that crime even if fresh evidence of the defendant's guilt comes to light later. It also means that a defendant who has been convicted of a crime cannot be re-tried to seek another conviction and, presumably, a harsher punishment. However, double jeopardy only applies to a single set of facts (a single incident). Just as it would be two separate offenses (and two distinct permissible prosecutions) to steal from someone on two different occasions, so it would be two separate offenses to murder someone twice (even though, of course, as a practical matter, one particular victim could not actually die twice). Surely if the husband in the movie *Double Jeopardy* remained alive and Libby killed him "again," that would be a different crime than the subject of the first trial. Libby cannot be re-tried for the original "killing" (where she allegedly stabbed hubby and dubbed him off their boat), but any other charges are fair game. Moreover, a parole board can revoke parole based on new information without violating double jeopardy, since parole is not a constitutional right.

Query: While we sympathize with anyone framed for murder, what if Libby's husband simply fell and gashed his head, left a bloody mess on the boat while falling overboard, and somehow survived (washing up on the proverbial deserted island and/or suffering amnesia); sounds far-fetched, but no more than any number of television and movie themes, including *Double Jeopardy* itself. The Fifth Amendment certainly speaks nothing of victims; in other words, whether it applies should not depend upon the merits or demerits of an alleged crime victim – a scoundrel such as Libby's husband who, as they say in Texas, "needed killing," or a true innocent – think Tom Hanks in "Castaway" (a 2000 movie) or Goldie Hawn in "Overboard" (a 1987 movie).

5. Enforcement of a Judgment (see pgs. 77-78; Emerson BL)

Many in the business world are more worried about enforcing judgments than in getting a judgment (e.g., consumer debts). The difficult part of a case may not be obtaining a judgment, but actually collecting money afterwards.[101]

So, most businesses try to get money upfront.

There is a judicial process for collecting on a judgment, but there are limits to that process. For example, in February 1999 Sears Roebuck & Co. pleaded guilty to criminal fraud charges and paid a $60 million fine for illegally collecting credit card debts from customers who had filed for personal bankruptcy. Sears' unlawful actions included: (1) failure to file, in court, 187,000 reaffirmation agreements that Sears entered with its customers, (2) telling debtors that their credit card debts were not dischargeable in bankruptcy, and (3) threatening to repossess goods purchased with the card. Sears also settled suits in this area with attorneys' general from all fifty states, the Federal Trade Commission, and lawyers representing customers and shareholders. So Sears paid about $185 million in reimbursements and penalties to cardholders, $40 million in state fines, and $12 million to settle shareholder suits; and Sears wrote off $120 million owed by cardholders under the reaffirmation agreements and had to spend about $56 million in related administrative costs and legal fees.

---

[100] The Casey Anthony acquittal for homicide charges concerning the death of her daughter, Caylee Anthony, in a Florida verdict on July 5, 2011 remains controversial. Although found not guilty of first degree murder, aggravated child abuse, and aggravated manslaughter of a child (but guilty of four misdemeanor counts of providing false information to a law enforcement office), Casey Anthony could possibly face civil suits.

[101] "A lean award [collecting money from the defendant] is better than a fat judgment [a right to collect money]," wrote Benjamin Franklin.

Government officials (e.g., sheriffs) may help a winning plaintiff collect: executing a judgment by confiscating property. Also helping in the repossessing of goods may be private helpers - "Repo" people.

Collecting on Judgments: Bankruptcy Can Interfere!

YOUTUBE – Bankruptcy 5mins45secs at robertwemersonufl (a man in a barrel)

In the bad old days, when people went bankrupt they often were reduced to, as they say, living in a barrel. All their clothes were gone; all their assets were gone; they had no recourse under the law. In fact, in England and a number of other locations, they actually put debtors in prison (they had a special type of jail called debtor's prison). Even sometimes the relatives of people that went bankrupt had to go to jail.

We have revised the laws tremendously. Now people are not required to wear barrels anymore, and, in fact, there are all sorts of protections for both individuals and businesses that are insolvent - that are unable to pay their debts as they become due. There is, for businesses, a reorganization that is available under Chapter 11 of the U.S. Bankruptcy Code. There is also a Chapter 13 readjustment, which is permitted for individuals having financial difficulties but who have not yet reached the point where really the only thing available is liquidation. And then there is Chapter 7 liquidation, which is what I believe most people think of vis-à-vis bankruptcy: you are completely discharged from a number of debts, there are some debts which are non-dischargeable, and of course there are some types of assets which cannot be collected upon during the course of bankruptcy.[102]

It is all an area of great interest, particularly to examine whether a defendant is worth suing. (That is not, by itself, enough.) There are three key things one wants in all litigation: first, one wants to find that there is a good cause of action that actually makes a real case against someone; secondly, one needs to show that there are damages (it's not enough that someone did something wrong, but also that you have been harmed); and, thirdly - and this is where bankruptcy law comes into question - you need to find a defendant who is not judgment-proof (but who, in fact, has assets sufficient to pay all or at least some judgment debt that you may have entered against that defendant).

Nowadays, it is not nearly as rough on those people that become insolvent. We have laws that afford some protections for people who decide that they need to declare bankruptcy. We also, of course, have involuntary bankruptcy petitions which are available for others (creditors) who need to proceed against a person who owes them and is not willing and/or able to pay their debts as they become due. That is the definition for bankruptcy. It is not simply calculating whether your debts exceed your assets; it is looking at, as your debts become due, are you able to pay them? And, if not, then you could well be insolvent and thus bankrupt.

We have laws now that permit businesses and individuals to either readjust their income stream and their debt payments, and this is typically Chapter 11 for businesses, where they can reorganize, or it is Chapter 13 for individuals who have a steady stream of income (so that they can readjust their debt), or, if that really is not practical, or if a business or an individual is too far gone,[103] then typically what they have invoked is Chapter 7, which is outright liquidation.

During a bankruptcy proceeding what you have is the discharge of the debts which are in fact dischargeable. One may end up paying little if anything to particular creditors, who are simply out of luck under the Bankruptcy Code. There are some debts which are non-dischargeable. For instance, child support payments are non-dischargeable, and there are some assets which cannot be collected upon in order to pay a bankruptcy award - in other words, that are free from any sort of creditor's grasp.

---

[102] E.g., recipients of child support cannot be made to pay something in bankruptcy proceedings due to those support payments (which are not "earnings").
[103] In a horrible financial bind.

> One reason this is so important is, if you think about litigation (and to reiterate what I said earlier), there are really three essential elements for anyone who considers bringing a lawsuit. The first step is that you actually have a good case, that you have some sort of cause of action, some legal wrong that has occurred to you. The second is that you have actually suffered damages. And the third is that there is some sort of defendant out there that is not judgment proof (i.e., not completely bankrupt, but actually has assets to pay the debt that you would be owed if you were to obtain a judgment against that particular defendant).

C. ALTERNATIVE DISPUTE RESOLUTION
(see pgs. 78-82; Emerson BL)

Everything in the post-World War II era seems to have sped up: do this, do that, file this, process that. The biggest legal developments of this time period, at least procedurally, may well be the burgeoning of administrative law and a tremendous increase in Alternate Dispute Resolution (ADR).

Litigation can be extremely costly and time-consuming. In response, alternative approaches have been considered, and some dispute resolution systems are not simply frequently used, but also well-established (with elaborate rules and principles for the older, most used systems, namely, arbitration and mediation). Indeed, businesses often prefer these alternatives over going to court and even insist on the use of contract clauses adopting these methods (e.g., arbitration) if there is a dispute.

The two most well-established forms of out-of-court dispute resolution are arbitration and mediation.[104] In mediation the mediator does not judge the case but merely facilitates discussion in hopes of gaining an eventual determination (http://library.findlaw.com/1999/Jun/1/129206.html). ADR may spur settlements, and it may foster quicker and less costly resolutions. Besides arbitration and mediation, there are numerous fairly recent ADR methods, such as mini-trials, summary jury trials, the use of ombudspersons, and early neutral evaluation.[105]

Typically, arbitration awards are very difficult to overturn. Appeals courts usually give even more leeway to arbitrators than they do to trial courts. For example, under the U.S. Arbitration Act, a federal court may vacate an arbitral award only "where the arbitrators exceeded their powers, or so imperfectly executed them that a mutual, final and definite award upon the subject matter submitted was not made." Most unfair awards will survive under this standard, so long as they are complete. An incomplete award is vulnerable.

YOUTUBE – ADR Compared to Litigation 3mins32secs at robertwemersonufl

> **Alternative Dispute Resolution: Arbitration and Mediation Compared To Litigation**
> When people feel aggrieved, often they think of filing a lawsuit or, as an alternative, at the very least they consider going through some form of alternative dispute resolution, such as arbitration or mediation. In such processes, it is often a foolish notion to expect that some sort of "magic resolution" will occur.
> Most litigators will comment to clients that the only reason to go to court is because of some actual pecuniary interest that can be met. In other words, you've got a situation wherein money can be paid to you or you've got money that you need to defend from someone else's claim. But to go to court

---

[104] Some special fields, such as alleged medical malpractice, have a combined system of mediation and arbitration.
[105] Early neutral arbitration involves an expert's reviewing the claims and giving a preliminary opinion as to the merits of the claim, so as to spur a possible settlement.

for a principle or to go to arbitration or mediation <u>simply</u> to be vindicated and told you were right (and the other person is wrong) is often a foolish proposition. Arbitrators, mediators and judges cannot really work magic; all that they can do is apply the law to those particular cases. All that an arbitrator <u>or</u> mediator is empowered to do is act within the scope or power of the arbitration or mediation that is presented to them. So in these fields[106] I think that sometimes people have unrealistic expectations.

There are many, many, many[107] processes that people will have to know about in litigation in particular. So one of the attractions of alternative dispute resolution is that it is often more informal: there are ways to avoid some of the technicalities and get to the heart of the matter in a quicker and often less costly and more private fashion. On the other hand, the big advantage of litigation over alternative dispute resolution is that you are more likely to have a "script" (a process) that definitely must be followed and if, for some reason, a trial judge or the jury does not act in compliance with that set of prescribed procedures, then, under the rules, there are better ways of appealing in litigation than there are in arbitration or mediation. The very informality of alternative dispute resolution, which attracts people, can also make it very difficult to challenge anything that you are actually upset about in the arbitration or mediation process. On the other hand, litigation and court rules provide all sorts of avenues for at least bringing forth an appeal; you may not win (you probably won't),[108] but at least you have more grounds to do so in litigation than in, say, arbitration.[109]

I. EMPIRICAL STUDIES

In a 2008 article, Professors Eisenberg (Cornell), Miller (NYU), and Sherwin (Cornell) conducted the first study of varying use of arbitration clauses across contracts within the same firms.[110] Using a sample of 26 consumer contracts and 164 nonconsumer contracts from large public corporations, the authors compared arbitration clause use in consumer contracts with their use in the same firms' nonconsumer contracts. Over three-quarters of the consumer agreements provided for mandatory arbitration but less than 10% of the firms' material nonconsumer, non-employment contracts included arbitration clauses. The absence of arbitration provisions in nearly all material contracts suggests that, ex ante, many firms value, even prefer, litigation over arbitration to resolve disputes with peers. The frequent use of arbitration clauses in the same firms' consumer contracts appears to be an effort to preclude aggregate consumer action rather than, as often claimed, an effort to promote fair and efficient dispute resolution. Civil litigation reform proposals also include (a) reduction or elimination of jury usage and (b) loser-pays attorney fee rules. However, Professors Eisenberg, Miller, and Sherwin find that these approaches were rarely adopted in the terms of the contracts they studied.

II. NEW ARBITRATION APPEALS PROCEDURES

The American Arbitration Association (AAA) Arbitration Rules used to allow appeals only to the courts, and only for very limited, rare reasons — generally, arbitrator bias or an arbitrator's refusal to allow a party to submit appropriate evidence. An arbitrator's ignoring the law or facts was not a basis for

---

[106] Common areas for arbitration include building construction disputes, stock brokerage controversies, and some employment or franchise disagreements. Mediation often occurs in, among other areas, labor law (e.g., bargaining) and family law (e.g., divorce).
[107] Mucho, trop, LOTS!
[108] Generally, the vast majority of appeals result in the upholding of the trial court's decision.
[109] The likelihood of overturning an arbitration award is even much smaller than for overturning a trial court judgment.
[110] Theodore Eisenberg, Geoffrey P. Miller & Emily Sherwin, "Arbitration's Summer Soldiers: An Empirical Study of Arbitration Clauses in Consumer and Nonconsumer Contracts" (May 30, 2008)), *New York University School of Law. New York University Law and Economics Working Papers.* Paper 136, at http://lsr.nellco.org/nyu/lewp/papers/136,

appeal. However, the AAA changed its Arbitration Rules to include new Optional Appellate Arbitration Rules (the OAAR), effective November 1, 2013. Parties can now appeal arbitration awards for an arbitrator's errors of law that are material and prejudicial or determinations of fact that are clearly erroneous.

The OAAR allow a party to appeal an arbitrator's underlying award to the AAA within 30 days after the award is submitted to the parties. Any party that does not appeal has seven days after receiving notice of another party's appeal to file a cross-appeal. When a Notice of Appeal is filed, the underlying arbitration award is not considered final, and the time to commence judicial enforcement proceedings of the award is tolled (stopped) while the appeal takes place.

Each party initiating an appeal or a cross-appeal must pay a $6,000 fee (a substantial sum compared to most other appeals, such as in courts); they also must pay the fees and costs of the appeal tribunal, and losing appellants may be ordered to pay the winner's costs and fees.

Under the OAAR, the appeals tribunal is composed of three arbitrators, none of whom can be the original arbitrator(s). The AAA provides the parties a list of ten prospective "Appellate Panel" arbitrators. If the parties cannot agree on who should be the three appeals arbitrators, each party has 14 days to strike names to which it objects and to number the remaining names in order of preference. The AAA then selects the tribunal from the lists returned to it. Parties also can request an appellate arbitrator with specific qualifications (e.g., franchise law experience).

The tribunal sets a schedule for parties to file written arguments, and rebuttals (general three to four months *in toto*), and it issues a ruling on the briefs – without holding a hearing - within 30 days after the final brief was filed. The tribunal has three choices: (1) to adopt the underlying award, (2) to substitute its own award, or (3) to request more information and extend the period for another 30 days. The appeals tribunal cannot order a new hearing or send the case back to the original arbitrator(s) for corrections or further review. This potential for delay in the process is still shorter than for a court appeal, and the cost of a delay may, of course, be much less than the cost of an unfair arbitration award.

The OAAR do not bind the parties unless the parties have opted for the appeals process.

Parties can opt in at any point in the arbitration process or in the initial agreement to have an arbitration procedure. Presumably, a party that thinks its position is correct factually and legally, then it should want to assure that an arbitrator cannot make an erroneous determination of fact, or a ruling counter to existing law, yet not be subject to an appeal on those grounds. Obviously, once a dispute arises one or both parties may realize that its/their positions are unsound or weak, so it is usually better to include arbitration provisions in the parties' initial agreement, including the OAAR appeal right. Indeed, the availability of an arbitration appeal right may encourage more such clauses.

III. COMPARATIVE LAW ON *ADR*

In many areas of the world, such as Africa, people may emphasize the forcing of a result rather than an individual right to sue. Yet, ironically, African countries – despite this anti-litigation tribal heritage – are far less likely than countries from elsewhere in the world to adopt the United Nations Convention on the Recognition and Enforcement of Foreign Arbitral Awards (1958). That convention binds signatory nations to uphold the validity of arbitration awards.

The 156 signatory nations as of October 2015 were: Afghanistan, Albania, Algeria, Andorra, Antigua and Barbuda, Argentina, Armenia, Australia, Austria, Azerbaijan, Bahamas, Bahrain, Bangladesh, Barbados, Belarus, Belgium, Benin, Bhutan, Bolivia, Bosnia and Herzegovina, Botswana, Brazil, Brunei, Bulgaria, Burkina Faso, Burundi, Cambodia, Cameroon, Canada, Central African Republic, Chile, China, Colombia, Comoros, Congo (Democratic Republic of) Cook Islands, Costa Rica, Côte d'Ivoire, Croatia, Cuba, Cyprus, Czech Republic, Denmark, Djibouti, Dominica, Dominican Republic, Ecuador, Egypt, El Salvador, Estonia, Fiji, Finland, France, Gabon, Georgia, Germany, Ghana, Greece, Guatemala, Guinea, Guyana, Haiti, Honduras, Hungary, Iceland, India, Indonesia, Iran, Ireland, Israel, Italy, Jamaica, Japan, Jordan, Kazakhstan, Kenya, Kuwait, Kyrgyzstan, Laos, Latvia, Lebanon,

Lesotho, Liberia, Liechtenstein, Lithuania, Luxembourg, Macedonia, Madagascar, Malaysia, Mali, Malta, Marshall Islands, Mauritania, Mauritius, Mexico, Moldova, Monaco, Mongolia, Montenegro, Morocco, Mozambique, Myanmar (Burma), Nepal, Netherlands, New Zealand, Nicaragua, Niger, Nigeria, Norway, Oman, Pakistan, Palestine "State," Panama, Paraguay, Peru, Philippines, Poland, Portugal, Qatar, Romania, Russia, Rwanda, Saint Vincent and the Grenadines, San Marino, Sao Tome and Principe, Saudi Arabia, Senegal, Serbia, Singapore, Slovakia, Slovenia, South Africa, South Korea, Spain, Sri Lanka, Sweden, Switzerland, Syria, Tajikistan, Tanzania, Thailand, Trinidad and Tobago, Tunisia, Turkey, Uganda, Ukraine, United Arab Emirates, United Kingdom, United States, Uruguay, Uzbekistan, Vatican City, Venezuela, Vietnam, Zambia, and Zimbabwe.

D. CRIMINAL LAW

I. TERMINOLOGY: THE GENERAL, LEGAL CATEGORIZATION OF CRIMES
(see pgs. 449–450; Emerson BL)

A. Treason

Treason is an extremely rare criminal charge. It is the only crime defined in the Constitution - (Article III, Section 3) - defined strictly – with a high standard of proof needed. Treason is restricted to levying war against the United States or giving aid and comfort to the United States' enemies; the prosecution needs the testimony of two witnesses to an overt act, or it needs a confession.

Dissent is not treason – the crime of treason involves much more than political opposition; there must be consorting with the enemy.

B. Felonies

Felonies are more serious crimes, with long prison sentences possible and convicts losing certain civil rights (e.g., perhaps losing voting rights).

<u>Capital</u> crimes: In medieval times, the basic punishments were death and banishment – <u>not</u> jail. Nowadays, felonies could be capital offenses (murder), but for most felonies one can just go to jail (no executions).

> CHANGING SOCIETAL CIRCUMSTANCES AFFECT DEFINITION OF CRIME
> The Burglary Example
> Burglary is trespassing for purposes of carrying out a felony. In traditional common law, there had to be a home, a breaking and entering at night.
> What has the test for burglary become? Almost any sort of trespass to commit a felony, day or night, of a residence or not.

C. Misdemeanors

Misdemeanor convictions often lead to no jail, or just short terms, and to lower fines. Convictions do not deprive defendants of their civil rights.

> Plea bargaining may lead to a reduction in the type of crime to be charged; such as from a low-level felony to a misdemeanor.

Misdemeanors usually can eventually be taken off the convicted person's record (if there are no subsequent convictions). Examples are simple trespass and disturbing the peace.

D. Offenses
Offenses are minor crimes (i.e., traffic violations, but <u>not</u> drunk driving) treated in administrative fashion, not criminal court proceedings.

E. Other Classifications
Crimes may also be classified by how they affect business (generally touching property rights), or by categories such as white-collar, organized, and victimless. Sometimes broad classifications are used, based on their victim – crimes against the person, the general public, the home, or other property.

F. The Constitutional Protections
There are many criminal defense protections in the Bill of Rights, specifically the 4th, 5th, 6th, and 8th Amendments.

The Bill of Rights originally applied solely to the national government. However, in the 1940s to 1960s, the process of incorporating almost the entire Bill of Rights into the U.S. Constitution's 14th Amendment due process clause[111] resulted, to a large extent, in the "nationalizing" of basic criminal procedure law. The criminal defense provisions of the Bill of Rights (the 4th, 5th, 6th, and 8th Amendments), as applied to the states in numerous court decisions, have set a minimum standard below which the states must not fall.

Criminal_law_4mins4secs is at robertwemersonufl - *a YOUTUBE video Introduction*
"A person was once introduced to another person as a lawyer, and the first person responded 'Are you a criminal lawyer?' to which a third person interjected 'Is there any other kind?' Well, that's a rather cynical view as to the ethics of lawyers or the wrongdoing propensities, perhaps, of some lawyers. But I do think it's true that when most people think of lawyers, they often gravitate toward criminal defense lawyers and the work of prosecutors and those who are representing people accused of crimes, in which there is nothing inappropriate about that at all.

"Criminal law is a focal point of the legal system. It is obviously a very significant area in terms of people's freedom and occasionally even their lives are at stake. It's so fundamental that when our bill of rights was enacted over 200 years ago, most of the provisions have something to do with criminal law. Our Constitution rests upon the notion that the power of the state is very, very strong and individuals need a number of protections to counter the power of the state, which can charge people with crimes, bring the full force of the state into a court, and to end up possibly convicting and incarcerating those individuals. That is really what so much of criminal law is about; it is procedural in orientation. Yes, the substance is also important, but in many ways we already have a sense of what the substantive law is. A lot of that we learn at a young age, in terms of basic concepts: don't steal, don't lie, don't cheat, don't do harm to others. A lot of these concepts are in the substantive law; they're more elaborated, the elements are much more defined than, say, what you learned from your third grade

---

[111] The unincorporated Bill of Rights provisions (not applied to the States via court opinion) include the entire Second (bearing of arms), Third (quartering of soldiers), and Seventh (jury trial in civil cases) Amendments, as well as parts of the Fifth (grand jury indictment) and Eighth Amendments (freedom from excessive bail). The other rights are considered so fundamental that they form part of the Fourteenth Amendment's Due Process restriction on state governments.

teacher, or in Sunday school, but it is really in the procedural law area where so much of criminal law has a lot of bearing and a lot of import.

"So what I hope for you is, while you're looking at various Internet sites, you bear in mind the reason for these protections, under the 4th, 5th, and 6th amendment or in various court decisions interpreting these various protections: It is much better for, as they say, a hundred guilty men to go free than one innocent person be incarcerated. That is the reason for these protections, the reason for the presumption of innocence, and the reason why we do not convict a person unless we are beyond a reasonable doubt and are convinced that, in fact, this person is guilty. It's an entirely different ball game than what we have in most areas of law, where there is a more even scale of preponderance of evidence standard. The reason is that we are worried about the state having overwhelming power, i.e. in the civil law context, and it is usually just private individuals slinging it out, we are much more content to kind of let them go at it and we are not worried nearly as much about one side taking advantage of the other.

Questions that might be explored in a criminal law class, such as in law school, are:

Does the criminal law cover behavior which, although immoral or at least inefficient or even harmful, should not be punished by society's laws? Give examples.

Does the criminal law fail to reach some behaviors that it should cover? Specify.

Do our courts protect criminal defendants too much? Too little? Explain.

How do you feel about the "guilty beyond a reasonable doubt" requirement? If you support it, do you see any conflict between that position and the notion that – in times of war, the government shouldn't have to seek a warrant to eavesdrop on conversations or carry out other "searches?"

> Joke – *Attorney: My client can't get a fair trial in this town!*
> *Judge: Then we will move it to another town.*
> *Attorney: Thank you, your honor.*
> *Judge: But we're coming back here for the hanging.*

II. CRIMINAL LAW COMPARED TO TORT LAW

A. Several Distinctions

■ "Guilt" in criminal law

A competent attorney should instruct the client about the elements for each crime the client allegedly committed, about the possible suppression of evidence or other key potential court rulings, about the client's strong presumption of innocence, and about the state's high burden of proof. The lawyer should do all that 'translating" of legal concepts into laymen's terms before a defendant might say he is culpable, *whatever* that term's meaning.

"Liability" in tort law

The laws (for crimes or torts) are very much tied into contemporary standards of what is or is not acceptable behavior. Circumstances, definitions, and society changes matters immensely.

■ Crime - a <u>public wrong</u> against society
■ Tort – a <u>private wrong</u> against an individual or business

• <u>Prosecutors/Plaintiffs</u> –Criminal cases are brought by the state (the prosecutors), with offended persons usually witnesses; tort cases are brought by plaintiff individuals or businesses.

Prosecutors at the federal level (U.S. Attorneys – one for each federal district court, with each generally having many Assistant U.S. Attorneys) are appointed by the President. Prosecutors at the state level (where the vast majority of criminal cases arise) often are elected, with a state's attorney for a county or some other judicial circuit (e.g., Florida's 20 circuit courts) elected, and assistant state's attorneys serving under him/her. Indeed, while the chief U.S. law enforcement officer (the U.S. Attorney General) is appointed by the President, the chief state law enforcement officer is elected by the voters in 43 states and in Guam.

That position is often a launching point for a political career (e.g., as governor, congressional representative, or U.S. Senator). But in five states the governor appoints the attorney general: Alaska, Hawaii, New Hampshire, New Jersey, and Wyoming. (Such gubernatorial appointments of the territorial attorney-general also occur for American Samoa, the Northern Mariana Islands, Puerto Rico, and the Virgin Islands.[112]) In Maine, the state legislature, via secret ballot, elects the attorney general, and in Tennessee, that state's supreme court appoints the attorney general.[113]

In many countries, other than the United States, the victim of a crime may commence a prosecution. Some examples where a victim may prosecute (although sometimes restricted to certain categories of offences or subject to other restrictions) are Argentina, China, England, France, Germany, Israel, and South Africa. In some countries where victims may commence a prosecution, such as Canada, the prosecution may be stopped or taken over by public prosecutors.

So who files?

Tort lawsuits are filed by private individuals (e.g., *Smith v. Jones*, or *Gonzales v. DEF Corporation*)

Criminal charges are brought by: *State v. Person* (Government vs. _____). The victim is a witness, not a party, in criminal cases; thus, the victim (or next-of-kin) does not control the criminal case, as he/she can in a civil matter, as a tort suit plaintiff. But there has been a trend toward recognition of victims' rights (appearances for sentencing and parole hearings, impact statements, conferences with prosecutors).

In criminal cases, the government itself is a party (it has brought charges against the defendant). The Prosecution is a.k.a. "the people."

- Burden of Proof: crimes – guilt beyond a reasonable doubt (a very high percentage for there being guilt – say, over 99%); torts (as with other civil cases) – preponderance of the evidence (just barely over 50% likelihood of liability – a slight tipping of the scale, such as to 51% probability)

- Jail/Damages
Damages ordinarily must be shown in tort cases; they are not usually needed in criminal cases.

---

[112] In the District of Columbia, the Mayor appoints the Corporation Counsel whose powers and duties are similar to a state attorney general.

[113] As chief legal officers of the states, commonwealths, and territories of the United States, the Attorneys General serve as counselors to state government agencies and legislatures, and as representatives of the public interest. Their duties occupy the intersection of law and public policy, dealing in areas as diverse as child support enforcement, drug policy, and environmental protection.

In many areas traditionally considered the U.S. government's exclusive responsibility, state Attorneys General now share enforcement power. State Attorneys General and their federal counterparts increasingly cooperate on many matters, particularly trade regulation, environmental enforcement, and criminal justice.

Typical powers of the Attorneys General, while varying from one jurisdiction to the next due to statutory and constitutional mandates, include the authority to: institute civil suits; represent state agencies; defend and/or challenge the constitutionality of legislative or administrative actions; enforce open meetings and records laws; revoke corporate charters; enforce antitrust prohibitions against monopolistic enterprises; enforce air pollution, water pollution, and hazardous waste laws; handle criminal appeals and serious state-wide criminal prosecutions; intervene in public utility rate cases; and enforce the provisions of charitable trusts.

Also, a *damages award* is the most typical remedy for a successful tort claim, while a successful criminal prosecution can lead to any number of punishments, including incarceration.

Four purposes of incarceration or other criminal penalties are punishment, prevention (the incarcerated person cannot, we hope, commit further crimes), deterrence (others who may be tempted to commit a crime are scared off), and rehabilitation.

Generally, the hallmarks of crime that may be grounds for stiff punishment are: deliberation, gross recklessness, stealth, and significant harm.

> "'Let the jury consider their verdict,' the King said, for about the twentieth time that day. 'No, no!' said the Queen. 'Sentence first – verdict afterwards.'" Lewis Carroll, Alice in Wonderland, Chapter 12.

Sentencing procedures open cases up to much more evidence than could be presented at trial. There is a battery of questions. Testimony may come from all sorts of sources - Victims, Defendant's mother, other relatives, friends, employers, or business colleagues; there may be accounts of the defendant's "finding" religion, suffering childhood abuse, or other supposedly extenuating circumstances.[114] There may be anguished cries for justice from the victim or next-of-kin. It is an opportunity for almost anything "relevant" to the crime, the defendant's life, the crime's impact upon the victim(s), and the prospective punishment to be put before the sentencing judge.[115]

> As a defendant, you should be very careful about what you say or do in sentencing, just as in any other stage of the proceedings. Often it would be better to just let a lawyer/your lawyer speak for you.

Most people that go to trial plead guilty or are found guilty: So the key thing is – what do we do with the convict? Sentencing guidelines call for sentences to fall within a range- it is easier to do that than to justify, in extensive writing, being outside the range. Probably the most important role of judges is sentencing. Most courses in criminology and law school emphasize other subjects than sentencing.

Sometimes, judges can be quite creative in sentencing.[116] An Ohio judge, for instance, is known to give unusual sentences. For a woman who failed to pay a cabdriver his fare for a 30-mile trip, the

---

[114] Perhaps the worst example of a defendant's plea for leniency was that of the young man who had been found guilty of murdering his parents. He supposedly asked the judge for mercy on the grounds that he now was an orphan!

[115] Of course, that can backfire on some defendants. As related in the Feb. 1989 ABA Journal, the late Wayne Superior Court Judge Harry Holtsclaw (an Indiana state judge) was known for his patient and clear explanations. An offender had just been found guilty of a repeat offense of drunk driving. Judge Holtsclaw suspended his license for two years and ordered him to serve several weekends in jail. The judge went to great lengths to explain to the defendant that he could not operate a motor vehicle until the suspension had expired. At the end, Judge Holtsclaw asked the defendant if he had any questions.

"Yes," the defendant said. "When I report to jail on weekends, where do I park my car?"

Clearly, that presented the judge with a chance to reconsider what the sentence should be!

[116] For example, in September 2002, a 20-year-old Santa Ana, California former high school basketball star, Alvaro Alvarez, convicted of the misdemeanor of marijuana possession, told Superior Court Judge Marc Kelly that he had smoked pot since he was 10 and that doing so made him a more relaxed, better player. So the 42-year-old Judge Kelly sentenced Alvarez to attend drug abuse classes and challenged Alvarez, the defensive player of the year as a sophomore at Santa Ana Valley High School, to a game of one-on-one. The judge stripped off his judicial robe and laced up his sneakers. At a basketball court outside the Orange County courthouse, Judge Steven L. Perk stepped up to referee and a half dozen court employees made up the cheering section. Although both players stood about 5-10 and appeared physically fit, it was no contest. In a game to see who could score the first ten baskets, the judge slam-dunked the former high school star 10 to 3. "Defensive player of the year, Alvarez? Come on," Kelly trash-talked at one point, then drove for two consecutive lay-ups. "The marijuana's getting to you, Alvarez. You're exhausted, aren't you?"

After the game, the two embraced. "You surprise me," a winded Alvarez told the judge. "You are quicker than

judge gave her the choice of 30 days in jail or a 30-mile hike.[117] However, sentencing statutes and guidelines are meant to reduce judicial discretion. Sentencing guidelines call for sentences to fall within a range, via a grid that considers mitigating and aggravating circumstances, including prior convictions or a "clean" record. Before the Guidelines were put into place in 1987, an armed bank robber could get from a federal judge a sentence ranging from probation to 25 years in prison. Now the typical sentence range for that crime is much narrower, between 70 to 87 months in prison. Indeed, a November 2004 study found that sentencing now is "more certain and predictable," with the average prison sentence today about 50 months, twice what it was in 1984, when lawmakers began calling for a uniform sentencing system. The difference, the study determined, is due mostly to the guidelines' elimination of parole for offenses such as drug trafficking.

> Problems with parole tend to be more with inadequate resources, than with the law itself: problems of staffing and supervision.

- <u>Basis for guilt or liability</u>: criminal guilt usually is due to an intentional act, but sometimes for gross negligence or recklessness; tort liability is possible for an intentional act, or negligence, or strict liability (without even requiring the defendant's "fault.")

> *Guilty Pleas*
> In most jurisdictions, <u>more than 95% of all criminal cases result in a guilty plea of some kind</u>. Plea bargaining handles the vast majority of cases going forward toward a trial, and thus most trials are avoided.[118] Of the small percentage that do go to trial, most defendants are found guilty.[119] Successful appeals are relatively rare (fewer than 10% of convictions are overturned).[120]

B. The Concepts of *Mens Rea* and *Actus Reus*

Two elements both generally needed to prove a crime are *mens rea* and *actus reus*.

1. *Mens Rea*

The Latin term, *mens rea* ("criminal mind") is a criminal law concept often stated in English as "wrongful intent."

---

most of the guys I play with." Perhaps that's because Kelly had played some ball himself, on a Notre Dame team that included future NBA players Orlando Woolridge and Bill Laimbeer. Alvarez acknowledged the marijuana was making him tired and that he might give up the drug.

[117] Aris Pinedo, Jasmine Brown & Alexa Valiente, *Why an Ohio Judge Is Using Unusual Punishments to Keep People Out of Jail*, ABC NEWS NIGHTLINE, Sept. 1, 2015, http://abcnews.go.com/US/ohio-judge-unusual-punishments-people-jail/story?id=33440871.

[118] Some European nations have adopted U.S. legal principles in changing their criminal law procedures. For example, France – in 2004-2005 - adopted American-style plea bargaining for criminal cases.

[119] In federal courts, statistics consistently show that about 85% of cases going to completion end up with conviction; of those convictions only about 9% were after a trial. Most come after a plea of guilt or no contest. At the state level, it seems that at least 76% of cases end in conviction.

Many other countries have incredibly high conviction rates. For example, China's is 99.7%, and Japan's is about the same.

[120] In M.J. Saks & J.J. Koehler, *The Coming Paradigm Shift in Forensic Identification Science*, 309 SCIENCE 892 (2005), factors associated with erroneous convictions were as follows: eyewitness errors (74%), erroneous forensic science (66%), police misconduct (44%), prosecutorial misconduct (40%), fraudulent or misleading forensic science (31%), bad lawyering (28%), false confessions (19%), dishonest informants (17%), and false witness testimony (17%).

Example: If one bounces a check, usually there is no *mens rea*. Unless you bounced it intentionally, and then it is a type of criminal fraud.

Mens rea does not necessarily mean cold-blooded or guilty "as sin."

It connotes purpose, knowledge, or awareness; that is the level of culpability required for conviction of most crimes (just behavior intentionally done- with knowledge of wrongfulness). Individual circumstances matter.

Just as some crimes are more serious than others (e.g., robbery is more serious than larceny (theft),[121] so the degree of culpability varies in relation to different crimes.

2. *Actus Reus*

The Latin term, *actus reus* ("criminal act") is a criminal law concept often stated in English as "wrongful act." Wrongful thoughts without acts are commonplace, but not criminal. Wrongful acts without intent also are usually not criminal.

There is a distinction between intending the criminal act (all that is usually necessary) and intending the actual harm (not usually necessary). One need not intend a result to be liable for the natural, foreseeable consequences of a wrongful act. The only necessity is intending the act; that itself creates responsibility for consequences.

Mens rea simply means that you intend the wrongful action, not necessarily the harm. So a professor could be held criminally responsible for shooting a machine gun in his/her classroom even though he/she intended no harm and was just trying to show how dangerous firearms are![122]

C. The Presumption of Innocence

The biggest reason guilty people go free is this: the law cloaks everyone in "innocence." Prosecutors must prove guilt beyond a reasonable doubt, not just that we "think he is guilty." "Not guilty" does not necessarily mean innocent, just that there was doubt. A fundamental notion is that it is better to let 100 guilty persons go free than to convict one innocent person. "It is far better that ten guilty persons escape than that one innocent suffers." Sir William Blackstone (1723-1780), Commentaries on the Laws of England, vol. 4, ch. 27 (1769). Indeed, the presumption certainly means that guilty people are found NOT guilty.

This presumption of innocence, although still missing in many countries (e.g., Mexico), increasingly a fundamental concept not just in common law countries, but worldwide. For example, the European Convention on Human Rights and Fundamental Freedoms (Rome, 1950) - now adopted by 47 nations - recognizes in its article 6(2) that "Everyone charged with a criminal offense shall be presumed innocent until proven guilty according to law." The adopting nations include Albania, Andorra, Armenia, Austria, Azerbaijan, Belgium, Bosnia, Bulgaria, Croatia, Cyprus, Czech Republic, Denmark, Estonia, Finland, France, Georgia, Germany, Greece, Hungary, Iceland, Ireland, Italy, Latvia, Liechtenstein, Lithuania, Luxembourg, Macedonia, Malta, Moldova, Monaco, Montenegro, Netherlands, Norway, Poland, Portugal, Romania, Russia, San Marino, Serbia, Slovakia, Slovenia, Spain, Sweden, Switzerland, Turkey, Ukraine, and the United Kingdom.

In the United States and many other nations, we have two possible findings: guilty and not guilty. One country, Scotland, adds a third category: innocent. In Scotland, both a "not proven" finding (the "not guilty" verdict) and a verdict of "innocent" mean that the charges against the defendant are dismissed (and both verdicts give rise to double jeopardy protections). But the latter verdict is a finding that the defendant was factually innocent, while "not proven" means that the defendant could be, in fact,

---

[121] Robbery involves force or the threat of force in order to perpetrate a theft; larceny (theft) involves just the unlawful taking of property, without force or threats –

[122] This same principle (focus on intending the act, not intending the harm) applies to intentional torts.

guilty, but sufficient proof of the charges was not sustained. So, Walter Scott, usually a zealous defender of all that was old and established in Scottish law, called it "that bastard verdict." He added, "Not proven: I hate that Caledonian medium quid." Perhaps mindful of that "half-way" status, Scottish judges and juries tend to grant more acquittals by an outright "innocent" verdict than by a "not proven" holding: "innocent" holdings tend to outnumber by 2 to 1 margins the "not proven" verdict (as usual, most cases going to trial end in a guilty verdict).

As in the United States, a Scottish criminal defendant acquitted via a "not proven" verdict may still be sued in tort law for the very same act, as the standard of proof in Scottish civil cases is merely "proof upon a balance of probability" (similar to America's "preponderance of evidence" standard).

- If there is consent, the "victim" probably cannot sue, but the state usually can still prosecute one of the few times consent is a criminal law defense: the alleged rape of an adult. For torts, the defense of Consent generally is possible unless the alleged victim has no capacity (e.g., the victim/plaintiff was a child or obviously demented). Why should people be able to sue if they consented to certain conduct? Ordinarily, tort law says: they should NOT be able to consent but later sue.
Contrast Crimes – consent usually is Not a Defense.
An exception is the crime of rape. As long as the alleged rape is of someone with capacity (e.g., an adult with no mental incapacity), then lack of consent is a required element for there to be a crime.

- Sources of Law – Tort (primarily common law) & Criminal (almost exclusively statutes, although the origins are the common law)

D. Two Separate Systems: Crimes and Torts

Criminal law and tort law are two separate systems, even if they concern the same underlying conduct. Crimes and torts are distinct, but may overlap. For most acts that are crimes, the same acts are also torts. (For example, the act that is the crime of larceny is also an action constituting the tort of conversion.) Vice-versa is not true: Most tortious acts (acts that constitute torts) are not also criminal acts.

1. Four Situations

a. Crime but No Tort

"Victimless" crimes – society is a victim, but generally no individual who could point to personal, compensable harm that he/she has suffered – e.g., tax evasion, illegal gambling, prostitution, illegal drug use. However, a number of states have enacted, or are considering, laws allowing people harmed by illegal drugs to sue drug dealers. But a problem, as with many suits, is that even if you win a claim, can you actually get money out of the defendant? Also, a number of Eastern states (e.g., Connecticut) permit private parties, such as law firms and collection agencies, to collect unpaid taxes. The private parties receive a percentage of what they obtain for the state.

What about an unsuccessful robbery? Assume that there is no personal damage, but it is still a crime. For example, intent to commit murder is a crime, but there may be no one who can sue about it (no tort). (If you actually commit the murder, of course, that conduct is both a crime (a wrong to society) and a tort, with individual victims – e.g., the next of kin – who can sue for damages.) That is the same for drunk driving where one causes no one else any property or personal injury (the defendant is guilty of a crime, but – because he did not hit anyone – cannot be successfully sued for a tort).

b. Tort But No Crime

Torts usually arise in one of three ways – most are negligence or strict liability, not the third type – intentional torts. So most tend not to overlap with crimes.

c. Crime *and* Tort

Here, the tort is almost always an intentional tort; and most intentional torts overlap with crimes.

> **Drunk driver example**
> When a defendant purposely gets drunk and then drives, that is a crime. Those actions also constitute a tort if someone is injured.

YOUTUBE - RicoReckonsWrongSkit5mins10secs.wmv at robertwemersonufl – A VIDEO - "**An Error Refuted -** *Rico Reckons Wrong* **- A reckless reprobate, Roger Ricardo Riggins, meets his match. Know the charges, or lack thereof, before you speak.**"

RICO: An Example of a Business Crime, and Possible Civil Suits
(see pgs. 470–471; Emerson BL)

As authorities are concerned about any disparity of treatment between white-collar crimes (e.g., embezzlement) versus blue-collar crime (<u>generally</u> viewed as violent and, therefore, worse), strong enforcement of RICO laws may be viewed as one move to address the disparity.

RICO is the Racketeer Influenced and Corrupt Organizations Act. This law is in the federal code at 18 U.S.C. §§ 1961-1968. A 1970 federal statute,[123] the national RICO law was intended to reach organized crime (e.g., the Mafia). But it can be invoked against all sorts of defendants (i.e., businesses generally).

RICO states that it is unlawful to: (a) Invest income derived from a pattern of racketeering activities, (b) Maintain ownership of an enterprise engaged in a pattern of racketeering activities, (c) Acquire an interest in a racketeering enterprise, (d) In any way participate in the affairs of an enterprise affecting interstate commerce through a pattern of racketeering activities. As with other white-collar crimes, often the people commit these illegal activities in a <u>lawful</u> occupation – e.g., as office workers or as business owners.

The RICO law makes it unlawful for a "person" employed by an enterprise to participate in a "pattern of racketeering." To constitute a pattern of racketeering activity, at least two acts of racketeering must have occurred in a ten-year period.

RICO involves both criminal and civil cases. RICO is <u>broadly construed</u> by the courts. Thus, RICO permits <u>criminal charges</u> in all sorts of cases; also, alleged victims (e.g., competitors) may file <u>lawsuits</u> under RICO and, as in antitrust law, win treble (triple) damages and other remedies such as injunctions. Predicate offenses (for RICO) are wrongs such as racketeering activities, unlawful gambling, mail fraud, extortion, running a brothel, bribery, criminally infringing upon intellectual property (e.g., knockoffs of patented inventions), kickbacks, making or selling illegal drugs and almost every felony under a state law. These underlying offenses are part of an ongoing enterprise.

d. Neither Tort nor Crime

Sometimes, life is just unfair, with no legal recourse available. *"A man cannot shift his misfortunes to his neighbor's shoulders."* Oliver Wendell Holmes, Jr. 1841-1935 (U.S. Supreme Justice, 1902 32).

> **Drowning kid example**
> Surely there exists a moral duty to furnish aid to a drowning child. However, unless special circumstances exist (e.g., one put the child in danger or worsened his situation), usually one has no legal duty to save people.[124]

---

[123] RICO was enacted under Title IX of the Organized Crime Control Act of 1970. Many states, including Florida (Fla. Stats., Ch. 895), have their own state version of RICO.

[124] An example of mandated surgery intended to benefit others is in *Curran v. Boszc*, 566 N.E.2d 1319 (Illinois, Dec. 20, 1990) (twin brothers; surgery on an incompetent or a minor for the benefit of a third party (e.g., the twin)); see also 4 ALR5th 1000 (1993) (by Lisa K. Gregory, J.D.).

> Most states do not impose a general duty to rescue. If a stranger is about to drown in a lake, most states will not charge someone who fails to rescue him with murder.

i. No Duty to Rescue

The "no duty to rescue" rule is found in common law countries, but generally is NOT the law elsewhere in the world. An article at 8 TOURO INT'L L. REV. 93 noted an example in which 38 neighbors heard or saw a woman being killed and no one was charged for their failure to act. In France, one example is that when Princess Diana died in a Paris traffic accident the Paparazzi (reporters) were investigated for not assisting; they could have been charged with crimes if they had indeed failed to act and that meant a difference.

Although very rarely applied, ten states now have laws modifying the common law and requiring some form of a duty to rescue if that does not pose a danger to the would-be rescuer: California, Florida, Hawaii, Massachusetts, Minnesota, Ohio, Rhode Island, Vermont, Washington, and Wisconsin. Generally, the duty is simply to notify law enforcement about criminal acts of violence (e.g., murder, rape, armed robbery). However, in Vermont, which in 1968 became the first state to enact a duty-to-rescue statute; the law is similar to laws in many Civil law countries because it requires ALL onlookers to come to the assistance of those who are endangered, as long as doing so poses no danger to the rescuer and would not interfere with others who are already rendering aid.[125]

> **Example: Dudley Do-Right Does Wrong?**
> Dudley Do-Right is walking along the road and sees Emeril, who is nearly passed out in the middle of the road. Emeril cries out, "Please! Help me out of the middle of the road!" Dudley rushes to Emeril and starts dragging him from the road when he sees a car coming. Dudley lets go of Emeril and barely jumps out of the way. But Emeril is run over and dies.
> Did Dudley have a duty to rescue Emeril? Yes. Once Dudley voluntarily began to rescue Emeril, he assumed a duty to help him in a non-negligent fashion.
> Dudley, now nervous from his experience with the late, lamented Emeril, walks farther. Around the bend, Dudley sees Gladys in the road. Gladys asks Dudley for help, but Dudley (who now knows that cars can run you over!) decides to leave her to her fate. Dudley walks by without doing anything. A bus later plows into Gladys.
> Did Dudley have a duty to rescue her?
> No generally, there is no duty to rescue.

---

[125]In 1968, Vermont became the first state to depart from the generally accepted rule that there is no duty to rescue, absent a special relationship. The Vermont rule provides the broadest duty to rescue of all of the states in the United States, as it requires. The other seven states listed above have not defined the duty to rescue as broadly as does the Vermont statute. For example, the relevant Massachusetts statute only applies to those who witness violent or sexual crimes.

Vt. St. Ann., tit. 12 § 519 (a) reads: "A person who knows that another is exposed to grave physical harm shall, to the extent that the same can be rendered without danger or peril to himself or without interference with important duties owed to others, give reasonable assistance to the exposed person unless that assistance or care is being provided by others.")

Mass. Gen. Laws Ann. ch. 268, § 40 reads: "Whoever knows that another person is a victim of aggravated rape, rape, murder, manslaughter or armed robbery and is at the scene of said crime shall, to the extent that said person can do so without danger or peril to himself or others, report said crime to an appropriate law enforcement official as soon as reasonably practicable. Any person who violates this section shall be punished by a fine of not less than five hundred nor more than two thousand and five hundred dollars."

> After these troubled, traumatic times, Dudley becomes quite happy to round the bend and enter his own neighborhood. Dudley sees his daughter, Little Nell, in the middle of the road. Little Nell screams, "Eyeh! Daddy! I am stuck in the road!" Dudley has 10 other children and concludes, "One less mouth to feed!" Dudley does not help Little Nell, or even tell others who might help her. A trucking fleet runs over Little Nell and injures her grievously.
>
> Did Dudley have a duty to rescue Little Nell?
>
> Yes. There is a special relationship — father and daughter — that creates a duty to rescue. Of course, in some situations courts will impose a duty. For instance, you must try to rescue members of your immediate family (e.g., your spouse or parent). Similarly, a nurse hired to care for someone who is ill is obliged to intervene if the patient seems to be having a heart attack.

ii. Duties Under Criminal Law and "Good Samaritan" Laws

The absence under tort law of a duty to act does not mean that one will be free from criminal liability. A few states have enacted statutes which provide that if a person, without substantial risk of personal harm or inconvenience to others, can provide assistance to one in peril, the person must do so or is subject to a fine, normally in a small amount, perhaps not exceeding $100. While theoretically a court, in a civil tort action, may rely upon criminal legislation to define the conduct of a reasonable person, it is unlikely that a court will do so under this type of statute, for there is often reason to conclude that the legislature intended the exclusive sanction for a violation to be a small fine.

Duty-creating statutes sometimes also contain provisions which confer immunities on persons who render aid at the scene of an accident. The statute may, for example, relieve the actor from liability for conduct undertaken in good faith, or may limit liability to cases of aggravated misconduct (i.e., something more than mere negligence). Laws conferring that kind of immunity are often referred to as "Good Samaritan" laws. They have been enacted in most states, many of which have not criminalized failure to act.

iii. Rescue as a Matter of Practice, Regardless of Law

Criminal law doctrine is often divorced from reality of criminal law practice. For example, most law school criminal law courses spend little time on narcotics prosecutions, even though drug cases are an important, if not dominant, feature in criminal law. Another example may be the duty to rescue, which is a narrow duty generally involving only the strongest of relationships or of contractually or professionally imposed duties, but which in practice seems not to matter. Many, many people try to rescue others regardless of the fact they have no legal duty to do so, and in spite of the fact (really, more just a perception) that an unsuccessful rescue could lead to their being sued.

In *Rescue Without Law: An Empirical Perspective on the Duty to Rescue*, 84 TEX. L. REV. 653-738 (2006), Prof. David A. Hyman finds that even in a world without a duty to rescue, rates of nonrescue are very low. Far more people die risking their lives to rescue strangers than die from failing to be rescued by someone who could have helped but did not. Hyman used more than twenty independent data sources to provide a "law and reality" perspective on rescue and non-rescue that complicates, if not outright contradicts, the positions of both proponents and opponents of a duty to rescue. His results paint a rich and largely reassuring picture of the behavior of ordinary Americans faced with circumstances requiring rescue. The data indicate that while the no-duty rule remains important for theoretical purposes, the ongoing debate should not obscure the reality that in practice, rescue is the rule - even if it is not the law. Perhaps the relatively aberrant nature of non-rescue should help shape and ground discussions of this issue.

iv. Comparing Punishment and Reward

While we ordinarily do not punish a failure to rescue, we do reward rescue (e.g., quasi-contract as a substitute for consideration). We take the same approach – financial or other rewards – for reporting crime and for service by cooperating witnesses. Even people accused of crimes may be rewarded – with reduced jail time – if they testify against co-defendants. Other than the rare case of *misprision* (e.g., concealment or nondisclosure of someone else's felony, 18 U.S. Code § 4) we do not, though, punish those who fail to report crime.

v. Comparative Law on the Duty to Rescue

Numerous Civil Law countries take an affirmative stance on the duty to rescue, including – perhaps uniformly – the European continent (nations such as the Netherlands, Portugal, Denmark, Germany, Hungary, Italy, Norway, Poland, Romania, and Russia) as well as many other countries, such as Turkey.[126] Also, most Latin American countries recognize a duty to rescue.[127] Finally, admiralty law (no matter the nation) finds that mariners have a duty to rescue on the seas.[128]

E. TORTS

The word "tort" comes from the French word for "wrong" and goes back to the Latin for "twisted"" or "crooked." (It is the root term for other English words such as "tortuous," bent in different directions; "torture"; and "torsion" - a torsion bar is part of a car's suspension.)

I. INTRODUCTION

Torts are somewhat difficult to define. A tort is <u>not</u> a crime, a breach of contract, or a French pastry! A tort is a civil, non-contractual wrong (a non-criminal wrong). A tort is not just a lapse in etiquette, but a violation of socially imposed sets of <u>civil duties</u>. Some torts might concern automobile accidents, burns from hot coffees, slip-and-fall accidents, dog attacks, fallen trees, food poisonings, trespasses, and baseballs breaking windows.

Not every harm is compensable. Besides perhaps not being worth pursuing (the possible damages award is not worth the cost of suing), the actions causing the harm may not even be a tort. For example, do you have much of a chance if a tiny stone comes flying out from a construction site and cracks your car windshield as you drive by? Perhaps not. And even if a tort is present, could you prove it, and would it be worthwhile to complain and, if still dissatisfied, to sue?

II. THREE MAIN DIVISIONS OF TORT LAW: NEGLIGENCE, INTENTIONAL TORTS, AND STRICT LIABILITY

<u>torts three main types 3mins3secs</u> is a YOUTUBE video at robertwemersonufl.[129]

---

[126] Jeanne A. Fugate, *Note: Who's Failing Whom? A Critical Look at Failure-To-Protect Laws*, 76 N.Y.U.L. Rev. 272 (2001).
[127] David N. Kelly, *A Psychological Approach to Understanding the Legal Basis of the No Duty to Rescue Rule*, 14 BYU J. Public Law 271, 278 (2000).
[128] Bernard H. Oxman, "*Human Rights and the United Nations Convention on the Law of the Sea*," 36 COLUMBIA J. TRANSNATIONAL L. 399 (1997).

[129] At the very end of this text, we consider warranties, particularly with respect to product liability. This actually tends to arise more out of contract law than torts, but warranties often arise in conjunction with other issues related to torts, such as negligence, possible strict liability, and allegations of fraud.

"When you read about a lawsuit, typically you're reading about either a case that is based on some sort of alleged contract and a breach of that contract, or you're reading about this topic, which is torts. Any sort of non-contractual wrong for which the law affords a civil remedy, in which people can sue and collect damages, tends to be called a tort. The word tort goes all the way back to Latin and old French for a word meaning to twist, to contort, to otherwise cause a wrong, and you can even say a wrong in the social fabric. The idea behind tort law is even though you have not agreed to something in the same sense that you would in contract law, we find that as a matter of social policy, if you cause harm to someone because of this breach of social etiquette or social norms, you should have to pay damages for the harms that you have caused.

"There are three main types of torts. One is negligence, and that's the biggest and most common of all torts. The most common of negligence torts is a car accident case. A second classification of torts is intentional torts and there are numerous types of intentional torts out there. There are cases involving, for instance, assault, or battery, or conversion of property, or defamation, or fraud. The third classification is strict liability. These cases do not require fault on the part of the defendant. All we're looking for is that the defendant's actions, his goods, his services, cause harm to a plaintiff, and as a matter of social policy, we have decided that the defendant should bear the risks and should have to pay for any of the harms from his goods or services. Now, torts come in many sizes and shapes. People are often, I believe, a little confused about this. I read of a case out of the state of Delaware in which a professor at the local law school, a professor of torts, was asked for her take on a particular case, and the journalist apparently was not even familiar with the word tort. She instead reported that she had talked to a professor of sorts."

Query: Torts cover as much as the mind of man, woman, or child can imagine. Is that good or bad?

III. NEGLIGENCE – "the Big Tort"

Examples of Negligence and other torts:
- A shopper backs his car into your car at a parking lot. (Negligence)
- An ogling male drives along Ft. Lauderdale Beach and watching women; he thus fails to see, and thereby hits, a pedestrian crossing the street (Negligence).
- Grocery clerk mopping entrance with no "wet floor" sign; customer falls and breaks her leg (Negligence).
- Tapping a partygoer's beer bottle so it foams up all over a guest's clothes. "Sorry, guess I forgot that was the beer we shook up." (Negligence, but how much in damages?)
- Without taking any precautions (and without seeking the help of a tree-cutting "expert"), a homeowner takes a chainsaw to a tree in his yard and the tree falls on his neighbor's house. (Negligence, perhaps also Trespass or Nuisance.)
- Two bags of luggage lost on an airline flight. The airline ticket (contract) certainly has a clause excusing the airline from any such negligence and limiting the amount of money (about $500 per bag under the Montreal Agreement) that could be recovered for such negligence. The airline had a duty to deliver the bags and their contents to the passenger when he arrived at his destination. It breached this duty by losing the luggage. Its action directly caused the passenger financial harm by the loss of clothes and whatever else was in the bags (Harm and Causation). So, theoretically, the airline acted negligently. However, the parties to a contract (such as the passenger and the airline, via a ticket) can agree to exclude or limit liability and/or the amount of damages for a breach. The Warsaw Convention bolsters the argument that the customer is limited in what he can recover. But a passenger may keep pestering the airline. He/she may still get his/her clothes back. Secondly, the squeaky wheel does often get the grease. The airline may offer other deals, besides just the money owed, to placate the passenger.

An introductory video (1:48) featuring a jester's hat, purple tie, and gold pom-pom, among other things, is at https://www.youtube.com/watch?v=d2pTWxqf01I&feature=youtu.be.

Negligence means that you have, in effect, proven as a plaintiff that the defendant has done four things. There are four elements; three out of four are not sufficient. You've got to prove all four – duty, breach of duty, causation, harm. If you show that the defendant breached a duty of care, and that breach caused harm, then you have a case of negligence. .

Imagine that you drive through a red light . . . .

A. Elements

There are four elements necessary to prove negligence. <u>All four elements are needed:</u> <u>Duty of Care</u>, <u>Breach of that Duty</u>, <u>Harm</u>, and <u>Causation</u>.

Speeding

Let's imagine you are driving your car at 65 miles an hour even though the speed limit is 45 miles per hour. 'Tis a stupid thing to do, something for which you could be charged with a traffic offense, given a ticket. Even though it is a breach of duty of care, it is not sufficient for anyone to sue you for negligence unless he/she can also show that your breach of duty (your speeding) caused him/her to be harmed.

There are plenty of actions in which people behave foolishly, but fortunately, since all of us are imperfect, we are not subject to the law of torts generally, or the law of negligence specifically, unless our foolish behavior, our acting like a crazed jester, actually causes harm to someone AND this injured person actually bothers to sue us. Studies show that most people who are harmed and might even have a case do not actually bother to sue.

Negligence can occur <u>via inaction as well as action</u>. In the <u>Humber Ferry</u> case (England, decided in 1348), a ferry operator was found liable when he overloaded his ferry with horses and the plaintiff's horse fell off the boat and drowned. Having held himself out as a ferryman, the defendant had a duty to do his job competently, and his failure to take the necessary measures to protect the horse (his inaction) rendered the defendant liable. Whether one calls the breach of duty a wrongful act or wrongful inaction does not matter; in either case, it is, in fact, a breach.

B. Duty of Care
1. A Duty to Whom?

A ga*s* leak injured or killed some New York City sewage treatment workers, in *Guarino v. Mine Safety Appliance Co.*, 255 N.E. 2d 173 (N.Y. Court of Appeals, 1969). Some had been in the tunnel where the leak occurred, and others had jumped into the tunnel to help their co-workers. The court quotes with approval the words of Judge Benjamin Cardozo: "<u>Danger invites rescue. The cry of distress is the summons to relief.</u>"

To whom did the gas company owe a duty of care? Besides just to the workers in the sewers/tunnels, there <u>also was a duty to people other than those in immediate danger</u>. So the duty extended also to the rescuers.

2. A Duty to Protect from Criminal Activity?

It seems from the news that more and more people with guns are blasting their former supervisors and co-workers and bystanders. How much should that be anticipated, deterred, dealt with, and – if it happens – mitigated? How expensive might the measures have to be?

Is there a duty to provide a place that is safe from criminals? Should a public park provide police patrols for people who may sleep there? If a business were to have a duty to protect against criminal activity, how far should that duty extend?

> **The Holiday Inn/ Criminal Gang Example – the need to warn patrons:**
> In *Crinkley v. Holiday Inns, Inc.*, 844 F.2d 156, 160 (4th Cir.1988), the U.S. Court of Appeals in Richmond held that an innkeeper could be liable for failing to inform guests of the potential for crimes. A gang of robbers was invading hotel rooms along that stretch of the interstate in North Carolina, but the hotelier defendant failed to warn its guests. That was a breach of a duty of care. Two guests who were assaulted and robbed in their hotel room thus brought a successful action against the hotel for its negligence in not warning or otherwise taking better safety measures.

C. Breach of Duty
1. Measured by an Objective, "Reasonable Person" Standard

Whether a breach occurred is, for adults, determined by an objective standard: What an adult reasonably should know to do or not do. The English writer, legal philosopher, humorist, and law reform advocate, A.P. Herbert (1890-1971), jokingly described the **reasonable person** as follows:

"The reasonable person invariably looks where he is going, and is careful to examine the immediate foreground before he executes a leap or a bound; he neither star-gazes nor is lost in meditation when approaching trapdoors or the end of a dock; ... He never mounts a moving train or plane and does not leave anything -car, bike, skateboard, golf cart- while it is still moving; He investigates exhaustively the sincerity of every beggar before giving even a quarter, and he will inform himself of the history and habits of a dog before patting her; the reasonable person believes no gossip, nor repeats it, without a firm basis for believing it to be true; she never drives her golf ball till those in front of her have definitely vacated the putting-green which is her own objective; she never from one year's end to another makes an excessive demand upon her family, her neighbors, her colleagues at work; she contemplates merchants, their agents, and their goods, with a strong degree of suspicion and distrust that the law deems admirable; the reasonable person never swears, rambles, or loses his temper, he uses nothing except in moderation, and even while he punishes his child is meditating on the golden mean. Devoid, in short, of any vice, and without prejudice, procrastination, ill-nature, greed, or absent-mindedness, as careful for his own safety as he is for that of others, this excellent but odious creature stands like a monument in our Courts of Justice, vainly appealing to his fellow-citizens to order their own lives after his own example."

Clearly, the "reasonable person" is a hypothetical person, just as the "economically efficient person" is a hypothetical concept.

> **A Breach of Duty of Care May Require Disclosures**
> In *Maurer v. Cerkvenik-Anderson Travel, Inc.*, 890 P.2d 69 (Ariz. App. 1994), defendant Cerkvenik-Anderson Travel, Inc. (CAT), a travel agency, sold and managed student package tours. A covenant in the agency's standard contract absolved it from liability for death, personal injury, or property damage sustained on a tour "whether due to [the agency's] own negligence or otherwise."
>
> A college student, Molly Marie Maurer, went on a student package tour of Mexico that the travel agent booked for her. She fell to her death between the cars of a poorly constructed "party train" from Nogales to Mazatlan. The court found the travel agents and tour operators to be fiduciaries, and the ride on that train was part of the tour. Molly's parents sued the travel agency for negligent failure to tell their daughter of a known danger: that there had been three deaths of touring college students in similar ways on that train.
>
> The Arizona Court of Appeals agreed with Molly's parents and held that the travel agency had a duty to disclose or warn of the tour's dangers about which it knew or should have known. That was, among other things, a violation of the Consumer Fraud Act. Whether the disclosure duty exists is a question of whether a party has a relationship-based obligation to use care and avoid or prevent injury to the other party. So, the Court held that summary judgment for the defendant would have been inappropriate because the release in CAT's standard contract was insufficiently specific to alert the student of the dangers she faced.

2. Breach of Duty Standard: Measured Subjectively for Children

Children are held to a subjective standard, based on a child's own knowledge and experience. Consider the case of a five-year-old boy and his neighbor's friend (*Garratt v. Dailey*, 279 P.2d 1091 (Washington Supreme Court, 1955)): At a neighbor's house, mischievous Brian Dailey pulled the chair out from under an elderly woman and hurt the woman. This five-year-old was found liable because the court determined that he knew it was unreasonable/wrong. So, perhaps ironically, the smarter or more experienced a child is, the more likely he/she is to be subject to tort liability.

A contrary point of view is found in *Baker v. Alt*, 132 N.W.2d 614 (1965), where the Supreme Court of Michigan upheld a common law standard that children under 7 years of age are incapable of contributory negligence. Here, Billy Parker, at the age of 6 years, 10 months, and 17 days, proceeded on his bicycle, at 7:00 a.m. Sunday, through a flashing red signal, racing after two nine-year old boys. Baker is still the law in Michigan, although "the child's conduct is, of course, admissible as it bears upon the question of whether defendant was guilty of any causal negligence." *Id*.

Parents are *not* automatically liable for the torts of their children. Thus, there is no *respondeat superior* for parents. To be liable, ordinarily parents must be negligent themselves in supervising the child.

It also remains very difficult to hold parents liable for the intentional torts of their children. While many state statutes specifically authorize civil damages against parents of kids who do harm, juries often disagree about what is appropriate behavior. And even when plaintiffs prevail in court, it can be extremely hard to collect damages from non-wealthy parents. Homeowners' insurance policies often provide little, if any, coverage. And school districts ordinarily are insulated from substantial damage awards under the legal doctrine of sovereign immunity, which limits suits against police and other governmental operations.

But there is a trend, albeit still a minority view, to hold parents liable. Parents may be liable under a negligent entrustment or family-purpose doctrine. E.g., the kid has the car in order to do things such as run errands - go to the grocery store, take Susie to ballet lessons, or whatever - and an accident ensues.

In addition, some states, including Florida, follow the dangerous instrumentality rule auto accidents. An auto is deemed inherently dangerous and the owner is liable along with anyone to whom the car was entrusted. So if Dad owns the car, he is probably on the hook, but there is a statue that limits liability to $100,000 per person or $300,000 per accident.[130]

An Ethics Question remains: Should parents pay, even if they have no legal responsibility?

3. Negligence *Per Se* (see pgs. 455-56; Emerson BL)

A number of municipalities have ordinances requiring all bicycles to be equipped with a bell to alert nearby pedestrians. However, in many instances the ordinances have been successfully challenged as facilitating selective enforcement by police officers – used to just stop some persons and then look for evidence of more serious infractions (e.g., illegal drugs or weapons).

Suppose that, in a town with a bike-bell ordinance, Basso Bicyclist rides his bike without a bell and hits Pedestrian Pamela. In a tort claim against Basso, what may Pamela argue about Basso's duty of care? Negligence *per se*. Pamela could argue that the ordinance puts a duty on Basso to equip his

---

[130] Florida also has a statute (322.09) that requires a father, mother or guardian to sign an application for a driver's license for any child under 18. Any negligence of driver under 18 is imputed to the person who signed the application and they are jointly and severally liable. Logic would indicate that an adult sitting in the front passenger seat next to an under-18 driver could be held jointly responsible for the negligence of that driver.

bicycle with a bell. Basso's not having a bell is a breach of that duty. If that breach caused Pamela harm, then negligence would be a winning claim![131]

D. Causation

One is responsible for the natural consequences of one's wrongful acts, whether intentional acts or negligent acts.

PAINTBALL TIME! VIDEO - about transference
Tortious negligence – recklessness (could rise to the level of a crime).

> DEGREES OF RESPONSIBILITY: The Homicide Example
> - Pushing victim into the water, and the victim drowns
> Motive - May go to "degrees," or mitigation, or level of wrongfulness
> Same reasoning toward possible punitive damages in tort law.

1. Responsibility for Consequences

You are responsible for the Natural, foreseeable consequences flowing from your wrongful act.

People have been charged with – and convicted for – deaths resulting from (1) a vociferous, in-your-face argument, (2) foolishly placing one's child on a plastic swimming pool raft in the back of a pick-up truck, and (3) dropping rocks off of a bridge onto I-75 (the defendant knew the rocks could hit a car and cause serious injury or even death).

If you put someone in a position where grievous injuries lead to pulling "the plug" on a severely injured person, then you can be found guilty of homicide. These examples illustrate that, if one intended to commit wrongful acts and those acts led to foreseeable consequences, one can be charged with a crime. One cannot do something bad (e.g., a lecturer spraying the classroom with machine gunfire) - carry out an actus reus, with the intent (mens rea) to do that wrongful act - yet say that one should not be held responsible for particular harms arising naturally from that act (on the grounds that "sure, I meant to spray the crowded room with gunfire but I didn't intend to hurt anyone!"). If you understand that, then you can also see how intended acts can be "transferred" from one intended victim to another, foreseeable, but unintended victim (see below).

Of course, intending the harm will increase the likelihood of a more serious punishment in criminal cases and of punitive damages in a tort case, but we do not want to let wrongdoers evade responsibility by requiring "proof" of intending harm. (Along these same lines, courts usually do not tolerate artificial distinctions between the harm admittedly intended and the more serious injury that the defendant caused but allegedly did not intend. If I maliciously hit you in the jaw, intending to hurt you a bit (bruise you), but somehow manage to break your jaw, I am accountable for that more serious injury even though I may not have intended that particular harm; I intended the wrongful act - hitting you - and I am liable for (guilty, in criminal law) the natural, foreseeable consequences.

> **Arson Leading to Felony-Murder: *State v. Veverka***
> Ronald Eric Veverka started a fire in his apartment unit. *State v. Veverka*, 271 N.W.2d 744 (Iowa 1978). He was convicted of five counts of felony-murder in connection with deaths which occurred during his perpetration of the arson.

---

[131] For a negligence *per* se flowchart, see Robert W. Emerson, *Business Law*. NY: Barron's Educational Series (6th ed., 2015), at 455.

> To convict Veverka, the jury was allowed to infer from other circumstantial evidence that he "willfully and maliciously" caused building to be burned to give attention to himself and gain reentry to a hospital for treatment of his alcoholism. Malice aforethought, an element of murder, does not necessarily require a specific intent to murder but may be implied from circumstances such as an intent to commit a felony from which death results.
>
> Veverka admitted that he had intended to burn some apartments. However, he did not know that other people were then in the apartment. Five of them died. While Veverka did not intend to murder anyone, the death of someone who is in a structure is a natural foreseeable consequence of burning down a house.

> ### A Grisly Example of Unintended Consequences
> In 1994, Desmon Venn, age 17, threw a single punch at a high school classmate, Zuhair ("Steve") Pattah, age 16, and put him in a coma. During a melee in the West Bloomfield High School, Michigan parking lot, the punch between Pattah's eyes forced Pattah backward so that Pattah hit his head on the pavement with such force that Pattah's brain stem was severed.
>
> According to prosecutors, the melee began after Pattah and another boy traded insults about their female relatives and acquaintances. Venn told authorities that he hit Pattah because he thought Pattah had struck him during the fray. Witnesses said Pattah did not hit him. Also, although Pattah was an Iraqi-American and Venn is black, the punch was not believed to be racially or culturally motivated.
>
> In 1995, Venn pleaded guilty to the misdemeanor of aggravated assault, spent two months in a boot camp, received two years of probation, and was fined $1000. He figured he had paid his debt to society. Meantime, after high school, Venn had more run-ins with the law, including current charges of cocaine possession and driving with a suspended license. In 2001, Venn was convicted of assaulting an Atlanta-area security guard.
>
> However, on January 8, 2003, nearly seven years after the assault, Steve Pattah died of his injuries without ever coming out of his coma. In February 2003, prosecutors in Oakland County, Michigan brought involuntary manslaughter charges against Desmon Venn.
>
> Venn could have received up to 15 years behind bars in Pattah's death. Venn's lawyer, Elbert Hatchett, said the charges violate Venn's constitutional protection against double jeopardy, or being prosecuted twice for the same crime. He also said the state's six-year window for filing an upgraded charge after such a crime has long since slammed shut. By prosecuting him then, prosecutors forfeited the right to prosecute him thereafter for the same behavior, Hatchett argues. But prosecutors contended that there was no double jeopardy because Pattah's death generated a new crime, which also rules out any statute-of-limitations argument.
>
> Ultimately, Venn was sentenced to 29 months in prison for the manslaughter.   Venn's lawyer, Elbert Hatchett, called that "the absolute bottom of the sentencing guidelines." Because Venn had previously been convicted on drug charges, a maximum sentence of 30 years was possible under the guidelines.

These types of cases have occurred from time to time in other states, and the federal courts have repeatedly ruled that the homicide charges do not constitute double jeopardy. The U.S. Supreme Court has ruled that double jeopardy exists only if the two crimes have the same elements. And in this case, death is an element of the manslaughter charge but not the assault charge.

2. **Transference**

> ### A Rock-Throwing Example: *Alteiri v. Colasso*
> A rock thrower, Stone, tosses a rock at his friend, Fritz. Stone says that he just intended to scare Fritz, not to hit him. Nevertheless, Stone hits Fritz in the eye, causing severe damage. What crime, if any, has Stone committed? Assault and battery. Stone admits that he intended to assault Fritzi. It is a natural

and foreseeable consequence that he might miss and hit him instead. Therefore, his intent to commit assault is transferred to the battery. *Alteiri v. Colasso*, 362 A.2d 789 (Conn. 1975). (The principle of "transferred intent" applies to an action for assault as well as an action for battery.)

At law, one may have a <u>transference of one intended act</u> (or one intended victim) <u>to what actually occurred.</u>

What if a person is "nodding off" (falling asleep) in class, and the professor, to teach that person a lesson, shoots a gun ("you better stay awake in my class!") in his direction but instead shoots "the wrong person" (someone else). The professor may say that was an "accident," but his act was intentional; only the consequences (hitting that person) were unintended. The professor's actions were both a crime and a tort (a battery upon the shot student; perhaps assault upon others in the classroom). So, you may be responsible for unwanted results; mens rea can be transferred from the intended felony to the one that actually occurred.

3. **Causation** is the <u>link between harm and breach of duty</u>.

There are two types of causation: (1) in fact, and (2) proximate cause (also called "legal causation").

Causation certainly is *not* intentional. Consider a man who pulls a hair from his nose and ultimately dies from an infection that started in the nose right where he yanked out that hair. His actions caused the harm, but was the harm intended? Was the harm ever foreseeable? There may be a continuum of labels from: (1) no tort, (2) negligence, (3) suicide. Would an insurance policy cover this scenario?

Factual Causation - Did the defendant act in the plaintiff's loss? This must be established before inquiring into legal causation, which often is a question of public policy. For legal causation, the question is profound: Is this the sort of situation in which, despite the outcome of the factual inquiry, we might nevertheless release the defendant from liability (or should we impose liability)?

When the connection between a breach and harm becomes long and attenuated, the courts may find there is insufficient cause to hold the defendant liable. So, causation involves both a factual component and a legal element.

In our torts system, factfinders first ask: Who caused the harm, and was it foreseeable? So we have "in fact" causation: <u>"But for"</u> that misconduct -> the harm would not have occurred. That is the test for <u>direct causation</u>. Put it another way: the defendant's conduct is the sine qua non – that without which the plaintiff's injury would not have happened.

4. *Palsgraf v. Long Island R.R. Co.*

The most famous proximate cause case (and one of the most famous case in all American legal history) is *Palsgraf v. Long Island R.R. Co.*, 162 N.E. 99 (N.Y. Ct. App. 1928) (**see pg. 458; Emerson BL**).[132] As reported by New York's highest court:

> Plaintiff was standing on a platform of defendant's railroad after buying a ticket to go to Rockaway Beach. A train stopped at the station, bound for another place. Two men ran forward to catch it. One of the men reached the platform of the car without mishap, though the train was already moving. The other man, carrying a package, jumped aboard the car, but seemed unsteady as if about to fall. A guard on the car, who had held the door open, reached forward to help him in, and another guard on the platform pushed him from behind. In this act, the package was dislodged, and fell upon the rails. It was a

---

[132] http://isites.harvard.edu/fs/docs/icb.topic960225.files/Readings%20by%20Number/Case%20-%20Palsgraf%20v.%20Long%20Island%20RR%20Co.pdf (the opinion with notes, summaries and other additional information); http://www.courts.state.ny.us/reporter/archives/palsgraf_lirr.htm (just the opinion).

package of small size, about fifteen inches long, and was covered by a newspaper. In fact it contained fireworks, but there was nothing in its appearance to give notice of its contents. The fireworks when they fell exploded. The shock of the explosion threw down some scales at the other end of the platform, many feet away. The scales struck the plaintiff, causing injuries for which she sues.[133]

So, railroad employees tried to help a man onto a moving train. At the train station, as Mrs. Palsgraf waited for another train with her young daughters, parts of decorative scales fell onto Mrs. Palsgraf. Yes, the railroad employees did breach a duty, and – yes – that did cause the accident, but the harm was so remote, so unforeseeable. There was *no* proximate cause, the court held.

The key proximate cause issue tends to be <u>foreseeability.</u>

<u>Foreseeability</u> is not the same as probability. In other words, something, to be foreseeable, need not be probable.

Here is a wacky example of foreseeability. On April 18, 2000, a hot dog promotion at the Toronto Sky Dome went awry as fans got splattered with bits of wiener when the hot dogs fell apart in mid air after being shot from the "Hot Dog Blaster." Although the hot dogs repeatedly disintegrated, promoters kept firing them into the stands. Conclusion: even if the hot dogs' disintegration was unforeseeable (that seems hard to believe), continuing to shoot the hot dogs seems willful, and the harmed fans might have had cases to pursue for battery.[134]

<u>Pumping Gasoline at the service station</u>

Gilbert is getting gas at the local gas station. He negligently lights a flame while pumping gas, which causes an explosion. Is his negligence a cause in fact? A proximate cause?

Yes — it is proximate cause. Cause in fact exists because, but for the flame, there would be no explosion. Proximate cause exists because an explosion is a reasonably foreseeable result of lighting a flame at a gas station.

The explosion spreads a fire to the house next to the gas station. Is his negligence a cause in fact of the destruction of the house? A proximate cause?

Again, yes to both. Cause in fact is present because, but for the flame. There would be no explosion, and if no explosion, no burning of the house. Proximate cause is present because an explosion that spreads to houses around the gas station is a reasonably foreseeable result of lighting a flame at a gas station.

The fire keeps spreading, and it destroys every tree and bush within a 500-mile radius. That means the extinction of the Western Wet Weed, a type of grass which is the main food for the Yuma Yak, which in turn is decimated. The Yucca-Yuma-Yorbalinda-Yankton Yak Society tracks Gilbert down; it can prove that, but for his negligent act, society members would still be able to enjoy stalking, photographing, and – in season - shooting this sacred Yak. Is Gilbert liable to society members?

Not under the *Palsgraf v. Long Island Railway Co.* standard. It appears to be a cause-in-fact, but not proximate cause. There is no foreseeability that negligently igniting a flame at a gas station could lead to these results.

---

[133] 162 N.E. at 99.

[134] By the way, at the game, Adam Kennedy tied an Anaheim Angels record by knocking in 8 runs, and Anaheim defeated the Toronto Blue Jays 16-10.

> Why should the tortfeasor be able to escape liability just because one could not reasonably foresee the actual injury? After all, the injury still occurred because of the act.
>
> Suppose you accidentally drop my textbook on the floor and the noise startles someone who drops dead of a heart attack? It was your mistake, and one could argue that you had a duty to hold the textbook carefully, so that you did not drop it and thereby hurt someone. But should you be accountable for everything associated with dropping the textbook? Dropping books on someone in a busy library as you hurry downstairs past a crowd of people going up the stairs seems different (more likely to lead to the harm that ensued) than the above example (a dropped book leading to a heart attack). Perhaps these distinctions explain the reasoning behind *Palsgraf*.

5. Comparative Law on Causation

An international comparison may reveal a different approach to causation.

In Sweden, reputedly, there was a child support case involving just one child, but five possible fathers, supposedly. Because any one of the five men <u>could have been</u> the father, each was ordered to pay a portion of child support. The American system would undertake paternity testing and simply require support from the one man who was actually the biological father. But is the American approach better? Might it not be fairer to hold each man accountable for behavior that could have resulted in his being the father? (Of course, visitation rights might, or might not, be a related issue. If you must pay for a child not actually your biological child, are you entitled to visitation rights, should you so desire? What is in the child's best interests?)

The French Civil Code, followed by many nations, reads, "Every human act that causes damages to another obliges the one through whose fault it has occurred to pay damages." The Civil Law system thus may not take into account "foreseeability". Also, that system allows greater latitude in recovering damages, such as granting restitution in criminal proceedings.

E. Harm

> *The plaintiff's decedent was killed by the defendant's negligence, but apparently his demise was more a cause of relief than grief; evidence indicated a nasty man, one little missed by those who knew him. The jury gave a **very low** damages award, except he won for burial expenses (even more than what the plaintiff requested). Refusing to overturn the jury's verdict as inconsistent, one appellate judge explained the jury's award this way: "maybe they just wanted to bury him a bit deeper!"*

Some damages are easily quantified - e.g., lost wages, hospital expenses. Other damages are more ephemeral. Hedonic (from the Greek word, "hedone," meaning "pleasure") damages concerns the lost pleasure in life: A broad interpretation of harm.

Economists can put an economic value on seeing the sunset, feeling a breeze, walking in the woods, hearing a bird singing, smelling a flower, residing with one's family, singing in a choir, gardening, playing tennis, etc. – a range of economic value some economic experts (for plaintiffs) have labeled a "zone of fairness."

> Aviation Damages Limitations
>
> In 1999, the member countries of the International Civil Aviation Organization (ICAO) agreed to an accord (known as the Montreal Convention) to replace the Warsaw Convention System, which is based on a 1929 pact. The accord removes the low caps - as little as $8,300 a passenger under the Warsaw Convention - that apply to airlines' liability for deaths or injuries. Under the two-tiered provisions of the new agreement, carriers will be liable for as much as $100,000 Special Drawing Rights

(about $140,000) per passenger, regardless of whether the airline was at fault in an accident. Beyond that, liability for damages will be unlimited unless a carrier proves that it was not at fault.[135]

The United States is an ICAO member, and the U.S. Senate ratified the Montreal Convention in 2003, bringing the number of ratifying nations to 30 and thus causing the Convention to reach enough ratifying "mass" and thus come into effect for those 30 countries.

One part of the Montreal Convention demanded by U.S. negotiators guarantees that plane-crash victims can sue an airline in their country of citizenship. This locks in the ability of U.S. victims' families to sue foreign carriers in American courts, even if the ticket was bought abroad and the airline was based in a foreign country. Also, under the accord all airlines would be required to prove they had liability insurance. Though this was already true for U.S. airlines and carriers that fly to the United States, it was not part of the Warsaw Convention.

F. Two Negligence Concepts: *Respondeat Superior* and *Res Ipsa Loquitur*

Among the most important negligence concepts are *respondeat superior* and *res ipsa loquitur*.

1. *Respondeat superior*

Respondeat superior is the doctrine by which the <u>employer is vicariously liable</u> for the negligence of its <u>employee acting within the scope of employment</u>. (The negligence of the employee is automatically ascribed to the employer.) This doctrine can explain why employers are liable when their employees engage in a negligent act even without their knowledge.

Two key questions are: (1) Was there an employment relationship? (2) Was the employee on the job, acting within the scope of his/her duties? These issues are, of course, important to resolving many agency issues and administrative disputes.

As an example, suppose that a department store allows its employees to dress up for holidays. An employee dresses as a clown, with a big wig, water-squirting flower, polka-dot pantsuit, and huge shoes. Because of her oversized shoes, she trips and knocks down a customer. Is the store liable for her negligence?

Yes. Under *respondeat superior*, the store is liable for its employee's negligence on the job.

Vicarious Liability Rules: Perverse Incentives for Business Organizations?
Professors Jennifer Arlen and Bentley McLeod note that, to be efficient, liability rules governing firms' liability for their agents' torts must ensure that organizations want their agents to take optimal precautions and thereby benefit from using cost-effective mechanisms to regulate agents. However, Arlen and McLeod believe that vicarious liability rules fail to satisfy these safety and monetary concerns. By holding organizations liable for torts committed by employees, but not by independent contractors, vicarious liability discourages organizations from asserting direct control over agents, even when control is an efficient way to regulate care. Indeed, Arlen and McLeod conclude, vicarious liability even encourages organizations to undermine the possibility of individual tort liability by hiring judgment-proof independent contractors – people who even on an individual basis cannot pay for harm they may cause.[136]

---

[135] Many major airlines, including all U.S. carriers, had already voluntarily waived any cap in cases where they were found to be at fault, but many carriers in Latin America, Africa, and Asia had not done so.
   Damage awards for lost luggage is another matter. There, the Montreal Convention limits payment for lost baggage to about $500 per bag (the passenger may have to provide proof of the lost contents), with the airline having just 21 days to locate the lost bag before having to compensate the passenger.

[136] Jennifer Arlen & W. Bentley McLeod, *Beyond Master-Servant: A Critique of Vicarious Liability*, an article in EXPLORING TORT LAW (Stuart Madden, ed., 2005).

2. Res Ipsa Loquitur

The Latin phrase, *res ipsa loquitur*, literally means, "The thing speaks for itself."

As a legal principle, *res ipsa loquitur* applies if: The instrumentality that caused the harm was under the exclusive control of the defendant(s) and the harm that occurred ordinarily only happens because of negligence.

In the great case of *Byrne v. Boadle*, 2 H. & C. 722 (England 1863), the plaintiff had walked past the defendant's warehouse, and a barrel of flour fell on the plaintiff's head. Although he was injured, the plaintiff could not prove any negligence; all the plaintiff knew was that the barrel fell and struck him on the head. Indeed, the plaintiff realized that he could not prove causation, and actually had no idea why the barrel just seemed to fall from the sky. The barrel presumably was under the exclusive control of the bakery. Ordinarily, barrels do not just fall from the stars. Thus, the obligation to come forward with evidence is put on the bakery.

The concept, *res ipsa loquitur*, thus was first put forth in this case of the of the mysterious, falling barrel: *Byrne v. Boadle*. The English high court, led by the Great Judge and Legal Scholar, Baron Pollock, wrote: "A barrel could not roll out of a warehouse without some negligence." The mere fact of the incident "spoke for itself" and made out a prima facie ("on its face") case of negligence. The burden thus shifted to the defendant; he had to put forth evidence that he was not at fault. Res ipsa loquitur means, in effect, "Let the defendant explain – the defendant should know what is going on (e.g., the plaintiff was under anesthetic while the defendant was conducting surgery on the plaintiff)." The defendant still has no burden of proof, but has the burden of introducing some evidence.

Here is another example from long ago. In the olden days (very early in the 20th Century), airplanes were so new that flight was still seen as unusual and, perhaps, unnatural. So airplane crashes were not presumed negligence in the very early stages of aviation. However, that soon changed. Now, under *res ipsa loquitur*, an airline defendant generally is given the burden to introduce evidence about the crashed plane's maintenance and the pilots' training and experience.

And here are three much more recent cases than the progenitor, *Byrne v. Boadle*. All three involve flying mammals (other than bats). In one case, a 16-year-old boy riding in a car near Gaston, Oregon, in August 2000 was killed by an airborne, 1,500-pound elk that had just been hit by a truck. In the second case, in April, 2000, another 16-year-old boy, on his bicycle, was killed by an airborne deer that had just been hit by a car in North Canton, Georgia. For the third case, in August 2000, Hida Yochikiata, 37, survived, but with major back injuries, after being hit by an airborne dog that had fallen from a ninth-floor window in a Paris suburb.

Could these be cases of negligence? By whom? Or were they simply acts of God? Are they similar to the Falling Barrel case? Only the last case seems to possibly invoke res ipsa loquitur (if res ipsa loquitur were in fact a principle of French law) because presumably the dog was a pet, hence subject to human control.

In the first two cases, presumably no one was in control of the animals, and if the elk and the deer simply bolted out onto the road, then, for the drivers of the truck and car that, respectively, hit these animals there was no breach of duty.

> The *res ipsa loquitur* doctrine bloomed in the last 100 years, as it proved useful to victims of wrecks, crashes, and explosions - those pursued by all manner of fallen or flying objects.

One type of hospital surgery example – a sponge or clamp or other item left in a patient's stomach – there are numerous cases that demonstrate these have always been the classic example of a res ipsa loquitur case. So leaving a sponge in a patient speaks for itself and does not require an expert witness to prove breach of duty.

Res Ipsa Loquitur: Video Re-Enactment -Ross Lucock of New South Wales, Australia (9:18), https://www.youtube.com/watch?v=8jIOy4aAJvo&list=UU_TuNN4AcpdLnoIdSTLx_MA

1. Ross' strange shoes, and bar patron Troy Bowron's lawsuit against Lucock and the Jannali Inn
2. Were the Inn/Ross in exclusive control of the "instrumentality?"

The reenactment is dedicated to an incredibly important common law tort concept, expressed in the Latin phrase *res ipsa loquitur*, which means "the thing speaks for itself." Although only developed in the past 150 years, this legal doctrine is redolent with venerable notions of fairness and evidence going back to the very birth of civilization. As with all sound precedents, the principle of *res ipsa loquitur* has been handed down as a treasure of law to each succeeding generation.[137]

G. Negligence in the Professional Context: Malpractice

Here is one way to avoid having a lot of people live to a ripe old age, or - if medical procedures don't work out - a bunch of malpractice claims! - **_"The abdomen, the chest, and the brain will forever be shut from the intrusion of the wise and humane surgeon."_** *Sir John Eric Ericksen, Surgeon-Extraordinary to Queen Victoria, 1873.* For more about the ideas, through the centuries, people had about the human body, see SHERWIN B. NULAND, THE MYSTERIES WITHIN (2000).

Malpractice is the failure to adhere to professional standards. It is negligence in a professional context. So malpractice is failing to do what a competent, reasonable doctor/attorney/accountant/etc. would have done. The failure is a breach of duty for *professionals in that field (not "what most people would/could do" – in other words, it is not enough for a brain surgeon sued for malpractice to say, "Hey, I performed better brain surgery than could 99% of the population!"*).

Malpractice can occur in any area where licensed, supposedly expert people practice or work. So, many malpractice actions have nothing to do with health care.

---

criticism tort lawsuits 2mins50secs (CRITICISM OF TORT LAWSUITS: MALPRACTICE AS AN EXAMPLE) is a YOUTUBE video at robertwemersonufl.

"Torts cover all sorts of things and we cannot go into all of them. Let me just give you one example, and that is malpractice, which is a special type of negligence (one of the three broad categories of torts). Malpractice is negligence in the professional context. It's an allegation that, say, a health care provider, a lawyer, an engineer, an accountant, some other professional, did not adhere to the standards for that profession and committed negligence in that professional setting. In other words, malpractice. Tort law is very, very controversial. We have all sorts of contentions that there are numerous frivolous lawsuits out there, that there are plaintiffs who are making a boatload of money, far beyond what they might deserve (assuming they deserve anything), and that they are getting substantial windfalls as are their lawyers. That's why I've got this sparkly gold head symbolizing the plaintiff who's seeking all the gold, having been injured. One sees this sometimes on bumper stickers or elsewhere where it says on a car, 'Don't brake for me; let's meet by accident; I could use the money.'

"The assumption that there are huge numbers of people making out like gangbusters through the tort system is probably erroneous. There certainly are some cases of people obtaining windfalls, but in most instances, the tort system is structured so that the most one will receive is simply compensation for actual, provable harm. Punitive damages are relatively rare; you're only going to get them in some egregious, intentional tort situation such as fraud. On the other hand, clearly there are sufficient indications that the system may be out of whack. We have many cases that are brought that do not reach fruition in terms of the judgment, but which cause businesses or professionals, particularly health care providers, to contend that there is a medical malpractice crisis. It requires a lot of defense, a lot of time, a lot of money, and a lot of lawyers (not necessarily paying on judgments); the ability of people to sue, even if they cannot win, can be troublesome."

---

[137] Much more on the Pork Chops as Shoes life example is discussed in the superseding causation defense part of this text.

> Questions for Self-Exploration:
> 1. Are there too many malpractice lawsuits? Too few? Or, ironically, both too many AND too few? (What am I asking?!)
> 2. Are doctors and others in the medical field needlessly subject to malpractice claims? What are solutions to the health care problems in America?

1. Medical Malpractice

One hospital patient to another patient: "Were you sick when you came in or did they make you sick after you got here?"

a. Informed Consent?

In medicine, generally malpractice involves wrongs in treatment, diagnosis, monitoring, prevention, and/or communication. Often the problem involves poor systems and failures of communication. An example of the latter is the lack of informed consent.

> In medical treatment decision-making, sometimes the main problem is a patient's not being told enough to make a sound choice of whether, and how, to undergo a particular treatment. An *informed consent* by patient P to treatment T occurs if and only if: (1) P receives a thorough <u>disclosure</u> concerning T; (2) P acts <u>voluntarily</u>; (3) P is <u>competent</u> to give consent; and (4) P <u>consents</u> to T. Five legally justifiable exceptions to the informed consent process are: public health emergency (e.g., a quarantine); medical emergency (imminent and life-threatening); patient waiver; an incompetent patient with no legal surrogate available; and therapeutic privilege (it would be detrimental to the patient to inform him/her).

b. Medical Errors

Medical errors are estimated to be responsible for about 200,000 deaths a year – far more than those caused by breast cancer, AIDS or motor vehicle accidents.[138]

2. Different Types of Malpractice

Different sorts of negligence (malpractice) are perhaps typical for particular professions - e.g., accounting, dentistry, psychiatry, and law.

a. Accounting

Inaccurate reading/analysis of financial records; mistakes re: taxes. In a leading case (*Ultramares Corp. v. Touche*, 174 N.E. 441 (N.Y. Ct. App. 1931)), New York's highest court refused to apply the foreseeability principles to damages based on an accountant's alleged negligence. The court limited claims for damages to persons receiving the *primary benefit* of the accountant's services, not creditors and other third parties who might incidentally rely on statements and documents certified to be correct. About ten states follow that approach.

A few states hold the accountant liable to any injured party whose existence and injury might reasonably have been foreseen. But over half of the states follow an intermediate standard – Restatement of Torts Section 552: accountant liability beyond his/her client to any class of persons the accountant knows will receive a copy of his/her work.

b. Dentistry

Dental malpractice often involves mistakes about a patient's teeth or gums, such as pulling the wrong tooth.

---

[138] This estimate has come from numerous studies, including the Institute of Medicine of the National Academy of Science. HealthGrades, a private company that rates hospitals for insurers and health plans, concludes that if hospital errors were included on the nation's list of the leading causes of death, they would show up as No. 6 - ahead of diabetes, pneumonia and Alzheimer's. Conversely, the workplace is apparently getting safer and safer, especially compared to the heyday of industrialization, when injuries and deaths were as much as a hundred times more common as today!

c. Psychiatry

Psychiatric malpractice involves cases such as: not controlling dangerous patients; or not informing at risk people about patients threatening harm (or not telling the authorities, the police). An interesting policy issue is Confidentiality vs. Public Safety (must a mental health care professional violate the duty of confidentiality to his/her patient in order to warn or otherwise protect a third party (e.g., the patient's employer or creditors, his ex-spouse) about whom the patient has issued threats; however, that is a rare problem. Much more frequent a concern, and one for whom an easier case against psychiatrists may be brought, is intentional wrongdoing – e.g., having sex with a patient (that is <u>beyond</u> malpractice, to an intentional tort).

d. Law

The most frequent type of legal malpractice, and easiest to prove, is missing deadlines.

A Side Note on Wills

Maryland, New York, Texas, and some other states adhere to the principle that the only person who can pursue a malpractice claim against a lawyer who allegedly made a mistake in drafting a will is the client (usually, the now deceased client). However, California, Florida, Hawaii and many other states permit claims by the living – typically, beneficiaries contending that the lawyer's mistake financially hurt them. Proponents of the more restrictive approach fear that to let disappointed beneficiaries sue - often decades after a will was written - opens a Pandora's box of potential liability and leads to open-ended prying into matters that should remain protected by attorney-client privilege (the communications between the testator/testatrix and his/her lawyer). On the other hand, why insulate estates-and-trusts lawyers from the litigation culture that hovers over other professionals, including other types of lawyers?

---

e. Translators

Few translation service firms or individual translators have been sued over their allegedly poor translations. Such suits probably could be brought as (1) matters of breach of contract (the translator had agreed to perform certain services, but breached his/her duty under the contract), or (2) torts (a type of malpractice – negligence in the professional context) – a breach of duty of care, measured by the standards of the translation profession, if that breach causes harm. Surely, as the need for and use of translators, including computer-based services, grows, translators will no longer continue to get "a free pass."

f. Ordinary people

Ordinary people cannot, as laypersons, commit malpractice. They can simply commit negligence (no professional standard).

Example: CAN A PATIENT COMMIT MALPRACTICE? Consider the urine sample story. There is no <u>professional</u> duty of care from a patient. Still, there could be liability as to ordinary negligence standards or for intentional wrongdoing.

3. Mere Mistakes Are Typically Insufficient for a Winning Malpractice Claim

It is hard to bring a case simply for questionable judgment calls. Much easier are claims involving clear breaches of ethics (e.g., violations of fiduciary duties, such as revealing confidential information) or even battery or infliction of emotional distress. Those intentional tort claims, which may coincide with malpractice allegations, usually are stronger than mere professional "negligence." Indeed, two areas in which courts have been extremely reluctant to permit malpractice claims are: (1) education (from pre-school all the way to graduate or professional school); and (2) religious counseling.

4. General Issues in Malpractice Law

These issues include: Society's interest versus an Individual's right to sue.

There is a balancing of various interests – A triad fighting about reforms: (1) Plaintiffs' Lawyers (often aligned with consumers' groups); (2) Insurers; and (3) Doctors. Each group has horror stories to tell

- of patients horribly injured or killed due to unbelievably poor diagnoses and/or treatment by repeatedly negligent health care providers;
- of worsening costs and administrative restrictions on better risk-assessment procedures;
- of medical doctors chased from their practice because of skyrocketing insurance costs, the need to practice "defensive medicine," and threats of frivolous lawsuits (all despite these doctors' exemplary records in much-needed fields such as obstetrics).[139]

Lawyers: Watch Your Phrasing!

Surely lawyers have sometimes increased their already poor reputation through (a) relentless advertising and (b) insensitive phrasing.

The author recalls a pamphlet he received in the mail, addressed to him as a member of the bar. It advertised for a seminar on brain injuries directed at trial lawyers handling accident, malpractice, or other tort cases. The pamphlet noted that brain injuries involve damages that may be far from direct economic losses, that the nature of the injury is often difficult to pinpoint, and yet the impact of such injuries can be very substantial. The "good news," the ad intoned, is that these injuries are "valuable" (i.e., high damage awards are possible), while the "bad news," according to the ad, was not that somebody's brain has been harmed but that "not handling these cases correctly can be costly" (little or no damage awards; in very poorly handled cases, perhaps malpractice claims against the lawyer).

With all that emphasis on getting money for a damaged brain, thereby making even some experienced lawyers feel uneasy, if not downright queasy, imagine how it would strike people unfamiliar with the legal system. The phrasing may be intended "for lawyers' eyes only," but the attitude certainly may be apparent to, and disturbing for, the public.

YOUTUBE – criticism_tort_lawsuits_2mins50secs at robertwemersonufl
(A Very Brief Set of Comments about Tort Suits, with Medical Malpractice the Focus)

Medical liability policy, according to William M. Sage, a physician and a law professor at Columbia University, should seek three goals: restraining overall costs, compensating the victims of medical mistakes, and providing incentives for doctors and hospitals to reduce medical errors. Malpractice reform measures called for – and some of which have been enacted in a number of states – include capping awards, tightening standards for expert witnesses, allowing judgments to be paid out over extended periods, partially shielding emergency room doctors from liability, and limiting lawyers' fees. The premise of most reforms is that insurance premiums will go down and that more doctors will thereby enter or remain in needed fields (e.g., in specialties such as obstetrics). However, the amount of premiums is derived not as much from claims as from insurers' pricing and accounting practices, including investment returns and circular business patterns (price wars to write more policies, inadequate premiums to cover losses, increasing premiums and loss of coverage, then eventually back to price wars).

---

[139] Surely lawyers have sometimes increased their already poor reputation through relentless advertising for new clients. Even fellow lawyers may be embarrassed by the drumbeat for new potential plaintiffs. The author recalls a pamphlet he received in the mail, addressed to him as a member of the bar. It advertised for a seminar on brain injuries directed at trial lawyers handling accident, malpractice, or other tort cases. The pamphlet noted that brain injuries involve damages that may be far from *direct* economic losses, that the nature of the injury is often difficult to pinpoint, and yet the impact of such injuries can be very substantial. The "good news," the ad intoned, is that these injuries are "valuable" (i.e., high damage awards are possible), while the "bad news," according to the ad, was not that somebody's brain has been harmed but that "not handling these cases correctly can be costly" (little or no damage awards; in very poorly handled cases, perhaps malpractice claims against the lawyer). With all that emphasis on getting money for a damaged brain, thereby making even some experienced lawyers feel uneasy, if not downright queasy, imagine how it must strike people not familiar with the legal system.

5. Good Samaritan Laws
These laws are designed to eliminate liability for ordinary negligence in certain situations. They exempt medical professionals from liability when they in good faith assist in emergency situations. (They would even shield passersby who just do what they can in using, for example, a portable defibrillator. See below, under "Negligence in Training and Resuscitation.")[140]

6. Suing for Malpractice: The Shotgun Approach
There are <u>various possible instances of negligence.</u>

The Shotgun Approach (like shooting a blast of shotgun pellets) is to assert many claims or defenses and hope at least one pellet hits the target.

> Suppose that Patti Patient sues her former doctor for malpractice. She might have five different theories to prove liability. Each one could suffice. She is just throwing forward, for possible acceptance by the judge, jury, or arbitrator, these theories:
> 1. Inadequate medical history: The doctor failed to find out information from the patient that might have led to a different, better approach.
> 2. Lack of informed consent: What did the doctor tell the patient? When it is purely elective surgery, should not the discussion of risks be especially detailed and informative?
> 3. Negligence in performing the operation - E.g., too much anesthesia?
> 4. Negligence in recognizing a cardiovascular collapse, or some other such problem. E.g., insufficient monitoring of pulse, breathing, etc.
> 5. Negligence in training and in resuscitation. Once it was recognized something was wrong, the health care providers failed to perform CPR properly or otherwise effectively treat the worsening condition.

However, some judges and others have severely criticized those pleadings, and have even punished attorneys or parties if it is decided that the shotgun approach was undertaken in bad faith or frivolously. For example, since the late 1990s, the U.S. Circuit Court of Appeals for the 11th Circuit (covering Alabama, Florida, and Georgia) has tried to fight "Shotgun Pleadings" that it believes permit marginal claims and turn lawsuits into fishing expeditions.

Sometimes the shotgun approach may undermine the better claims/defenses because the more dubious claims/defenses leave people questioning everything the "shotgunner" says. For example, in the 1998-2000 antitrust trial against Microsoft, the defense counsel – instead of concentrating on the defenses that consumers were not harmed and that competition was not foreclosed from the market – also argued a more dubious proposition – that Microsoft is not a monopoly; they thus undermined in the judge's eye (and in the "court" of public opinion) even their more promising arguments. It sometimes is better to give an inch and not risk losing a mile.

H. Topical Lecture: Defenses Unique to Negligence Cases (<u>Not</u> defenses to crime or intentional torts)

Introduction to Topical Lecture:

Defenses to negligence, but not applicable to intentional torts, include: Act of God, superseding causation, assumption of risk, comparative negligence, and contributory negligence. To assume a risk, one must know of that risk, so plain, conspicuous warnings to potential plaintiffs often help a defendant establish this defense. For Workers' Compensation claims, the injured worker's (or co-worker's) own negligence is no defense to liability

---

[140] For the Florida Good Samaritan law, see Florida Statutes § 768.13(2). (It also protects licensed veterinarians for aiding injured animals at the scene of an emergency).

1. Act of God

a. Elements and Examples

Act of God is a defense to negligence when purely natural forces such as lightning, earthquakes, or hurricanes are the proximate cause of injury that could not have been prevented by any amount of foresight reasonably to be expected of a defendant. For example, if Sam rents a sailboat which sinks when struck by a tsunami, ordinarily he would have no decent claim based on the boat's failure to withstand this onslaught of Mother Nature.

In *O'Neill v. Hemenway*, 3 So.2d 210 (La. App. Ct. 1941), a pile driver machine was left on a public street in New Orleans. It was not grounded, and several youths, including Thomas O'Neill, age 18, took advantage of the shade afforded by the pile driver and sat beneath it on a piece of timber. Shortly after O'Neill sat down, an electric storm arose and he was struck and killed by a bolt of lightning. The court found that the machine's owners committed no negligence in view of the fact that the machine had been stored in the manner usual and customary in the business, and the further fact that the lightning strike was extraordinary. Pointing out that a defendant can only be required to guard against an anticipated danger, not every possibility of harm but only such harmful contingencies as might reasonably be expected, and noting that it had been shown by two experienced pile driver operators that lightning very rarely struck pile drivers, the court declared that the defendants were, consequently, not obliged to ground the driver. So Thomas O'Neill's parents lost their suit on account of an act of God.

However, when a person negligently creates a situation whereby a foreseeable act of God could cause damage, no defense is available to foreseeable damages. For example, the "act of God" defense was used when a condominium homeowners association sued the developer/builder of the building following a hurricane. Serious damages resulted from the hurricane. While the builder used the act of God defense, engineers were able to provide evidence that the building had not been built to code. Likewise, a Texas church was held accountable for the injuries to a parishioner struck by lightning as he left the church; the church argue (what else?!) act of God, but lost because the lightning rod had been negligently constructed and had, in fact, taken the lightning directly from the steeple to the exit door - where supposed precautionary measures actually and foreseeably *increase* the likelihood of a potentially lethal natural phenomenon and enhance the risk of injury, the negligent third party will not be excused from liability in any resulting accident simply because an act of God was involved.[141]

And here is another possible act of God example -

FABIO AND A GOOSE AT BUSCH GARDENS

On March 30, 1999, the male supermodel Fabio (famous for formerly gracing the covers of many romance novels and for his saying, in a television commercial with his European accent, "I can't believe it's not butter) was left bloody by an "act of nature."

At the Williamsburg, Virginia Busch Gardens, the theme park had touted Fabio's ride on a new roller coaster called Apollo's Chariot as a "Modern-Day Adonis vs. Ancient-Day Sun God." But a bird upstaged the supermodel during the ride. The animal hit Fabio on the face and left him with a one-inch cut on the bridge of his nose. Blood streamed down Fabio's chin and cheeks. Several female models sitting near him in white tunics, portraying goddesses, were splattered with blood.

Fabio was soon released from a hospital, with no serious injuries. No one was sure about the bird's plight, although its prospects seem to have been poor.

Although it was an "act of god," negligence may have been present after all.

Fabio later said: "Building a roller coaster on a lake inhabited by geese could cause more serious accidents or possibly a child's death. I'm glad the results were much less significant."

---

b. Lightning and Golf Courses

---

[141] *Macedonia Baptist Church v. Gibson*, 833 S.W.2d 557 (Tex. Ct. App. 1992).

While a number of states have had cases holding that the obvious risks of lightning from an impending thunderstorm tend to protect golf course operators from liability for lightning strike deaths or injuries to their patrons,[142] circumstances can lead to potential liability. In *Maussner v. Atlantic City Country Club, Inc.*, 691 A.2d 826, 835 (N.J. Super. Ct., App. Div. 1997), the New Jersey appeals court held:

"[W]hen a golf course has taken steps to protect golfers from lightning strikes, it owes the golfers a duty of reasonable care to implement its safety precautions properly. We do not go so far as to hold that golf course operators have an absolute duty to protect their patrons from lightning strikes. We refrain from finding this greater duty because it may still be cost-prohibitive to make all golf courses adopt particular safety procedures. Our holding has the following consequences. All golf courses have a duty to post a sign that details what, if any, safety procedures are being utilized by the golf course to protect its patrons from lightning. If a particular golf course uses no safety precautions, its sign must inform golfers that they play at their own risk and that no safety procedures are being utilized to protect golfers from lightning strikes. If, however, a golf course chooses to utilize a particular safety feature, it owes a duty of reasonable care to its patrons to utilize it correctly. This latter standard means, for example, that if a golf course builds shelters, it must build lightning-proof shelters; if a golf course has an evacuation plan, the evacuation plan must be reasonable and must be posted; if a golf course uses a siren or horn system, the golfers must be able to hear it and must know what the signals mean; and if the golf course uses a weather forecasting system, it must use one that is reasonable under the circumstances."

The trend may be toward undermining the viability of act of God as a defense when protective measures could deal with specifically unpredictable, but generally foreseeable harms stemming from lightning, hurricanes, earthquakes, volcanoes, and other forces of nature.

2. Superseding (Intervening) Causation

> Fulgencia Fuego is pumping gas into her car when she negligently spills some. A pyromaniac then puts some highly flammable rags and cardboard by the spilled gas and lights it. The gas spill now aflame, the fire spreads to the gas station's gas tanks, which are soon ablaze. Within minutes, the gas station explodes in flames.
>
> Fulgencia's best defense to a negligence claim against her is that the pyromaniac's action was a superseding event — an unforeseeable act that broke any chain of causation.

This is a defense that "Whatever we did, something/someone interrupted the chain of causation"; it was an unforeseeable (foreseeable is not the same as probable or likely) interruption. This is not a question of physics but, as with proximate cause, a question of responsibility. For example, even if you were negligent to leave something in the rain, others who subsequently could easily have brought the item in from the rain (but did not do so) could be held to have superseded your negligence.

Here is a superseding causation example, from the author's legal practice, involving misdelivered bank securities. An armored courier had misdelivered securities, but the bank that received them negligently retained the securities for years (and informed no one until pressed to do so because of a lawsuit). In the lawsuit against the courier, the courier defendant raised the defense that its own negligence was superseded by the receiving bank's negligence. After a trial, the case settled with the courier, the bank, and a couple other defendants each agreeing to pay a portion of the plaintiff's damages for not being able to exercise its rights in the lost securities. While superseding causation may have left the last defendant fully responsible for the plaintiff's harm, it also is quite possible that a judge or jury will simply find more than one defendant jointly responsible for the harms, so that becomes a factor in parties compromising a claim.

---

[142] See, e.g., *Patton v. United States of America Rugby Football*, 851 A.2d 566 (Md. 2004).

3. Assumption of Risk

Examples

a. Numerous cartoons
   1. Throwing darts at someone with an apple on his head
   2. Ben Franklin and his Kite-in-the-Storm Experiment
   3. At the Circus, standing on a galloping horse
   4. "Bending Her Beau"- shooting arrows at a target and hitting her nearby boyfriend
   5. Cavemen shouting, "Eat it, Zok!" to a fellow caveman holding a nasty-looking critter
   6. The lion-tamer with his head inside the open mouth of Ernie the lion, as fellow lions say, "Ernie is a chicken. Ernie is a chicken."

b. Big-Mouth child swallowing whole some huge cookies, on a dare. (Can a child assume a risk? Probably not.)

c. Prof. David Laude of U Texas at Austin – "My greatest invention ever, the indoor thunderstorm - surely you can use it to teach something about the law, like how to get sued from doing a dangerous demonstration in front of unsuspecting students:
i. Borrow about 20 liters of liquid nitrogen from a chemist and put it in a plastic tub.
ii. Have about 10 gallons of water heated to boiling, and then throw the boiling water with a little bit of force into the liquid nitrogen? With luck you are standing in the middle of a thunderstorm that soaks half the class and sends a vapor cloud 30 feet in the air. The person who creates the storm ends up looking like the guys they dig out of the ice age.
   Did that student know, and thus assume, the risk? <u>To assume a risk, one must know the risk. So potential defendants should give information to possible plaintiffs.</u>

   i. Perhaps there is no need to warn about incredibly obvious risks. For example, on the sidelines of a football game: The "Bubba Factor" (that a 300-pound sprinting lineman will crash into you).
   ii. Do you know about the risk of foul balls and splintered bats at a baseball stadium? (How many games have you seen, attended, played?)
   iii. Dangerous Fishing? The "Where Is Wally?" missing fisherman example. Do you assume the risk of a "Jaws" incident on the wharf?

This defense depends upon a plaintiff's knowingly, voluntarily taking a risk. A plaintiff who does that may not recover for an injury arising out of the known risks inherent to that situation. (An exception to this defense is a rescuer acting in an emergency situation.)

Several state courts have barred suits stemming from acts of ordinary negligence in voluntary games - acts such as accidentally tripping or running into someone, hurting someone with a thrown ball, or offhandedly tossing a bat after hitting. These courts are, in essence, saying that the participants assumed these risks. Of course, even these states would permit suits involving intentional or reckless "rough play" (the sort of behavior considered outside the range of ordinary activity for a sport).

Assumption of risk is likely to be implied, but it could be express. Releases of liability, placed in writing, constitute forms to prove a potential plaintiff's express assumption of risk. Here is an example of such a form:

RELEASE OF LIABILITY, WAIVER OF CLAIMS, EXPRESS ASSUMPTION OF RISKS, AND HOLD HARMLESS AGREEMENT

In consideration of my being allowed to participate in the _____ Program (the "Program"), I hereby agree:

> I, _____, for myself and my estate, heirs, administrators, executors, and assigns, hereby release and hold harmless the Program, and its officers, directors, employees, representatives, agents, and volunteers (collectively, the "Releasees"), from any and all liability and responsibility whatsoever, however caused, for any and all damages, claims, or causes of action that I, my estate, heirs, administrators, executors, and assigns may have for any loss, illness, personal injury, death, or property damage arising out of, connected with, or in any manner pertaining to the Program, WHETHER CAUSED BY THE NEGLIGENCE OF RELEASEES or otherwise.
>
> I fully understand that there are potential risks associated with my participation in the Program, including, but not limited to, possible injury or loss of life. Despite the potential hazards associated with this activity, I wish to proceed, and freely accept and assume all risks, dangers, or property damage to me or to my property, WHETHER CAUSED BY THE NEGLIGENCE OF RELEASEES or otherwise. I acknowledge that I am freely participating and that I am not required to participate in the Program. I further agree to indemnify and hold harmless the Releasees from any judgment, settlement loss, liability, damage, or costs, including court costs and attorney fees for both the trial and appellate levels, that Releasees may incur as a proximate result of any negligent or deliberate act or omission on my part during my participation in the Program.
>
> In signing this agreement, I acknowledge and represent that I have read and understand it; that I sign voluntarily and for full and adequate consideration, fully intending to be bound by the same; and that I am at least eighteen (18) years of age and fully competent.
>
> I HAVE READ THIS AGREEMENT, UNDERSTAND THAT I AM GIVING UP SUBSTANTIAL RIGHTS BY SIGNING IT, AND VOLUNTARILY AGREE TO BE BOUND BY IT.
>
> NAME (PRINTED) _____ SIGNATURE _____ DATE _____
>
> WITNESS NAME (PRINTED) _____ WITNESS SIGNATURE _____ DATE _____

Many American courts have found that a spectator hit by a baseball had assumed the risk and could not recover from the baseball team or the stadium's owners. Some cases have been settled with payments to fans. For example, the Houston Astros paid an injured female spectator from England who had never before seen a baseball game and was unfamiliar with the sport. One court decision for the fan was *Uzbavines v. Metropolitan Baseball Club, Inc.*, 454 N.Y.S.2d 238 (N.Y. 1982). There, though, the circumstances were unusual. A foul ball went through a poorly-repaired screen at the New York Mets' Shea Stadium and hit a spectator behind home plate.

<u>There is no assumption of risk or comparative negligence (e.g., the plaintiff's alleged foolishness) concerning intentional misconduct (intentional torts, or crimes)</u>. For example, assume that it is 2:00 a.m., and someone is inebriated and waving his/her wallet in the air while stumbling around in a "bad" part of town. A robbery is not legally assumed just because the victim's behavior was tremendously stupid![143]

> ### The Impact of Administratively or Statutorily Compelled Warnings
> Ironically, a warning that legislators or regulators force upon businesses may legally protect the businesses, even though the warning was not voluntarily put on a product. The classic example is the warning found on cigarette packages. Smokers may be found to have assumed the risk, as the dangers of smoking are well known. So tobacco companies that fought these compelled warnings later used the warnings to argue against their alleged liability for a negligently produced or otherwise tortious product. These defenses tended to be impervious to successful challenge until the late 1990s. Then, claims about

---

[143] The author discusses the case of former NBA star Dennis Rodman kicking a cameraman at Robert W. Emerson, *Editor's Corner: The Business Law Team Brand*, 52 AMERICAN BUSINESS LAW JOURNAL v, vii-viii, at n.9 (Fall 2015)., available at http://ssrn.com/author=86449.

warranties or disclaimers may have been rendered moot in many American lawsuits by a new element since the late 1990s: Evidence (internal tobacco industry documents) pointing beyond negligence or breach of warranties or disclaimers, to <u>fraud</u> by the tobacco industries.

Here is a humorous look at the classic disclaimers concerning tobacco:
Evolution of Tobacco Industry Warning Labels
- "Smoke 'em—It's better to *LOOK GOOD* than *FEEL* good. (1955)
- "Rumors about cigarette smoking may be hazardous to your health." (1965)
- "The fascist, anti-business surgeon general has determined that cigarette smoking is ha-ha-ha hazardous to your health. So go ahead and **TRY** to quit (wink wink)." (1975)
- "Hey—Don't sue US! We **WARNED** you about smoking!" (1995).

AN EXAMINATION OF PACKAGING AND WARNINGS WORLD-WIDE

In Canada, no cigarette advertising is allowed. In the United States, the broadcast advertising of cigarettes is prohibited. More important in both countries may be the extensive efforts to dissuade people from smoking, via warnings about its deleterious effects. The Need is for *effective* warnings.

Over time, there have been much stronger health warnings about tobacco, in the United States and elsewhere. Most, of course, were mandated by government action: statutes or regulations. The U.S. Surgeon General's warning contains only text (no photos), appears on the side of the package, and is smaller than that found in some other countries. There have been Congressional proposals to have the warnings cover half of the front panel of packages and also half of cigarette advertisements, with the text messages supported by color photographs. So far they have not been enacted. The idea is for cigarette packs to make you sick before what is inside the packs can kill you! The effect is to say to someone pulling out a cigarette – "you're stupid and a low-life."

Canada has very strong health warnings, requiring that over half the cigarette packet is covered with warnings. These warnings cover the top half of the front and back of a pack and use graphics such as color photographs of diseased lungs, hearts, and mouths. For example, one cover features photos of some really nasty looking teeth and gums with the large warning that "Cigarettes Cause Mouth Diseases: Cigarette smoke causes oral cancer, gum diseases and tooth loss." Other pictures include those of diseased arteries causing a stroke; and a foot turned gangrenous from poor circulation. Some simply include the phrase, "Smoking can kill you."

Other text warnings include: "Cigarettes make it harder for your saliva to remove germs in your mouth"; and "Smoking can cause a slow and painful death." Appealing to people's vanity and sexual concerns, warnings may note smoking-related problems with skin (premature wrinkling) and that smoking increases the chances of impotence.[144]

Brazil likewise has strong, graphic warnings on cigarette packages. And most countries at least have gone toward requiring some warning labels for tobacco products.

The European Union (EU) has very large warnings. A law taking effect in the EU in October 2002 significantly enlarged health warnings on cigarette packets and made them much more explicit. The warnings must cover at least 30% of the pack's front and 40% of the back, up from what had been as little as 4%. The more graphic warnings now include, "Smokers die younger." Individual EU governments can even require manufacturers place on cigarette packs color photos showing how smoking-related diseases can ravage the body with stained teeth, diseased lungs, and other smoking-induced impacts.

The EU law is the first one in the world to ban the use of such terms as "light," "mild," and "low tar" on the grounds that they are misleading. The law's passage was smoothed by U.S. tobacco trials, which gave documentary evidence of bad faith among tobacco companies.

---

[144] Canadian law also mandates that many packs carry information about quitting smoking.

4. Comparative or Contributory Negligence

These two distinct defenses have important effects on a lawsuit for negligence.

Under *contributory negligence*, a plaintiff who contributes to his/her own harm is barred from any recovery.

Under *comparative negligence*, the plaintiff's own negligence does not bar his/her recovery but instead reduces the plaintiff's damages award by the percentage of the fault attributed to the plaintiff.

All states first adopted contributory negligence. But, especially in the 1970s and early 1980s, almost every state switched to comparative negligence. Only four states now have contributory negligence: Alabama, Maryland, North Carolina, and Virginia.

These defenses offset (remove or erase) a defendant's liability for negligence, but not for intentional wrongdoing. For a car accident, suppose that person A was "at fault" (acted negligently) while person B intentionally, or at least recklessly, committed a wrongful act (e.g., in a rage, rams his car into A because A had failed to use a turn signal). Neither comparative negligence nor contributory negligence would apply; B would be out of luck, and A presumably could collect for damages that A suffered (even though A was negligent). Mere negligence is not comparable to intentional or reckless misbehavior. But if B's wrongful behavior was a minor traffic offense constituting simply a type of negligence (e.g., speeding 8 miles per hour over the limit), then the rules of comparative negligence should apply. Obviously, the facts of a particular case are paramount. And, of course, the law is often more complex than can be explained briefly in class or a textbook.

A policy question is: Does comparative negligence encourage lawsuits? As for contributory negligence, it is not as "harsh" on plaintiffs as it might appear; it is tempered by doctrines/approaches such as Last Clear Chance - even if the plaintiff was contributory negligent, a court may hold that the defendant had a "last clear chance" to avoid causing the harm and should have done so (thus was negligent and liable to the plaintiff).

5. A Student's Hypothetical Example - Is This Superseding Causation?

"The other day I was walking in front of Kotobuki restaurant, and there were some empty beer kegs on the balcony. I thought to myself: If someone grabbed those kegs and tossed them on a car below, would Kotobuki be liable on grounds of foreseeability?"

The professor's response: Using the reasonableness standard, a reasonable person would not perform such an act as throwing the kegs off the balcony, so Kotobuki would probably not be liable. But that others might behave unreasonably, especially inebriated folks, is not that foreseeable?

Australian Ross Lucock and His Foolish Behavior

See YOUTUBE – PorkChopsAsShoesDownUnder_ResIpsaLoquitur9mins18secs.wmv at robertwemersonufl

Twenty-seven-year-old Ross Lucock and his "mates" were downing numerous drinks at a "rowdy drinks night" at the Jannali Inn, in Sydney, Australia.

In between pints, Ross won the meat tray raffle.

Now Ross was drunk, and barefoot! The Inn's Assistant Manager told a barefoot Ross that customers must wear shoes. The Inn refused to serve Ross any more drinks unless he put on some footwear. So Ross improvised.

From the meat tray that he had just won, Ross picked a pair of pork chops. Ross and his mates had a big chuckle, until another patron – Ross' friend, Troy Bowron - proceeded past the bar. He slipped and suffered, on his left side, a severe hematoma to his humerus, leaky synovial fluid in the membrane sac of the capitulum, and compound fractures of both the radius and ulna. The doctor found that Troy Bowron suffered in his left arm a "clicking sensation," scarring, and pain and suffering. Unable to lift heavy weights, Troy might continue to have disabilities in his left arm and later need elbow replacement.

> Troy Bowron was an upholsterer of furniture. He claimed to have lost past and future earnings as well as various medical expenses. Bowron sued the Jannali Inn, its licensee, and Ross in Australia's District Court for New South Wales.
>
> Bowron won a damages award of what would be almost 35,000 in American dollars. The whole gist of the case was that the bar should have known that Ross was inebriated. Ross Lucock had created a hazard for everyone in the vicinity. The Inn should have, for safety's sake, removed from the premises both Ross Lucock and his slippery pork chops.
>
> In June 2002, Judge Anthony Puckeridge found that the Jannali Inn and its licensee had breached their duty of care by failing to clean the area that Lucock had made a greasy, meaty mess. However, Ross Lucock was so drunk that he did not even remember placing the pork chops on his feet; he owed no duty of care, Judge Puckeridge ruled, and the judge actually ordered Troy Bowron to pay his former friend Ross Lucock's legal costs defending Troy's lawsuit.
>
> Note: The common law principles of negligence used in American also apply Down Under.

End of Topical Lecture on "Defenses Unique to Negligence Cases"

I. Criminal Defenses

1. Alibis

What are alibis? Alibis are facts. In Latin, the word "alibi" means "elsewhere." Thus, at law, an alibi is a plea or fact that an accused person was somewhere else when an offense was committed. (So the defendant could not have committed the crime.) (So here is the word used in a sentence: "Immediately after the robbery the gang scattered to establish alibis!" (to claim, with witnesses, that they were elsewhere).

2. Defenses

There are many defenses to crimes. Most also usually apply, in some manner, to intentional torts. Defenses are <u>excuses</u> – "I did something that seems bad, but here is my explanation/excuse for why the act is not really a crime, a wrong."

In essence, an excuse may be a legal defense and thus keep an otherwise criminal act from constituting a crime. That is because the defense ordinarily meant that an element needed for conviction – <u>mens rea</u> (criminal intent) – is missing.

> **Some Examples of Criminal Excuses (just Jokes)**
>
> The classic excuse – blame the Judge himself. For example, a teenager was arrested for joyriding. His excuse for why he led police on a reckless chase. He'd been in trouble before. "Judge, when I saw the flashing red lights, I thought of the time before when I was in trouble! You were the judge, and you let me go, after telling me, that you never wanted to see me in this courtroom again. And if I'd just gotten away from the police, I wouldn't be here, your honor."
>
> Is the following a good excuse? I doubt it.
>
> A client of Deputy Public Defender George F. Bird, Jr., in Compton, California, pled guilty to reckless driving. The police report stated that Bird's client was traveling 45 m.p.h. in a 25 m.p.h. zone and had run a stop sign, all with a man clinging onto the hood of his car. Traffic Court Commissioner Ronald Tisch accepted the guilty plea and asked the defendant who was that man on his hood.
>
> My brother-in-law, he answered.
>
> What happened? Tisch asked.
>
> My brother-in-law owed me money, I asked for it, he said no, and he hit me in the face. I was on my way to the police station when he jumped onto the front of my car.
>
> Tisch asked, If I let you out of jail, how can I be sure this won't happen again?
>
> Oh, said the defendant, I think he learned his lesson.

ABA J., Oct. 1, 1987, at 166.

What about this series of defenses: In 1990, Florence Schreiber Powers, age 44, a Ewing, New Jersey administrative law judge on trial for shoplifting two watches, called her psychiatrist to testify that Powers was under stress at the time of the incidents. The doctor said that Powers did not know what she was doing from one minute to the next, for the following 19 reasons

    a recent car accident,
    a traffic ticket,
    a new-car purchase,
    overwork,
    husband's kidney stones,
    husband's asthma and breathing machine (which occupies their bedroom),
    menopausal hot flashes,
    an ungodly vaginal itch,
    a bad rash,
    fear of breast and anal cancer,
    fear of dental surgery,
    son's need for an asthma breathing machine,
    mother's and aunt's illnesses,
    need to organize her parents' 50th wedding anniversary,
    need to cook Thanksgiving dinner for 20 relatives,
    purchase of 200 gifts for Christmas and Hanukkah,
    attempt to sell her house without a Realtor,
    lawsuit against wallpaper cleaners,
    purchase of furniture that had to be returned,
    and a toilet in her house that was constantly running.

She was convicted. There is such a thing as invoking too many excuses and ticking off the judge.

And Some Excuses for Traffic Accidents

Many people have experienced the confusion of traffic accidents and have then tried to summarize, very briefly, what happened on an insurance/accident form. These were answers provided on such forms:

    I collided with a stationary truck coming the other way.
    A truck backed through my windshield into my wife's face.
    A pedestrian hit me and went under my car.
    The guy was all over the road. I had to swerve a number of times before I hit him.
    I pulled away from the side of the road, glanced at my mother-in-law and headed over the embankment.
    In my attempt to kill a fly, I drove into a telephone pole.
    I had been shopping for plants all day, and was on my way home. As I reached an intersection, a hedge sprang up, obscuring my vision. I did not see the other car.
    I had been driving my car for 40 years when I fell asleep at the wheel and had an accident.
    I was on my way to the doctors with rear end trouble when my universal joints gave way, causing me to have an accident.
    As I approached an intersection, a stop sign suddenly appeared in a place where no stop sign had ever appeared before. I was unable to stop in time to avoid the accident.
    To avoid hitting the bumper of the car in front, I struck the pedestrian. {Good choice!}
    Coming home, I drove into the wrong house and collided with a tree I don't have.
    The other car collided with mine without giving warning of its intentions.
    I thought my window was down, but I found out it was up when I put my hand through it.

> An invisible car came out of nowhere, struck my vehicle, and vanished.
> I told the police that I was not injured, but on removing my hat, I found that I had a skull fracture.
> I was sure that the old fellow would never make it to the other side of the street when I struck him.
> The pedestrian had no idea which direction to go so I ran over him.
> I saw the slow-moving, sad-faced gentleman as he bounced off the hood of my car. {He was sad. Imagine that!}
> The indirect cause of the accident was a little guy in a small car with a big mouth.
> I was thrown from my car as it left the road. I was later found in a ditch by some stray cows (who evidently called for help!).
> The telephone pole was approaching fast! I attempted to swerve out of its way, when it struck the front of my car.

The following are some specific defenses.

a. Intoxication

Is intoxication a defense? Only if it deprives you of mens rea. Voluntary intoxication generally is <u>not</u> a defense, while Involuntary intoxication (accidentally, by force) is a defense.

Example – Drew gets drunk, hits Sara, and puts her in a coma. Drew claims he could not have had the mens rea needed to be convicted of a crime, because he was drunk. He cannot even remember what he did. However, Drew can be prosecuted for his battering of Sara; voluntary intoxication is generally NOT a criminal defense.

> **"THE TEDDY BEARS' PICNIC"** (just for your interest's sake)
>
> Featuring bear dancers!   Music by John W. Bratton   Words by Jimmy Kennedy
> Dancing by Christina Reagan Greene & Nicole Srur
> Directed by Robert Emerson
>
> If you go down in the woods today,
> You're sure of a big surprise.
> If you go down in the woods today
> You'd better go in disguise;
>
> For ev'ry Bear that ever was
> Will gather there for certain, because
> Today's the day the Teddy Bears
> Have their picnic.
>
> [Ev'ry Teddy Bear who's been good
> Is sure of a treat today.
> There's lots of marvelous things to eat,
> and wonderful games to play.
>
> Beneath the trees where nobody sees
> They'll hide & seek as long as they please
> Cause that's the way Teddy Bears
> Have their picnic.
>
> If you go down in the woods today,
> You'd better not go alone.

> It's lovely down in the woods today,
> But safer to stay at home.
>
> So watch them there, so unaware
> Having a picnic holiday
> A lovely time to dance and play
> For every bear.
>
> See them gaily gad about,
> They love to hop and shout;
> They never have any care;
> At six o'clock their Mummies & Daddies will take them home to bed,
> Because they're tired little Teddy Bears.

b. Infancy

Even a child, with no Capacity, can commit a crime. The test for judging whether infancy excuses a defendant is a subjective test.

Courts look at knowledge/foresight/conscience. The Common Law standard provides that ages 7 and 14 are key divides.

Under age 7, a defendant was held absolutely to be too young to form the requisite <u>mens rea</u>. From age 7 until the child is 14, there is a rebuttable presumption that the child's infancy should act as a defense. These children were presumed to lack the mens rea due to "infancy." But that presumption could be overcome (and the child thus charged with, and perhaps convicted of, a crime).

From the age 14 until 18 (or some other age of adulthood), the rebuttable presumption is that the child should be charged as if he/she were an adult. These older minors were presumed to have the mens rea needed to be charged with and convicted of a crime. But that presumption could be overcome, this time with evidence brought forth by the minor's side.

So, in general, there are presumptions, but they are shiftable. Most states have moved to a sliding scale, based on experience, <u>not</u> a more rigid "age 7 or 14" common-law approach.[145] And all states permit (but do not require) children under 16 to be tried as adults.[146] Around 25,000 children a year have their cases sent to adult courts instead of being tried in juvenile courts (whose convicted defendants normally are set free by the time they turn 21).

In criminal law, it is better that a child <u>not</u> be "gifted." The more precocious a child is (the greater experience and aptitude), the more likely it is that he/she is subject to criminal charges as an adult.[147]

c. Entrapment

---

[145] Fourteen states, and the District of Columbia, expressly allow prosecutors to file charges against juveniles in criminal court. Twenty-three states have no minimum age. And two, Kansas and Vermont, even explicitly permit the trying of 10-year-olds as adults.

[146] Between 1992 and 1999, every state except Nebraska enacted laws making it easier for juveniles to be tried as adults.

[147] A MacArthur Foundation study (led by Temple University psychology professor Laurence Steinberg) released on March 2, 2003 concluded that many children under age 16 had as much difficulty grasping the complex legal proceedings as adults who had been ruled incompetent to go to court. The study looked at more than 1,400 people between the ages of 11 and 24 in Los Angeles, Philadelphia, northern Florida, and northern and eastern Virginia. Subjects were given intelligence tests and asked to respond to several hypothetical legal situations (e.g., whether to confess to a police officer). The study found that one-third of children age 11 to 13 and one-fifth of those 14 or 15 could not understand the proceedings or help lawyers defend them.

Entrapment is not simply clever police work. A prerequisite for the entrapment defense is <u>no predisposition to commit the crime</u>.

> THE $10 BILL EXAMPLE: IS IT ENTRAPMENT?
> a. You see it lying on the ground with no way of identifying whose it is.
> b. You take it.
> c. You were not predisposed to commit a crime.
> CONCLUSION: Due to c, this is entrapment.

d. Duress

> Examples of bad behavior by Robby Robber:
> 1. Places gun to your head and says, "I'll shoot you unless you turn over the employer's bank account number or open the company safe!" Duress? YES.
> 2. Puts gun to your head and shouts, "I'll shoot you unless you break Johnny's legs!" Duress? YES.
> 3. Points his foot at your groin and yells, "I'll kick you in the groin unless you break Johnny's legs." Duress? MAYBE (how would we compare a really nasty kick to the privates versus broken legs?)
> 4. Pins a gun to your head and proclaims, "I'll shoot you unless you shoot Johnny." This is the Bibi and Bill example immediately below).
>
> Suppose that a robber takes bank teller Bibi and her co-worker, Bill, hostage. The robber gives Bibi a gun and tells Bibi that she has a choice: the robber will either shoot Bibi, or Bibi can shoot Bill. Ordinarily, duress would not work as a defense, because the threatened harm to Bibi is no greater than the harm she is supposed to inflict.

Duress occurs only when more serious, <u>imminent</u> harm is threatened to the defendant than the harm he/she was allegedly forced to commit. Harm to you has to be greater than the harm you are forced to commit.

e. Use of Reasonably Necessary Force

Justifiable self-defense concerns the right to protect one's self and others (our loved ones), especially if in a dwelling. This defense focuses on preventing a crime. There is probably no right to take deadly force on a fleeing subject, because you are not in danger.

So, when force is used, what is reasonable? Surely the following was <u>not</u>: On September 13, 2000, Craig Holtzman, 31, returned to his Norristown, Pennsylvania (suburban Philadelphia) home from a night of drinking. He took off his clothes before going to sleep and later walked into his backyard to relieve himself. Holtzman then mistakenly walked into his neighbor Paul Bellina's home basement; Holtzman thought it was his home. Bellina, age 52, did not recognize this naked intruder as his neighbor. He was justified in firing the first shot at Holtzman. But Bellina committed crimes when he chased the wounded Holtzman into another neighbor's backyard and shot him three times in the head. On June 4, 2001, Bellina pleaded guilty to voluntary manslaughter and was sentenced to 15 years in prison.

> Maury is playing basketball with his daughter Dora when angry passerby Pixie yells at them, "You're too shrimpy, and you cannot jump." Pixie starts throwing fists full of pebbles at Maury and Dora. Infuriated, Maury takes his switch-blade, charges Pixie and stabs her in the chest. While Maury is entitled to use reasonable force in self-defense and in defending another person such as Dora, Maury's force was excessive given that he used deadly force to repel something that was not life-threatening. If Pixie had been flinging buckets of hydrochloric acid, shooting bullets, or lobbing grenades, then charging with a knife would have been a reasonable response.

f. Legal Realism in Evaluating Self-Defense Allegations

What if a kid is running out of your house, dropping items he was stealing from your home? You cry out, "Stop, Thief!" But he is now climbing over the fence at the back of your yard. Can you lawfully get out your Magnum 45 and blast away because the kid still has some of your property and he is fleeing the scene?

What would a jury in many jurisdictions (e.g., North Florida, South Georgia, Lower Alabama, etc.) say? Would the jury strictly follow the law in a case against you for shooting the fleeing thief?

g. Other Defenses

Some additional, possible defenses are consent, immunity, insanity, mistake of fact or of law, and the statute of limitations.   **(see pgs. 472–476; Emerson BL)**

IV. INTENTIONAL TORTS (see pgs. 462-468; Emerson BL)

"Torts are infinitely various, not limited or confined, for there is nothing in nature but may be an instrument of mischief." Chief Justice Pratt, Kings Bench (England), <u>Chapman v. Pickersgill</u>, 95 English Reports 734, 2 Wils. Kings Bench 145 (1762).

A. Introduction

> "FROM FOOLISHNESS TO BATTERY, BEYOND JUST NEGLIGENCE TO INTENT" (1:25 long) is a YouTube video:
> https://www.youtube.com/watch?v=OUdrn4w_A6E&list=UU_TuNN4AcpdLnoIdSTLx_MA&index=47
>
> There are many lawsuits involving disagreements over music, dance, and other esthetics at bars, discos, and dance halls - Problems spill over from foolishness and perhaps "fraud" into intentional torts (such as battery)
>
> A local example would be arguments between rabidly opposed football fans that escalate into misconduct - what "fool" would wear an FSU shirt in Gainesville?!

What is "intent?" An intended wrong is, legally, far worse than is "mere" negligence. As a great American jurist wrote, *"Even a dog distinguishes between being stumbled over and being kicked."* Oliver Wendell Holmes, Jr., THE COMMON LAW 3 (1881). So if dogs can do that, certainly our laws can! Almost nothing - certainly not mere stupidity/negligence – justifies intentional physical contact upon another person – a battery.

Each type of intentional tort has different elements. All have certain recurring themes; all involve <u>an intended wrong</u> (<u>while the harm itself may not have been intended</u>). But each has a distinct definition. So, while negligence is just one type of tort, with the same four elements all of the time, for intentional torts each type is different. And, for intentional torts, punitive damages are much more likely to be awarded than for "mere" negligence.

Here are some <u>examples of intentional torts</u>:
- A drunk punches you in the nose (Battery).
- An angry person violently swings a baseball bat at you and comes very close to hitting you (Assault).
- Landlord to tenant, "I didn't tell you about the asbestos in your apartment because I thought you'd get used to it!" (Negligence, Fraud, Battery, Breach of Covenant of Habitability).
- "Oh yeah, I should have told you about the broken stair…Sorry" (Negligence).

- "I thought I told her I had herpes" (Negligence, perhaps Battery, Intentional Infliction of Mental/Emotional Distress).[148]
- Waving on a faster, car from behind - into oncoming traffic! (Battery, Fraud, Intentional Infliction of Mental/Emotional Distress).
- A truck overturns and spills gasoline that pollutes your land (Negligence, Trespass, and Strict liability re: hazardous substances).
- Children getting off school bus have worn a path over a corner of your yard (Trespass, but if done for years an easement may have been created).
- "Hey - your elephant thinks my yard is a bathroom!" (Trespass).
- A nearby country club erects rainwater deterrent around its golf course's 14th hole; the discharged water destroys your "happy petunia garden" (Trespass, Nuisance).
- An incredibly loud party (Nuisance to neighbors).
- Repeatedly telling someone that she is fat; leaving messages on her home phone, cell phone, and office answering machine telling her she is fat; having feedbags delivered to her at work; and renting a billboard along a well-travelled roadway with the person's name and saying "She's Fat"; the victim suffers extreme physical and mental anguish, misses much work, and requires much psychiatric assistance (Intentional Infliction of Mental or Emotional Distress).
- Secretly taping you and another person having sex and then, again without the other person's knowledge, distributing copies of the tape to others (Invasion of privacy (public disclosure of private facts)).
- A competing business "bugs" your office with listening devices (Trespass, Invasion of Privacy).
- A newspaper improperly identifies you as the shoplifter picked up yesterday in a local store (Defamation).
- Standing on the street corner and screaming to all passersby, "Paula P. Plaintiff is a communist, Satan-worshipping pedophile!" These are all false statements, and they cause serious harm to Paula's great reputation at work, in her neighborhood, and at her church (Slander - a type of defamation).
- A doctor improperly diagnoses your problem as stomach flu when you actually have appendicitis (Malpractice).
- A lawyer improperly advises you, causing a $10,000 loss (Malpractice).
- "Sorry, I guess those WERE my killer dogs I forgot to lock up" (Negligence; Strict Liability for keeping dangerous, wild animals).
- Dragster explodes on starting line - pieces kill a spectator (Negligence, Strict Liability, and Product Liability).

To understand the main types of intentional torts (the basic elements), we have four broad categories: (1) Interference with Property, (2) Interference with the Person, (3) Fraud, and (4) Interference with Business Relations.

B. Interference with Property

1. Four types of property-related torts **(see pgs. 465-466; Emerson BL)** are conversion, trespass, nuisance, and attractive nuisance.

Conversion is unjustified control over another's personal property. The tort of conversion is committed when a party wrongfully commits a distinct act of dominion over the property of another which is inconsistent with the owner's rights. *Dillard v. Wade*, 45 S.W.3d 848 (Ark. App. 2001).

Trespass is wrongful encroachment on, or other offense against, real or personal property

---

[148] E.g., if you have HIV you must tell your sex partners. http://www.theindychannel.com/news/22621928/detail.html

If a building's overhang extends over another's property line (although the ground floor does not), that overhanging extension is a trespass. Trespass also occurs when someone throws or places any unwanted item onto another's property (e.g., places dirt on the other person's property, shoots a bullet or arrow onto the other person's property).

Nuisance is improper use of one's own property to disturb other persons' use of their property; substantially interfering with the plaintiff's right to use and enjoy his/her property (private nuisance) or with rights common to all (public nuisance). Examples of nuisance include: Obnoxious (hence, objectionable) music, smells, and other harmful impacts (e.g., a brothel or a crack house), or – a real Florida case – a pig farmer playing music to calm his swine, but disturbing the owners of a nearby golf course. Now, zoning often helps with these land use matters, as does other statutory law. But the common law of nuisance is still available, also.

Example: A. Mazon "Jaws" Fishman loves piranhas (as his name implies). On Fishman's property is a small, man-made pond that he has stocked with piranhas. Valerie and Victor Victims are 8-year-old twins living nearby who see that no fence around the pond, and decide to take a dip. The Piranhas bite them both, and they suffer grievous injuries. That sounds as if it is likely to be attractive nuisance. That the children were trespassers is not a defense.

YOUTUBE - attractive nuisance2mins8secs is at robertwemersonufl – a vignette on attractive nuisance - swimming pools, edibles, and mulch piles. (There are special responsibilities for pool owners and for homeowners; and food preparation\inattention may create liabilities.)

Attractive nuisance is a dangerous condition, even on private property, that may constitute a nuisance because it attracts trespassers (e.g., children) unaware of the dangers. These are several examples: unsecured construction sites (big bulldozers with keys in them), outdoor trampolines (possible broken limbs), unsecure swimming pools (possible drowning), and unfenced trees (climbing and falling). To protect oneself, property owners should: fence in and otherwise keep people out of swimming pools; remove doors from old refrigerators (e.g., keep children from getting trapped); remove keys from motor vehicles; lock up any firearms; keep fruit trees picked/harvested and the property barricaded (e.g., to prevent people from sneaking in and harming themselves in search of fruit).

ENVIRONMENTAL LAW, a YOUTUBE video – "Environmental Law4mins40secs" – is at robertwemersonufl.

Welcome to the environmental world of Professor Robert Emerson and his friends, friend monkeys, friend parrot, friend llama, friend panda bear, and friend porpoise.

Environmental regulation was present before the 1960's, but this type of regulation was essentially a very private type of regulation. In other words, you as a landowner had a right to pursue someone who you believed was violating your right to enjoy and to use your property. It could be, for instance, through pollution. This might be a form of trespass, someone intruding onto your property or discharging something onto your property, or it could well be simply a nuisance, that is a person's use of his own property in a way that disturbs your rightful expectation to use and enjoy your own property. There have also been protections for landowners through zoning regulations, and again, in a way, this could constitute a form of environmental protection on behalf of landowners who feel that their property interests have been agreed. The problem was that by the 1960s, with the growth of the environmental movement, the notion of the earth as a precious body being violated by mankind's own pollution, were not very protective on a systemic fashion, so environmental laws were enacted.

Chief among all these laws is, in essence, the law that created the Environmental Protection Agency and authorized it to implement and enforce most of the federal environmental protection laws. At the state level there are comparable agencies that attempt to protect our natural resources. The goal behind these laws is of course to deter events that degrade the environment and also to implement standards for actually improving the environment. The goal is to set up a system which systematically attacks pollution and other degradations in a way that private lawsuits may not be able to accomplish.

Having said that, though, I must acknowledge that lawsuits are still a primary instrument of plaintiffs, of environmental groups, of others and often these people will, in effect, say 'trust me, I'm a lawyer'. I am simply - as a lawyer on behalf of Earth First or whatever, implementing the federal laws. We are doing what needs to be done through lawsuits because the EPA or other agencies are understaffed, or underfunded, or sometimes they are simply refusing to carry out the policy that they were directed to carry out by our private initiative.

The counter to that is, of course, that these lawsuits are often leading to ineffective measures. They are not cost-effective, they are forcing landowners and businesses to do things which really are not the best method for dealing with pollution, for protecting the environment, and that is the criticism that is often bandied about. We certainly will not see the end of lawsuits anytime in the near future, and it is an area for continual debate as to what really is the best method for improving our environment, for staving off pollution, and for otherwise dealing with the problems in this area.

C. Interference with the Person (see pgs. 462-464; Emerson BL)

1. Assault

Assault is the reasonable apprehension of imminent unjustified (harmful or offensive) contact. The expectation of harm is sufficient for a court to hold that an assault has occurred <u>if</u> the plaintiff was reasonable in imagining what he/she thought was going to happen. For example, when a defendant brandishes a "weapon," does that supposed weapon reasonably seem to be a real switchblade? A real chainsaw? A real gun?

About switchblades – these knives are illegal to carry in 37 states; and most states ban their sale unless they are manufactured in that state. Also, U.S. customs law prohibits the import of switchblade knives. But sales are soaring, typically over the Internet.

2. Battery

Battery is an unjustified contact: the contact itself does not have to be harmful, just offensive. For example, an unwanted kiss is generally deemed to be a battery.

<u>Here, arising out of a battery, is an example of the intertwining of Negligence Law and Criminal Law</u> (Employer accountability for the allegedly negligent acts of employees in not complying with third persons' criminal demands?). In a 1995 California appellate decision, *Kentucky Fried Chicken of California Inc. v. Superior Court,*, 14 Cal.4th 814 (Cal. App. 1997), the court found that businesses owe customers a duty to comply with the demands of robbers. In rejecting the *KFC* decision, a Florida appellate court held that a restaurant customer who was shot by a robber during a hold-up could not recover damages despite his argument that the restaurant employee failed to protect him properly. The Illinois Supreme Court likewise has held that imposing a duty on businesses to surrender to hostage-takers would only punish the blameless and encourage robbers to take hostages. While most courts have ruled against liability (the Florida and Illinois approach), the issue remains open in a number of states (i.e., no court rulings yet).

> Assault Compared to Battery
> Assault involves apprehension, while battery requires contact. Cory Creep sneaks up on Sleeping Sylvia and kisses her. That is, if unwanted behavior, a battery. If Sylvia woke up five seconds before the foul deed was to occur, and she sees Cory's creepy lips coming toward her, that is assault. She runs away, to avoid battery, but assault (the apprehension) did take place.
> One Can Claim Assault Without Battery or Battery Without Assault
> Battery example: Static electricity babies

> Assault example: With what is he about to attack me? What does the alleged victim apprehend?

3. False Arrest
False arrest is detention of plaintiff, without his consent, under falsely asserted authority (e.g., an insurance claims adjuster pretends to be a cop in order to get information from someone).

4. False Imprisonment
False imprisonment is the wrongful use of force, physical barriers, or threats to restrain plaintiff's movements.

If <u>not</u> a merchant, you had better be right when you detain someone. For merchants, an "honest mistake" may excuse an erroneous detention.

a. Merchants' Protection Statutes
To assist shop owners in fighting shoplifting, most states have passed merchants' protection statutes. To apply, there must be <u>probable cause</u> (reasonable grounds) <u>and reasonable confinement</u> - place, time, etc. These statutes give to merchants limited (not an absolute) right to detain, more than just a citizen's right to detain.

<u>What if the store does not let the detained person go until he/she signs a release?</u> (That is not permissible. One can ask the person to sign, but once one no longer has cause to hold a person, one must release a person even if that person will not sign a release.)

<u>What if the store personnel detain a person, but say that they cannot do anything else until the manager returns from lunch? No, that is not reasonable.</u>

What if store signs say: "No students Allowed" or "No more than 2 students Allowed" (profile, etc. -> opening up the store to a legal challenge)? That may show that the store personnel are predisposed against young people. So, if a young person is erroneously detained, these circumstances (e.g., the signs) may support the contention that the store personnel were biased – that they failed to look at the young person as an individual and simply – without probable cause – detained him because he is young (or a minority, etc.).

> "TROUBLESOME TOOTHPASTE: A SHOPPER'S REAL-LIFE NIGHTMARE" (Skit is 4:24 long, and then discussion is 13:28 long) – this is on YouTube:
> https://www.youtube.com/watch?v=jF4y97nvnxg&list=UU_TuNN4AcpdLnoIdSTLx_MA
>
> a. Anna buys toothpaste at one store, without getting a receipt.
>
> b. She later is detained at another store for alleged shoplifting.
>
> c. "Stop, Thief!"
>
> d. Battery? A privilege? Use of reasonable force?
>
> e. False arrest? What authority?
>
> f. False imprisonment? Reasonable detention?
>
> g. Damages.

b. An Example: The Florida Law
Florida Statutes § 812.015(3)) permits a law enforcement officer, farmer, merchant, or merchant's employee to detain a person suspected of unlawfully taking farm produce or store merchandise. There must be <u>probable cause</u> to believe that the items were taken unlawfully and that the items may be recovered by taking the person into custody. Detention may only be for a reasonable time and only for the purpose of recovering the produce/merchandise or for prosecution (a law enforcement

officer is to be called to the scene immediately). Florida's statute also specifies that the activation (e.g., buzzing noise, closing of doors) of an inventory control device constitutes probable cause to detain a person, if the merchant posted notification to customers about the use of such devices.

D. Malicious Prosecution (see pg. 468; Emerson BL)

> *"If a man accuses a man, and charge him with murder, but cannot convict him, the accuser shall be put to death."* A law in Hammurabi's Code.

Modern law is not so severe towards false or unproven allegations. Lawsuits for malicious prosecution are an option. An example would be the ultimately dropped case for rape brought in 2006 against three Duke University lacrosse players.[149]

E. Intentional Infliction of Mental or Emotional Distress

There is a relatively new tort involving interference with the person: intentional infliction of mental or emotional distress. It is a tort for which one could win punitive damages – e.g., an airline pilot's outrageous "joke" – indicating an imminent crash - that frightens and even physically traumatizes some of the airline's passengers.

Intentional infliction of mental or emotional distress is a 20th Century Tort. It only covers extreme, outrageous behavior, with physical manifestations of real harm. E.g., the plaintiff needed psychiatric counseling, suffered ulcers, missed work, etc. Because the behavior must be outrageous, it is usually insufficient to complain of just one or two bad acts; it generally is much better for a plaintiff to point to a pattern – a series of planned bad acts (perhaps an organized campaign).

This tort is usually not the focal point of the plaintiff's case if there are good arguments to be made for more "traditional" intentional torts, such as assault, battery, false imprisonment, defamation, or fraud. Because it must be outrageous and involve physical manifestations of harm, this tort claim is still relatively rarely asserted.

An example of how this tort is so narrowly interpreted is the case, "Little Amazons Attack Boys." In *Fudge v. Penthouse International, Ltd.*, 840 F.2d 1012 (1988), Penthouse magazine had published a photograph of several elementary school girls with a statement that the school principal had segregated the boys and girls at recess. The title of the photo (which was not obscene - the kids were clothed) was, "Little Amazons Attack Boys," and there was some mildly offensive language. The trial court's dismissal of the children's and their parents' lawsuit for intentional infliction of emotional distress was upheld on appeal because publication of the photo and the article was insufficiently "extreme and outrageous."

The term, "emotional distress," covers a wide range of human suffering, including: fright and shock at the time of an accident; humiliation due to disfigurement or disability; unhappiness and depression over not being able to return to the activities of one's prior life (e.g., inability to work, play sports, or have sex); anxiety about the future; and anger over the vicissitudes of life. The law awards compensation for this kind of harm in a number of ways. It permits an action for intentional or reckless infliction of severe emotional distress (the tort of outrage). It also allows emotional distress damages to be recovered as parasitic damages in cases of physical injury. In addition, mental suffering is frequently treated as an element of recoverable damages in connection with certain non-physical injury torts, such as defamation, invasion of privacy, and assault.

A Joke Gone Bad? A Lifeguard at the Pool

---

[149] "Abuse of process" is wrongful use of a court process. *See* Robert W. Emerson, *Business Law*. NY: Barron's Educational Series (6th ed., 2015), at 467.

> This could be more than just trespass, let alone negligence! Intentional infliction of mental/emotional distress, as one thinks about how he must have done that before.
>
> A Radio Contest
>
> Would the following be intentional infliction of mental or emotional distress? And/or defamation or invasion of privacy (discussed shortly)?
>
> Twenty-year-old Adrienne Breidigan of Naples, Florida on June 19, 2002 sued disc jockey Bruce Da Moose and the parent company of radio station WBTT in Florida's Circuit Court. Asleep with the flu, Breidigan was awakened around 6:45 p.m. on June 12, 2002 when her cell phone rang. In his prank call to Breidigan, the DJ allegedly identified himself as a Fort Myers doctor treating Breidigan's ex-boyfriend; he told Breidigan that her ex-boyfriend had been diagnosed with an incurable, potentially life-threatening sexually-transmitted disease, and she might have been infected. The DJ broadcast Breidigan's full name and Breidigan cried. Only when the caller started to ask graphic questions about her sex life did Breidigan suspect a hoax. Breidigan, a licensed bondsman and private investigator (she is a co-owner of Collier County Bail Bonds), claimed that the prank was set up by one of her friends, that the statements made by the DJ were untrue, and that her reputation may have been harmed.
>
> Does the fact that at first Breidigan laughed and felt relief when she discovered it was a "joke" mean that a case for intentional infliction of mental or emotional distress is undermined? Adrienne Breidigan's suit against DJ Bruce Perry ("Bruce Da Moose") and the parent company, Clear Channel Broadcasting, owners of Fort Myers' WBTT, was settled on January 10, 2003 for $100,000. Specifics of the agreement were confidential. Attorneys for Clear Channel declined to say anything about the settlement, including whether the station admitted wrongdoing. The wrongful behavior, though, clearly may be considered an intentional infliction of mental or emotional distress.

F. Negligent Infliction of Emotional Distress?

This tort has been recognized as a lawful claim in most states, but it has been quite restricted in its scope. One reason for the reluctance to allow these claims is the realization that plaintiffs would be tempted to miscast what is really an intentional tort – willful infliction of mental or emotional distress – into a case of negligence because only in the latter situation may liability insurance be available.

Recovery for negligent infliction of emotional distress will never be permitted unless the distress is severe, which is ordinarily judged by an objective standard. In *Lewis v. Westinghouse Electric Corp.*, 487 N.E.2d 1071 (Ill. App. Ct. 1985), the court held that an ordinary person would not have suffered severe distress from being trapped in an elevator for forty minutes. Consequently, the plaintiff's claim was dismissed.

Most courts hold that negligent harm to property, by itself, is an insufficient predicate for an award of emotional-distress damages, at least if the harm occurs outside the plaintiff's presence and is the result of mere negligence.

G. Defamation

> "A good name smells sweeter than the finest ointment."   THE BIBLE, ECCLESIASTES 7:1.

This tort often overlaps with other areas. One example would be a lawsuit by a former employee against his former employer because of adverse references. The suit could be on these grounds: defamation, blacklisting (e.g., antitrust violations, such as boycotts), discrimination, invasion of privacy, interference with contract or prospective contract (e.g., with employment), and intentional infliction of mental or emotional distress. Thirty-six states, including Florida, have enacted laws protecting from civil liability those employers who in good faith provided job references to others. "Job Reference Shield Laws," www.crimcheck.com/resources/job-reference-shield-laws.htm

Defamation is either slander (purely oral) or libel (written or otherwise recorded).

Elements of defamation include:

(1) "Publication" to another person - put forth, transmitted (not necessarily in writing) to a third person (someone other than the plaintiff or the defendant);
(2) False statement of fact (not mere opinion) –
"I believe Joe is a loathsome scum sucker" (opinion), compared to "Last Thursday, while walking past a pond, I saw Joe loathsomely sucking scum from a pond." (fact statement, whether true or not); and
(3) Harm to reputation (held up to contempt, ridicule, hatred).

1. Defamation Examples: The Second of Three Elements - False Statement of Fact

Gator Growl Program "Joke"
In late August 1999, Florida Blue Key agreed to pay an undisclosed settlement to a former University of Florida student, Jen Cardon, who sued the UF honorary society for damaging her reputation in its 1998 Gator Growl program. Cardon filed a suit in the circuit court for Alachua County (Florida's 8th Circuit) after reading the phrase, "I've never had sex with Jen Cardon," on a page of jokes in the printed program for the homecoming pep rally. The suit claimed the joke implied that Cardon was a "sexually promiscuous woman."
The society's president for fall 1999, Ashley Moody, said that Blue Key settled the suit so members could start the new school year with a clean slate, not because the organization was at fault.

2. Defamation Examples: The Third of Three Elements - Harm to Reputation

For most alleged defamation, a plaintiff must introduce evidence to show that the supposedly defamatory statement harmed the plaintiff (slander or libel *per quod*). But some statements, in and of themselves, are presumed to be so injurious that, if false and published, the third and final element of defamation need not be proven: Damages are assumed (this is slander or libel *per se* - **see pg. 751; Emerson BL**).

Libel suits filed by fired employees against their former employers account for about one-third of all defamation actions.

Example: A web posting states that George was responsible for a poor product rollout – a form of Employee Disparagement

Fred, Ed and George all work for the same company. George is an engineering manager for a new product. Ed posts on Fred's Facebook page a statement disparaging both George and the new product.

What if it were not a post, but email exchanges between Fred and Ed AND it was for a performance review of George. Does this condition eliminate defamation? Does Fred have qualified privilege?

Emails based on a subject in which all parties have an interest are protected by a qualified privilege – so defamation would be difficult to prove, even if George were fired.
For emails, when would the email be considered defamation?
It was published, but was George harmed?
It would be quite different if the e-mail were sent to the whole company.
George could have a case if he proved defamation per se: the e-mail accused George of a serious criminal offense, has a loathsome disease, abuses alcohol or other drugs, is insane, is incompetent or dishonest in his profession, or is unchaste (especially if George were – like the great writer George Sand - actually a woman).[150] George could have a case for defamation per se if these posts (clearly "published") were provably false.

---

[150] This is a relic of old-fashioned double standards about sex: that a woman willingly engaged in sexual relations may be considered promiscuous for the very behavior that earns applause (from some) or at least little criticism for a man.

Watch out for E-Mail Chains! And "Reply to All." What if the e-mail made it to the inbox of recruiter? In this case the company opens itself up to a defamation suit. George would still have to prove his case but courts are sympathetic to former employees that are prevented from pursuing their profession by slanderous or libel statements.

Two Quotations

"Reputation, reputation, reputation! Oh, I have lost my reputation! I have lost the immortal part of myself, and what remains is bestial."
William Shakespeare, 1564-1616, in Othello, Act II, Scene 3.

Basketball player Charles Barkley: "I heard Tonya Harding [the skater who hired people to bash the knees of her competitor, Nancy Kerrigan] is calling herself the Charles Barkley of figure skating. I was going to sue her for defamation of character, but then I realized I have no character."

---

3. Constitutional Law and Defamation Allegations: A Higher Threshold for Plaintiffs to Meet When They Are Public Officials or Figures

There is a constitutional law concern about fears of defamation actions leading to a "chilling" of free speech. The worry is that the press will pull back from undertaking its function of governmental oversight and investigative and reporting work. To counter this concern, the courts have created a harsher standard for defamation plaintiffs to meet when they are public officials or public figures - the very people about whom the press should be especially ready and willing to undertake excellent, fearless works of journalism. This standard is not simply proof of a falsehood, but also of *malice* (malicious falsehood).[151]

The *Bartnicki* Case: Public Issues Versus Privacy Issues

A recurring issue is the right to privacy versus the right to disseminate information about public issues. In *Bartnicki v. Vopper*, 532 U.S. 514 (2001), the U.S. Supreme Court ruled 6-3 that, "In this case, privacy concerns give way when balanced against the interest in publishing matters of public importance."

The case involved collective-bargaining negotiations during 1992 and 1993 between the Pennsylvania State Education Association, a teachers union, and the Wyoming Valley West High School board. In May 1993, the union's acting chief negotiator, Gloria Bartnicki, and Anthony Kane Jr., the union's president, had a lengthy cell-phone conversation about the talks.

Some months later, after a collective bargaining settlement was reached, a radio commentator broadcast a tape of the conversation. Commentator Frederick Vopper, who was generally a union critic, had received the tape from another union critic, Jack Yocum, who said it had been dropped anonymously in his mailbox.

Bartnicki and Kane sued Vopper and alleged that Vopper's broadcast broke state and federal wiretap laws by broadcasting a tape he knew - or should have known - was made illegally. Vopper countered that he had nothing to do with the illegal interception and, in any case, his broadcast was protected by the First Amendment.

Writing the majority opinion, Justice John Paul Stevens said the court was addressing a narrow question: May the government punish the publication of information legally obtained by the publisher, but from someone who obtained it illegally?

Addressing one of the arguments supporting the wiretap law - that it would discourage illegal wiretapping - Justice Stevens concluded: "It would be quite remarkable to hold that speech by a law-

---

[151] When the issue is one of punitive damages, then, for all defamation plaintiffs (even those who are not public officials or figures), malice must be proven.

abiding possessor of information can be suppressed in order to deter conduct by a non-law-abiding third party."

Writing in dissent, Chief Justice William Rehnquist, joined by Clarence Thomas and Antonin Scalia, came down on the side of privacy. The majority's opinion will diminish the First Amendment by "chilling the speech" of Americans who rely on "electronic technology to communicate," Rehnquist wrote.

4. Ethics and Defamation

Ethical issues associated with strongly derogatory comments: Just because one legally can say some things, does that mean one <u>should</u> say those things? At an early age, are not most children taught that sometimes a "little white lie" beats telling the complete truth? (E.g., "No, you don't look overweight"; "You look younger than ever"; "Your child seems so smart.") Furthermore, remember what your mother or others often advised: "If you cannot say something nice about someone, just don't say anything at all." (If people listened to Mom, there would be a lot more silence! And less need for lawyers.)

5. Defenses to Defamation

The usual <u>Defenses to Defamation</u> are truth and privileged statements.

If a representation is true, then it simply cannot be defamatory (falsehood is an element of the tort of defamation).

<u>Privilege</u> is a protection for "core" judicial/legislative functions: the statements of judges and lawyers <u>in the courtroom</u> (although lawyers may be in contempt of court for what they do or say in court), and the statements of legislators while <u>in the legislature</u> (e.g., in Congress debating a bill, but <u>not</u> while appearing on a television talk show). Even if a judge has a tirade as he/she gives his/her opinion, even if a lawyer's closing statement is "over the top" or outrageous, we do not want to "chill" that speech. Thus, the statements are absolutely protected, even if we prove that the judge or lawyer knew they were false. Indeed, this complete protection, entitling the legislator, lawyer, or judge to say or write anything in those limited core functions without fear of a libel or slander suit, is to help prevent any chilling of the person's vital role. Note: he or she still might be subject to other sanctions for a deliberately or recklessly false statement, such as the trial judge's holding the lawyer in contempt or a legislative or judicial body taking measures against its own member.

<u>The Legislative Privilege:</u> Not Present for Sen. Proxmire's Golden Fleece Award

Hutchinson v. Proxmire, 443 U.S. 111 (1979), is a famous case involving the privilege for legislators. There, the Supreme Court upheld a defamation judgment against Senator William F. Proxmire (D-Wis.), who served from 1957 to 1988. Proxmire, with his "Golden Fleece of the Month Award" for government waste, had publicized the federal funding of Professor Ronald Hutchinson's research on animal emotional behavior, such as the clenching of jaws upon exposure to aggravating stressful stimuli. The National Aeronautics and Space Agency (NASA) and the Navy were interested in the potential of this research for resolving problems associated with confining humans in close quarters for extended periods of time in space and undersea exploration.

The U.S. Supreme Court, in an 8-1 decision, held: (1) the Constitution's speech or debate clause did not protect transmittal of the allegedly defamatory material in Proxmire's press releases and newsletters, and (2) Hutchinson was not a "public figure" so as to make a showing of actual malice necessary.

In contrast to voting and preparing committee reports, which are part of Congress' function to inform itself (and thus absolutely immunized from defamation claims), newsletters and press releases are primarily means of informing those outside the legislative forum and simply represent the views and will of a single Member. The Court stated, "A speech by Proxmire in the Senate would be wholly immune and would be available to other Members of Congress and the public in the Congressional Record. But

> neither the newsletters nor the press release was 'essential to the deliberations of the Senate' and neither was part of the deliberative process."[152]

The "telegraph" privilege has been extended, sometimes, to Internet-service providers because they perform no editorial functions (not like publishing a letter to the editor – there, a newspaper could be accountable). For example, in *Lunney v. Prodigy Communications Corp.*, 94 N.Y.2d at 242, cert. denied, 529 U.S. 1098 (2000), New York's highest court held that the trial judge should have granted a summary judgment in defendant Prodigy's favor. Alexander Lunney, a teenager in Westchester County, New York, sued after someone opened a bogus Prodigy account in Lunney's name and e-mailed a death threat to his Boy Scout troop leader. To the relief of Internet providers, the high court affirmed that e-mail service providers are not responsible for the messages sent by their subscribers. "Prodigy's role in transmitting e-mail is akin to that of a telephone company, which one neither wants nor expects to superintend the content of its subscribers' conversation," the Court wrote.

6. British and European Law on Defamation

British libel law is much more pro-plaintiff than American law. European law generally, however, may be more in line with American defamation law.

Under British libel, allegedly defamatory statements are presumed false and defendants must prove they are true. Also, public officials or figures need not show malice. In the United States, plaintiffs, to win, must prove the allegedly defamatory statement was false; and, again, plaintiffs who are public officials or public figures must show malice.

However, the European Court of Human Rights, in Strasbourg, France, in July 1995 overturned the largest British damages award for libel. It was $2.4 million that Lord Aldington won from Count Nicolai Tolstoy over a March 1987 pamphlet written by Tolstoy and distributed by a co-defendant, Nigel Watts, alleging that Aldington, a brigadier in occupied Austria after World War II, knowingly sent more than 70,000 Cossacks and anti-Tito Yugoslavs to their deaths in Communist hands. The Human Rights Court agreed with Tolstoy that the scale of the British High Court jury award in 1989 violated Tolstoy's freedom of expression, as guaranteed in the European Convention on Human Rights. So European law is more like American, pro-defendant defamation law and may trump British, pro-plaintiff defamation law.

7. Internet Service Providers

Cases also are brought against media or Internet Service Providers (ISPs), with more chances to achieve compensation against the ISP. The business response, to protect itself, has been better compliance with more privacy laws, upgraded usage policies in business, legal disclaimers in websites, and to emphasize, whenever possible, that ISPs and e-Media servers are different from brick and mortar media. Under the Communications Decency Act (1996), ISPs do not qualify as publishers of third party content.

> **Torts Come and Torts Go: New or Defunct Torts**
> A brooding, jurisprudential question always lurks in tort law: Are there some other, new torts that the courts (or legislatures) should recognize? One that courts so far have declined is "Malparenting."
> <u>Some now defunct or close-to-defunct torts</u> are criminal conversation and alienation of affections ("You lothario! You stole her affections!). As of October 2011, only eight states still recognized criminal conversation and alienation of affection claims: Hawaii, Illinois, Mississippi, New Hampshire, New Mexico, North Carolina, South Dakota, and Utah.

---

[152] 443 U.S. at 130.

H. Invasion of Privacy (see pgs. 463-464; Emerson BL)

Invasion of privacy is a 20th-21st Century Tort. An extremely influential law review article advocated a right of privacy to meet changes in technology, which then concerned newspapers and photography. Two Harvard law professors, Charles Warren and Louis D. Brandeis, wrote: "The Right to Privacy," 4 HARVARD LAW REVIEW 193 (1890), http://groups.csail.mit.edu/mac/classes/6.805/articles/privacy/Privacy_brand_warr2.html.

Unlike in defamation, for invasion of privacy, truth is not a defense. But here, honor – or damage to it – still matters;[153] and intrusions may be a tort.

"It is perfectly monstrous the way people go about nowadays saying things behind one's back that are absolutely true." *Oscar Wilde (1854-1900), Anglo-Irish playwright and author (words of the character Lord Henry, in the novel, The Picture of Dorian Gray).*

. **INVASION OF PRIVACY: CONTEXT & WARNINGS (BALLET AND LOCKER ROOMS)**
Context Matters, for Time, Place, and Subject
Ballet

Context really matters. In ballet, the male dancer holds the ballerina high in the air, holding her in an area usually viewed as rather private. Yet it is done live in front of hundreds or perhaps thousands of observers who even applaud what has taken place. It is quite another thing to come up to someone on the street and try to hoist someone over your head holding him/her in that dancin' way!

A Child's Perspective (versus that of an Adult)
Grandma Nana (trying to shut the bathroom door) - "Laura, ladies like privacy."
3-year-old Laura (coming in, anyway) - "Yes, but little girls like to watch."

---

1. Computers, the Government, and Private Companies

Perhaps the most serious legal problem created by computers is their encroachment upon the individual's right to privacy. Through the use of national and worldwide networks, computers have provided numerous businesses and governments with the means to gain a large amount of information about many individuals.

a. Government Intrusion on an Individual's Privacy

Just because government authorities violate a citizen's right of privacy does not mean that the citizen is entitled to damages. For example, Ru Paster sued his college, Gonzaga University, for disclosing to the state teacher certification agency that Paster had been accused of date-rape. Gonzaga had thus refused to issue a "moral character" certificate that Paster needed to get a state teaching license. (That was even though both Paster and the alleged victim denied the allegations against Paster, which were investigated when a college employee heard a third student imply that Paster had sexually assaulted the "victim.")

---

[153] "The purest treasure mortal times afford
Is spotless reputation; that away,
Men are but gilded loam or painted clay.
A Jewel in a ten-times-barr'd-up chest
Is a bold spirit in a loyal breast.
Mine honour is my life; both grow in one;
Take honour from me, and my life is done." William Shakespeare, *Richard II*.
  One may contend that honor is focused on what is within, while any damages award concerns the objectively manifested outward self – the harm to reputation – i.e., what people can glean, can see when they look at or hear about you. As Lady Macbeth said in Shakespeare's *Macbeth*, "Out, out, damned spot – out, I say."

Paster sued Gonzaga for allegedly violating a 1974 privacy law (the federal Family Educational Rights and Privacy Act) by releasing this personal information about Paster without his permission. A jury ordered Gonzaga to pay Paster about $1.1 million for defamation and other claims, including some $450,000 for violating the 1974 law. That grew to nearly $2 million with interest, and the Washington State Supreme Court upheld the verdict.

But, on appeal of that decision, in a 7-2 ruling, *Gonzaga University v. Doe,* 536 U.S. 273 (2002), the U.S. Supreme Court held that the privacy act gives "no specific, individually enforceable rights." For the Court, Chief Justice William Rehnquist wrote that only the federal government can punish a school for violating the law, with a cutoff in federal funding.

Gonzaga conceded that it erred in telling the state agency about the allegations against Paster. And it still had to pay Paster for the damages accorded to him under the defamation and related state law claims. But the Supreme Court's opinion meant that Gonzaga need not pay Paster the $450,000 plus interest awarded under the 1974 federal privacy law.

b. Private Companies' Privacy Policies

A rapidly increasing number of companies now have CPOs (Chief Privacy Officers). A CPO's skills should include: understanding of law and (typically) a background in regulatory compliance, familiarity with security technology, ability at public relations, and capacity to navigate various departments within an organization.

2. Criminal Context and Possible Invasion of Privacy

The 4th Amendment: Search, Seizures, and Probable Cause

"The right of the people to be secure in their persons, houses, papers, and effects, against unreasonable searches and seizures, shall not be violated, and no Warrants shall issue, but upon probable cause, supported by Oath or affirmation, and particularly describing the place to be searched, and the persons or things to be seized."

<u>Searches and seizures</u>: Generally, warrants are needed for both searches and arrests.

Warrants are issued upon <u>Probable Cause</u> - Not definite proof, but <u>more than "You Look Like Trouble."</u> One needs more than a hunch, a gut feeling that you cannot articulate. But random or systematic searches may be okay. For example, in *Illinois v. Caballes,* 543 U.S. 405 (2005), in a 6-2 decision, the Court ruled that it is constitutional for police to use drug-sniffing dogs to check stopped cars whose drivers have given police no particular reason to suspect illegal activity.

BALANCING TEST: SOCIETY'S INTERESTS VS. INDIVIDUAL RIGHTS
"IN SEARCH OF . . . A BULLET IN THE GUT *(based on actual events)"* – would that be a constitutional *search*? At http://www.youtube.com/watch?v=WmofPuA5ydI
- *skit featuring a shopkeeper, a customer, a dog (very briefly), a robber, some violence, a hospital patient, a doctor, and a police detective.*

a. Facts: <u>Not</u> medically necessary to remove bullet. Police want to extract it as evidence.

b. Constitutional Law: Hair, blood sample, and handwriting – compelling their submission does not violate the 5th Amendment. But compelled <u>testimony</u> does (a violation of one's right not to be compelled to testify against oneself).

c. Defendant's argument: The balance of interests sides with the defendant; prosecutors can use other evidence, but not force a bullet extraction.

Bullet in chest – Decide not to remove the Bullet

- **State seeks Search Warrant of Suspect's Stomach—**
- **Defenses against the Surgery**
- **5th Amendment?—No; this amendment is a testimonial privilege, about words.** It is NOT about physical traits--- fingernails, blood, semen, hair

  - Even a handwriting sample can be required, but not "I am the murderer"
  - E.g. Patsy Ramsey (born Dec. 1956 - died June 2006) gave about five such samples re her murdered 6-year-old beauty queen daughter, JonBenet Ramsey (who was murdered in 1996).

- **4th Amendment— Probable Cause, Privacy issues**

Example: Imagine a man talking on the phone, in a low voice: "Hmmm, baby, that was so good last night. I haven't had something like that in a long, long, long time."

The man pauses, then laughs as if he knows a dirty secret to which no one else but the two on the phone are privy.

He then continues to speak: "I love how you spiced it up, like you never did before. Just thinking about it makes me want it again."

Licking his lips, he says, "And the taste – it felt like it melted in my mouth and I wanted it over, and over, and over again."

Now smiling broadly, the man says, "When all was said and done, I was exhausted and tired like never before. I slept like a baby… with a big fat smile on my face."

Talk about a hot topic! Sounds risky, sounds dirty, and sounds like something you would only want to say to your "honey" (spouse, girlfriend, boyfriend, significant other). But you might sound the same if your loved one prepared a perfect turkey dinner! How would you feel if someone eavesdropped on your conversation and immediately assumed you are just plain kinky? What if you were a schoolteacher or otherwise worked around children? This would seem to be an invasion of privacy is someone takes this private conversation and publishes it or otherwise uses it against the speaker. On the other hand, if this conversation did take place in the presence of third parties, who drew reasonable inferences from what they heard, then that would be "probable cause" for reasonable actions to deal with the conversation – for example, to tell a schoolteacher to not have conversations like that at work, which may be misconstrued!

The totality of evidence: In *United States v. Arvizu*, 534 U.S. 266 (2002), the U.S. Supreme Court unanimously held that a border patrol officer had probable cause to stop Ralph Arvizu's van (which had in it 128 pounds of marijuana). For the Court, Chief Justice Rehnquist wrote that while each of Arvizu's actions, such as not looking directly at the border patrol agent as he drove by, could be interpreted as innocent behavior, "taken together, we believe they sufficed to form a particularized and objective basis" for stopping the van.

Comparative Law: Searches and Seizures

While the United States, Canada, and some other nations ordinarily require that warrants must be preceded by the approval of judicial authorities, other countries (e.g. China, Italy, and South Africa) permit warrants simply to be issued by prosecutors or the police. Not in the United States but in many nations (e.g., Argentina, China, France, Israel, Russia), during the search of a dwelling, witnesses are required. Again, not in the United States but, in a number of nations (e.g., Argentina, England, France), searches may *not* - absent special circumstances — occur at night.

3. Employers Spying on Their Employees

Employers may monitor employees' job performance without being engaged in an unconstitutional "search"[154] or the tort of invasion of privacy. Clearly, since workers can be disciplined, demoted or fired based on poor job performance, that performance can, within reason,[155] be monitored. It is the prediction of bad work or higher employer costs, based upon tests or other corporate "spying," that is harder for some legislatures, courts, and individuals to condone. Workers are successfully suing employers who knowingly listen to workers' personal phone calls or who engage in otherwise unduly intrusive behavior. An ordinarily acceptable purpose for employers to engage in surveillance methods is to: (1) ensure that employees not carry out illegal activities; (2) deter disgruntled or dishonest workers from passing along confidential information; or (3) measure productivity and quality.

As for firing an employee because of his/her off-the-job activities (e.g., smoking, drinking, sky-diving, living with someone of the opposite sex without being married to him/her), presently the tort of invasion of privacy - while growing in use and success - still is not used as much by fired employees as are marriage discrimination status, lifestyle protection status, and Title VII's protection against religious discrimination. Over 30 states have enacted some version of "off-the-job privacy protection laws." And some companies have adopted their own codes of privacy. There are private free speech concerns, e-mail protection issues, and other privacy problems and possible legislative reforms that still have been addressed only sporadically in some states and by some employers.

4. Four Different Ways to Make a Civil Case for Invasion of Privacy:

The four ways are public disclosure of private facts, false light, intrusion upon private life, and unauthorized appropriation of name or likeness.

a. Public Disclosure of Private Facts (must be outrageous)

There is often a question of conduct. Did the plaintiff agree to the behavior? How much expectation does the plaintiff have that his/her behavior will be kept out of the public eye, and how reasonable is his/her expectation, given the circumstances?

Suppose that an ex-spouse tells others that his/her spouse cheated on taxes 20 years ago. That is not really pertinent, unless he/she is running for public office, or set to be a corporate comptroller. Does the ex-spouse have a privacy interest? Yes, especially if his/her arrest/conviction is now under seal or if it was removed from the records because of time lapse.

Another example is a large sign in a store stating that a customer is a deadbeat. That is not for a legitimate public purpose - preventing more crime - but to humiliate the customer. A claim could very well lead to the store's liability to and punitive damages to the customer.

And here is a third example: A man's frequent searching of internet adult porn sites on his own time and his own computer, is more likely to be given some expectation of privacy than if the searches were done on government owned or employer-monitored computers while at work, let alone if the searches were of child porn sites (especially searches by a teacher, coach, or someone else supervising children).

---

[154] Although the Constitution's 4th Amendment comes into play only when government actions threaten an individual's "reasonable expectations of privacy" (*Terry v. Ohio*, 392 U.S. 1, 9 (1968)), developments under this Constitutional standard may shed some light on social expectations recognized in lawsuits alleging invasion of privacy. After all, Fourth Amendment threshold tests have asked: (1) did the Defendant subjectively expect privacy, and (2) is that expectation "one that society is prepared to recognize as 'reasonable.'" *Katz v. United States*, 389 U.S. 347, 361 (1967) (Harlan, J., concurring). In a Fourth Amendment challenge to an employer's search of an employee's desk and file cabinets, the Supreme Court held that an employee had a reasonable expectation of privacy when the employee did not share the desk or file cabinets, had occupied his office for more than 17 years, and had kept personal materials in his office. *O'Connor v. Ortega*, 480 U.S. 709, 718-719 (1987).

[155] The employer's having an acceptable purpose does not necessarily mean that its methods for attaining that purpose are permitted.

Finally, consider the case of *Sipple v. Chronicle Publishing Co.* 154 Cal. App. 3d 1040, 201 Cal. Rptr. 665 **(**1984) concerned Oliver ("Bill") Sipple, an ex-marine, who, in San Francisco on September 23, 1975, lunged at Sara Jane Moore. Sipple may have deflected Moore's gun and saved Pres. Gerald Ford, the target of this would-be assassin. At the very least, Sipple's quick thinking may have saved Pres. Ford from additional shots. Sipple was already a politically active and well-known gay man in the community, and his homosexuality became part of the world-wide story about his heroism. Sipple sued the San Francisco Chronicle for revealing what Sipple wanted to keep private; but Sipple lost because he had become a public figure and questions about his character were deemed newsworthy. The court noted, "There can be no privacy with respect to a matter which is already public or which has previously become part of the 'public domain.' Once the information is released, unlike a physical object, it cannot be recaptured and sealed."

"Florida woman sues makers of 'Girls Gone Wild' videos"

In 2001 a Florida State University student sued after being taped topless by Girls Gone Wild employees without her consent. She was celebrating Mardi Gras. Her image was used in television advertisements and on a billboard in Italy. Although case law generally recognizes no privacy claims in public places,[156] the case settled in 2003 for about $20,000. Surely it is issues of fraud,[157] apparent intoxication and thereby lack of consent,[158] and –generally – unethical business practices that may have colored the case in the plaintiff's favor and thus led the case to a fairly sizeable payoff, with implications for other suits.

---

b. Publication of Information Placing a Person in a False Light
(must be outrageous)

An example is *Wood v. Hustler Magazine, Inc.*, 736 F.2d 1084 (5th Cir. 1984), cert. denied, 469 U.S. 1107 (1985), a case involving "nonprofessional models" in Hustler Magazine.

A neighbor burglarized the Woods' home and stole nude photographs of Mrs. Woods, which he later sent to Hustler Magazine. Hustler published the photographs, and the Woods sued Hustler.

Was there defamation? Some statements in Hustler about Mrs. Wood were false, but the photograph itself was accurate.

It was false light because publication of the photos created an appearance that she consented to the submission of the photos and because it wrongly attributed to her debauched fantasies (about herself and bikers, and – at a very simple level - that she, in fact, wanted to be in Hustler).

While it was also public disclosure of private facts – Mrs. Wood's nude appearance – the appeals court's opinion emphasized *false light* and noted that the damages for public disclosure would just be duplicative of the damages for false light.

Incidentally, there was no libel claim because it was barred by a shorter statute of limitations. Such limitations periods (e.g., one year) usually are shorter for defamation (and a few other intentional torts, e.g., assault and battery) than for most other torts. And while, of course, Wood could have sued the burglar-neighbor and Hustler could have brought a third-part claim against the burglar-neighbor (for any damages Hustler incurred, such as to pay Wood), this most culpable party – as is typical – probably had little or no assets to satisfy any judgment.

c. Intruding Upon a Person's Private Life (must be outrageous)

---

[156] A Mardi Gras celebration on the streets of New Orleans is certainly in a public place, as even an FSU student should know!

[157] Typically, the photographed females were inadequately informed about the possible exposure worldwide of their own bodily exposure.

[158] In some cases, the Girls Gone Wild personnel obtained photos from person who could not give consent because the disseminated photographs were of females under age 18.

This is often a question of perspective on what people consider private (Is it a celebrity's private estate or is he/she walking on a public street?). For example, journalists or others may be snapping pictures of celebrities even when doing so entails intruding upon a space the celebrity has a right to consider private.

A royal example of such a gross intrusion was, in 1994, when a German newspaper published nude photos (taken with a powerful telephoto lens) of Britain's Prince Charles drying off after a bath in his own bathroom.

Here is another example: On May 24, 1999, in *Hanlon v. Berger*, 526 U.S. 808 (1999), and *Wilson v. Layne*, 526 U.S. 603 (1999), the U.S. Supreme Court unanimously held that police can be sued for violating privacy rights by allowing "media ride-alongs" in which television crews or reporters accompany police as observers into people's homes. That any videotape is not broadcast does not protect the police from liability for the intrusion upon privacy by having these non-police present during an arrest or search.

Warnings Help to Ensure There Is No Right of Privacy
"NOTICE TO STUDENTS: SEARCH OF LOCKERS OR STORAGE AREAS
School authorities may search student lockers, vehicles, or other storage areas upon reasonable suspicion that a prohibited or illegally possessed substance or object is contained within the area. [F.S. (Florida Statutes) 232.256]"

---

d. Unauthorized Appropriation of Name or Likeness
for Commercial Purpose

The <u>first three forms</u> of invasion of privacy <u>must be</u> <u>highly offensive</u> to reasonable persons (with presumably some deep and long-lasting damage). Therefore, posting on the Internet, without permission, a video of two people briefly kissing is less likely to constitute an invasion of privacy than posting on the Internet a video of the same two people, again without permission, but this time engaged in sexual intercourse.

The fourth form - **Unauthorized Appropriation of Name or Likeness for Commercial Purpose** – has no requirement that the defendant's behavior must be highly offensive (outrageous). A classic example is that of baseball cards from the early 1900s, with Future Hall of Famer Honus Wagner and others winning against the tobacco companies because no permission was given. The cards were flattering, but used for commercial purposes. Honus Wagner's card, one of the most valuable in existence today, was recalled in 1909. At the time, the card was distributed along with tobacco, and Wagner – a nonsmoker – objected to his image being included with the product; he did not want to set a bad example for children, and the American Tobacco Company did stop selling the card.
Pictures in Advertisements (e.g., for ads for "irregularity" - names were not used, but photographs of people were prominently displayed).

Here is a separate issue: <u>Even if permission was given for the use of name or likeness, governmental authorities may pursue allegedly unfair, misleading advertising</u>. For example, in 1997, the Food and Drug Administration (FDA) ordered the pharmaceutical giant, Merck & Co., to stop using blood-pressure medicine ads which featured pictures of Cal Ripken, Jr. The pictures, taken with the paid permission of Ripken's business agents, and the ad, whose copy was approved by those agents, showed the Baltimore Orioles' third baseman in action accompanied by the words, "Cal Ripken, Jr. and Prinivil. . . . Both on the job. Everyday." Ripken also wore a baseball cap with a Prinivil logo, and the caption, "[he's the] hardest working man in baseball, . . . [and] in many patients . . . Prinivil is hard at work against hypertension."

Cal Ripken, Jr.'s blood pressure was fine, though, and he did not use Prinivil. Small print in the ad said, "Cal Ripken, Jr. is not hypertensive and is not taking Prinivil." The FDA ruled that the disclaimer "lacks significant prominence and does not balance or clarify the misrepresentation of the product endorsement." Merck, to comply with the FDA order, enlarged the type of the disclaimer and moved it higher up in the ad.

>
> **Comparative Law: The European Law on Name and Likeness**
>
> European Law tends to more strongly protect the name and likeness of dead people than does American Law. For example, in Europe successful actions were brought against the publication of photographs taken of Otto von Bismarck's death and of a famous French actress dying. In America, similar cases have gone all the way up to the U.S. Supreme Court. But in the United States these attempts to bar the publishing of intrusive photos of a now deceased person have failed.
>
> Also, the European Union (EU) tends to try to protect Internet users' privacy more so than is the case in the United States. Some American companies have decided to abide by EU standards.
>
> Microsoft, Intel, Hewlett-Packard, Procter & Gamble and over a hundred other companies decided in 2001 to apply the tough EU data-privacy rules to its global business. What impeded such sign-ups is a consensus among many American companies, and the United States government, that the "model contracts" in which data can be transferred between companies on both sides of the Atlantic is incompatible with "real world operations." But the EU contends that any problems with the model contract can be ironed out over time and practice.
>
> The European Commission Directive on Data Protection (EU Directive) prohibits online transfers of personally identifiable information to non-EU countries unless an "adequate" level of privacy protection is observed. The EU Directive applies to every organization in the U.S. collecting or receiving personal data about EU nationals online.
>
> Because the patchwork of U.S. privacy laws do not conform to the EU's privacy standards, they are not deemed an "adequate" level of protection. As a result, the EU Directive can potentially interrupt the flow of critical business data, and may expose U.S. companies to prosecution by European authorities for failure to protect the privacy of EU nationals.

I. Fraud: A Very Important Intentional Tort, Often Arising in the Contractual Context

Fraud has six elements: MKIRDC (material misrepresentation, knowingly made, intended to induce reliance, producing justifiable reliance, damages, and causation - **see pgs. 118-121; Emerson BL**).

Fraud is a tort. Because fraud often arises in the context of contract formation, it was outlined in this text's Second Section, on Contracts.

Commercial fraud is well established in the law. What about sexual fraud? Prof. Jane Larson of Northwestern University Law School says it should also be recognized. Intimate relations are, in most instances, more important than commercial transactions, and the courts ought to find a way to permit people to sue for being misled (lied to) all the way into bed. That is what Larson writes. But the courts traditionally shy away from claims involving such personal matters.

Just because the government has a right to pursue fraud does not mean that individuals necessarily can sue as well. For example, in *Buckman Co. v. Plaintiffs' Legal Committee*, 531 U.S. 341 (2001), the U.S. Supreme Court unanimously ruled that only the Food and Drug Administration (FDA) can sue companies that allegedly defrauded the government to get a medical device approved. (By analogy, the decision could easily apply to any federal agency where plaintiffs claim that the agency was defrauded.) In 1984, Buckman Company, a regulatory consulting firm that helps businesses seek FDA approvals, applied on behalf of spinal-implant maker AcroMed Corp., now a unit of Johnson & Johnson, for marketing approval of the bone-screw device. Prompted in part by a television report, some 5,000 people filed state lawsuits claiming injuries from the device and alleging that Buckman used misrepresentation to win FDA approval. Writing for the Court, Chief Justice Rehnquist held that federal authority pre-empted these state-court lawsuits. "The FDA is empowered to investigate suspected fraud (and has) a variety of enforcement options that allow it to make a measured response to suspected fraud upon the agency."

J. Interference with Business Relations

These torts include abusive discharge, disparagement, infringement of intellectual property, tortious interference with contract, tortious interference with prospective economic advantage, unfair competition, and various antitrust law violations.

> Extreme Cases of "Competition"
> Some extreme cases of "competition" are unlawful. However, generally, high hurdles (high thresholds) are imposed on claims of unlawful "competition" because we like competition. We tend to say, "let businesses fight it out in the marketplace, NOT in the courts." Rough, aggressive practices - absent anything else – tend to be okay.

> AntiTrust and AntiCompetitive Practices 2mins8secs - http://www.youtube.com/watch?v=S97zBjjo9xs – a YOUTUBE video at robertwemersonufl, features a lecturer in a black/rainbow hat with yellow yarn/hair.

1. Tortious Interference with Contract

Three things must be shown to prove tortious interference with contract. Let us illustrate that with the *Paul (P), Daniel (D) and Laura (L) example:*

    1. Valid Contract between P & L;
    2. D knows about the P - L Contract; and
    3. D intentionally causes L (or P) to breach the Contract or otherwise prevents performance.

Here, there are two distinct causes of action:
(1)   a <u>tort claim</u> (tortious interference with contract) - P sues D to recover damages stemming from D's interfering with the contract P had with L (from D's inducing L to breach the P-L contract).
(2)   a <u>breach of contract claim</u> - P sues L for breaching the contract between P and L.

a. Two Examples of Tortious Interference

1. A "Turkey of a Case!" A turkey raiser who contracted with a major food processing company to raise and provide flocks of turkeys to the processor, sued the processor for contractual interference. The processor, upon the collapse of a contract between the parties, had written to nine other major turkey processors urging them, apparently on false pretenses, not to buy the plaintiff's turkeys. Such <u>tortious interference</u> with contract supported an award of $200,000 in punitive damages. *Rusk Farms, Inc. v Ralston Purina Co.*, 689 SW2d 671 (Mo. App. 1985).

2. *The divorce/suicide example*: In a Delaware case, *Wilmington Trust Co. v. Clark*, 325 A.2d 283 (Del. Ch. 1974), a divorce agreement included alimony, which, per the divorce agreement, was to cease upon either party's death (or the alimony recipient's re-marriage). The party responsible for paying the alimony (the ex-husband) committed suicide. No clause in the divorce agreement concerned the cause of a party's death, so the ex-husband's estate had a contractual right to stop paying alimony. The estate was discharged from the alimony obligation so the discontinuance of alimony was NO breach of contract. But was the ex-husband's suicide, as the ex-wife contended, tortious <u>interference</u>? The court said, "No."

b. Privilege

Some inducements for others to breach are lawful. These inducements are "privileged" if they use reasonable methods and have proper purposes.

Privileged behavior is a defense from claims of tortious interference. Two examples are advertising and labor union activities.

<u>Advertising campaigns, including truthful ads mentioning the other business by name</u>. (Typically, the party carrying out the advertising does not even know who will be influenced by it and whether they have any contracts they may be persuaded to breach.)

<u>Labor union activities, such as strikes</u>. For example, in *International Ass'n of Machinists v. Southard*, 459 P.2d 570 (Colorado Supreme Court, 1969), due to a strike, a Colorado businessman was stuck on business and could not get to his return location, Denver, without having to pay an additional $52.19 for a flight with another airline . The businessman sued the airline for breach, but the airline ticket had numerous clauses exculpating the airline for canceled flights, including due to strikes. The businessman also sued the union for tortious interference with the businessman's contract with the airline. He lost. Although clearly the union knew its actions would cause flights to be canceled, its actions were privileged. Otherwise, the right to strike would, in effect, be nullified by tort law. (It surely did not help the businessman that he was trapped, in of all places, Hawaii!)

YOUTUBE – yellow_dog_contracts3mins25secs is at robertwemersonufl

2. Tortious Interference with Prospective Economic Advantage

Tortious interference with prospective economic advantage can involve subtler behaviors or results than an outright interference with a contract. Here, there is: not a contract, but a known relationship (perhaps on the verge of becoming a contract). The alleged tortfeasor knowingly interferes with the plaintiff's rightful expectations concerning that relationship.

Strong competition, by itself, is insufficient to constitute a tort. Generally, one must show <u>misrepresentation, intimidation or malice.</u>

<u>Tortious interference can occur even though the interferers were engaged neither in competition with one another nor in a business relationship with each other</u>.

Thus, in *Guillory v. Godfrey,* 286 P.2d 474 (Cal. App. 1955), a California appeals court held that the evidence was sufficient to establish that a liquor store proprietor and one of his employees had maliciously interfered with a restaurant owner's business by intimidating the restaurant's customers to such an extent that the restaurant was forced out of business. The evidence showed that after the restaurant had hired an African-American cook, the liquor store proprietor and his employee asked patrons entering the restaurant if they were "n----- lovers," made disparaging remarks about the café and the food, performed antics in front of the restaurant, some of them obscene, and yelled at the customers that the place was not fit to eat in.

It was also proven that the employee had entered the restaurant and forcibly ejected a patron, causing him to bleed at the mouth. This evidence, the court concluded, amply supported a finding of malicious disruption of the restaurant owner's business and damages proximately flowing therefrom. The court observed that in California the wrongful or malicious interference with formation of a contract or the right to pursue a lawful business, calling, trade, or occupation constitutes a tort.

An Example of Real Estate Promotions to Snowbirds, with Competition by a Former Employee:
Azar v. Lehigh Corp., 364 So. 2d 860 (Fla. Dist. Ct. App. 1978)

At its expense, a real estate firm, Lehigh Corporation, brought to Florida snowbirds (people from the North who live in Florida seasonally and "migrate" to Florida for the winter). Lehigh paid airfare, put the snowbirds in hotels, and paid for their meals. A former Lehigh employee, Azar, would show up and sponge off Lehigh's efforts. Therefore, once Lehigh had identified prospective real property purchasers and brought them down, Azar would then make his pitch to sell property to these snowbirds from his property listings rather than Lehigh's.

For the Florida District Court of Appeals, Judge Grimes wrote (underlining added by author): There is a narrow line between what constitutes vigorous competition in a free enterprise society and malicious interference with a favorable business relationship. Under the heading of "Interference with prospective advantage," Prosser states: "Though trade warfare may be waged to the bitter end, there are certain rules of combat which must be observed. . ." W. Prosser, Law of Torts (4th ed. 1971) at 956.

[Prosser] goes on to say that the courts have generally prohibited such activities as defamation of the competitor, disparagement of his goods and his business methods, and intimidation, harassment and annoyance of his customers. In the final analysis, the issue seems to turn upon whether the subject conduct is considered to be "unfair" according to contemporary business standards.

So what activities are "going overboard?"

The appeals court decided that the trial judge was right to hold Azar's acts to be tortious interference. And it upheld the trial judge's order as being "precise enough for [Azar] to understand what he cannot do. Considering [Azar's] knowledge of Lehigh's operation, we are confident that he will have no difficulty in ascertaining which of the motel patrons constitute [Lehigh's] guests as defined in the temporary restraining order [injunction]." Thus, the injunction against Azar was upheld, and Azar remained under court order not to solicit business from the customers that Lehigh Corporation brought to Lehigh Acres.

K. Other Interference with Business Relations Torts

1. Disparagement (also called "trade libel" or "commercial disparagement")

Disparagement is any unprivileged false statement concerning the quality of a business' service or product that is intended to and does cause that business financial hardship. Disparagement is thus a type of defamation - in a business context (defaming a competitor's products, services, or general reputation)

2. Unfair Competition (including remedies under the federal Lanham Act, http://topics.law.cornell.edu/wex/Lanham_Act)

Often unfair competition is a claim based on alleged unfair, false, or deceptive advertising. A general concern is basic fairness.

If in doubt, one should give even more information, more warnings. More specifically, unfair competition may be in the confusing of names or identities as to deceive or mislead the public about a product's or service's source. Thus unfair competition is a deceptive trade practice.

a. Court Decisions and Statutes

Courts are frequently asked to intervene when one business uses unfair tactics to compete with another business. Among the unfair tactics the courts have condemned is a business trying to lure customers away from a competing business by confusing customers as to which business or products they are dealing with. The most common way to confuse customers is for a second business to market its goods or services under a name or other mark that is confusingly similar to that used by the first business on its goods or services.

Although courts originally decided these types of disputes without the benefit of a legislative enactment, Congress and most state legislatures have now codified the principles developed by the courts to deal with unfair business practices. Altogether, these court decisions and statutes are termed *unfair competition law*. Under this body of law, a business may obtain a court order preventing a competitor from engaging in unfair business practices.

Unfair competition is not usually considered a separate branch of intellectual property law, as it targets general business practices rather than intellectual property as such. However, because the use of misleading names and marks to improperly lure customers away from another business is also very much what trademark law is concerned with, the two types of law often overlap. Example: The name used by Joe's Pizza is very ordinary and not distinctive enough to be considered a trademark. If, however, another business opens up down the street under a "Joe's Pizza" sign, the courts may use unfair competition laws to force the second user to modify the name to distinguish it from the first.

Lawsuits and Administrative Remedies

Injunctions and even, in very rare cases, court-mandated corrective advertising may be ordered. An example is the Federal Trade Commission (FTC) and the Ramses condom maker. Ramses was advertised as being 30% stronger than other brands. The FTC told the Ramses **manufacturer to show the proof that their condoms are quantitatively stronger, as advertised.**

> Antitrust Liability2mins27secs - http://www.youtube.com/watch?v=7Dm8suXGncQ - is a YOUTUBE video at robertwemersonufl.

b. Predatory Business Practices Constitute a Type of Unfair Competition

An example of unfair competition in this broader context is: an entirely predatory business practice. E.g., a Bank President, upset with a disastrous catered event at his/her home, persuades the Bank's Board of Directors that the Bank should diversify and go into catering. The sole goal of this new Bank "venture" is to "do in" the caterer.

But it is very difficult to prove that a business venture was entirely predatory. The following is a rare example from case law: *Tuttle v. Buck*, 119 N.W. 946 (Supreme Court of Minnesota, 1909). This case, concerning a bank's alleged unfair competition against a barber, sets forth the general legal principles:

"[We must] preserve the principle of competition and yet guard against its abuse to the unnecessary injury to the individual. So the principal that man may use his own property according to his own needs and desires, while true in the abstract, is subject to many limitations in the concrete. Men cannot always, in civilized society, be allowed to use their own property as their interests or desires may dictate without reference to the fact that they have neighbors whose rights are as sacred as their own. The existence and well-being of society requires that each and every person shall conduct himself consistently with the fact that he is a social and reasonable person.

"To divert to one's self the customers of a business rival by the offer of goods at lower prices is in general a legitimate mode of serving one's own interest, and justifiable as fair competition. But when a man starts an opposition place of business, not for the sake of profit to himself, but regardless of loss to himself, and for the sole purpose of driving his competitor out of business, and with the intention of himself retiring upon the accomplishment of his malevolent purpose, he is guilty of a wanton wrong and an actionable tort. In such a case he would not be exercising his legal right, or doing an act which can be judged separately from the motive which actuated him. . . Such conduct in its moral quality may be no better than highway robbery."

In *Tuttle v. Buck*, a barber (Edward Tuttle) had for ten years in the small village of Howard Lake, Minnesota, maintained himself and his family comfortably from his barbershop income. The defendant, Cassius Buck, was a wealthy, very prominent banker in the same community who "maliciously" established a competitive barbershop. The defendant employed a barber to carry on the business and used his personal influence to attract customers away from the plaintiff's barbershop. Apparently, for 12 months, the defendant circulated false and malicious reports and accusations about the plaintiff and personally solicited many of the plaintiff's patrons, persuading them to stop using the plaintiff's services. Indeed, the defendant used his personal power as the town's banker to coerce some customers into using the defendant's shop, instead. The plaintiff charged that the defendant undertook this entire plan with the sole design of injuring the plaintiff and destroying his business, not for serving any legitimate business interest. The lower appeals court and the Minnesota Supreme Court affirmed the trial court's decision for the plaintiff (to not grant the defendant's demurrer).

The Minnesota Supreme Court held that it was not at all correct to say that the motive with which an act is done is always immaterial, providing the act itself is lawful. Motives need not be pure, but completely malicious or otherwise wicked purposes need not be cloaked by freedom of competition.

c. Antitrust Law: An Example Looking at the Robinson-Patman Act
1. Antitrust Law Generally

Antitrust law is meant to foster and protect competition. The American economy is a compromise between two ends of a spectrum: At one end lies complete laissez-faire and at the opposite end lies socialism, with the concept of an intermediate "regulated competition" coming to fruition in America. "Beware of that profound enemy of the free enterprise system who pays lip service to free competition - but also labels every anti-trust prosecution as a 'persecution.' You know, it depends a good deal on whose baby has the measles." Franklin D. Roosevelt (1882-1945), U.S. President.

What is the greatest enemy of business? Many people reflexively answer, "the government." However, while government regulation can be quite burdensome on, even onerous for, businesses, the statistics are clear: Most business failures stem from *competition*, from a competitor's out-marketing, out-managing, out-financing, out manufacturing a product. *Therefore, human nature being what it is,* some competitors naturally want to gather to reduce their "cutthroat competition." "Can't we all get along?" they say. But what they seek to do – dividing the market and trying to eliminate any "price wars" – is anticompetitive behavior at or near its worst.

2. Robinson-Patman Act (1936)

Charging different prices for a commodity without a legally justified reason for the difference is price discrimination. The Robinson-Patman Act tends to make it unlawful. Generally, there must be a real difference in costs (e.g., shipping). Simply claiming that one was trying to boost sales is not generally a lawful excuse.

Federal predatory pricing laws require that alleged harm must be to overall competition, not just to an individual competitor. Pricing some items below costs, at a large retail establishment, is not a Robinson-Patman violation: To prove a violation, one must show pricing for an entire market; only that truly affects overall competition (not just impacts particular persons).

It is <u>not</u> ordinarily a Robinson-Patman violation to reduce prices simply to meet competition. The question is whether the price arrangement conforms to economic reality. However, some state antitrust laws are more pro-plaintiff than Robinson-Patman is. They sometimes permit successful predatory pricing claims that could not succeed at the federal level. **(see pgs. 541-542; Emerson BL).**

VIDEO SKIT - J.D. JEOPARDY: AN ANTITRUST AND COMPETITION LAW GAME SHOW (with Alex Trebledamages, Shelly Sherman, Clyde Clayton, and the irrepressible Vanna, along with two Crew members) – 15:47 long – is in Part 3 of the Resources section of the course website.

The skit comes with a few simple questions on antitrust law and related topics –see also Barron's book chapter 22.

---

d. Some Specific Antitrust Concepts

Tying, market divisions, production quotas, competitors' agreeing upon prices, and boycotts are <u>per se violations</u>.

Groups usually <u>excused from the antitrust laws</u> include Farmers, Fishermen, Labor Unions, Federally-regulated industries, and State-regulated insurance companies. Also, choices about how to proceed, and against whom, in some antitrust cases are very much tied to political philosophies and concerns. One President's Justice Department may have a very different approach, say, toward Microsoft, industry pricing standards, or other matters than another Presidential administration does. Also, a person who is the director of several small, non-competing companies is not in violation of the Clayton Act's provisions against interlocking directorates.

<u>Unjustified Price Discrimination</u>. Robinson-Patman violations occur when a business charges different prices for the same commodity without a legally justified reason for that difference. Different transportation costs or other expenses, but not simply trying to boost sales, may excuse a price differential.

<u>Mergers and Monopolies</u>. Ordinarily, the Justice Department or the Federal Trade Commission investigates the potential merger of large corporations. Unrelated companies can form a conglomerate, which is legally acceptable (although sometimes foolish business).

Currently, in order to determine <u>whether a business has monopoly power</u> allowing it to exercise significant control over prices, courts focus on the answer to <u>two questions</u>: what is the <u>relevant market</u> in which to consider questions of monopolization, and what is the <u>market share</u> of the business/defendant within the relevant market? In antitrust case law, *relevant market* means the total demand for the product or service allegedly being monopolized as well as the interchangeable products or services within the geographic area in question. [The relevant market is the demand for interchangeable products within a geographic area.]

A business cannot be liable for a violation merely for holding monopoly power. The business must also exhibit monopolizing conduct. If charges were directed against a power lawn mower manufacturer for trying to monopolize, the court would first have to determine the relevant market. First, the court would look at the sales of the defendant's mowers within the geographic area. Second, it would add the sales, within that area, of reasonably interchangeable products: other power lawn mowers, push lawn mowers, garden tractors with mower attachments, and the like. Third, the court would divide the defendant's sales by the total sales in the relevant market to determine the defendant's <u>market share</u> (<u>the percentage of the relevant market under the defendant's control</u>).

This percentage is matched to a "market power" scale provided by Judges Learned Hand and Augustus Hand when they decided *United States v. Aluminum Company of America,* 148 F.2d 416 (1945): "[O]ver 90[%] … is enough to constitute a monopoly; it is doubtful whether 60 or 64 percent would be enough, and certainly 33 percent is not."

With these percentage guidelines in mind, courts and businesses alike can determine whether monopolizing power (indicated by a market share of more than 90 percent according to the above) exists with reasonable certainty. As the market share slides toward the 33 percent level, so too does the possibility that such power will not be held to exist.

---

e. Advertising, Warnings, and the FTC

To defend yourself from possible claims of unfair competition (e.g., deceptive advertising), **GIVE EFFECTIVE WARNINGS.** Be able to prove what you say, or issue *disclaimers*
BEWARE! The warnings had better work, or there will be threats of lawsuits and regulation.

When you advertise, you must be prepared to back up your claims. You may have to issue a disclaimer unless you can prove what you are saying.

A way to defend yourself from claims of unfair competition/deceptive advertising is to <u>GIVE WARNINGS</u> - warn the consumer about what he/she is getting and not getting. In a larger sense of the word, unfair competition can be any unlawful business practice. It is thus often combined with allegations of tortious interference with contract, fraud, and infringing of intellectual property.

In its findings on deceptive advertising, **the FTC considers the effect, not the intent, of communication**. The FTC may hold an advertiser liable for implied claims discerned by as little as 14% of a consumer audience. The criteria by which an advertisement is judged to determine whether it is highly likely to mislead <u>reasonable consumers under the circumstances</u>, are:
(1) substantiation, by the advertiser, of claims made in the advertisement;
(2) disclosure, to the consumer, of material information; and

(3) disclosure of any material connection between an endorser and the product or manufacturer endorsed.

Under its 1983 Policy Statement on Deception, the FTC put forth standards for what is deceptive advertising under Section 5 of the Federal Trade Commission Act. It is essentially a looser common-law fraud standard: a deceptive ad has, for instance, a material representation, omission, act, or practice (e.g., "material" means anything about a product's performance, features, safety, price, or effectiveness – whether that thing is express or implied; by including or omitting information from an ad, the advertiser admits its materiality!)

It is no defense to a consumer protection action that the conduct is widely practiced within an industry. See, e.g., *Commonwealth v. DeCotis*, 316 N.E.2d 748 (Mass. 1974). So do not rely on industry convention as comfort for the acceptability of conduct that is unfair or deceptive to consumers. There are always a few state Attorneys General looking to reform what they believe to be improper, but widely practiced or tolerated, marketplace activity.

f. Comparative Advertising

Ordinarily, comparative advertising is okay. Comparisons simply must be supported by the facts. And opinions generally are okay. It might simply be puffing/puffery, such as use of the words "better than" or "superior."

In *Pizza Hut, Inc. v. Papa John's International, Inc.*, 227 F.3d 489 (5h Cir. 2000), the court held that the Papa John's advertising slogan - "Better Ingredients. Better Pizza" - standing alone, is not an "objectifiable statement of fact" upon which consumers would be justified in relying. Thus, it did not constitute a false or misleading statement of fact that violates Section 43(a) of the federal Lanham Act (against unfair competition). The slogan, when appearing in comparative advertising — specifically, comparing Papa's John's allegedly fresh sauce and well-prepared dough to the "lesser" ingredients of Pizza Hut - became misleading; but Pizza Hut failed to show that the misleading facts conveyed by the slogan actually mattered to the consumers to which the ad was directed. Therefore, Pizza Hut failed to produce evidence of a Lanham Act violation.

g. Required Disclosures

The federal Truth-in-Lending Act mandates comprehensive disclosure of credit terms. Generally, state consumer protection is more stringent and substantive than is federal law, which is more devoted simply to information disclosures. Sometimes, disclosures are by the governing authorities themselves. Sometimes disclosures are ordered by courts or administrators, or are trumpeted by the winning party.

h. The International Realm

At the international level, the International Chamber of Commerce, an independent organization, has promoted self-regulation by developing voluntary codes of marketing practices for businesses.

In many European (especially Scandinavian) countries, there is more government assistance for consumers than in the United States: European ombudsmen, advisory councils, and agencies coordinating private consumer organizations generally pursue options not mandated by law much more than do American corporate officials (e.g., vice-presidents for consumer affairs) who usually have no company or industry mandate to order relief. However, the United States leads the world in providing post purchase legal remedies: product liability legislation, cooling-off periods, and strict liability all arose first in the U.S. Moreover, Americans' freedom of expression leads to advertising that would be restricted or outright banned in European nations.

In less-developed countries, the consumer movement is also less developed. Caveat emptor ("buyer beware") still reigns on almost every occasion. Sometimes the most effective consumer protection is something as simple as a properly calibrated scale.

V. STRICT LIABILITY, PRODUCT LIABILITY, AND WARRANTIES

We have discussed Negligence and Intentional Torts. Now to the third (and last!) area of torts: Strict Liability.

A. Public Policy Debates over Strict Liability

Strict liability concerns: (1) dangerous activities, and (2) products.[159] To impose strict liability, fault is <u>not</u> necessary, but one must always show causation and harm.

Strict liability, as a basis for imposing burdens/costs upon defendants, is often disparaged. Insurance companies, manufacturers, and others criticize strict liability for stifling innovation and long-term productivity. A competing view is that strict liability laws (and the lawsuits emanating therefrom) serve as a necessary restraint upon business; it induces businesses to behave more responsibly – to make products and services safer. Almost everyone agrees: Products should be made as safe as practical, given the circumstances. The argument is over what those circumstances are, and what is practical.

B. The Test for Strict Liability Concerning Dangerous Activities

Strict liability covers <u>dangerous activities</u> (sometimes called ultra-hazardous activities, and defined as "a risk of serious harm to the person, land, or other property of others that cannot be eliminated by the use of the utmost care"). Such activities include: keeping dangerous (wild) animals; storing gas in underground tanks; transporting hazardous waste; (perhaps) manufacturing, marketing, and/or sales of assault weapons.

VIGNETTE: SPECIAL RESPONSIBILITIES – DUTIES AND BREACHES ARE BASED ON CIRCUMSTANCES (1:11 long) - Special_Responsibilities.wmv is on YOUTUBE at robertwmersonufl - E.g., Control of Animals, and Vehicles (Special responsibilities concerning animals, especially pets; Special duties re: heavy equipment, especially motor vehicles).

The Test for Strict Liability concerning Dangerous Activities is: <u>Strict liability if these 3 questions are answered (1) Yes, (2) No, and (3) Yes</u>:
1. Is there a high level of danger from the activity?   Yes
2. Can the risk in the activity be reduced by reasonable (non-extraordinary) measures?   No
3. Is the activity unusual in that locale?   Yes

Many contract and tort law concepts developed before there were modern methods of mass production and distribution. So the law may, as usual, be playing "catch up" to the technological and social changes.

---

[159] The concern about harmful products long predates the rise of the legal doctrine of strict liability. For example, a Girard, Pennsylvania tombstone from 1870 warns consumers:
>Ellen Shannon
>Who was fatally burned
>March 21, 1870
>By the explosion of a lamp filled with "R.E. Danforth's
>Non-Explosive Burning Fluid."

C. Product Liability

Product liability is often <u>a matter of public policy</u>: how should these matters be resolved -courts, ballots, or expertise? Our legal system values the competing concepts of Liberty and Individualism versus Security and Constraint. But here is a Bottom line: Torts sometimes simply arise from or are defended against based on stupid actions - if you behave stupidly, just hope no harm was done; and if you are harmed, just hope you did not behave stupidly![160]

So here are the three main groups of decision makers, with advantages and disadvantages –
1. Jurors and Judges - apply common sense approach. But it is ad hoc (case by case), thus not as efficient as a comprehensive legislative or regulatory approach.
2. Legislatures – can hold hearings and enact systematic approaches (statutes). Lawmakers are representative (elected), but often are influenced by lobbyists (so-called special interests).
3. Bureaucrats – conduct investigations, bring in experts (e.g., about consumer safety); can put in time to hold hearings. Can promulgate rules, but - compared to juries and legislature - these administrative agencies are least representative of the populace.
More on product liability is at http://www.personalinjuryfyi.com/product_liability.html

D. Broad Class of Potential Plaintiffs/Defendants

In product liability law, one can use negligence, strict liability, and/or warranties (the last is a type of breach of contract claim).

Product liability cases receive far more attention from business and government than is proportionate to their share of tort cases (product liability cases are only 4% of all tort cases). However, the impact of product liability cases on individual businesses, industries, employees, and consumers is often far greater than those low numbers might indicate. Many of the large, important cases concerning manufacturing and marketing involve businesses' alleged liability for harm supposedly caused by the business' <u>products</u>.

E. Who Is Liable for a Defective Product?

Each party in the chain of distribution may be liable.
- *Manufacturers*, particularly of end-products (not just component parts), may be liable even if a subsequent party (e.g., a distributor) is responsible for final inspections of, and possible corrections of, the product.
- *Component-part manufacturers* are liable if it is their defective manufacturing or design of the part that is the basis for the suit; but, unless they had reason to believe the manufacturer was in error, component-part makers ordinarily are not liable for design defects in a part that they simply made per the manufacturer's erroneous specifications.
- *Wholesalers* usually are liable for defective products they sell, except that some states relieve them of liability for latent or hidden defects when the wholesaler merely sold the product in the same condition that it received them.
- *Retailers* often are liable, but some jurisdictions excuse from responsibility a retailer who did not in any way help cause the product's defective condition.

---

[160] A Video Vignette - Product Liability and Public Policy: Freedom to Play Rough and to be Stupid? (Liberty/Individualism Versus Security/Constraint) (2:48 long) on YouTube at Product_Liab_and_Pub_Policy.wmv (robertwemersonufl):
https://www.youtube.com/watch?v=sO7k0mSO9Tg&list=UU_TuNN4AcpdLnoIdSTLx_MA&index=23

- *Successor corporations* tend to be liable for the acquired company's debts, including product liability judgments or claims stemming from the acquired business' actions before it was acquired.

Because they usually extend no warranties and buyers generally have no great expectations when dealing with them, *sellers of used goods* are rarely liable except for (1) some states' special laws requiring warranties from used-car salesmen and (2) their own conduct in poorly making, replacing, or repairing a part.

> In many complex cases, experts frequently assist the factfinder (judge or jury) in determining the facts, especially concerning duties, breaches, defects, and damages. Usually the parties (through their lawyers) hire the experts, although the Federal Rules of Evidence (and comparable state rules) permit judges to hire neutral experts (and charge the parties for these costs). They can even hire special masters, under Federal Rule of Civil Procedure 53, as, in a sense, "junior judges." *See* Robert W. Emerson, *The French Huissier as a Model for U.S. Civil Procedure Reform*, 43 U. MICHIGAN JOURNAL OF LAW REFORM 1043, 1115-1118 (2010), available at http://ssrn.com/author=86449. For information about use of experts to prove one's case – key U.S. Supreme Court cases, *Daubert v. Merrell Dow Pharmaceuticals, Inc.*, 509 U.S. (1993), and *Kumho Tire Co. v. Carmichael*, 526 U.S. 137 (1999); **(see pg. 458; Emerson BL).**

F. Strict Liability, Negligence, Breach of Warranties

Strict liability (without needing to prove fault) is imposed as a matter of public policy. Reasons given for imposing strict liability on a manufacturer or other seller: (1) Make it the insurer of its product; (2) It has control over product quality; (3) It can distribute costs; (4) It can bear burdens better than others (e.g., the consumer) can; and (5) Morality - it has special responsibilities.

G. Strict Liability for a Product: Section 402A of the Restatement of Torts

To win a strict liability case involving products, a plaintiff must establish these six factors to show liability under Second Restatement of Torts §402A:

Defective Product, with the defendant
Engaged in the business of making or selling such a product;
and the product - in its defective condition - was
Unreasonably dangerous to the user;
No substantial change to the product after it left the defendant's control;
Causation (a causal link between the defect and the alleged harm); AND
Harm to the plaintiff.

Four states do NOT apply this strict liability standard (Restatement Section 402A or a similar approach) for product cases. North Carolina and Virginia have never adopted strict liability, via court cases or legislation. Delaware only applies strict liability in bailment cases; and Michigan has strict liability, but not in product cases. All other states have strict liability in some form for products cases.

So, to reiterate, for 46 of the states the six elements are **D**efect, **E**ngaged in the Business, **U**nreasonably Dangerous, **N**o Substantial Changes, **C**ausation, and **H**arm. Take the first letter, and the mnemonic is **DEUNCH**. Each of these six elements will now be considered. **See also pg. 484; Emerson BL.**

1. Defect

A defect is something that leaves a product <u>unreasonably dangerous</u>. Defects may exist when products are/were: poorly made; badly designed; or with insufficient or nonexistent warnings.

a. Problems in Manufacture, Design, or Marketing

Manufacturing

Here is a manufacturing defect: example - *Shoeshine Coca-Cola Bottling Co. v. Dolinski*, 420 P.2d 855 (Nevada Supreme Court, 1967). A bottling company was held strictly liable when Dolinski bought a soda from a vending machine and got very ill from drinking a portion of the soda. The bottle's contents included a decomposing mouse and also mouse feces.

Design

The defects associated with some of the most notorious transportation catastrophes have been design defects. For example, the O-ring sealant on the Challenger Space Shuttle was not designed to withstand unusually cold weather; this failure resulted in the explosion of that spaceship (and the deaths of the seven astronauts) shortly after the Challenger's launch in 1986. For automobiles, one can point to design defects such as seatbelts with faulty latching mechanisms or with shoulder-only belts. As the seatbelt examples indicate, a defect could be not something that causes an "accident," but that fails to deal with the problem (the "accident") after it occurs. That is what is called the <u>Crashworthiness Doctrine</u>. The lack of "crashworthiness" has been defined as a defect that did not cause a vehicular accident, but that increased the plaintiff's injuries from that accident.

Ordinarily, the defendant is <u>not required</u> to provide an accident-proof product. For example, if a car or truck rolls over, that may be chargeable to misuse by the driver - misuse that was not reasonably foreseeable and thus something for which the defendant cannot be held responsible. However, manufacturers need to do as much as they reasonably can to prevent an unintended, possibly harmful use. For example, pharmaceutical makers are constantly seeking to engineer and re-engineer bottles – to design with twists and turns or other schemes the "Perfect Pill Bottle": one toddlers cannot open, but elderly folks can![161]

> YOUTUBE – Medicines_and_Defects.wmv is at RobertWEmerson. This video vignette on inadequate warnings and bad designs concerns only one field, albeit very important – medicine. The problems with medicines include that they can be the wrong kind or the wrong dosage, they can produce allergic reactions, there can be bad interactions of multiple medicines, and a consumer may fail to follow directions.

b. Consumer Expectations and Risk-Benefits Analysis

There are <u>two tests</u> for determining whether a product is defective under the law of strict product liability in the United States.

The first test (<u>consumer expectations</u>) inquires whether the product meets reasonable consumer expectations of safety. <u>This test considers the average consumer's viewpoint (his/her reasonable, fairly definite expectations) in deciding defect issues</u>. Implicit in the test is something akin to a negligence calculus: jurors typically are instructed to find a product defective if it was "dangerous to an extent beyond that which would be contemplated by the ordinary consumer who purchases it, with the ordinary knowledge common to the community as to its characteristics." The standard first arose in consumer warranty cases (see UCC 2-314 – Implied Warranty of Merchantability). Later, it was applied to product liability cases involving consumer goods and thus has rarely been applied to product liability cases concerning non-consumer goods.

> A video vignette, SOME ORDINARY ACTIONS (ACTIVITIES OR USES) (32 seconds long), SomeOrdinaryActions32secs (http://www.youtube.com/watch?v=RBi8gWpUHO0), is on YOUTUBE at robertwemersonufl
> Even ordinary activities or use of a product can occasionally produce harm –

---

[161] In 1970, Congress passed the Poison-Prevention Packaging Act, ushering into American homes the line-up-the-arrows bottles for aspirin and prescription drugs. Some medicine bottles now feature key-like devices that must be inserted into grooves, or slide-button "trapdoor" tops, or quarter-turn tops into anchor-lock grooves.

> e.g., while using play equipment.

The second test (risk-benefits analysis) assesses the alleged product defect from the manufacturer's viewpoint. This test mandates a balancing of the product's risks against its benefits. (E.g., on balance, do the benefits of the challenged product outweigh its inherent dangers.) Criteria to examine in developing the risk-benefit analysis include: (a) Consumer expectations of the danger of the product;[162] (b) the usefulness and desirability of the product (its utility to the user and to the public); (c) the safety aspects of the product (the likelihood that it will cause injury, and the probable seriousness of the injury); (d) the availability of a substitute product which would meet the same needs, yet be safer; (e) the manufacturer's ability to eliminate the unsafe characteristics of the product without impairing its usefulness or making it too expensive to maintain its utility; (f) the user's ability to avoid danger by exercising due care in using the product; and (g) the feasibility of spreading the loss in setting the product's price or by carrying liability insurance.

Courts around the nation are divided over which test to use when a design defect is alleged in a non-consumer product. Four states (Illinois, Louisiana, Mississippi, and Texas) have, via legislation, explicitly rejected consumer expectations as part of tort reform and instead use the "reasonable alternative design" (RAD) requirement of the newest Restatement on Torts. RESTATEMENT (THIRD) OF TORTS: PRODUCTS LIABILITY § 2(b) (1998). Which other states do so via case law, or otherwise have some combination of the two standards, is not at all clear. Alabama, Maine, and Michigan courts seem to have replaced consumer expectations with RAD, but legal scholars continue to debate what the courts throughout the United States have held.

2. Engaged in the Business of Selling/Making that Product
(A Merchant-Manufacturer or an Expert)

If you do not make or ordinarily sell the product, then you are not engaged in the business.

3. Unreasonably Dangerous Product
(When the Product Is Used for Ordinary Purposes)

Sometimes this requirement is treated as being the "Consumer Expectations Test" - *the consumer has a right to expect a product to perform as safely as an ordinary consumer would assume should be the case, when the product is used in an intended or reasonably foreseeable manner.*

The "unreasonably dangerous"/consumer expectations test is: do the circumstances of the product's failure permit an inference that the product's design performed below the legitimate, commonly accepted [minimal] safety assumptions of its ordinary consumers?[163]

This test creates a higher, more pro-plaintiff standard than does a "reasonable manufacturer" test. The latter, court-developed test presumes that a manufacturer, supplier, or seller knows of the harmful characteristics of its product; therefore, a product is unreasonably dangerous if it is so harmful to persons that a reasonably prudent manufacturer/supplier/seller with this knowledge would not have placed it on the market.

> A video vignette, PRODUCT LIABILITY AND OTHER TORTS IN THE MAKING (2:39), is on YOUTUBE, product_liability_torts.wmv (http://www.youtube.com/watch?v=7V6T_95GllM) at robertwemersonufl

---

[162] So consumer expectations are a part of this test (the risk-benefits analysis), but are not the whole approach, as in the consumer-expectations test.

[163] Just as Florida follows Restatement § 402A as the standard for product liability cases – *West v. Caterpillar,* 336 So.2d 80 (Fla. 1976) – so Florida also uses the consumer expectations test in manufacturing defect cases (*Cassisi v. Maytag,* 396 So.2d 1140 (Fla. Dist. Ct. App. 1981)).

> Consider the Consumer Expectations Test. In the vignette, we see a refrigerator, microwave oven, water heaters, aquarium, and plants and other objects. Even ordinary products can be dangerous (e.g., appliances, toys, plants, picnic benches).
> A Question to Consider: Should the courts focus more on what consumers expect or what the so-called reality may be – what manufacturers realistically (e.g., given profit margins) can produce?

4. No Substantial (Material) Changes to the Product Since It Left the Defendant's Control?

Ordinarily, a merely decorative alteration would not be a material change, while an alteration of a product's working components would be a material change. So, if a buyer simply paints a product with a new color, that normally would *not* be a material change. On the other hand, if a buyer takes his/her new hedge trimmer and tinkers with it, by adding a hose, to use it as a water pick (a dental tool), that would constitute a substantial change. If the buyer uses that hedge trimmer-pick as his/her new toothbrush and ends up losing a few bicuspids, the buyer would have no case for strict liability.

What about a product improvement?[164] As a matter of policy, the plaintiff cannot use the defendant's subsequent improvements to a product to prove a defect for strict liability purposes or to prove a breach of duty for purposes of negligence. That policy is intended to encourage product innovation, and it has the same rationale as does the typical approach of not letting us place information about a settlement offer into evidence as an admission of liability (the policy reasoning: to encourage settlements). [Tangential warning: if you extend a settlement offer, make sure that it is structured as simply an offer, not admitting any facts.]

In *Geier v. American Honda*, 529 U.S. 861 (2000), the U.S. Supreme Court held 5-4 that a lawsuit in state court was pre-empted by a 1984 U.S. Transportation Department rule requiring auto makers to equip some, but not all, of their vehicles with airbags. Because the federal rule did not require side airbags, it would not be appropriate to let auto makers be held liable in a state court for that "failure."

Many states have enacted consumer protection statues providing for specific remedies for a variety of product defects. The best known example: lemon laws, which became widespread because automobiles are often an American citizen's second largest investment after buying a home. Some commentators say that the Supreme Court unfairly slants a narrow law into a broadside against plaintiffs and personal injury lawyers.

5. Causation and Harm

As with all tort suits, for a successful strict liability suit there must be harm and a causal link between the alleged problem (here, the defect) and that harm.

a. *MacPherson v. Buick Motor Co.* (see pg. 482; Emerson BL)

In *MacPherson v. Buick Motor Co.*, 111 N.E. 1050 (N.Y. Ct. App. 1916), Donald C. MacPherson purchased a new Buick automobile from a dealer of Buick Motor Company vehicles. Later, he was injured when the car ran into a ditch after one of its wheels crumbled into fragments because the spokes were made from defective wood. The wheel had been made by another manufacturer and then put on the car by Buick. MacPherson sued all the way up the chain, not the dealer (the seller of the product), but the manufacturer of the car - Buick.[165] New York's highest court found that placing a product in the

---

[164] Sometimes an advertisement trumpets a product as "new and improved." Is a natural inference to be drawn: that the product used to be "old and lousy?" The public policy is not to draw that conclusion as a matter of law.
[165] MacPherson could also have sued wholesalers, suppliers to the manufacturer (e.g., of the defective tire), and others.

"stream of commerce" creates a responsibility to ultimate buyers as well as to other injured parties.

Privity thus was found to NOT be required for MacPherson to have a claim against Buick. Privity is the requirement that a person should be one of the parties in the contract, in order for that person to have a legal interest in the contract or to have damages allegedly stemming therefrom.
At trial, the evidence indicated that the defects could have been discovered by reasonable inspection, but that Buick undertook no such inspection. Judge Benjamin Cardozo, for the highest court in New York (the Court of Appeals), delivered an opinion for MacPherson: Buick's duty to exercise reasonable care (not behave negligently) extended to MacPherson even though MacPherson and the company were not in privity of contract.

> Cardozo wrote:
> We [will not limit liability] to poisons, explosives, and things of like nature, to things which in their normal operation are implements of destruction. If the nature of a thing is such that it is reasonably certain to place life and limb in peril when negligently made, it is then a thing of danger. Its nature gives warning of the consequences to be expected. If to the element of danger there is added knowledge that the thing will be used by persons other than the purchaser, and used without new tests, then, irrespective of contract, the manufacturer of this thing of danger is under a duty to make it carefully. The proximity or remoteness of the relation is a factor to be considered. We are dealing now with the liability of the manufacturer of the finished product, who puts it on the market to be used without inspection by his customers. If he is negligent, where danger is to be foreseen, a liability will follow.
> Beyond all question, the nature of an automobile gives warning of probable danger if its construction is defective. This automobile was designed to go 50 miles an hour. Unless its wheels were sound and strong, injury was almost certain. It was as much a thing of danger as a defective engine for a railroad. The defendant [Buick] knew the danger.
> It knew also that the car would be used by persons other than the buyer. This was apparent from its size; there were seats for three persons. It was apparent also from the fact that the buyer was a dealer in cars, who bought to resell. The maker of this car supplied it for the use of purchasers from the dealer. [Indeed, that dealer was] the one person of whom it might be said with some approach to certainty that by him the car would not be used.
> It is true that an automobile is not an inherently dangerous vehicle. The meaning, however, is that danger is not to be expected when the vehicle is well constructed. If danger was to be expected as reasonably certain, there was a duty of vigilance, and this whether you call the danger inherent or imminent [e.g., from a faulty wheel]. We think the defendant was not absolved from a duty of inspection because it bought the wheels from a reputable manufacturer. It was not merely a dealer in automobiles. It was responsible for the finished product.
> *MacPherson v. Buick Motor Co.*, 111 N.E. 1050, 1053-1054 (N.Y. 1916).

b. Privity: Comparative Law **(see pg. 482; Emerson BL)**

Where jurisdictions insist on privity, only immediate buyers (or lessees) can sue only immediate sellers (or lessors) of the product. Others further down the chain of distribution cannot sue for lack of vertical privity, and anyone outside of the chain, such as other users of the product, cannot sue for lack of horizontal privity. This is the rule in many jurisdictions, e.g., Germany, Malaysia, Poland, South Africa, Taiwan, and the United Kingdom.

Many countries, however, have either seriously weakened or virtually abolished the privity limitation in the product liability context. In France and the jurisdictions following its lead (e.g., Belgium, Luxembourg, and Quebec) every buyer in the chain of distribution has a direct action against the original (professional) seller for hidden defects (vices cachés). In Austria and Liechtenstein warranties may extend a protective effect to third party users. [Besides just the United States, Australia as well as] several other common law systems provide important statutory exceptions from [privity, such as Canadian provinces extending warranties to the ultimate user, and India extending warranties for inherently dangerous products marketed without adequate warning].

c. *Truck v. Tree*: A Product Liability Example Illustrating Theories of Recovery

"Beefy" Beeferino attempts to assist his neighbor, "Sweet-Cakes," in removing a large tree from Sweet-Cake's yard. Instead of employing more conventional methods of tree removal such as using a chain saw or hiring a tree service, Beefy insists on using his Ford pick-up truck to tackle the job. Despite Sweet-Cake's skepticism, Beefy's cavalier attitude gets the best of him as he attempts to remove the tree by hooking the tree trunk to his vehicle and towing relentlessly. When the epic struggle between machine and nature ends, Beefy is injured and his truck is destroyed.

To add insult to injury, the tree stands tall and overshadows its defeated challenger. Drew is convinced Ford is at fault for the mishap and vows to bring suit against the automaker to compensate him for his ruined truck and hospital costs.

Let us apply product liability concepts to Beefy's arguably asinine behavior and lack of common sense. Is it reasonable that Ford bear the responsibility of protecting its customers from improper and perhaps unforeseeable uses of its vehicles? Should Ford have foreseen this use and warned against it? Can Beefy prove Ford's truck was defective and therefore was the proximate cause of the accident? These are just a few of the questions to consider when analyzing this product liability case.

1. Theories of Recovery

The three primary theories on which a product liability claim can be brought are breach of warranty, negligence, and strict liability. The breach of warranty action is concerned with whether the quality, characteristics, and safety of the product were consistent with the implied or expressed representations made by the seller at the time of the purchase. The action requires that the injured party be in a contractual relationship, either expressed or implied, with the seller. This notion of privity of contract is intended to prevent recovery in the suit by anyone who was not in privity with the seller. In our example, Beefy, the plaintiff, could claim breach of warranty and attempt to prove his truck failed to meet the standards communicated by the Ford dealership where he made the purchase.

Secondly, the plaintiff could claim the theory of negligence by the truck's manufacturer. The key difference between the breach of warranty theory and the negligence theory is that the negligence theory requires no privity of contract between the buyer and the seller. Instead, our injured party would only need to show that Ford did not use reasonable care in designing or manufacturing the truck or in providing adequate warnings. This is certainly not an easy point for our plaintiff to prove. In addition, the claim can be weakened if the plaintiff is found to have been negligent themselves in their misuse of the product. In our case, is it reasonable to assume Beefy was misusing his truck by attempting to tow down a large tree?

The final, and historically the easiest product liability theory to prove, is strict liability. Under strict liability, the injured party does not have to prove negligence, nor do they have to be in privity with the defendant seller. For our defendant, Ford, to be held strictly liable for the truck mishap, the plaintiff must prove:

(1) The plaintiff, or his property, was harmed by the product.
(2) The injury was caused by a defect in the product.
(3) The defect existed at the time the product left the defendant and did not substantially change along the way.

More specifically, the second and third criteria above must be accompanied by the fact the defect made the product unreasonably dangerous. The plaintiff, Beefy, has a number of alternatives to consider for proving strict liability against Ford.

Working with his attorney, Beefy must decide which theory(s) of recovery to pursue. Can you, as a burgeoning legal expert(!), decide which theory is most viable for Beefy? Here are some possibilities.

- *Manufacturing Defect* – A flaw in a product that occurs during production whereby the product is fundamentally different than the others rolling off the same production line. In our case, the plaintiff could argue his Ford truck had a manufacturing defect which led to the truck's structural failure when attempting to pull down the tree.

- *Design Defect* – Despite the product being manufactured according to the specifications, a product can be defective if inadequate design or poor choice of materials makes it dangerous to users. In the case of *Mason v. Ford Motor Co.*, 307 F.3d 1271 (11th Cir. 2002), Richard Mason sued Ford Motor Company in the death of his son for a design defect in Ford Explorers. Evidence showed that his son survived a crash in the Explorer but was subsequently killed when the fuel tank exploded. Ford was found liable for the faulty design and testing of the fuel tank. Similarly in the case of *Muth v. Ford Motor Co.*, 461 F.3d 557 (5th Cir. 2006), Barry Muth sued Ford Motor Company for injuries he sustained in an accident in 1996. He won on the basis the design contained "inadequate rollover/roof crush protection" and an "inadequate occupant restraint system." In our case, the plaintiff may contend his truck's frame was improperly designed or inadequate materials were used such that the truck should have instead been able to withstand the rigors of towing down the tree.

- *Inadequate Warnings* – A product must carry adequate warnings of the risks involved in its normal use. To prevail on the basis of failure-to-warn, the plaintiff must prove the defendant breached a duty to warn and that the failure to warn was the proximate cause of the injury. In our scenario, Beefy would have to prove that pulling down a tree was a normal use for the truck and that he was not warned of the risks involved with this use.

2. Liable Parties and Potential Damages

After consulting his attorney, Beefy is overjoyed to find out he may sue not only Ford but also other parties in the chain of distribution. Under product liability laws, the auto maker, component parts manufacturer, and retailer may all be strictly liable for any defects discovered with the Ford pick-up. Now that Beefy understands the theories of recovery upon which to build his case and the parties whom he will target in his suit, a final step in building the case is to evaluate the damages sought.

Product liability laws provide an array of compensatory and punitive damage possibilities. However, more than thirty states, including Florida, have enacted legislation limiting the punitive damages awards. Since Beefy's case would be heard in Florida, state law limits punitive damages to the greater of three times the compensatory damages or $500,000.

3. Defenses

If you were a manager at Ford, which defense would you employ?

To battle Beefy's claims, Ford and its potentially liable distribution partners have a number of defenses to raise on their own behalf. However, there are three product liability defenses most applicable to the case.

- *Assumption of Risk* – This defense holds that the manufacturer is not liable for any resulting injury when the injured party voluntarily and unreasonably assumes the risk of a known danger. In our case, Ford may contend their pick-up was never intended to be used for towing fixed objects such as trees. In fact, the owner's manual warns against it and provides specific instructions as to the truck's towing purposes and thresholds.

- *Obvious Risk* – If the use of the product carries an obvious risk, the manufacturer cannot be held liable for any injuries resulting from ignoring the risk. Despite our plaintiff's assertion that Ford should have warned of the dangers of using the truck to pull down a tree, the courts often apply the standard that a manufacturer need not warn if the danger is generally known and recognized. Arguably, Ford could build a strong case on the grounds that using their product to pull down a tree is a generally accepted dangerous behavior.

- _Unforeseeable Misuse of the Product_ – This defense holds that a manufacturer or seller is entitled to assume its product will be used in a normal manner, thus they will not be liable for injuries resulting from abnormal usage. It is reasonable to assume Ford will contend that using its pick-up to pull down a large, planted tree was not a foreseeable use of its product, thereby removing any liability.

4. Conclusion

In the case of _Truck v. Tree_, Ford would not be responsible for Beefy's injuries or the loss of his truck if Beefy's attempt to pull the tree down with his truck was an unforeseeable misuse of the product.

In order to win on strict liability, Beefy would have to prove the Ford truck was defective. But Ford, as well as many other truck manufacturers, often shows its trucks in advertisements ripping large stumps out of the ground, towing semi-tractor trailers, or pulling airliners down a runway. What, if anything, does this do to Ford's ability to limit the foreseeable uses of its pick-up trucks when it is advertising to the contrary?

H. Ethical Issues in Product Liability

1. A Skit Example: "An Alarming Alarm Clock"

YOUTUBE – Alarming_Alarm_Clocks_10mins10secs -

http://www.youtube.com/watch?v=a47Z5JVY5ao - at robertwemersonufl

> _Narrator:_ It's 7 a.m. on a typical workday, and we find our future plaintiff, Stacey Pillow Casey, deep asleep….. Until now.
> **Alarm sounds.**
> **Stacey (getting up from her pillow): Oh, I hate that alarm clock!**
> **Stacey tries to turn the alarm off – then, a high voltage sound goes "zzzzzzzzzzzz." Stacey tries to turn it off, but she lets go of the clock in pain. .**
> _Stacey:_ Good gosh! That electric shock almost made me forget that ridiculous dream I was having. I dreamt I was trapped taking a business law test and every time I finished the last problem another one would appear! What a nightmare!"
> _Narrator:_ Or, you find yourself dressed nearly naked – just your jammies! - in front of thousands of people!"
> **Alarm sounds again. Then, after Stacey tries to turn it off, the clock starts to spark, almost like a firecracker! Stacey beats the clock with her pillow. It finally stops.**
> _Stacey:_ What was that? That's one messed-up alarm clock. There's got to be a better way to wake you up than with a clock that sputters and hisses and shoots sparks like it's the Fourth of July!
> **Alarm sounds a third time. Stacey again tries to turn the alarm off, but fails. Soon it becomes an eerie, ear-splitting sound seemingly from a bad, bad Sci-Fi movie. Stacey this time persists in holding the clock, fighting through the pain as she shakes the clock and puts the clock on the ground and stomps on it. Stacey sits in exhaustion, with things finally quiet. But now a lawyer appears!**
> _Narrator:_ Quickly entering the room is Stacey's lawyer, Slick Suer.
> _Slick:_ What's wrong, Stacey?
> _Stacey:_ Gee, Slick, you're fast. I hadn't called you. I hadn't even <u>thought</u> of calling you.
> _Slick:_ Well, any lawyer worth his salt knows when his client SHOULD be calling him. I'm very proactive.
> _Narrator:_ Some would call it ambulance-chasing.
> _Slick:_ Mr. Narrator, I'd advise you to watch your language. I got a subpoena right here in my pocket, and I know how to use it!
> _Stacey:_ Yesterday I purchased that alarm clock from the store, Here Today Gone Tomorrow. When the alarm went off this morning I tried to shut it off but it kept shocking me. I'm not sure, but – maybe - I ought to take that clock back and get it replaced.
> _Narrator_: Maybe? Maybe!

> *Slick:* (to Narrator) Now you're thinking. Mr. Narrator, welcome to the bar association!
> (to Stacey) Now, Stacey, is that all you really want to do? Return the clock for a replacement?
> *Stacey*: Well, uh . . .
> *Slick:* Stacey, you <u>could</u> do that, but is that enough? As you know, I'm a lawyer at Dewy Cheatham & Howe, and I can tell just by looking at you that you have suffered immensely as a result of the defective alarm clock. I'm sure we can prove negligence in that the manufacturer and everyone else associated with the product or any of its components failed to use reasonable care in <u>designing</u> or <u>making</u> that alarm clock.
> And there's more. When you took the alarm clock out of the box, Stacey, did you see any warning about the risk of electrocution from using the product?
> *Stacey*: No.
> *Slick:* Any warnings at the store?
> *Stacey:* I don't think so.
> *Slick*: So, wouldn't you agree, Stacey, that something was <u>dreadfully wrong</u> with that clock?
> *Stacey:* It was pretty dreadful.
> *Slick:* That's right, Stacey. <u>Dreadful!</u> When we sue every business that sent onward this defective product, all we gotta prove is that you just took the clock out, started it up, and then were horribly injured from a defect rendering the clock unreasonably dangerous. It's a case of Strict Liability. Honey, I smell cash!
> *Stacey:* Wow, you're right. I do feel sort of <u>funny</u> after that horrific experience.
> *Slick:* Funny? No I don't think so. Maybe sick. Yes, <u>grievously</u> ill, Stacey. Don't you have a headache that won't go away? And I can tell by the way your arm looks that you lost some feeling in it. I bet you will get duh willies – duh cold sweats - every night you go to bed, afraid that in the morning you'll have to turn off, and perhaps be <u>electra-fried</u> by, another alarm clock. Undoubtedly, this will <u>affect</u> you for the <u>rest</u> of your natural born days, with you never able to, uh, keep a job.
> *Stacey:* Really, why?
> *Slick:* Because you cannot get up on time.
> *Stacey*: Huh?
> *Slick:* Because you are afraid of alarm clocks!
> *Stacey*: (At first she is perplexed. Then she finally gets it. She now completely sees the light.)
> Those poopy-heads! How could they do this to me! I just want to cry; my life is over.
> *Slick*: YES, YES, Stacey, please cry. I will do the rest!
>   THE END

2. Discussion of Law and Ethics

Does simply obeying statutes, common law decisions, and administrative regulations exhaust the moral duties businesses owe to consumers? Ethics may demand more.

Mohandas Gandhi is credited with saying:
"Your beliefs become your thoughts,
Your thoughts become your words,
Your words become your actions,
Your actions become your habits,
Your habits become your values,
Your values become your destiny."[166]

---

[166] Also note how language can influence how we think. *See* GUY DEUTSCHER, THROUGH THE LANGUAGE GLASS: WHY THE WORLD LOOKS DIFFERENT IN OTHER LANGUAGES (2010) (discusses how language can influence cognition, which is known as weak linguistic relativity, while rejecting the

In the end, adherence to high ethical standards may be better for one's conscience, soul, or mental health.[167] And this adherence may, in the end, redound to the economic benefit of a business.

> "CUSTOMER SERVICE, WHERE ARE YOU?" - a *video skit* - is in Part Three of the Resources section of the course website.
> **"Uh, huh; uh huh, okay; so what is it?"**
> The audience never finds out what is in the box and exactly what is wrong with it. We just know that it evidently does not work *and* that the customer relations representative apparently is stalling; he is not prepared to do very much to placate the customer.
> Even if the business has no legal duty to reimburse the customer, the business' failure to do so may not make business sense, anyway. If it is all a close question (i.e., the law or facts are unclear), the safe approach is to reimburse the consumer. Obviously, sometimes businesses have a legal obligation to refund money. One can get in big trouble for NOT obeying warranty law, say, by putting customers on hold without really accommodating them.
> **Ultimately > Angry Customers > Poor Public Relations & Lawsuits.**
> Even if one was legally justified to do what one did, those actions may have so angered others that your actions were counterproductive, for they led to lawsuits. One's acts started the downward spiral > poor communications, putting people on hold > poor customer relations.

Concerning product liability, one can put forth several standards that businesses should meet regardless of whether the law requires such action. Note that the following seven principles present more a series of ethical duties than they posit a legal mandate:

a. Businesses must monitor all manufacturing processes. For example, there should be rigorous safety testing procedures.

b. Businesses must have their safety specialists review their marketing strategies and their advertising for possible safety problems. Inasmuch as the marketing and advertising influence how a product is ultimately used, and by whom, the marketing and advertising affect the likelihood and severity of particular safety problems.

c. Businesses must provide consumers with specific, understandable written information about their products, including clear operating instructions, a description of the product's safety features, a complete list of how the product can be used, a strong warning about the conditions that tend to cause the product to fail or malfunction, and a specific admonition listing the ways in which the product should not be used.

> Failure to Follow Instructions, or to Take Safety Measures or Otherwise to Behave Sensibly – failuretofollowdisrections2mins21secs (http://www.youtube.com/watch?v=UhFtfc25xM0) is a YOUTUBE video at robertwemersonufl.
> Examples include: no loosening up before or warming down after exercising; improper loading; using a product without heeding warnings; playing sports without use of protective equipment; traveling without using a seat belt or helmet.

d. Businesses must anticipate and minimize the ways in which their products can cause harm, even harm involving product misuse. If a type of "misuse" is foreseeable, particularly misuse that could cause serious bodily harm to the consumer or third parties, the business may need to take extraordinary measures to ensure continued safe use of the product.

---

hypothesis of Benjamin Lee Whorf that language controls cognition); JOHN LEAVITT, LINGUISTIC RELATIVITY (2011) (applying both anthropological and historical analyses to how language influences thought).

[167] One's values may actually affect what word one uses to refer to this benefit to the self.

> INSIDE A BICYCLE HELMET
> "Shell of injection molded thermoplastic, liner of expanded polystyrene.
> WARNING! No protective headgear can protect the wearer against all foreseeable impacts. However, for maximum protection this helmet must be of good fit and all retention straps must be securely fastened.
> Helmet can be seriously damaged by many common substances including solvents, paints and adhesives without damage being visible to the user. Use only mild soap and water to clean shell, liner and pads. Make no modifications. If helmet experiences a severe blow, return to the manufacturer for inspection or destroy and replace it."
> Several features related to that warning.
> <u>Why destroy a helmet that "experiences a severe blow," and not just throw it away? A mechanical engineer and UF grad who regularly watches my class explains in a letter he wrote to me:</u>
> "The reason for destroying the helmet is to keep anyone from using the helmet that he/she might reclaim from the trash or a dump. A lawn mower was thrown away by three different owners, and a fourth owner injured himself and sued the manufacturer for his injury. The design engineer - who knows the hazards, should write the warning because the marketing people may tone down the warning's severity to not scare the consumer and to help sell the product. The warning should clearly disclose ALL possible dangers, including death. Good warning!
> "BTW, I really enjoy your class."

e. Businesses must investigate consumer complaints. Those complaints which are not frivolous may serve as a spur to prevent future injuries via improved warnings, designs, and manufacturing processes.

> Improving the warning design, and Some Consumer Protection Laws
> If one does not read a warning or other disclaimer, then one may not deal with it. Studies often show people do not read warnings or even notice them. It may be better to put warnings in assembly directions rather than in a separate area of the papers, which people often do not read.
> A number of jurisdictions have statutes that prohibit or otherwise restrict the use of limitations on implied warranties or on remedies for their breach. These prohibitions/restrictions typically are intended to protect consumers. These jurisdictions include Alabama, California, Connecticut, the District of Columbia, Kansas, Maine, Maryland, Massachusetts, Minnesota, Mississippi, New Hampshire, Oregon, Rhode Island, South Carolina, Vermont, Washington, West Virginia, and Wisconsin.

f. Businesses must give safety the priority called for by a particular product. While cost cannot be ignored, businesses must bear in mind the severity of potential injuries as well as the frequency of a mishap. Strict budgetary calculations of costs versus savings can easily be thrown out of kilter by unforeseen factors, so - even assuming that bottom-line economic balancing (e.g., weighing how much a life is worth) is morally permissible, it may not prove fiscally sound in the long run. The ethically responsible approach is to err a bit on the side of increased safety rather than stick to strict "bean counting."

g. Businesses should carefully evaluate the morality (or lack thereof) of selling products abroad which cannot be so easily sold in the domestic market because of stricter laws protecting the consumer. Examples of products "easier" to sell abroad include: products (e.g., toys, drugs, equipment) requiring expensive testing and, perhaps, also expensive modifications to meet federal or state safety standards; cigarettes[168] or other products requiring dramatic warning labels if sold in the United States.

Of course, one may disagree with these positions, or at least seek to clarify them further through the use of difficult examples.

I. The Inconsistent Positions on Product Liability

Most Republicans support a national uniform law to deal with product liability, while most Democrats prefer to keep this area a matter of state law. These are results-oriented positions, because most of the states permit a tort system more favorable to plaintiffs, and Democrats are more likely to be "pro-consumer" than are the more typically "pro-business" Republicans.

These positions do not align with the positions normally taken by the two political parties. In most other areas, such as corporate law, environmental law, labor law, and employment law, Republicans usually have favored state rights and Democrats have favored national legislation.

J. Product Liability Proposals

Many reforms have been enacted in a number of states. These new approaches often have one or more of the following measures:

1. no strict liability for just passing a product along without changing it;
2. limits on punitive damages, enacted so far in 34 states (Alabama, Alaska, Arizona, Arkansas, California, Colorado, Connecticut, Florida, Georgia, Idaho, Indiana, Iowa, Kansas, Kentucky, Louisiana, Minnesota, Mississippi, Missouri, Montana, Nevada, New Hampshire, New Jersey, New York, North Carolina, North Dakota, Ohio, Oklahoma, Oregon, South Carolina, South Dakota, Texas, Utah, Virginia and Wisconsin);
3. permitting the defendant to use negligence defenses, such as comparative negligence and assumption of risk, in strict liability cases.

No national reforms have been enacted. Among the proposed reforms are:
(1) to allow federal courts to hear most class-action suits (federal courts generally are considered more friendly to business in tort cases than are most state courts);
(2) provide more scrutiny of lawyers who reach settlements offering their clients "coupons" for goods or services, instead of cash (while the attorney, of course, gets paid in cash!);
(3) protect companies from the discovery process when they have dismissal motions pending;
(4) require plaintiffs to more clearly specify the relief they seek; and
(5) permit an immediate appeal when a court certifies a case as a class action.[169]

These constraints on liability findings and caps on damages awards have raised due process concerns for plaintiffs, just as – from the opposite perspective – high punitive damages awards relative to low compensatory damages has led the Supreme Court to acknowledge due process rights for the defendant.[170] Some state courts have struck down the tort reform legislation as unconstitutional, but other state courts have upheld these laws.

Beware of *Caveat Emptor*

Historically, the standard was *caveat emptor* (As stated by George Herbert (1593-1633), English clergyman and poet: "The Buyer needs a hundred eyes, the Seller not one." *Caveat emptor* ("Buyer

---

[168] Some economists have argued that – for society as a whole – cigarettes may not cost us much. The reason is that, while it increases some medical costs, the premature deaths save billions of dollars that otherwise would be paid in social security and Medicare.

[169] A state-of-the-art standard is found now in some states. If the defendant follows all of the highest standards or procedures available at the time of manufacture (operates at the "cutting edge"), *then* it may not be liable.

[170] State Farm Mutual Automobile Ins. Co. v. Campbell, 538 US 408 (2003).

Beware") was and is a seller's defense: so the buyer should inspect, ask questions, mull it over, make sure he/she knows what he/she is getting before he/she lays down money and walks off with the item.

TOPICAL LECTURE ON "Warranties"
Introduction to Topical Lecture:
Warranties are either express (e.g., UCC 2-313 – a seller's explicit guarantee that the goods have certain qualities) or implied (e.g., UCC 2-314 - *merchantability* - a guarantee that goods are reasonably fit for the general purpose for which they are sold). To be effective, a warning must be read and understood. Disclaimers of a warranty can eradicate or at least limit potential implied warranties, but usually are ineffective against express warranties (which, to be avoided, simply should not have been given in the first place). Much of warranties and disclaimers law is related to consumer protection law, which may aid consumer purchasers or users (the law may prohibit or limit the scope of disclaimers). For a similar transaction involving a business purchaser or user of goods, that customer would receive no such legal protection against restricted warranties or broadly worded disclaimers.

K. Warnings and Disclaimers
We have already seen that the warnings a business issues to consumers may help to meet regulatory disclosure requirements, negate possible liability for defectiveness of a product, and even increase the likelihood that a potential plaintiff assumed a risk or otherwise behaved negligently.

Warnings also may disclaim warranties. Here, we discuss disclaimers, and then consider some examples of disclaimers.

Disclaimers eliminate or, via modification, restrict warranty obligations. "As Is" is the classic disclaimer.[171]

If you really want people to read warranties, disclaimers, etc., then put them in the instructions. People evidently are more likely to read instructions - e.g., for installation or operation - than to read separate statements (e.g., Warnings) elsewhere in a product's packaging and documents. Of course, the Law ordinarily assumes that you have read a warning if it has been provided to you.

Disclaimers and the law of disclaimers are geared towards implied warranties. Disclaimers can wipe out, or limit, implied warranties. It is <u>very difficult (practically impossible) to disclaim an express warranty</u>. There is a practical and moral notion that one should not give with one hand and take away with the other hand. (You should not be able to express a warranty and later disclaim it.) Instead, just do <u>not</u> give an express warranty in the first place.

1. Parking Disclaimer: An Example
CLAIM CHECK, Scupper Valet Inc. (SVI), Anytown, Florida, USA
THIS CONTRACT LIMITS OUR LIABILITY – PLEASE READ IT:

---

[171] Here are two joke examples of disclaimers
Joke One: A pig sold "as is" might or might not oink.
Another Joke: A Disclaimed Birthday card, written by the Law Firm of Letz, Milkem & Cheatum: "Have a Happy Birthday! Disclaimer: The aforementioned wish for birthday happiness neither expresses nor implies responsibility on the card sender's part for said happiness. Furthermore, the undersigned is hereby indemnified, released, and otherwise absolved of any and all liability for any preexisting condition of sadness, grumpiness, or abject misery suffered by the recipient on the day heretofore specified. . . . Thank you. That will be 900 dollars . . . at least. Please remit at your earliest convenience."

Car is accepted for parking only. The vehicles parked by SVI will not be delivered without the surrender of the customers claim ticket. SVI hereby declares it is not responsible for fire, theft, damage to or loss of such vehicle or any articles left therein while operating or not operating services, except through our own negligence. All vehicles driven, requested for or delivered at the owners risk and any so person so driving shall be the exclusive servant of the owner. In no event will SVI assume liability for damage sustained through faulty brakes or other faulty equipment. SVI is not responsible for damage or claims whatsoever once the vehicle has left the premises. SVI reserves the right to choose the person and place for repairs. Any claims resulting from negligence of the valet will be handled by SVI, independent from the establishment. No employee has authority to vary or increase our liability or change the above terms and conditions.

2. An Example from Maryland Law: A Defective Heat Pump, Parts and Labor, Manufacturer's Disclaimer, and a Special State Law

There may be some special state laws affecting warranties and disclaimers, beyond the UCC and in addition to federal laws such as the Magnuson-Moss Act. That knowledge proved useful for your author long ago when his townhouse heat pump failed. The warranty/disclaimer language for the heat pump and related parts stated that the warranty for parts was four years, but for labor was just one year. The state law (Maryland UCC provision 2-316.1) was that when a warranty is extended to cover a consumer purchase, that warranty must cover both the price of parts and of labor.

L. Warranties Fundamentals (see pgs. 478-483; Emerson BL)

For all sales (UCC) there are a set of promises incidental or collateral to the sale (the contract) – warranties. The seller may not even know he/she is giving these promises, these warranties.

1. Introduction

Warranties are either express or implied. If you want a warranty to exist, it is generally better to make an express promise (and to put it in writing) than simply to hope a warranty is implied. Warranties are about character, quality, and time (how long).
Warranties usually go down the chain (down the stream of commerce) - lawsuits can go back up the chain (to everyone all the way up - in reverse chronological order).

Reliance is not needed for warranty claims under UCC Article 2 (Sales). Warranties for other types of contracts require reliance.

2. The Express Warranty (UCC 2-313) (see pgs. 461-62; Emerson BL)

Uniform Commercial Code Section 2-313 concerns the express warranty, which is about the quality, condition, and performance of goods. This warranty can be made by any seller (to the buyer, or perhaps others who take the goods from the buyer).

Usually the express warranty is in words, but it does not have to be in words. It does not have to be any particular words. It could be words such as "guarantee" or "promise" or "warrant."

Examples of statements that make, or do not make, an express warranty:
-new [Yes][172]   -gets good gas mileage [No][173]   -gets 48 miles per gallon [Yes][174]

---

[172] In the 1990s, a number of claims were made against Chrysler Corporation because some demonstrator models used at dealerships had disconnected odometers. People had purchased these cars as "new" when in fact they had been driven thousands of miles – many as much as 12,000 to 20,000 miles. The cars had been sold as having very few miles of driving (e.g., just 50 miles on the odometer), with that certainly being close enough to constitute "new"; but, in fact, the cars had been driven for far too many miles to be "new." So the sale of such cars was a breach of warranty.

[173] That is just opinion. What is *good* gas mileage has such a range of possibilities that it is too speculative. It is not an affirmation of fact, and is thus not a warranty.

-makes you sexy [No][175]   -Model ABC [Yes][176]   -seaworthy [Yes - industry standards][177]
-this little baby really hums! [No][178]

Opinions (such as statements of value), unless by an expert, in his/her area of expertise, are *not* warranties.

Puffing is not a warranty, nor a disclaimer.

Are Words Necessary? No. Warranties can arise from models, blueprints, diagrams, or photographs. A picture, indeed, is worth a thousand words.[179] So to use a picture can be, just like using words, an affirmation of the fact of conformance, or a description, or an expression by reference to a sample or model, and thus constitute a warranty.

Text of UCC 2-313: Express Warranties by Affirmation, Promise, Description, Sample

"1. Express warranties by the seller are created as follows:

(a) Any affirmation of fact or promise made by the seller to the buyer which relates to the goods and becomes part of the basis of the bargain creates an express warranty that the goods shall conform to the affirmation or promise.

(b) Any description of the goods which is made part of the basis of the bargain creates an express warranty that the goods shall conform to the description.

(c) Any sample or model which is made part of the basis of the bargain creates an express warranty that the whole of the goods shall conform to the sample or model.

2. It is not necessary to the creation of an express warranty that the seller use formal words such as "warrant" or "guarantee" or that he have a specific intention to make a warranty, but an affirmation merely of the value of the goods or a statement purporting to be merely the seller's opinion or commendation of the goods does not create a warranty."

---

[174] That is specific enough to be a guarantee. While some variance would probably not be a breach – mileage may vary, depending upon one's driving habits and the type of driving involved (e.g., city or highway traffic) – if the car got considerably below 48 miles per gallon that would likely be a breach of warranty.

[175] That is just opinion. The premise of most advertising is the overt or implied promise that you will be made richer, smarter, more popular, or attractive to others – all conditions that are difficult to quantify and that, especially for the nature of attractiveness ("Beauty is in the eye of the beholder") – courts would be extremely reluctant to view as a guarantee.

[176] It is an affirmation of fact – that you will receive a particular good (in this case, a specific brand – the ABC model). If you end up with a different brand, notably one of a lesser quality (e.g., the XYZ model), then that would constitute a breach of warranty.

[177] At first blush, the word "seaworthy" may seem to be a rather vague. But a long tradition in an industry (here, the maritime world) and a series of court opinions (or legislative or regulatory determinations) may have fleshed out the meaning of a term that would otherwise appear indefinite. "Seaworthy" is not mere opinion because of the longstanding court holdings and industry standards: there might be room to argue, but clearly a ship that is sold as "seaworthy" ought to be able to venture onto the ocean without succumbing to (sinking because of) even a minor storm. The *seaworthy* boat ought to be able to go to sea (e.g., into the Gulf of Mexico), not just onto a lake or slow-moving river.

[178] That statement, such as about an automobile, is an opinion. It is puffing, similar to statements claiming a purchaser would be rendered sexier. What exactly does it mean to say that a vehicle will "hum?" While the implication is that the car will drive smoothly (or in some other satisfactory manner), that does not lead to a sufficiently particular affirmation of fact to guarantee something to the purchaser. So there is no warranty.

[179] There are, for example, professors or other teachers who employ all sorts of visuals (e.g., drawings, skits, hats, costumes) to drive a point home to a class. The author is personally aware of such a business law professor! The idea is that these visuals make lectures more vivid and thus more memorable. That increases learning. Certainly, if visuals help students to acquire and retain knowledge, then visuals also should help someone to recognize and understand the creation of a warranty about the characteristics of a particular product.

3. Implied Warranties   (see pgs. 479-480; Emerson BL)

<u>Implied warranties</u> are warranties that the law derives by implication or <u>inference from the nature of the transaction</u> or the relative situations or circumstances of the parties.

The <u>trend</u> is for implied warranties replace caveat emptor ("buyer beware"). The justification is essentially the same as for having strict liability as a public policy for consumer purchases.

Still, the practical advice to a buyer, even nowadays, is: Inspect; you want a good product, not a lawsuit.

a. UCC 2-314

The warranty of merchantability is implied, unless expressly disclaimed by name, or the sale is identified with the phrase "as is" or "with all faults." Under UCC 2-314,[180] if you are a merchant or an expert, then you are responsible for (expected to provide a good with) the qualities associated with that good.

i. Trade Customs and Warranties: An Example

In defining and refining warranties and disclaimers, courts may consider trade customs.

For example, it is customary for car dealers to check new cars before delivering them to customers. Suppose that a dealership, Jumbled Jaguar, fails to make those checks. If the checks had been done, Jumbled Jaguar would have discovered that, in one of the automobiles, the car engine's exhaust gas leaked into the passenger compartment. While driving the car, the buyer of that defective car is overcome by carbon monoxide fumes and, as he passes out, his car hits a tree. Jumbled Jaguar may be liable to the buyer for the damages caused by its breach of an implied warranty arising from trade usage (UCC 2-314 and its Official Comments). If Jumbled Jaguar had performed according to trade custom, the problem would have been found and repaired before the buyer even received the car.

ii. UCC 2-314 Extending to All in the Chain: Another Example

Assume that you purchase a shirt from a merchant. Under UCC 2-314 (warranty of merchantability), the shirt's seams should NOT unravel right away. The warranty extends to everyone in the chain (buyers and sellers – all transferors and transferees) who obtains the shirt. As discussed shortly, there is probably no claim under UCC 2-315 unless there was a representation to the buyer of a specific or extraordinary use for the shirt – e.g., to help the wearer fly. (Buyer - "I thought it was a superhuman shirt" and would help me fly or win the triathlon or carry out some other amazing physical feat.)

The UCC 2-314 and CISG Article 35 are very similar. The only notable difference is that the UCC restricts the extent to which the parties to a contract can limit its implied warranties. Under the

---

[180] Text of UCC 2-314 - Implied Warranty of Merchantability; Usage of Trade (italics added by author to emphasize certain language):

"1.Unless excluded or modified (Section 2-316), a warranty that the goods shall be merchantable is implied in a contract for their sale *if the seller is a merchant* [defined in UCC 2-104(1)] *with respect to the goods* of that kind. [That means that retailers, manufacturers, and/or experts concerning the goods in question.] Under this section the serving for value of food or drink to be consumed either on the premises or elsewhere is a sale.

2. *Goods to be merchantable* must be at least such as:
(a) pass without objection in the trade under the contract description; and
(b) in the case of fungible goods, are of fair average quality within the description; and
(c) *are fit for the ordinary purposes for which such goods are used*; and
(d) run, within the variations permitted by the agreement, of even kind, quality and quantity within each unit and among all units involved; and
(e) are adequately contained, packaged, and labeled as the agreement may require; and
(f) conform to the promises or affirmations of fact made on the container or label if any.

3. Unless excluded or modified (Section 2-316), other implied warranties may arise from course of dealing or usage of trade."

> implied "warranty of merchantability" provision, a disclaimer must be conspicuous. According to UCC 1-201(10), conspicuous is "a term or clause that is so written that a reasonable person against whom it is to operate ought to have noticed it."
>
> The CISG, on the other hand, does not limit disclaimers of implied warranties. It assumes that the parties in an international transaction are more sophisticated than the average buyer and need, therefore, fewer legal protections.

b. UCC 2-315

The warranty of fitness for a particular purpose is implied when a buyer relies upon the seller to select the goods to fit the specific request.

Uniform Commercial Code Section 2-315 (UCC 2-315)[181] applies only when the seller (any seller, whether a merchant or nonmerchant) knows or should know the buyer's purpose and knows that the buyer is relying on the seller's skills/judgment to obtain **suitable goods**.

Assume that you enter a store and announce, "I need motor oil for my xyz car; what do you recommend?" If you end up buying Motor Oil at the store, a number of conclusions may be drawn:

(1) If the motor oil does not do what the package says it does, then there is a breach of express warranty (UCC 2-313);

(2) There is a breach of warranty of merchantability (UCC 2-314) if the oil does not do what you would normally expect the oil to do.

(3) Did the purchaser tell the seller the specific type of motor for which the oil is needed? Was saying "for my xyz car" sufficient? Did the store personnel give recommendations, based on that specific intended use (i.e., the particular engine/machinery)? If so, then that establishes a possible warranty under UCC 2-315 (warranty of a specific purpose), for which a breach is possible.

A key question is: What did the seller know about the buyer's prospective use?[182]

Consider the computer industry as an example. Critics contend that computer makers and retailers frequently misstate the memory, Internet readiness, screen size, laptop weight, battery life, CD-ROM speed, printer speed, abilities of high-speed modems, on-site warranties, and what constitutes the bundled software. As with any product, in any industry, it almost always is better for a buyer simply to avoid these problems entirely - by avoiding the product - than to buy the product and acquire both the product AND its problems.

c. Comparison to the Civil Law

In France, rather than having the same implied warranties as in American law, sellers are held liable for latent defects. French Civil Code, Article 1641. French law looks to the actual intentions of the parties, but also has a tradition of regulating contracts once they are made. As stated in the French

---

[181] Text of UCC 2-315 (Implied Warranty: Fitness for Particular Purpose): "Where the seller at the time of contracting has reason to know any particular purpose for which the goods are required and that the buyer is relying on the seller's skill or judgment to select or furnish suitable goods, there is unless excluded or modified under the next section [2-316] an implied warranty that the goods shall be fit for such purpose."

[182] If a person in a farming community walks into a store to buy some rope, that rope purchase will involve possible express warranties (e.g., guarantees in the labeling or packaging of the rope) and perhaps an implied warranty of merchantability (for ordinary farm uses of the rope), but no implied warranty of fitness for a particular purpose that is unknown to the store employees. If the rope were to be used on the farm, but for, say, Helicopter cow lassoing – with branding of steers in mid-air(!) – that presumably is not a normal usage and the employees would have to know of that use in order to make a recommendation for which the 2-315 warranty might apply. Even a UCC 2-314 merchantability breach is unlikely to be found if the rope breaks and Bovine Bessie plummets to the ground from the hovercraft.

Civil Code, Article 1135, "Contracts create obligations not merely in relation to what they expressly provide, but also to all the consequences which equity, custom, or legislation give to them according to their nature." Some French laws supplement the parties' contractual terms (*loi supplétive*), which the parties can overcome by simply being more precise in their language. But increasingly the Civil Code of the past few decades has moved toward the *loi imperative* – a law governing contracts that the parties cannot alter.

4. Overlapping Warranties

The law ordinarily permits several different overlapping warranties. One can use all of these warranties, if they are consistent. If the warranties are inconsistent, then the UCC resolves it (i.e., it determines which warranty is given priority).

5. UCC 2-318 and Breach of Warranty Lawsuits

Privity is not an issue for negligence and strict liability cases and often not much of an issue for alleged breaches of warranty. The latter is the case because of UCC 2-318, which concerns liability based on warranties. (One might try, as plaintiff, to use all 3 approaches: Negligence, Strict Liability, and Warranties.)

Text of Uniform Commercial Code Section **2-318 (Third Party Beneficiaries of Warranties Express or Implied)** *(States to select one of three alternatives)*:

Alternative A:
"A seller's warranty whether express or implied extends to any natural person who is in the family or household of his buyer or who is a guest in his home [in Florida, this is added here - "or who is an employee, servant, or agent of his buyer"] if it is reasonable to expect that such person may use, consume or be affected by the goods and who is injured in person by breach of the warranty. A seller may not exclude or limit the operation of this section."

Alternative B:
"A seller's warranty whether express or implied extends to any natural person who may reasonably be expected to use, consume or be affected by the goods and who is injured in person by breach of the warranty. A seller may not exclude or limit the operation of this section." Alternative B is slightly broader than Alternative A.

Alternative C:
"A seller's warranty whether express or implied extends to any person who may reasonably be expected to use, consume or be affected by the goods and who is injured by breach of the warranty. A seller may not exclude or limit the operation of this section with respect to injury to the person of an individual to whom the warranty extends." Alternative C is the broadest in coverage of the three alternatives. It covers not just natural persons (as Alternatives A and B are restricted), but any persons (including corporations).

So, if a blade comes whirling off a lawnmower and strikes a passerby, the passerby has a warranty claim against the manufacturers/wholesalers/retailers under Alternative C, probably has a warranty claim under Alternative B (e.g., a neighbor walking by could "reasonably be expected to É be affected by the goods") and only has a warranty claim under Alternative A if the passerby also happens to be a family member, household member, or guest of the people operating/owning the lawnmower.

Note that Alternative C simply says "injured"; unlike Alternatives A & B, Alternative C is not limited to physical injuries. It can cover property damage. But here, too, the seller can exclude or limit property damage claims. (The last sentence of C simply says that the seller cannot exclude or limit claims arising out of personal injury. Also, the last sentence in each of Alternatives A & B means that the personal injuries alleged under those Alternatives cannot be disclaimed.)

6. A Practice Question

To understand better both warranties and strict liability, consider the following hypothetical question, with all names taken from William Shakespeare's *Romeo and Juliet.*

Mercutio Merchant owns and operates a retail outlet that sells equipment to grocery stores. He carries new Montague Manufacturers meat slicers, one of which is sold to Benvolio's Butchering Boutique (BBB). A few days after the purchase, Juliet, a BBB employee, was slicing meat for a customer when the blade flew off the slicer and injured Romeo, who was strolling by. If Romeo can establish that Montague Manufacturers provided defective parts to Mercutio Merchant, but asserts a claim against Mercutio Merchant for the injury, what is Romeo's best theory of liability?

Factual Chronology of the Hypothetical Example

Montague Manufacturers > Mercutio Merchant > BBB (with Juliet, a BBB employee) > Customer

- - - - - Injury to Romeo from Juliet using blade that flies off]

Choices for Answer

Romeo's best theory of liability is:

i. Express warranty.
[Nothing in the facts of the question indicates anything about warranties. That must be right based on the facts. So, NOT THE CORRECT ANSWER.]

ii. Negligence, relying on res ipsa loquitur.
[Hint: Who was in control of the instrumentality when harm was caused? Since Mercutio was not in control when the harm happened, the res ipsa loquitur case could be against BBB but not Mercutio. So, NOT THE CORRECT ANSWER.]

iii. Negligence relying on respondeat superior.
[Hint: for whom was Juliet working? Since she was working for BBB, respondeat superior could work against BBB, but not against Mercutio. So, NOT THE CORRECT ANSWER.]

iv. Comparative/Contributory Negligence.
Irrelevant: these are used as defenses, just as act of God and Assumption of Risk are. SO, DEFINITELY NOT THE CORRECT ANSWER! These are not claims or causes of actions. The answer is total nonsense]

v. Strict liability.
[YES – see the six elements of strict liability – the mnemonic DEUNCH discussed above concerning strict liability for defects]

End of Topical Lecture on "Warranties"

THE END OF PART THREE OF THE TEXT

END OF THE TEXT (EXCEPT FOR THE INDEX)

Index

10-K.... 147
10-Q.... 147
14Th Amendment.... 25, 52, 245, 414
1St Amendment.... 25
4Th Amendment.... 25, 52, 245, 414, 464, 465, 466
5Th Amendment.... 25, 296, 341, 395, 399, 400, 406, 464, 465
8-K.... 147
8Th Amendment.... 17, 25, 414
A. Bartlett Giamatti.... 4
A.p. Herbert.... 427
Abe Fortas.... 337, 361
Ability Tests.... 313
Abortion.... 10, 306
Abraham Lincoln.... 64, 330, 368, 397
Abuse Of Discretion.... 151
Abuse Of Power.... 298, 318
Abuse Of Process.... 336, 457
Abusive Discharge.... 106, 299, 300, 304, 305, 307, 321, 470
Abusive Working Environment.... 320
Academia.... 329
Academic Background.... 354
Acceptance.... 37, 132, 171, 172, 176, 177, 179, 184, 185, 187, 196, 200, 203, 204, 205, 208, 209, 210, 211, 212, 213, 217, 242, 276, 277, 281, 367, 440
Access To Information.... 30, 379
Accidents.... 100, 272, 424, 428, 437, 441, 448
Accommodation.... 290, 307, 310, 315, 323, 324, 325
Accountant.... 91, 139, 140, 141, 186, 187, 226, 234, 235, 238, 250, 300, 345, 346, 347, 396, 399, 436, 437
Accounting.... 4, 106, 110, 119, 121, 135, 147, 148, 152, 207, 235, 250, 299, 339, 341, 437, 439
Act Of God.... 440, 441, 442, 497
Act Of Parliament.... 43
Active Misrepresentation.... 233

Actual Agency.... 90, 95
Actual Authority.... 90, 91, 97, 110
Actual Harm.... 75, 87, 153, 227, 419
Actual Notice.... 95, 96, 374
Actual Termination.... 180, 304
Actus Reus.... 418, 419, 429
Adam & Berthunia Example.... 188
ADEA.... 301
Adequacy Of Consideration.... 217, 218, 294
Adequate Consideration.... 217, 219, 444
Adhesion Clause.... 248, 257, 258
Adhesion Contract.... 257
Administrative Agencies.... 31, 103, 104, 111, 329, 392, 478
Administrative Code.... 13
Administrative Law.... 30, 31, 36, 358, 410, 448
Administrative Remedies.... 473
Administrators.... 311, 312, 318, 444, 476
Admiralty Law.... 424
Admission.... 22, 50, 72, 257, 262, 328, 339, 340, 341, 381, 384, 386, 391, 392, 482
Adr.... 13, 53, 143, 300, 410, 412, 458
Adrienne Breidigan.... 458
Adversarial Approach.... 60, 62, 344
Adverse Impact.... 310, 311, 313, 314, 376
Adverse Treatment.... 302
Advertisements.... 8, 92, 199, 200, 230, 313, 357, 445, 467, 468, 486
Advice.... 45, 109, 111, 115, 148, 223, 227, 237, 241, 310, 329, 343, 344, 345, 348, 349, 350, 388, 398, 399, 494
Advocate.... 10, 38, 48, 53, 62, 63, 297, 333, 340, 341, 342, 343, 344, 347, 385, 427, 463
Affection.... 218, 462
Affirm The Contract.... 232
Affirmation.... 8, 25, 408, 464, 492, 493, 494
Affirmative Defenses.... 150, 377
AGBG.... 255

Age Discrimination Employment Act.... 303
Agency By Estoppel.... 93, 121
Agency Costs.... 137, 211
Agency Law.... 90, 105, 116, 121, 236, 257, 323, 336
Agency Relationship.... 103, 107, 110, 336
Agent's Duties.... 106
Agent's Powers.... 110
Agents Of The Corporation.... 145, 150
Aggrieved Party's Behavior.... 294
Agravio Morat.... 183, 289
Agreements To Agree.... 199
AICPA.... 347
AIDS.... 393, 437
Airbags.... 482
Airline Ticket.... 240, 425, 471
Akzo Nobel V. Commission.... 350
Alabama.... 16, 22, 45, 46, 52, 88, 247, 328, 351, 356, 369, 440, 446, 452, 481, 489, 490
Alaska Packers Ass'n v. Domenico..... 220
Albert Einstein.... 128
Alexander Hamilton.... 31
Alexis De Tocqueville.... 4
Alibis.... 447
Alienation Of Affections.... 462
Alleged Discrimination.... 188, 303, 308
Alleged Misrepresentation.... 242
Alleged Retaliation.... 301, 319
Alteiri V. Colasso.... 430, 431
Alter Ego.... 27, 152, 153, 154, 155
Alternate Jurors.... 45
Alternative A.... 410, 496
Alternative Dispute Resolution.... 410, 411
Alternative Pleadings.... 378
Amazon.... 369, 457
Ambiguity Of Terms.... 200
Amending The Constitution.... 33
Amendments.... 20, 23, 25, 30, 33, 74, 141, 142, 167, 341, 414
American Association Of Retired Persons.... 332

American Bar Association.... 144, 334, 342, 345, 356, 363
American Institute Of Certified Public Accountants.... 347
American Law Institute.... 4, 144, 248
American Revolution.... 7, 22, 76
American Tobacco Company V. State.... 348
Americans With Disabilities Act.... 102, 104, 303, 306, 310, 315, 316, 323, 325
Analytical Skills.... 4
Anarchy.... 27, 30, 33, 54
Anatole France.... 42
Ancient Professions.... 63, 335
Ancillary.... 133, 193
Anderson V. Regents Of University Of California.... 270
Andrei Marmor.... 37, 38
Animal Rights.... 41
Anita Hill.... 365
Announcements.... 199, 277
Annulments.... 293
Anthony Kennedy.... 86, 365, 381
Anti-Discrimination Laws.... 299, 303, 313, 314, 315
Anti-Retaliation Provisions.... 301
Anti-Takeover Defenses.... 142
Anticipatory Breach.... 279, 280
Anticompetitive Behavior.... 343, 474
Anticompetitive Practices.... 470
Antitrust Law.... 36, 114, 132, 138, 421, 470, 474
Antitrust Violations.... 458
Antonin Scalia.... 84, 296, 364, 365, 461
Apparent Agency.... 93, 95
Apparent Assent.... 222
Apparent Authority.... 92, 93, 95, 96, 97, 98, 115, 116, 121
Apparent Principal.... 93
Appeals Court.... 4, 16, 48, 55, 98, 108, 110, 159, 207, 254, 299, 301, 302, 323, 325, 351, 352, 354, 356, 359, 360, 363, 365, 366, 403, 404, 405, 406, 407, 410, 442, 467, 471, 472, 473
Appearance Of Truth.... 397
Appellant.... 3, 403, 412

Appellate Courts.... 353, 359, 392
Applicable Law.... 6, 397
Appointed Federal Judges.... 353
Approaches.... 5, 11, 38, 40, 124, 179, 205, 259, 274, 283, 308, 391, 398, 410, 411, 446, 478, 490, 496
Appropriate Training.... 100
Arbitration.... 160, 211, 213, 220, 228, 320, 330, 391, 406, 410, 411, 412
Argentina.... 24, 28, 74, 124, 183, 194, 264, 289, 375, 407, 412, 416, 465
Aristotle.... 5, 18, 337, 338
Arizona.... 2, 45, 50, 53, 144, 156, 159, 351, 356, 359, 427, 490
Arm's Length Transaction.... 118
Arson.... 169, 285, 407, 429, 469
Article I.... 1, 21, 84, 99, 110, 169, 327, 360, 361, 413, 434
Article II.... 99, 110, 169, 327, 360, 361, 413
Article V.... 21, 33
Articles Of Confederation.... 21, 30
Articles Of Incorporation.... 140, 141, 142, 155, 201
Artificial Being.... 125, 126, 131
As Much As Deserved.... 187
As Much As You Earned.... 295
Asbestos.... 452
Ascertainable.... 167, 287
Aspirin.... 84, 87, 480
Assault.... 20, 108, 228, 307, 346, 401, 404, 405, 425, 427, 430, 431, 452, 455, 456, 457, 463, 467, 477
Assent.... 140, 177, 184, 198, 212, 222, 225, 230, 232, 235, 252, 266
Assignability.... 271, 272
Assignment.... 201, 268, 270, 271, 272, 319
Assisting Compromises.... 17, 18
Associate Justices.... 360, 361, 363
Associated Press V. Walker.... 162
Association Plans.... 332
Associations.... 80, 98, 105, 113, 156, 334, 343, 357
Assumption Of Risk.... 377, 440, 443, 444, 485, 490, 497
At Equal Fault.... 251

At-Will Doctrine.... 299
Athens.... 5, 12
Attachment.... 17, 119, 388, 475
Attorney Advertising.... 159
Attorney Client Privilege.... 349
Attorney-At-Law.... 111
Attorneys General.... 416, 476
Attorneys' Fees.... 256, 371
Attractive Nuisance.... 453, 454
At-Will Doctrine..... 299
Audit.... 104, 115, 136, 139, 146, 147, 152, 188, 309, 347
Auditors.... 139, 147, 347
Augustus.... 13, 84, 475
Auntie Nolo.... 344
Australia.... 14, 23, 54, 143, 194, 245, 256, 263, 264, 333, 375, 407, 412, 435, 446, 447
Authenticated Documents.... 386, 390
Authorized Act.... 89, 91, 95, 96, 99, 336, 351
Authors.... 31, 55, 64, 65, 68, 75, 76, 77, 78, 79, 162, 280, 380, 411
Auto Accident.... 238, 333, 341, 384, 428
Automatically Renewed Insurance Policy.... 210
Aviation Damages Limitations.... 433
Avocat.... 329, 330
Avocati.... 330
Avoidance.... 129, 195, 241, 292
AWCSE.... 101
Azar V. Lehigh Corp.... 471
Babylon.... 12, 130, 393
Back Pay.... 302
Bailment.... 257, 479
Baker V. Alt.... 428
Balance Of Equities.... 188
Balancing Of Interests.... 33, 79
Balancing Test.... 2, 34, 297, 464
Banishment.... 413
Bank Accounts.... 141, 188
Bank Deposits And Collections.... 191
Bankruptcy.... 114, 124, 132, 184, 185, 219, 221, 227, 281, 300, 328, 385, 408, 409
Bankruptcy Law.... 409

Banks.... 121, 130, 146, 196, 229, 324, 337, 380
Banque Indosuez.... 235
Bar Exam.... 327, 328, 339, 340
Bar Mitzvah Singer.... 273
Bargain Sale.... 130
Bargaining Power.... 172, 191, 227, 251, 252, 254, 255, 256, 257, 288, 388
Barney V. San Diego Chicken.... 79
Barristers.... 55, 329, 398
Bartnicki V. Vopper.... 460
Bates V. State Bar Of Arizona.... 159
Batson V. Kennedy.... 52
Battery.... 14, 19, 108, 109, 136, 169, 307, 417, 425, 430, 431, 432, 438, 452, 453, 455, 456, 457, 467, 495
Battle Of Hastings.... 14
Battle Of The Forms.... 211, 212, 213
Baumgartner V. United States.... 167
Belgium.... 23, 124, 184, 194, 263, 375, 412, 419, 483
Belief Of Impending Death.... 391
Bench Trials.... 47, 48, 376
Beneficiary Contracts.... 268
Bengoshi.... 329, 333
Benjamin Cardozo.... 35, 43, 118, 398, 426, 483
Benjamin Franklin.... 31, 111, 408
Berne Convention.... 76, 80, 81
Bespokoistvo.... 183, 286
Best Efforts.... 197
Better Business Bureau.... 82
Beyond A Reasonable Doubt.... 41, 233, 402, 415, 416, 419
BFOQ (Bona Fide Occupational Qualification), 315
Bias.... 49, 50, 52, 54, 61, 79, 134, 156, 170, 312, 359, 373, 375, 387, 411, 456
Bible.... 12, 218, 306, 400, 405, 458
Bids.... 42, 199, 316, 330, 331, 373
Big Picture.... 1, 58, 176, 197, 208, 390, 403
Big Tort.... 425
Bike-Bell Ordinance.... 428
Bilateral Contract.... 185, 186, 205, 210
Bill Gates.... 115

Bill Of Rights.... 22, 25, 30, 33, 341, 389, 414
Binding Contract.... 178, 179, 223, 240
BJR.... 150, 151
Black Armbands.... 165
Blacklisting.... 458
Bleak House.... 371
Blind.... 15, 173, 231, 232, 258, 313, 324, 325, 339
Blogs.... 162, 163, 164
Blue Laws.... 17
Blue Sky Laws.... 191
Blueprints.... 493
Board Certification.... 328
Board Of Directors.... 11, 96, 114, 127, 132, 135, 137, 140, 141, 144, 145, 146, 150, 207, 307, 473
BOARDSCAM.... 146
Bob Hill.... 407
Body Language.... 62
Body Politic.... 7, 167
Boilerplate Language.... 181, 197
Boise Dodge, Inc. V. Clark.... 286
Bolivia.... 24, 183, 289, 412
Bona Fide Occupational Qualification (BFOQ), 314, 316
Bonds.... 263, 458
Bonuses.... 122, 220, 362, 385
Boumediene V. Bush.... 381
Bourne Co. V. Twentieth Century Fox Film Corp.... 80
Boycotts.... 458, 474
Bragdon V. Abbott.... 324
Braunstein V. Jason Tarantella, Inc.... 246
Brazil.... 21, 23, 24, 124, 183, 194, 195, 287, 292, 334, 412, 445
Breach Of Duty.... 100, 109, 271, 426, 427, 428, 431, 435, 436, 438, 482
Breach Of Fiduciary Duty.... 118, 149
Breach Of Good Faith.... 163
Breach Of Warranty.... 484, 492, 493, 495, 496
Breaching Party.... 278, 280, 288, 290, 291
Brennan V. Bally Total Fitness.... 320
Bribery.... 47, 48, 133, 251, 421
Bribes.... 49, 107
Briefs.... 338, 350, 403, 412

Britain.... 9, 13, 22, 31, 60, 127, 131, 162, 329, 331, 337, 468
British Courts.... 31, 355, 391
Brokers.... 122
Brown V. Board Of Education.... 3, 9, 15
Bucerius Law School.... 329
Bull.... 41, 63, 77, 146, 158, 263, 279, 343, 370, 372, 451, 454, 464
Bundle Of Entrusted Gold.... 278
Burden Of Proof.... 75, 139, 257, 319, 390, 402, 415, 416, 435
Bureaucracy.... 31, 127, 128
Burglary.... 2, 413
Burlington Northern & Santa Fe Railway Co. V. White.... 302
Burma.... 413
Business Contracts.... 195, 254, 255
Business Deals.... 170, 185, 193
Business Decision Making.... 151
Business Entities19, 111, 114, 116, 124, 126, 127, 192, 384
Business Ethics.... 4, 337
Business Format1, 112, 114, 117, 119, 123, 124, 125, 128, 138
Business Judgment Rule.... 143, 148, 150
Business Necessity.... 313, 314, 316
Business Organizations.... 434
Business Records.... 391
Business Transactions.... 189, 194, 263, 283, 335, 338
Business-To-Business Contracts.... 254
Businesspersons.... 1, 58, 169, 180, 335
But For.... 49, 103, 129, 134, 152, 214, 224, 227, 310, 359, 384, 387, 413, 426, 431, 432, 486, 492, 495
Buy/Sell Agreement.... 119
Buyer Beware.... 147, 174, 477, 494
Buying Out A Partner.... 119
Bylaws.... 141, 146, 150
Byrne V. Boadle.... 435
Cal Ripken.... 468
Calendars.... 92
California Dental Association V. Ftc.... 343
California Supreme Court.... 53, 167, 247
Calvin Coolidge.... 138, 330
Cameron Stracher.... 330
Campaign Buttons.... 165, 277

Campaign Contributions.... 356, 357
Canada.... 14, 16, 20, 23, 24, 28, 84, 131, 143, 180, 194, 245, 264, 313, 329, 337, 351, 367, 375, 406, 407, 412, 416, 445, 465
Canadian Supreme Court.... 353
Cancellation.... 241, 254, 294
Canon Law.... 293
Cantons.... 23
Capacity..... 64, 87, 89, 98, 99, 115, 148, 170, 172, 182, 183, 184, 224, 239, 240, 241, 242, 243, 244, 245, 252, 253, 267, 269, 352, 391, 420, 450, 464
Capdodfwep.... 161
Capital Contributions.... 122
Capital Crimes.... 413
Card Shark.... 224
Carrie Chapman Catt.... 35
Cartoon Characters.... 76, 315
Carve Out.... 23, 368
Case Law.... 20, 29, 30, 31, 33, 60, 76, 90, 115, 303, 318, 358, 467, 473, 475, 481
Catalogues.... 199
Categorical Imperative.... 40, 57
Categorical Taking.... 296, 297
Categories Of Contracts.... 184
Categories Of Law.... 34
Categorization Of Crimes.... 413
Categorizing Contracts By How They Are Formed.... 186
Causation.... 229, 231, 232, 238, 425, 426, 429, 431, 433, 435, 436, 440, 442, 446, 469, 477, 479, 482
Cause Of Action.... 371, 409, 410
Caution.... 96, 425, 434, 441, 442
Caveat Emptor.... 147, 174, 477, 490, 494
Cellophane.... 84
Censure Of Judges.... 357
Center On Wrongful Convictions.... 398
Cert. Denied.... 78, 79, 93, 161, 299, 340, 350, 366, 462, 467
Certain Amount.... 172, 292
Certainty.... 4, 5, 18, 35, 132, 133, 189, 195, 281, 287, 475, 483
Certification Marks.... 82

Certified Mail.... 136, 374
Certiorari.... 340, 357, 360, 362, 363, 365, 366
Chaplinsky V. New Hampshire.... 167
Chapman V. Pickersgill.... 452
Chapter 11, 409
Character Checks.... 339
Character Witnesses.... 396
Charities.... 206, 209
Charles Barkley.... 460
Charles De Secondant.... 6
Charles Dickens.... 371
Charles Lamb.... 397
Charter.... 5, 33, 43, 98, 126, 130, 132, 133, 134, 135, 136, 138, 140, 142, 152, 155, 416
Chartering.... 133, 138
Chattel.... 389
Chaucer.... 331
Check The Box.... 111, 128
Checks And Balances.... 6, 24, 25, 26, 32
Ch'en Tu-Hsiu.... 18
Cherokee Nation V. Georgia.... 367
Chicken Tenders.... 85
Chief Justice John Marshall.... 126
Chores.... 183
Christine Jolls.... 170
Christopher D. Stone.... 41
Chung V. Kaonobi.... 290
Church Law.... 293
Cigarettes.... 69, 276, 277, 445, 490
Circuit Courts.... 24, 105, 352, 353, 359, 416
Circulars.... 84, 199
Circumstantial Evidence.... 338, 401, 402, 430
Cisg.... 193, 194, 195, 196, 204, 213, 246, 264, 267, 291, 297, 494, 495
Civil Cases.... 45, 46, 47, 48, 52, 63, 232, 353, 366, 414, 416, 420, 421
Civil Code.... 6, 240, 262, 267, 283, 297, 433, 495, 496
Civil Disobedience.... 9
Civil Law Judges.... 60, 263
Civil Law Nations.... 47, 61, 143, 183, 286, 289, 333, 392, 407
Civil Lawsuit.... 395, 402, 406

Civil Liberties.... 365
Civil Procedure.... 61, 63, 143, 368, 373, 374, 381, 386, 479
Civil Rights Act.... 104, 301, 303, 305, 312, 323
Civil Rights Movement.... 9
Civil War.... 24, 25, 33, 228, 344, 367, 405
Clackamas Gastroenterology Associates, P.c. V. Wells.... 102
Clams.... 126
Clarence Thomas.... 364, 365, 461
Clarification Of Ambiguity.... 266
Clark County School District V. Breeden.... 319
Class Actions.... 174, 333, 378, 379
Classifications Of Law19
Clauses.... 22, 94, 119, 157, 196, 203, 248, 254, 255, 256, 257, 258, 260, 271, 283, 284, 292, 320, 410, 411, 412, 471
Clayton Act.... 132, 138, 474
Clean House.... 239
Clear And Present Danger.... 161
Clerical Error.... 266
Close Corporation.... 123, 133, 135, 136, 137, 144, 154
Close Relations.... 52, 249
Close Relationship.... 249
Closely Held.... 128, 144
Closing Arguments.... 402
Clothing.... 86, 220, 243, 254
Clout.... 170
Co-Determination.... 145
Co-Owners.... 114, 116, 117, 119, 120, 121, 125
Coaching.... 398, 399
Coca Cola.... 87
Code Civil.... 13
Code Law.... 11, 19, 60, 286
Code Napoleon.... 13, 60
Code Of Commerce.... 13, 297
Code Of Hammurabi.... 12
Code Of Solon.... 12
Codes Of Ethics.... 237
Cohen V. California.... 165
Collections.... 191
Collective Membership Marks.... 82

Colorado Republican Federal Campaign Committee V. Fec.... 157
Commenda.... 122, 144, 207, 324, 360, 493, 495
Commentaries On The Common Law.... 7, 16
Commentaries On The Laws Of England.... 419
Commentators.... 63, 103, 146, 318, 341, 343, 367, 482
Commerce Clause.... 21
Commercial Code.... 20, 132, 189, 194, 195, 208, 212, 246, 253, 255, 262, 263, 492, 495, 496
Commercial Disparagement.... 472
Commercial Fraud.... 469
Commercial Free Speech.... 158, 160
Commercial Impracticability.... 281, 282, 283, 284
Commercial Law.... 20, 60, 189
Commercial Paper.... 19, 221
Commercial Purpose.... 79, 468
Commercial Speech.... 159, 160
Commingling.... 107, 154
Commissions.... 23, 94, 109, 110, 126, 196, 356, 362, 367, 374
Committees.... 146, 356
Common Knowledge.... 93, 94
Common Law Copyrights.... 75
Common Law Countries.... 20, 60, 127, 263, 264, 385, 419, 422
Common Law Doctrine.... 14, 117
Common Law Fraud.... 140
Common Law Heritage.... 286
Common Law Judges.... 60, 392
Common Law Marriage.... 247
Common Law Principles.... 60, 447
Common Law System.... 13, 16, 20, 353, 358, 407, 484
Common Ownership.... 117, 125
Commonality.... 13
Commonly Performed.... 101
Commonsense Rules.... 175
Communal Standard.... 208
Communications To Clergy.... 347
Communism.... 17, 32

Community.... 9, 40, 54, 114, 137, 141, 161, 396, 467, 473, 480, 495
Commuting.... 100
Company Rule.... 73, 300
Comparable Worth.... 312, 313
Comparative Advertising.... 476
Comparative Negligence.... 440, 444, 446, 490
Compelled Self-Incrimination.... 395
Compensatory Damages.... 285, 287, 288, 292, 306, 323, 386, 485, 490
Competence.... 8, 61, 250, 337, 342
Competent Attorney.... 415
Competent Lawyer.... 63, 339
Competent Tribunal.... 389
Competing Themes.... 298
Complete Lawsuits.... 406
Completed.... 106, 136, 184, 201, 210, 235, 261, 263, 271, 279, 356
Complex Civil Litigation.... 372
Complexity.... 4, 27, 194, 380, 391
Composition.... 72, 221, 389
Composition With Creditors.... 221
Compositions Of Matter.... 72
Compromise.... 13, 17, 18, 27, 37, 174, 195, 368, 369, 372, 381, 390, 474
Compulsion To Win.... 236, 237
Compulsory Self-Disclosure.... 400
Computer Programs.... 69
Concealment.... 424
Concurrent.... 198, 273, 352, 360
Condominium.... 172, 441
Confederacy.... 24, 228, 344
Confessions.... 2, 3, 50, 418
Confidences.... 11
Confidentiality.... 10, 345, 346, 347, 349, 438
Confirmation.... 96, 212, 263, 365, 389
Confirming Letter.... 263, 280
Conflict Of Interest.... 109, 148, 149, 361
Conflicting Terms.... 201, 203
Conscience.... 8, 219, 246, 254, 450, 488
Consequential Damages.... 287, 288, 289, 293
Consequentialism.... 40

Conservative.... 8, 54, 158, 161, 356, 360, 363, 364, 365
Consideration.... 28, 52, 65, 75, 76, 90, 150, 169, 171, 172, 182, 190, 196, 197, 204, 205, 206, 207, 214, 215, 216, 217, 218, 219, 220, 221, 241, 243, 247, 250, 259, 267, 269, 270, 294, 311, 423, 443, 444
Consistency.... 27, 343, 396
Conspiracy.... 20, 249, 348
Constantine.... 13
Constitutional Amendment.... 17, 20, 25, 33, 54, 158
Constitutional Court.... 351, 366
Constitutional Interpretation.... 30, 367, 368
Constitutional Law.... 2, 29, 30, 31, 351, 460, 464
Constitutional Protections.... 22, 414
Constitutional Question.... 340
Constitutional Rights.... 23, 27, 156, 340, 389
Construction.... 20, 113, 179, 279, 311, 361, 396, 411, 424, 454, 483
Constructive Notice.... 95, 96
Construe.... 26, 32, 78, 166, 196, 197, 202, 212, 284, 306, 315, 353, 369, 381, 421, 465
Consultants.... 44, 51, 147, 241, 312
Consumer Complaints.... 489
Consumer Debts.... 408
Consumer Expectations.... 480, 481, 482
Consumer Protection.... 174, 223, 238, 248, 251, 330, 476, 477, 482, 489, 491
Consumer Purpose.... 248
Consumer Transactions.... 238
Contemporaneous Words.... 266
Contemporary Community Standards.... 161
Contempt.... 48, 85, 165, 295, 359, 373, 459, 461
Contempt Of Court.... 48, 165, 295, 373, 461
Context Matters.... 166, 302, 463
Contingency Fees.... 332, 333, 334
Contract Clause.... 95, 110, 157, 190, 256, 271, 277, 410

Contract Duties.... 255, 271, 272, 273, 278, 281
Contract For Sale.... 190, 208, 212, 262
Contract Formation.... 173, 208, 469
Contract Of Adhesion.... 388
Contract Of Sale.... 179, 221
Contract Privity.... 268
Contract Suit.... 284
Contract Terms.... 93, 191, 213, 227, 266, 275, 285, 292, 295
Contractual Clauses.... 94
Contractual Elements.... 172
Contractual Obligation.... 207, 276, 280, 281, 282, 358
Contractual Rights.... 186
Contractual Stipulations.... 292
Contractual Terms.... 295, 496
Contrast Crimes.... 420
Contrast Offers.... 198
Contributions To Judicial Campaigns.... 356
Contributory Negligence.... 377, 399, 428, 440, 446, 497
Controlling Shareholder.... 148
Convenience.... 7, 315, 423, 491
Convention On Contracts For The International Sale Of Goods.... 194, 264
Conversion.... 188, 420, 425, 453
Convicted Felons.... 51
Convictions.... 6, 53, 55, 61, 228, 311, 396, 398, 399, 404, 413, 414, 418
Convicts.... 243, 245, 311, 413
Cooperatives.... 113
Copperheads.... 344
Copyright.... 65, 67, 68, 69, 72, 74, 75, 76, 77, 78, 79, 80, 81, 82, 83, 84, 87, 89, 160, 162, 290
Copyright Infringement.... 78, 79, 160
Copyright Office.... 75
Copyrightable.... 76, 78
Cornwall.... 14, 73
Corporate Attorney.... 338, 342, 348
Corporate Authority.... 95, 140
Corporate Charter.... 5, 132, 133, 152, 416
Corporate Data Sheet.... 141
Corporate Format.... 127, 129, 133, 137, 154

Corporate Governance.... 128, 137, 144, 147
Corporate Hierarchy.... 211
Corporate Law.... 27, 113, 131, 132, 133, 134, 135, 137, 138, 139, 144, 151, 154, 155, 159, 235, 251, 329, 342, 348, 490
Corporate Managers.... 90, 151
Corporate Marketplaces.... 192
Corporate Opportunity.... 143, 145, 148, 149, 150
Corporate Opportunity Doctrine.... 143, 145, 148, 149, 150
Corporate Records.... 146, 399
Corporate Seal.... 215
Corporate Standards Of Conduct.... 152
Corporate Structure.... 126, 139, 155
Corporate Veil.... 152, 153, 154, 155
Corporate Veneer.... 113
Corporation By Estoppel.... 201
Corporations.... 1, 19, 21, 41, 44, 64, 65, 89, 104, 111, 112, 113, 114, 117, 123, 124, 125, 126, 127, 128, 129, 130, 131, 132, 133, 134, 135, 136, 137, 138, 139, 140, 141, 143, 145, 146, 148, 152, 153, 154, 156, 158, 169, 211, 284, 313, 329, 331, 348, 349, 388, 399, 400, 411, 475, 479, 496
Corpus.... 125, 130, 338
Corrective Advertising.... 473
Cost-Management Procedure.... 331
Counselor.... 329, 341, 342, 344, 346, 405, 416
Counterclaim.... 70, 188, 378
Counteroffer.... 172, 203, 212, 213, 238, 265
Country Of Origin.... 81, 305
Course And Scope Of Employment.... 101
Course Of Dealings.... 209
Court Approaches.... 205, 283
Court Cases.... 3, 13, 16, 20, 47, 60, 159, 162, 223, 281, 320, 336, 345, 352, 369, 371, 387, 405, 479
Court Of Appeals.... 3, 4, 15, 53, 58, 92, 118, 166, 299, 303, 311, 312, 337, 348, 350, 351, 353, 355, 359, 360, 366, 426, 427, 440, 472, 483

Coverage.... 32, 81, 94, 102, 192, 210, 256, 308, 428, 439, 496
CPA.... 147, 347, 350
Craig Holtzman.... 451
Crashworthiness.... 480
Creation Of Agency.... 89
Creations.... 76, 130
Creativity.... 64, 76, 77, 79, 374
Creditor Beneficiaries.... 268
Creditors.... 95, 119, 121, 124, 126, 135, 137, 146, 151, 152, 153, 154, 155, 191, 221, 227, 268, 269, 388, 389, 409, 437, 438
Creed Of Omerta.... 362
Crime And A Tort.... 431
Crime But No Tort.... 420
Crime-Fraud Exception.... 345, 348
Criminal Act.... 11, 107, 340, 419, 420, 422, 426, 447
Criminal Activity.... 340, 426
Criminal Appeals.... 416
Criminal Cases.... 29, 45, 46, 47, 51, 53, 334, 347, 366, 396, 402, 404, 415, 416, 418, 429
Criminal Charges.... 66, 188, 227, 239, 359, 407, 416, 421, 450
Criminal Conversation.... 462
Criminal Defendants.... 22, 23, 25, 29, 54, 403, 415
Criminal Defense Attorneys.... 336
Criminal Defenses.... 447
Criminal Fraud.... 408, 419
Criminal Intent.... 11, 447
Criminal Law.... 4, 19, 20, 29, 46, 60, 138, 173, 227, 247, 334, 336, 347, 368, 380, 395, 399, 402, 403, 406, 413, 414, 415, 418, 419, 420, 423, 429, 450, 455
Criminal Law Defense.... 420
Criminal Liability.... 152, 423
Criminal Mind.... 418
Criminal Procedure.... 20, 414
Criminal Prosecution.... 26, 227, 347, 380, 416, 417
Criminal Sentencing.... 239
Criminal Trials.... 45, 51, 392, 396, 400
Criminal Violations.... 342

Crinkley V. Holiday Inns, Inc.... 427
Critical Thinking.... 4
Criticism.... 27, 36, 46, 79, 167, 213, 312, 323, 327, 329, 330, 333, 344, 436, 439, 455, 459
Criticism Of Tort Lawsuits.... 436
Cross-Claim.... 378
Cross-Examination.... 390, 392, 398, 399, 400, 401
Crucial.... 1, 26, 63, 64, 101, 173, 191, 193, 212, 253, 277, 358, 366, 372, 380, 381, 402, 405
Cruel And Unusual Punishment.... 2, 26
CSM.... 354
Culpability.... 419
Cults.... 226
Cunning.... 11, 180
Customer Lists.... 50
Customer Preference.... 316
Customer Recognition.... 82
Customer Service.... 223, 488
Customs.... 5, 6, 9, 11, 13, 14, 31, 83, 193, 213, 337, 351, 358, 455, 494
Cutting Edge.... 490
Cyber Piracy.... 66
Cyberfakes.... 66
Cycle Of Effects.... 10
Daily V. Minnick.... 219
Damage Awards.... 143, 183, 369, 428, 434, 439
Danger Invites Rescue.... 426
Dangerous Activities.... 106, 477
Daniel.... 48, 108, 131, 219, 224, 225, 287, 288, 289, 316, 394, 470
Daniel Defoe.... 131
Dartmouth College V. Woodward.... 126
Database.... 69, 72, 82, 83, 385
Daubert V. Merrell Dow Pharmaceuticals, Inc.... 479
Dave Flood.... 245
David A. Hyman.... 423
David Souter.... 365
De Facto.... 141
De Facto Corporation.... 141
De Jure.... 141
De Jure Corporation.... 141
De Minimis Non Curat Lex.... 292

Deadlines.... 277, 438
Deadly Force.... 451
Death Of Offers.... 203
Debtor-Friendly Courts.... 132
Deceit.... 120, 229, 348
Deception.... 113, 476
Deceptive Advertising.... 230, 472, 475, 476
Decision Making.... 4, 43, 47, 151, 348, 350
Declaration Of Independence.... 39, 40
Deductions.... 18, 59, 115, 129, 256
Deep Pockets.... 99
Defamation.... 108, 160, 161, 162, 163, 164, 307, 321, 369, 385, 425, 453, 457, 458, 459, 460, 461, 462, 463, 464, 467, 472
Defamation Claims.... 461
Default Judgment.... 59, 377
Defect.... 65, 107, 211, 222, 229, 234, 252, 281, 288, 385, 478, 479, 480, 481, 482, 483, 484, 485, 486, 487, 491, 492, 494, 495, 497
Defective Product.... 385, 478, 479, 487
Defense Attorneys.... 10, 51, 336
Defenses.... 55, 139, 142, 150, 172, 231, 281, 284, 314, 315, 371, 375, 377, 378, 390, 440, 444, 446, 447, 448, 449, 452, 461, 465, 485, 490, 497
Defenses To Defamation.... 461
Defenses Unique To Negligence Cases.... 440, 447
Defensive Medicine.... 439
Definite.... 29, 38, 54, 68, 83, 86, 87, 120, 136, 171, 198, 199, 200, 208, 212, 261, 279, 280, 281, 292, 328, 362, 380, 381, 397, 410, 411, 427, 464, 480, 493, 497
Definition Clauses.... 203
Defraud.... 184, 217, 224, 231, 232, 236, 305, 348, 469
Defrauded Party.... 232
Defunct Torts.... 462
Degree Of Completion.... 184
Delaware.... 23, 46, 50, 124, 132, 133, 134, 135, 136, 144, 148, 151, 307, 351, 355, 369, 425, 470, 479
Delegability.... 271

Delegates.... 271
Delegation.... 128, 271
Delegation Of Authority.... 128
Deliberation.... 45, 46, 47, 48, 50, 53, 376, 403, 404, 417, 462
Delineation Of Duties.... 183
Delivery Terms.... 190
Delta.... 162, 164
Demand Letter.... 227, 370, 373
Demeanor Of The Witness.... 396
Democracy.... 4, 12, 22, 43, 142, 361
Demographic Data.... 51
Demurrer (Motion To Dismiss), 376
Dennis Rodman.... 444
Dentistry.... 250, 437
Deontological.... 40, 56, 57
Department Of Justice.... 47
Deposit Acceptance Rule.... 210
Deposition.... 63, 94, 224, 312, 373, 379, 380, 381, 382, 383, 384, 386
Der Spiegel.... 233
Derivative Suit.... 143, 144, 155
Derogatory Comments.... 461
Description.... 3, 73, 254, 258, 302, 311, 313, 325, 387, 488, 493, 494
Design Defect.... 478, 480, 481, 485
Design Patents.... 70, 71
Deunch.... 479, 497
Development Of Evidence.... 379
Dicta.... 15, 20, 32, 114, 134, 170, 183, 213, 240, 246, 295, 304, 342, 363, 418, 442, 473
Dictator.... 114
Digital Millennium Copyright Act.... 81
Dignity.... 246, 320, 400
Dilemmas For Attorneys.... 10
Diligence.... 139, 342
Dilution.... 86, 87
Direct Causation.... 431
Direct Evidence.... 309, 401, 402
Direct Examination.... 398, 399, 401, 402
Direct Liability.... 89, 100, 106
Direct Losses.... 288
Directed Verdict.... 386, 402
Disability.... 163, 245, 300, 304, 306, 308, 310, 324, 325, 357, 457

Disaffirm.... 240, 241, 242, 243, 244
Disaffirmance.... 241, 242, 243, 244
Discharge By Agreement.... 280
Discharge Of Contracts.... 275
Disclaimers.... 163, 445, 462, 475, 491, 492, 494, 495
Disclosed Agency.... 89, 101, 102
Disclosed Principal.... 97, 102
Disclosure Requirements.... 123, 491
Discovery.... 27, 29, 70, 72, 224, 309, 348, 352, 372, 378, 379, 380, 381, 384, 385, 386, 391, 490
Discretionary Authority.... 91
Discrimination Law.... 102, 103, 169, 218, 298, 299, 303, 304, 313, 314, 315, 319, 323, 325
Discrimination Statutes.... 301, 303, 304, 323
Disgrace.... 227
Disinterestedness.... 151
Disloyal Agent.... 89, 109
Dismissal.... 49, 50, 108, 311, 319, 321, 376, 377, 457, 490
Disney Extension.... 76
Disorder.... 324
Disparagement.... 459, 470, 472
Disparate Treatment.... 311, 312, 325
Dispute Resolution.... 390, 410, 411
Disputes.... 18, 160, 174, 183, 211, 220, 267, 336, 346, 355, 360, 368, 369, 381, 390, 411, 434, 472
Dissent.... 22, 23, 29, 76, 102, 118, 129, 132, 158, 167, 301, 340, 346, 361, 365, 366, 381, 389, 395, 413, 461
Dissolution.... 119, 120, 124, 135, 352
Distinct Entity.... 126, 131
Distinctions.... 33, 167, 310, 359, 415, 429, 433
Distinctive Packaging.... 86
Distinctive Symbols.... 82
District Courts.... 16, 24, 351, 352, 353, 360
Disturbing The Peace.... 165, 414
Diversify.... 255, 473
Diversity Jurisdiction.... 135
Dividend Substitutes.... 129
Dividends.... 129, 130, 144, 146

Division Of Powers.... 23
Divorce.... 17, 119, 135, 148, 193, 222, 247, 248, 250, 260, 293, 294, 334, 339, 345, 349, 368, 385, 411, 423, 470
DNA.... 20, 56, 189, 228, 274, 359, 398, 407
Doctors.... 214, 229, 396, 437, 438, 439, 448
Document Production.... 380
Document Requests.... 384
Documentation.... 61, 127, 176, 187, 274, 309, 349, 382
Doing Before Paying.... 273
Doing Business.... 100, 113, 136
Domestic Corporation.... 135, 136
Dominican Republic.... 183, 195, 250, 333, 412
Domino Effect.... 32
Donee Beneficiaries.... 268, 269
Door-To-Door Sales Rule.... 238
Double Billing.... 330
Double Jeopardy.... 406, 407, 408, 419, 430
Double Taxation.... 123, 128, 129, 136
Douglas Ginsburg.... 365
Dr. Pepper.... 193
Dress Code.... 44
Driving.... 9, 30, 41, 55, 64, 128, 152, 252, 276, 280, 302, 370, 378, 384, 396, 401, 414, 417, 420, 426, 430, 447, 448, 473, 492, 493, 494
Drug Use.... 325, 420
Drug-Sniffing Dogs.... 464
Drunk Driving.... 9, 414, 417, 420
Drunks.... 178, 243
Dual Sovereignty.... 23
Dual-Purpose Document.... 350
Duces Tecum.... 380
Dudley.... 54, 56, 422, 423
Due Care.... 151, 481
Due Diligence.... 139
Due Process.... 25, 26, 365, 373, 374, 385, 387, 388, 389, 414, 490
Due Process Clause.... 25, 365, 388, 414
Dumping.... 300

Duress.... 172, 173, 184, 217, 221, 224, 227, 228, 260, 267, 285, 451
Dutch Cv.... 124
Duty Of Care.... 110, 118, 148, 426, 427, 428, 438, 447
Duty Of Exclusivity.... 110
Duty Of Loyalty.... 109, 110, 118
Duty Of Mitigation.... 290, 291
Duty Of Obedience.... 110
Duty To Act.... 423
Duty To Control.... 99
Duty To Know The Industry Standard.... 213
Duty To Rescue.... 422, 423, 424
E-Mail.... 67, 141, 163, 176, 184, 308, 380, 459, 460, 462, 466
Early Settlement.... 334
Earnings.... 32, 73, 129, 235, 409, 447
Ease Of Formation.... 114, 119
Ease Of Ownership Transferability.... 126, 130
Ecclesia Universalis.... 130
Economic Efficiency.... 36
Economic Inequalities.... 41
Economic Interest.... 249
Economic Loss.... 227, 439
Economic Realities Test.... 105
Economic Value.... 37, 79, 87, 218, 289, 433
Economically Efficient Person.... 36, 427
Economically Viable.... 122, 296
Economics.... 4, 34, 35, 36, 37, 38, 54, 56, 57, 105, 137, 141, 147, 170, 255, 276, 336, 411
Economists.... 37, 90, 292, 396, 433, 490
Economy.... 56, 103, 105, 128, 298, 330, 474
Edmund Burke.... 4, 39
Educational Purpose.... 79
Edward Levi.... 358
EEOC.... 301, 302, 303, 305, 306, 309, 313, 315, 316, 317, 318, 320, 325, 399
Efficiency.... 4, 18, 24, 27, 36, 38, 128, 212, 266, 313, 387
Egalitarianism.... 40
Egoism.... 36, 40
Egregious Cases.... 48

Egypt.... 195, 375, 412
Elbert Hatchett.... 430
Elder V. Ashcroft.... 76
Elected.... 25, 43, 48, 95, 156, 182, 211, 336, 350, 351, 352, 353, 355, 357, 363, 364, 405, 415, 416, 478
Elected State Judges.... 353
Elections For Board Of Directors.... 132
Electricity.... 377, 455
Electronic Contract.... 175
Electronic Filing.... 372
Electronic Transactions.... 192
Element Of Intent.... 175
Elements Necessary To Prove.... 237, 426
Elements Of A Contract.... 171, 183
Elena Kagan.... 363, 364
Ellen Simonetti.... 162, 164
Elvin Martinez.... 44
Emancipation.... 240
Embarrassment.... 108, 373
Embezzlement.... 169, 188, 421
Emergency Situations.... 389, 440
Eminent Domain.... 45, 296
Emotional Distress.... 289, 290, 307, 438, 453, 457, 458
Emotional Statements.... 199
Empanelling A Jury.... 50
Empanelling: Challenges And Jury Consultants.... 51
Emperor Justinian.... 13
Empirical Studies.... 411
Employer Contributions.... 129
Employer Liability.... 100, 164
Employer's Interests.... 101
Employment Agreements.... 171
Employment At Will.... 163, 298, 299, 303
Employment At-Will Doctrine.... 299
Employment Conditions.... 107, 308
Employment Contract.... 108, 240, 291, 307, 411
Employment Discrimination.... 102, 103, 132, 290, 298, 303, 305, 307, 312, 323, 325, 399
Employment Interviews.... 310
Employment Law.... 169, 192, 298, 303, 304, 490

Employment Test.... 313, 325
Encroachment.... 33, 453, 463
Endorsed.... 41, 238, 315, 476
Enemy Aliens.... 243, 245
Enforceability.... 177, 184, 215
Enforceable Contract.... 176, 177, 184, 264
Enforceable Rules.... 5
Engineer.... 66, 67, 68, 82, 87, 235, 250, 256, 350, 436, 441, 459, 480, 489
English Case.... 20, 369
English Common Law.... 116
Enjoined.... 295
Enrichment.... 179, 187, 188, 295
Enron.... 139, 147, 148
Enslen V. Village Of Lombard.... 227
Enterprise.... 58, 102, 105, 106, 118, 130, 139, 149, 191, 192, 298, 367, 416, 421, 472, 474
Entertainment.... 76, 82, 100, 105, 107, 158, 316, 327
Entire Agreement.... 258, 266
Entity.... 89, 98, 99, 102, 112, 113, 115, 123, 124, 125, 126, 127, 130, 131, 136, 139, 141, 154, 155, 202, 224, 225, 226, 282, 332, 345, 400
Entrapment.... 450, 451
Environmental Law.... 328, 454, 490
Equal Bargaining Power.... 254, 255, 256, 388
Equal Employment Opportunity Commission (EEOC), 301, 399
Equal Management Rights.... 120
Equal Pay Act.... 306, 312, 313
Equal Protection.... 52, 245, 365
Equal Rights Amendments.... 33
Equality Of Access.... 158
Equitable Concept.... 292
Equitable Relief.... 217
Equitable Remedies.... 284, 293, 294
Equity.... 4, 39, 122, 129, 142, 143, 147, 151, 179, 188, 198, 205, 208, 217, 280, 291, 293, 294, 295, 297, 313, 352, 361, 496
Equity Remedies.... 294, 295
Ernesto Miranda.... 359
Essential Characteristics Of General Partnerships.... 117

Essential Elements.... 284, 410
Essential Terms.... 200, 211
Establishing A Business.... 111
Estates.... 19, 41, 214, 216, 329, 352, 438
Estes V. Texas.... 61
Estoppel.... 93, 121, 172, 201, 204, 205, 206, 207, 221, 262, 377
Estoppel Doctrine.... 201
Ethical And Practical Dilemmas For Attorneys.... 10
Ethical Concerns.... 138
Ethical Duties.... 335, 337, 488
Ethical Egoism.... 36
Ethical Ramifications.... 262
Ethical Restraints.... 170
Ethical Standards.... 8, 335, 337, 341, 488
Ethics.... 4, 5, 7, 8, 10, 12, 20, 40, 55, 98, 101, 114, 138, 141, 161, 219, 223, 236, 237, 238, 239, 241, 267, 298, 330, 334, 335, 336, 337, 338, 339, 341, 342, 345, 349, 359, 369, 398, 414, 428, 438, 461, 487
Ethics Question.... 101, 267, 428
Etiquette.... 5, 9, 183, 368, 424, 425
European Convention On Human Rights And Fundamental Freedoms.... 419
European Court Of Human Rights.... 370, 462
European Law.... 76, 462, 469
European Union.... 31, 102, 350, 366, 445, 469
Evidence Of Contract.... 267
Evidence Rule.... 176, 180, 259, 260, 265, 266, 267, 268
Evidentiary Mistakes.... 392
Exaggeration.... 230, 237, 253
Exceptions To Free Speech.... 161
Exceptions To The Statute Of Frauds.... 262
Excess Rent.... 130
Excessive Interest.... 129
Excited Utterances.... 391, 392
Excitement.... 198, 392
Exclusionary Rule.... 28, 29
Exclusive Control.... 114, 435, 436
Exclusive Rights To Sell.... 69
Exclusivity.... 23, 88, 110

Exculpatory Clause.... 248, 255, 256, 257, 258, 267
Excuses.... 144, 166, 281, 447, 448, 450
Executed.... 61, 140, 175, 178, 184, 185, 214, 264, 279, 287, 369, 410
Executed Contracts.... 287
Executive Branch.... 25, 26, 350, 368
Executor.... 44, 155, 171, 184, 185, 259, 260, 261, 264, 271, 280, 287, 444
Executory.... 155, 171, 184, 185, 264, 280, 287
Executory Agreement.... 185, 280
Executory Contracts.... 184, 185, 287
Exemplary Damages.... 286
Exercising Rights.... 274, 301
Exodus.... 12
Exorbitant Damage Awards.... 183
Expanded Functions Of Juries.... 53
Expectation Of Confidentiality.... 345, 346
Expectations.... 17, 18, 19, 114, 166, 170, 171, 181, 182, 185, 193, 286, 287, 297, 335, 346, 411, 466, 471, 479, 480, 481, 482
Expenses.... 18, 99, 100, 113, 114, 129, 144, 146, 182, 190, 194, 199, 205, 206, 219, 234, 256, 288, 291, 332, 371, 372, 377, 381, 433, 447, 475
Experience.... 1, 10, 14, 30, 35, 54, 56, 63, 89, 109, 114, 115, 129, 132, 134, 160, 170, 183, 239, 241, 255, 310, 319, 328, 335, 343, 354, 355, 358, 399, 412, 422, 428, 435, 439, 441, 448, 450, 487, 489
Experimentation.... 42, 89
Expert Testimony.... 87
Expert Witness.... 332, 382, 396, 398, 435, 439
Expertise.... 27, 91, 150, 152, 230, 324, 325, 328, 335, 354, 355, 390, 478, 493
Experts.... 53, 61, 134, 139, 147, 204, 235, 309, 316, 332, 341, 345, 362, 381, 396, 397, 398, 433, 478, 479, 494
Expired Copyright.... 83
Explanations.... 266, 417
Express Agency.... 90
Express Authority.... 95, 97, 130
Express Conditions.... 273

Express Contracts.... 273
Express Partnerships.... 120
Express Ratification.... 96
Express Warranties.... 491, 493, 495
Expression Plus.... 164
Extensible Markup Language (Xml), 211
Externalities.... 90, 292
Extortion.... 228, 421
Extradition.... 228
Eyewitness.... 3, 396, 397, 398, 402, 418
Factual Analysis.... 359
Failure To File.... 408
Failure To Warn.... 143, 485
Failures.... 38, 49, 64, 129, 437, 474
Fair Dealing.... 163, 190, 246, 298
Fair Labor Standards Act.... 105
Fair Market Value.... 217, 252, 296
Fair Use.... 74, 78, 79, 87
Fairness Opinions.... 139
False Arrest.... 456
False Claims Act.... 229
False Imprisonment.... 456, 457
False Light.... 466, 467
False Representation.... 229, 231
False Statement Of Fact.... 162, 459
Family Guy.... 80
Family Law.... 12, 13, 19, 248, 293, 334, 353, 411
Family Matters.... 183, 246
Family-Owned Businesses.... 135
Family-Purpose Doctrine.... 428
Farmers.... 36, 71, 474
Father Of The Constitution.... 16, 33
Fault.... 21, 59, 121, 237, 239, 251, 287, 312, 370, 371, 377, 387, 398, 403, 418, 425, 433, 434, 435, 446, 459, 477, 479, 480, 483, 484, 485, 492, 494
Fax.... 141, 184, 192
FDA.... 75, 468, 469, 470
Federal Approach.... 375
Federal Communications Commission.... 180, 358, 359
Federal Constitution.... 15, 22, 23, 353
Federal Corporate Law.... 138

Federal Courts.... 15, 50, 52, 69, 308, 347, 351, 353, 372, 386, 418, 430, 490
Federal Diversity.... 135
Federal Government.... 22, 24, 134, 146, 301, 341, 351, 361, 380, 389, 464
Federal Judges.... 25, 353, 354, 360
Federal Judicial Oversight.... 357
Federal Law.... 21, 22, 23, 79, 105, 132, 137, 154, 158, 207, 248, 323, 390, 455, 476, 492
Federal Level.... 132, 135, 174, 312, 360, 415, 474
Federal Rules Of Civil Procedure.... 143, 368, 381
Federal Rules Of Evidence.... 61, 479
Federal Statutes.... 301, 307
Federal System.... 22, 44, 83, 174, 351, 357, 359
Federal Trade Commission.... 132, 138, 209, 230, 343, 408, 473, 475, 476
Federal Trademark Dilution Act.... 87
Federalism.... 23, 24
Federalist Papers.... 31
Fee Arrangement.... 330, 331, 332, 333, 334
Feinberg V. Pfeiffer.... 207
Feinberg V. Pfeiffer Co.... 207
Feist Publications, Inc. V. Rural Telephone Service Co.... 78
Felonies.... 19, 45, 352, 353, 413
Felony-Murder.... 429
Ferries.... 133
Fictitious Business Name.... 140
Fictitious Name.... 114
Fiduciaries.... 98, 116, 118, 146, 150, 226, 227, 286, 427
Fiduciary.... 89, 90, 107, 110, 118, 119, 124, 125, 144, 145, 148, 149, 151, 226, 227, 234, 236, 338, 438
Fiduciary Duties.... 89, 110, 119, 124, 125, 144, 145, 148, 149, 438
Fiduciary Relationship.... 107, 118, 234, 236
Fifth Amendment.... 395, 407, 408
Fighting.... 68, 132, 161, 164, 166, 321, 344, 367, 438, 456, 486
Fighting Words.... 161, 164, 166
Filing Fees.... 332, 372

Filing Requirements.... 114, 116
Final Agreement.... 199, 265
Financial Institutions.... 135
Findings Of Fact.... 47
Findlaw.... 7, 345, 410
Fine Print.... 175, 211, 213, 257, 388
Fines.... 6, 26, 36, 104, 116, 129, 169, 173, 347, 353, 369, 377, 390, 408, 413, 458
Fired Hospital Doctor Example.... 188
Firewall.... 346
Firm League Of Friendship.... 21
Firm Offers.... 204
First Amendment.... 34, 52, 76, 79, 156, 157, 158, 159, 160, 163, 165, 166, 167, 315, 319, 340, 341, 460, 461
First Priority.... 335
Fishing Expedition.... 380, 440
Fitness.... 278, 320, 325, 339, 340, 341, 495
Fitness For A Particular Purpose.... 495
Fitness For Duty.... 325
Fitness For Particular Purpose.... 495
Flag Burning.... 158
Flags.... 158
Flat Fee.... 334
Flexibility.... 111, 112, 123, 128, 134, 135, 140, 191, 380
Flexible Management.... 114
Flexible Operations.... 119
Flirtation.... 321
Florida Supreme Court.... 121, 124, 352, 353, 358, 371
FLSA.... 104
Food And Drug Administration.... 75, 468, 469
Food Labels.... 234
Football.... 19, 77, 78, 85, 270, 321, 442, 443, 452
Forbearance.... 185, 186, 210, 215
Force Majeure Clause.... 281, 282, 283, 284
Foreclosure.... 124
Foreign Arbitral Awards.... 412
Foreign Corporations.... 135, 136
Foreign Country.... 72, 192, 434
Foreign Policy.... 23
Foreseeability.... 287, 432, 433, 437, 446

Foreseeable Consequences.... 419, 429
Foresight.... 441, 450
Formal Requirements.... 116, 262, 263
Formalism.... 215, 217
Formalities.... 120, 135, 154, 215
Formality.... 81, 137, 267, 411
Former Executives.... 300
Forum Clause.... 196
Founders.... 31, 130
Four Situations.... 204, 420
Fourteenth Amendment.... 167, 365, 388, 414
Fourth Amendment.... 389, 466
Franchise.... 1, 65, 76, 89, 93, 105, 107, 113, 114, 116, 134, 156, 164, 170, 181, 190, 235, 248, 256, 267, 299, 322, 323, 411, 412
Franchise Tax.... 134
Franchise Termination.... 190, 299
Franchisee.... 1, 65, 89, 93, 105, 107, 114, 116, 156, 164, 170, 181, 248, 256, 267, 299, 323
Franchising.... 65, 88, 89, 93, 105, 156, 190, 234, 267, 299
Franchisor.... 1, 65, 89, 93, 105, 107, 114, 164, 170, 181, 248, 256, 267, 299
Francis Bacon.... 5, 12, 162
Fraud.... 10, 47, 65, 67, 95, 101, 113, 118, 119, 121, 136, 140, 143, 147, 153, 154, 155, 160, 169, 172, 173, 179, 182, 184, 198, 217, 221, 223, 224, 228, 229, 230, 231, 232, 233, 236, 237, 238, 239, 242, 251, 253, 258, 259, 260, 261, 262, 263, 264, 265, 266, 267, 277, 285, 286, 294, 301, 305, 345, 348, 349, 380, 385, 398, 408, 418, 419, 421, 424, 425, 427, 436, 445, 452, 453, 457, 467, 469, 470, 475, 476
Fraud Cases.... 229, 231
Fraudulent.... 143, 155, 229, 237, 266, 348, 385, 418
FRCP.... 373, 381
Free Enterprise System.... 474
Free Exercise Clause.... 34
Free Speech.... 52, 156, 157, 158, 160, 161, 162, 163, 165, 166, 340, 356, 369, 460, 466
Free Speech Concerns.... 466

Free Speech Rights.... 52, 158, 162, 166
Free Will.... 5, 226, 227
Freedom Of Contract.... 169, 245, 298, 299
Freedom Of Expression.... 158, 166, 370, 462, 476
Freelancers.... 104
French Civil Code.... 262, 267, 283, 297, 433, 495
French Courts.... 179, 246, 355
Frivolous Lawsuits.... 436, 439
Frolic And Detour.... 100
FTC.... 124, 230, 238, 343, 473, 475, 476
FTC Door-To-Door Sales Rule.... 238
FTDA.... 87
Fuentes V. Shevin.... 387, 389
Full Faith And Credit Clause.... 406
Fully Built.... 288
Fully Disclose.... 109, 149, 227
Fully Informed Jury Association.... 53
Functional Law And Economics.... 38
Fundamental Breach.... 292
Fundamental Notion.... 39, 246, 419
Fundamental Right.... 27, 29, 298, 316, 365
Gambling.... 32, 66, 249, 250, 324, 420, 421
Gamesmanship.... 336
Gandhi.... 9, 315, 487
Garratt V. Dailey.... 428
Gary V. Helmerich.... 15
Gas.... 19, 83, 93, 102, 182, 195, 227, 292, 387, 408, 413, 426, 432, 435, 442, 453, 477, 492, 494
Gator Growl Program.... 459
Gays.... 307
Geler V. American Honda.... 482
Gender Norms.... 308
General Conflict.... 298
General Issues.... 101, 438
General Laborers.... 300
General Language.... 202, 238
General Partnership.... 116, 117, 119, 120, 122, 125, 136, 137
General Principles.... 14, 194
Generic Term.... 84, 85
Genericide.... 84, 85
Geneva Convention.... 395

Genocide.... 39
Genuine.... 27, 29, 61, 67, 83, 100, 127, 131, 212, 220, 222, 245, 321, 327, 381, 384, 386, 397
Geographic Area.... 87, 475
Geography.... 161
George Bernard Shaw.... 8
George Herbert.... 490
Georgia.... 15, 16, 24, 45, 46, 136, 144, 178, 184, 195, 351, 356, 364, 367, 397, 412, 419, 435, 440, 452, 490
Gerber.... 193
German Gmbh.... 124
German Nachfrist Notice.... 291
German States.... 23
Gestures.... 62, 223
Get The Big Picture.... 1, 208
Gifted.... 450
Gifts.... 107, 109, 169, 171, 202, 207, 214, 226, 448
Glass Ceiling.... 317
Global Business.... 293, 469
Global Copyright Protection.... 80
Goals.... 35, 104, 239, 335, 343, 386, 439
Golden Spike Little League.... 98
Goldman V. Allyn & Bacon, Inc.... 280
Golf Courses.... 41, 441, 442
Gomez V. Potter.... 301
Gonzaga University V. Doe.... 464
Good Business.... 8, 264
Good Samaritan Laws.... 440
Good Will.... 223
Google.... 7, 58, 162
Government Agencies.... 311, 416
Government Officials.... 31, 344, 409
Government Regulations.... 160
Governmental Administrative Agencies.... 111
Governmental Intervention.... 298
Grand Jury.... 26, 28, 414
Grandfather Clause.... 282
Granting Summary Judgment.... 59
Grants.... 69, 81, 133, 146, 362, 380
Greatness.... 387
Greece.... 5, 12, 124, 195, 278, 350, 375, 412, 419

Gross Recklessness.... 417
Gross Unfairness.... 236
Grossly Unfair Terms.... 251
Grounds For Appeal.... 50
Guarantee.... 22, 23, 41, 64, 65, 67, 126, 135, 154, 215, 234, 235, 263, 276, 316, 365, 376, 387, 434, 462, 491, 492, 493, 495
Guarantor.... 241, 261
Guardianships.... 293
Guarino V. Mine Safety Appliance Co.... 426
Guatemala.... 412
Guidance.... 14, 15, 16, 42, 132, 194, 247, 359
Guidelines.... 139, 152, 163, 174, 239, 304, 313, 318, 320, 322, 324, 335, 349, 417, 418, 430, 475
Guidelines For Multinational Enterprises.... 139
Guild Member.... 341, 342
Guilds.... 127, 130, 342
Guillory V. Godfrey.... 471
Guilty Pleas.... 418
H.L.A. Hart.... 4, 5, 37, 42
Habitual Drunkard Statutes.... 244
Hadley V. Baxendale.... 289
Hadrian.... 13
Hague Service Convention.... 375
Hale V. Committee On Character And Fitness Of The Illinois Bar.... 340
Hallmark.... 287, 417
Hamdi V. Rumsfeld.... 381
Hammurabi.... 12, 110, 117, 457
Hammurabi's Code.... 12, 110, 117, 457
Handwriting.... 202, 464, 465
Hans Kelsen.... 37
Harasser.... 312, 318, 321, 322
Harassment.... 9, 300, 302, 306, 307, 311, 312, 317, 318, 319, 320, 321, 322, 345, 376, 399, 406, 472
Harm To Reputation.... 459, 463
Harmless.... 255, 256, 392, 443, 444
Harmless Error.... 392
Harris V. Forklift Systems, Inc.... 319
Haumont V. Security State Bank.... 227
Hawaii Housing Authority V. Midkiff.... 296
Hawkins V. United States.... 347

Hazardous Waste.... 416, 477
Health Clubs.... 314
Hearings.... 25, 228, 301, 389, 391, 416, 478
Hearsay.... 386, 390, 391, 392
Hebraic Law.... 12
Hedonic.... 433
Hedonism.... 40
Heirs.... 33, 121, 208, 346, 444
Henningsen V. Bloomfield Motors, Inc.... 252
Henry David Thoreau.... 9
Henry Vi.... 82, 327
Herbert M. Kritzer.... 333
Heretic.... 12
Hewlett-Packard.... 469
Hickman V. Taylor.... 350
Hierarchies.... 11
Higher Law.... 31, 39, 42
Highest Court.... 4, 14, 118, 158, 355, 360, 431, 437, 462, 482, 483
Highly Offensive.... 158, 161, 468
Hire And Train.... 101
Hired Guns.... 62, 342
Hirers.... 104
Hiring.... 90, 100, 103, 104, 105, 106, 110, 114, 144, 146, 273, 305, 308, 309, 310, 311, 312, 313, 315, 316, 317, 325, 372, 399, 434, 484
Historical School.... 35, 57
History Of Law11
Hmong.... 130, 342, 404, 405
Hold Harmless Agreement.... 443
Holy Blood.... 78
Holy Grail.... 78
Home Purchase.... 274
Homer.... 17, 212, 231, 244, 249
Homer Simpson.... 17, 212, 231, 244, 249
Homosexual.... 226, 307, 317, 324, 467
Honest Mistake.... 456
Hong Kong.... 158
Honoring Expectations.... 17, 18
Honus Wagner.... 468
Hooters.... 86, 198, 316
Horizontal Privity.... 483
Horror Stories.... 438

510

Hospital Expenses.... 433
Hostile Witnesses.... 399
Hostile Work Environment.... 318, 323
Hotels.... 82, 324, 471
Hourly Fees.... 331
House Of Representatives.... 25, 182
Huissier.... 61, 63, 479
Human Cannonball.... 79
Human Nature.... 6, 39, 43, 285, 287, 474
Human Reason.... 12
Humber Ferry.... 426
Hume.... 5, 446
Hung Jury.... 46, 50, 53
Hungary.... 195, 375, 412, 419, 424
Hustler Magazine.... 467
Hutchinson V. Proxmire.... 461
Hybrid Business.... 113
Hybrid Business Categories.... 113
IBM.... 64, 69, 153, 192
Ice Caps.... 199
Identity.... 102, 113, 224, 225, 226
Ignorance.... 27, 30, 40, 57, 58, 63, 94, 222, 407
Illegal Act.... 113, 163, 348, 349, 421, 464, 466
Illegal Aliens.... 243
Illegal Discrimination.... 310, 312, 316
Illegal Drug Use.... 325, 420
Illegal Gambling.... 420
Illegality.... 28, 248, 251, 267, 282
Illegality/Public Policy.... 248
Illinois.... 4, 29, 46, 50, 84, 189, 227, 253, 307, 339, 340, 351, 356, 421, 455, 462, 464, 481
Illinois Bar.... 339, 340
Illinois Supreme Court.... 4, 340, 455
Illinois V. Caballes.... 464
Illinois V. Wardlow.... 29
Illusion Of Bigness.... 113
Illusory Promises.... 220
Imbalance Of Power.... 298
Immanuel Kant.... 40
Immunity.... 135, 143, 228, 313, 347, 348, 423, 428, 452
Impact Adverse.... 149
Impeachment.... 357, 360

Implemented.... 152, 163, 290, 303, 345
Implements Of Destruction.... 483
Implication.... 17, 71, 75, 134, 163, 181, 193, 277, 323, 467, 493, 494
Implicit Repudiation.... 280
Implied Agency.... 90
Implied Authority.... 90, 91, 94, 95, 97
Implied Conditions.... 274
Implied Contract.... 106, 163, 186, 188, 298, 299
Implied Contractual Restraints.... 106, 299
Implied Partnerships.... 120
Implied Terms.... 200
Implied Warning.... 10
Implied Warranties.... 489, 491, 494, 495
Implied Warranty Of Merchantability.... 252, 480, 494, 495
Implied-In-Fact.... 187
Imposing.... 100, 124, 137, 245, 246, 353, 455, 477, 479
Impossibility.... 253, 281, 282, 283, 284, 285, 295
Impossibility Of Performance.... 253, 295
Impracticability.... 281, 282, 283, 284
Imprisonment.... 6, 20, 52, 165, 169, 367, 456, 457
Improper Purpose.... 152, 154
Improper Use.... 84, 454
In Good Faith.... 130, 141, 144, 148, 150, 199, 221, 274, 276, 278, 341, 399, 423, 440, 458
In Pari Delicto.... 248, 251
In Re Matter Of Matthew F. Hale.... 340
Inaction.... 151, 321, 426
Inadequacy Of Consideration.... 217, 218
Inadequate Funds Or Insurance.... 101
Inadequate Warnings.... 480, 485
Inadvertent Admissions.... 50
Inalienable Rights.... 7, 293, 298
Inappropriate Behavior.... 8, 108, 300, 404
Incapacity.... 115, 172, 182, 241, 244, 267, 352, 420
Incentives.... 13, 29, 61, 104, 128, 134, 160, 212, 330, 434, 439
Incidental Beneficiaries.... 269
Incidental Damages.... 291
Incompetence.... 61

Incompetent.... 41, 117, 203, 244, 343, 375, 380, 421, 437, 450, 459
Incomplete Agreement.... 267, 268
Incorporation.... 128, 133, 135, 140, 141, 142, 155, 195, 201
Incorporators.... 133, 140, 141, 154
Increased Costs.... 282, 284, 293
Indemnification.... 92, 99, 132, 148, 256
Indemnity.... 255, 256
Indemnity Clause.... 256
Independent Advice.... 227
Independent Contractor.... 103, 104, 105, 106, 110, 114, 163, 434
Indictment.... 26, 414
Indirect Costs.... 293
Indirect Losses.... 288
Individual Level.... 27, 112, 129
Individual Property Interest.... 65
Individual Right To Sue.... 412
Individual Rights.... 12, 62, 126, 157, 464
Individualism.... 292, 327, 372, 478
Industrialization.... 211, 437
Industry Custom.... 209, 210
Inebriated.... 172, 202, 444, 446, 447
Infancy.... 239, 243, 450
Infant.... 41, 169, 240, 241, 243, 375
Infliction Of Emotional Distress.... 307, 438, 457, 458
Influencing Conduct.... 18
Informality.... 137, 411
Informed Consent.... 437, 440
Infractions.... 428
Infringement Of Intellectual Property.... 67, 470
Inherently Distinctive.... 86, 87
Initial Public Offerings.... 127, 133
Injunction.... 87, 155, 217, 294, 295, 297, 421, 472, 473
Innocent Third Party.... 95, 101, 224
Inoculations.... 34
Inquiries.... 203, 292, 390
Inquisitorial Approach.... 60, 61, 344
Inquisitorial System.... 60, 61, 63
Insane Persons.... 241, 243, 244
Insanity.... 55, 203, 452
Insider.... 10, 107, 145, 147, 160, 380

Insider Trading.... 10, 107
Insiders.... 145, 147, 380
Insolvent Firm.... 151
Inspect.... 110, 142, 146, 194, 237, 252, 274, 280, 291, 385, 386, 478, 483, 489, 491, 494
Inspection Condition.... 274
Inspections.... 110, 142, 386, 478
Inspections Of Corporate Books.... 142
Installment Payments.... 387
Instances Of Negligence.... 440
Instincts.... 6, 43
Institute Of Certified Public Accountants.... 347
Institutional Authority.... 30
Institutional Investors.... 141, 142
Institutionalism.... 5
Insufficient Evidence.... 252
Insurable Interest.... 249, 250
Insurance Claims.... 456
Insurance Companies.... 135, 196, 315, 474, 477
Insurance Policy.... 202, 210, 249, 273, 431
Insurance Requirement.... 255
Insurers.... 44, 211, 256, 274, 334, 369, 437, 438, 439
Intangibles.... 64
Integrated Contract.... 266
Integrated Written Agreement.... 266
Integrity.... 28, 192, 250, 279, 337, 373, 396
Intel Corp. V. Advanced Micro Devices.... 379
Intellectual Property.... 64, 65, 67, 68, 69, 71, 73, 74, 80, 84, 85, 86, 87, 88, 89, 140, 190, 328, 421, 470, 472, 475
Intended Donee Beneficiaries.... 268, 269
Intending The Criminal Act.... 419
Intent To Discriminate.... 312, 313, 314
Intent To Induce Reliance.... 230, 231
Intentional Act.... 418, 429
Intentional Infliction Of Mental Or Emotional Distress.... 453, 457, 458
Intentional Infliction Of Mental/Emotional Distress.... 453, 458

Intentional Misconduct.... 108, 255, 444
Intentional Torts.... 109, 419, 420, 424, 425, 428, 440, 444, 447, 452, 453, 457, 467, 477
Intentional Wrongdoing.... 438, 446
Interference With Business Relations.... 453, 470, 472
Interference With Contract.... 458, 470, 475
Interference With Property.... 453
Interference With Prospective Economic Advantage.... 470, 471
Interference With The Person.... 453, 455, 457
Intermediate Standard.... 437
Internal Revenue Service.... 104, 105, 111, 136, 137, 198
International Chamber Of Commerce.... 237, 476
International Civil Aviation Organization.... 433
International Comparison.... 307, 333, 433
International Law.... 21, 114, 194, 228, 291, 328, 375, 406
International Law On Service Of Process.... 375
International Military Comparison.... 395
International Sale Of Goods.... 194, 264
International Sales.... 193, 195, 264
Internet Age.... 385
Internet Exchanges.... 192
Internet Legal Information And Documents.... 344
Interpreting Terms.... 179, 201
Interrogatories.... 381, 384, 386
Interrogatory.... 384
Intersection Of Intellectual Property Laws
Interstate Commerce.... 421
Interviewing.... 309, 310
Intimidation.... 310, 318, 471, 472
Intoxication.... 449, 467
Introduction.... 1, 60, 64, 89, 91, 111, 116, 126, 132, 133, 145, 152, 155, 169, 174, 189, 198, 237, 239, 265, 266, 271, 293, 298, 306, 317, 323, 330, 345, 355, 414, 424, 440, 452, 491, 492
Intruding Upon A Person's Private Life.... 467

Intrusion.... 193, 380, 436, 463, 466, 468
Intrusion Upon Private Life.... 466
Invasion Of Privacy.... 169, 307, 453, 457, 458, 463, 464, 465, 466, 468
Inventions.... 69, 73, 74, 421
Inventory.... 87, 117, 191, 211, 237, 288, 457
Investigating.... 321
Investment Securities.... 191
Investor Responsibility Center.... 142
Investors.... 59, 122, 123, 125, 127, 130, 141, 142, 143, 147, 149, 191, 192, 229, 233, 249
Invitation.... 182, 183, 199, 200
Involuntary.... 244, 318, 347, 352, 409, 430, 449
Involuntary Intoxication.... 449
Iowa.... 45, 193, 219, 247, 307, 351, 356, 429, 490
IPO.... 74, 76, 80, 81, 127, 143, 324, 335
Iran.... 2, 3, 24, 60, 195, 228, 282, 359, 412, 454
Iraq.... 12, 24, 195, 282, 430
Ireland.... 46, 195, 245, 263, 333, 350, 375, 385, 412, 419
Irreparable Harm.... 144
Irrevocable Offers.... 204, 221
IRS.... 6, 10, 11, 12, 14, 21, 25, 32, 33, 34, 48, 52, 54, 62, 64, 66, 67, 70, 72, 73, 74, 76, 79, 81, 82, 96, 104, 105, 107, 111, 112, 113, 114, 115, 119, 121, 123, 124, 126, 129, 130, 131, 132, 133, 134, 136, 137, 138, 141, 142, 143, 144, 145, 146, 148, 149, 150, 151, 154, 155, 156, 157, 158, 159, 160, 163, 165, 166, 167, 169, 172, 175, 176, 178, 179, 181, 182, 186, 187, 191, 192, 198, 200, 201, 207, 208, 209, 217, 218, 220, 226, 228, 237, 238, 242, 251, 252, 259, 261, 264, 271, 284, 291, 296, 304, 308, 309, 315, 319, 320, 327, 329, 330, 332, 334, 335, 338, 340, 341, 343, 346, 348, 351, 354, 356, 357, 358, 360, 361, 364, 365, 366, 368, 371, 372, 382, 383, 387, 388, 398, 407, 408, 409, 410, 411, 414, 417, 421, 422, 431, 433, 435, 444, 445, 446, 451, 455, 458, 460, 461, 468,

472, 473, 475, 476, 479, 480, 487, 491, 492, 493
Isaac Newton.... 72
Islamic Law.... 60, 358
James Baldwin.... 41
James Fitzjames Stephen.... 36
Jeremy Bentham.... 36
Jewelry Store Example.... 204
Jimmy Carter.... 228, 330, 364
Job Description.... 73, 302, 311, 313, 325
Job Performance.... 313, 466
Joe Dimaggio.... 269
John Adams.... 330, 344, 366
John Austin.... 5, 37
John D. Rockefeller.... 309
John Dewey.... 42
John Donne.... 40
John Hart Ely.... 361
John Jay.... 31
John Paul Stevens.... 296, 364, 460
John Stuart Mill.... 36
Joint Venture.... 113, 118
Joint Ventures.... 113
Jointly Owned.... 120
Joke Gone Bad.... 457
Jokes.... 304, 392, 399, 447, 459
Jonathan Swift.... 63
Journalists.... 468
Judge Judy.... 357
Judge-Made Law.... 13, 14
Judges.... 1, 6, 7, 13, 14, 15, 16, 25, 30, 31, 33, 38, 41, 43, 44, 47, 48, 50, 51, 52, 53, 54, 55, 56, 58, 60, 62, 63, 93, 134, 189, 191, 193, 248, 263, 287, 301, 303, 304, 312, 327, 336, 341, 347, 350, 351, 352, 353, 354, 355, 356, 357, 358, 359, 360, 361, 362, 363, 366, 368, 373, 376, 380, 381, 384, 388, 392, 393, 394, 396, 402, 403, 404, 405, 406, 411, 417, 420, 440, 461, 475, 478, 479
Judgment Calls.... 438
Judgment Proof.... 410
Judgments.... 39, 124, 162, 293, 318, 367, 393, 406, 408, 409, 436, 439, 479
Judicial Bias.... 61
Judicial Campaigns.... 356, 357

Judicial Decisions.... 396
Judicial Power.... 6, 361
Judicial Process.... 43, 58, 408
Judicial Review.... 25, 43, 361, 366, 367
Judicial Selection Process.... 354, 355
Jurisprudence.... 34, 55, 58, 363, 400
Juriste.... 329
Jurors.... 44, 45, 46, 48, 49, 50, 51, 52, 53, 54, 303, 376, 395, 404, 478, 480
Jury Duty.... 49, 51, 110, 373
Jury Instructions.... 50, 53, 395, 402
Jury Nullification.... 53, 54
Jury Trials.... 45, 46, 47, 48, 52, 376, 410
Jury Verdict Research.... 300
Just Compensation.... 26, 176, 177, 296
Just Words.... 164, 186, 231
Justice.... 5, 7, 8, 12, 14, 17, 18, 19, 20, 22, 26, 27, 28, 29, 30, 33, 35, 37, 39, 40, 41, 43, 47, 50, 51, 52, 53, 58, 61, 63, 69, 76, 82, 84, 86, 102, 118, 126, 154, 156, 158, 161, 162, 165, 166, 167, 173, 205, 221, 252, 273, 296, 297, 302, 320, 321, 329, 330, 333, 336, 337, 340, 341, 343, 344, 345, 350, 352, 353, 354, 355, 356, 357, 358, 360, 361, 362, 363, 364, 365, 366, 367, 381, 387, 389, 395, 398, 400, 402, 404, 407, 416, 417, 421, 427, 452, 460, 461, 464, 465, 469, 474, 475
Justice And Fairness.... 40
Justice Department.... 474, 475
Justifiable Reliance.... 205, 206, 229, 230, 231, 232, 242, 469
Justifiable Self-Defense.... 451
Justinian.... 6, 13, 406
Justinian Code.... 13
Kellogg Company V. National Biscuit Company.... 84
Kelo V. City Of New London.... 296
Key Concepts.... 172, 239
Key Employee.... 249
Key Terms.... 89
Key Topics.... 237
KFC.... 88, 100, 455
Kickbacks.... 107, 109, 110, 229, 421
Kingseely Thermos Co. V. Aladdin Industries, Inc.... 84

Knockoffs.... 66, 67, 68, 83, 421
Know-how.... 69, 88, 89
Known Integrity.... 396
Kodak.... 70, 85, 87
Kumho Tire Co. V. Carmichael.... 479
Labor Contributions.... 122
Labor Department.... 317
Labor Law.... 21, 104, 132, 138, 157, 411, 490
Labor Union Activities.... 471
Laboratories Of Democracy.... 22
Laches.... 294
Lack Of Character.... 339
Lack Of Consideration.... 204, 205, 221
Lack Of Informed Consent.... 437, 440
Lacking Capacity.... 172, 241, 242, 243, 245
Laesio Enormis.... 217
Lake Tahoe.... 296
Lakeside V. Oregon.... 395
Lander.... 23, 453, 458, 459, 460, 461
Lanfier V. Lanfier.... 219
Lanham Act.... 82, 83, 84, 86, 472, 476
Lapse Of Trademark.... 84
Larceny.... 419, 420
Large Print.... 202, 203, 257
Last Clear Chance.... 446
Latin America.... 13, 39, 59, 60, 116, 124, 183, 193, 195, 289, 366, 424, 434
Law And Economics.... 36, 38, 56, 57, 170, 255, 411
Law And Morality.... 315
Law Approach.... 11, 21, 60, 105, 221, 347, 450
Law Firm.... 110, 119, 121, 135, 159, 324, 329, 332, 333, 339, 340, 373, 420, 491
Law School.... 4, 7, 37, 38, 42, 137, 327, 328, 329, 339, 343, 345, 361, 364, 365, 415, 417, 423, 425, 469
Lawrence V. Fox.... 269
Laws Of Nature.... 72
Lawsuit Chronology.... 368
Lawyers.... 1, 6, 7, 10, 11, 15, 27, 40, 41, 42, 44, 45, 46, 47, 48, 50, 51, 52, 53, 54, 58, 60, 62, 63, 85, 99, 103, 105, 114, 115, 121, 127, 128, 139,

148, 159, 166, 171, 174, 181, 214, 223, 232, 233, 248, 250, 262, 293, 299, 300, 301, 305, 327, 328, 329, 330, 331, 332, 333, 334, 335, 336, 337, 338, 339, 341, 342, 343, 344, 345, 346, 347, 348, 349, 350, 351, 354, 356, 357, 359, 361, 366, 368, 369, 371, 372, 373, 376, 377, 380, 381, 382, 384, 385, 388, 390, 392, 396, 398, 400, 401, 405, 408, 414, 436, 438, 439, 450, 461, 479, 482, 490

Lawyers Training.... 327
Lay Judges.... 355
Laypeople.... 350
Laypersons.... 1, 43, 342, 438
Leading Questions.... 399, 400, 401
Lean Award.... 408
Learned Hand.... 84, 156, 475
Leases Of Goods.... 191
Lebanon.... 115, 195, 412
Lefkowitz V. Great Minneapolis Surplus Store, Inc.... 200
Legal Advertising.... 372
Legal Alphabet.... 215
Legal Analysis And Reasoning.... 358
Legal Defense.... 237, 447
Legal Detriment.... 215
Legal Entity.... 89, 98, 99, 126
Legal Errors.... 403
Legal Ethics.... 7, 8, 114, 330, 342
Legal Foundations.... 60, 113
Legal Games.... 63
Legal Norms.... 192
Legal Notice.... 374
Legal Realism.... 42, 43, 55, 56, 452
Legal Relations.... 26, 183
Legal Requirements.... 8, 152, 335, 358
Legal Scholars.... 13, 134, 213, 344, 366, 481
Legal Structure.... 126
Legal Systems In The World.... 59
Legal Tasks.... 110
Legality.... 28, 172, 173, 236, 245, 246, 248, 250, 251, 267, 282, 352
Legality/Public Policy.... 248
Legally Distinct Entities.... 112, 125

Legally Enforceable.... 170, 171, 176, 177, 181, 182, 197
Legislation.... 14, 20, 31, 35, 76, 116, 133, 174, 197, 198, 282, 304, 356, 367, 389, 423, 476, 479, 481, 485, 490, 496
Legislative.... 6, 20, 24, 31, 133, 197, 245, 296, 363, 367, 416, 461, 466, 472, 478, 493
Leibniz.... 5
Leibovitz V. Paramount Pictures Corp.... 79
Lemon Laws.... 160, 482
Leon.... 13, 29, 60, 161, 367, 388
Lesion.... 253
Lesser Courts.... 329
Letters Of Credit.... 191
Letters Of Intent.... 199
Level Of Culpability.... 419
Level Playing Field.... 298
Leverage.... 223, 239, 242, 243, 257, 369
Leviathan.... 6
Lewis Carroll.... 417
Lex Civilis.... 13
Lex Talionis.... 12
Liabilities.... 99, 102, 112, 115, 124, 454
Liability Judgment.... 479
Libel.... 162, 163, 164, 369, 370, 381, 458, 459, 460, 461, 462, 467, 472
Liberal Right To Amend Pleadings.... 378
Liberty.... 6, 7, 26, 33, 36, 40, 156, 344, 407, 478
Library Of Congress.... 7
Licensing.... 65, 72, 73, 78, 83, 156, 248, 250, 251, 258, 341
Licensing Agreement.... 258
Licensing Fees.... 72, 73
Lifetime Appointments.... 353, 360, 362
Lifting.... 153, 448, 456
Lightning.... 283, 285, 314, 441, 442
Limitations Period.... 215, 467
Limited Contractual Capacity.... 245
Limited Liability Companies.... 111, 112, 113, 114, 116, 124, 137
Limited Liability Company.... 112, 115, 117, 123, 124, 125, 129, 201, 332
Limited Liability Partnership.... 111, 117, 123, 125

Limited Life Span.... 117
Limited Partnership.... 111, 116, 117, 122, 123, 124, 125, 129
Limits On All Types Of Speech.... 161
Limits On Discovery.... 381
Limits On The Attorney-Client Privilege.... 349
Lincoln.... 64, 127, 330, 367, 368, 397
Lingering Authority.... 95, 98, 116
Liquidated Damages.... 292, 293
Liquidated Sum.... 217
Liquidation.... 409
Listings.... 78, 472
Litigation.... 13, 27, 43, 70, 141, 144, 147, 170, 181, 183, 313, 322, 325, 330, 331, 332, 348, 350, 368, 369, 371, 372, 377, 379, 380, 381, 385, 386, 388, 390, 409, 410, 411, 412, 438
Little Amazons Attack Boys.... 457
Little League Baseball Sponsors.... 98
LLC.... 93, 94, 112, 123, 124, 125, 131, 411
LLP.... 123, 244, 272, 374, 448
Loan Sharking.... 248
Lobbying.... 350
Lockard V. Pizza Hut, Inc.... 322
Lockers.... 468
Lon Fuller.... 5, 38, 42, 215
Longest Trial.... 369
Look And Feel.... 86
Lost Profits.... 287, 289, 293
Lost Wages.... 293, 433
Lottery.... 175, 249, 250
Louis D. Brandeis.... 22, 463
Louisiana.... 13, 23, 45, 108, 148, 189, 351, 356, 389, 481, 490
Lower Appeals Courts.... 4, 351, 352
Lower Federal Appeals Courts.... 359
Lowest Common Denominator.... 8
Loyalty.... 106, 107, 108, 109, 110, 118, 145, 298, 299, 310, 340, 342, 363
Lrn Inc.... 345
Lucas V. South Carolina Coastal Council.... 296
Lucy V. Zehmer.... 177
Lunney V. Prodigy Communications Corp.... 462

Lydia G. Cochrane.... 342
Lyons Partnership, L.p. V. Giannoulas.... 79
Macbeth.... 463
Macpherson V. Buick Motor Co.... 482, 483
Mafia.... 421
Magistrate.... 61, 62, 352, 381
Mail Fraud.... 421
Mailbox Rule.... 210, 211
Mailing Address.... 140
Major League Baseball.... 4
Malice.... 162, 430, 460, 461, 462, 471
Malicious Falsehood.... 460
Malicious Prosecution.... 457
Malpractice.... 135, 148, 181, 290, 332, 392, 410, 436, 437, 438, 439, 440, 453
Management Flexibility.... 135
Managerial Approach.... 299
Managerial Rigidity.... 128
Mandamus.... 297
Mandatory Retirement.... 353, 355, 357
Manipulations.... 63
Manner Of Performance.... 200
Manufacturers.... 75, 97, 116, 160, 223, 252, 445, 477, 478, 480, 482, 486, 494, 496, 497
Manufacturing Defect.... 480, 481, 485
Marbury V. Madison.... 366, 367
March Madness.... 84
Marijuana.... 44, 165, 417, 418, 465
Market Analysis.... 36
Market Failure.... 38
Market Forces.... 298
Market Freedom Vs. Level Playing Field.... 298
Marriage.... 21, 32, 117, 121, 214, 247, 259, 260, 269, 290, 352, 365, 382, 466, 470
Martin Luther King, Jr.... 9, 18
Marvin V. Marvin.... 247, 248
Mary Carter Agreements.... 369
Maryland.... 46, 78, 133, 148, 156, 157, 172, 189, 307, 309, 351, 356, 369, 398, 438, 446, 489, 492
Mason V. Ford Motor Co.... 485
Mass Marketing.... 211
Mass Production.... 477

Massachusetts.... 23, 39, 45, 47, 50, 53, 188, 290, 307, 308, 343, 351, 355, 406, 422, 489
Master/Servant Relationship.... 102
Masters Of Law.... 328
Material Breach.... 110, 275, 276, 278, 292
Material Fact.... 222, 230, 231, 234, 386
Material Misrepresentation.... 230, 231, 469
Material Mistake.... 223
Material Nonconsensual Alteration Of Written Agreement.... 281
Material Omission.... 139
Matthew Hale.... 339, 340, 341
Max Stirner.... 40
Max Weber.... 5
Maximize Profit.... 37
MBCA.... 132, 144
Mcbryde V. Committee To Review Circuit Council Conduct.... 357
Mccall V. Frampton.... 247
Mcdonald's Corp. V. Steel & Morris.... 369
Mckune V. Lile.... 395
Mclibel Case.... 369
Media Ride-Alongs.... 468
Mediation.... 391, 410, 411
Medical Bills.... 293
Medical Malpractice.... 410, 436, 437, 439
Medicine.... 60, 62, 63, 229, 250, 335, 339, 437, 439, 468, 480
Medieval Commenda.... 122
Medieval England.... 13, 216
Meetings.... 127, 128, 141, 142, 145, 146, 150, 154, 345, 416
Meinhard V. Salmon.... 118
Memorandum.... 177
Mens Rea.... 418, 419, 429, 431, 447, 449, 450
Mental Anguish.... 286, 385, 453
Mental Duress.... 184
Mental Examinations.... 385
Mental Impairments.... 324
Mental Steps.... 70, 72
Mentally Ill.... 172
Merchantable.... 494
Merchants' Protection Statutes.... 456

Mercutio Merchant.... 497
Mere Negligence.... 423, 446, 458
Merger.... 5, 124, 132, 139, 146, 233, 251, 266, 475
Merging Companies.... 139
Merit Pay.... 220, 314
Meritor Savings Bank V. Vinson.... 321
Mesaros V. United States.... 200
Mesopotamia.... 12
Method Of Payment.... 105, 106
Methodologies.... 390
Mexican Curse.... 327
Mexico.... 24, 45, 115, 124, 144, 183, 195, 236, 289, 305, 307, 351, 356, 375, 413, 419, 427, 462, 493
Michael Hoffman.... 337
Michigan.... 4, 22, 45, 61, 63, 86, 144, 223, 254, 351, 356, 396, 405, 428, 430, 479, 481
Microsoft.... 64, 66, 69, 104, 148, 160, 162, 380, 440, 469, 474
Middle Ages.... 5, 38, 127, 216, 293, 342
Middle East.... 26, 39, 193
Miller V. California.... 161
Miller-El V. Dretke.... 53
Million-Dollar Comma.... 180
Mills V. Wyman.... 219
Mini-Trials.... 410
Minimal Contacts.... 94
Ministry.... 63, 116, 335
Minitenders For Securities.... 217
Minnesota.... 45, 135, 201, 220, 307, 348, 351, 356, 405, 422, 473, 474, 489, 490
Miranda V. Arizona.... 2, 359
Mirror Image Rule.... 211, 212
Mischief.... 12, 61, 452
Misconduct.... 11, 28, 54, 108, 154, 242, 255, 257, 301, 324, 340, 343, 368, 418, 423, 431, 444, 452
Misdelivered Bank Securities.... 442
Misdemeanor Convictions.... 413
Misdemeanors.... 45, 352, 353, 413, 414
Misleading Conduct.... 170
Misleading Marks.... 83
Misprision.... 423

Misrepresentation.... 154, 179, 229, 230, 231, 233, 234, 235, 236, 237, 242, 256, 469, 471
Misrepresentation Of Material Fact.... 230
Mississippi.... 45, 53, 144, 284, 351, 356, 406, 462, 481, 489, 490
Mistake Of Fact.... 452
Mitigate Damages.... 280
Mitigation.... 290, 291, 429
MKIRDC.... 229, 235, 237, 469
Model Business Corporation Act.... 132, 144
Model Rules Of Professional Conduct.... 11, 334, 342, 348, 398
Moderate.... 346, 363, 364, 365
Modern Corporation Statutes.... 133
Modern Law.... 457
Modification.... 76, 123, 221, 256, 267, 489, 490, 491
Monday Night Poker Club.... 98
Monetary Damages.... 245, 294
Monopolies.... 76, 475
Montana.... 45, 46, 144, 247, 351, 356, 490
Montesquieu.... 6, 39
Montreal Convention.... 433, 434
Moral Climate.... 246, 247
Moral Damages.... 183, 184, 287, 289
Moral Issues.... 239
Moral Obligation.... 7, 209, 218, 219
Moral Problems.... 171
Moral Rights.... 75, 76
Morally Wrong.... 9, 40
Mortgage.... 18, 96, 216, 227, 249, 261, 263, 274, 314
Moseley V. V Secret Catalogue, Inc.... 86
Motion For Summary Judgment.... 198, 385, 386
Motions For Directed Verdict.... 402
Motivation.... 56, 57, 64, 396
Motive.... 67, 167, 212, 219, 302, 303, 371, 429, 473, 474
Multinational Corporations.... 65, 127, 139
Munaf V. Geren.... 381
Municipal Corporations.... 135
Murder.... 19, 45, 48, 52, 54, 193, 249, 338, 339, 341, 349, 397, 407, 408, 413, 417, 420, 422, 429, 430, 457, 465
Mutual Agency.... 117
Mutual Agreement.... 144
Mutual Mistake.... 222, 223, 224, 225, 226
Mutual Rescission.... 280
Mutuality.... 140, 172, 173, 184, 222, 225, 232, 235
Mutuality Of Assent.... 140, 184, 225, 232, 235
Myanmar.... 24, 413
Mylegs.... 259, 260
N.y. Times V. Sullivan.... 162
Nachfrist Notice.... 291, 292
NAFTA.... 24, 406
Naked Gun.... 79
Name Or Likeness.... 466, 468
Napoleon.... 13, 60, 367
National Association Of Realtors.... 238
National Center For State Courts.... 46, 47
National Constitutions.... 20, 366
National Government.... 21, 22, 24, 25, 371, 406, 414
National Labor Relations Act.... 21, 105, 157
National Labor Relations Board.... 323
National Origin.... 53, 305, 309, 310, 312, 315
Native American Tribes.... 367
Native Americans.... 21, 85
Natural Consequences.... 283, 429
Natural Forces.... 441
Natural Law.... 38, 39, 40, 41, 42, 54, 55, 56, 208
Natural Phenomena.... 72
Natural Rights.... 76
Naturally Occurring.... 69
Nature Of Work.... 106
Nazi War Criminals.... 344
Nazis.... 32, 228, 344
Necessaries.... 239, 242, 243, 244, 245
Need For Governmental Intervention.... 298
Need To Compromise.... 368
Negligence.... 99, 100, 101, 104, 106, 135, 143, 150, 164, 169, 235, 238, 252, 255, 256, 257, 283, 372, 377, 399, 418, 420, 423, 424, 425, 426, 427, 428, 429, 431, 432, 433, 434, 435, 436, 437, 438, 440, 441, 442, 443, 444, 445, 446, 447, 452, 453, 455, 458, 477, 478, 479, 480, 482, 484, 487, 490, 492, 496, 497
Negligence Concepts.... 434
Negligence Law.... 455
Negligence Per Se.... 428, 429
Negligent Acts.... 255, 429, 455
Negligent Hiring.... 106
Negligent Infliction Of Emotional Distress.... 307, 458
Negligent Misrepresentation.... 235, 236
Negotiable Instrument.... 189, 190, 191
Negotiation.... 170, 173, 174, 177, 199, 200, 204, 211, 241, 246, 255, 258, 265, 267, 295, 341, 368, 460
Negotiation Costs.... 170
Negotiator.... 172, 228, 267, 434, 460
Neither Tort Nor Crime.... 421
Netherlands.... 116, 131, 195, 262, 350, 375, 407, 413, 419, 424
Nevada.... 20, 45, 46, 148, 296, 307, 319, 351, 356, 480, 490
New Business.... 118, 287
New Dea.... 31
New Jersey.... 23, 50, 53, 94, 133, 148, 252, 307, 332, 351, 355, 364, 416, 442, 448, 490
New Trial.... 48, 404
New York Court Of Appeals.... 58, 118
New Zealand.... 14, 195, 263, 333, 413
Newspapers.... 31, 79, 96, 463
Nicaragua.... 24, 413
Nigeria.... 24, 116, 195, 413
Ninth Circuit.... 351
NLRA.... 104
No Substantial Change.... 479
Nolo.com.... 344, 345
Non-Compete Covenants.... 114
Non-Consumer Goods.... 480
Non-Dischargeable.... 409
Non-Employment Arrangement.... 103
Noncompetition.... 109
Noncriminal.... 19, 49
Nonmerchants.... 213
Nonobvious.... 72, 77

Nonobviousness.... 72, 77
Nonparty.... 380
Nonverbal Conduct.... 400
Norman Invasion.... 13
Norms.... 4, 5, 9, 10, 15, 65, 183, 192, 193, 247, 307, 308, 342, 344, 425
North American Free Trade Agreement.... 406
Nose Job.... 290
Not Consideration.... 219
Not Guilty.... 46, 52, 402, 403, 404, 407, 408, 419
Not Liable.... 46, 99, 100, 101, 106, 111, 127, 312, 478, 485
Not Offers.... 199
Notaire.... 329
Notarized Seal.... 215
Novation.... 65, 69, 72, 73, 88, 268, 272, 280, 477, 482
Novelty.... 72
Novelty And Nonobviousness.... 72
Nudum Pactum.... 220
Nuisance.... 9, 391, 425, 453, 454
Number Of Jurors.... 45
Nuremberg Trials.... 39, 40
O.J. Simpson.... 19, 408
Obamacare.... 364
Obedience.... 9, 17, 38, 107, 108, 110
Obfuscation.... 341
Obiter Dicta.... 15
Objections.... 34, 79, 177, 237, 380
Objective Indication.... 198
Objective Intent.... 190, 208
Objective Standard.... 208, 278, 427, 458
Objective Theory Of Contracts.... 175, 179
Obligations.... 26, 40, 106, 107, 122, 174, 181, 215, 219, 257, 271, 273, 279, 280, 281, 282, 286, 301, 358, 491, 496
Obscenity.... 161, 166
Observations.... 156
Obstetrics.... 247, 439
Obtainable.... 291, 292
Obvious Risk.... 442, 443, 485
Odorizzi V. Bloomfield School District.... 226
OECD.... 138, 139

Off-The-Job Activities.... 466
Offenses.... 352, 408, 413, 414, 418, 421
Offer.... 2, 15, 18, 37, 45, 53, 72, 73, 84, 88, 109, 118, 121, 122, 126, 127, 133, 134, 142, 143, 145, 149, 152, 160, 171, 172, 176, 177, 179, 182, 184, 185, 186, 188, 193, 196, 198, 199, 200, 201, 203, 204, 205, 206, 207, 208, 209, 210, 211, 212, 213, 217, 219, 220, 221, 225, 229, 235, 238, 258, 265, 270, 271, 273, 275, 276, 277, 306, 307, 308, 311, 323, 324, 325, 332, 333, 334, 335, 344, 390, 391, 395, 399, 402, 425, 473, 482, 490
Offeree.... 171, 172, 185, 186, 198, 199, 201, 203, 204, 205, 210, 225, 271, 273
Offeree Accepted Benefits.... 210
Offeree's Rejection.... 203
Offeror.... 37, 198, 201, 203, 204, 205, 210, 213, 225
Offeror's Revocation.... 203
Officer Of The Court.... 10, 340, 341, 342, 343, 344
Official List.... 300
Ohio.... 45, 53, 79, 228, 351, 356, 417, 418, 422, 466, 490
Old Testament.... 12
Olmstead V. Ftc.... 124
On The Job.... 304, 314, 321, 434, 468
Oncale V. Sundowner Offshore Services, Inc.... 320
Ontario.... 313, 333
Open Courts.... 385
Open Records.... 385
Open-Ended Questions.... 399
Operation Of Law.... 281
Operative Words.... 215
Opportunity To Be Heard.... 373, 387, 389
Options.... 112, 128, 204, 205, 233, 271, 325, 470, 476
Oral Agreement.... 174, 258, 261, 265, 358
Oral Arguments.... 365, 403
Oral Changes.... 267
Oral Contract.... 258, 259, 261, 263, 264, 265, 358
Ordinances.... 352, 428

Ordinary People.... 43, 44, 438
Oregon.... 45, 307, 351, 356, 395, 435, 489, 490
Organization For Economic Cooperation And Development.... 139
Organized Crime.... 17, 421
Orientation.... 11, 306, 307, 317, 359, 363, 406, 414
Original Jurisdiction.... 352, 360
Original Position.... 40, 41
Oscar Wilde.... 463
Ostrowski V. Avery.... 149
Othello.... 460
Otto Von Bismarck.... 145, 469
Ouija Board.... 48, 269
Out-Of-Court Statement.... 390
Outside Directors.... 143, 145, 148
Outside Interference.... 298
Overboard.... 44, 285, 321, 408, 472
Overlapping Warranties.... 496
Overreaching Bargaining.... 239
Overturning On Appeal.... 404
Ownership Of Property.... 40
Oxford University.... 7, 130
Pack Of Lies.... 376, 377
Palimony.... 247
Palming Off.... 66, 67, 68
Parachutes.... 142
Paralegals.... 345, 380
Parent Corporation.... 154
Parliament.... 31, 43, 131, 259
Parody.... 79, 80
Parol Evidence Rule 176, 180, 259, 260, 265, 266, 267
Parole.... 20, 51, 228, 268, 408, 416, 418
Partial Performance.... 262
Partially Disclosed.... 102
Participation.... 303, 348, 354, 359, 444
Parties' Actions.... 104
Partisan Election.... 356
Partly Built.... 289
Partnership Agreement.... 115, 119, 120, 121, 122, 125
Partnership Format.... 120, 128, 129
Partnership Law.... 116, 117, 118, 120

517

Partnerships.... 12, 19, 21, 89, 111, 112, 113, 114, 115, 116, 117, 119, 120, 121, 122, 123, 124, 125, 126, 129, 130, 133, 135, 137, 145, 169

Party's Intent.... 175

Past Consideration.... 219

Patent And Trademark Office.... 69, 82, 83, 86

Patent Holders.... 11, 75, 86

Patent Law.... 64, 67, 69, 73, 74, 77, 86

Patent Office.... 74, 85

Patents.... 64, 67, 68, 69, 70, 71, 72, 73, 74, 77, 79, 82, 84, 86, 87, 88, 89, 351

Pathological Behavior.... 335

Patron Of Justice.... 12

Patrons.... 91, 108, 245, 427, 442, 471, 472, 473

Pattern Of Racketeering.... 421

Pattern Or Practice Of Discrimination.... 314

Paul Butler.... 53

Paul M. Romer.... 65

Payroll Taxes.... 104, 129

Pc.... 74, 102, 123, 136, 214

Penal Code.... 13, 165, 166

Pennsylvania.... 45, 47, 77, 144, 247, 351, 356, 388, 389, 451, 460, 477

Pennsylvania Supreme Court.... 144

Pension Funds.... 142

Pension Plan.... 145, 207

Per Capita.... 329

Per Se.... 297, 338, 428, 429, 459, 474

Perceived Injury.... 368

Peremptory Challenges.... 52, 53

Perfect Pill Bottle.... 480

Perfect Tender.... 275, 291

Perjury.... 6, 10, 259, 384, 395, 398, 399, 400

Perpetual Existence.... 126, 130

Personal Areas.... 183

Personal Duties.... 110, 271

Personal Jurisdiction.... 59, 94, 373

Personal Matters.... 110, 272, 290, 469

Personal Privacy.... 316

Personal Property.... 134, 190, 262, 293, 453

Personal Services Contract.... 273, 282

Personal Values.... 218

Personnel Manual.... 299

Perspectives On Blogs.... 162

Persuade.... 31, 49, 62, 96, 236, 361, 367, 390, 398, 400, 402, 471, 473

Peru.... 116, 183, 195, 229, 289, 384, 413

Pervasive.... 4, 318, 319, 320

Perverse Incentives.... 212, 434

Petit Jury.... 45, 46, 390

Petitioner.... 59, 340

Pets.... 100, 106, 203, 477, 482

Philippines.... 24, 184, 195, 286, 413

Philosophy.... 4, 8, 12, 34, 40, 42, 222

Phrasing.... 3, 32, 78, 273, 294, 361, 439

Physical Duress.... 227

Physical Evidence.... 400

Physical Harm.... 227, 422

Physical Injuries.... 496

Piehl V. Norwegian Old People's Home.... 254

Piercing The Corporate Veil.... 152, 153, 154, 155

Pinned Down.... 379

Pinocchio.... 80

Piracy.... 20, 66, 117, 249, 348

Pizza Hut.... 322, 476

Pj.... 348, 349

Place Of Incorporation.... 195

Plain English.... 267

Plain Language Legislation.... 174

Plant Patents.... 71

Plato.... 5, 34

Play The Game.... 27, 37

Players.... 43, 63, 134, 175, 193, 287, 327, 417, 418, 457

Plea Bargaining.... 413, 418

Pleadings.... 330, 368, 376, 378, 386, 440

Plumber.... 90, 396

PMB.... 113

Poison Pill.... 142

Poison-Prevention Packaging Act.... 480

Poland.... 195, 350, 375, 413, 419, 424, 483

Police.... 2, 17, 28, 29, 38, 41, 43, 136, 165, 220, 227, 290, 365, 405, 407, 418, 426, 428, 438, 447, 449, 450, 451, 464, 465, 468

Policy Statement On Deception.... 476

Political Speech.... 157, 158, 159, 160, 161

Politicians.... 30, 32, 44, 128

Politics.... 4, 18, 35, 128, 156, 159, 164, 333, 363, 405

Polygamy.... 34

Polygraphs.... 395

Poor Business Judgment.... 143

Pope.... 367

Pornographic Movies.... 246

Portugal.... 334, 350, 375, 413, 419, 424

Positive Law.... 37, 38, 39, 42, 57

Positivism.... 37, 38, 42, 54, 56

Postal Reorganization Act.... 209

Postal Service.... 7, 21, 113

Potential Defendants.... 443

Potential Disadvantages.... 61, 63

Potential Settlement.... 368

Powers Of Observation.... 396

Practical Advice.... 223, 227, 241, 494

Practical Dilemmas.... 10

Practical Obscurity.... 385

Practicality.... 171, 243, 287

Practice Of Discrimination.... 314, 318

Pre-History.... 11

Preamble.... 196, 197

Precedent.... 14, 15, 16, 20, 35, 60, 71, 76, 131, 247, 267, 272, 273, 274, 277, 330, 363, 366, 436

Predatory Business Practices.... 473

Predatory Pricing.... 474

Predicate Offenses.... 421

Preemptive Rights.... 140, 142

Prefatory Language.... 181, 197

Pregnancy.... 300, 305, 320

Pregnancy Discrimination Act.... 305

Preliminary Negotiations.... 199

Preparation.... 336, 337, 378, 379, 398, 399, 454

Preponderance Of Evidence.... 75, 232, 402, 415, 420

President Gerald Ford.... 362

Presidential Election Controversy.... 358

Presumption Of Innocence.... 407, 415, 419
Presumptions.... 450
Pretense.... 128, 470
Pretrial Conference.... 352, 384, 386
Prevarication.... 399, 400
Prevent Harassment.... 406
Preventative Law.... 342
Prevention.... 18, 164, 417, 437, 480
Price Discrimination.... 474, 475
Price Quotations.... 199
Pricing.... 88, 211, 439, 474
Prima Facie.... 312, 435
Prima Facie Case.... 312
Prime Minister.... 387
Princess Diana.... 422
Principal Office.... 140
Principals.... 98, 99, 102, 110, 116, 120, 336
Principles Of Corporate Governance.... 144
Printing.... 21, 78, 79, 443
Prior Agreement.... 266
Prior Convictions.... 396, 418
Prior Course Of Dealings.... 209
Prison Litigation.... 371
Prison Litigation Reform Act Of.... 371
Prison Rehabilitation.... 395
Prison Revolt.... 227
Prisoners Of War.... 395
Prisoners Suing The State.... 371
Privacy Concerns.... 385, 460
Private Clubs.... 314
Private Corporation.... 132, 135
Private Employers.... 157
Private Exchanges.... 192
Private Facts.... 453, 466, 467
Private Helpers.... 409
Private Insurance.... 94
Private Law.... 19, 329, 358, 454
Private Nuisance.... 454
Private Process Servers.... 373, 374
Private Securities Litigation Reform Act.... 141, 147
Private Wrong.... 99, 415
Privileged Statements.... 461
Privity.... 268, 269, 483, 484, 496

Privity Of Contract.... 268, 269, 483, 484
Pro Se.... 43, 44, 45, 390, 401, 403
Pro Se Briefs.... 403
Probability.... 416, 420, 432
Probable Cause.... 25, 456, 457, 464, 465
Probate.... 44, 185, 328, 352, 353, 421
Probation.... 418, 430
Procedural Due Process.... 387
Procedural Fairness.... 387
Procedural Law.... 19, 27, 415
Procedural Protections.... 26, 124, 387
Procedural Rules.... 90, 309
Procedural Unconscionability.... 236, 252, 255
Process Of Codification.... 60
Processors.... 470
Procuratori.... 330
Product Liability.... 65, 380, 424, 453, 476, 477, 478, 479, 480, 481, 483, 484, 485, 486, 488, 490
Production.... 18, 56, 64, 66, 75, 77, 81, 85, 87, 88, 93, 137, 263, 281, 284, 292, 316, 324, 337, 380, 381, 400, 474, 477, 485
Prof. Jane Larson.... 469
Professional Codes Of Ethics.... 237
Professional Context.... 436, 438
Professional Corporation.... 102, 135
Professional Relationship.... 345, 346
Professional Standards.... 238, 436
Professionals.... 6, 43, 58, 99, 105, 135, 148, 238, 250, 300, 329, 331, 335, 336, 337, 341, 342, 343, 355, 405, 436, 438, 440
Professions.... 63, 159, 214, 238, 313, 335, 337, 339, 341, 437
Profit Expectations.... 185
Prohibition Era.... 49
Prominent Proponents.... 35, 36, 37
Promisee.... 185, 186, 206, 207, 220
Promisor.... 172, 182, 185, 186, 206, 219, 220, 221
Promissory Estoppel.... 172, 204, 205, 206, 207, 221, 262
Promissory Notes.... 191

Promote.... 7, 39, 45, 64, 76, 79, 94, 139, 197, 213, 237, 246, 313, 316, 320, 368, 376, 411, 432, 476
Promoters.... 139, 432
Promoting Equality.... 17, 18
Proof Of Intent.... 311
Property Interest.... 65, 87, 216, 249, 454
Property Law.... 4, 64, 216, 472
Property Rights.... 64, 68, 73, 74, 86, 192, 193, 297, 414
Prosecuting.... 43, 350, 430
Prosecutors.... 3, 29, 51, 54, 227, 330, 346, 400, 407, 414, 415, 416, 419, 430, 450, 464, 465
Prospective Economic Advantage.... 470, 471
Prostitution.... 66, 177, 246, 420
Protected Group.... 312
Protecting Confidential Information.... 106
Protestants.... 364
Protests.... 160, 165
Protests Against A Business.... 160
Provinces.... 22, 23, 24, 263, 333, 484
Provincial.... 23, 24, 351, 355
Proximate Cause.... 431, 432, 441, 442, 484, 485
Proxy.... 142
Psychiatry.... 437, 438
Psychologists.... 62
Psychology.... 4, 34, 44, 251, 309, 450
Public Corporation.... 131, 135, 411
Public Disclosure.... 74, 453, 466, 467
Public Disclosure Of Private Facts.... 453, 466, 467
Public Figure.... 162, 460, 461, 462, 467
Public Good.... 64, 65, 334, 337
Public Interest.... 45, 133, 237, 245, 416
Public Law.... 19, 424
Public Nuisance.... 454
Public Officials.... 162, 287, 374, 460, 462
Public Relations.... 76, 77, 206, 223, 317, 370, 464, 488
Public Safety.... 438
Public Trial.... 26
Public Use.... 26, 296
Public Wrong.... 169, 299, 415

Publication.... 72, 73, 78, 80, 114, 199, 374, 380, 457, 459, 460, 467, 469
Publication Of Information Placing A Person In A False Light.... 467
Publishers Clearing House.... 232
Puffing.... 223, 230, 236, 237, 476, 493
Pumping Salesmanship.... 253
Punishment.... 2, 18, 25, 26, 29, 39, 52, 164, 227, 246, 292, 307, 371, 408, 413, 417, 418, 423, 429
Punitive Damages.... 42, 108, 153, 162, 232, 285, 286, 289, 290, 306, 322, 386, 429, 436, 452, 457, 460, 466, 470, 485, 490
Purpose Becomes Illegal.... 203
Purposes Of Law.... 17
Qualifications.... 22, 141, 310, 311, 314, 325, 361, 412
Qualitex Co. V. Jacobson Products Co.... 82
Quantity.... 200, 211, 212, 257, 259, 262, 275, 494
Quantum Meruit.... 187, 295
Quartz.... 225, 226
Quasi-Contract.... 179, 187, 188, 295, 423
Quebec.... 24, 184, 189, 263, 329, 483
Queen Victoria.... 55, 436
Quid Pro Quo.... 171, 215, 216, 318
Quintilian.... 400
R&D.... 72
Racial Discrimination.... 303
Racism.... 340
Racketeer Influenced And Corrupt Organizations Act.... 421
Racketeering.... 248, 421
Raffles V. Wickelhaus.... 224, 226
Range Of Discovery.... 380
Rape.... 49, 61, 208, 320, 359, 405, 407, 420, 422, 437, 457, 463
Rasul V. Bush.... 381
Ratification.... 23, 25, 96, 97, 242
Rational Basis.... 151
Re-Cross Examination.... 402
Re-Direct Examination.... 402
Reaffirmation Agreements.... 408
Real Dispute.... 31, 281
Real Estate.... 105, 110, 117, 119, 190, 201, 214, 215, 216, 217, 231, 232, 234, 249, 261, 267, 274, 291, 297, 328, 332, 341, 471
Real Estate Deeds.... 215
Real Estate Promotions.... 471
Real Life.... 2, 355
Realists.... 42, 43
Realtors.... 237, 238
Reasonable Accommodation.... 307, 310, 324, 325
Reasonable Alternative Design.... 481
Reasonable Apprehension.... 455
Reasonable Care.... 108, 442, 483, 484, 487
Reasonable Cause.... 302
Reasonable Doubt.... 41, 233, 402, 415, 416, 419
Reasonable Expectations.... 287, 346, 466
Reasonable Foundation.... 296
Reasonable Grounds.... 139, 246, 456
Reasonable Manufacturer.... 481
Reasonable Measures.... 107
Reasonable Period.... 203
Reasonable Person.... 37, 93, 175, 176, 198, 203, 208, 222, 252, 319, 423, 427, 446, 468, 473, 495
Reasonable Reliance.... 230, 232, 235
Reasonable Suspicion.... 29, 468
Reasonable Time.... 203, 204, 205, 210, 212, 213, 241, 244, 263, 275, 456
Reasonable Value.... 187, 243, 244
Reasonableness.... 98, 110, 232, 276, 323, 446
Reasonably Necessary Force.... 451
Reasoning.... 12, 14, 15, 32, 43, 46, 220, 231, 254, 315, 358, 363, 365, 429, 433, 482
Rebuttable Presumption.... 450
Recalls.... 308, 439
Rechtsanwalt.... 329
Reciprocal Rights.... 268
Recitals.... 181, 196, 197
Recklessness.... 150, 256, 257, 417, 418, 429
Recorded.... 2, 11, 12, 14, 47, 75, 77, 80, 115, 203, 216, 380, 458
Recovery.... 92, 93, 99, 143, 271, 277, 290, 332, 333, 334, 446, 458, 484, 485
Reebok.... 383
Reference To A Sample Or Model.... 493
Reform Proposals.... 333, 411
Reformation.... 284, 294, 295
Registered Agent.... 136, 140
Registration Statement.... 139, 140
Regulation Of Business.... 4
Regulatory Areas.... 234
Regulatory Licensing.... 250
Regulatory Taking.... 296, 297
Reimbursement.... 97, 99, 100, 146, 209, 229, 241, 293, 332, 370, 371, 408
Reinventing The Wheel.... 14, 212
Rejection.... 149, 172, 203, 210, 241
Release.... 51, 70, 163, 216, 228, 255, 280, 281, 303, 371, 381, 427, 431, 441, 443, 444, 450, 456, 461, 462, 467, 491
Release Of Liability.... 443
Relevant Legal Principle.... 358
Reliance.... 6, 81, 82, 92, 94, 121, 140, 155, 205, 206, 207, 226, 229, 230, 231, 232, 235, 242, 267, 277, 290, 469, 492
Religion.... 12, 18, 25, 34, 51, 53, 156, 298, 300, 303, 304, 306, 311, 312, 315, 405, 417
Religious Discrimination.... 303, 306, 466
Remand.... 149, 150, 167, 404
Remedies For Breach.... 275, 284
Remedy At Law.... 294
Removal.... 52, 209, 285, 357, 358, 362, 363, 385, 484
Removal Of Judges.... 357
Rental Amount.... 203, 243
Reorganization.... 209, 409
Repair.... 160, 179, 288, 291, 337, 370, 371, 444, 479, 492, 494
Replacement.... 65, 94, 187, 249, 252, 284, 288, 291, 362, 446, 487
Repossess Goods.... 408
Republican Party Of Minnesota V. White.... 356
Republicans.... 157, 161, 182, 490
Repudiation.... 262, 279, 280
Reputations Of Lawyers.... 327
Request For Jury Trial.... 376

Requests For Admissions.... 381, 384
Requests For Bids.... 199
Requests For Documents.... 384
Required Disclosures.... 234, 476
Res Ipsa Loquitur.... 434, 435, 436, 497
Res Judicata.... 27, 406
Rescind The Contract.... 232, 275
Rescission.... 155, 207, 221, 223, 226, 236, 243, 253, 280, 294, 295
Research And Development.... 72, 296
Resources.... 7, 17, 21, 45, 61, 63, 66, 225, 257, 298, 318, 330, 345, 374, 381, 386, 418, 454, 458, 474, 488
Respect For Private Autonomy.... 295
Respondeat Superior.... 89, 100, 101, 104, 106, 115, 117, 125, 164, 428, 434, 497
Responsibility For Consequences.... 419, 429
Restatement (Second) Of Agency.... 101
Restatement (Second) Of Contracts.... 206, 286, 289
Restatements.... 101, 264
Restitution.... 244, 294, 295, 433
Restoration.... 51, 241
Restraint.... 13, 14, 32, 106, 146, 170, 299, 477, 485
Resuscitation.... 440
Retailers.... 220, 223, 478, 494, 495, 496
Retainers.... 331
Retaliation.... 12, 163, 301, 302, 303, 319
Retention.... 177, 352, 354, 355, 356, 489
Retiree Example.... 188
Retirement.... 207, 308, 353, 355, 357, 361, 362, 363, 364
Retirement Of Judges.... 357
Revenue Licensing.... 250, 251
Reverse.... 8, 50, 61, 87, 167, 249, 321, 341, 378, 404, 492
Reverse Discrimination.... 321
Reverse Engineering.... 87
Reviewing.... 43, 111, 120, 172, 309, 319, 320, 351, 366, 406, 410
Revised Model Business Corporation Act.... 132
Revised Uniform Limited Partnership Act.... 123

Revised Uniform Partnership Act.... 118, 119
Revocation.... 203, 208
Reward.... 18, 64, 69, 119, 137, 163, 185, 200, 212, 219, 220, 229, 332, 374, 423
Reynolds V. United States.... 34
RICO.... 30, 45, 46, 351, 416, 421
Right Of Control.... 106
Right Of Privacy.... 166, 463, 468
Right Of Refusal.... 145
Right To An Accounting.... 110
Right To Control.... 78, 105, 117
Right To Counsel.... 63
Right To Disaffirm.... 242
Right To Know.... 159, 174, 274, 309, 380
Right-To-Sue Letter.... 320
Rights Of Contract.... 298
Risk Of Loss.... 101, 117, 128, 190, 200, 211
Risk Of Losses.... 117, 128
Risk-Benefits Analysis.... 480, 481
RMBCA.... 132
Robbery.... 3, 20, 169, 359, 419, 420, 422, 444, 447, 473
Robert Bork.... 365
Robert Jackson.... 344
Robert Louis Stevenson.... 189
Robinson-Patman Act.... 132, 138, 474
Roe V. Wade.... 10, 365
Roger B. Taney.... 367
Rogers Communications.... 180
Roman Law.... 6, 13, 20, 60, 406
Roman Times.... 100, 125, 127, 130, 215
Romero V. Allstate Ins.... 303
Roprahs.... 305
Roscoe Pound.... 170
Royal Cows.... 223
Royal Society.... 72
Royalties.... 65, 69, 70, 78
RRRIQS.... 294
Rule Of Law.... 11, 13, 14, 15, 43, 54, 171, 192
Rules Of Civil Procedure.... 143, 368, 373, 374, 381
Rules Of Evidence.... 27, 61, 390, 391, 479

Rules Of Professional Conduct.... 11, 334, 338, 340, 342, 348, 398
RULPA.... 123
RUPA.... 118, 119
Russian Law.... 172
Ruth Bader Ginsburg.... 364
S Corporation.... 79, 112, 123, 124, 125, 127, 129, 132, 134, 135, 136, 137, 139, 141, 144, 145, 154
Safe Harbor.... 149
Sale Of Goods.... 89, 184, 190, 194, 208, 211, 212, 221, 259, 262, 264, 275
Sale Of Present Home Contingencies.... 274
Sales Contract.... 190, 195, 208, 212, 221, 252, 262, 264, 275, 387, 388
Sales Contract Formation.... 208
Sales Contracts.... 190, 212, 264
Sales Representative Agreement.... 196, 256
Sales Talk.... 230
Salespeople.... 237, 300
Same-Sex Marriage.... 365
Sample Contract.... 110, 196, 271
Sample Settlement Agreement.... 369
Samuel Butler.... 185
Sanction For Breach.... 170
Sanctions.... 10, 12, 28, 37, 347, 384, 461
Sarbanes-Oxley Act.... 10, 11, 147, 346, 349
Satisfaction.... 37, 108, 276, 277, 278, 281, 299, 390
Satisfaction Standards.... 277
Saturday Morning Tennis Group.... 98
Saudi Arabia.... 60, 115, 116, 195, 413
SBA.... 32, 112, 121, 177, 188, 222, 245, 248, 264, 289, 322, 334, 339, 340, 342, 347, 348, 383, 393, 394, 407, 408, 448, 470
Scandals.... 131, 147, 148
Schenck V. United States.... 161
Schlunk.... 375
Schools.... 4, 8, 9, 15, 30, 43, 130, 171, 306, 327, 328, 361
Science.... 1, 6, 8, 14, 15, 19, 34, 51, 64, 65, 68, 70, 72, 76, 219, 246, 254, 396, 418, 437, 450, 488
Scienter.... 231, 233, 234, 235

Scientific Speech.... 159
Scientists.... 5, 62, 66, 70
Scope Of Employment.... 73, 101, 164, 434
Scotland.... 45, 333, 419
Scott Turow.... 397
Seal.... 3, 206, 214, 215, 216, 260, 385, 466, 467, 480
Seals.... 206, 214, 215, 216
Searches.... 1, 7, 25, 28, 29, 69, 82, 415, 464, 465, 466
Searches And Seizures.... 25, 28, 464, 465
Sears.... 199, 299, 408
Seaworthy.... 493
Secession.... 24
Second Restatement Of Torts.... 479
Secondary Authority.... 361
Secondary Market.... 122, 218
Secondhand Smoke.... 9
Secretaries.... 345
Section 402A Of The Restatement.... 479
Secured Transactions.... 189, 191
Securities Act.... 132, 138, 140, 147
Securities And Exchange Commission.... 147, 198, 347
Securities Exchange Act.... 132, 138, 234
Security.... 6, 25, 104, 105, 123, 129, 189, 191, 207, 227, 290, 385, 388, 389, 396, 430, 464, 478, 490
Segregation.... 9, 15, 321
Seizures.... 25, 28, 464, 465
Self-Defense.... 54, 451, 452
Self-Esteem.... 236, 237
Self-Help.... 45, 285, 290
Self-Imposed Duties.... 169
Self-Incriminating Testimony.... 399
Self-Interest.... 36, 145, 170, 238, 388
Self-Regulation.... 343, 476
Sellers.... 105, 109, 177, 222, 225, 233, 278, 291, 479, 483, 494, 495
Selling Illegal Drugs.... 421
Selling Product.... 489
Senate.... 24, 25, 182, 353, 360, 363, 365, 434, 461, 462
Seniority Systems.... 314
Sentencing.... 49, 54, 152, 239, 335, 396, 416, 417, 418, 430

Sentencing Guidelines.... 152, 239, 335, 417, 418, 430
Separate But Equal.... 9, 15
Separation Of Powers.... 26, 31
Sequestering The Jury.... 376
Sequestration.... 376, 392
Serbin V. Walt Disney World.... 94
Servanthood.... 103
Serve Process.... 59, 136, 373, 375
Service Marks.... 82
Service Of Process.... 94, 140, 197, 372, 373, 374, 375
Set Fees.... 331
Severability.... 197, 198
Severance.... 206, 309
Sex Discrimination.... 305, 306, 316, 317
Sexual Assault Counselor.... 346
Sexual Behavior.... 318, 324
Sexual Discrimination.... 303
Sexual Fraud.... 469
Sexual Harassment.... 9, 306, 307, 312, 317, 318, 319, 320, 321, 322, 345, 399
Sexual Orientation.... 306, 307, 317
Shamash.... 12
Shared Profits.... 118, 125
Shareholder Meetings.... 142
Shareholder Rights.... 142
Shareholder Suits.... 143, 408
Shares Of Corporation.... 140
Sharia.... 60, 115
Sheff V. O'neill.... 22
Shell Corporation.... 154, 155
Shelter.... 57, 79, 122, 243, 442
Shepard V. Maxwell.... 61
Sheriff.... 55, 373, 374, 387, 388, 409
Sherman Act.... 132, 138
Shihoh-Shoshi.... 329, 330
Shipping.... 162, 190, 282, 453, 474
Shipping And Risk Of Loss.... 190
Shotgun Approach.... 285, 440
Shredded Wheat.... 84
Side Deals.... 369
Side Morals.... 209
Sierra Club V. Morton.... 41

Sierra Preservation Council, Inc. V. Tahoe Regional Planning.... 296
Signatures.... 140, 177, 198, 203, 216, 259
Significant Harm.... 417
Significant Performance.... 205
Significant Terms.... 202
Silence.... 30, 166, 208, 209, 210, 233, 234, 235, 264, 362, 461
Silence As Acceptance.... 210
Silence As Fraud.... 233
Simple Trespass.... 414
Singapore.... 19, 195, 413
Single-Sex Health Clubs.... 314
Sipple V. Chronicle Publishing Co.... 467
Sir John Eric Ericksen.... 436
Sir Walter Scott.... 58
Sir William Blackstone.... 7, 419
Sixth Amendment.... 53
Sj.... 37, 385, 386
Slander.... 453, 458, 459, 460, 461
Slavery.... 9, 24, 39
Slippery Pork Chops.... 447
Slippery Slope.... 31, 32, 33, 341, 398
Small Business.... 112, 113, 114, 115, 128, 129, 137
Small Claims Court.... 182, 352, 392
Small Fry.... 245
Small Print.... 94, 176, 177, 202, 203, 468
Smith And Edwards V. Golden Spike Little League.... 98
Smith V. Van Gorkom.... 148, 151, 152
SMLLC.... 124
Smoking.... 9, 10, 69, 160, 348, 444, 445, 466
Snowbirds.... 471, 472
Sobhani V. @Radical.media, Inc.... 78
Social Contract.... 7
Social Invitations.... 199
Social Justice.... 53
Social Order.... 5, 18, 170
Social Security Act.... 105
Social Welfare Maximization.... 38
Social Worker.... 346
Sociology.... 4, 34
Sole Proprietorships.... 112, 114, 116, 121, 129, 130

522

Solicitor General.... 343, 364

Solicitors.... 329

Solon.... 12

Solvency.... 115, 194

Something For Something.... 215

Sonny Bono Copyright Term Extension Act.... 76

Sorites Arguments.... 32

Sources Of Law.... 20, 190, 420

South Africa.... 20, 28, 60, 195, 256, 263, 366, 367, 413, 416, 465, 483

South Carolina.... 45, 46, 53, 124, 189, 247, 296, 351, 355, 489, 490

South Dakota.... 45, 47, 54, 351, 356, 462, 490

South Korea.... 70, 116, 143, 195, 375, 413

South Sea Company.... 131

Sovereign Immunity.... 135, 428

Sovereign States.... 21, 22

Sovereignty.... 21, 22, 23, 24

Soviet Union.... 24, 26, 65, 263

SOX.... 11, 152, 229

Spain.... 23, 195, 264, 300, 366, 375, 413, 419

Spam.... 67

Spanish.... 6, 13, 61, 183, 193, 229, 235, 264, 300, 315, 354

Speak The Law.... 23

Special Appearance.... 373

Specialized Commercial And Labor Courts.... 355

Specific Language.... 202

Specific Performance.... 179, 217, 280, 294, 296, 297

Speech Rights.... 52, 156, 158, 162, 166

Speeding.... 42, 426, 446

Speedy And Public Trial.... 26

Spinoza.... 5

Spying.... 465, 466

St. Thomas Aquinas.... 38, 56

Stability.... 6, 14, 17, 19, 35, 85, 119, 170, 192, 213

Staggered Elections.... 132

Stakeholders.... 137, 141, 142

Standard Of Proof.... 232, 390, 413, 420

Standard Spiel.... 10

Standardized Forms.... 211, 212, 213, 257

Star Trek.... 192

Starbucks.... 103

Stare Decisis.... 14, 15, 60, 363

State Constitutions.... 22, 23

State Corporate Law.... 134

State Courts.... 15, 22, 23, 46, 47, 53, 61, 136, 144, 201, 299, 351, 352, 357, 372, 373, 386, 443, 490

State Government.... 22, 23, 24, 51, 311, 313, 414, 416

State Judges.... 352, 353, 356

State Legislature.... 33, 133, 148, 355, 367, 416, 472

State Retiree Example.... 188

State Statutes.... 428

State Trial Courts.... 3, 16, 352

State V. New Chue Her.... 403, 405

State V. Veverka.... 429

Statistics.... 47, 70, 137, 223, 300, 302, 305, 306, 314, 337, 366, 418, 474

Status Quo.... 185, 223, 286, 287, 390

Statute Of Frauds.... 119, 121, 173, 184, 198, 258, 259, 260, 261, 262, 263, 264, 265, 285

Statute Of Limitations.... 27, 184, 219, 221, 281, 377, 452, 467

Statutory Confidentiality Privileges.... 346

Statutory Law.... 20, 29, 31, 454

Statutory Question.... 366

Statutory Requirements.... 202

Stay.... 29, 32, 38, 129, 134, 202, 216, 221, 304, 328, 361, 362, 372, 393, 431, 450

Stealth.... 417

Stephen G. Breyer.... 302, 364

Stipulations.... 292, 384, 386

Stock Options.... 128, 205

Stocks.... 132, 147, 288, 313

Storage.... 191, 291, 468

Storage Areas.... 468

Strategies To Reduce Or Eliminate Double Taxation.... 129

Stream Of Commerce.... 483, 492

Street Address.... 113, 140

Street Name.... 141

Strength Tests.... 325

Stress.... 109, 219, 289, 290, 307, 324, 392, 426, 438, 448, 453, 457, 458, 461

Strict Liability.... 418, 420, 424, 425, 453, 476, 477, 478, 479, 482, 484, 486, 487, 490, 494, 496, 497

Strict Liability Standard.... 479

Strikes.... 145, 283, 442, 471, 496

Style.... 3, 51, 67, 86, 102, 120, 137, 167, 173, 359, 418, 466

Subjective Standard.... 239, 277, 278, 428

Suborning Perjury.... 398

Subpoena.... 349, 373, 379, 380, 384, 386, 486

Subpoena Duces Tecum.... 380

Subsequent Illegality.... 282

Subsequent Trial.... 207

Subsidiaries.... 123, 125, 141

Subsidiary.... 154

Substantial Change.... 479, 482

Substantial Compliance.... 273

Substantial Performance.... 276

Substantive Law.... 26, 27, 134, 270, 372, 414

Substitute.... 83, 129, 205, 215, 235, 271, 280, 291, 292, 374, 388, 412, 423, 481

Substituted Agreement.... 280

Substituted Service.... 374

Successor Corporations.... 479

Sudan.... 24, 60

Sue Yerpantzoff.... 371, 373

Sufficient Evidence.... 252, 258, 386

Sufficiently Definite.... 171, 199

Suitable Goods.... 495

Summary Judgment.... 50, 188, 198, 233, 234, 301, 352, 385, 386, 427, 462

Summary Jury Trials.... 410

Summoning Jurors.... 51

Summons.... 49, 373, 374, 375, 387, 426

Sun God.... 12, 441

Superior Court.... 3, 94, 228, 352, 417, 455

Superior Risk Bearer.... 255

Superseding (Intervening) Causation.... 442

Superseding Causation.... 436, 440, 442, 446

Suppliers.... 88, 107, 137, 139, 141, 144, 154, 191, 192, 249, 482
Supply Disappears.... 281
Supremacy Clause.... 21
Supreme Court Justices.... 41, 352, 353, 356, 360, 361
Surprise Approach.... 379
Surveillance Methods.... 466
Survivorship.... 116, 121
Susa.... 12, 265, 300, 383, 393, 394
Susanna.... 265, 300, 393, 394
Sweden.... 46, 195, 375, 413, 419, 433
Swidler & Berlin V. United States.... 346
Swierkiewicz V. Sorema N.A.... 309
Swing Vote.... 365
Switzerland.... 23, 124, 195, 246, 337, 355, 375, 413, 419
Symbolic Function.... 216
Symbolic Speech.... 165
Syndicates.... 66, 113
T.S. Eliot.... 1
Taiwan.... 74, 116, 483
Take It Or Leave It.... 252, 257
Takeover Talks.... 233
Takeovers.... 132, 251
Talent.... 271, 330
Talis Juror.... 49
Tangible Goods.... 84
Tangible Result.... 297
Tapia V. Banque Indosuez.... 235
Tardiness.... 287, 293
Tarnishment.... 87
Tax Advantages.... 129, 134, 135
Tax Evasion.... 420
Tax Law.... 18, 19, 23, 217, 300, 328
Tax Principles.... 128
Tax Purposes.... 111, 122, 123, 124, 136, 234
Taxation.... 27, 122, 123, 128, 129, 136, 179
Teaching.... 4, 315, 335, 463
Technicalities.... 29, 336, 411
Technicality.... 29
Technology.... 15, 60, 64, 65, 71, 87, 296, 308, 461, 463, 464
Teleologica.... 40, 56, 57, 58

Temporary Employees.... 104
Temporary Workers.... 104, 105
Ten Amendments.... 25
Tenants In Partnership.... 121
Tender Of Performance.... 275
Tender Offer.... 152, 217
Tennessee.... 45, 46, 52, 228, 302, 351, 356, 398, 416
Tenure.... 25, 206
Terminology.... 13, 169, 171, 184, 294, 373, 405, 413
Territory.... 17, 22, 196, 197, 367, 389
Terrorism.... 283, 346
Terry V. Ohio.... 466
Test For Strict Liability.... 477
Testimony.... 41, 51, 53, 61, 62, 87, 120, 176, 178, 254, 259, 262, 263, 265, 329, 346, 347, 348, 359, 379, 381, 390, 391, 396, 397, 398, 399, 400, 401, 402, 404, 405, 413, 417, 418, 464
Texas.... 45, 47, 50, 51, 61, 104, 124, 158, 247, 252, 301, 345, 351, 356, 357, 398, 408, 438, 441, 443, 481, 490
The Chain.... 318, 442, 478, 482, 483, 485, 492, 494
The Thing.... 273, 317, 393, 406, 435, 436, 483
Theft.... 65, 79, 88, 113, 188, 228, 229, 324, 419, 492
Theodore Levitt.... 335
Theories.... 4, 34, 35, 36, 54, 307, 311, 330, 379, 440, 484, 485
Theories Of Law34
Theory Of Tax Shelters.... 122
Thermos.... 84
Thing Decided.... 406
Third Party.... 91, 92, 93, 94, 95, 96, 97, 101, 121, 152, 153, 224, 268, 269, 270, 274, 290, 292, 421, 438, 441, 461, 462, 483, 496
Third Party Beneficiaries.... 496
Third Party's Rights.... 270
Third-Party Claim.... 378
This For That.... 215, 318
Thomas Hobbes.... 6, 7
Thomas Jefferson.... 1, 40, 329, 330, 331
Thomas Lewis Ingram.... 331

Thoughts Without Acts.... 419
Threats As Duress.... 227
Threats Of Retaliation.... 303
Three Main Concepts Concerning Corporations.... 130
Thrift-Paradox.... 336
Throw Out.... 54, 198, 239, 295
Thurgood Marshall.... 361, 362, 365
Time Of Performance.... 200
Timing.... 71, 273
Tinker V. Des Moines School District.... 165
Title IX.... 421
Title VI.... 104, 300, 301, 302, 303, 305, 306, 307, 308, 309, 310, 311, 312, 313, 314, 316, 317, 319, 320, 321, 323, 466
Title VII.... 104, 300, 301, 302, 303, 305, 306, 307, 308, 309, 310, 311, 312, 313, 314, 316, 317, 319, 320, 321, 323, 466
Title VII Defenses.... 314
Title VII Of The Civil Rights Act Of.... 301, 323
Title VII Violation.... 308, 311, 320
Tobacco Cases.... 385
Tobacco Companies.... 160, 348, 444, 445, 468
Tone.... 7, 14, 15, 16, 41, 44, 61, 80, 102, 149, 225, 229, 231, 254, 312, 316, 356, 358, 387, 388, 400, 419, 424, 430, 439, 448, 477, 489
Too Clever.... 327
Toothless Maid.... 315
Topics.... 1, 12, 23, 27, 36, 114, 189, 237, 306, 385, 472, 474
Tort But No Crime.... 420
Tort Cases.... 155, 415, 416, 439, 478, 490
Tort Claim.... 417, 428, 438, 457, 470
Tort Law.... 23, 36, 101, 104, 415, 416, 420, 423, 424, 425, 429, 434, 436, 462, 471, 477
Tort Liability.... 59, 106, 418, 428, 434
Tort Liability Of Hirer.... 106
Tort Reform.... 481, 490
Tortious Actions.... 100
Tortious Interference With Contract.... 470, 475
Total Independence.... 40

Totality Of Evidence.... 465
Totally Undisclosed Principals.... 102
Towne V. Eisner.... 165, 173
Trade Customs.... 494
Trade Dress.... 70, 86, 87
Trade Journals.... 96
Trade Libel.... 472
Trade Names.... 84
Trade Secret.... 67, 68, 87, 88, 89, 290, 345, 347
Trademark Lawsuits.... 83
Trademarks.... 67, 68, 74, 79, 81, 82, 83, 84, 85, 87, 88, 89, 114, 163
Training.... 6, 14, 43, 100, 169, 229, 272, 308, 311, 322, 323, 327, 328, 329, 330, 335, 337, 341, 345, 350, 351, 354, 355, 435, 439, 440, 472
Training Of Lawyers.... 327
Trammel V. United States.... 347
Transactional Costs.... 27
Transferability.... 121, 126, 130
Transference.... 429, 430, 431
Transformative.... 79
Translators.... 193, 403, 405, 438
Transportation.... 17, 234, 235, 240, 281, 290, 291, 475, 480, 482
Travel.... 63, 94, 100, 122, 188, 332, 381, 427, 447, 453, 488
Treason.... 413
Treaties.... 34, 76, 80, 81, 361, 406
Trespass.... 14, 99, 216, 413, 414, 424, 425, 453, 454, 458
Triad Fighting About Reforms.... 438
Trial Courts.... 3, 16, 45, 351, 352, 353, 359, 360, 410
Trial Judge.... 54, 58, 61, 78, 109, 253, 354, 355, 356, 359, 360, 376, 392, 395, 404, 405, 406, 411, 461, 462, 472
Trial Lawyers.... 329, 405, 439
Trial Proceedings.... 397
Trier Of Fact.... 312, 402
Trips.... 231, 236, 434
Trivial.... 70, 182, 292
Trusts.... 19, 111, 214, 226, 293, 416, 438
Truth.... 34, 51, 62, 63, 139, 162, 164, 167, 231, 236, 275, 340, 342, 343, 376, 384, 390, 391, 394, 396, 397, 400, 461, 463, 471, 476
Truth-In-Lending Act.... 476
Truthfulness.... 400
Truthiness.... 397
Turnpikes.... 133
Tuttle V. Buck.... 473
Two Less Used Types Of Discovery.... 385
Types Of Corporations.... 135
Types Of Intentional Torts.... 425, 453
Tyranny.... 6, 17, 30
U.S. Arbitration Act.... 410
U.S. Bankruptcy Code.... 409
U.S. Constitution.... 6, 7, 22, 23, 30, 64, 156, 360, 361, 389, 406, 414
U.S. Court Of Appeals.... 92, 303, 311, 312, 337, 351, 359, 427
U.S. Patent And Trademark.... 69, 82, 83
UCC -, 20
UCC Approach.... 205
UCCl.... 35, 191, 383
Ukraine.... 23, 24, 184, 195, 375, 413, 419
Ultimate Goals.... 104
Ultra-Hazardous Activities.... 477
Um Nammar.... 12
Unauthorized Appropriation.... 466, 468
Unauthorized Contracts.... 91
Unconscionability.... 172, 236, 248, 251, 252, 253, 254, 255, 257, 267, 285, 320
Unconscionable Contract.... 253
Unconstitutional.... 8, 31, 63, 158, 160, 356, 367, 466, 490
Uncopyrightable Facts.... 78
Uncustomary.... 213
Under Duress.... 173, 217, 227, 228, 260
Under Oath.... 224, 381, 384, 390, 395
Undercapitalization.... 154, 155
Underlying Contract.... 221
Undisclosed Agency.... 89, 102
Undisclosed Principal.... 97, 102
Undue Hardship.... 307
Undue Influence.... 172, 173, 184, 224, 226, 236, 267, 338
Unemployment Compensation.... 104, 129
Unenforceability.... 184
Unenforceable.... 84, 184, 220, 228, 245, 257, 258, 259, 320
Unequal Bargaining Power.... 254
Unfair Behavior.... 399
Unfair Competition.... 70, 83, 86, 230, 470, 472, 473, 475, 476
Unfair Questions.... 401
Unforeseeable.... 221, 282, 283, 287, 432, 442, 484, 486
Unforeseeable Misuse Of The Product.... 486
Unforeseen Event.... 282, 295
Uniform Commercial Code.... 20, 132, 189, 194, 195, 208, 212, 246, 253, 262, 263, 492, 495, 496
Uniform Laws.... 124, 189
Uniform Partnership Act (Upa).... 117
Unilateral Contract.... 185, 186, 204, 205, 210
Unilateral Mistake.... 222, 223, 224, 225
Unincorporated Bill Of Rights Provisions.... 414
Unintended Consequences.... 238, 430
Union Plans.... 332
Unions.... 103, 114, 137, 142, 145, 156, 157, 474
Uniqueness.... 297
Unitary System.... 22, 23, 24
United Kingdom.... 14, 23, 31, 48, 84, 143, 175, 194, 195, 245, 329, 350, 375, 413, 419, 483
United States Federal Organizational Sentencing Guidelines.... 335
United States V. Arvizu.... 465
United States V. Doe.... 400
United States V. Frederick.... 350
United States V. Leon.... 29
United States V. Scheffer.... 395
United States V. White.... 399, 400
Universal Copyright Convention.... 80
Universitas.... 130
Unjust Enrichment.... 179, 187, 188, 295
Unlawful Interest Charges.... 248
Unlawful Retaliation.... 301, 302
Unlimited Liability.... 115, 119
Unlimited Personal Liability.... 112, 115, 125

525

Unpopular Persons Or Causes.... 344
Unreasonable Searches.... 25, 464
Unreasonably Dangerous Product.... 481
Unstable Business Format.... 114
Unstable Business Life.... 119
Unstricken Alternative Language.... 203
Unsworn Testimony.... 62
UPA.... 3, 40, 92, 105, 106, 117, 118, 119, 314, 315, 316, 372, 421, 471, 485
Upjohn Test.... 348
Urban Decay.... 83
Url.... 106, 123, 162, 302, 316, 330, 331, 334
Use Of Experts.... 479
Use Of Reasonably Necessary Force.... 451
Useful.... 1, 6, 7, 16, 22, 29, 36, 64, 72, 84, 89, 144, 164, 171, 179, 236, 274, 327, 345, 361, 385, 435, 481, 492
Usefulness.... 36, 236, 481
Usury.... 248
Utah Appeals Court.... 98
Utilitarianism.... 35, 36, 38, 40, 41, 54, 56, 57, 58
Utilities.... 130, 249, 337
Utility.... 4, 36, 37, 50, 58, 70, 71, 72, 298, 353, 377, 416, 481
Utility Of Market Forces.... 298
Utility Patent.... 70, 71, 72
Vacate.... 291, 404, 410, 427
Vacate And Remand.... 404
Valid Contract.... 177, 184, 204, 240, 470
Values.... 31, 37, 38, 39, 145, 151, 164, 167, 218, 297, 306, 335, 340, 361, 362, 478, 487, 488
Van Gorkom.... 148, 151, 152
Variation.... 73, 105, 140, 212, 389, 494
Various Antitrust Law Violations.... 470
Various Possible Instances Of Negligence.... 440
Vaughn V. Edel.... 312
Verdict.... 9, 44, 45, 46, 47, 48, 49, 50, 54, 61, 70, 71, 85, 299, 300, 350, 376, 386, 402, 403, 404, 408, 417, 419, 420, 433, 464
Vertical Privity.... 483
Veto.... 24, 25, 31, 53, 367
Victimless.... 414, 420

Vietnam War Protests.... 165
Viewing Of Property.... 386
Vikings.... 13, 46
Village.... 43, 227, 284, 285, 473
Virginia.... 45, 46, 133, 144, 148, 156, 177, 228, 316, 328, 351, 355, 356, 369, 381, 398, 441, 446, 450, 479, 489, 490
Vivid Language.... 398
Voidability.... 267
Voiding Party.... 244
Voir Dire.... 48, 49, 50, 51, 52, 54, 138
Vokes V. Arthur Murray.... 235, 253
Volkswagen Aktiengesellschaft V. Schlunk.... 375
Voltaire.... 19
Voluntary.... 2, 32, 98, 115, 170, 237, 244, 318, 323, 347, 352, 357, 409, 430, 443, 449, 451, 476
Voluntary Intoxication.... 449
Voluntary Retirement.... 357
Waiter's Discretionary Authority.... 91
Waiver.... 2, 197, 227, 280, 281, 336, 388, 437, 443
Wal-Mart.... 49
Wales.... 28, 333, 407, 435, 447
Walt Disney.... 76, 80, 94
War Crimes.... 39, 407
Warning.... 2, 10, 158, 216, 222, 257, 323, 348, 359, 379, 400, 427, 440, 444, 445, 448, 463, 468, 472, 475, 479, 480, 482, 483, 484, 485, 487, 488, 489, 490, 491
Warranties.... 174, 191, 232, 424, 445, 477, 478, 479, 483, 484, 489, 491, 492, 493, 494, 495, 496, 497
Warrantless Searches.... 25
Warranty Of Fitness.... 495
Warranty Of Merchantability.... 252, 480, 494, 495
Warsaw Convention.... 425, 433, 434
Washington Redskins.... 85
Weasel Out.... 212
Wedding Announcements.... 277
Wedge Argument.... 32
Weight Requirements.... 313
Wendt V. Beardmore Suburban Chevrolet, Inc.... 232

Western Nations.... 6, 65
Whistleblowing.... 10, 11, 147, 163, 301, 346, 347
White Pages.... 78
White-Collar Crime.... 143, 421
Wholesalers.... 97, 220, 478, 482, 496
Wild Animals.... 453
William Brennan.... 158
William F. Gladstone.... 387
William Howard Taft.... 330, 362
William Lloyd Garrison.... 39
William Penn.... 204
William Rehnquist.... 389, 461, 464
William Shakespeare.... 89, 111, 327, 460, 463, 497
William The Conqueror.... 13, 46
Wills.... 19, 214, 244, 245, 293, 332, 438
Wilmington Trust Co. V. Clark.... 470
Winding Up.... 119
Wiretapping.... 460
Witchcraft.... 12, 61
Witches.... 61, 195
Without Cause.... 254, 298
Witnesseth.... 181, 196, 197, 369
Wood V. Hustler Magazine.... 467
Woodrow Wilson.... 1, 133, 330
Worcester V. Georgia.... 367
Work Environment.... 318, 323
Work Incentives.... 128
Work Product.... 381
Workers' Compensation.... 104, 108, 247, 328
Workers' Councils.... 145, 146
Workplace Environment.... 318
Workplace Harassment.... 319, 321
World Comparison.... 65
World Intellectual Property Organization.... 74, 80
World Trade Organization.... 83, 406
World War.... 39, 43, 83, 161, 228, 245, 344, 410, 462
Writ Of Certiorari.... 340, 360, 365, 366
Writ Of Mandamus.... 297
Writs Of Certiorari.... 365
Written Agreements.... 102, 185, 258, 295
Written Constitution.... 31

Written Contract.... 115, 266, 267
Written Demand.... 142
Written Evidence.... 173, 175, 184, 258, 259, 261, 263, 264, 267, 358
Written Offer.... 184, 203, 204, 221
Wrongful Act.... 9, 99, 143, 151, 323, 419, 426, 429, 446
Wrongful Behavior.... 49, 335, 446, 458
Wrongful Death.... 19, 408
Wrongful Discharge.... 299, 300
Wrongful Encroachment.... 453
Wrongful Intent.... 418
Wrongful Termination.... 163, 164, 300, 307, 321
Wrongfulness.... 246, 419, 429
WTO.... 24, 72, 406
Year Books.... 14
Yugoslavia.... 24
Zacchini V. Scripps Howard.... 79
Zadvydas V. Davis.... 380
Zealous Advocate.... 10, 343
Zone Of Control.... 100, 256
Zone Of Fairness.... 433
Zoning.... 103, 232, 235, 273, 282, 296, 454